Advance Praise for
Hands on the Freedom Plow

"This collection provides the texture and tone of that eclectic group of women who joined together in common cause, still debating and disagreeing along the way but united by overlapping values, newfound courage, and the ambitious dream of changing the political face of the nation, which, in large part, they did. A treasure trove of stories and reflections by an amazing group of women activists."

— **BARBARA RANSBY,** author of *Ella Baker and the Black Radical Tradition*

"An extraordinary contribution to historical understanding of the Civil Rights Movement, this work illuminates the ground swell that was SNCC. It's a complex story, well told by the participants, whose real voices bestow this collection with remarkable authority. These gripping narratives by tough, resilient women, these tales of courage, perseverance, hope, and dedication to a cause, portray an amazing time in America."

— **ORVILLE VERNON BURTON,** author of *The Age of Lincoln*

"This marvelously broad and deep collection of SNCC women's voices gives the reader a rare insight into the trials and triumphs of the black freedom struggle of the 1960s. These stories related by women at the center of the struggle are simultaneously simple and complex, diverse and united. At the same time, as they relate their own personal struggles for freedom, their voices are punctuated by passion and pain, and frustration and determination."

— **CYNTHIA GRIGGS FLEMING,** author of *Yes We Did? From King's Dream to Obama's Promise*

"*Hands on the Freedom Plow* is, quite simply, a stunning collection. These stories of courage, hope, and, yes, conflict, will inspire all Americans who believe in the possibilities of democracy. This volume belongs on that short shelf of books on the Movement that must be read."

— **JOHN DITTMER,** author of *Local People: The Struggle for Civil Rights in Mississippi*

"These women's lives, spent in the freedom struggle, call to us. Their political insight and creativity make them American heroines; their strategic vision allows them to point a better way forward for all, worldwide, who aspire to equality and democracy."

— **WESLEY C. HOGAN,** author of *Many Minds, One Heart: SNCC's Dream for a New America*

"A remarkable achievement, sweeping in scope, rich with detail, and infinitely readable. Without question, this is the new starting point for learning about the central role that SNCC, and women, played in the African American freedom struggle."

— **HASAN KWAME JEFFRIES,** author of *Bloody Lowndes: Civil Rights and Black Power in Alabama's Black Belt*

HANDS ON THE
FREEDOM
PLOW

UNIVERSITY OF ILLINOIS PRESS

URBANA, CHICAGO, AND SPRINGFIELD

edited by

FAITH S. HOLSAERT

MARTHA PRESCOD NORMAN NOONAN

JUDY RICHARDSON

BETTY GARMAN ROBINSON

JEAN SMITH YOUNG

and DOROTHY M. ZELLNER

HANDS ON THE
FREEDOM
PLOW

**PERSONAL
ACCOUNTS
BY WOMEN
IN SNCC**

First Illinois paperback, 2012
Manufactured in the United States of America
4 5 6 7 8 C P 5 4 3 2 1
∞ This book is printed on acid-free paper.
Danny Lyon/Magnum Photos courtesy of Edwynn Houk Gallery.

The Library of Congress cataloged the cloth edition as follows:
Hands on the freedom plow : personal accounts by women in SNCC /
edited by Faith S. Holsaert . . . [et al.].
p.   cm.
Includes index.
ISBN 978-0-252-03557-9 (cloth : acid-free paper)
1. African American women civil rights workers—Biography. 2. African
American women political activists—Biography. 3. Student Nonviolent
Coordinating Committee (U.S.)—Biography. 4. African Americans—
Civil rights—History—20th century. 5. Civil rights movements—United
States—History—20th century. 6. Civil rights movements—Southern
States—History—20th century. 7. United States—Race relations—
History—20th century. 8. Southern States—Race relations—History—
20th century. I. Holsaert, Faith S.
E185.96.H24   2010
305.43'323092—dc22   2010020850

PAPERBACK ISBN 978-0-252-07888-0

To all the women past
who have devoted their lives
to the freedom struggle, including
our mentor, Miss Ella Jo Baker;
our heroine, Mrs. Fannie Lou Hamer;
and our colleague, Ruby Doris Smith Robinson.

To our sister contributors who did not
live to see this book's publication:
Mrs. Victoria Gray Adams, Joanne Grant,
Prathia Hall, McCree Harris,
and Hellen O'Neal-McCray.

And to all those who organize
for social justice.

Contents

We Are Soldiers

We are soldiers in the army
We got to fight although we have to cry
We got to hold up the freedom banner
We got to hold it up until we die

My mother was a soldier
She had her hands on the freedom plow
She said, "One day I'll get old, I can't fight on anymore
But Lord I'll stand here and fight on anyhow"

We are soldiers in the army
We got to fight although we have to cry
We got to hold up the freedom banner
We got to hold it up until we die

I'm glad I'm a soldier
I got my hands on the freedom plow
One day I'll get old, can't fight on anymore
But Lord I'll stand here and fight on anyhow

We are soldiers in the army
We got to fight although we have to cry
We got to hold up the freedom banner
We got to hold it up until we die

—— FREEDOM SONG based on a popular
   gospel song recorded by the Caravans
   led by Albertina Walker, also featuring
   James Cleveland as pianist, arranger,
   and singer

PART 5

**Get on Board: The Mississippi Movement through
the Atlantic City Challenge, 1961–1964**   211

PART 6

Cambridge, Maryland: The Movement under Attack, 1961–1964   271

PART 7

A Sense of Family: The National SNCC Office, 1960–1964   299

PART 8

Illustrations follow pages 84, 156, and 270.

HANDS ON THE
FREEDOM
PLOW

Introduction

The book you are holding in your hands will open the door to a special world. It is a book by women who, now mostly in our sixties and seventies, are teachers, organizers, doctors, nursing home workers, singers, farmers, television documentary producers, nurses, homebodies, and professors. But in the 1960s some of us leaped over the expectations of our families and communities while others acted out of family and community traditions of social justice—all to become organizers and agitators in the Civil Rights Movement.

We worked with the Student Nonviolent Coordinating Committee (SNCC), which grew out of the wave of student sit-ins that swept across the South in the winter and spring of 1960. Established as a coordinating committee for southern student activists, SNCC soon became the more radical and confrontational arm of the Civil Rights Movement.

In this book we women explain why we did what we did—why we traveled directly toward danger. These stories explore how we overcame fear, acquired new skills, and experienced personal growth in this crucible of change. We organized in dangerous rural communities, registered voters, led mass meetings, and marched, all under the constant threat of arrests and beatings at the hands of hostile white southerners. The writers recount their experiences in southern jails, the victims of beatings and sexual harassment. These are accounts of strength and endurance.

The fifty-two women speaking in this book represent a wide variety of movement participants—black, white, and Latina; young and old; southern and northern—reflecting the composition of the Movement itself. SNCC's college-age staff organizers are here, alongside southern community women whose activism began in their hometowns.

This volume fills in the civil rights picture by presenting the stories of women, the majority of movement participants. Their accounts represent the incredible breadth of a movement that encompassed hundreds of thousands of people, each of whom would have sworn up and down that she was not unusual in the least. In fact, we hope this book will affirm that you don't have to be special or especially brave to start a movement or participate in it.

Though only women's narratives are included here, the men of SNCC are ever present. In SNCC we referred to ourselves as being "a band of brothers [and sisters] and a circle of trust," and we meant it. The men of SNCC shared with us the dangers, the joys, and the pain of everyday movement life. And many of those bonds continue to this day.

Here is an in-depth look at women activists and our backgrounds. Who were we, and why did we choose to participate in the Movement? How did our civil rights activism transform us and affect the rest of our lives? Was the effect mostly political, moral, or spiritual? How did our time in the Movement influence our concept of ourselves as women? Did we continue to live the Movement throughout the rest of our lives?

The contributors chose what they would write about. This personal approach is one reason this book is so unusual. It reflects the spirit and feelings of those of us who actually experienced the Movement and the many sources of strength that nurtured us as activists, allowing us to move through our fears.

Like the real history of a tumultuous movement, this book is full of debates and disagreements. After four decades our recall may not be perfect; our interpretations may differ. Like movement-building itself, the contradictions can be messy.

The idea of doing this project had been floating around for some time, but we were spurred into action by reunions and meetings we attended in the 1990s. Some of us hadn't seen each other since the 1960s. For some of us, the aftermath of SNCC's dissolution was painful. But at these reunions and retrospectives some of us met again, not as strangers, but as old friends renewing the deep bonds that had been forged in struggle. We shared stories and remembered what we had meant to each other—and what SNCC had meant to all of us.

At these moments of coming together we also met exceptional young people who could have been us forty years ago: insightful students working on their dissertations; wonderful young filmmakers conducting interviews; enthusiastic sons and daughters of former SNCC workers, who'd heard all our tales and had ideas of their own about what the next movement should be like. These young people energized us and reminded us of the necessity—and urgency—of documenting this amazing time in our lives for those coming behind us.

So in 1995 a few of us began to talk about putting together a book that would capture those feelings and the importance of our work, particularly as women in the organization. We became a committee of six women, all former SNCC staff members: three African American, three white. One year later, in January 1996, we sent out our first solicitation to women who had worked in SNCC-related projects throughout the South for a prolonged period. Most importantly, we insisted that the local women who formed and grounded the Movement must be reflected in this book. We conducted oral interviews to provide a starting point for several authors who then went on to complete their own manuscripts.

Creating this book has sometimes been difficult, but we stayed together—because we knew we had to. The result—this book—was worth all our hard work and struggle.

There are accounts here from women active during different times and phases of movement activity. Some were present at SNCC's founding in 1960; others were involved in programs that flourished closer to the end of the decade. Some participated mostly in direct action efforts, others in voter registration and community organizing, yet others in offices or in cultural activities like song leading and the Free Southern Theater. Some believed in nonviolence as a way of life while others viewed it only as a useful tactic and saw no contradiction between that tactic and their strong belief in self-defense.

These first-person narratives provide perhaps the broadest base yet from which to paint a picture of what it was like to be a female SNCC worker in the 1960s, describing the overall environment the Civil Rights Movement provided for women and how women responded to and influenced their surroundings. This period was so important in our lives that more than forty years later we remember many of our thoughts and actions with great clarity and detail.

Some of the women in this book played pivotal roles in the Movement, making decisions and promoting activities that changed the course and character of the civil rights struggle. Others conceived, built, and directed movement projects while others were involved in the daily repetitive, yet still challenging tasks of movement building. Most took their places on the front lines, but some chose to remain more in the background or in more supportive activities. The same woman, at one time or another, may have done all of these things.

Our contributors provide a glimpse into their backgrounds and personal lives, answering questions such as how their time in the Movement influenced their concept of themselves as women and affected their life visions and goals. They revisit movement debates and disagreements as they present their thoughts and analyses, held during those years when they were conducting a search for the best way to move forward. They express their views on the overall direction of the Movement, its tactics, strategies, and underlying philosophies, including the role of white people in a black-led movement, as well as the role of women within the Movement and the society at large.

The organizing in SNCC was often based on female leaders, some of whom were prominent in their communities before SNCC ever arrived. The dynamic interaction between SNCC organizers and local community activists is a recurring topic. Southern community women—some of whom were themselves on SNCC staff—and SNCC's female college-age staff energized and supported one another. Usually it was the local women who made it possible for the students to operate in these dangerous areas, offering food, shelter, and meeting places and providing protection and guidance along with a readiness to fight for freedom beside the students.

From these amazing women we SNCC staff workers gained lessons and strength that we called upon the rest of our lives. To use author Mary Helen Washington's phrase, they were "the strong black bridges we crossed over on." These are the women who nurtured and sustained their families, their churches, and us; the ones whose courage and intelligence allowed us and the men of SNCC to go on when the days were darkest—because this is what they had always done. Our book is a testament to them: women like Mama Dolly Raines, Victoria Gray Adams, Unita Blackwell, Gloria Richardson, Carolyn Daniels, and all those too numerous to mention.

In the more than fifteen years it has taken to compile this anthology, five of our contributors have passed away: Victoria Gray Adams, Joanne Grant, McCree Harris, Prathia Hall, and Hellen O'Neal-McCray. However, we are fortunate to have their work in the Movement recorded in this book.

As the contributors relate, going to jail in the South—a break from many previous civil rights efforts—was an expected part of SNCC workers' activism. Even though they would never have imagined serving jail time before their decision to take a stand for equality, they chose to enter southern prisons memorialized for their brutality in legends and songs. Denied basic necessities, placed on death row or in isolation, crowded together, subjected to beatings and sexual harassment, they still found ways to offset the jailers' tactics and to stage protests in jail.

Unlike most other civil rights organizations in the sixties, from 1961 on SNCC focused on building organizations and introducing new concepts of leadership in the Deep South, where the harshest forms of racial segregation, economic oppression, and terrorism held sway. This meant we SNCC workers lived and worked in communities where earlier civil rights activists had been run out of town or killed. We stayed and kept working, even though we were the victims of random attacks and even after some of our associates were also murdered. Sometimes we walked the same streets as the killers.

When we made the choice to walk such dangerous paths, we helped create, sustain, and direct one of the most important social protest movements in American history. We felt the power and responsibility of being major players on history's stage. We took on the task of dismantling an ingrained system of social and political oppression that was then almost a century old and fought to replace it with a more just and egalitarian society. In so doing, our contributors not only challenged the power of local and state southern governments, but also changed some of the basic premises and underlying power bases of the national government and of the country's established social order.

Most of our contributors were influenced by the events of the preceding decade, the 1950s: the 1955 lynching of fourteen-year-old Emmett Till, the repression of the McCarthy era, the Montgomery Bus Boycott of 1956–1957, the bravery of the Little Rock Nine in 1957, the determination of the African liberation struggles against colonialism. The influence of this finally positive reflection of Africa could be seen in SNCC's slogan, "One Man, One Vote," taken directly from these anti-colonial struggles.

The individual stories tell one central story: that of the growth and development of a movement for freedom and equality. It is this larger narrative that dictates the arrangement of this book. In the course of this history, the authors describe much about how this movement for social and political change was developed, supported, and maintained. They show how this central objective gave purpose and meaning to all that they did and created enduring bonds among the participants.

Except for the first piece, "Little Memphis Girl" by Gwendolyn Zoharah Simmons, the narratives in this collection are arranged roughly by chronology and geography to follow the story of SNCC from its formation in 1960, through the early sit-ins, and continuing through the SNCC projects of the late 1960s. Introductory material for each part, written largely by Faith S. Holsaert and Martha Prescod Norman Noonan, begins each section. The postscript was also written by Faith S. Holsaert and Martha Prescod Norman Noonan. We were helped and sustained through these years by our friends, colleagues, family, historians, participants in this book, and women in SNCC, and we thank them all.

When you open this book you will enter a different world, a world where danger is ever present. Beatings, shootings, bombings, and church burnings happen all too frequently. The issue of the day is always: how to make social and political change, how to press forward, how to keep going—in short, how to make a movement. In this world, freedom and justice are real, solid, and tangible. Freedom and justice are the reasons for being and doing and the reasons for dying.

Though the voices are different, they all tell the same story—of women bursting out of constraints, leaving school, leaving their hometowns, meeting new people, talking into the night, laughing, going to jail, being afraid, teaching in Freedom Schools, working in "the field," dancing at the Elks Hall, working the WATS line to relay horror story after horror story, telling the press, telling the story, telling the word. And making a difference in this world.

—The Editors

PART 1

Fighting for My Rights
One SNCC Woman's Experience, 1961–1964

Gwendolyn Zoharah Simmons's account spans several years of SNCC history and incorporates themes found in the remaining fifty-four contributions. Her story introduces memories of courage, conflict, and fear and expresses the hope and commitment of every woman who chose to act on her conviction that equality and freedom were worth any price.

Steeped in a family history that included recollections of slavery, Simmons lived a comfortable and protected life in her hometown of Memphis, Tennessee, until, as a high school student, she left the black community to look for work. Her quest to understand and protest racism brought her into the sit-in movement and later to the front lines of struggle in the Mississippi Movement. Here she chronicles her personal growth from a gradual and somewhat timid entrance into activism to becoming a self-assured project director.

"Fighting for My Rights" is the title of a freedom song written by Freedom Singer Chuck Neblett in a Charleston, Missouri, jailhouse and set to the Ray Charles tune "Lonely Avenue." The song begins, "Well, I'm tired of segregation / And I want my equal rights / Respect and education / Total desegregation" and is followed by the chorus, "That's why I'm fighting for my rights / Fighting for my rights / Fighting for my rights."

From Little Memphis Girl to Mississippi Amazon

Gwendolyn Zoharah Simmons aka Gwendolyn Robinson

A college student is torn between meeting her high academic goals and her growing commitment to the Movement. Her activism is met with fierce opposition from black college administrators and her family.

The Early Years

My paternal grandmother, Rhoda Bell Temple-Robinson-Hudson-Douglas (she was married three times and outlived them all), who reared me from the age of three (she was "Mama" to me), told me a lot about the ways of the world for a black girl-child in the heart of the Deep South. My grandmother had been raised by her grandmother, who spent her youth and early adulthood in slavery. The product of a white "master" and an enslaved African American mother, Grandma Lucy was blonde and blue-eyed (hard to believe if you saw my grandmother or me). Grandma Lucy hated the color of her skin because of all the suffering it had caused her. When she was eleven or twelve years old, her slave master/father gave her as a wedding gift to her half "all white" sister. This sister hated her immensely, presumably because she knew that her father was Lucy's father, too. The punishments the new "mistress" meted out to her half-sister for any infractions of her draconian codes included lashes with a buggy whip and, most cruel of all, the insertion of long darning needles between Grandma Lucy's fingernails and nail beds while my great-great-grandmother bled profusely and begged for mercy. Grandma Lucy told my grandmother the stories of slavery as she grew up. My grandmother then told them to me. I have told them to my daughter, Aishah Shahidah Simmons (may the circle be unbroken!).

Mama was a great storyteller. I learned about the harsh realities she had faced under the sharecropping system, trying to eke out a meager living from the soil from year to year in the face of harrowing racism and an economic system stacked against the sharecropper. She had spent all of her early life on different farms in Arkansas, and although the conditions in each place were none too good, she said she always gave thanks for not living in Mississippi, which was the worst "hell hole" in the whole wide world for black folks.

I can remember being terrified by the stories she told about Negroes still living at that time under a virtual form of slavery in Mississippi. She knew people who had recently escaped from Mississippi plantations where they had been held for years at gunpoint because of their so-called indebtedness to their white landowners. She said she thanked God every day that she had not had to set foot into the state of Mississippi, and she warned me never to land there if I knew what was good for me. Of course I promised myself that I would never, ever go there! Memphis was bad enough; I certainly didn't want it any worse.

For the most part, growing up was joyful. I lived happily in my all-black world, surrounded by a loving family and wonderful teachers and church members; they showered me with tender care, support, and encouragement to reach the highest goals that I could imagine, in spite of the obstacles of race and gender. Mama was a happy person by nature, kind and loving and full of the joy of life. I guess our temperaments and personalities meshed well, and life with my grandparents was a happy one. Although my mother (Juanita Cranford-Robinson-Watson) and father (Major Lewis Robinson) were separated when I was three and a half, they were loving, affirming, and actively involved in my life. After my parents' breakup, Mama asked if she could keep me, since my mother had to return to work full-time. I did spend many weekends with my sweet mother, who was like a big sister to me, and my father lived in the house off and on with my grandparents and me for most of my growing up. Though he wasn't one to express much affection verbally, he clearly loved me, and as I grew up to be a leader at school and at church, he was visibly proud.

My aunts Jessie (Jessie Neal Hudson) and Ollie Bee (Ollie B. Smith) both took great interest in me and encouraged me to excel. Both were strong women who took their destinies into their own hands and carved out rich and wonderful lives. My aunt Jessie was especially attractive, lived in Chicago, and boasted a wardrobe and colognes that I thought only movie stars owned. With her high school diploma in hand, she migrated to Chicago, as so many Memphians did, and pushed her way into the white preserve of retail window design. On her biyearly treks home to Memphis, she regaled me with stories of her life in the Windy City. She made my whole community come to life when she came to town. She was all of my friends' "Aunt Jessie" too. She brought many of them presents and baked for everyone.

There was music and dancing in the house when she came. She taught me how to dance. And the clothes that she brought or sent me twice a year made my eyes bug out. *Bold, audacious, daring,* and *a pioneering spirit* are terms that best describe her. It was through her that I learned that while the North did offer more opportunities to black people than did the South, it was still no Promised Land!

I was blessed with many excellent women role models: there was Miss Willa McWilliams-Walker—my second-grade teacher—who was the first black person to run for the Memphis school board. At my church there were Dr. Clara Brawner, the first black woman doctor I ever saw; her sister Alpha Brawner, a world-renowned opera singer; and Ophelia Little, another internationally known opera singer. There were so many good teachers at my school and mentors at my church home who made special efforts to help me develop my leadership potential. By and large it was these womenfolk who made indelible impressions on me during my developing years. They told me constantly that I should reach for the stars. I studied hard, played hard, did well in school, and set my sights upon attaining a full tuition scholarship from either Howard University or Spelman College, two of the most prestigious historically black colleges in the United States.

Yes, I was subjected to the daily indignities that all black people were exposed to. But for the most part, these things were the gray background to the Technicolor life that I was busily leading at the time. For the most part it only minimally intruded upon my happy, busy, event-filled, and purposeful life.

The Realization

At the end of my junior year in high school, it was clear that I had to get a job and save money for college. A number of my peers, particularly the boys, had begun working during the summers long before me. Many of them worked in nearby cotton fields, being paid meagerly for their backbreaking efforts. I had been spared this exhausting work by my grandmother, who said, "I have picked enough cotton for the both of us." Fortunately, our family could afford to live without my adding to the family's income, since both my father and grandfather were working. My granddad, Henry "Lev" Douglas, worked at a whiskey distillery that even unionized. He was proud to be a union man.

For some reason I got it into my head that I wanted a "nice" job (read, white folks–type job) working in an office or in a department store. I answered several want ads, only to be told by the irate and anxious clerks that this was not a job for a "colored girl." I began to feel a bit depressed about securing a good summer job. One day in early June, I was again rebuffed. It was hot, and the air was so thick and humid that you could have cut it with a knife. I was standing outside a commercial establishment wondering if I should answer some of the other ads or just call it quits for the day. Quite suddenly a violent thunderstorm blew up, and before I could collect myself, I was caught in torrential rains with thunder and lightning flashing all around. I was quite disturbed about being caught out in the open in a thunderstorm with no shelter. As I looked around at the glass-and-concrete buildings and at the white people standing in the windows looking out at the storm—and me in it—I was seized by the feeling of being stranded in an alien land. I was in my homeland, yet somehow I did not know the place. I stood there on the street, soaked to my skin, with thunder and lightning playing all around. I began to cry as I looked at all the cold buildings with their white inhabitants surrounding me. There was no shelter for me in this storm. I felt foreign and alone. For the first time, I think I realized what it meant to be black in the American South. Mama and all the loving ones who had shielded me from the harsh realities were not there. This was the real South for a black girl. I was afraid and angry. For the first time, I felt hatred for the white South and all the white southerners in it. Dripping wet and seething with a feeling I had not known before, I made my way to the bus stop where I would catch a bus to take me back to my part of town.

As I boarded the number 31 cross-town bus, I was steaming and mad as hell. I glared at the bus driver, and after dropping my coins into the fare box, I sat down on the front seat across from the driver as rivulets of water dripped from the hem of my skirt onto the floor and water seeped out from my squishy shoes. The driver, obviously shocked, looked at me and said, "Gal, I don't want no trouble; you better git on to the back, where you belong." I responded with a stony silence and a hate-filled gaze. There were no white passengers on the bus, but there were a scattering of black riders seated in the extreme rear, who were quite agitated by my actions. Several of them began hissing at me. They began to gesture in exaggerated movements, urging me to "come on to the back" and "don't start any trouble." There was fear for themselves and concern for my safety in their expressions. I looked away from them, unmoved, and stared straight ahead. I had no plan, no rational thoughts. I did not know what I was going to do. All I knew was that I was not going to give up my seat without a struggle. I didn't know how far I was prepared to go. I thought, *I am a human being, not a dog. I am a person just as good as they are.* Gone were all the sheltering adults who had done their best to protect me from the bitter realities of being black and female in the Jim Crow South. It was just *me* and *them.* For the first time in my life, I was being an "uppity nigger," and it felt good. Who the hell did white people think they were? I didn't give a damn what the next moment would bring. All I felt was that I was a "nigger" to be reckoned with!

I was lucky that day. They say that God looks after fools and angels. Clearly I had committed a dangerous act and, fortunately, did not have to pay for it. The driver didn't call the police or physically throw me off the bus. The few white passengers who boarded the bus didn't insist on their "skin privilege" that day, but cursed and muttered and stood over me in anger. A few sat down on the opposite side of the bus, glaring menacingly at me all the while. I returned their glares. The black passengers in the back looked on in fear and astonishment and seemed to breathe with a sigh of relief when their stops approached. I reached my destination and got off with tired and heavy steps as the bus sped away.

I stopped trying to find a job in white Memphis after that. A dear neighbor got me a summer job at the Harlem House, a chain of hamburger joints scattered across black Memphis, where I washed dishes until my hands became raw and, when I was lucky, flipped burgers.

I didn't pull off any other daring acts of courage in Memphis, but I did join the NAACP youth organization and their choir; things were pretty tame in Memphis in the early '6os, compared to what was going on in other parts of the state and across the South, with the sit-ins and the Freedom Rides. There was no doubt about it: change was in the air. No black person with breath in his or her body was unaware of the rising tide of resistance that was gripping black America.

Spelman College: A Dream Come True

I did get that scholarship to Spelman College. I also received offers from Bennett College (the other black women's college), Morgan State University, and a small white college in the Midwest that was integrating its campus. I chose Spelman. In my mind it was the most prestigious, and several of my role models—Clara and Alpha Brawner and Mrs. Epps, my pastor's wife, were alumnae. I graduated third in my high school class of more than two hundred and beamed with pride when my name was called and they read my lists of scholarships and honors. I was really on my way. I had reached for the stars and they were coming closer.

My grandmother was so proud of me. Of course everyone in my family, my school, and my church were, too. But this was so special for Mama, as she had wanted to go off to boarding school when she was a girl so long ago in Arkansas. I was living out her dream of going to college. Mama, my mother, and my stepfather (Rev. Granville Watson) drove me to the campus in Atlanta. I was thrilled as we pulled onto the beautiful tree-lined campus with all of its old, stately buildings. I had to pinch myself to see if I was dreaming. I was assigned to a room in Packard Hall, one of the older buildings on campus. It was like heaven to me and a long, long way from the four-room shotgun house in which I had grown up. Everything was spotless, and the beautiful wooden floors and magnificent wood trim shone like burnished brass. My dream had come true; I was a freshman at Spelman College.

My folks stayed a couple of days for the parents' orientation. I could see in Mama's eyes how thrilled she was for me and herself. I promised her that I would do well for her—that I would be good, study hard, and not let *anything* or *anyone* come between me and my studies. Her parting words to me were to not get into any trouble with boys or to let *anything* pull me away from my school work. I promised!

I was so thoroughly caught up in my new life on campus that it was some time before I really noticed that there was a movement going on right outside the tall brick walls that separated Spelman from the housing project. Outside of my Spelman utopia was the same ugly reality I had experienced all my life. In this city with the motto "too busy to hate" was the same Jim Crow. Downtown Atlanta was all white except for the menial laborers. SNCC (Student Nonviolent Coordinating Committee) and SCLC (Southern Christian Leadership Conference) had headquarters in Atlanta and were actively working to destroy legal racism in the city. The Spelman administrators warned us Spelman women to stay clear of any involvement with the Movement. We were there, we were told often, to get an education, not to get involved in demonstrations and protests. They made it clear that any young ladies who got involved would be summarily dismissed, especially those of us who were on scholarships. I heard that! I certainly had no intention of getting involved. I had my priorities straight. This was an opportunity of a lifetime for me; I certainly wasn't going to blow it.

The Conflict

As fate would have it, I was assigned to an experimental class combining history and American literature. The two faculty members, Dr. Staughton Lynd and Ms. Esta Seaton, were northern white liberals who were well acquainted with the African American struggle for freedom. They set out to awaken us to that incredible history. Throughout my first semester, I became acquainted for the first time with the history and protest writings of my people, and pride in them and their long struggle for justice was awakened. In addition, I met others who fanned the flame of black pride and identity. Vincent and Rosemary Freeny Harding were codirectors of the Mennonite House in

Atlanta. Howard Zinn was head of Spelman's history department. I heard many of his illuminating lectures on the African American contribution to the expansion of democracy in the United States. Another very important factor in my burgeoning transformation was my membership in the West Hunter Street Baptist Church. I joined, following my grandmother's orders and without knowing of its significance to the Movement: Rev. Ralph Abernathy was its pastor. The church's first lady, Juanita Abernathy, had a sister who was in my class and invited me to attend church with her. It was somewhat like my own church back in Memphis, the Gospel Temple Baptist Church. Plus it was just a few blocks from the campus. Staying true to my upbringing, I went every Sunday and joined the choir, something that I knew Mama would approve of—and I loved to sing.

While I was totally unaware of it, the stage was being set. What I was learning in my classes, hearing in church about the Movement—mass meetings and even the opportunity to see and hear eloquent sermons from Dr. Martin Luther King Jr. himself in my newfound church—began to erode the defense I had constructed against anything that would come between me and my precious college education. At the same time there were regular visits to the campus by SNCC recruiters, who would alternate between cajoling and lambasting us for not joining demonstrations or sit-ins. They loved to say that we were the next generation of "handkerchief-head-Negroes" who, with all our college degrees, would still be bowing and scraping to "Mr. Charlie," saying, "yassir boss," "nawsu boss," following the white man's orders 'til the day we died. They would ask, "What is a black man with a PhD?" and answer, "A nigger!" They had some really effective recruiters. One of the best was Willie Ricks, sometimes called "Reverend" Ricks. He'd stand on the campus in his blue-jean overalls (the SNCC uniform) and talk about how the SNCC folks were making history while we studied it.

Many of their barbs hit their target with me. The more I learned about this great "River of Black Protest," so named and eloquently described by my beloved Vincent Harding in his seminal work, *There Is a River,* I yearned to become involved.

It wasn't an overnight change that I went through, however. It was gradual. I began to wear my hair natural. After I appeared on campus with my new Afro, I was called into the dean of students' office. "What have you done to your hair?" she asked. "I washed it," I replied. Angrily she responded, "Don't get smart with me, young lady!" She informed me that I was an embarrassment to the school, as all Spelman women were expected to be well-groomed. But there were no other repercussions and I kept my new hairstyle.

Second, I went against Spelman's rules and dared to visit SNCC's headquarters at 8½ Raymond Street. It was within walking distance of the campus, just two blocks from my church home. Not very impressive, rather cluttered and chaotic. But, boy, was the place jumping. There was James "Jim" Forman, SNCC's executive secretary, whom I later came to idolize. He is truly one of the unsung heroes of the Civil Rights Movement. Always frantically working to hold the place together was Ruby Doris Smith Robinson, a powerhouse of a woman, who brought so much talent, energy, leadership, and commitment to her job. She put her college education on hold to work full-time in the Movement. And of course there was dear Rev. John Lewis, so pious, so committed, and really very shy. Mildred Forman, Jim's second wife, was there, a quiet and calm force in the storm; Mark Suckle, a Jewish student from the North; and, to my amazement, there were two Japanese Americans, Edmond "Ed" Nakawatase and Tom Wakayama. I couldn't believe my eyes when I first saw them. They were the first Asians I had ever met. Early on in my furtive and clandestine visits to the SNCC office, I asked them what they were doing working in a black people's movement. This is when I learned about the Japanese internment camps (concentration camps). I could not believe it. It had been completely written out of our history books! There were many others: Jack Minnis, an older white lefty in charge of research; Casey Hayden, a white southerner from Texas; and Mary King, another white southern woman, who looked like what she was with her mohair sweaters, penny loafers, soft perm, and just-right makeup. I was truly shocked to see these white ladies fraternizing with black men in the Deep South. Boy, did I admire them and all the rest of the SNCC gang who were defying all the southern norms and building a movement for deep changes in the social order.

At first I just volunteered to type press releases, stuff envelopes, and help mimeograph. I tried to pick work that was useful but out of the limelight and definitely away from any news cameras or police paddy wagons. I assured myself that I was just going to do a little support work, nothing heavy that might cause me to be discovered by Spelman or, even worse, Mama. I convinced myself that I would never participate in any demonstrations or marches and that I would study doubly hard to make sure that I kept my grades up and did not endanger my scholarship, lest I be sent home in ruin and disgrace.

This worked my freshman year. I did not demonstrate; I kept my involvement secret from my family and the school; I kept my grades up so that my scholarship was renewed. I didn't do so well, however, during my second year. Returning to Atlanta in the fall of 1963, I was changed by the great March on Washington. I had watched every televised moment, read everything I could get my hands on, and been lifted to unbelievable heights as I listened to the soaring rhetoric of Dr. King's "I Have a Dream" speech.

My heart trembled and my skin was covered with goose bumps, not only during Dr. King's speech but also when John Lewis, Bayard Rustin, Roy Wilkins, and many others spoke so passionately during that historic event. I had wanted to go so badly. Buses were going from Memphis, but Mama would not let me go.

We were one of the few families on our little street with a TV. So our living room was filled with adults and children watching the march together. I took this occasion to brag about the fact that I had met and shaken Dr. King's hand and that I had even been to his house and met Mrs. King. Boy, did that get me some Brownie points! Everybody kept saying, "You've met Dr. King?" "You've been to Ebenezer Baptist Church?" "You've been to his house?" I beamed with pride, but was careful about what I did and did not tell. I didn't want Mama to know that I was getting "mixed up" in the Movement.

When I got back to school, I resumed my SNCC volunteer work and started quietly trying to recruit other Spelman women to volunteer. I succeeded in getting a few. That fall I was elected by the Atlanta University Student University organization—the Committee on Appeal for Human Rights (COAHR)—to serve on SNCC's board, its coordinating committee, from the Atlanta University Complex (the six traditional black colleges in Atlanta: Atlanta University; Clark, Morehouse, Morris Brown, and Spelman colleges; and the Interdenominational Theological Center). A part of me knew I should not have accepted that nomination and run for that office, as it would be hard to keep my deepening involvement with SNCC a secret from the school and, by extension, Mama if I were elected. My growing commitment to SNCC and my pride at being selected by my peers got the best of me.

Secret No Longer

In many ways you could say that this was the beginning of my new life. I did my best to balance my schoolwork with my new SNCC duties, but it was becoming harder not to participate in the demonstrations, which were increasing in number and intensity. SNCC was targeting several downtown restaurants, including Shoney's Big Boy restaurant, Lester Maddox's Pickrick restaurant, and the Krystal chain. When I first decided to join the line along with several of my Spelman sisters, we marched with the demonstrators, triumphantly singing, "Ain't gonna let nobody turn me around," through the AU Center, the black neighborhoods, and into white-dominated Atlanta. I calmed my fears by promising myself that I would not get arrested, no matter what. I convinced myself that if the police ordered us to leave or be arrested, I would quietly excuse myself, without guilt, as my future hinged on Spelman's not becoming aware of my involvement. I was committed, but I wasn't crazy! *No one should expect me to give up my future,* I angrily told myself, irritated that fate had put me into such a bind in the first place. At that moment, and as my involvement deepened, I hated whites—at least some of them—for what they were doing to me and to my people. *Why do white people put other human beings who happen to be of a different skin hue in this predicament? Why are they so mean and low down,* I wondered. *Why do they hate Negroes, who have always been so loyal to them and this country?* It was such a dilemma, because the Spelman women who had joined me on the demonstration included three white exchange students: Pam Parker and Karen Haberman from Carleton College in Minnesota and Mardi Walker from the Connecticut College for Women. They also were volunteering at SNCC. It was all so damn complicated; the contradictions were too great.

My strategy worked for a while, but alas, I wasn't able to leave one of the demonstrations in front of Maddox's restaurant. A bunch of us were arrested, including Spelman friend Barbara Simon, a wild black woman who feared no one and nothing! It was comforting to be with her. *Well,* I thought, *This is it!* But I didn't give a damn at that moment. I had stood up to those cops with their German shepherds and to white Atlanta. We black people were going to get our freedom, our rights, and our dignity, no matter what! What the hell if I lost the scholarship and got thrown out of school? *Sometimes a woman has got to take a stand and do what she's got to do,* I thought, consoling myself as I looked through the bars of the paddy wagon. *I'm going to jail! I'm really going to jail!* This, too, was a first in my family. First college and now jail. The paddy wagon literally shook with our singing, clapping, stomping, and shouting, "Oh, freedom, Oh, freedom, and before I'll be a slave, I'll be buried in my grave!" The white cops snarled, "You niggers better keep it down back there before we give you something to shout about." Undaunted, we sang even louder. For the moment it was fun.

We arrived at the jail and were ushered in none too politely. One by one we were booked and led off to the bullpen with the other women already incarcerated there. This was a sobering sight. I think I would have died from fright if I had been in there alone. We sang freedom songs, told jokes, smoked cigarettes, and huddled together for safety throughout the night as we awaited word from SNCC's lawyer. As well as I can remember, we Spelman women were locked up just overnight before attorney Howard Moore's lovely smiling face appeared with the papers that secured our release. Boy, was I glad to see him. Now came the really scary part—returning to campus to face the music there. Howard grinningly told us that we had made the front page of the *Atlanta Constitution* that morning: "Spelman Girls Arrested for Disorderly Conduct in Desegregation Attempt at Local

Restaurant." He said, "You're famous!" I groaned in disbelief. This was definitely not good news. As expected, there was trouble. I was called into the dean's office and asked why I had left the campus without permission, lied on the dorm sign-out sheet, and disobeyed the school's regulations regarding participating in civil rights demonstrations. She reminded me that I was there on scholarship, which I was putting in serious jeopardy. Last, but certainly not least, she had called my grandmother. My record would be reviewed, and I was to call home immediately!

Making that call was one of the worst moments of my life. Of course Mama was very upset. She said that I had disgraced the family and reminded me that I was the first person in our family ever to be arrested. She sounded so sad, so pained. Her voice was low and husky. It was the same tone she had used all my life just before she would go out to the backyard and cut a strong switch from a peach tree to give me a whipping. Thank God there was more than four hundred miles between us! She said that the dean had told her I could lose my scholarship and be expelled from school. She told me that if the school didn't kick me out and send me home in disgrace, I had better mend my ways and stay clear of those marches and this "SNICK" organization (she said it with such venom), whatever it was. Clearly my wee hope that Mama would be proud of me for going to jail for Negroes' rights was dashed. I had seen her stand up to some white policemen (with a shotgun across her forearm) who were roaming around without authorization in our backyard late one night "looking for a suspect." Hadn't she told me the stories about Grandma Lucy during slavery and her own struggles as a sharecropper with unscrupulous white landowners? Hadn't she told me all my life, "White people are dirty; they'll kill a Negro just as soon as look at them"? Why wasn't she proud that I was standing up to them and fighting for what was rightfully ours? I knew that if she didn't support me, my mother and father, who had questioned my going off to school in the first place, certainly would not understand. I was heartbroken. I went to my room, got in my bed, and cried until my pillow was wet. When I went to dinner at Chadwick Hall that night, my legs felt like lead, and my heart was quivering with fear and anxiety over being thrown off campus and forced to go back home to Mama in disgrace.

No one can imagine my joy and surprise when I entered the dining hall and many of my Spelman classmates stood up and cheered, singing "For She's a Jolly Good Fellow." "Speech, speech!" they shouted. Now I knew why my roommate, Smithy Tuggle, had made me get out of bed and go to dinner instead of bringing my meal to me as I had requested so that I could hide in my room awaiting the news of my fate. I felt better knowing that many of my friends and others I knew only slightly thought I had done a good thing.

By the grace of God, I was spared. The administration put me on probation for "lying" and "bringing dishonor" to the college. From then on I really tried to hide my ongoing activities, but my conflict was worse than ever. I had been bitten by the bug of resistance. There was no turning back for me, but I still wanted to finish college and make something of myself. For the most part, I went to the demonstrations but stayed out of jail. But later, several of us Spelman women launched our own campaign against the Krystal chain in downtown Atlanta over a two- or three-day period. We talked it over with Jim Forman and others at SNCC, who thought it was a good plan. As soon as black people went in, the restaurants would put a Closed sign in the window and even lock the doors so that no one else could enter. Our strategy was to go from Krystal to Krystal with white students first and Barbara and me following. After they would close, we would leave and go to another one and do the same thing, and then we would repeat this, beginning early in the morning right through the lunch hour, when the restaurants did most of their business. The plan was to hurt them financially and to hurt them badly. We thought that since they were a national chain, affecting their bottom line would make them give up their segregationist policies. Jim Forman assigned two or three of the local Atlanta male regulars to accompany us at a distance in case we were attacked.

By our third day, we had been able to keep all three of the Krystals closed for most of the two previous days. On this day when we went in and sat down, they announced, as usual, "We are closed; please pay the cashier for your purchases and leave as quickly as possible." The waitresses were livid. So was the manager, who immediately put the Closed sign up. What was different was that they steamed the windows so that no one could see in or out of the all-glass front. The waitresses had a "cat that swallowed the canary" look. All of a sudden several young white men came running from the back with sticks and clubs in their hands, attacking us with a fury. The manager and the waitresses joined the fray. Before I could think, I had jumped across the counter, trying to get away from one of the male attackers, only to be jumped by one of the waitresses. When she grabbed one of my arms and embedded her fingernails into my flesh with such fury that I began to bleed, I punched her with all my might and shoved her away from me. Then I began throwing cups, saucers, and dishes at the attackers, trying to keep them off of me. My sisters were also attempting to defend themselves. Suddenly there was a loud crash, and the three SNCC guys who had been assigned to us crashed through the plate-glass door and began to beat our attackers. The place was in a shambles, and a bloody row was in progress when "Atlanta's Finest" came in. They arrested all of us, but none of our attackers.

Needless to say, we were charged with a number of crimes, including: inciting to riot, rioting, disorderly conduct, assault and battery, and destruction of private property. I had been only slightly injured, but my heart was pounding so hard, I felt as if I were going to have a heart attack as I sat in the paddy wagon with my Spelman sisters. This was really *it*. I couldn't imagine what the headlines would read this time—or, rather, I could. It was really going to be "bye-bye Spelman."

Attorney Howard Moore really had to struggle to get some of the charges dropped and our bail reduced. He also called upon the Spelman administration to intervene on our behalf. We languished for three days while negotiations were in process. It seemed like a lifetime. Sleeping on the iron slabs with no mattresses and no blankets, carrying out our bodily functions in full view of all the others in the pen, and trying to stay clear of the amorous advances of some of the female inmates was a trying experience. We survived on the half-rotten bologna-on-white-bread sandwiches and Kool-Aid. We were unable to shower and had no change of clothes, so we were very rank when we finally tumbled out of those dank quarters into the bright Atlanta sunlight.

Somehow I had kept my mind off the fate that I knew awaited me. My probationary period had just ended, and here I was, in trouble all over again. Plus, I had been getting some unwanted attention from Spelman's administration because of the rallies I had been helping to promote on campus related to more campus freedoms. We were kept on a very tight leash in those days. Up until junior year, coeds could only sign out to the library or another dorm after 6:00 P.M. on weekdays, and only to social events on the Morehouse or Spelman campuses or to the one neighborhood theater on weekends. You had to get special permission to do anything else! So, tired, smelly, and scared, I arrived on campus and went right to my room, but not before seeing that look of disapproval on the face of Mrs. Gordon, our housemother. We had of course made the newspapers again. You would have thought we had been caught trying to rob a bank from the way the story was written.

At least they let me have a good night's rest before I was hauled in before both the dean and the president. Ironically, Spelman's president, Dr. Albert E. Manley, a distinguished-looking black man, asked me if I were a Communist and if I had been sent to foment dissent and chaos on the campus. A Communist? I hardly knew what that was. A *paid* instigator? Boy, I was as poor as Job's turkey with hardly a penny to my name. I wished somebody *were* paying me to catch the hell I was catching. It was left to the dean to tell me that my scholarship had been suspended and that I should start packing my things. Her office would call my parents to find out if they would be able to pick me up. While I expected the worst, hearing it for real caused me unimaginable pain. A part of me wanted to throw myself at her feet, sobbing and begging for another chance. Another part, however, wouldn't let me grovel. That part won out, and so I rose slowly when dismissed, mumbling something unintelligible as I exited her office. I hardly remember making it back to my room. I felt numb, hollow, frightened. The tears fell in torrents once I was safely in my room with only Smithy Tuggle, my room-mate, to hear my sobs. Word spread like wildfire, and unbeknownst to me, Smithy and some of my friends began planning a protest march demanding that Spelman reinstate the women who had been arrested—with no loss of scholarship money. The next day more than a hundred students and SNCC workers marched to the president's house and held a rally singing freedom songs and making speeches about our bravery. They threatened to organize a boycott of classes and to get their brothers over at Morehouse College to do the same if all of us were not reinstated. A number of Morehouse men and SNCC organizers joined the rally. In particular, the SNCC folks declared they would turn the campus out if Barbara Simon and I weren't reinstated. The exchange students were not in the same kind of trouble. In fact, they would most likely be seen as heroes on their liberal campuses. Some of the folks sat in on the president's lawn, and others burned him in effigy. It was a hell of a time on the ole campus. I could hardly believe what I was seeing. My sisters and friends had come to my defense, even when, in the case of the Spelman women, they were endangering themselves!

While I didn't think I would be reinstated, I was so proud of my sisters and grateful to my SNCC pals. Plus, Jim Forman assured me that I did not have to go home if I didn't want to. I was over eighteen, and I could stay and work with SNCC and move into the freedom house where many of the SNCC staff lived. Miraculously, both Barbara and I were permitted to stay, but under strict probation. The exchange students were not expelled either. My friends had saved the day.

The Big Decision

Something bigger was on the horizon for me, though I was only faintly aware of it. During the months I had served on SNCC's coordinating committee, a plan was being finalized for the Mississippi Freedom Summer Project scheduled for the summer of 1964 across the state. I was so excited about the project. In my joint history/English class, which had continued into my sophomore year, Staughton Lynd was working on developing some of the curricula for the Freedom Schools, so I had an opportunity to help both in and out of class. I wanted to go, knowing I would be one of the relatively few black college students to participate. I was terrified at the prospect of spending three months in Mississippi. I could visualize being caught by some rednecks, raped and tortured before being shot, and thrown into a creek tied to a bale of cotton to keep my body from floating to the top. Those gruesome pictures of Emmett Till's remains in *JET* magazine's centerfold haunted my thoughts and my dreams as I tried to figure out how I could persuade Mama to let me go. I talked to Vincent Harding, Staughton Lynd, and some of the Spelman women who were also thinking of going. I also talked to SNCC's Mississippi staff about the conditions in the state and how they were surviving. Deep in my heart, I knew I had to go, even though my rational mind was still objecting and my fear was great. I needed them to tell me that it was going to be one of the greatest events in the history of black people in my lifetime and in the struggle for the expansion of democracy in America. Jim Forman, Vincent and Rosemary Harding, Staughton Lynd, Ruby Doris Robinson, and many others whom I loved and trusted encouraged me to go. I was convinced.

The next challenge was getting Mama to let me go. After much thought I decided she would never agree to it, given her fear and hatred of Mississippi. But I was nineteen and legally an adult; I didn't really need her permission. SNCC folks said I could stay at the SNCC freedom house or with one of the staff after my final exams and then go with the crew to the orientation session in Oxford, Ohio, where I would be assigned to a project for the summer. After that I could go home safe and sound and all would be forgiven. *Yes,* I thought, *all would be forgiven, and there is a tooth fairy.* I quietly shared my plans with a few trusted friends on campus, swearing everyone to secrecy. I filled out the application and was accepted. Yes! I would be a part of this history-making event. I reassured myself that I would stay just for the summer and be back at school in time for the fall 1964 semester.

The Big Break

Somehow I got through the remainder of my second semester and took my exams while running over to the SNCC office every chance I had, to keep abreast of the preparations for the summer project. Things were really jumping, and they needed all the help they could get with every conceivable task. I helped with typing, mimeographing (this was before the days of the photocopier), and working in the print shop, helping with the pamphlets, ballots, registration forms, Freedom School primers, Mississippi Freedom Democratic Party (MFDP) posters, signs, and so forth. It was exhilarating to be a part of this important moment. Command Central was 8½ Raymond Street, and I was there helping to make it happen.

After my exams I began packing my trunk and suitcases in preparation for my move-in with SNCC friends. Early one morning, before either Smithy or I was out of bed, there was a knock on our dorm door. Mrs. Gordon was calling, "Miss Robinson, Miss Robinson, get up and get dressed; you have guests." I couldn't imagine. Then a voice I knew all too well called out, "Gwen, it's Mama. Your mother, Reverend Watson, and I have come to take you home. Hurry up and get dressed!" My heart began to race. What on earth were they doing here? I had already packed to move in with SNCC friends. I meekly said, "Yessum, I'm coming." I was fighting back the tears. Everything was ruined. They must have found out. Oh, my God, what could I do? I had to tell the folks at SNCC. But the only phone in the dorm was in Mrs. Gordon's office, and she would be guarding that like a hawk. My only recourse was to hurriedly write notes for Smithy to deliver to Jim Forman and Staughton to let them know what had happened and that I still wanted to go. Fighting tears and humiliation, I finished packing my things, got dressed, and met Mama and the others in the office. They were all somber. Mama told me that the dean had learned of my plans and had alerted them, advising them to come and get me. She told me how ashamed she was that I was planning to run off with these SNICK people to "God-awful-Mississippi!" She couldn't believe it. She said she thought those "SNICK Negroes" had hypnotized me, possibly putting something in my food to make me go crazy. "Thank God," she said, "the dean found out and alerted us so that we could bring you home before you take your fool self off to Mississippi and get killed trying to get Negroes to vote. Don't you know that those Mississippi crackers are going to kill up a bunch of you crazy kids?" she asked, her voice breaking. I rolled my eyes and said nothing. I rode all the way back to Memphis in stony silence. Mama said that I still wasn't too big to get a beating! She assured me that when I looked back on that day, I would thank her for saving me from those Mississippi peckerwoods.

I was literally kept a prisoner when we got home. Mama intercepted all of my mail, monitored all of my phone calls, and I was practically penniless. One girlfriend, Geraldine Shaw, had her own phone and car and let me call the SNCC office and Professor Lynd. SNCC agreed to send a money order to cover the bus fare, but Mama opened it and destroyed the money order. When she told me about it later, I was really angry. Tension had been building in the house since our return from Atlanta. I had been sulking the whole time and saying very little. I called Dr. Lynd and asked if he would send another money order, this time to Geraldine's house. When that money order came, I told Mama that I was over eighteen and she could not stop me. She, my mother, and my dad all threatened, begged, and pleaded with me not to go. Both Mama and my mother cried. My dad was angrier than I could remember. His position was to let me go. "She'll see," he said, "she has a hard head! Two years of college have turned her into a fool." As she continued to cry, Mama said that I would be raped and killed. Both my mom and my dad blamed my grandmother. In their opinion, I should have stayed right there at home and gone to LeMoyne College.

When Geraldine came to pick me up to take me to the bus station, Mama said that if I left I could never come back! This was it, as far as she was concerned. With a heavy heart, I put my bags into Geraldine's car and, as we drove off, looked at the angry and sad faces of Mama, my mother, and my dad. While I had stuck to my guns at the house, once Geraldine backed out of McComb Street and started up Pearce en route to the bus station, all of my bravado began to crumble. I began imagining all of the horrible things that most likely awaited me. After purchasing my bus ticket, I had a little less than ten dollars left. Ten dollars between me and the cruel world, without the love and support of my family. Doubt assailed me from all sides. I cried all the way to Atlanta. Clearly I had embarked upon a major new phase in my life, a bleak one, it seemed, which could lead to my death.

I was met at the bus station by Dr. and Mrs. Lynd, who warmly welcomed me to their home on Spelman's campus, until the Freedom Summer orientation. I was put on staff and began receiving my ten-dollar-a-week salary. As SNCC staff I was given a job as an assistant trainer for the orientation. The first week's daytime hours were filled with workshops on issues ranging from African American history, to the philosophy and strategic use of nonviolent resistance, to practical issues like what to do if you're stopped by lawmen, how to use walkie-talkies, and other important lessons. The SNCC organizers were dead serious and tried to convey that to all the participants. But many of the white students couldn't believe they would really be in any danger. Several of them asked, "How bad can it be? This is still America." Our evenings were filled with cookouts, songfests, and all-night parties. During the workshop breaks, we lay out on the lawns getting to know one another as we absorbed the Ohio sun.

Many Ohio white people were disturbed by the gatherings. Headlines both in and out of state screamed, "Black Men and White Women Engaged in Orgies at the Mississippi Freedom Summer Orientation." Interestingly, there was no mention of black women and white men. My white Spelman friend, Karen Haberman, and I were physically attacked at a convenience store by several burly white men. They chased us, hurling expletives, and we barely made it to her Volkswagen Bug and locked the doors. They beat on the car, calling us "nigger" and "nigger lover." We were terrified as they tried to overturn the car. By the grace of God, some men from the orientation showed up at the store and faced off with these big bullies, who backed off rather than fight. How could this be? We were up north!

Around the third day of the second orientation, we were pulled away from our training and called into the auditorium. Some of the leaders (I remember Bob Moses, Vincent Harding, and James Forman in particular) were on the stage with very grim expressions. They told us that three of the civil rights workers had disappeared in Mississippi. I remember Bob speaking barely above a whisper. If they were missing, we were told, they were most likely dead! The room became extremely still. The shock of what Bob had said sent us all reeling. Oh, my God, many of us had just seen them, watched them pull off, and wished them well. I had met James Chaney, his mother, and his sister at the first week's orientation. The men couldn't be dead! We all became very serious from that moment on. I imagined that the white students in the room could not believe that two white men had been killed by other white men for trying to help black folks get the vote! They had said earlier; "This is still America, isn't it?" Even I was shocked that they had killed white men!

Bob, Jim, and the others gave all of us the option to go home with no questions asked. After that session, many of us milled around talking about whether we should leave and go home or continue on our mission. Only one or two people left. I felt that I didn't have an option. I couldn't go home after what Mama had said.

I was assigned to Laurel, Mississippi, along with Jimmy Garrett, a black college student from Los Angeles, and Lester McKinney, a SNCC field secretary from Washington, D.C., who had worked in Laurel before. Only three of us, all black. Because Laurel was a stronghold for the Ku Klux Klan, with little to no infrastructure, it was too dangerous to send in white people, as they would attract too much attention. I couldn't believe that I was one of three people going to work in an all-black project because it was too dangerous for white volunteers! The whole idea, I thought, was to bring in white students so as to open up the state and in some sense let them act like shields against the violence. I was none too happy at the prospects for the three of us.

That was one scary ride into the state. Since I couldn't drive a car at the time, I sat in the back while Lester and Jimmy sat up front. My way of dealing with the terror of entering Mississippi was to sleep almost all the way there. It was an un-refreshing sleep, as I had nightmares about Emmett Till and the three missing workers. This was the most frightening experience of my life so far. When the guys woke me up to tell me we were in Mississippi, I could hardly believe it. It was so green and beautiful. To my amazement, from its physical appearance there was no indication of the evil that lurked there. It was a pretty place.

Mississippi Project Director

Initially, no residents in Laurel agreed to house us, so we had to sleep in Hattiesburg, thirty miles south, for the first two or three weeks, driving up to Laurel every day to scout out the prospects. We had the names of three people who had been active in the Laurel NAACP: Mrs. Suzie Ruffin, a Mr. Richardson, and a Mr. Simmons. We began meeting secretly with them and a few others. A number of black residents in Laurel wanted their city to be a part of the summer project. Two brave women, Mrs. Carrie Clayton and Mrs. Eberta Spinks, came forward and offered to house the three of us. We began looking for building space for our headquarters.

At first, many people were quite afraid. Everybody said that there was only one black landowner in town who owned a property large enough for what we needed. When we approached him about renting an old boarded-up nightclub, he flatly refused, so Mrs. Clayton said we could put the office in her house, too. We were reluctant to clutter up her lovely home, which we knew represented years of hard work, but she insisted. We compromised and used her back porch for more than half of the summer.

Jimmy, Lester, and I began walking the hot, dusty roads canvassing and soliciting people's participation in the summer project. A few days later, when Lester, the project director disappeared, everyone in our fledgling group feared the worst. After some of the black ministers intervened at our request, law officials admitted they were holding Lester on an old warrant. Lester had neglected to tell any of us he had violated a bond by missing a court appearance; the authorities had arrested him now and refused to let him out on a new bond. Jimmy and I were terribly upset for Lester and for the project. Lester was the seasoned SNCC worker; Jimmy was a California college student with no southern organizing experience. What little I knew I had learned in Atlanta attempting to desegregate lunch counters. Clearly, in my mind, neither of us could carry on the project without Lester or someone of his experience. A lawyer was sent in to get Lester out. The lawyer for the Council of Federated Organizations (COFO) got Lester out on the condition that he leave the county permanently or face five years in prison.*

I kept asking SNCC to send a replacement for Lester. I was told they had no one to send and I would have to be project director until they could find someone else. I couldn't believe what I was hearing! Jim Forman kept assuring me that I could do it. And do it I did, but not without a lot of fear and trepidation in the beginning.

* COFO was the sponsoring organization for the Mississippi Summer Project. The organizations involved in COFO included CORE (Congress of Racial Equality), NAACP, SCLC, and SNCC.

By the grace of God, the job was done. After Jimmy and I stabilized the project, we began recruiting housing for additional volunteers and urging COFO and SNCC to send us more people. And send them they did. All told, we had twenty-three volunteers, including two additional black college students. While handicapped in the beginning, the Laurel Project established a Freedom School, with a satellite freedom day-care center, held successful mock voter registration campaigns in which we registered hundreds of black residents, and had a good turnout for the mock elections. We built a strong Laurel chapter of the MFDP and selected the delegates for the state convention.

Mr. Golden, the wealthy black realtor who owned the boarded-up night-club, relented and offered his place to us "as is" at an exorbitant rent. I reluctantly agreed, as we had long outgrown our back porch office. Plus we had to close our office every time it rained! Although I agreed to the rent, I was furious that Golden thought nothing of ripping off the Movement. He kept saying, "It's just business. After all, I'm taking a real chance renting to you folks. Suppose crackers decide to burn the place down? I'll lose everything." As the place was in shambles, I thought he didn't have very much to lose. The local community helped us refurbish the old dump and turn it into a fairly nice office space, including a classroom/meeting room/library. We made the place operational in a couple of weeks.

One of our crowning achievements was the establishment of a fifteen-hundred-volume lending library. The volunteers got their families and friends involved in a book drive. We received books from many places in the country. Children and adults began to visit the library and borrow books. For many of the adults it was their first time ever in a library, because the Laurel Public Library was closed to the black community.

The project picked up momentum as the summer progressed. Many who were afraid at first began coming out to the meetings, all of which were first held in the smaller churches. Ironically those churches with the largest congregations and the most wealth were the most reluctant to open their doors to us. But as more people began participating in our activities, the larger churches were pushed by their members to let us in. The widely acclaimed New Orleans–based Free Southern Theater performed with their fantastic rendition of *Purlie Victorious* and *Waiting for Godot* at a number of project sites, including Laurel. I am fairly certain that this was a first for black people in Laurel, and these wonderful artists performed to packed audiences several times during their stay. Nationally known folk singers Len Chandler and Julius Lester also performed to packed churches in Laurel. I could hardly believe that the Laurel Project was not only surviving but also flourishing and with a relatively small amount of rancor and discord.

Although I was not aware of the concept for many years to come, I now know that I naturally used what some theorists call a "feminist style" of leadership, which was extremely democratic (sometimes to a fault). There were few top-down edicts from me as director. Some of my male codirectors in other projects were noted for their authoritarian leadership styles. As one of the few women project directors in the state, I was particularly sensitive to sexual harassment. One of my few nonnegotiable edicts was to disallow all forms of sexual harassment and to declare all underage local women off-limits to project males. There would be one warning and one warning only. If it happened again, out you went. Given the conservative nature of the community and our need to gain and maintain approval, I did insist on a dress code of no shorts in the streets and generally modest dress. Since the church was such a strong and respected institution in the community, we all had to attend church regularly, generally with our host families. Gender relations were difficult, to say the least. For many white Mississippi males this was the thing that galled them the most. They thought all black men wanted to rape all white women, so they were livid over the fact that white women were living in black homes where black men lived. Also, there was a mutual attraction between the black men and white women. I am sure that the forbidden nature of those relationships, even in the North, made the urge even more irresistible. Becoming a sexual relations counselor was another one of the tasks that was in my unwritten job description. Often this issue took up an inordinate amount of my time and taxed me the most.

Courtships among COFO volunteers were permitted but were to be carried out in a low-key way with no public displays of affection. We had to respect the moral code of the community, which was very strict in comparison to the lifestyles of most of the volunteers. As a black southerner, I was much more acquainted with these mores and therefore insisted that my insights on these matters had to be respected. I can recall one amusing episode when I reluctantly agreed to the volunteers' pleas to have a party at the Gores' house (where two of the volunteers lived) while the Gores were out of town. I agreed only after everybody promised not to get drunk or be loud. Well, given the pressure that we were all under, it was too much to expect that any of us could or would stick to that promise. We didn't. Folks got drunk, loud, and some even went out onto the lawn scantily clad, frolicking around and having a good time. The neighbors saw and heard us, and of course they reported it to the Gores. The word spread like wildfire about our all-night party, and we were practically run out of town. I caught most of the heat, as I was blamed for participating and letting it happen. Needless to say, we never did that again. We started driving to Jackson or Gulfport for our partying.

Though I was just a girl, I had to grow up real fast and assume an air of authority, especially with the white male volunteers, who could not believe that a black girl younger than they were was the project director. Boy, did I learn a lot about the northern liberal brand of racism and about male sexism. I had been thrown into a fast-moving river, and I had to learn to swim the rapids. I nearly drowned many times. Allah alone sustained me.

There are so many examples of God's grace throughout my time in Mississippi. I basically taught myself to drive on one of our donated cars, an old 1953 Chevy sedan, with a stick shift, of course. So many times I ran into ditches and would have to crawl out, leave the car, and walk back to town or to a nearby farm to get some men to help me pull the car out. One of the volunteers, who came late in the summer, was a race car driver who taught me how to drive, and I do mean drive. I am sure this is why I survived several high-speed chases, driving close to a hundred miles an hour while being chased by rednecks with guns.

I remember facing off with the sheriff at a sit-in at a small diner downtown. He leveled a gun at my chest and told me to turn the demonstrators around or he would fire. I was so afraid, but the demonstrators were mostly kids, and I felt that I had to stand up to him, not show my fear. I kept walking toward him, whispering a prayer as I walked. For some unknown reason, he let me and the scraggly line of demonstrators pass him and carry out our demonstration until we dispersed. He laughed and, holstering his gun, said, "Gal, you sure is crazy; you gonna git your damn self kilt one of these days." I thought, *I'm working God overtime today!*

Our work was possible because of Laurel's strong indigenous leadership, which was central to our recruitment efforts. Of course we faced strong opposition from many white people. This was Ku Klux Klan territory. One of the most devastating acts was their firebombing of our offices and beautiful fifteen-hundred-volume library. What Golden had predicted actually occurred, and they did burn his building, which was uninsured. Over the summer, crosses were burned, people's jobs were threatened and lost, and all of us were harassed by both city and county officials. There were arrests and death threats. On more than one occasion the Klan held counter-demonstrations. For some of the older black people, seeing Klansmen in their robes was a frightening thing, as historically someone was lynched whenever the Klan paraded. Also, the FBI agents who were supposed to be our protectors acted more like spies than protectors. The threats were so intense that Mrs. Spinks had begun sitting up all night with her shotgun at the ready in case there was an attack upon her or Mrs. Clayton, who lived across the street. She would laugh and say, "They might get me, but I'm going to get one or two of them first." She was so wonderful; she would tell me, "Sleep soundly, honey. Mrs. Spinks ain't going to let no one harm you. They'll get to you over my dead body!" She and so many others in Laurel and across that state were willing to give their lives for us and the Movement.

The summer sped by, and all of us who had come as volunteers had to decide whether we would go or stay in Laurel to continue the work that we had begun. It was a difficult issue for all of us. I knew that the white reactionary forces were just waiting for the COFO volunteers to leave, especially the white ones, so that they could step up their reign of unfettered terror. While Mrs. Spinks, Mrs. Clayton, and all the others would not ask us to put our educations on hold, I could see their concern for the future without all the human and material resources that we brought with us. I felt a real commitment to this community.

Staughton Lynd, knowing of my difficulties at Spelman, had gotten me into Antioch College in Yellow Springs, Ohio. So here I was in Laurel, Mississippi, trying to decide whether I should avail myself of a full scholarship to Antioch or stay in Laurel. With a heavy heart, I decided to stay; I couldn't do otherwise. I asked Antioch for a semester extension, which they granted. Two of the white female volunteers, Marian Davidson from Pasadena, California, and Linnel Barrett from Compton, California, also stayed. The three of us would spend a total of eighteen months in Laurel.

Somehow during the summer I acquired a reputation of being an "Amazon," which meant "She don't take no shit, especially off of men!" My sexual harassment policy was converted to "She hates men" by some of my male colleagues. A "car incident" added to my Amazon notoriety. SNCC was given a fleet of more than twenty-five brand-new cars. I had been begging for a good fast car, as the two or three that we had were old ones, donated to the project. I had hoped that we might have gotten some special consideration during the car distribution, given the amount of Klan activity in Jones County. After I had harassed the Atlanta and Jackson offices for weeks over our need for a car, they told me there was a 1964 Plymouth Valiant that had been seized by the sheriff in Holly Springs. I was told, "If you've got the nerve to go get it, it's yours." One of the local Laurel male activists (who said he was afraid of nothing and nobody) and I went to get it. He reluctantly agreed that I should actually go into the sheriff's office and ask for the car, thinking that because I was a woman, they might not beat me up or throw me in jail. I recalled the two earlier attacks on me by white males when the fact that I was a woman sure didn't seem to mean a thing.

So I was really afraid when I went in with the duplicate papers to try to retrieve the car. I decided to try to use my heaviest southern drawl and act like a "dumb colored girl," with the hope that I could soothe the sheriff's ire, perhaps retrieve the car, and not end up in jail. By the grace of God, it worked. I tolerated a lot of sexual innuendoes and racial slurring, but I walked out with the keys and the original papers to the car. The sheriff told me that I had better know what I was doing getting caught up with these "outside agitators." He said he just couldn't understand how a nice girl like me had gotten my fool self involved in this mess, since I knew as well as he did that "Nigras" didn't know nothing about voting and running for office. I said enough yassirs and nawsirs to get out of there with my hide and my car.

On the way back to Laurel, I stopped in the COFO office in Jackson to show them the car they had challenged me to try to get. The male worker whose car it had been made some threatening noises about taking it away from me. I let him know in no uncertain terms that anybody who tried to take that car away from me was going to have to leave the state to keep it, as I would go after him across the state to get "my" car back. I implied that I would be packing. Of course my threat was backed up by my Laurel comrade who had risked his life by going with me to get the car. He was a big, burly dude with a serious attitude. It helped that he also had a serious crush on me. With my ire and his backing, I kept the car!

In reality I was really a little proud of the title Amazon. To me it meant that I had come of age. I had proven myself worthy of being called a SNCC field secretary, and, more impressively, I had joined the ranks of those known as the Mississippi field staff, considered the baddest, baddest, baddest organizers in SNCC.

GWENDOLYN ZOHARAH SIMMONS continued to work for SNCC until 1968. Immediately afterward she worked for the National Council of Negro Women (NCNW) as their Midwest field representative for Project WomenPower. After two years with NCNW, Simmons worked on the staff of the American Friends Service Committee (AFSC) for more than twenty years, traveling to war-torn areas of the world, including Cambodia immediately after the fall of the Pol Pot regime, and Vietnam and Laos after the end of the Vietnam War. At AFSC she also worked on civil liberty issues, helping to expose the illegal activities of various U.S. intelligence agencies. She also returned to college in the 1980s to finish the education she interrupted to work full-time in the Movement. She received her BA from Antioch University and her MA and PhD degrees from Temple University in Philadelphia. She is currently an assistant professor of religion at the University of Florida. Trained in Islamic studies, Simmons lived in the Middle East for two years researching the impact of Islamic law on the lives of women in this area, which became the topic of her dissertation. She is a seventeen-year student of Sufism and the mother of a feminist daughter, Aishah Shahidah Simmons, who produces documentary films.

PART 2

Entering Troubled Waters

Sit-ins, the Founding of SNCC,
and the Freedom Rides, 1960–1963

> Wade in the water. Wade in the water, children.
> Wade in the water. God's gonna trouble the water.
>
> —Spiritual/Freedom song

Women participated in all phases of the early sixties Civil Rights Movement, playing key roles in the sit-ins, the formation of the Student Nonviolent Coordinating Committee (SNCC), and the Freedom Rides. The February 1, 1960, sit-in that took place in Greensboro, North Carolina, is usually cited as the start of the modern southern student movement. Although four young men carried out that sit-in, some young women, like Angeline Butler, had already participated in earlier, less publicized sit-ins and were in training to take part in similar civil disobedience against southern segregation laws. Sit-ins were not a new tactic. Civil rights activists were sitting in during the 1940s, and quite a few groups in the Midwest and Upper South sponsored such protests in the late 1950s.

The beginning stories in this section, along with portions of the opening piece, focus on the sit-ins. In the year after Greensboro, more than fifty thousand people across the South participated in sit-ins and similar demonstrations. The overwhelming majority of the participants were students at black colleges and universities. They were supported by sympathy pickets in the North and in certain locations joined by southern white college students. The sit-inners opposed southern laws and practices that prevented black customers from sitting down in eating establishments yet required that they pay the same prices for the food as the seated white customers. Some places did not allow black customers inside the premises but had a walk-up window for them at the back. These rules were enforced even at the five-and-dime stores like Woolworth's, which were heavily patronized by black people. The students demonstrated their displeasure with this kind of segregation literally by sitting down and demanding service. Most sit-in efforts were backed up by a boycott of the stores in question as well as a boycott of all the downtown merchants. The establishments and institutions that took black people's money with one hand and doled out inequitable and demeaning treatment with the other remained targets of protests throughout the sixties movement.

These narratives suggest that black educational institutions and their surroundings provided fertile ground for the growth of the Movement, even when the administrations vigorously opposed their students' participation. In addition to bringing large groups of students together in close proximity, some schools provided grounding in black achievement, culture, and history. Some had their own history of civil rights activism or were located in cities with active movements. And some had one or more professors on campus with the kind of social consciousness that made them willing to encourage and support black student activism.

Quite soon after the sit-ins began, a number of students discussed the need for an organization to bring the various southern sit-in groups together. Ella Baker, then executive secretary of the Southern Christian Leadership Conference (SCLC), headed by Dr. Martin Luther King Jr., organized the April conference that resulted in the formation of SNCC, at her alma mater, Shaw University located in Raleigh, North Carolina. Miss Baker played a significant role in the southern black students' decision to remain independent of existing civil rights organizations, most notably, SCLC. The first year the students elected a Fisk graduate student, Marion Barry, as chairman; a year later they chose Chuck McDew, a South Carolina State student, as head. At first SNCC was primarily an information clearinghouse, providing a means of communication and sharing news about ongoing organizational activities among member groups. In 1961 SNCC began taking charge of projects and giving direction to the Movement as a whole, assisting various sit-in efforts and promoting a "jail, no bail" policy, most notably in support of the Rock Hill, South Carolina, Movement.

In the spring of 1961, SNCC's major project was the continuation of the Freedom Rides. The last three stories in this section focus on these rides, held after the U.S. Supreme Court banned segregated terminal facilities for interstate bus and train passengers in a December 1960 decision, *Boynton v. Virginia*. To test compliance with that decision, two small groups of black and white civil rights activists boarded buses in

Washington, D.C., in May 1961 and headed for New Orleans under the sponsorship of the Congress of Racial Equality (CORE). An interracial group founded in 1942, CORE advocated applying nonviolent civil disobedience tactics to civil rights activities and had sponsored an earlier ride, called a "Journey of Reconciliation," through the Upper South in the spring of 1947. Even before this organizational effort, black southerners, individually and in groups, had opposed segregation on trains and buses that traveled across state lines. The 1961 Freedom Riders were viciously attacked in Alabama by Klan-based mobs that bombed one of the buses and closed the Birmingham airport when some of the Freedom Riders tried to fly to New Orleans. Fearing that someone would be killed, CORE called off the rides.

Diane Nash, who had been chairman of the Nashville sit-in movement and was the first of the sit-in activists to leave school to work as a full-time civil rights organizer, became the prime mover in the effort to continue the rides. She insisted that valuable civil rights momentum would be lost if the rides did not continue. Allowing white mobs to stop movement activities, she predicted, would encourage even more mob action, resulting in even more bloodshed. A small group of Nashville students felt the same way. Certain they were facing death, about twenty young men and women made their way to Birmingham to restart the rides. This group included a more balanced proportion of women than the first two rides. In spite of being arrested by Birmingham chief of police Bull Connor, hassled and beaten by Klansmen along the way, and surrounded by a menacing white mob in Montgomery, most members of this group were able to make the trip into Jackson, Mississippi.

They were immediately arrested in Jackson, where the police beat several riders in the city jail. Following the "jail, no bail" principle, the Freedom Riders chose to remain in prison and invited other riders to follow, hoping to fill the jails. It is at this juncture that the Freedom Ride activities described in this section begin. As the city and county jails became overcrowded, Freedom Riders were sent to the Mississippi State Penitentiary, known as Parchman Farm, in the Mississippi Delta, one of the most-feared jails in the country. Over the next few months more than three hundred riders were arrested in Jackson. Many continued their protests in jail, using hunger strikes and other tactics. In addition to keeping the Freedom Rides alive, SNCC and CORE workers expanded the rides' impact by using them as a base to establish other kinds of civil rights projects in Jackson and other places in Mississippi.

The stories in this section and throughout the book describe the soul-searching young women underwent when deciding to participate in movement activities. Family relationships and academic goals had to be considered. Besides mob violence from the white community, black student activists might face adamant opposition from their families and from black college administrators. White women might discover their overall relationship to their families and communities permanently and drastically altered. For all, there was a sense of leaving the familiar and the comfortable and entering into the unknown.

Once in the Movement, women did face new social situations such as participating in interracial groups or interacting with local prisoners. At the same time, the Movement and SNCC immediately provided a solid base, a network, a community, and much camaraderie for female activists, who moved not in individual isolation but in the midst of an open, welcoming, and growing Civil Rights Movement.

Movement women also took on new and quite different activities. Usually the protests they held were not spur-of-the-moment actions but involved planning, organization, training sessions, support efforts, and a constant rethinking of strategies and tactics. Yet, even with considerable preparation, some women in the thick of the action were unable to maintain nonviolent discipline. Movement women who were not directly involved in confrontational actions still had to deal with the hate-charged environment and make courageous choices.

The Movement as a whole, and SNCC in particular, provided an entirely new context for women activists, dramatically expanding their notions of what they could do. In essence, they took on the task of changing their world. Their participation, in turn, immediately quickened the pace and intensity of struggle. Human relations talk sessions, Connie Curry notes, were replaced with direct action. Instead of an occasional bus boycott here one year and another somewhere else several years later, more confrontational and riskier activism was taking place on a daily basis all across the South. Making gradual change in liberal southern areas changed to attacking the unrepentant Deep South at its Black Belt core. The early southern black student movement altered the agendas of established civil rights advocates like the Southern Regional Council and inspired white student groups like the National Student Association and the fledgling Students for a Democratic Society toward a more active and powerful politics.

It was years before the segregation of public accommodations facilities was ended in most places in the South. Some of the sit-in activists in this book were picketing the same places in 1963 that had been targets in 1960, yet the writers express considerable exhilaration and a sense of power regarding their actions. The sit-ins and the Freedom Rides were particularly effective tactics. Whether the stools were taken out or the waiting room was closed rather than integrated, the place was no longer as it had been before and no longer labeled white only, and the white South, with all its methods of enforcement, had been unable to prevent the change. Even in the early experimental movement forays, segregation was shaken at its center. Most important, when the students entered the troubled waters of activism, they radically altered the southern scene by establishing a dynamic in which they were the actors and the white southern opposition the reactors.

What We Were Talking about Was Our Future

Angeline Butler

*A member of the Nashville Student Coordinating Committee
and founding member of SNCC participates in the discussions
and meetings that surrounded the nonviolent student movement.*

A New Phase of My Life

I grew up on a farm in Eastover, South Carolina, the adopted daughter of a
Baptist minister, Rev. Isaac Bartley Butler, and his wife, Emma. The early
part of my life was heavily influenced by nature—the woods that surrounded
me, the natural rivers, fishing streams, the fields in which we played. We all
walked many miles to school. After school and in the summers we worked
in the fields. White people lived all around us, and their children played
with me and my five sisters freely, without any regard to the color of our
skin or any other kind of differences. Those differences were taught to us
as we grew older and began to go to separate schools; then we began to ask
questions of our parents and eventually of the society.

In the fall of 1957 I left my rural home to attend Fisk University in
Nashville, Tennessee. That first year was psychologically and academically
challenging for me. When I boarded the Greyhound bus to go to college,
my father had to put me at the back of bus for the first time in my life after I
innocently plopped down on a second-row seat. Having been sheltered from
the more demeaning aspects of segregation, I experienced an emotional
shock that lasted throughout the year. Secondly, although I was chosen as a
soloist by Dennis Cowan, the conductor of the Fisk University Choir, which
was quite an honor for a first-year student, my heart was elsewhere. Since I
excelled in music, I had wanted to attend the Oberlin Conservatory of Music
rather than a liberal arts college. The conservatory had admitted me and
given me a scholarship, but someone accidentally took my father's briefcase
with the admissions material in it while he was attending a principals' meet-

ing in Charleston, South Carolina, at the end of August. It was just too late to contact all the offices involved and get the paperwork sent again before classes began at Oberlin. As a result, I ended up at Fisk pursuing a general curriculum instead of music. I was required to take classes in which I had no interest, like Western civilization, and other classes, like remedial math, to make up for the deficits of South Carolina's rural black schools.

In my sophomore year I developed other interests. I began attending the Nashville Friends Sunday morning discussions and other informal meetings and events at the home of Quaker faculty member Dr. Nelson Fuson and his wife, Marian. Discovering the larger world outside the small world we had known, we began to open our minds to new ideas regarding American politics and race relations. Here we began the process of intellectual and spiritual exploration that led us into social activism.

Some of my classmates—Peggy Alexander, Jean Fleming, Elena Gouch, Luther Harris, King Holland, Eleanor Jones, Jean McCray, Julia Moore, Joseph Rooks, and Maxine and Matthew Walker—along with upperclassmen Janiece Cochran (Miss Fisk) and Julius Lester, attended these meetings as well as three young men—James Bevel, Bernard Lafayette, and John Lewis—from the nearby American Baptist Theological Seminary, who were studying with activist theologian Kelly Miller Smith. Later, white exchange students Carolyn Anderson, Laura Greene, and John Nye along with transfer students Paul LaPrad, Diane Nash, and graduate student Marion Barry Jr. joined us at the Fusons' home. All of these students soon became active in the Nashville Movement. Shortly afterward, Carolyn, nicknamed Candy, married Guy Carawan, movement activist and folksinger, and Marion Barry Jr. became the first chairman of SNCC. I had met the three theology students at Fisk University's International Student Center. Through films and lectures held at the center, we learned about places outside the United States and discussed international issues. At the Fusons' we focused on a wide range of social problems within this country and how people with a certain kind of consciousness had dealt with these conditions as a model for what we could do to bring about social change and justice.

The Fusons were connected to Highlander Folk School in Monteagle, Tennessee. Founded in the thirties, Highlander was a center for exchanging ideas related to making social change. The center encouraged labor organizing and civil rights efforts among both black and white southerners. In the spring of 1959 the Fusons took a group of Fisk students to Highlander. There we discussed the South, race relations, and the change that needed to come to the South and met long-time activists like Septima Poinsette Clark, founder and organizer of the Citizenship Schools; Esau Jenkins, a Charleston, South

Carolina, community worker who had set up a bus service to help nearby Sea Islanders find employment and to try to get them registered to vote; and Myles Horton, labor activist and founder and director of Highlander. In the company of these older activists, we held informal self-exploratory discussions that allowed us to see ourselves in the larger scheme of things in the South and the world. We also discussed more democratic ways of organizing. The central idea of Highlander was that people needed to talk and listen to one another until they could discover some common ground, some agreement on what changes needed to be made. Once a consensus was reached, only then could a method be applied.

Highlander provided an opportunity for black folks and white folks to sit down together, to experience communication as human beings. We had dinner together, washed dishes together, slept in bunk beds in the same room side by side, laughed, and shared humorous stories. We were able to touch one another and to see up close the obvious differences. We had to realize we each had God's light within us, that we were all from the same source and deserved to share the same opportunity in life.

In the fall of 1959, also through the Fusons, I heard about the workshops on nonviolence at Clark Memorial Church. With the help of members of the Nashville Christian Leadership Council—Rev. Alexander Malachi Anderson, Rev. Metz Rollins, Rev. Kelly Miller Smith, Rev. C. T. Vivian, and others— Rev. James Morris Lawson Jr. organized and conducted the workshops. Lawson was a divinity student at Vanderbilt University and a field-worker with the pacifist organization called the Fellowship of Reconciliation. He had traveled to India as a Methodist missionary; while there he studied the philosophy of Mahatma Gandhi and had already served time in jail as a conscientious objector to the Korean War. I recruited other students from Fisk to attend the workshops: Peggy Alexander and Diane Nash were among the female students who responded. Mary Anne Morgan from Meharry Medical College in Nashville came also.

In these workshops what we were all talking about was our future. A new phase of my life began as we addressed the truth about our place in the society and how the society looked upon us as a people. We studied Mahatma Gandhi, the life of Jesus Christ, and Thoreau. Pretty soon we applied their teachings of nonviolence and civil disobedience to the fundamental inequality of people in Nashville's segregated society. We began to define clear targets that needed changing. We wanted access to all services in establishments where we spent money: lunch counters in five-and-dime stores, department stores, bus stations, and drugstores. We expected this would lead to changes in employment practices and economic change in the community. Then we felt the need to place our bodies and minds on the line and began the sit-ins and other demonstrations. We all knew that this was a new beginning and that our efforts would have an impact on our lives and the lives of Americans for all time.

In October and November 1959, small groups of students who attended the workshops also held test demonstrations and sat in at lunch counters to see what would happen and to bring the results back to the workshop for discussion. When we were threatened with arrests, we would leave peacefully. Then a week after the February first Greensboro sit-in, in response to calls from Greensboro activists, three hundred students sat in all over downtown Nashville. This caught the authorities by surprise and so no one was arrested. Before our third massive sit-in on the twenty-seventh of February, we received word from the chief of police that we would be arrested if we went downtown. The thirteen members of the Nashville Student Nonviolent Coordinating Committee canvassed the dorms for sit-inners the night before and met in the basement of Rev. Kelly Miller Smith's First Baptist Church early on the morning of the thirteenth. This committee included students from all the black colleges in Nashville—Fisk University, Meharry Medical College, Tennessee A & I University, and the American Baptist Theological Seminary.

There were many feelings, many issues to iron out before we could make the decision to go downtown. This was a difficult moment for all of us. We had to think about the repercussions for our parents and for ourselves. We would surely face expulsion from school, our only avenue to a decent living. We might have a criminal record, and we might be beaten or worse once inside the jail. Since all decisions were rendered collectively, it took several hours before the members of the committee reached consensus; we all agreed to hold the sit-ins. Those who did not want to be arrested would serve as runners between the various sit-in locations. We went upstairs to the sanctuary, where only forty-one students were waiting. We explained the situation and gave each student the choice of whether or not to join us.

One by one each of the students present raised a hand, choosing to go downtown and be arrested. I had tears in my eyes. We divided into small groups of six or seven. The group I led to McClelland's five-and-dime's counter included Maxine Walker, Paul LaPrad, John Lewis, Leslie Green, and Jean Fleming. We faced almost instant violence as the store filled up with shoppers and spectators. They threw things at us, yelled insulting remarks, and put burning cigarettes out on our backs. Paul LaPrad, a white transfer student to Fisk from DePauw University, was badly beaten by two young white men.

The police put the two white youths out of the store, arrested Paul, and made us leave the counter. Once outside, when I realized only Paul was under arrest, I gathered my group and Bernard Lafayette, who was on the outside coordinating from store to store, and we all went back into

McClelland's. Finding the lunch counter roped off, we stepped over the ropes, took a seat, and did not move until all of us were arrested. The chief of police himself put us in the paddy wagon, making ours the first arrests of the Nashville sit-in movement.

On that day, group after group was arrested until there was no more room in the Nashville jail. In the morning only the thirteen members of the coordinating committee and forty-one students in the church sanctuary were involved in the sit-ins. But when students on the different campuses heard of our arrests, they headed down to the First Baptist Church, and James Bevel, Rev. C. T. Vivian, and Rev. Kelly Miller Smith sent them downtown to various business establishments, such as Walgreen's drugstore, Kress's five-and-ten, Harvey's department store, and Cain and Sloan's department store, and by the end of the day at least one hundred students had gone to jail. Pictures of some of the students peering out from behind jail bars appeared in the local newspaper and in *Life* magazine. Filmmakers Robert Young and Michael Roemer made a one-hour documentary about our activities for NBC television titled "White Paper Series Number 2, Nashville Sit-In," narrated by Chet Huntley and David Brinkley. Some parts of this early 1960 documentary were featured in more recent efforts, including the PBS series *Eyes on the Prize*.

Soldiers in the Army

Throughout the course of the Nashville demonstrations, Tennessee A & I, a state university, provided the greatest number of participants. Paul Brooks, Lucretia Collins, Kenneth Frasier, William Harbour, Lonnie Hubbard, Pauline Knight, Catherine Burke, and Rip Patton were some of the activists from there. In February 1960, after facing continuous arrests, jailings, court dates, and threats to bomb the dorms, sit-in demonstrators from all four schools retreated to Highlander Folk School for a weekend. The idea for SNCC was born at this weekend. Peggy Alexander, Marion Barry, James Bevel, Paul Brooks, Kenneth Frasier, Eleanor Jones, Bernard Lafayette, John Lewis, Mary Anne Morgan, Curtis Murphy, Diane Nash, me, and other members of the Nashville Student Coordinating Committee—along with Ella Baker, Septima Clark, the Fusons, Myles Horton, and several northern supporters, and Andrew Young—discussed, among other things, the need for a South-wide student organization. In April as many as five hundred of us met in Raleigh, North Carolina, to build a structure and to express some common concerns, goals, and direction for this phase of the Movement. A little later we met as SNCC in Atlanta. By this time more arrests had occurred, more legal issues had come up—for instance, students had been rearrested on state charges of conspiracy to obstruct trade and common commerce—and more questions had arisen about how to deal with the enlarging situation. Problem solving was required. How could we provide legal support and bonds for local student groups and develop better communications? How would we deal with violence committed toward us, and where would we go from there?

No matter where we were, we were always talking about the same thing: what was happening in the different areas, what we were going do when we got back to our state, and how we weren't going to let the white man stop us. How happy we were to be able to do this work. How close we felt to one another.

It amazed me how we got around then. Our trips were mainly on weekends and holidays, as we had to go to class during the week. Most of us had modest allowances of three to five dollars a week from our parents or our part-time work. Usually we pooled our resources to buy gasoline for the few small cars we owned. Sometimes adults volunteered to drive us.

When we traveled to Raleigh and to Atlanta for the first two SNCC meetings, we slept as many as forty people on a living room floor volunteered by local families. We would talk most of the night. Many times we would go to the school cafeterias and ask for the leftovers to pack lunches for our travels. Sometimes our hostesses would cook large pots of food for us. Julian Bond's family cooked for and entertained students after the first SNCC meeting in Atlanta.

During three years of demonstrations in Nashville, we all felt as one. There was equality of women and men. I don't believe we ever felt a difference between us. Though many romances occurred between males and females, when it came to who we were in our movement voices, the male/female distinction never came up. Human beings were speaking to each other around our common goals to get something done.

The Movement made each of us into a "one-person army" strong enough to take the lead wherever we could visualize that change was needed. Through our consciousness, developed in struggle, we could see the specific things to do, then design a course of action, and stand up for our beliefs. Change and revolution are created by individuals who react to a given situation, study it, envision a solution, then step forward and set activity in motion.

ANGELINE BUTLER continued going to jail for civil rights and played significant organizing roles in Miami CORE's Summer Project, the Freedom Rides, Route 40 demonstrations, and the March on Washington. She graduated from Fisk University, studied at Juilliard on scholarship, and earned a master's degree from Columbia University in ethnomusicology. She sang and recorded the folk album *The Pilgrims/Just Arrived* on Columbia Records and a solo album, *Angeline Butler Impressions,* on Co-Burt-MGM. She has played major roles in live New York theater productions. Early in her career she made frequent appearances on Johnny Carson's *Tonight Show,* the *Dick Cavett Show,* and Hugh Hefner's *Playboy after Dark* series.

She has written and produced a documentary play, *Voices of a Sit-in,* and her autobiographical scrapbook project is on permanent display in the Nashville Room at the Davidson County Library. She has taught in the ethnic studies department at the University of California and currently teaches in the African American studies department of John Jay College for Criminal Justice. In 2005 she worked on four of CBS's *La Nueva Estrella Awards* shows and is now a company member at the Metropolitan Opera. She received a Freedom Flame Award at the 2010 Selma Bridge Crossing Jubilee.

"What We Were Talking about Was Our Future" © 2010 by Angeline Butler

An Official Observer

Constance Curry

The first white member of SNCC's executive committee gathers the stories used to make the American public aware of the realities of segregation.

Nashville and Atlanta

On a cold afternoon in mid-February 1960, I stood outside Woolworth's five-and-ten-cent store in downtown Nashville, Tennessee. A group of African American students from Fisk University, Tennessee State, and the American Baptist Seminary had just sat on stools at the store's lunch counter and asked for service. I didn't know what to expect, but I was totally unprepared for the strange quiet and then the rush of angry white people from the streets into the store, followed by a swarm of police who arrested the students. It was my first experience with mob violence. I felt sick, sorry, and sad; mostly I wanted to run away.

Later I read in the newspaper that white hecklers had actually put burning cigarettes onto the backs and arms of the students. I was thankful I had not been stationed inside the store and witnessed the violence. The students, well trained in the techniques and philosophy of nonviolence, had remained seated and not responded to the jeers, threats, and burns. Thus began my career as an observer for many of the sit-ins, marches, and jail-ins that marked the early days of the Civil Rights Movement. As a young white southerner, I could observe without attracting much attention.

Early SNCC demonstrations were highly structured and strategically timed. People had designated roles, including captains, monitors, and observers. Captains kept the demonstrators organized. Monitors, usually the physically larger students or members of the community, provided a measure of security. In addition to watching and following each protest, observers alerted the SNCC office, the U.S. Justice Department, and the press when the demonstrators were arrested. Observers might also witness or testify at the subsequent trials. Although observers were supposed to be a safe distance from the action, sometimes they also faced danger.

In the fall of 1960 I was stationed by an elevator near the Magnolia Room restaurant in the downtown Rich's department store. Inside the restaurant, students from the Atlanta Committee on Appeal of Human Rights (COAHR) were holding a sit-in. I recognized the white man standing next to me, cursing and muttering invectives, as Calvin Craig, the local head of the Ku Klux Klan. When the students were arrested and marched past us, I prayed, "Dear God, please don't let any of the students look at me or show any recognition, because this man will surely do me harm." Thankfully, all of the students held their dignified composure and none of them even glanced at me.

Augusta, Georgia

In the spring of 1961, in Augusta, Georgia, I witnessed the most frightening attack of all at a demonstration held by Paine College students. Since the 1930s, Paine, a historically black college, had hosted an interracial annual statewide Christian conference. This conference was clandestine, since interracial gatherings were banned by the state's segregation laws. A few faithful white and black college ministers secretly took their students to the conference. Early in the spring of 1961, Paine students had formed the Paine College Steering Committee and had been conducting sit-ins in downtown Augusta. Silas Norman Jr., who later became a SNCC project director in Selma, Alabama, chaired the student committee. Rev. Richard Stenhouse,* an African American professor of religion, a Quaker, and a conscientious objector, was one of the group's three advisers and a conference host.

* Editors' Note: Reverend Stenhouse was the uncle of Janet Jemmott, whose story appears in part 5: "Get on Board." Jemmott also worked on SNCC's Alabama Project during some of the same time Paine College Steering Committee chair Silas Norman Jr. worked there. Jemmott later married Bob Moses, director of SNCC's Mississippi Project.

The students who came to the weekend conference that spring had a growing knowledge of the Freedom Movement because of the civil rights demonstrations taking place all across the South and were reinterpreting their duty as Christians to include political activism. Rev. James Lawson, a strong teacher and advocate for nonviolent training, was one of the conference speakers. On the Saturday of the conference, an integrated group of sixty students from the conference went downtown to sit in at the H. L. Green store.

The Augusta police, notified as usual shortly before the demonstration, did not put any security in place and withdrew all the regular police from the area, including traffic police. The police evidently informed enough local white people of the impending demonstration for a mob to assemble. Walking on the sidewalk in front of the store as a designated observer, I saw a white man emerge from the gathering white crowd directly in front of me, pull a knife, and stab William Didley, vice chair of the Paine student movement, in the chest. This happened so quickly that the movement security monitors did not have a chance to react. Didley had been stabbed right next to his heart, but he was rushed to the hospital and survived. I went into a state of shock, wandering down the street, looking into store windows, trying to assimilate what I had just witnessed. The police arrived shortly after the violence. Though he had been unarmed, Didley was charged with carrying a concealed weapon and inciting a riot. His attacker from nearby Bennettsville, South Carolina, was never charged. The last Paine College Christian Conference was held in 1963. By then, options for student involvement in social change included sit-ins, picketing, marching, voter registration—a wider vision—so that interracial conferences alone seemed to have outlived their usefulness.

At the same time that I was observing demonstrations for SNCC, I was establishing and directing the Southern Student Human Relations Project for the National Student Association (NSA). The project was funded by a Field Foundation grant and based in Atlanta. "Promoting better human relations between southern black and white college students" was the stated focus. With students taking part in direct action for social change, however, the initial goal of my project, "getting black and white students together to talk" about "common issues," suddenly became outmoded. I consulted the project's advisory committee, which consisted of eminent southerners who believed that some southern college students, both black and white, wanted an alternative to the segregation and racism that engulfed their lives. The committee included Rev. Will Campbell of the National Council of Churches; Dr. Rufus Clement, president of Atlanta University; Ruby Hurley, southeastern director of the NAACP; Dr. Benjamin Mays, president of Morehouse

College; and Ralph McGill, publisher and editor of the *Atlanta Constitution*. Understanding the importance of the burgeoning student movement and wanting to preserve the goals of the grant, the committee recommended that I should observe and report on the southern student movement to areas and associations outside the South. In this capacity I published a monthly newsletter chronicling movement events that went out to groups like the NSA and the National Federation of Christian College Students; some of their members then assisted the southern movement with northern support demonstrations and finances.

My role as an observer did not put me in the same kind of jeopardy that SNCC workers faced. I sometimes felt bad as I saw my friends being physically hurt or carted off to jail, but not once did I feel disdain or anger from them. This acceptance of one another was the basis of the beloved community that we were trying to build in those early days. It is also the bond that, for many of us, endures over the years and, no matter the length of separation, quickens our hearts.

A native of North Carolina, **CONSTANCE CURRY** attended SNCC's founding meeting in April 1960 with Ella Baker, whom she had recently met. After the conference both were made adult advisers and, as such, members of SNCC's executive committee. After directing the National Student Association project through 1964, she was southern field representative for the American Friends Service Committee for nine years, working for peaceful school desegregation in Mississippi. She also served as director of human services for the City of Atlanta from 1975 to 1990. An attorney and writer, she has authored *Silver Rights* (1995), *Aaron Henry: The Fire Ever Burning* (2000), and *Mississippi Harmony: Memoirs of a Freedom Fighter* (2002), and coedited *Deep in Our Hearts: Nine White Women in the Freedom Movement* (2000). More recently she produced a documentary film, *The Intolerable Burden* (2002), about public school resegregation and incarceration of youth of color. Currently an Institute for Women's Studies fellow at Emory University, she recently edited the memoirs of Bob Zellner, SNCC's first white male field secretary.

"An Official Observer" © 2010 by Constance Curry

Onto Open Ground

Casey Hayden

A white movement participant's oratory creates
a watershed experience for white college students.

Besides the sit-ins and the formation of the Student Nonviolent Coordinating Committee, the largest and most significant student political event of 1960 was the United States National Student Association (USNSA) Congress, held that summer at the University of Minnesota campus in Minneapolis and attended by about five hundred delegates. NSA was a national association of college student governments, whose primary concern in the United States at this time was campus issues. At the congress Connie Curry and NSA staff were working to pass legislation for NSA empowering the new officers to use the considerable resources of the organization to publicize and raise money for the southern student movement, which was using civil disobedience to protest segregation. It was rough sledding. These delegates were student government folk, mostly white, many from the South and all for law and order. The idea of supporting civil disobedience was not catching on.

SNCC folk tried to create the feeling of a mass meeting at their panel, but were unsuccessful. Southern white delegates demanded equal time. Desperate, NSA's national affairs vice president asked Connie if she knew a pro sit-in white southerner he could add to their panel. She suggested me.

The night before the plenary, I stayed up late writing and rewriting. My words then, as today, sound moderate and calm. I had thought this out before entering the movement in Austin the previous spring. I addressed the objections being raised about the sit-ins, emphasized how we whites were also limited by segregation laws, and made a moral appeal.

I was the last of the panelists to speak the next day. Twenty-two years old, I had a strong southern drawl and hardly spoke above a whisper. Using the gender and ethnic language of the day, wearing my cotton shirtwaist dress with the round collar, I stood at the front of the auditorium before a microphone, and said:

> I understand we on this panel are to represent different shades
> of opinion on the sit-ins. While I may fall within a certain shade of
> opinion, I speak neither for the sit-inners nor the southern white, but
> only for myself. I find the sit-in question to be essentially an ethical
> question, not a question of expediency or emotion. I do not mean

this to be abstract, for an ethical question means a personal decision. None of you can make this decision for me, nor would I attempt to make it for any of you.

Now, an ethical question is both utterly simple and confusingly complex. On this particular question, I only hope we do not lose its essential simplicity in the complexity. I would touch on the first point first—its simplicity. When an individual human being is not allowed by the legal system and the social mores of his community to *be* a human being, does he have the right to peaceably protest? Yes. No "buts," just "yes." Perhaps in this situation, protest is the only way to maintain his humanity.

I feel sure that everyone concurs with the statement I have just made. However, we may say this and add "but," and the complexities arise. First, the fear of violence. I can understand this. We certainly feared violence in Austin after hearing of Marshall.* But should a person who does not strike back be blamed because he is struck? I simply fail to understand why, if the presence of Negro students sitting quietly or white and Negro students sitting together is so infuriating to a mob that they resort to violence, the students should be blamed for the sickness of the mob.

Another complexity may be that you agree with this but simply do not think the sit-ins are *wise*. Well, wise in terms of what? The amount of discomfort caused? I do not choose to live my life in terms of comfort. Or perhaps unwise because it will cause the segregationists to harden in their attitudes? Here I can only say that I do feel some pity for the segregationists and realize it will be difficult to accept the changes that *must come*. But I am not free as long as he keeps me from going where I please with whom I please, and I do not think that fear of him should keep me and others from trying to right the wrong for which he stands.

Still further, we may raise the question of the relation of protest and the law. In the first place, most of the laws applied are old laws obviously revived to enforce the segregationist mores of a community. Secondly, I believe the patently discriminatory laws are illegal under the Fourteenth Amendment. However, students are breaking state laws. As I see it, a person suffering under an unjust law has several choices. He can do nothing; we have never advocated this in a democracy. He can use legal means; this has been done and will

* Marshall, Texas, was the scene of police violence against peaceful student protesters, ending in the spring of 1960.

be done. However, if he sees the slowness of the legal means and realizes he is a human being *now* and the law is unjust *now*, he has other choices. He can revolt; I think we should all be proud and glad that this has not been the course of the southern Negro. Or he can protest actively, as southern students have chosen to do, and he must take the consequences. I do not see the law as immutable, but rather as an agreed-upon pattern for relations between people. If the pattern is unjust or a person doesn't agree with the relations, a person must at times choose to do the right rather than the legal. I do not consider this anarchy, but responsibility.

But the things I have been discussing I discuss only in order to converse with the other panelists. It seems to me now that these questions disturbed me because I'm so used to giving lip service to an ideal. We would all quote the slogan that segregation is wrong, but we would condemn the method used to bring people's attention to its wrongness. An ideal can be transmuted into action . . . a just decision can become a reality in students walking and sitting and acting together.

I cannot say to a person who suffers injustice, "Wait." Perhaps you can; I can't. And having decided that I cannot urge caution, I must stand with him. If I had known that not a single lunch counter would open as a result of my action, I could not have done differently than I did. I am thankful for the sit-ins if for no other reason than that they provided me with an opportunity for making a slogan into a reality by making a decision an action. It seems to me that this is what life is all about. While I would hope that the NSA Congress will pass a strong sit-in resolution, I am more concerned that all of us, Negro and white, realize the possibility of becoming less inhuman humans through commitment and action with all their frightening complexities.

When Thoreau was jailed for refusing to pay taxes to a government which supported slavery, Emerson went to visit him. "Henry David," said Emerson, "what are you doing in there?" Thoreau looked at him and replied, "Ralph Waldo, what are *you* doing out *there?*"

What are *you* doing out there?

There was silence for a moment, and I thought my audience was going to stonewall me. Then there was an outburst, applause and cheers, and people leaping to their feet in a long standing ovation. Thus, despite the flaws of my effort, it stands as representative of the thinking of white supporters of the sit-ins and of SNCC at our beginnings. Present were the germinal elements of what would become a national radical student movement: ethics and existentialism, impatience with hypocrisy, a search for meaning, American idealism, and a vision of young African Americans as the heroic vanguard.

The legislation passed, with significant political implications. In this one act the center of campus politics moved left dramatically. Student governments of member colleges could now support morally right and legally wrong activity on the part of their black southern counterparts, a huge change. The vote also paved the way for personal involvement by these campus leaders, middle-of-the-roaders mostly, changing their lives in big ways and laying a foundation for our Friends of SNCC groups later.

The victory empowered NSA's tiny Liberal Caucus, the very beginnings of the New Left and Students for a Democratic Society, which would later lead the fight against the Vietnam War. Suddenly the position of this minority had won and they were legitimate, even sought after by other delegates. Here was where many of us who would be colleagues and comrades in years to come first found one another. I met Tom Hayden there, whom I would later marry. The caucus supported Timothy Jenkins from Howard University for national affairs vice president, and he was elected. That initial nexus now included the powerful and moneyed USNSA.

For the girl I was, this talk, and this whole event—this convergence, if you will—gave me a chance to step out onto the open ground of my own life. In doing so, I followed the path broken by those thousands of kids sitting at lunch counters and filling the jails across the South, so very young and so very brave.

CASEY HAYDEN initiated the book *Deep in Our Hearts: Nine White Women in the Freedom Movement*. Her memoir, *Fields of Blue*, appears in that volume. *Body on the Line*, an autobiographical essay on Satyagraha, was published in *Being Bodies: Buddhist Women on the Paradox of Embodiment*, edited by Lenore Friedman and Susan Moon. Today she is close to her children and lives with her partner, Episcopal priest and community organizer Paul W. Buckwalter, in Tucson, Arizona. She says, "Our home is large and funky and old, and our neighborhood is home both to Tucson's historic black churches and school and to an assortment of today's young radicals. The peaceful back porch looks out over the distant mountains."

"Onto Open Ground" © 2010 by Casey Hayden

Two Variations on Nonviolence

Mildred Forman Page

*While demonstrating in Atlanta, a Chicago
woman questions the validity of nonviolence.*

Moving South

One day in the fall of 1961 when I came home from working at the gas
company, I found Diane Nash and other students from the sit-in movement
in my Chicago living room. I wasn't surprised. My husband, Jim Forman, a
schoolteacher, had spent several summers in the South working with local
Civil Rights Movements, including the Nashville Movement. Together we
had raised money and collected food and clothing for black sharecroppers
in Fayette County, Tennessee, who had been evicted from their homes after
trying to register to vote.

The students were asking Jim to come south for one year to help get
SNCC organized. I was not anxious to pack up and move south. Both
our families lived in Chicago and were active members of Coppin Chapel
A.M.E. (African Methodist Episcopal) Church, which is where Jim and
I met. We had been married just a little less than two years. After much
deliberation and debate, I agreed to go, because I didn't want to keep him
from going, and I couldn't imagine being apart from my new husband for a
whole year. We separated three years later, but despite my early reservations
I stayed with SNCC for a total of five years. During that time I participated
in so many protests and demonstrations that most run together as a blur,
except for the two demonstrations I describe below, when I was unable to
remain nonviolent.

"Somehow . . . my fists balled up"

One warm summer night in Atlanta in 1962, I was part of a group that
went to the Fulton County Jail to hold a pray-in for SCLC officer Rev. Fred
Shuttlesworth and several students who had been arrested for demonstrating at Lester Maddox's restaurant. The police allowed us to pray and sing
for about ten minutes before they told us to disperse or be arrested.

Our orders from movement training were to hold fast even if we were
arrested, so we began to sit down. We were approximately eight rows deep
with six or seven people in a row. The officers began with the first row,

dragging demonstrators across the pavement to the door of the jailhouse. I was in the second-to-last row. I watched as the students and staff members went limp. My mind began to race as I looked down at my bare legs, my *new* leather thong sandals, and crisp blue-jean skirt. Vanity took over. I did not want my skirt torn or my legs or heels scratched on the pavement, so I stood up and crossed one wrist over the other, implying that I surrendered. But as fate had it, a young rookie officer arrested me. He was determined to drag me as the other policemen had dragged their prisoners. He pushed me down to the pavement, and I sprang up, crossing my arms again. He pushed me again and I stood up, telling him I surrendered and would go with him peaceably.

The young officer was having none of that. He pushed me again, this time with more force. His eyes were filled with hate and determination to harm me. At that moment I remembered that nonviolence was only a tactic, not my Chicago way of life. Somehow my arms became uncrossed, my limp wrists became rigid, and my fists balled up. I proceeded to fight him. I fought him all the way to the jailhouse door, where other officers restrained me.

After we were released the next day, we drove to Albany, Georgia, for a demonstration there. While my husband, Jim, John Lewis, Dr. Martin Luther King Jr., Andrew Young, and others were having breakfast at the home of one of the community people, I sat out front in one of the lawn chairs, eating nuts that had fallen from a large pecan tree in the yard. Soon Dr. King, Jim, and the others came outside. Dr. King walked over, greeting me with, "Good morning, daughter, and how are you today?" Then he said to Jim, "I think you are going to have to keep your wife in the office. Did you see the Atlanta news last night? She is going to ruin our nonviolent concept!" They laughed. I totally agreed.

Rescued

A few weeks later I was with about ten demonstrators who were standing in the doorway of Maddox's Peachtree Street restaurant holding signs and singing when Ku Klux Klan members appeared. Dressed in their robes, they looked very frightening. They circled us, saying nasty and threatening things. Although scared, we did not move. After about ten minutes, another group of Klan members, with Lester Maddox in the lead, appeared, waving sticks. I knew it was all over for us until we heard a faint chant in the distance. A group of black youngsters were running in our direction, brandishing sticks and other objects and shouting, "Freedom! Freedom!" They came upon the Klansmen and began to hit them.

The Klansmen broke out running away, again with Maddox in the lead. His robe was open and flying in the wind. His hood was hanging around his neck. I got a good look at him and he was scared. The black youths gave chase, and the Klansmen ran back up Peachtree Street, jumped in their cars and trucks, and left. All the while, the press was filming. We began to laugh, and I thanked God for looking out for us. As I look back over the many times we have put our lives on the line and came out unharmed, I say only God could have saved us.

In addition to working in the Atlanta office and participating in numerous demonstrations, **MILDRED FORMAN PAGE** traveled with the Freedom Singers as a kind of den mother, keeping track of their itinerary and appearances. After her years with SNCC, she returned to Chicago, remarried, and raised a family of three children. She worked for the Chicago Board of Education for ten years and in the social service field for twenty, retiring in 2000. She remains active in her church, Trinity United Church of Christ, pastored for thirty-six years by the Rev. Jeremiah Wright, and is on the board of directors of Chicago Area Friends of SNCC, which is still an active group. The members are working to preserve movement history by holding conferences, conducting interviews, and establishing a civil rights archive at the Carter G. Woodson Library in Chicago.

"Two Variations on Nonviolence" © 2010 by Mildred Forman Page

A Young Communist Joins SNCC

Debbie Amis Bell

*A young American leftist seeks a place
in the Civil Rights Movement.*

My Communist Genes

Like a divining rod leads to water, my background led me to the Civil Rights Movement, specifically to SNCC. I am the child of American Communists. My father, an African American, born in Chicago to a missionary family, attributed his left politics and activism to Ida B. Wells, whom he knew from belonging to the NAACP there. From the NAACP, he went to the Communist Party and in the 1930s played a significant role in bringing together the defense team for the nine Scottsboro Boys, who were falsely accused of raping two white women in Alabama. My father also worked with the committee to free Angelo Herndon, another Communist Party activist, who was charged with "attempting to incite an insurrection" for organizing the poor in Georgia under the slogan "Jobs or Relief."

My mother, a white member of the party, made a considerable contribution to fighting racism through her community work. She was ostracized by her family for marrying my father in the 1930s at a time when interracial marriages were frowned upon and were actually illegal in many states. She raised her children with this same spirit, and all five of us played some part in the Civil Rights Movement. Although my parents were party stalwarts, I made my own decision to join the party in the 1950s, judging it to be the only organization addressing and interrelating the multitude of issues I considered important: racism, jobs, peace, health, and the general quality of life in our country. I had decided that it was important for me to devote my life to trying to ensure that these American ideals became a reality.

Introduction to SNCC

In April 1960, my senior year at West Chester College in Pennsylvania, I eagerly accepted when the Communist Party asked me to attend a student civil rights conference in Raleigh, North Carolina, as an observer. This meeting turned out to be the founding conference of SNCC. As a northerner attending an overwhelmingly white college, I had never been south, or in the intellectual or social company of a large gathering of African Americans who were running the show.

The conferees were serious and purposeful. The attendees represented a well-integrated tapestry of college students: black and white, female and male, working-class and the more privileged. The sessions I attended focused on what we as students could contribute to undermining the entrenched system of segregation in the South. Virtually all of the strategy centered on equal access to all public facilities. There was also a fierce sentiment that we students were capable not only of contributing our bodies to the Movement but also of directing and coordinating our own programs. The conference was spirited and emotional; the community participated in rallies, and there were inspiring accounts by those who had been in the sit-ins. Singing was everywhere. Amid this heady atmosphere, SNCC was born.

The conference ended with clear tasks for both southerners and those of us from the rest of the country. Recruiting and fund-raising were among the many tasks northerners might choose. I left Raleigh with a sense of urgency, knowing I could not fail to fulfill a role. I was determined to make a difference.

Facing my future, I wondered, how would I financially support myself? What would be the risks? What skills or talent could I offer? What about my Communist Party affiliation? Almost three years after the founding conference, I decided to apply to work for SNCC. My experience told me that as soon as I came out of the political "closet," my skills, talents, and contributions would take a backseat to prejudices against the party. I decided not to disclose my party affiliation.

I was ecstatic when in March 1963 Ruby Doris Smith wrote from the Atlanta office, accepted my application, and offered to arrange housing for me. Two months later I left my Philadelphia home and drove straight to Atlanta, stopping only to refuel my car. When I finally located the SNCC office on Raymond Street, I chuckled, because emblazoned on the facade of the building was its name: the Marx Building.

Eager to accept virtually any assignment, I entered the office holding Ruby Doris's letter to me and my response. Young people scurried everywhere, and it took several minutes—which seemed like hours—for anyone to notice my presence. As I looked around the office, most of the flurry was in a spacious room with all types of office machinery and numerous desks laden with papers, packages, and assorted materials. Finally I was led past a couple of cubicles to meet Ruby Doris. In one cubicle a young man was bent over a typewriter, with a cigarette hanging out of his mouth. He was typing faster with two fingers than anyone I had ever seen typing with all ten. I later learned this was SNCC press secretary Julian Bond.

Ruby Doris welcomed me, but it was clear that my arrival was a surprise. To honor the letter, I was expediently assigned to secretarial duties. Objectively, I had no secretarial skills. I could not type, nor did I know anything about stenography, bookkeeping, filing, duplicating, or collating. Subjectively, I didn't want to be cast in the typical women's role.

Having worked with the Philadelphia NAACP, I thought I had some organizational and leadership skills that could be useful if I were given a community assignment. An impatient person, I immediately immersed myself in the local sit-ins sponsored by the Atlanta Committee on Appeal for Human Rights (COAHR) and enrolled in an Atlanta University Negro history class. I thought taking the class would both enhance my knowledge of our people's history and be a constructive way to acclimate myself and develop a base in the community.

Eventually Jim Forman noticed my activity and discussed work options with me. I could be a field secretary in Selma, Alabama; a campus traveler;

or the coordinator of the four-person campus team who recruited students to the Movement and helped student groups with their tactics and strategies. After much deliberation and discussion, we agreed that I would remain in Atlanta, where I had established ties with students and organizations involved in the local movement. I worked with the various Atlanta community groups, especially COAHR. COAHR chair Larry Fox and I met regularly with SCLC leadership at Dr. Martin Luther King Jr.'s office in Ebenezer Baptist Church to discuss overall strategy for the Atlanta Movement.

At that time there was a fragile coalition between the demonstrating students and the more conservative black business and religious community, which provided bail, health care, and other essential resources to the demonstrators. The businesspeople would tell the students, "Give the mayor more time," or "These tactics are too confrontational." Still, these two groups managed to work together, achieving some semblance of unity and a program of action.

I felt welcomed into this informal association of community activists. To meet my SNCC responsibilities, I needed to participate in the diverse civil rights, religious, and business community activities in Atlanta. I became a regular attendee at West Hunter Street Baptist Church, pastored by Ralph Abernathy, whose inspirational sermons used biblical texts to urge involvement in the Civil Rights Movement. Several times Reverend Abernathy and his wife, Juanita, invited me to join them for dinner after church. When we learned that President Kennedy had been shot, Abernathy brought Larry Fox and me back to his church, turned on the lights, and gave the two of us the most moving oration I have ever heard on the subject of violence and intolerance.

A local doctor regularly treated me to breakfast at Paschal's, a local black-owned restaurant near the SNCC office, when I conveniently showed up each morning not only to be fed but also to engage in stimulating discussions with him on a broad range of topics. Once, Dr. King asked Prathia Hall and me to spend an evening "sitting" with his mother while he and other family members were out of town. Mrs. King was gracious and kind. It was akin to being at home with my mother. This was one of my most memorable moments. Still, when we met with the local ministers or other established black leaders, usually only one or two females were present, and the women and youth, usually SNCC members, had to struggle for their ideas to be heard.

Working with the Atlanta Movement, I demonstrated frequently and went to jail quite a few times. On a typical day, we Atlanta field secretaries and COAHR representatives would march downtown, recruiting local residents along the way. We would go from one restaurant to another picketing and sitting in. Our demonstrations brought out the KKK in full regalia. One of the restaurants we targeted belonged to Lester Maddox and was famous for its chicken. Maddox and his employees used baseball bats, which they called "drumsticks," to intimidate and hit sit-inners.* Both the KKK and Maddox targeted the women and the girls for attack. Needless to say, the assailants were never arrested, but the demonstrators were, often, by the black officers of the Atlanta Police Department. We were usually charged with disturbing the peace. Sometimes our bail was posted immediately and we were released. Other times we spent hours or days awaiting release, or we chose jail without bail.

Jail Lessons

After one arrest, without any explanation, we were removed from the city jail and spirited off in the dark of night on buses rather than being released as we had expected. After a long ride we arrived at the Fulton County Jail, a facility for hardened criminals. I was the only African American woman arrested, so I faced imprisonment separated from all the other civil rights workers. The guards turned me over to a black female trusty, who issued me a loose green top; oversized, green men's boxer shorts for underwear; and extra-large shoes with no shoelaces. No personal or sanitary supplies were included. The trusty escorted me into a cavernous dormitory room with bunk beds and pointed to where I would sleep at the end of a long row of bunks.

Alone and frightened, I lay down and hugged the pillow, discovering someone else's personal items were already there. The trusty explained that the prison was a round-the-clock work facility with two shifts. Those inmates who worked during the day slept in the same beds as those who worked at night. She was sharing her bed with me, which I understood to be quite an honor, since she was one of the highest-ranking prisoners. The trusty continued to look out for me during my stay. One day she pulled me from my work duty, saying, "You are wanted in the medical suites to be examined internally. You don't want this to happen, and I don't want you to have to go through this, Freedom Rider." She escorted me back to the bunk room, where she and the other inmates maneuvered around the bureaucracy by moving me from bed to bed with precision for the two weeks until our group was released on bail. The white female SNCC demonstrators were not as fortunate and had to endure the degrading assault of the internal search, not to mention the hostility of the white female inmates.

Here, as in most of the jails I was in, everything was out in the open and most of the guards and trusties were men. There was no privacy for female

* Editors' Note: Maddox became so well known and so well thought of throughout the state for these kinds of segregationist antics that he was elected governor in 1966.

inmates to dress, sleep, or use the toilet. The matrons in this county jail brought no feminine relief; they were as harsh as their male counterparts. Hardened white women who rarely spoke in modulated tones, they preferred instead to constantly bark orders to their African American charges. The black female inmates, however, generally befriended me and shared some of their personal stories and fantasies.

I came from a very cloistered environment, and my civil rights arrests introduced me to people accused of regular crimes. Most of these women viewed their incarceration only as a detour in the road, and many had set themselves high goals. I came to feel that if they were fortunate enough to receive even minimal support, they could succeed once they were released.

During another jail confinement, I decided to fast. Although I drew no attention to my self-imposed fast, the moment the matron determined that I wasn't eating breakfast, an uproar ensued. I was removed to solitary confinement. It hadn't dawned on me that as a Freedom Rider my mere presence represented a threat to the jail authority and that they did not want some young protester putting ideas of resistance into the heads of their carefully managed prisoners.

The solitary cell was isolated and absolutely empty. There were no accommodations—no bed, no sink, only a cold, hard concrete floor. In the corner of the cell there was a recessed hole in the floor that served as the toilet. I was miserable. For the three days I was there, I heard and saw no other human beings except the black male trusty who befriended me. He risked his own standing to bring me toilet paper and candy. He also gave me pencils and paper and mailed the notes that I had written my parents. I spent my time writing letters and singing freedom songs to myself. When I ran out of the precious paper, I wrote on the toilet paper. This experience fortified me, and I continued to demonstrate and work for equality.

About SNCC

The most appealing quality of SNCC for me was that it gave its field-workers plenty of latitude to establish their own style of work to accomplish the stated goals of the organization. Strategy and tactics were collectively discussed, but the individual field secretary had plenty of room to exploit his or her talents. Women were generally accepted for their intelligence as well as their organizational skills. At the same time, it was not unusual for me to participate in a meeting dominated by men where it was impossible to interject a word.

In March 1964 I was asked to leave SNCC. I felt certain it was because the organization learned of my affiliation with the Communist Party, which also meant southern movement lawyers did not want to take my case. After I left, SNCC was never far from my mind or activities. Apparently the organization had no qualms about my being active in the north, and I participated in a Philadelphia SNCC support group that held numerous fund-raising affairs. I had the opportunity to travel around the area and speak, and, of course, raise money, but it wasn't the same as being in a southern project that put me on the streets daily.

I particularly treasure the special relationships I had in SNCC. I feel euphoric every time I meet or even read about the special heroes and heroines with whom I worked or met in the Movement. I remember my work with SNCC as challenging and very gratifying. It gave me a feeling of accomplishment, of making some small contribution toward changing our country for the better.

DEBBIE AMIS BELL is still a member of the Communist Party, serving on its national board and as district chairperson. She taught in the Philadelphia public school system for thirty years and remains active with the Philadelphia Federation of Teachers' political and unionizing activities. She is a past officer and current member of the Black Radical Congress. Over the years, she has continued to be arrested for union organizing and peace activities, including recent actions to end the Iraq War. In 2006 she gave the keynote address at Monmouth University's fortieth anniversary of Dr. Martin Luther King Jr.'s speech there.

Watching, Waiting, and Resisting

Hellen O'Neal-McCray

A young woman describes the dangerous and fearful atmosphere in Mississippi, where she lived, and her entry into the Civil Rights Movement.

Mississippi Justice

Growing up in the Delta, time seemed endless, nothing moved. For black folks Mississippi was sitting-on-the-porch summertime days—a chair rocked, a fan waved, a soft voice hummed, a chinaberry dropped, the sharp crack of a fly swatter broke the stillness. We were always sitting, waiting for something to happen. Clarksdale, Mississippi, the soul of the Delta, is my home. My aunt Mrs. Susie Long still lives on a farm about seventeen miles outside of Clarksdale between Tutweiler and Dublin. Clarksdale is where legendary blues singer Robert Johnson met the devil at the crossroads.

When our lives were the bleakest and our burdens the heaviest, stories were told about southern black heroes, like Eddie Noel, a marksman who had returned to the state after fighting in the Korean War. His wife told him that when she went to the store, the shopkeeper, who was also a part-time deputy sheriff, had said, "Nigger woman, you git your uppity self out of the way so I can wait on this white woman," and pushed her. Noel exploded and stormed the store. This was it. After fighting in the war, no white man was ever going to insult him or his wife again. Noel shot and killed the store-keeper. When the sheriff and his deputy came, guns drawn and blazing, Noel killed both of them, sent his wife home, and headed for the woods.

A posse of more than a hundred white men from surrounding coun-ties formed and burned Eddie Noel's house. According to the story, posse members beat his wife and forced her to walk in front of them to keep Noel from shooting them. He was such an excellent marksman, however, that each time they approached the clearing in the woods where he had gone, he shot around or over his wife, leaving another one bleeding in the dust. The total number killed depended on who was telling the story. But all agreed he had slipped away to the North, perhaps even taking his wife. Eddie Noel was a hero in the cotton fields, juke houses, front porches, barbershops, and in all the other places where poor and disenfranchised black folk gathered. He had fought back and lived.

In addition to recounting heroic tales, there was active resistance in my hometown of Clarksdale. When fourteen-year-old Emmett Till was lynched in Money, Mississippi, we looked at his mutilated body in *JET* magazine with horror. He was our age. We knew awful things happened in Missis-sippi. Our parents reminded us often enough. Till's case was also discussed in churches, pool halls, beauty shops, anyplace where more than one black person gathered. We shared tears of bitter disappointment with Emmett Till's mother as Roy Bryant, one of the two men who later admitted kill-ing Till, and his wife celebrated his acquittal with a long, slow kiss on the courthouse steps. Sadness swept over our community like a shroud. Bryant and his wife moved to Clarksdale. She got a job at the Dallas department store, a store where most of the shoppers were black. Immediately black people stopped shopping there. Bryant was hired at the local bottling plant, working with black men, and they refused to work with him. The Bryant family finally moved on.

The people in my family were small landowners, farmers, tradesmen, and skilled craftsmen, who did their best to avoid segregation. As a child I had no contact with white people, and family members discouraged me from going anyplace with "white" and "colored" doors. My stepfather taught my sister Inez and me to patronize black businesses and not spend our money anywhere we were not respected. As a result, I shopped only at those stores where I was treated well. We used white services only when no comparable black services existed. When my stepfather took my sister to a white doctor and a white woman was called in before them, he took Inez home without seeing the doctor. "Better body sick than head sick," he explained. Usually we went to Mound Bayou, Mississippi, an all-black town, if our local black doctor, Dr. McCaskill, was not in his office.

On our porches, we read the *Chicago Defender,* the only news that black people in Clarksdale could read and believe. Our local newspaper, the *Clarksdale Press Register,* dripped race hatred and contempt; black men and women were criminals or didn't exist within its pages. My stepfather always read them both. Most of the people in Clarksdale were connected to Chicago by blood ties. The *Chicago Defender* allowed us to read about successful black people and their lives. When the news was about a civil rights victory there, my neighbor Miss Gert, usually a quiet, thoughtful woman, would get excited and exclaim, "Them colored folks in Chicago are somethin'. They don't take no white folks' mess."

We also followed the growing national Civil Rights Movement in the *Defender's* pages and on our little television set. We knew that something was going to happen somewhere soon. We tried to figure out if the 1954 Supreme Court decision meant we would be going to Clarksdale's white schools. The *Register's* editorials said, "Our colored are happy; they don't want to go to our schools." We watched from our porches as the scramble took place to build new schools for African Americans. It was a puzzle to us. We watched our television with our neighbors when the Little Rock Nine started to school. We couldn't get enough of it. We cheered when President Eisenhower nationalized the National Guard for the Little Rock Nine. Arkansas was just across the river; certainly we would be next.

In the 1950s, with each victory that took place in another state, we suffered a great loss in Mississippi. Voting rights activist Rev. George Lee was killed in Belzoni. Before a trial, Mack Parker, accused of rape in Poplarville, was taken from his jail cell and lynched. In our city a local boy accused of raping a white woman was arrested and beaten in the county jail until blood and water ran from his ears. Churches organized and collected money for a lawyer, but there were no black lawyers in Clarksdale. Finally, after weeks of beating and no confession, the young man was released and the money was used to send him and his family to Chicago.

Freedom Rides, Protests, and Jail

The sit-ins started and we watched with utter amazement as people our age sat at lunch counters in North Carolina and, especially, Nashville. People my age were exhilarated and felt a sense of power. We could hardly wait for the day our friends from Tennessee State came home and told us about Nashville. We decided that we couldn't be nonviolent, especially in Clarksdale. Besides, our parents warned us against trying that in Mississippi. Whenever we looked in our parents' eyes, we saw terror. But pictures and news of sit-ins made us tremble with excitement.

When the first Freedom Riders rode into Jackson, we wondered if something was finally going to change in Mississippi or if this was just another false start. By this time I was a student at Jackson State, where I met James Bevel and Bernard Lafayette, who were trying, unsuccessfully, to recruit students from Jackson State College to take part in the Freedom Rides. Several local high school students did go, including Luvaughn Brown, Charles Cox, Jesse Harris, and two or three high school girls. They were immediately arrested at the bus stations and kept separately from the Freedom Riders who had come from out of the state. Most of the Freedom Riders stayed in jail, usually at Parchman Penitentiary, for thirty days, but some served the entire six months. It was Mrs. Claire Harvey, Mrs. A. M. E. Logan, and their fellow club women who found places for the released Freedom Riders to get cleaned up and fed. I met SNCC activists Stokely Carmichael and Ruby Doris Smith shortly after they were released from Parchman Penitentiary. I was absolutely overwhelmed by their presence. It really made me want to do something. I talked about them all night with my friends Mary Felice Lovelace and Brenda Morman.

By the summer of 1961 I was ready to participate in my first demonstration. I withdrew from summer school and went with Dick Haley from CORE to picket the Southern Governors Conference that was being held in the city. Unable to recruit other students for this demonstration, I was terrified I was going to be alone. The thought of jail was so very scary to me, especially the idea of being there by myself. I worried about my parents' reaction and what they were going to do to me. I wrote them a letter explaining why I felt I had to do this and mailed it just before I went downtown. When we got out of the car in front of the Heidelberg Hotel, where the conference was being held, the press and police were already there. We got our signs and started to walk back and forth in front of the hotel. Soon Police Captain

Ray walked over to us and said, "You are disturbing the peace; now, move on." We continued to picket and were immediately arrested. This was the first time in my life that I had come in contact with the police and the first time I had ever disobeyed a person in authority.

In the beginning I was housed with the regular women prisoners in the city jail. Most of them were in for petty crimes, but some were there just for being "uppity." They taught me how to smoke, play cards, and cuss. The thing I found amazing was that the other prisoners sang freedom songs with me, even though it was very risky for them, and asked the trusties to slip me reading material. I was in the city jail for two or three days before we went to court with William Kunstler as our attorney to enter our "not guilty" pleas. Next, I was taken to the county jail and placed in a cell alone. The trusties brought our meals, and occasionally they would slip me things to read. A woman who was in for the murder of her husband was let out of her cell to bring the rest of us some water from a bucket and dipper. I spent a lot of time talking with her.

In the cell next to me was an alcoholic white woman whom I called Jessie Mae. She had a little hand mirror, and we used it to stare at each other when she placed it outside her cell. She taught me how to blow smoke rings and swallow a lighted cigarette. We played cards and listened for the jangle of the jailer's keys, which would make us scramble to our bunks. There was no mattress on my bed, just a wool army blanket. There were no screens on the windows, and every morning when I woke up I was covered with mosquito bites as well as circles about the size of a quarter from the holes in the metal bed frame.

After my jail stay, since I knew my mother was very upset with me, I was afraid to go home. Brenda Morman and I had become good friends, so I lived with her family that summer while recruiting other college students and working in the CORE/SNCC office, which was buzzing with activity. Now Marion Barry, Paul Brooks, and Bob Moses were there; Diane Nash, who had been in Jackson earlier that summer, returned. I had to strain to hear Bob when he spoke; he seemed to burn with intensity cooled by gentleness, a combination I have not seen again. Someone rented a house on Rose Street, creating the first freedom house in Mississippi. A number of Freedom Riders chose to stay in Mississippi; some of them followed Bob Moses to McComb. I knew the breeze of change was blowing.

At the end of the summer I took the bus home. It was Labor Day, which Mississippians didn't celebrate, because they considered it a Communist holiday. When I boarded the bus for Clarksdale, I sat up front in the second seat. I was arrested, jailed, and discharged that night. Being released at night scared me, because I didn't know what they were planning to do with me and no one knew where I was. The police took me back to the bus station and waited with me outside until the bus came. Other policemen blocked the white-only waiting room door to make sure I could not enter. When the bus arrived, I again sat down in the second seat. A young black man sat down next to me. I was worried that something might happen to him, but we were not bothered at all.

My mother was furious with me for dropping out of summer school and wasting that money, but all of my kinfolk and neighbors were proud of my involvement, and this eased the way with my mother. After arguments and tears, she agreed to pay for my education that coming year. When I returned to Jackson in the fall, there were organizers in the Delta and in Amite and Pike counties. At the CORE/SNCC office we heard their stories and the horror stories of white folks' responses to movement activity around the state. Together these were the stories of the change I had waited for all of my life.

When I think of SNCC and the Mississippi Movement, it is as if I watched a great drama unfolding with me on the edge. After my SNCC experience I have been disappointed, because I have not come in contact with people of such dazzling brightness.

HELLEN O'NEAL-McCRAY did graduate from Jackson State in 1963, making her the first person in her family to graduate from a four-year college. Afterward she joined the SNCC staff in Mississippi and worked on the organization's literacy project with Doris Derby, Casey Hayden, Lee Jack Morton, and John O'Neal. In 1964 she taught at a Freedom School in McComb, Mississippi, and the following summer she worked for the Lawyers Constitutional Defense Committee in Shreveport, Louisiana. She taught elementary school in Springfield, Ohio, for twenty-nine years, English and literature courses at Wilberforce University for nine years, and occasionally taught similar classes at the McGregor School at Antioch College. She married another former SNCC worker, Willie McCray, and they had two sons. Willie McCray died in 2006; Hellen died in 2010.

"Watching, Waiting, and Resisting" © 2010 by Malcolm McCray

Diary of a Freedom Rider

Joan Trumpauer Mulholland

A white southerner makes the unusual choices of attending a small black college in Mississippi and of going on a Freedom Ride, knowing her final destination will be a Mississippi jail.

Putting Our Own House in Order

I am Southern and White—as southern as the red clay of Georgia, as southern as Lee's Mansion overlooking the Potomac. Northern Virginia is where I lived; rural Georgia was "down home." My grandmother used to say, "The only foreigner we ever had in the family was a Yankee." As a teenager witnessing Virginia's campaign of Massive Resistance to court-ordered school desegregation, I knew something was terribly wrong in the South. Both as a Christian and as a southerner, I felt that when I had a chance to do something to change things, I should do it. We southerners needed to put our own house in order.

In 1960, when I was a student at Duke University in Durham, North Carolina, my chance came with the sit-ins. A few other white Duke students and I joined the black North Carolina college students at the lunch counters and in the jails. The repercussions were such that I dropped out of Duke at the end of the year and returned to the Washington, D.C., area. There, I held an office job and participated in the local movement led by the Nonviolent Action Group (NAG), a SNCC affiliate based at Howard University. Howard students as well as black and white residents of the Washington, D.C., area participated in these demonstrations.

I shuddered at the news pictures as Charlayne Hunter integrated the University of Georgia, and thought, *She should not have to go through all that.* Integration shouldn't be a one-way street—whites had to make the journey, too. I decided to apply to Negro colleges. Not in Georgia—that was too close to home. My family shouldn't have to suffer reprisals for me. The sit-ins hadn't reached Mississippi. SNCC people were talking about organizing there, and someone recommended that I apply to a school in Mississippi. I was accepted at Tougaloo Southern Christian College. Since the school's charter was older than the state's Jim Crow laws, the black college decided to accept white students, and I made plans to head south to school.

That same spring, the Freedom Rides turned bloody and students on different campuses mobilized to keep the rides going. NAG members had kidded Henry Thomas that he was taking a vacation when he left on the ride, but then news photos of him, stunned and bleeding by the burning bus near Anniston, Alabama, appeared. Among southern students, NAG was second only to the Nashville students in supplying Freedom Riders. Paul Deitrich and John Moody were the first NAG members to go. Others followed. Paul's late-night call from the besieged church in Montgomery galvanized us.

The original plan was to continue the ride from Alabama, where the first Freedom Riders had been savagely attacked. The plan quickly expanded, and riders came into Jackson, Mississippi, from other directions. The idea was to challenge segregation in all interstate transportation (not just buses) and to keep things interesting and unpredictable in order to garner media attention. Small groups of Freedom Riders arrived in Jackson every day or two to keep the police busy there. In early June 1961 I was in a group that flew from D.C. to New Orleans to catch the train to Jackson.

We were also trying to "fill the jails." Most riders remained behind bars for weeks. Because I had no plans and no place to go until school opened in the fall, I served my two-month sentence and additional time to work off my two-hundred-dollar fine. Each day in prison took three dollars off the fine. I paid up just in time to enroll at Tougaloo that fall.

Our imprisonment began in the Jackson City Jail and ended on death row at the notorious Parchman Penitentiary in the Mississippi Delta. I kept a diary from June 8 through June 23, from the beginning of my Freedom Ride until my transfer to the penitentiary. During the two weeks when I was in the Hinds County Jail in Jackson, I kept the diary hidden inside the hem of my checkered skirt, which was covered by heavy crochet and ruffles, crumpling and re-crumpling the pages to conceal them. They are hard to read now. Time and a broken water pipe have also taken their toll, but I was able to review the diary with the help of a magnifying glass. Expectations of a shakedown and dwindling paper supplies contribute to an increasingly abbreviated writing style.

The diary, now with titles added, reflects accurately our daily routines and my feelings, but may be occasionally misleading. Sometimes what we thought we knew in the white women's cell was wrong. Still, I believe these old pages will bring you close to my real jail experience. There was such monotony that the plain prison meals were often the noteworthy highlights of the day. At the same time, the singing, worship, and the continual flow of new Freedom Riders made it one of the most inspirational times of my life.

Other NAG members—Travis Britt, Stokely Carmichael, Gwen Green, Jane Rosett, Jan Triggs, and Helene Wilson—were with me on the ride. Attracted by the southern movement, Travis had moved down from New York City. Stokely, Jan, and Gwen were Howard students, Stokely and Jan from

New York, Gwen from D.C. Helene and Jane were also white residents of D.C., but originally from the North. Jane had just spent a year or so living with relatives in North Carolina, attending high school there, and participating in the Durham sit-in movement. We were joined by Robert Wesby, an African American minister from Aurora, Illinois, and Terry Pearlman, another young white woman, from the Bronx. I was the only white southerner. We were the second Freedom Ride by train into Jackson.

My Freedom Ride: An Uneventful Event

JUNE 8, 1961

Around 6:50 we arrived at the train station. Reporters spotted us as we came in and were real eager beavers. The girls all came together and Gwen bought the tickets. Unfortunately, the man gave us round-trip tickets and we didn't realize it until we were on the train. While we were in line, the guys came in. Jane gave the reporters [our] . . . names and a few non-committal statements. The girls ran the gauntlet of reporters to the train.

In [to] one car which was too full, through the dining car and into the next. A bunch of rowdy college kids were in the front and there were eight seats together in the back so we took them. A Negro man turned them together for us. . . . By and large, the trip was uneventful. The college kids had some comments to make but didn't try to start anything. Tony, Terry, Jane and I ate together—pretty good service. A young woman and her two little girls were very nice. She said she might not agree with us but she had to admire our courage. A young female reporter from New Orleans on her day off talked to us.

Every place we stopped there were at least two or three police— usually clustered around the entrance to the "white" waiting room. At one place the sign read, "White waiting room by orders of the police." The man who turned our seats around took our letters to mail in Memphis. When we got off, all the Negroes wished us luck, smiled, waved, etc.—including the waiters. I began to feel slightly nervous but at this point I was probably the calmest. I was in the back of the girls. A rough, burly man followed us and we expected violence.

Arrest and Trial

We went down steps to the waiting rooms. Signs with arrows were prominently displayed pointing to the different waiting rooms and with police all over. We walked to the back and around a bit to some seats—police following. When we sat down they asked us to move "on and out." Gwen said she didn't see any reason to and we all sat down. They asked if we'd all heard and then said we were under arrest. The boys had gone slightly past us and about the same thing happened to them.

We were all marched off to a sweat-box of a paddy wagon. We were told not to sing or demonstrate—for our own safety, but the doors were no more than closed when we started. [When we were getting out of the paddy wagon at the city jail], an officer took my elbow and said to be careful. "We don't want you chillun to get hurt." First we were segregated—boys in one hall, girls in the other. One cop was nasty. "We got nine: five black niggers and four white niggers." . . . We were booked, fingerprinted, photoed and had our stuff checked. . . .

There was . . . [another Freedom Rider]—Carol—already in [the cell]. It was a large, two-room cell. One room with four clean cots. The other room with table, sink, shower, and toilet. Across the hall were two [white] divinity students from Yale. After awhile everyone went down to see the lawyer. There was a white Canadian guy who came on his own, head of NY NAACP, and a NY state Senator. Later [the police] took us individually to the inquisition—a general grilling session covering everything from religion to intermarriage. Lunch was o.k.—cornbread, greens and spaghetti.

At 3 was our trial. Ha!! The prosecuting attorney had a printed set of questions. One police testified for the state. Our lawyer asked him if his answers would be substantially the same as in previous trials. He said yes and that was it. Four months with two suspended and $200 fine. [This was an increase from earlier sentences. Soon the sentence was six months and $500.] The courtroom is beautiful. Modern, wood paneled.

Jail

Around 4:30 we got our things and were taken across the street to the county jail. We're in the basement with Negro girl riders [in cells] on either side. Ruby [Doris] Smith is on my right. Betsy [Wyckoff, a white college professor] was already here—since Friday. We've adopted her as cell mother. A really wonderful woman. Two [regular prisoners] . . . are here: Betty (5 days for drinking . . .) and "Grand-mother" (an alcoholic and dope addict who the police . . . beat to bring in). "Grandmother" was asleep and we were expecting trouble when she woke up. All she did was sway on the bars once and beg cigarettes and aspirins (neither of which she's supposed to have).

The time was spent sleeping, reading, writing, and singing. I wrote until my eyes hurt and then slept a while. There are four cots on the walls and four mattresses on the floor. The place is pretty clean, light yellow and comparatively cool since it's in the basement. The toilet is partially stopped, the shower is cool—which is good. Shortly before the lights go out, the "store" comes: two cardboard boxes with cigarettes, candy bars, paper and envelopes. We aren't supposed to have anything to read or anything glass. However, we were able to bring in everything we were carrying (out of our bags). Birdie (on the left) gets along with one of the trustees and he brings the paper nearly every day. Things can be passed fairly easily from one cell to the next. The food is plain but better than some campuses. The boys are upstairs but if we call to them the windows will be closed. We can hear them sing tho!

Settling In

JUNE 9, 1961

They were bringing in food as I was waking up. Jane and Betty were still asleep but we woke them up about half way through breakfast. Grits & gravy, four stewed prunes, three hot biscuits. We roll the beds up and put them around the spare wall space. They give us a broom and a mop with disinfectant. We've got a clothesline strung up—camera straps + ripped up handkerchief. They collect mail in the morning. Also, today some of us are making phone calls and getting our clothes. Helene went first, then Terry. After breakfast some of us did exercises. Five more [Freedom Riders] from Nashville have been arrested and should be over tonight. . . .

[Rev. C. T.] Vivian was in the sweat box—he got fresh. The jailer CAN be very nice when he wants. Vivian's posted bond. The jailer says they're going to have shake-downs. Therefore, read while you can. On our left there aren't any freedom riders but we think that the second cell on the right is. We got a *JET* from Birdie but had to pass it on before we could read it. Gwen was put next door last night—also another girl. They brought them over after dinner but we gave them some cornbread.

Last night they brought around papers with our sentences on them. Jane promptly made hers into an airplane. There's a guy who once lived in D.C. upstairs—seven years for robbery. I talked to him for awhile last night. Betty is letting us wear her pedal pushers & blouse. Terry wore them till she got her clothes & then Helene took them. Around 10:15 the jailer came by to say "Grandmother's" going to the mental hospital—Whitfield . . .

Lunch: cornbread, kidney beans, greens. . . . In the afternoon two more . . . [female Freedom Riders] joined us—on the floor. From up North: Dell and Winona. They came down with two white boys & one Negro girl (Pat, next door) by train. They don't smoke either. When we were tried yesterday, it was with two sets of bus arrests & one plane set. Carol was able to get her clothes and several books.

There was a rain storm—much thunder & water in here till we closed the windows [high up and hard to close]. I slept a good deal this afternoon and read some of my book on Gandhi. Dinner: potatoes & gravy, fish, cornbread. After dinner came mail. Jane, Gwen & I got telegrams from Gloria [Bouknight, my D.C. roommate]. This evening I wrote Gloria, & the office [Senator Claire Engle's office (D-CA), where I had been working]. I'm wearing a white sleeveless blouse of Terry's. Washed out pants & blouse.

More Singing in Jail

JUNE 10, 1961

. . . I woke up as they were bringing breakfast. No salt in the COLD grits this morning, three prunes & three biscuits. The biscuits were better than yesterday. One girl from each cell got to go after clothes. I went for ours. No opportunity to make phone calls yet.

The Boys State [outstanding white high school students, selected on the basis of merit to participate in a two-week study of Mississippi state government in Jackson] came by—about four or five of them. Our first reaction was laughter, then [wise] cracks. They got real uneasy. After they went on to the other cells we decided we should be more dignified. When they came back we sang two verses of "We Shall Overcome," then a pause & a third verse. Someone wolf whistled and that almost broke us up, but we made it through. We're writing (uncensored) to the NY Times. Notes for Helene and Terry came from Jan. We've sent some back. . . . Lunch: hominy, black-eyed peas & cornbread. After I got our clothes, I started copying over my diary for Betty to mail The Fox [a contact in the Durham, North Carolina, Movement].

In the afternoon I slept (wrote a little after lunch). The jailer was talking when I woke up. He says more will be over tonight or tomorrow. Sometimes he says 3, sometimes 5. Also, he says this is the only cell for white women. Washed my hair. Dinner: spaghetti with 2 little chunks of hot dogs & cornbread. Ugh! Pat can't take it & Win is trying to call the lawyer. Lovely little article in yesterday's paper about me. Wrote Paul [another rider in the same jail], but got it back. He's bailed out & so has Frank [Hunt, a newspaper reporter who ended up joining the rides].

This evening we sang a lot. Most girls did folk dancing, but since I'd just washed I didn't want to get all sweaty. . . . I think all the girls in here are gems but I feel more in common with the Negro girls & wish I was locked with them instead of these atheist Yankees—particularly when they sing. The boys have devotions twice a day. Sigh!

. . . Almost as soon as the lights went out the singing started—till about 11. The boys would sing some & we'd sing some. A man named Charles (non-rider) has a beautiful voice and sang several solos. Someone further away sang "How Great Thou Art" for Betty. Some white guy kept cursing us out. One guy answered back a little and everyone sang the louder. We quit around 11. It was one of the most uplifting experiences I've ever had.

Protest and More Yearning for Religion

JUNE 11, 1961

Woke up as they were bringing in breakfast. Very good: two slices white bread, apple sauce, scrambled eggs. Some girls didn't particularly like them because they were powdered, but I didn't see that much difference. After breakfast & clean-up: exercise, including ballet lessons from Dell. I dressed up: flowered outfit, curly hair, polished shoes, lip stick. The jailer said (when we asked) that we couldn't make phone calls or couldn't call our lawyer because of our singing "way past midnight." However, we can see the lawyer if he comes to see us. Real nice. We're singing again tonight. Betty's calling the lawyer when she gets out. When we started putting the mats up, a lot of stuffing fell out. We dumped it in the hall in protest . . .

. . . . The Salvation Army woman came around. At first the girls said "no" but then they thought of me. I tried to hear her talking to the girls next door but couldn't, so they stopped her on her way out. A comparison of Solomon & Saul stressing doing things for others.

The girls asked me to read a passage & after I told them the words to "Jacob's Ladder" they sang that. They're TRYING to be nice, but as they jokingly said, I'm "square." . . . By using the mirror we can see who we're talking to next door. Wrote a while then read Gandhi while walking till lunch.

Lunch: saltless noodles and potatoes with a couple hunks of meat; cornbread. . . . Visiting hours. Two colored ministers came by to give the Negro girls communion—but of course they couldn't give me any. I was mad enough to cry. . . . Read some more.

Dinner was a laugh: 3 tough biscuits, tiny piece of bacon & molasses. Find out we're on the fourth floor. . . . Played charades. Ugh. Jailer told Betty total of seventeen arrested since Del & Win. Surprise—turned the lights out at 9. We sang some but they left the fans on & we couldn't hear. Bobby [a trusty] says [they're] trying to send us to pen [Parchman Penitentiary]. Some girl cried [in anguish], "Please, Mr. Kennedy."

Unsuccessful Smuggle, a Beating

JUNE 12, 1961

Woke up as they were bringing in the food. Grits, prunes, biscuits. Ballet and exercises. I participated. We had a meeting: organized a schedule . . . Washed out some things. Read & slept. Betty left about 9:30. They shook her down and returned our letters [concealed in her underwear]. If we try it again: no mail. Lunch: beans, cabbage & cornbread. We got this at the same time as the letters so spirits were low and not much eating. We talked with the boys a while. John got it started by calling Gwen. We talked to Stokely & Dion [Diamond] (Helene, Gwen & I). . . . Unfortunately, Hutto [the jailer] came by & we had to stop. After that we never got "connected" again.

Fell asleep after lunch. 2:30 before [they] came for plates, then devotions. I read about Paul before Agrippa for devotions. This is Terry's idea. Three new [Freedom Riders]—Chicago & Minnesota—Kit, Lee & Claire [O'Conner]. Kit got beaten up in the other jail by a drunk. Newspaper. Saturday: four white and two Negro [Freedom Riders arrive]. Sunday: six white [riders]. Also Polly—the drunk that beat up Kit. We think she's a plant. Very O.K. so far . . . the new white boys are being sent to the pen. Betsy got a letter, towel, two washcloths & white sneakers. Dell got a letter from her father. New LONG clothesline—right over my bed. Dinner: grits, hot dog, cornbread. About the worst yet. Lots of singing.

Attorney Visits

JUNE 13, 1961

. . . Sang late last nite. Watch [out] for Polly . . . last time lifted $4. To farm this a.m. Sentence to late Aug. [NAACP attorney Jack] Young came. Great welcome. Sizes for clothes and other needs. Hunger strike in wind since Monday P.M.

We Become a Tourist Attraction, Again

JUNE 14, 1961

Many Girls State [delegates touring the jail]. I made a sign: Attention Tourists: I'm not a Yankee. I'm from Georgia. Guard took (upset). Girl has as souvenir. Much sewing & writing. Talk of NY Jewish food & sick songs. By the time I get out I'll know how a minority feels.

Another CARE Package

JUNE 15, 1961

Slept most time till about 3:30. Letter from parents. . . . Meeting while I slept: meditation at nite. I lead discussion on NV [nonviolence]. Kelley [jailer] and four T [trusties] came down with toiletries and flip-flops [sent] for us [from Woman Power Unlimited, a group of black church women in Jackson headed by Claire Collins Harvey and supported surreptitiously by a few white church ladies]. Much trading later. Tongs [flip-flops], shorts, T shirt, pants. Raised spirits much.

Crowded In

JUNE 21, 1961

Usual break. Exercise & ballet. Little read & write. So many [seventeen in cell meant for four], not much peace. Haven't slept well last two nights. Meeting on what to do with cigarettes—no ration. Win taken to sleep[ing] in shower. Sleeps most of day. Jailers getting worse. Drunk taken out this morning. Stew. Slept. Jane got package from Don—picture book. . . . Letters may be rationed. Wrote letters & read. Long day. . . . Dinner. Long evening. Danced. Learning cha-cha. Lights out early. Boy called that 10 more [were] arrested.

* * *

Two days later, we were sent off to Parchman.

JOAN TRUMPAUER MULHOLLAND spent the remainder of the summer in Parchman Penitentiary. Arrested numerous other times, she spent the next three years in Mississippi going to school at Tougaloo, working with both SNCC and CORE, and participating in the Jackson Movement's direct action campaigns. Later she returned to the D.C. area and raised a family. She worked in the public school system with children outside the American mainstream for more than thirty years. Her involvement in local community activities and approach to her job were shaped by her experiences in the Civil Rights Movement.

"Diary of a Freedom Rider" © 2010 by Joan Trumpauer Mulholland

They Are the Ones Who Got Scared

Diane Nash

Organizing in Mississippi in the wake of the Freedom Rides, SNCC's first female field secretary discovers her own strengths.

The Charge

How was it that I was in jail pregnant with my first child? It all began the summer of 1961 when the Freedom Rides came to Mississippi. I was based in Jackson as a SNCC staff member. SNCC and I were in agreement that it was crucial for people to be educated in how to carry on liberation struggles and make decisions themselves rather than simply follow what "leaders" told them to do. Since I had been educated in nonviolence while a student at Fisk University, I was providing workshops for young black people from Mississippi to help them prepare to join the Freedom Rides.

The workshops consisted of learning the reasons for remaining nonviolent and the philosophy that Mohandas Gandhi developed, which provided the moral framework that underlay the earlier movements in India and our current movement in the southern United States. We also discussed nonviolent strategy and tactics—for example, how to execute a nonviolent campaign or what physical position offered the maximum protection possible if a demonstrator was being attacked. We showed how if a demonstrator was being very severely beaten, other demonstrators could come to his or her aid by putting their bodies between the threatened demonstrator and the attackers. These classes also covered measures one could take to avoid becoming demoralized in jail and other related topics.

I was twenty-three years old, and some of the young people who attended the workshops were under twenty-one. Since it was against state law for Negro and white people to ride buses in a desegregated fashion, I was charged with contributing to the delinquency of minors for conducting workshops encouraging young people to desegregate the buses. Five minors who had participated in the workshops were named, and I was charged with five counts of "contributing."

At the trial, I pled not guilty, and it took only a few minutes for the judge to find me guilty. Each count carried a sentence of six months, giving me a total sentence of two and one-half years. I appealed my case, and while still in the courtroom I read my appeal bond carefully before I signed it. This document said I was to report to the appeals court when it came into session. The NAACP Legal Defense Fund in New York had already sent the twenty-five hundred dollars for my bond, so I was free to leave.

Sometime later I saw an article in the newspaper stating that the appeals court would come into session the following Monday morning. I called my attorney in Jackson, saying, "I understand that I'm supposed to be in court next Monday." He replied, "No, I'll notify you when." I called him the next day and every couple of days after that, insisting that I was required to appear, but I always received the same answer. Finally his attitude became unpleasant and he said, "Look, I *told* you, I'll let you know when you have to appear."

Three or four months later, my lawyer contacted me and said, "You *were* supposed to be there. Now there is a warrant out for your arrest, and you stand to forfeit your bond." Ordinarily, the judge or someone in the court told him when his clients were supposed to appear, but they had not done so in my case. They probably wanted to get my husband, James Bevel, and me out of the state, because by that time we were doing voter registration work in the Mississippi Delta and were receiving a good response from the black community there.

The Decision

This warrant for my arrest presented me with quite a dilemma: I did not like either of the two choices the warrant left me. I neither wished to go to jail as a civil rights worker in Mississippi, nor did I want to leave the state to escape the warrant, which would mean I would always face the possibility of arrest if I returned. To begin with, my husband and I had planned to spend the rest of our lives in Mississippi working for the liberation of black people. It was what both of us wanted to do—together—and what we thought God wanted us to do. It would have broken up our family and/or negated our plans if I or both of us had left. Also, I didn't want Mississippi white men or anybody else to be able to decide where we could live and work. I didn't want anybody to run me anywhere that I did not want to go. Further, if I left, the NAACP stood to lose the twenty-five hundred dollars in bond money. Twenty-five hundred dollars was worth a great deal more in 1961 than it is now.

Bevel and I felt a responsibility connected with encouraging black citizens to try to register to vote. Many black Delta residents lived and worked on plantations and often had large families. When a black plantation resident went to the courthouse to try to register to vote, often the white registrar or another white person at the courthouse would call the plantation owner and say "your Mary" or "your John" has come here trying to register to vote. By the time the voter applicants got back home, they found they had instantly lost their jobs and the places where they lived. It would have been wrong to encourage people to make such tremendous sacrifices, to put themselves in such jeopardy and then leave them before we reached the goal of getting the right to vote. If I left, I knew I would never again be able to look at myself in the mirror and respect the person I saw.

Lastly and quite importantly, Bevel and I were expecting our first child. I was already six months pregnant. Serving a two-and-a-half-year sentence would mean our first child would be born in jail and I wouldn't even know her for the first two years of her life. It was a dreadful, dreadful position in which to be. So I retreated to my bedroom. Bevel accommodated my request that I not be disturbed and did not let anyone bother me. I did nothing but eat, sleep, think, and pray. After three days I made the decision to surrender and serve the term.

With intense meditation I had tapped in to a very powerful force that I can't totally explain. But after I made that decision and emerged from my bedroom, I was invincible. There was really nothing anybody could do to hurt me. If they had killed me, I was ready. I knew I could handle it. I had thought over every eventuality and was prepared to face anything. I had come to a place of strength and peace.

Bevel was impressed with my decision and was very supportive. I felt he admired me for it and understood that I had to go where the Spirit led me. Soon I started to feel sorry for him, because when a number of people discovered that I was getting ready to go and serve the sentence, they would say, "Oh, Reverend Bevel, you shouldn't make your wife do that. That's too much." Even though both of us would say that he wasn't making me do it, some people remained convinced that he was. I imagine these people thought a woman was incapable of making a decision like that on her own. Instead of considering me a person with a brain and my own relationship to the Creator, they thought of me only as "the Reverend's wife."

My Baby Will Be Born in Jail

The decision made, my husband drove me to Jackson to turn myself in. I was unquestionably pregnant with an absolutely huge abdomen. I reported to the sheriff of Hinds County on Friday, April 27, 1962. I told him who I was and said, "I understand you have a warrant for my arrest; I am here to surrender. I wish to drop my appeal and serve the sentence." The authorities had not known I was pregnant when they issued the warrant, and the sheriff was clearly amused. He had a twinkle in his eye when he looked at my bulging midsection and responded, "This is Judge Moore's problem, not mine. Surrender to him." But that Friday afternoon, no one was in Judge Russell Moore's court. I had to wait until the following Monday. Many years later, when I saw the movie *Ghosts of Mississippi,* I learned that this was the same Judge Moore who was the judge in the trial of Byron De La Beckwith, the murderer of Medgar Evers. According to the movie, the rifle that was used to murder Evers was eventually found in Judge Moore's home. I went to his court that Monday in April 1962 as directed.

When I got to the courtroom, I thought, *I'm here to serve two and a half years; I'm not going to move to the back of the courtroom, too.* So I sat in the front row in defiance of local segregation laws. Jesse Harris and Luvaughn Brown, two fellow SNCC workers, who had only planned to accompany me to court, joined my protest and also sat in the front row. This spirit of unity and camaraderie, of not leaving each other to face the adversity of segregation alone, was one of the most valuable things about SNCC. The judge sentenced me to ten days in the Jackson County Jail for contempt of court and Jesse and Luvaughn to forty days on the Hinds County prison farm, where they were beaten repeatedly by prison guards.

The Jail

In the spring of 1962, when I entered that Mississippi jail to serve the ten-day sentence, not the least accommodation was made for my advanced pregnancy, and it was clear that the jail administrators intended to make my stay as difficult as possible. They did not allow me to take anything with me to jail, not even vitamin pills or a toothbrush or a change of clothes. The only clothes I had throughout my stay were the clothes I wore in—a cotton maternity blouse and skirt. In my cell there was a washbowl, a commode, and a shower. There was no door on the shower or partition around the commode. I tried to time the use of these facilities to gain some degree of privacy. I combed my hair and brushed my teeth with my fingers. I'd wash my underwear and wear my outer clothes when I was awake. When I prepared to sleep, I'd wash my outer clothes. While I slept, I'd wear my underwear and wrap myself securely in a sheet, leaving my outer clothes to dry. This way I had clean clothes every day.

I developed a routine to deal with the amazing number of cockroaches in my cell. At night they made what seemed to be a deliberate march toward me. They would start from many different locations in the cell, climb the walls, walk up to the ceiling, position themselves right over my cot, and drop down onto it. I sat up all night so I could dodge the roaches. When one began to drop, I would get up until it landed on the cot, then I'd scoot it off with a piece of paper or something. I slept during the day, when not nearly as many roaches walked around. There was another type of insect that was so big that when everything was quiet late at night, I could hear it walk across the floor.

The Mississippi jailers kept me isolated. I'm sure they were afraid that I would influence other Negro "residents" of the jail with freedom-fighting ideas. No one else was put in my cell, although it was designed to hold several people. I was not allowed to have any visits from family or friends. All of the other prisoners had been instructed not to talk to me, though the trusty, a white woman from New York, occasionally broke that rule and also passed me some *Reader's Digest Condensed Books,* one at a time. It was our practice to engage in conversation with prison personnel, arresting policemen, lunch counter managers, and anyone in the opposition. We would talk to them in a calm, constructive manner designed to urge them to consider the morality of segregation.

I did engage the trusty, and we had conversations when she thought she would not be discovered. She was aware of the existence of prejudice and discrimination, but she thought it was a minor thing, not presenting any serious problems for black people in Mississippi. Among the many things I shared with her were statistics from a current report from the state's Department of Education printed in the *New Orleans Times-Picayune* showing the vast discrepancies in money spent on children's yearly education. Overall, school districts spent $81.86 per white child and $21.77 per Negro child. Quite a few districts had huge differences—for example, Holly Bluff spent

$191.77 for white children and only $1.26 for black; Noxubee County spent $113.29 and $1.21 respectively. Our conversations, she told me, made her see how difficult the situation was for black people in Mississippi.

Then there was a local white woman who visited a couple of times and was really funny. I heard her before I saw her. She stood at the end of the hall and shouted, "Yoo-hoo, I just came to bring a little sunshine." I thought, *Who is this?* She wore a hat with a flower on it; the stem was a spiral that held the flower six or seven inches above the hat. She looked as if she had stepped out of a comic strip. She was doing her Christian duty, visiting prisoners, including the black prisoners. When she came to my cell, she said, "God loves you, even though you're in jail." I answered, "I believe that is true." I engaged her also and told her why I was there. I challenged her on the morality of segregation, suggesting that as a Christian she should protest my being there to the judge and to the prison authorities. At first she said that God didn't intend for the races to be mixing. Naturally, I disagreed with that. We had a couple of exchanges and she took flight. When she visited the next time, she muttered a brief greeting and did not stop at my cell.

The Case Vanishes

Upon my release from jail, I came before Judge Moore again. He indicated that the matter of contempt of court was finished and that I was free to leave. I asked, "Are you going to hear the case about contributing to the delinquency of minors?" "No," he said. That surprised me. I wanted the matter resolved. I did not want to be in a position where court officials could call up the case at a time of their choosing, so I pointed out, "Well, Judge Moore, if you let me go, I am going to go right back and resume what I was doing." Moore insisted, "The court is not going to hear that case at this time." I continued, "I live at 614 Chrisman Avenue in Cleveland, Mississippi. I want you to know I am not hiding from you. When you get ready to hear the case, that's where you can find me." I was released. When I returned home I sent him a certified letter repeating the same information.

What had happened? Why hadn't the court prosecuted me on the charge of contributing to the delinquency of minors? Before appearing in court, I had launched my own support campaign and contacted all the major national civil rights organizations and some of their local chapters. I was part of SNCC, so the SNCC national office and SNCC personnel were on alert. Bevel was on the staff of the Southern Christian Leadership Conference, so I knew I would have SCLC's assistance. I telephoned the Congress of Racial Equality's national office and every CORE chapter where I knew someone, likewise with the NAACP. I called well-known entertainer Harry Belafonte, who had been very supportive of SNCC. I also contacted journalists, which resulted in a considerable amount of publicity for my case. *JET* magazine, based in my hometown of Chicago, had pictured me on its cover three times and had written accompanying stories. They printed a quote of mine that attracted considerable attention and sympathy in the black community. I had said, "This will be a Negro child born in Mississippi, and so wherever he is born, he will be born in jail."

The night before I was to appear in court to surrender, I desperately wanted to prepare a press release as well as a longer statement for movement people explaining the necessity for my surrendering and serving the sentence. I saw an opportunity to address the "jail-no-bail" issue. Staying in jail focuses attention on the injustice. It puts the financial burden on the state, making the state pay the cost for enforcing unjust laws. Posting bond puts the financial burden on our community of supporters and takes the authorities off the hook, defeating much of the purpose for going to jail.

When I needed to prepare the press release and the piece for movement people that night, I was tired, tired in a way that only a pregnant woman can be. While I was expecting, it seemed that physical functions took on a compelling dimension. I was lying, fully clothed, on top of a bed at the Jackson freedom house with a blanket covering me, so sleepy that sleep seemed all-consuming. I was in a deep, deep sleep.

Fortunately, Anne Braden had come to Jackson to help with my campaign. She prepared the press release and the longer statement for movement people regarding "jail-no-bail." I was incapable of doing it. She sat down at the typewriter and worked late that night into the wee hours. When she needed a quote from me or other information, she would shake me and ask me what she had to ask. I answered and went right back to sleep. I believe having those documents in circulation also played a major part in keeping me from spending the two and a half years in jail. The organization in which Anne was prominent, the Southern Conference Educational Fund (SCEF), and the newspaper she edited with her husband Carl, the *Southern Patriot*, followed and championed my case.

The fact that our phones were tapped worked to my advantage in this situation. The Mississippi authorities were aware of the phone calls I made and of the positive responses I received and probably decided that putting me in jail was more of a public relations liability than they wanted to assume. I was glad I didn't have to forego the deeply fulfilling experience of mothering my first child during her babyhood.

I came away from this whole experience much strengthened. I grew spiritually through tapping in to the power of an extraordinary force through meditation. In jail I learned that I could live with very little. The oppressive authorities imprisoned me and withheld basic necessities to frighten and control me, but it backfired. They are the ones who got scared. In the end, I was freer, more determined, and stronger than ever.

A founding member of SNCC, **DIANE NASH** had already served thirty days in jail in Rock Hill, South Carolina, before going to jail in Mississippi. She went to jail many more times during the course of the Movement. After the birth of her daughter and a son a few years later, she remained a full-time movement activist. Valued by the staffs of both SNCC and SCLC as a dedicated believer in the philosophy of nonviolence and as an expert strategist in civil disobedience, she was one of the two major strategists for the SCLC's 1965 voting rights campaign in Selma, Alabama. A peace activist, she worked in opposition to the war in Vietnam and still instructs groups around the country in Gandhian philosophies and nonviolent strategies.

Danny Lyon first photographed the Movement in Cairo, Illinois, in the summer of 1962. Encouraged by James Forman, he continued to photograph the Movement and joined the SNCC staff in 1963.

Ella Baker, who called the 1960 meeting of student activists in Raleigh, North Carolina, out of which SNCC was created. Her grassroots organizing philosophy grounded SNCC's strategies; she is considered the "godmother" of SNCC. Danny Lyon/Magnum Photos

Dottie Miller Zellner, who lost her shoes to high-pressure fire hoses after being clubbed, gives an affidavit to SNCC executive secretary James Forman (Danville, Virginia, 1963). Danny Lyon/Magnum Photos

SNCC field secretary Prathia Hall speaking at a mass meeting. Hall was a key organizer of SNCC projects in both Southwest Georgia and Alabama (Alabama, 1963). Danny Lyon/Magnum Photos

SNCC worker Martha Prescod (foreground, third from left) accompanying a group of residents for a voter registration attempt (Greenwood, Mississippi, 1963). Danny Lyon/Magnum Photos

Sit-in at Toddle House, a segregated southern restaurant chain, during
a national SNCC staff meeting. Following the demonstration, the group
was arrested and jailed. Seated, right to left: Chuck Neblett (facing), Judy
Richardson (facing with papers), Joyce Ladner (speaking with man behind
her), Taylor Washington (looking out window). Standing, right to left: George
Greene (foreground, looking out window, behind Chuck Neblett), Ivanhoe
Donaldson (background, looking out window) (Atlanta, December 1963).
Danny Lyon/Magnum Photos

SNCC staff singing in Atlanta office during a national staff meeting: Joyce Ladner, Judy Richardson, Jean Wheeler Smith (left to right), with Charles Sherrod pointing with amusement at a young boy (Atlanta, 1963–1964). Danny Lyon/Magnum Photos

Cambridge, Maryland, leader Gloria Richardson and other demonstrators are led to jail by Maryland State Police. SNCC demonstrators (left to right): Stanley Wise (second from left); Gloria Richardson; Stokely Carmichael (short sleeves); Cleve Sellers (denim jacket) (Cambridge, Maryland, spring 1964). Danny Lyon/ Magnum Photos

Hattiesburg, Mississippi, Freedom Day demonstration. The mass registration attempt was organized to gain national publicity for the beating and murders of those attempting to register to vote (center foreground: SNCC worker Dona Richards) (Hattiesburg, Mississippi, January 22, 1964). Danny Lyon/ Magnum Photos

Jean Wheeler Smith standing in aisle during SNCC national staff meeting. Also pictured: Dorie Ladner (left rear, sitting in cubbyhole at back of hall) and Jack Minnis (far right with glasses) (Waveland, Mississippi, November 1964). Danny Lyon/Magnum Photos

During World War II, Tamio Wakayama was part of the Japanese Canadian community that was dispossessed and sent into internment camps in British Columbia. After the war, his family was forced to relocate and settled in the black community of the southern Ontario town of Chatham, which was once a terminus on the Underground Railroad. In 1963 Tamio drove to the funeral for the four little girls in Birmingham, where he met Jim Forman, John Lewis, Julian Bond, and Danny Lyon. After driving them to Atlanta, he was put on SNCC staff and, with the encouragement of Danny Lyon, eventually became a SNCC photographer.

Gwen Robinson leading a mass meeting in a church in Laurel, Mississippi, during a voter registration campaign as part of Mississippi Freedom Summer in 1964 (Laurel, Mississippi, summer 1964). Tamio Wakayama

Betty Garman working the WATS telephone line in Jackson during Freedom Summer to maintain communications between the SNCC/COFO campaign and the outside world via SNCC's many national networks: Friends of SNCC, Campus Friends of SNCC, et al. (Jackson, Mississippi, summer 1964). Tamio Wakayama

PART 3

Movement Leaning Posts

The Heart and Soul of the Southwest Georgia Movement, 1961–1963

> The women were the leaning posts that
> everyone relied on. We were the strength
> of the Albany Movement.
>
> —Joann Christian Mants

In this section women born and raised in Southwest Georgia share their stories of living with segregation and participating in civil rights activities. In the latter half of 1961, SNCC began organizing in parts of the South known as the Black Belt. Former cotton-growing lands, these were primarily rural areas where black residents usually outnumbered white residents, presenting a potential for substantial black political power. Portions of the old cotton kingdom were located in a cluster of counties in Southwest Georgia with the town of Albany at the center. In the fall of 1961, three male SNCC field secretaries—Charles Sherrod, Cordell Reagon, and Charles Jones—entered Albany, joining with local participants in the already ongoing fight against segregation.

The contributors' firsthand accounts of growing up in the Deep South offer a glimpse into the nature of segregation that, in turn, provides valuable background to understanding the Civil Rights Movement. The system of segregation was much more than a set of state and local laws designed to keep the races apart. It was a fundamentally unjust system, intended to demean and terrorize black people while maintaining white supremacy.

The separate facilities provided for black patrons were usually significantly inferior to those provided for their white counterparts. The white waiting rooms at train and bus stations were large indoor rooms while the black waiting area might be an open porch outdoors with no indoor bathroom facilities. Educational facilities for black students were similarly inferior. The schools for white children were usually substantial brick buildings; the same school board, particularly in rural counties, usually provided rickety wooden buildings without central heat or indoor plumbing for black children. Everywhere southern school boards allocated much less for each black child's education than for that of each white student. On rare occasions, such as in McCree Harris's case, a state might pay for a black graduate student's education out of state to avoid integrating a white university. Quite frequently, though, white officials decided it was unnecessary to offer any cultural or recreational institutions at all for the black population in their jurisdiction, designating public facilities such as museums, libraries, parks, and swimming pools as white only.

What might seem to be individual acts of meanness in the following narratives actually reflect some of the unwritten social requirements that accompanied legal segregation. For example, all store clerks in the Deep South, not just the ones described here, routinely took care of all white customers before waiting on black ones, including the white customers who arrived after the black patrons. White southerners, young and old, called black people by first names, but black people were required to address whites with a title and use the last name for adults. So a mature black woman would be called "Janie" by her employer's five-year-old child, whom the older woman would have to call "Miss." Black men especially were never to look a white person in the eye and had to remove their hats when standing in the presence of a white person.

Two of the stories in this section and several others throughout the book deal with the sexual oppression that was also a part of segregation in the Deep South. If a white person perceived any imagined or real sexual contact between a black man and a white woman, the black man could be severely punished, castrated, or killed. Black women, not exempt from other forms of physical punishment, could also be sexually exploited by white men without much legal recourse. Subjecting black women to sexual innuendos, sexual touching, even rape, was permissible under this system. Sexual objectification of black women was so common, Annette Jones White recalls, that school-age white children felt free to sing sexually charged rhymes to young black girls.

Verbal and physical brutality was also an integral part of the Deep South's system of segregation. White southerners were free to push, shove, slap, and kick black people. White racists routinely employed more severe attacks and terrorist methods of enforcement to keep black people "in their place." The local sheriffs or police chiefs, often Ku Klux Klan members themselves, were always the point men for maintaining segregation and initiating the suppression of "uppity" or activist black people. Southern law officers, as already seen in the sit-in stories, could notify the white townspeople most likely to form an angry mob when civil rights actions were taking place and make police protection scarce. In Southwest Georgia, as in other southern locales, law enforcement officials might give the names of black people who attended mass meetings or participated in voter registration efforts to employers and white supremacists. As a result, movement participants might lose their jobs and find themselves subject to attacks by night riders.

Seeing segregation as a whole allows for a clearer understanding of the Civil Rights Movement. For women in Southwest Georgia, attaining dignity, equality, and an end to sexual oppression, brutality, and terrorism were important aspects of their fight against segregation. In Albany and other locations where SNCC established projects, local women of all ages provided the central support for civil rights activities. In Joann Christian Mants' words, women were the Movement's "leaning posts," helping the organization to establish itself and maintain various programs. Their stories disclose how, linked by interconnected ties of family, friendship, and institutional memberships, they used their existing social relationships to create a core of dedicated freedom fighters, to bring in greater numbers, and to augment the Movement's strength. For many movement women, participation was an intergenerational family undertaking.

Many of Albany's female activists also brought to the Movement individual as well as organizational protest experience. Familiar with the NAACP and introduced to SNCC and SCLC in the sixties, they made choices about the best way to stay active. They understood how little protection they had and just how risky their civil rights actions were. They felt that changing the terms and circumstances of their lives rested with them alone, that no one else was going to come along and make things better for them. The sheer volume of local women's efforts, as well as the audacity and boldness of their actions, helped propel the Movement forward.

Family and community traditions of everyday struggle in Southwest Georgia's black community, along with a solid religious faith, nurtured and strengthened the Civil Rights Movement. A special contribution of the Southwest Georgia Movement derived from the area's deep and intense musical culture, which stretched back into previous centuries. When connected to a freedom struggle and occasionally touched by other musical influences, this music was especially inspirational and sustained black and white participants, who were taking great risks. It was the power of the congregational singing in Albany's mass meetings that was the genesis of the effort to take the music to a national audience as a means of securing support for southern-based movement organizing. Albany's music became the music of the Movement when Cordell Reagon organized the first group of SNCC Freedom Singers in 1962. This group was comprised of Reagon; two Albany student activists, Rutha Harris and Bernice Johnson; and an experienced SNCC field secretary from Carbondale, Illinois, Chuck Neblett. Booked by Toshi Seeger, Pete Seeger's wife and manager, the Freedom Singers took the story of the Movement through the singing of freedom songs to audiences all over the country.

SNCC workers entered Albany with an approach to civil rights activism that was fundamentally different from that of Dr. King's organization, SCLC. The goal for SNCC was the creation of long-term, democratically run grassroots movements headed by local people. SNCC staff decried SCLC's tendency to launch short-term campaigns run authoritatively by its national staff. The issues of whether to support or participate in SCLC campaigns and whether SNCC should take time away from community organizing to sponsor demonstrations at all were matters of debate in national and local SNCC meetings throughout the Movement.

Although encouraged by Dr. King's participation in the Albany Movement, many local participants neither approved of his moratorium on demonstrations nor accepted his view of the Albany Movement as a failure. As Diane Nash was during the Freedom Rides, they were concerned about maintaining movement momentum and wished to continue demonstrations. Though their demands were not met and there was no immediate desegregation of public facilities, they judged their movement a victory. They found success in the coming together of community members from all walks of life and of all ages and in showing that it was possible to build and sustain a mass movement for racial justice in the Deep South. In addition, they knew that their movement was the model for many subsequent citywide protests across the South. Several of the writers in this section also take ownership of the Albany Movement, making it very clear that they see it as their movement rather than Dr. King's.

The authors are aware that by standing fast in the face of economic and physical reprisals, jail terms, bombs, and death threats, they had served notice that the most powerful weapons of terror in the southern segregationist arsenal would not stop their fight for freedom. Instead of just a few individuals fighting oppression, when black Albany protesters marched, they marched by the hundreds. When they decided to fill the jails, they not only filled them in Albany but also in the surrounding counties. Like the sit-inners and Freedom Riders, they felt strengthened and emboldened by their movement experiences. The white South retaliated with everything it had, but when it was over, black Southwest Georgia residents were still marching and protesting. In Carolyn Daniels's words, "We just kept going."

Ripe for the Picking

Janie Culbreth Rambeau

One of the students expelled from Albany State College for participating in the Civil Rights Movement describes the mounting grievances that ripened into a mass movement in Albany, Georgia.

A Gradual Accumulation

I cannot say exactly when I noticed the strong trees bending with the fruit of unrest. I do know that from as far back as I can remember there were repeated accounts of events that brought fear, anger, and wonder as my parents told various stories in deliberate, sometimes whetted voices. These events were told with such frequency that I can remember them verbatim. My parents spoke about the murder of a northern white man who was friendly to black people and the subsequent framing and lynching for the crime of a crippled and slightly retarded black man called Buddy. I often heard accounts of hangings and property burnings. Jail and prison cruelties were commonplace. Older people often talked about events that occurred at the prison on Newton Road in the area where the youth detention center and the State Department of Transportation are now.

The man in charge of the prison was called Cap'n Penson. Prisoners on his chain gang were beaten and often killed for little or no reason. One of my uncles had worked on Penson's chain gang and talked about how Cap'n Penson would make them dig a grave. Next, Penson would hit a prisoner in the head with an ax or a shovel, throw the prisoner over into the hole, and order the other prisoners to cover him up. My uncle said there were times when the prisoners were not completely dead when they covered them.

Later a modern housing project, Dennis Homes, was built along this same road. One lady, Mrs. Evelyn Jones, who died in the 1980s at the age of 104, refused to move there even though they had all the modern conveniences that her house lacked. Explaining that no amount of luxury could make her move, she said, "When Cap'n Penson had that chain gang, he had so many folks buried all up and down that Newton Road that they called it Freedom Town Cemetery. Some of my folks is buried there, so I can't move there."

I used to hear my mom and dad talk about the early 1930s when they moved off the white man's plantation in south Dougherty County and into town, resulting in their being harassed and threatened. When black people moved off the plantation, white landowners considered it an act of defiance and often falsified documents or made unfounded accusations to force their laborers to remain. One Saturday evening, as my father was riding his bike home from his job in town, the son of the plantation owners, a young white man, stopped his car with the intention of beating my dad into going back to the farm. He knocked my father off the bike, but my dad jumped back up and beat that young man to the ground. Later that night my father was arrested, but a day or two later he was released, and my parents never went back to the plantation.

My parents were very staunch Baptists, and this provided me with moral leadership. My sisters and I used to laugh about my dad's being a "starched and ironed" Baptist deacon, benign but staunch. My parents reared me in a rural church in a community where church life was a serious part of my upbringing. It took all the neighbors and everybody else to raise one child. They all encouraged us to do well, expecting that we would go on to get a college education.

I grew up in a segregated situation, and even before I knew what prejudice was, I had experienced it. Once, as a very small child, I got on the bus and just sat down. I was very excited, because I was going downtown to get some new shoes. My mom took me by my arm and carried me to the back of the bus to the "black" section. I simply did not understand, but I knew she loved me. In elementary school we went on our first school picnic in Tift Park. At the park a group of us ran for the playground where the swings were, not knowing that there were areas where black children were not allowed to play. The teacher, who was black, came at us with her strap and drove us back to the designated area. I can still hear her saying, "You colored children got to learn to stay in your place." Again I did not understand. I did not know at the time that my mother and the teacher were protecting me and that the teacher might have lost her job if she had not kept us in "our place."

I don't know exactly when my awareness started, but each experience renewed within me the experience that had come before. Over the years there was an accumulation. My first act of rebellion or fighting back occurred downtown when I was in high school. My mom used to chew Apple Sun Cured Tobacco. I went downtown on Saturdays to get her supply at the Silver five-and-ten-cent store. The sales clerk there was really mean to black customers. She would make us wait until she finished helping all the white customers. When she came to me, she always threw the package and the change across the counter at me.

One Saturday I said to myself, "I don't have time to fool with this." I took a can full of pennies, the exact amount that I needed for the purchase, and I waited. When she put the tobacco in a bag and threw it across the counter, with all my force I threw the can full of pennies at her—pennies scattered everywhere. In order to avoid arrest, I headed for the back door and out through a little alley.

Other things started to come into focus, such as segregated water fountains that had been there all the while, but all of a sudden, as I was in high school, these things were becoming more and more a target in my eyes.

Praying in Jail

By the time SNCC came, many people felt the way I did. We had begun to get tired. All this was ripe for picking. I remember the mass meetings and people like Charles Sherrod going around talking to kids about going swimming and having a watermelon party at Tift Park, things we could not do in segregated Albany. Being able to do those things sounded good to us. Then a lot of the black people in Albany started saying things like, "You're as good as they are. Why do you have to go to the back door to get food, and why do you have to drink from the 'colored' water fountain. Why do you have to go to the 'colored' restrooms?" These questions sounded very good, too.

Soon we decided to demonstrate against these conditions, even though it meant going to jail. One of the main reasons we went to jail was to remove the hammer that the power structure held over our heads. For years, black people were threatened with jail. Jail became the representation of fear. The trumped-up charges, unfair trials, and regular beatings in jail were weapons in the white South's arsenal of oppression. Thus, in an effort to maintain control of an already oppressed people, the hammer of jail hung heavily. To remove the threat, people moved against it. Hear God's people singing, "We are not afraid."

So we marched knowing we faced certain arrest and jail. I marched in the first large Albany demonstration on a cold, rainy morning in December 1961. Several hundred—old and young—marched down Jackson Street toward the jail, singing, "We Shall Overcome." Policemen tried to break up the demonstrations, but the people were determined. Chief Laurie Pritchett came on the bullhorn, yelling in frustration, "You are all under arrest." We continued to march and sing.

The jail at that time was on the south side of Pine Avenue next to the fire station. A small breezeway separated the two. When we reached the jail, we were herded in like cattle. People were being pushed, and from time to time someone would trip or be pushed to the ground. One teenage girl was literally dragged across the graveled way. Inside, a white policeman shoved her into the iron bars. Her head bled profusely. We looked on helplessly. Although we were wet and cold, nobody wanted to leave.

I stood there that morning, an insignificant prisoner, mentally noting the unfolding events and remembering the stories that I had heard from my youth. Inside, the jail conditions were deplorable. Water fountains were directly over the toilet stools; to add to our discomfort, some of the germ-infested mattresses had been removed from the metal bunks, and we were housed in overcrowded cells.

Later that day, many people were transferred to jails in surrounding counties, because Albany could not hold all of the movement prisoners. I was with the group remaining in Albany. We sang and prayed. After three days some people became very ill. Some had chronic illnesses, such as high blood pressure and diabetes; others were ill from the damp and cold, especially because they had no change of clothing, after having been wet and cold during the march. It was then that I wrote the lyrics asking the mayor, Asa Kelley, and Chief Pritchett to release us. I set the words to the tune of the Negro spiritual "Rockin' Jerusalem." I couldn't sing, but Bertha Gober, a fellow Albany State student, who had already been expelled for her civil rights activity, could. She took the lead and we sang out:

> Oh Pritchett, Oh Kelley, Oh Pritchett
> Open them cells
> Oh Pritchett, Oh Kelley, Oh Pritchett
> Open them cells
> I hear God's children
> Crying for mercy
> I hear God's children
> Praying in jail
> Freedom, Freedom, Freedom
> (*Sung in background*)
> Bond's getting higher
> Praying in jail
> Bond's getting higher
> Praying in jail

Others started to sing Negro spirituals. Each song led to another and to frequent prayers. Word came to us in jail that Dr. Martin Luther King Jr.

was coming to Albany. Excitement resounded through the jail: "Martin Luther King is coming to Albany. Martin Luther King is coming to Albany." Demonstrations continued and so did the jail-ins.

When I was released from jail, I had a letter from Albany State College informing me that I had been expelled because of my participation in the demonstrations. There were more than fifty other students who faced the same situation. These were not troublemakers, but upstanding students, including Miss Albany State, Annette Jones, who lost her scholarship. We were expelled for the cause of human dignity.

The Albany Movement

When the Albany Movement leaders called a halt to the marches and the demonstrations during a "cooling-off period," I got angry. Many other students were disappointed also. I said, "This is one of the biggest stunts Satan ever pulled." Everything had been going full steam, but we lost the momentum. During that time there were still some people in jail suffering; some even laid down their lives, and I don't think the cooling-off period was an effective way to deal with that. In addition, we were never able to get people together with as much zeal after we called that halt. Though angry, most of us students complied with the Albany Movement leaders, because we had such high respect for Dr. William G. Anderson, the president of the Albany Movement. Likewise, when we had the boycott during the Movement, if we had just kept it going a little longer, it could really have done the job. There were some black people with money who were having clothing and other items delivered to their homes while the Movement was boycotting downtown. Over the years I have had to deal with my own prejudices and anger. After the Movement I would see people who had been strongly against us, who paid lip service to the Movement but broke the boycott, people who had not lost their jobs or made sacrifices for the Movement. They would be in restaurants and other places where we could not go before the Movement, and it was a very painful experience for me. Painful because often those students, women, and children who had helped to open the doors were the ones who did not have the money to enjoy the fruits of their labor, to patronize the very places they had helped desegregate. Very gently, the Lord guided me through that stage of my life.

There was a time when some people thought those of us in the Movement were a bunch of renegades. Some of the professional people even thought this, but other local people supported us in some very nice ways. Sometimes after mass meetings, we young people would go to Nastie Sallie's, a small local black eatery. At her place, for two dollars we could get enough food to feed four or five people—shrimp box, chicken box, sausage sandwiches. She would pile ice cream on top of the cones until it just fell off, because she was such a strong supporter of the Movement. It would all be so good.

After we'd been expelled from Albany State College, we started focusing on voter registration. Some ministers from SCLC came down to Albany. I remember Rev. Fred Bennett in particular. We worked on voter registration, canvassing from house to house, in the summertime. It was very hot and dusty. Our goal was to cover every house in our district. Some folks wouldn't even give us a glass of water. Many people flat-out refused to register to vote. I'm not sure why. Maybe fear played into this, or not understanding, or seriously feeling inferior, or a combination of all three. Sometimes there'd be a thunderstorm, and because we were from the Movement, people wouldn't let us take shelter on their porches. Some people told us that we should stay in our places. One lady told me her white lady voted for her. Another didn't want to talk with me, and when I insisted, she said, "Come on in the house." When I got inside, she threw hot grease at me, barely missing me.

What could I do? I picked up and went on. I get emotional about this: getting people to register was not as easy as some people think. It might seem that all you had to do is tell someone, "If you vote, you can elect your officials. You get the right people in office, and you can have a voice." Until then we had not had a voice. We lived in a time when black people did not even think about things that we take for granted now. Looking back I wonder, how did we achieve all this? We didn't have any black city officials, black county commissioners, black police officers, no one to identify with. Some people thought, "Why vote? It's not going to do any good anyway." There were some places in the South where white people tampered with the vote. It's not easy to get people to register to vote, because you have to convince them that voting will bring about a change.

I still have the mental picture of one woman, bending over a washtub, sleeves rolled up to her elbows, using a washboard. She was visibly oppressed and worn, but afraid to register to vote. When I returned home that evening, I wrote about the event in poetic form, as I often did to relieve the stress:

> One day as I was walking down the long, hot dusty road,
> I saw a woman bending down beneath a heavy load.
> She turned her head to look at me, and then she said,
>   "My Dear,
> Whatever you are looking for you will not find it here."
> You won't find it here.
> I said, "I want to help you with that heavy load you tote

But first you must lift up your head and register and vote."
She said, "My child, I know that you are doing your very best,
But leave it to the Lord, my child, and He will do the rest."
He will do the rest.
I said the Lord will never come and put it in your hand.
If Freedom is a-coming, we must take a firmer stand.
We gotta take a stand, my friend, we gotta take a stand.
If Freedom is a-coming, we must take a firmer stand.
We have to take a stand.

The reality of the Movement and the demonstrations was that we were all hyped up. It was so exciting. Everything was sounding good, and we felt sure we were going forward. After all, we were singing "We Shall Overcome" and "Oh, Freedom"—"Oh, freedom over me. Before I'll be a slave, I'll be buried in my grave, . . ." We were so sure that everything we wanted would be accomplished in a short period of time. But when it came to something very basic and simple like registering to vote and following through with actually voting, it was not as easy as a lot of people thought. Another thing that kept people from registering was that they were told by white folks, "They're gonna cut off your check," meaning a pension or Social Security. Of course it was a hoax, a fraud, but some older people didn't know that.

In essence, what I went through in the Movement is the very same thing I have gone through in the ministry. I told one male minister, "You know, there was a time when we worked as maids in white people's houses. I would go in their houses through the back door and clean all the way to the front, wash, iron, cook, and see about their children, but I was not good enough to sit down to the table with them. Now I'm seeing the same thing here. I can clean your house from the back to the front, but I'm not good enough to sit in the pulpit." It comes down to the same kind of prejudice. I'm sure the Lord took me through some of my past experiences becoming a minister so that I would know how to handle the present ones. When the time came, I had help from a lot of my brethren in the ministry, and they have stood by me through the years.

Albany's Finest Citizens

Many people paid a dear price for the cause of human justice. There were some students who got so involved that they never finished college and gave up possible lifetime careers for the Movement. Some were not mentally, emotionally, or physically able to return. Some have since suffered mental breakdowns and nervous disorders. There were people who lost their jobs because their children or other family members were involved. I do not feel that anyone can go through a movement like that without being affected by it. In some ways I was not ready for everything that happened to me—jail, being expelled, canvassing. I don't think anyone was, but it was time and there was no turning back. The call was a compelling force.

Often students are not given credit for the things they started and the sacrifices they made in the Movement. The NAACP and the Albany Movement Committee were very important entities, but what made Albany stand out was the fact that overall it was the people's movement. I'm pained when I read books or see articles that call Albany Dr. Martin Luther King Jr.'s Waterloo. It can't be your Waterloo unless it was your fight in the beginning. It was the people's movement, not his. He came and he did a lot of good, but he came because the Albany Movement *invited* him to join *us*. The Movement was already under way with several hundred people in jail when Dr. King first came to Albany.

A majority of Albany Movement participants were women, some of them very young. There was the Christian family and all their girls. Many mothers marched holding their little children by the hand. When our Avon lady, a strong, soldier-type woman, Mrs. Corene Watkins, went to jail, she went prepared with everything she needed in the line of toiletries. Dear Dear and Pa Papa Berry, the grandparents of Annette Jones White, opened their doors and were great supporters of the Albany Movement. Annette's mother, Mrs. Delores Jones, welcomed the Movement. My parents, Mr. and Mrs. Ross Culbreth, were serious supporters of the cause and were encouragers of those who were actively involved. Mrs. Katie B. Harris sheltered many who came to Albany with the struggle. Eighteen-year-old Ola Mae Quartimon actually started the bus boycott in Albany when she refused to give up her seat. Every policeman in Albany, it seemed, came to arrest her: one black person—a student. Mary Tolson Jones, Mrs. Alice Porter, Mrs. Lorenzo Gaines, and her entire family, and many, many more carried the torch for freedom. I am sometimes grieved that so little is written about these fine people of Albany. I tell you, the time was ripe for the picking.

Even the news media was antiblack. At that time, Albany's Channel 10 (WALB) was the only station that most people could get on television. It was horrible the way newscasters and city officials spoke of black people. At the beginning of the Albany Movement, and of Civil Rights Movements around the nation, words like "niggers," "nigras," and other inflammatory remarks were commonplace on the air. White people used to ask, "Why do y'all want to be called black instead of Negroes?" The answer was simple: it's hard to mispronounce black.

The Albany Movement was very diverse. There were students from everywhere, people of every color, ministers and leaders from various religions, Jews, Gentiles, Catholics, black and white who came here. Those marches were really something to behold. Just the idea of seeing that many people hand in hand sends chills all up and down my spine. After our original marches, people came from all over the country and joined us to show their support. Those who couldn't come held prayer vigils for us in cities all across the nation.

One night someone was throwing those little handmade bombs in the street between Shiloh and Mt. Zion. Mass meetings were being held simultaneously in both churches directly across the street from each other. This was one of those times when Dr. Martin Luther King Jr. was speaking. We didn't know where the small bombs were coming from, whether it was from black folks or white folks, but the small bombs were causing loud explosions and making large fires in the middle of the street. Still, we were so caught up in the moment, we were not afraid of anything. We would have walked through those bombs if called to do so. We could have marched through fire, just to let everyone know we weren't scared of fire.

I needed to go through what I went through in the Civil Rights Movement. I needed to be expelled from school, I needed to go through the threats of voter registration in order to stand now, because a tree that doesn't get any rain, or any storm, or any wind will not grow to be a strong tree. I tell students about some of the things that we lived through, and they say, "I don't believe that." We have not done a lot of informing our young people about the Albany Movement. Why haven't we? It is a legacy that should have been passed on from day one, because that boldness, that calling that we had then is what we need today. We need the same kind of feeling in our meetings today. After those meetings we were ready to go anywhere and do anything. Some people say we got closer to the Lord during the Movement. I do know we got closer to one another, thereby getting closer to God.

I don't know where that feeling came from or what was different then, but our spirit was strong and it could be heard in our songs. You sing the same songs now, and it won't move you the same way it did then. It was time. It was ripe. It *was* harvest time. And when it's ripe, you had better pick it. There was fire in our singing; those songs touched you way down inside until you shook. It was more than singing. It has got to be that it was harvest time. Those were harvest songs and we were ripe for the picking.

An honors graduate of Monroe High School, **JANIE CULBRETH RAMBEAU** returned to and graduated from Albany State College with a degree in French. She went on to earn several master's degrees and two doctorates. Returning to Albany, she taught secondary school for thirty-eight years and college-level classes for two. She is the first black female to be ordained in the Baptist Church in Albany and serves as pastor of the House of Refuge Baptist Church, Inc., whose major mission is to save the lost and minister to the poor.

Finding Form for the Expression of My Discontent

Annette Jones White

Miss Albany State's familiarity with racial oppression leads her into the struggle for equality.

Growing Up in Segregated Albany

I was born August 29, 1939, in Albany, Georgia, at a time when most whites called us "nigger" or "nigra," and we called ourselves "Negro" or "colored." My father, Paul Lawrence Jones, was a carpenter who could find work only as a laborer because of his color. He struggled to support us, and it was not until many years later, when he was hired to help build the U.S. Marine Corps Supply Center in Albany, that he had a steady job with a decent salary and benefits. My mother, Delores Berry Jones, washed and ironed at home for several white doctors and their families. My parents, brothers and sisters, and I lived with my maternal grandparents. My grandfather, Asa Berry, worked for millionaires as a chauffeur, yardman, butler, and occasional cook. My grandmother, Willie Mae, whom everybody called Mamie, baked cakes during holidays for Negro and white clientele.

As far back as I can remember, I had heard about injustices suffered by Negroes at the hands of whites, including the murder of my great-great-uncle Peter. In winter, when we sat around the fireplace, the adults' talk always turned to Jim Crow laws and to how each generation of Negroes had to make things better for the next generation. They also said that even though there was no NAACP chapter in Albany, they were all members of the NAACP, sending their dues off to the main office "for our protection."

When I was young, Albany was a quiet, racially segregated city. Every now and then a few prominent Negro men tried, to no avail, to persuade the city commission to desegregate public facilities, but mostly Negroes in

Albany stayed in the place to which they were relegated. They were unhappy, angry, and frustrated, but not ready to take the bull by the horns.

The only jobs available to Negroes were as maids, laborers, chauffeurs, and cooks, except for those who were self-employed or worked at the all-Negro Albany State College, the all-Negro public schools, or Turner Air Force Base. Policemen entered the homes of Negroes without knocking and without warrants. They gave billy-club beatings at the drop of a hat to Negro men and women and arrested Negroes at the whims of white people. Negro parents were often forced to whip their children on the orders of policemen. The law of the land was posted everywhere: White Only at bus and train stations, at the library, the playground, the zoo, movie theaters, restaurants, drinking fountains, and doctors' offices.

On the other hand, when destitute and brutalized black men and their families on the run from beatings or the lynch rope passed through Albany, there was an underground railroad. Certain members of Albany's black community supplied many a desperate person with food, lodging, medical attention, bus tickets to other cities or states, money, and hope.

In Albany white male offenders between the ages of eighteen and twenty-four were called "youths," especially if they committed offenses against Negroes, such as driving by with car doors open to knock Negroes down or flinging urine-filled balloons at them. Then these acts were defined as "pranks," not subject to prosecution. Negro male offenders in the same age group were called "men" when they committed minor offenses, especially offenses that only Negroes could commit, such as "sassing" whites, "reckless eyeballing" (looking at white women), or acting "suspicious" or "uppity." These acts were considered crimes and resulted in prosecution and jail.

Growing up I was humiliated, harassed, and threatened by white people. Shopping downtown was so unpleasant that my mother often traced the outlines of my feet on paper and shopped for my shoes without me. On one of the few times she took me along, when I was four years old, a clerk in the Belk-Smith department store refused my mother's request to let me use the store's bathroom. I could not "hold it," so I urinated on myself. A crowd of white shoppers, both children and adults, laughed and pointed at me. Then I had to walk home visibly wet and embarrassed with my urine-soaked oxfords squishing with every step I took.

In December of that same year, I was downtown again when my father reluctantly allowed me to get in a line to see Santa Claus. When Santa sat the girl in front of me on his lap, I became excited because I knew I was next. When the girl slid from his lap, I moved up, smiling. Santa reached around me and pulled a white boy onto his lap. When he was finished, Santa pulled another white child from behind me. I seemed to grow smaller and smaller as I stood there. How could this be happening when Santa had brought me something every Christmas? Why was he acting this way now? My father took my hand and led me out of the store, telling me that was not the real Santa, just a helper. But nothing could change how I felt. Something exciting and wonderful had been spoiled. Although I could not name the emotions at that age, resentment and anger stirred in me with each such incident.

Every day as I walked to and from junior high school, a bus passed me on Newton Road carrying poor white children from their homes near me to all-white schools across town. As the bus went by, the white girls would say, "Hey, little nigger," and the boys would say, "Wanna wallow for a dollar?" I was just at that insecure age where I was neither a child nor a woman. It was a difficult time to hear this daily litany of put-downs, but I was able to rise above their ignorance mainly because my mother said that, in the long run, it was not what *they* thought of me that mattered; it was what *I* thought of me that was important.

After I entered junior high school, my mother felt that she had instructed me enough that I could go downtown by myself. There was an unwritten law in Albany that if a Negro and a white person met on the sidewalk, the Negro was to step off in deference. My parents and I had never done this, and I had no intention of ever doing it. One day I was downtown when a tall, brown-haired white "youth" came toward me on the sidewalk. So I braced myself, held my head high, and kept walking. He slammed his bent elbow into my side. The force of the blow lifted me up and moved me off the side-walk, but I refused to fall. I continued walking and did not look back. My side was sore and bruised for days from the blow I received. I have thought of that "youth" often over the years and wondered if he is still proud of his actions that day.

As I got older, these kinds of incidents made me determined to try to change things. It had been drummed into me around the fireplace that it was up to me to make things better for the next generation. I took that charge seriously, and I did find other ways to protest the way things were besides holding my place on the sidewalk. I drank from every white-only fountain I could find downtown and smiled at the indignant clerks or outraged citizens who were anxious to tell me what my place was. The smile seemed to infuriate them even more than the drinking did. In my senior year in high school, I became a registered voter. My teacher Benjamin (B. B.) White took each of his students to register to vote as soon as they turned eighteen. Even though there were not enough Negroes registered to have any significant political impact, I felt that voting under such conditions was a message to the power structure that I would exercise this right until it *did* make a difference.

Miss Albany State

Voted most likely to succeed when I graduated from Monroe High School in 1958, I received partial scholarships to Paine, Bennett, and Spelman colleges. Because my parents could not make up the amount required in addition to these scholarships, my only choice was to attend local Albany State College. Disappointed, I decided to work and save money to go to the college of my choice. As a result of a program at Monroe High put in place by B. B. White, I was employed as secretary to attorney C. B. King. King suggested I was wasting my time doing secretarial work and urged me to attend Albany State. I planned to make the most of it by excelling in academics, becoming a leader on campus, and being a member of every organization open to females.

My plan worked; I was an honor student; English and French were my best subjects. I was involved in a wide range of campus activities and elected to a variety of offices: Basileus of Alpha Kappa Alpha Sorority, secretary and Miss Drama of the drama club, senior editor of the yearbook, business manager for the college choir, and sports editor of the college newspaper. I was also elected to be the sweetheart of Alpha Phi Alpha Fraternity, Miss Charm, and Miss Albany State. Since my fellow students had entrusted me with so much responsibility, I felt I should do all I could to address the needs of the students on campus.

Being a college student did not protect me from racial harassment. One spring day as I was walking to campus, a white man tried to force me off the Flint River Bridge to the embankment below, where, using sexually explicit language, he made it clear he intended to "have a good time" with me. There was a white motorcycle policeman at the other end of the bridge, talking to a female motorist. I ran to him for help, but he told me he was busy. He and the motorist continued chatting for several minutes, laughing and flirting, and the man who had approached me turned and slowly walked away, looking over his shoulder. When the woman left, I told the policeman what the man had said and tried to do. The policeman looked me up and down several times and asked what I'd said to the man. When I told him I had said nothing, the policeman responded, in an exaggerated drawl, "When he *does* something to you, let me know." Then he took off on his motorcycle as the man headed back toward me. Fortunately, a classmate drove by at that moment and gave me a ride. At great risk to his own safety, my father reported the incident and the officer's behavior to the police, but nothing was done. Once again I was left with resentment and anger.

From my sophomore year on, I was also a civil rights activist. I sat in at a fast-food place called the Arctic Bear along with two reluctant friends.

There were no white-only signs, but we knew the expected procedure for black patrons was to go to the window, get their food, and then leave the premises. Instead we took our food and sat down at the outdoor tables customarily reserved for white customers. The proprietor did not call the police and asked us to leave only when passers-by complained. We left when we finished our meals. Seeing what happened a year later to students who sat-in in Greensboro and other places, I realized that we could have been beaten, spat upon, and jailed.

That same year, 1959, I became a member of the newly formed NAACP Youth Council along with other college and high school students. Bobby Burch was president, and Bernice Johnson, my best friend, was secretary. Anne Booyer, Janie Culbreth, Julian Carswell, Evelyn Toney, Andrew Williams, and James Wilson were also members. Our first effort was to get Negroes hired at a white-owned drugstore in a Negro neighborhood. We were not successful.

The following year, Mrs. Irene Asbury became the dean of students. She captured the hearts of the student body right away, because she was a warm and sincere person who took a keen interest in our opinions and needs. She listened to us, investigated, and tried to effect change. She held the first leadership workshop for campus leaders and members of the Student Government Association (SGA), of which I was the secretary. As a result of her efforts, for the first time the SGA had a working budget.

Honor student Leviticus Roberts, a dynamic and outspoken senior, was president of the Student Government Association. Under his leadership, SGA charted a new course and sought to make changes on campus. We organized the off-campus students and brought to light the facts that there was little or no security at the girls' dormitories, that the dining hall food was inadequate, and that nothing was being done about the "pranks" being played by white "youths" who sped through the campus side-swiping students; throwing eggs, ice, and urine on students; or who sneaked around the girls' dormitories and later burned a cross in front of Gibson Hall. We asked for redress of these grievances and received hostility and "Who do you think you are?" attitudes from campus personnel.

There was definitely a movement brewing on campus. Excited, I wrote a poem. Actually I submitted two poems for publication in the college's newspaper, the *Students' Voice*. One poem, a bit of fluff called "Spring Fever," was accepted and published. The other, "If I Could Speak for the World," dealt with human rights, ethics, and world peace and was rejected. The newspaper's faculty adviser told me that the college's president felt the poem was too controversial and might offend the all-white board of regents. All my life I had faced discrimination and embarrassment, had known the violence done to my race and family, and had seen fear and despair in the eyes of grown men. I thought things would be different at Albany State, but once again I felt resentment boiling around inside me. It had become my constant companion.

In January 1961 a local radio station, WALB, which often issued racial diatribes against black people, made insulting remarks about Charlayne Hunter and Hamilton Holmes, who had just desegregated the University of Georgia. One comment was that because of their presence, the university was changing its "Who's Who" to "Who Dat." Some of us in the SGA, including Olivia Blaylock and Weyman Patterson, decided to write a letter of protest to WALB and send a copy to the *Albany Herald* to be published in a section called, "The People's Forum." I helped write the letter, denouncing WALB for its racist statements and demanding the comments cease. I typed it, and Lewis Carter signed it with a fictitious name, "Leonard Carson, Albany State College." Melvin Webb, president of the junior class and a dear friend, hand-delivered the letter as he had done others we had written in the past.

When the letter was published in the Sunday edition of the paper, Albany State president William Dennis called an emergency meeting of the student body the next day in Caroline Hall. He denounced the letter, stating that there was no Albany State student named Leonard Carson. Bernice Johnson rose and gestured toward the students assembled. "There are five hundred Leonard Carsons here," she said. We all cheered. President Dennis told us to discontinue such actions. He disbanded the SGA for the rest of the year and put the office under lock and key. In a further attempt to defuse the campus movement, Dennis also assigned Leviticus and other education students active on campus to student teaching positions out of town. Dean Asbury resigned in protest. At the end of the year I was elected Miss Albany State College for the following school year. If college officials thought they had squashed student activism, they were mistaken. Frank Shaw and Margaret Worthy, outspoken and influential students, were elected president and vice president of SGA and planned to take up where the previous officers had left off.

In the fall of 1961, Cordell Reagon and Charles Sherrod from SNCC came on campus asking for Bernice Johnson and me, because we had been identified as student leaders by members of the Lincoln Heights Improvement Association, a group of local black leaders who had unsuccessfully tried to persuade the city commission to desegregate public facilities, pave streets, install streetlights, and generally improve conditions in the black community. Cordell was slight of frame, very young, and filled with suppressed energy. Sherrod, a tad larger than Cordell, was soft-spoken but intense and immediately evoked a feeling of trust. Almost every day for several days the SNCC workers walked around campus with Bernice and me, and later Janie Culbreth, talking about events—the Montgomery Bus Boycott, the sit-ins, voter registration, and conditions on campus and in Albany. They also talked to other students, including Bertha Gober and Blanton Hall, who would play a major role in events to come. I noticed that we were being watched and followed by college officials. Joined by SNCC worker Charles Jones, a gifted orator and thinker, Cordell and Sherrod also came to a meeting of the NAACP Youth Council describing SNCC's voter registration project. Speaking of direct action, nonviolence, and jail without bail, they explained how their organization differed from the NAACP.

The three also talked to high school students and to people in the community. In October 1961 they organized the first community meeting and held it in the basement of Bethel A.M.E. Church, where Rev. Ben Gay was pastor. Community people and leaders, high school students, and a few ministers attended. Most of the student leaders from Albany State were there, and one student we recognized immediately as a spy for the administration. Sherrod and Cordell, who had beautiful tenor voices, taught us freedom songs, and we talked about voter registration and conditions in Albany. A week or two later they began small group meetings and workshops on nonviolent tactics, one of which was held at my house. The day after the first meeting, the new dean of students, Charles Minor, called me into his office and told me that I had been seen at a meeting held by people who were harmful to me and to the college. He insisted that I disassociate myself from these outside forces and identify the other students who attended the meeting. Of course, without a second thought, I refused.

On the first of November the Interstate Commerce Commission's ruling barring segregation in interstate transportation terminals went into effect. Jones, Reagon, and Sherrod planned to test the ruling along with SNCC's executive secretary, Jim Forman, by riding a bus from Atlanta to Albany, but they postponed the plan, thinking they would be arrested before reaching the white waiting room. Members of the NAACP Youth Council also planned to test the ruling, but Mrs. Ruby Hurley, the NAACP's Southeast regional secretary, denounced SNCC for supporting the youth council plan, saying SNCC had no money for bail and would leave us in jail if we were arrested. She suggested that we wait before doing anything until we received approval from the NAACP's national office. Although we agreed with SNCC's "jail-without-bail" policy because it kept issues at the forefront, since she was our adviser we reluctantly followed Mrs. Hurley's wishes and postponed our plans. Several Albany State students did enter the white waiting room at the bus station, were asked to leave, but were not arrested. SNCC workers informed the U.S. Justice Department of the incident. The high school and college members of the youth council continued to follow policies set by the NAACP, but our leanings were more toward SNCC policies and the SNCC people with whom we worked on a daily basis.

On the second of November I was called into Dean Minor's office again and told once more to stay away from SNCC, mass meetings, and demonstrations because I was putting students' lives in danger. The director of field services, Rev. Osmond H. Brown, told me that as Miss Albany State College I owed it to the other students to do all I could for them. I agreed and said that was exactly what I was trying to do. He warned me that I might not be crowned Miss Albany State College the next day if I did not tell him when the next meeting would take place. I told him I honestly did not know, which was the truth.

My coronation went on as scheduled in Sanford Hall Gymnasium on the third of November. Since Miss Albany State was also the sweetheart of the football team, Frank Shaw, co-captain of the football team and SGA president, escorted me to the platform where my throne sat in blue and gold splendor. When the time came for me to be crowned by President Dennis, he avoided my eyes. While holding the crown, he said nice things about me without much sincerity, things that once I would have been happy to hear and that once he would have been happy to say. I looked at my parents standing proudly and realized this was their moment. Then President Dennis held the crown up high with only one hand and let it *drop* onto my head. A murmur went through the crowd: "Did you see how he crowned her? Did you see that?" Then Dennis turned and left the platform. As I gave my acceptance speech, it rang hollow. I was sad because I felt so little for something about which my parents felt so much.

As Miss Albany State College I would receive a full scholarship for that school year and a fellowship for the graduate school of my choice from a pool of four, including Villanova University. My parents were ecstatic, and I felt a sense of satisfaction and pride that my future education was secure, but I had become completely disillusioned by the president's behavior toward campus activism and toward me personally.

Strutting and Stepping All the Way to City Hall

Later that month, after a series of meetings, the NAACP Youth Council, SNCC, the Lincoln Heights Improvement Association, the Federated Women's Clubs, the Baptist Ministers' Alliance, and other groups came together to form the Albany Movement. Dr. William G. Anderson, an osteopath, was president; Slater King, a real estate broker, was vice president; and Marion Page, a retired railroad worker, was secretary. Attorney C. B. King, Slater's brother, was legal counsel for the organization. The Albany Movement's agenda was to attack discrimination and segregation.

As members of the program committee, Bernice Johnson and I helped plan meetings and provide music. Bernice, Anne Booyer, Janie Culbreth, Brenda Darten, Bertha Gober, Rutha and Emory Harris, and Andrew Reid; SNCC workers Cordell Reagon and Charles Sherrod; and I sang freedom songs and spirituals during the mass meetings. In the summer of 1962 we made the album *Freedom in the Air: A Documentary on Albany, Georgia, 1961–2*, which was produced by Guy Carawan of Highlander Folk School and Alan Lomax and included a movement sermon by Rev. Ben Gay.

On November 22, 1961, three members of the NAACP Youth Council— Evelyn Toney, Julian Carswell, and James Wilson—attempted to be served in the restaurant at the Trailways bus station and were arrested. Thirty minutes later, just as Mrs. Hurley had promised, the NAACP posted bond and they were released. Later that same day, other Albany State students were also at the bus station, going home for the Thanksgiving holidays. Dean Minor was there, too, making sure the students went to the "colored" side of the station and preventing them from going to the white side. However, Bertha Gober and Blanton Hall, both Albany State students and SNCC supporters, succeeded in going to the white side and even got to the ticket window before they were arrested. While serving several days in jail, Bertha and Blanton were suspended from Albany State without any kind of a hearing or procedure for appeal.

The first mass meeting of the Albany Movement took place immediately after Bertha and Blanton were released from jail. It was held at Mt. Zion Baptist Church, where Rev. E. James Grant, a respected high school principal, was pastor. I was amazed at the diversity of the people present: college professors, public school teachers, doctors, ministers, maids, laborers, the elderly, high school students, and college students. A well-known and well-loved mentally challenged member of our community who went by the name of Slim was also in attendance. Everyone there rallied behind the students arrested at the bus station, who were the main speakers. Bertha Gober's speech relating her arrest and jail experience brought tears to the eyes of many. I felt exhilarated. It was a night to remember. I went home and could not sleep at all. I felt as if my whole being was on fire. Now there was something positive I could do with the anger and resentment that had built up over the years. At last, in the words of the Albany Movement's lawyer, C. B. King, I had "found form for the expression of my discontent."

On Sunday, November 26, the night before the trial of the students arrested at the bus station, Bobby Burch, Janie Culbreth, Bernice Johnson, Frank Shaw, Evelyn Toney, Melvin Webb, Margaret Worthy, Stanley Jones, and I went from dormitory to dormitory at Albany State urging students to participate in a protest march the next morning. Most students agreed that an injustice had been done, but they seemed apprehensive and uncertain as to what the course of action should be. When I finally left for home, I was not sure of what to expect the next day.

Bernice was already on campus when I arrived the next morning. We waited around but saw only a handful of students, mostly those who had been trying to organize the march. Disappointed beyond words, we started out on our own. We walked in silence up Hazard Drive and then left onto Oglethorpe, toward the Flint River Bridge. At first we walked together, each lost in thought. Then Bernice assumed the lead, stepping with urgency and taking long strides, her head high against a light wind. I was trying to keep pace with her, and the other few students were a step or two behind me. Halfway over the bridge, I looked back. "Bernice," I said. "Look back!"

She kept walking and would not look back. I told her again to look and she did. We both stopped and stared. There was a long, long line of students marching five and six abreast strung out along Hazard Drive and onto Oglethorpe Avenue. We looked at each other and laughed, our eyes full of unshed tears. Then we both started strutting and stepping all the way to city hall. We were joined by other people from the community and students from Monroe High School as we went along. It was one of the most moving experiences of my life—seeing those students marching in silence, heads high and shoulders back, making an eloquent statement without speaking. At city hall, hundreds of us encircled the block, singing. A policeman asked us to leave, but Charles Jones led us in prayer. After we sang another song or two, we marched several times around the block before marching back across the bridge to Union Baptist Church, which was pastored by Rev. William Boyd. There we discussed the day's events and planned further strategy. We decided to stage a demonstration on campus in order to involve even more students.

After many speeches by students, members of SNCC, and ministers, we left for the campus, which was right down the hill from the church. We marched through the library, the administration building, and the science building, but the students there only dropped their heads when they saw us. Disappointed, Bernice, Janie, and I left the campus and went to the SNCC office. The next morning President Dennis fired me from a volunteer position of secretary to the English department. Other students were fired from salaried jobs or threatened with dismissal or the loss of financial aid. The students became fearful, and that day marked the end of mass involvement in the Movement by students at Albany State College. It also marked the day my father lost all respect for President Dennis.

Jailed and Expelled

Undeterred, a group of us, all students at Albany State, continued to participate in movement activities. On Sunday, December 10, members of SNCC and others tested the Interstate Commerce Commission's ruling again in Albany. SNCC members Norma Collins, James Forman, Lenora Taitt, Bob Zellner, and several other people came to Albany by train from Atlanta, accompanied by Tom and Casey Hayden of Students for a Democratic Society. They were arrested after they went into the white waiting room. Outside the train station, Bertha Gober and Charles Jones stood in a crowd that had gathered to greet the group. The police pulled both of them from the crowd and arrested them. A young woman named Willie Mae Jones, who was not part of the Movement, happened to be at the station to meet relatives. The police also pulled her from the crowd and arrested her. Thereafter she was a faithful member of the Movement.

At the next evening's mass meeting, we planned to march to city hall the following day when the trials were being held to protest the arrests and the city's disregard for the Interstate Commerce Commission's ruling. Early Tuesday morning Janie Culbreth and I went to campus hoping to join other students who would also be marching to city hall, but there were no students in sight. Bernice was taking a final examination, so Janie and I took a taxi to SNCC's office, where a crowd was already beginning to move toward city hall. Joined by Anne Booyer, we found a place in line just as a light drizzle started, a drizzle that turned into rain that did not stop for a week.

Slim, who was almost seven feet tall and towered over the crowd, also joined the line. Several well-meaning ladies, concerned that he was mentally challenged, told him he could not go and removed him from the march. He did not resist them, but he stood looking disappointed as the line moved away. I was disappointed, too, since I felt he should have been allowed to march.

As I walked along, I thought of my parents and some of the people who had touched my life as I struggled to become me, such as C. B. King; his mother, Mrs. Margaret King; and my teacher B. B. White, and I wondered if I would be arrested. When I reached the corner of Pine and Jackson streets, I saw police chief Laurie Pritchett looking like a bright balloon as he strode about in one of those yellow slickers and caps worn by policemen on rainy days. "Disperse and go about your normal way," he said repeatedly. We continued to march, circling the block again, and I thought, *What does he mean by "normal way?" That we should go home and continue to live as second-class citizens?* I had news for him: "Never again."

"You are under arrest," he said loudly as he herded us into an alley on the right side of the Albany city jail. As the first mass arrests in Albany began, I felt as though my whole life had been geared toward that moment. Fearing that the cells would fill before I could be booked, I kept moving toward the beginning of the line, asking person after person if I could get in front of them, because I wanted to be certain I would be arrested. I wanted to make my personal statement.

I got to the front of the line, but still I remained in the alley for quite a while before I was finally taken inside the jail. On the way to my cell, I could hear someone faintly calling my name. I looked around and finally located Cordell Reagon, who was lying on his stomach under a steel bunk in an extremely overcrowded cell. Knowing that jail was foreign to me and that I was anemic, he asked if I was all right. I assured him that I had never felt better.

First I was placed with twenty-three other women in a filthy cell that was built to hold four. As the white jailer put more and more people in the cell, he kept saying apologetically that he was just doing his job. We were packed in like sardines, with the last person pressed against the bars. One young girl was standing on the commode. We could barely breathe. Shortly after the mass arrests, all of the toilets and water fountains in the cells were turned off.

The arrests began in the morning and continued for hours. At one point all the women were placed in the men's bull pen, a huge, filthy cell with steel bunks almost to the ceiling. About three o'clock some white men in business suits were allowed to look us over. While they were there, some-one in another cell called out, "Miss Albany State is in here," and my fellow prisoners cheered. I learned later that one of the men in suits was James H. Gray, editor of the *Albany Herald, who* reported in his paper the next day that we looked like "monkeys in cages." White people made threatening phone calls to the college; at least one of them mentioned that Miss Albany State was in jail, which suggested that members of my family and myself could become the target of this anger.

Later a trusty served us a meal of cabbage, beets, and Spam that she crammed into one cup per person with her hands. I refused to eat it. The prisoners were separated: some remained in the city jail while others were taken to the county jail, my friends Janie and Anne among them. I hated to see them go, since I had known them longer than any of my other friends. Finally we were taken out of the bull pen. Seven other women and I were put in another cell designed to hold four people. Since there were no mat-tresses on any of the steel bunks, I gave my coat to seventy-three-year-old

Mrs. Mary Williams to sleep on. The rest of us talked and sang all night, cheering as prisoners refused bail that had been posted by loved ones. The whole time we were in the jail, we had no privacy from either the male prisoners or the white policemen. The male prisoners averted their eyes, but the policemen kept coming back to look us over. We held up our coats in front of us whenever we used the toilet.

Before dawn the next morning, after refusing a breakfast of cold congealed grits with chunks of egg whites tinged blue, I was put on a city bus along with thirty-eight other women, including my classmates Brenda Darten, Olivia Josey, and Annie Ruth Williams. Mrs. Marian King, wife of Albany Movement vice president Slater King, and the elderly Mrs. Mary Williams, were on the bus also. The policeman accompanying us said we were going to Newton, Georgia, located in Baker County. Our hearts fell, because Baker was one of the worst counties in Southwest Georgia in terms of its treatment of black people. I felt apprehensive, because with no one knowing our whereabouts, anything could happen to us. In Baker County there was a reception committee of about one hundred white men yelling at us, calling us names, and labeling us as Freedom Riders. My cousin Paul Phipps was there also, to see if any of his Albany relatives had been jailed. He did not see me, and I did not call out to him, because I was afraid he would be in danger if the county power structure knew he had a Freedom Rider relative in its jail. My parents did not know where I was until a day and a half later, when the FBI, summoned by movement leaders, arrived in Albany and forced officials to release information concerning the whereabouts of all the prisoners.

In contrast to the jail in Albany, the jail in Newton had been freshly cleaned, and the water fountain and toilets worked. Once in the cell, some of us decided to bathe. We were half clad when, without warning, the Newton police brought a dozen men into the cell block to "look us over." They were there for about fifteen minutes, walking around and staring at us. Two of the men did not want to leave until forced to by the police. "We may have to defend ourselves tonight," Mrs. King whispered when the men finally left. That afternoon, dinner arrived with a flourish: a policeman flung open the cell door, placed a large cardboard box in the doorway, and kicked it into the cell block. The box contained individual plates of peas, raw onions, and cornbread. We discarded the peas and onions and armed ourselves with the cornbread, which was as hard as a rock. I had not eaten in two days, but I felt fine.

The Albany policeman who brought us to Baker County was nicer there than he had been in Albany around his fellow officers. At nightfall he came to "tuck us in," as he put it, and we told him about the men brought in to look at us. He ordered a spotlight that when put up lit the dark areas around the building. He told us not to worry, that he would be in the building across the street. He asked us if we needed anything, so we gave him a list that included soft drinks, aspirin, toothpaste and toothbrushes, and other personal items. He bought everything and refused to take the money we had hidden on our persons.

While others slept I chose to keep watch, positioned myself at the window, and kept my eyes on the road outside in front of the jail. Cars passed the jail all night, slowing as they approached, but we weren't attacked. I could also hear the heavy rumble of buses rolling, and I knew they were buses from Albany carrying other prisoners to Camilla, in nearby Mitchell County. The breakfast of grits topped with grease and a generous portion of pork belly complete with nipples, like dinner the night before, was inedible. I was beginning my third day without food, and I had also missed my weekly vitamin shots. I drank a great deal of water and wondered how long I could go on without eating, since I had begun to feel a little nauseated every now and then. At times tempers flared and voices rose in the cell block. To make the time pass more quickly, we sang, did house-cleaning chores, took baths, combed our hair, and wrote down our thoughts with pencils and paper furnished by the Albany policeman who had taken on the role of protector. Although we were in accord about why we were incarcerated, the close living conditions wore on some nerves. Those who could not stand the constant noise retreated to the back of the cell block.

At that time there were more than five hundred of us filling the jails not only in Albany but in all the surrounding counties as well. Then, in order to give impetus to the Movement and garner more publicity, the adult leaders of the Albany Movement invited Dr. Martin Luther King Jr. to Albany to give a speech. He and his friend and co-worker Rev. Ralph Abernathy led a march. Both of them were arrested, along with two hundred Albany residents. Rev. Andrew Young, also from SCLC, arrived in Albany. He soon became extremely popular with the demonstrating students. Later that week the three members of SCLC, accompanied by the adult leaders of the Albany Movement, entered into negotiations with city officials. There were four provisions in the resulting agreement: the Trailways bus station, the train station, and city buses would be desegregated; all demonstrators would be released from jail on property bonds provided by family and friends; all mass demonstrations would be called off; and the newly elected city commission would meet with Albany Movement leaders sometime "in the future."

One week after the mass arrests we were all released on bond. We still faced charges, but we had not been told what they were. The "cooling-off period" of no more mass demonstrations began. Many of us felt that nothing concrete had been gained and that it was a mistake to end the marches, but we did not go against the agreement. As it turned out, only the train station was desegregated. Mass meetings continued and the voter registration drive intensified, but mass demonstrations ceased. We began a boycott of the downtown stores, requesting that black people be employed in other than menial positions. The boycott went into effect before Christmas and took its toll on merchants. My family and I and most of the black community shopped in other cities. When Albany State student Ola Mae Quartimon was arrested for sitting at the front of a city bus, the black community boycotted the buses, forcing the entire bus system to shut down.

When I went back to Albany State to arrange to take the exams I had missed while I was in jail, I was asked to leave the campus. Soon afterward thirty-nine student activists were suspended from the college; five of us who were considered leaders and a danger to the college were expelled: Anne Booyer, Bertha Gober, Blanton Hall, Bernice Reagon, and me. Parents and community members—Emma Jean Berry; Rev. J. D. Bolden, Annie Mae Culbreth, Beatrice Johnson, Delores Jones, and A. C. Searles—formed a committee. They went to Albany State and questioned our being suspended without a hearing. As a result, the college had a hearing and upheld the suspensions and expulsions. Three of the Atlanta University colleges—Spelman, Morehouse, and Morris Brown—offered scholarships to the suspended and expelled students who met those schools' qualifications. I accepted the invitation and chose to attend Spelman.

While waiting for classes to begin at Spelman in January, I went with a group from Albany to SCLC's citizenship training school in Dorchester, Georgia, for a week to learn how to set up Citizenship Schools. I was very impressed by our instructors, especially Mrs. Septima Clark, Dorothy Cotton, and Rev. Andrew Young. They treated us respectfully, listened to us, and valued our opinions. When I left Dorchester, William Porter, coordinator for the Citizenship Schools in Albany, told me to set up a Citizenship School in the C. K. Smith Presbyterian Church, where the NAACP Youth Council had held its meetings. Since I was leaving soon to go to Spelman, there was little time to organize, but a few people did come to the sessions. One of my elderly pupils, whom I tutored at the church and in her home, had difficulty reading. She went down to register but failed the test because she left a syllable out of the word "Constitution" when asked to read. One of the happiest moments in the Movement for me came that summer. I was walking down Odum Street distributing leaflets when all of a sudden this same elderly lady grabbed me and hugged and kissed me. She told me that she had finally registered to vote, saying, "Now, ain't you proud of me?" I assured her that I was and gave her a big hug. One woman, one vote.

I spent almost every other waking minute at SNCC's office on Jackson Street, typing, cleaning, running off flyers, participating in strategy meetings, and hearing about courageous students in the Movement like Julian Bond, Diane Nash, and Ruby Doris Smith. Since a truce was in effect, there were no mass demonstrations, but each day several groups of us participated in small attempts to desegregate the lunch counters, the movie theaters, and the public library. At each site, when we were directed to use the colored counterpart or be arrested, we chose to leave.

The 1963 Albany Summer Project

When I went to Spelman in Atlanta along with Bernice Johnson and Janie Culbreth, every chance we got we would come back to Albany to work with the Movement and in the Citizenship Schools. In Atlanta we spent many hours at the SNCC office at 6 Raymond Street, only a stone's throw from the Spelman campus. There I met Ruby Doris Smith, who attended Spelman but spent most of her time with SNCC. I also met Mary King, Sam Shirah, Norma Collins, Mildred Forman, and John Lewis, as well as many others who were always passing through. I marched with a group of SNCC people and Atlanta University Center students to Grady Hospital in a demonstration led by a Dr. Bell, an African American Atlanta dentist, to demand that more black people be hired in all departments.

Spring break marked our first trip home from Spelman. Bernice, Janie, and I decided to make a statement. We each embroidered one word—*freedom, justice,* or *equality*—on the left side of the white blouses we wore. As we tried to board the Trailways bus in Atlanta, the driver refused to take our tickets until he had taken the white passengers' tickets and directed them to the front of the bus so we could not sit there. We were met with hostile stares at our blouses all the way to Albany. We could have been pulled from the bus in any of the small towns where the bus made stops, but we felt no fear. I think we fed off each other's courage and audacity.

During the summer, when school was out and I was at home, I often went to meetings in Atlanta, other folks and I often stayed at Bobbi Yancy's apartment; Bobbi was away in Paris, so I never had a chance to meet her or thank her.

In the summer of 1963, SNCC sponsored its second summer project in Albany. Dozens of college students, mostly white, came to participate in the Albany Movement. Other students who were on their way to civil rights work in other states also stopped off in Albany to receive training and survival skills from SNCC. An orientation session was held at Koinonia, an interracial cooperative farm in nearby Americus, Georgia. While the summer volunteers worked in Albany, I helped sixty-three-year-old Miss Dora White prepare breakfast and dinner for them. After Miss Dora suffered a stroke brought on by the stress of being a defendant in the federal case against the Albany Movement, I prepared both meals myself.

Between meals I canvassed a very large area every day, trying to get as many black people as possible to attempt to register to vote. As I canvassed, I found people in need of assistance and gave their names to attorney C. B. King. Some needed medical attention and food; others needed repairs done on the white-owned shacks in which they lived. Janie Culbreth, Marva Berry, and I continued working with the voter registration project in Albany even when it came under the direction of SCLC and Rev. Fred Bennett. We canvassed together until Sherrod asked me to be responsible for the all-black neighborhood referred to as C.M.E., so named because of the C.M.E (Christian Methodist Episcopal) church there. This was an area that even the police did not frequent. It was dangerous to be in that community unless you lived there, knew someone there, or were a member of a gang there. One of the gang leaders, Blue, was active in the Movement, and Sherrod asked him to accompany me everywhere I went in C.M.E., protecting me so that I would not be attacked by gang members considering me an intruder. I was both terrified of and fascinated by Blue and his many battle scars. He was a stranger to me, an outcast to many, and yet he treated me like a lady. I thought him a gentleman and trusted that part of him; he did not disappoint me.

Unknown to my parents, I would travel out to meetings in surrounding cities—Americus, Leesburg, Moultrie, and Dawson—with SNCC workers. We would be in cars with black males and white and black females. One night we left Dawson after the town's 10:00 P.M. curfew for black residents. Fortunately we encountered no police officers or angry white citizens. Although danger lurked everywhere, I never felt afraid to do what was needed. After I did it, though, I would feel afraid when I thought about what could have happened to me.

One of the worst times in the Movement—one of the worst times of my life—was when Sherrod told me about the treatment of civil rights demonstrators in Danville, Virginia. Arriving at 5:00 A.M. one morning to take me to the orientation session at Koinonia, he sat on my porch, at first unable to speak. Finally he said that high-powered water hoses had been turned on the demonstrators, forcing them against cars and walls, where they then were beaten bloody with baseball bats. Sherrod seemed to be in shock as he questioned how people could do such things to other people. He expressed his feelings about this incident at length. When he was talked out, we just sat there and watched the sun come up, our thoughts with the people in Danville.

At one point the Albany police tried to arrest all of the SNCC workers. When there were only twelve left, Sherrod called a meeting at the Women's Federated Club House, where a few workers were staying. By that time I was included in all of the meetings, although I was not officially a member of the organization. What I remember most about this particular meeting is that Sherrod announced that they had all agreed that from that day on I would be considered a member of SNCC. I was moved beyond words. I am sure that not one of them knew how much that meant to me.

The summer of 1963 was eventful. Every day there were pickets, swim-ins, sit-ins, and many other small group demonstrations. We wore the police out, and they decided to arrest the remaining members of SNCC to prevent any further activity. The word was out; someone called me at home and said the police were closing in on SNCC's office, which was now on Madison Street. It was dusk when I walked over to the office, and I found it surrounded by police cars, some parked, some cruising as if waiting for an order to come down. Taking a deep breath, I walked up the steps. Inside there were about six SNCC staffers and summer volunteers, expecting to be arrested at any moment. They urged me to go home, saying that I did not have to be involved. I refused to go, however, because I *was* involved. All of the students in that room were from other cities. They had come to help Albany, and I was an Albanian. There was no way I could leave them.

Finally a coded message came by telephone from other Albany Movement members, informing us that we were to go to the home of Aurelia Noble for safety. It was up to us to get there. We had to protect the office files, so I took them next door to Mrs. Mary Booyer, whose daughter Anne was active in the Movement and a close friend of mine.

I suggested to the white students that they disguise themselves by putting on the dark coats that were in the boxes of clothes collected by the Friends of SNCC in New York and smear soot from the stove on their faces so that they would not be seen. We left via the back door, walking in the absolute dark, for there were few streetlights in the black community. We felt our way across the yards. We ran into a fence and my heart sank. It was too high to scale. After searching for nearly ten minutes, I discovered a way around it. We could see police cars speeding up and down the alley near us, their lights sweeping across the SNCC office; we stopped until they had passed.

Someone laughed nervously. Then a dog barked at us. Although afraid of the dog, we kept walking. The dog's owners turned on their backyard lights. We ran back into the darkness and stood there frozen for nearly an hour until they decided to turn off the lights. Finally we ran past the dog and made our way to the safe house. After fifteen or twenty minutes a phone call came saying we had been offered sanctuary in Beulah Baptist Church. Cars came for us, and the white students had to lie down on the seats as Rev. Samuel Wells and schoolteacher McCree Harris drove slowly to Beulah. Joined by the other SNCC students coming from other safe houses, we settled down for the night, male students in a room on one side of the church with the deacons, females on the other side with the deaconesses. Suddenly from the church proper came the sound of a jazzy blues piano played by one of the northern volunteers. As a result, the next morning, we were "evicted" to Shiloh Church, where the twelve SNCC members stayed until they were eventually arrested, one or two at a time, as they ventured out.

There are so many events that will probably go untold and so many people who will go unnamed: the time Felicia Oldfather and I were arrested for passing out leaflets; the time, during a news blackout in Albany, we called the white women of the city to tell them how their husbands, fathers, and sons were treating the black citizenry, and some of the women cried; the night two thousand marched spontaneously; the Molotov cocktails thrown outside of Mt. Zion Church; the time Chief Pritchett came inside Shiloh Church; and the stories of people like local SNCC volunteer Eddie Brown, shot in the arm when night riders fired randomly into the SNCC office.

During the time of the Albany Movement, I thought that if people in this country really knew how cruelly and unfairly some others were being treated, their consciences and sense of fair play would move them to join us in affecting change, in righting wrongs. I thought that if I could help bring some of the injustices to light, then the voices of the "whole world watching" would ring out as one and a change would come. As time passed, I knew I had hoped for too much. Yet, I still hold fast to the idea that each generation of people on earth must make things better for the next generation.

ANNETTE JONES WHITE graduated from Spelman in 1964, two years later than her expected graduation date from Albany State. From 1966 on she taught young children, emphasizing tolerance, concern for the environment and its creatures, and social responsibility. She worked for seventeen years at Spelman College as a kindergarten teacher, child care center director, and lecturer in early childhood development. For her master's degree in early childhood education from Virginia State University (1980), she created a curriculum to teach standard English to nonstandard-English-speaking black children without denigrating their existing speech patterns. Her poetry and essays have appeared in a number of magazines and journals, including *American Visions* and *Sage*, as well as in the book *Doublestitch*. Recently she assisted in doing research, writing, and editing for the Albany Civil Rights Institute Museum, where part of her story is included in some of the museum's exhibits. Now retired, she is completing a novel about growing up in a segregated environment. She has two daughters and two grandchildren.

Uncovered and Without Shelter, I Joined This Movement for Freedom

Bernice Johnson Reagon

A student counselor in a freshman dorm for women sets up a sting to catch a sexual predator. The effort and its failure reshift her sense of herself as a woman in the fight for justice through the Movement.

The Peace Hall phone rang and I picked it up. Peace Hall was the freshman dorm at Albany State College in Albany, Georgia. I did not live on campus, and I was not a freshman. I was a junior, and the year had started great because I had a job as student counselor at the freshman dorm. I had also gotten a temporary job helping with registration at the beginning of the fall quarter. It was 1961; I was the third of eight children of Beatrice Wise and Rev. Jessie Johnson, on full tuition scholarship; and I needed all the help I could get.

On the other hand, some things were not good at all. During the previous spring quarter, student government had been suspended and the fall semester opened with a new dean of students. Our previous dean, Irene Asbury, the best dean we had ever had, strongly supported our efforts to organize around campus safety and health issues and understood that as student leaders we would also be involved in larger issues challenging racism in our communities. Dean Asbury had resigned in protest after receiving no support from the administration in her role to protect students who were being harassed by some whites who often violated the integrity of the campus.*

* There had been repeated incidents of white males driving through the campus and shouting obscenities and throwing objects at female students as they walked on the main sidewalk of the campus. In one incident a student was injured, and with the license number and the assistance of attorney C. B. King, charges were filed against the driver of the car. As the case was being heard in court, a representative of the

Student government was suspended after an assembly where student government leaders asked college president William H. Dennis to respond to a number of issues on campus and in the South that affected our daily lives as Black people and as students. Julian Bond, a Morehouse College student leader of the Atlanta Sit-in Movement, had called and asked Albany State students to support the sit-in demonstrations led by Black college and sometimes high school students going on throughout the South. The February 1, 1960, sit-in at the Woolworth's lunch counter by four students from North Carolina A & T had started a wonderful firestorm that was still sweeping the South. Everybody, everywhere was talking about what mostly Black students were doing and asking, "Shouldn't we be doing something here? Where can we sit in?"

After the call from Julian, we met in the Student Government Association's office and discussed what we could do. All of us were excited about the sit-ins and wanted to be involved. It made a difference that we had a number of students, like Lewis Carter, who were veterans continuing their education under the GI Bill. Another member of our group was Olivia Blaylock, a senior who the year before had been Miss Albany State. I was the youngest member of that group and felt good about the weight and range of our collective voice.

At this meeting we decided that we would combine campus issues with issues raised by the growing sit-in movement and take them to the administration. One evening after classes, a group of students gathered at the home of President Dennis and presented our joint concerns and asked for his response. He received our list and agreed to meet in a full assembly before the campus. On the day of the assembly, we all gathered in Caroline Hall, the campus auditorium. The room was packed with students and faculty. Each of the officers of student government had one question to put before the president about the sit-ins in particular and a longer list about conditions on campus. When the assembly began, President Dennis came to the podium and said, "Please read all of your questions first, and then I will give my response." We had not thought about this. We had envisioned a session where he would respond to each issue separately. Not knowing what to do, we read our questions one by one. Then he came to the podium and read a prewritten statement, and the assembly was over.

---

administration came in and informed the judge that the college wished the case to be dropped. After numerous requests to President Dennis to discuss the matter, Dean Asbury resigned under protest. Irene Asbury became one of the leaders of the Albany Movement organization.

To this day, I do not remember what President Dennis said. I only remember feeling that we had been outmaneuvered. Afterward some sympathetic faculty members volunteered that they thought we had been rather ineffective and that President Dennis had won the day by not responding to our specific questions. Soon after this assembly, the president suspended student government. In our last meeting, where we received the news from Dean Asbury, I suggested that we go around with black armbands to protest the suspension.

Looking back on this event, I now see how far we still had to go. I find it interesting that one of our earliest moves involved asking the administration of a state-supported school to respond to the growing struggle for change against racism. We did not really believe that the president would actually take a stand, but we believed he should be asked to speak to this important movement, which was centered in communities where Black colleges were located. It also became increasingly clear that our actions would not always get an immediate response and that we had to be willing to come back together and try to work out what the next step should be.

It was not an ordinary time. The fall quarter opened with no student government. During registration a young man came up to my desk and introduced himself as Charles Sherrod. He asked me what I thought of Terrell County. I remember being flippant and responding, thinking of Dawson, the county seat, "It is a little bitty town." I remember feeling small when I heard Otis Turner, a student from Terrell, answer the question by describing how difficult it was for Black people to live there because of how hateful and oppressive white people were. He said it was sometimes called "Tombstone Territory" and that it was generally open season on Black people, even though we made up most of the people who lived in the county. I remember wishing I had not been trying to be cute and had also been serious about the question.

I would soon learn that Charles Sherrod was Rev. Charles Sherrod, a native of Petersburg, Virginia, and a field secretary for the Student Nonviolent Coordinating Committee, SNCC (pronounced "Snick"). I told Sherrod that they needed to find another name for the organization, because it didn't say anything. I understood the terms *student, coordinating,* and *committee,* but the term *nonviolent* did not name anything in my experience. I understood *non* acting on the word *violent* meant "not engaging in violence." But the combination of all those terms did not register for me. It certainly did not give me anything to wrap myself around. Charles Sherrod had participated in demonstrations led by Rev. Wyatt T. Walker in Petersburg, Virginia. He had gone to jail in Rock Hill, South Carolina, and for the first time those arrested refused bail. Sherrod had also participated in the Freedom Rides. He had come to Southwest Georgia with another SNCC field secretary, Cordell Hull Reagon, from Nashville, Tennessee, who as a high school student at Pearl High had participated in the Nashville sit-ins. Cordell had also been a Freedom Rider, spending time in Parchman Penitentiary, and was the youngest staff member of the organization.

Albany, the county seat of Dougherty County, was the largest city in Southwest Georgia. In 1961 the city was 40 percent Black. However, it was surrounded by several counties—Terrell, Mitchell, and Baker—where Black people outnumbered whites three to one. The theory that supported the strategy of SNCC was to focus on those Black Belt areas of the South to get Black people registered to vote. If Black people voted in those counties, they could control political power in the counties where they lived. If Black people in Georgia voted in large numbers, we would probably not vote for racist federal and state representatives like Herman Talmadge.

At the time the phone rang in Peace Dormitory in the fall of 1961, I was a member of the youth chapter of the NAACP. Our adviser was Thomas Chatmon, and I was the secretary. In Albany there was a two-block section of Jackson Street with a lot of Black-owned businesses. The Harlem Drug Store located on that strip was owned by a white man. In 1959 we had sent a delegation from the chapter to the drugstore to ask if Blacks could be hired there, since we made up 100 percent of the clientele. Our delegation, all high school seniors, was turned down flat.

In our meetings we continued to talk about what we could do to change conditions for Black people in Albany. We also discussed what we were seeing on television about the spreading sit-in movement. We normally would be singing "Lift Every Voice and Sing," the Negro National Anthem, but looking at the televised accounts of students organizing from Nashville, Atlanta, and Greensboro, I noticed they were singing other songs, freedom songs, and we began to sing them in our meetings. One of the songs they sang was "This Little Light of Mine." During one story out of Nashville, I heard them sing a song we sang in church:

> I'll overcome, I'll overcome
> I'll overcome, someday.
> Oh, if in my heart, I do not yield,
> I'll overcome, someday.

I realized that what I heard in the news account was a little different, but it was the same song, so I led it at the next meeting in the same style and with the text we used in church in Southwest Georgia. At the first chapter meeting that Charles Sherrod and Cordell Reagon attended, they asked if we sang any freedom songs. I started this song, and Cordell stopped me in the middle of the song, saying, "This song is the theme song of the Movement. Whenever we sing it, we stand, and we join hands right over left. And we don't say, 'I'll overcome'; we say, 'We shall overcome,' because *I* is individualistic and *we* expresses community, and we are in this struggle for freedom together." He then raised his tenor voice and led us in "We Shall Overcome," a more staid revision of the church version we had grown up with. Even though this new version did not grab me as much as the traditional one, I loved the idea of being in a movement that had a theme song and a ritual about singing it. I stood next to Cordell, hands crossed and linked, singing alto to his tenor, and felt great.

I would work out later that while *we* might express a collective, it was not always a wise replacement for *I*. When Black people sang "I'll Overcome" in a group, the collective was expressed, because with all present singing "*I*," the group was there, formed by individuals stating their commitment or condition. One song that did not go through this revision was "This Little Light of Mine, I'm Gonna Let It Shine." There was rarely a gathering during the Movement when this song was not heard, and sometimes it was sung several times during a mass meeting. "I'm gonna let it shine" had to do with the need to witness specifically about what *I*, the person singing, was going to do with his or her light, or his or her life. *I* was going to march and demonstrate and protest; *I* was willing to go to jail. And *I* was never singing that song alone, so there was a group and the collective was expressed. Another song that was shifted was "I Shall Not Be Moved." The freedom song version was always sung as "We Shall Not Be Moved." If singing *we* helped to pull us together, then so be it. There was no big discussion about the shift; we just moved with the change.

When the phone rang in Peace Hall, I was a changed person looking for expanded ways to be in the Movement. I said hello, and a white male voice asked, "Do you want twenty dollars?" I thought it was a radio program and that I was going to have a chance to win a prize, so I said yes and waited to see if I could answer what I thought would be a quiz question. The voice said, "There is twenty dollars on the front seat of my car for you." I felt as if I had been hit with a bolt of lightning! My mind was racing! The head counselor was out of the dorm, and I could not believe what I had heard! "Pardon?" I said, and he repeated it. "There'll be twenty dollars on the front seat of my car for you if you want it."

Then I knew it was not a radio quiz show. This man was asking me to have sex with him for twenty dollars! My mind was working so fast; I was thinking, *He is calling the freshmen dorm! I am the student counselor and the only counselor present, what shall I do?* I had watched too much TV, so I decided I would catch him. I made a date with him for 6:00 P.M. off campus at the nearest gas station.

Shaken and dazed, I walked across campus to my adviser. I told him about the call and the appointment. He looked at me and then said, "Lord, child." He told me to go to my classes and that he would talk to the dean and to the president. He told me later that the administration did not want him to call the police but finally agreed to it. I had made the appointment off campus in Albany to make sure this was not just a campus issue. I actually thought that it was against the law to do what he was doing. My adviser told me that I could go ahead and that they were going to catch the caller.

When I told my boyfriend what I was planning to do, he shook his head. At 6:00 P.M. I was at the appointed corner and my boyfriend walked by, still worried and angry with me. A few minutes later up comes this Volkswagen, and through his window the driver, a white male, said, "Get in the car." I didn't see the police; I didn't hear any sirens, *no* flashing red lights, so I stalled: "Where is the twenty dollars?" He insisted, "Get in." Thinking that any girl who would do this would have to be kind of rough, I responded, "I am not getting in this damn car until I see the damn money." It was the first time I had said "damn" out loud. I was nineteen. He said, "I have to get a check cashed." I thought to myself, *It's a good thing I asked.*

He then drove across the street to another gas station. I was still looking for the police. He started back! Still no police. I began to think that the police were not going to show up and that I was on my own. So as he drove back to the gas station where I was waiting, I began to walk back toward the campus. He drove alongside me, constantly asking me to get in the car. Suddenly my adviser's car came into view—still no police. My adviser swung his car around the corner and behind the Volkswagen. The head of campus security jumped out the passenger's front side, slammed his hands on the back of the man's car, shouting, "What the hell do you think you are doing?" The car sped off, and I got into the car with my rescuers, who drove me back to the campus. They told me I had done a good job and that they had gotten his tag number.

The next morning the dean of students took me down to the police station to see Chief of Police Laurie Pritchett, whom I'd never met before. Pritchett had informed the campus administration that this was a campus matter best handled by campus security. (I found out later that the head of campus security had had a shotgun in the car.) When we arrived in his office, Pritchett thanked me. He said they had used the tag number to identify the man in the car and went to his home, but the man's wife said he was out of town. Pritchett said they would catch him later. I was shocked! The man who called Peace Hall looking for sex for twenty dollars with young Black women had a wife! I wondered what this woman felt, or even if the police had told her what he had done. With the dean, I filed a complaint and left.

When I left the police station that morning, I left some of my innocence behind. I went back to the campus getting more pieces of what had gone on between the time I first spoke about the incident to my adviser and when he told me that everything had been set up to catch this guy. It was years before I could put into some perspective what it might have been like for the Black men who took up the question that afternoon. They had been faced with a naïve student who had set up a sting operation. What should or could they do about it? Was there sex between students and white men? How pervasive was it? What would it cost for them to get involved? How did they feel when the administration wanted to drop the matter? How did they feel when the Albany city police decided not to show up? Why did they decide not to tell me I was not going to be covered by the police? Why the hell were they late?

A short time later I was participating in nonviolent workshops led by Cordell and Sherrod. When we asked what *nonviolence* meant, Cordell answered, "Nonviolence is love—love for your fellow man, love as sisters and brothers—no matter who they are and what they are doing, you come in 'love.'" It still did not compute for me, so I settled for nonviolence meaning that no matter who hit me, I was not going to hit them back, because I wanted to be in the Movement.

I was with Cordell and Sherrod when the same dean of students tried to run them off the campus, threatening that he would call the police. I wondered if the same Albany police who would not apprehend a man trying to buy sex over the phone from the freshman dorm would come to the campus to run Sherrod and Cordell off.

Later that quarter I went on the first demonstration in Albany in support of two students, Bertha Gober and Blanton Hall, who had been arrested for trying to purchase tickets at the white-only ticket window of the Trailways bus station. Other members of the NAACP Youth Chapter had been arrested, but they had been bailed out. Blanton and Bertha refused to post bail and remained locked up. These actions tested the ICC (Interstate Commerce Commission) ruling, effective November 1, 1961, making it unlawful for commerce crossing state lines to utilize segregated facilities. The arrests and this demonstration were followed by the formal organization of the Albany Movement and the first of many powerful mass meetings.

A second test of the ruling was organized as a train ride by SNCC's national office. The integrated group of Freedom Riders were all arrested in Albany, and, for the second time, so was Bertha Gober, who was not among the riders but was standing in the crowd gathered to greet and support them. When the riders were arraigned, there was a demonstration in support of them; all of those who marched were arrested. I was not on that march. On the second day, I was among those who marched and spent more than two weeks in jail.

As the Movement got under way, there were daily marches and mass meetings outside the police station. On one march, when we got to the police station we prayed and sang. Pritchett came up to me and asked, "Weren't you in my office a little while ago?" I answered, "Yes." He said, "Didn't we try to help you?" I said, "You didn't catch him, did you?" Pritchett walked away.

When I think about my journey as a fighter for justice, there are sign-posts—events that happened in my life that helped me to understand more clearly where I was in reality as a person living within the larger American society. These experiences let me know that being Black made a difference and that if I was going to be effective, I had to really revise the way I myself visualized my current status, or I would have no chance of effectively choosing strategies to transform that status. This was a transformative experience that shattered the facade of school civics lessons, the *Highway Patrol* and *Lone Ranger* TV and radio shows that influenced my culture.

Also there was this tiny but growing awareness that being female was different. It was something you knew and that you had ingrained in you as a girl. It was something you lived with; it was like the floor you walked on, the walls of your house—it was just there. If you were a girl, some really bad things could happen to you—and often there was not one thing you could do about it. It seemed to come with being female. I mean it was there when I first knew I was a girl. I knew I was prey and that protection for me was weak or nonexistent. I also knew at the same time that I must go on anyway. I still remember the instructions we received about rape in high school: if someone tries to rape you, don't struggle, and maybe he won't kill you.

It took Joan Little to crash that prison I was locked up in. In 1975, when Joan Little in her jail cell killed the jailer who forced her sexually, she set me free. That's why I wrote the song about her: "Joan Little, she's my sister, Joan Little, she's our mama, Joan Little, she's your lover, Joan's the woman who's going to carry your child." It was key to my counting myself as a part of the Women's Movement. But this was not 1975; this was 1961, and I was not there yet.

However, there was a little light peeking through the crack created by my efforts to stop this white man that time, and it was shining on a place in me that said, *This doesn't have to be a given. There might just be another way to be Black and female in this universe.*

As I review this particular event, the fact that females were being preyed upon by white men looms large. Sometimes when people interview me about the Movement they ask about sex. What they are asking is, did we, the activists, have sex? Was there cross-racial sex? How were white women treated if they had sex with Black men? Thinking through this story, I am aware that no one has asked me about the sexual practices that were a constant thread through too many Black women's and girls' lives in the South.

My experience was not an isolated case. I came through this experience understanding that the officials of Albany State College would not protect me against white men and would often not stand and be counted in the Movement that was sweeping the South. My trusted faculty adviser would also not be able to deliver the police to bring justice or protect me. They would come late to the corner and I would be on my own. My boyfriend would not like what I did. My parents later said to me that they had heard what I had done, that it was a brave thing to do, but that it was too dangerous and I should not do it again. I told them I was just doing my job to try to stop someone calling the freshman dorm for sex for pay while I was on duty. I came out knowing that when I was really pressed and up against white men and sex, I was not going to be protected by the system.

It has been more than forty years since this event happened, and I still feel the loss of innocence that made me know that as a Black-female-sexual life, I was in trouble everywhere in this society, with nowhere to hide, nowhere to run. So, uncovered, without shelter, with every ounce of strength I had, and all my heart and soul, I joined this Movement for FREEDOM!

Expelled from Albany State College because of her activism, **BERNICE JOHNSON REAGON** graduated from Spelman College and earned a doctoral degree in history from Howard University. A founding member of the SNCC Freedom Singers, she married SNCC field secretary and organizer of the group, Cordell Reagon. She organized and performed for more than thirty years with Sweet Honey in the Rock, an a cappella musical ensemble. Currently she is curator emeritus at the Smithsonian National Museum of American History and distinguished professor emeritus at American University. A historian, author, composer, and music producer, she is the recipient of the MacArthur Fellowship and Presidential Medal for the Humanities. She has created sound tracks for various film projects, such as *Eyes on the Prize, Africans in America: America's Journey through Slavery, Freedom Never Dies: The Legacy of Harry T.*

Moore, and *Beah: A Black Woman Speaks;* compiled African American musical history, including documenting the music of the Freedom Movement in a CD collection, *Voices of the Civil Rights Movement,* and Black church music in the Peabody Award–winning 1994 radio series *Wade in the Water: African American Sacred Music Traditions.*

We Turned This Upside-Down Country Right Side Up

Joann Christian Mants

Following family traditions, a teenager repeatedly defies brutal treatment by southern policemen.
[Editors' note: Based on an oral history interview.]

When SNCC Came to Albany

Every generation has its race to run. We were reared with a calling, in the way that preachers are called. I do believe our commitment to the uplift of our community is our calling; it is part of what we must do. When I was growing up, our grandmothers and grandfathers, our mothers and fathers established criteria for how we were to be, showing us by example in the way they carried themselves. They were very proud people, working for themselves, insisting on ownership of things, on workmanship of things. I saw in them a strength that I think I have inherited. As I look back over the years, I see that the older folk, who were more conservative than the young activists, were radical in their own way—radical to the point of not allowing others to take away their dignity.

I became interested in the Movement long before the SNCC workers came to Southwest Georgia. When I was only eight years old, I followed the bus boycott in Montgomery, Alabama, on the news, watching on a black-and-white television. I saw what was happening there, but I did not quite understand what I saw or what courage it took to take part in those events. But I knew that something was wrong. On the news I continued to hear the words "Freedom Riders . . . Freedom Riders." The only thought that came to my mind each time I heard those words was "I wish those Freedom Riders would come to Albany, Georgia." There were wrongs that existed in Albany, and we needed those wrongs righted. I watched the news religiously, every day, just to see what was happening throughout this country and wishing that the Freedom Riders would hurry up and come to Albany, Georgia.

In the 1950s and 1960s people walked everywhere. One day in 1961, while walking toward downtown Albany with my sister, Lavetta (whom we called "Dear")—I remember it being a sunny, fall evening—I saw Charles Sherrod and Cordell Reagon near the old Trailways bus station. They were crossing Oglethorpe, the dividing line between the white business section of Albany and the black business community. I remember Sherrod and Cordell saying to us with a smile, "Don't forget to come to the mass meeting." I remember that someone had whispered to me, "Those are some of those Freedom Riders," and that they had come to Albany. I thought, *The Freedom Riders are here!* I felt my prayers had been answered, not understanding that this would be the beginning of a new lifestyle for me and my family and friends. When Sherrod and Cordell came to Albany, I was in the ninth grade, my last year of junior high school. Therefore, I was not sure what I expected from them; however, I knew I was just happy they had made it to Albany. We were going to be free, because the Freedom Riders had come.

The day after my sister and I saw them on the street, they came to my school (then called Carver Junior High School, now Monroe High School), asking students on campus to come to the mass meeting at Shiloh Missionary Baptist Church, which was only one block from the school. I was afraid to go without permission from my mama or my daddy, because we could not tarry after school. So I went home and asked my daddy if I could go to the mass meeting, and he said, "Yes, Sugar." I went to the meeting and thought it was the best thing that had ever happened in my life. I felt that freedom was just right over the hill, not understanding that the cost would be great and the time would be long.

After that mass meeting, my sister and I would leave school every day and go by the office to see what people had to say, to hear the plans, all the details. We worked in the Movement! The first SNCC office was in the black downtown, called Harlem. At that time it was strange to see the white SNCC folks in Harlem. White people from Albany almost never came to Harlem except to pick up their maids. Seeing people of both races interacting in a friendly and equal way was so unusual that white Albany residents driving by would almost have accidents. Besides, these white SNCC folks walking around with long hair and sandals were a strange sight to southerners. All this was new to my sister and me, too. Sitting around the office and just listening to what everyone was saying was an entirely new experience to us as well.

I remember SNCC workers Charles Jones, Bill Hansen, Charles Sherrod, Cordell Reagon, and others just sitting around and discussing the issues of the day—how would they deal with a particular situation, and what would be the consequences of their actions? My sister and I sort of huddled behind the older SNCC folks, and they sort of patted us on the head as though they thought we were very cute. I was fourteen years old. I kept thinking, *This is something else. We are going to be free.* I was not sure where I would fit in, what my niche would be, but I knew I would do *something*. I didn't understand all their words and language then. I was naïve and just wanting to be free, wanting all of us to be free. I continued to listen. I learned a great deal about these strange, new-thinking, new-talking, and new-acting SNCC folk. I continued to listen. Eventually I was able to understand them; some of their ideas became my ideas, and then I was able to create some of my own new ideas and concepts.

This was the summer of 1961. Along came the autumn. Mass meetings were happening weekly, mostly at the Shiloh Missionary Baptist Church and the Mt. Zion Baptist Church. Any time you heard the words *mass meeting* you would know that meeting would be held at one of these churches. All summer long we had heard many of our local community leaders speak about the injustices that existed in Albany and that plans were being made to find ways to correct these injustices.

After much discussion with the all-white members of the local government and our local leaders—since no agreement had been reached—Dr. Martin Luther King Jr. and workers from SCLC were asked to come to Albany to bring up a greater awareness. Dr. King came, but the local authorities still refused to agree to any of the concerns of the local leaders, so the black community was forced to follow through on their plans to march through the streets of Albany.

Those of us who attended the mass meeting were asked to commit to marching—and most people agreed. I agreed, but I knew I had to go through my parents before I could make such a move. I finally got enough nerve to go home and ask my father and mother if I could march with the Freedom Riders. I had heard those Freedom Riders say that we might go to jail, but for some reason the consequences did not register with me. So I still asked Daddy if I could march. He said, "Yeah, Sugar. Lead the line." I believe he said that just to get me out of his way.

The Beginning of a New Me

The next day we met at the church (I think it was Shiloh) and prepared to march. The mass meeting was very high in spirit, and the sun was just about to set. Dr. King presented one of his soul-elevating speeches, and we were ready to face dangers seen and unseen. We were asked to line up and given some additional instructions about what might happen, but we were so ready to move that we would allow nothing to get in our way, not even the threat of jail. I believe I was number six in line—just following my father's instructions—and marching right behind Dr. King. We marched off to downtown Albany and were met by the Albany police. We were told to dismiss or go to jail. No one moved. And off to jail we went.

Mama said that when she saw the news that night, she saw me pass by with all the people who'd been arrested. She didn't know what to say. She knew Daddy would be coming home and he'd count heads. If he didn't see one of us, he'd be really upset. When he came in, they were all sitting by the fire, hoping he would not ask about me, but of course he asked, "Where's Joe [my nickname]?"

Mama said, "She didn't come home." That got him sort of upset, so Mama told him, "I think she's in jail." He said, "She's in jail?" "Yeah, I saw her on TV."

I later found out that he called all of our family about my being in jail. It was the talk of the family. It was degrading for anyone to go to jail during my early life, and every effort was made to avoid this, but this time jail became almost a badge of honor, because it was related to something that, hopefully, would be for the betterment of all.

I had the pleasure of being carted off to the jail in Camilla, about twenty miles from Albany. The night of our arrest it was estimated that seven hundred people were arrested.

That night in jail was something! It was strange, frightening, funny, and enlightening—all at the same time. People who had never prayed before, prayed. The police harassed us all night long, beating on the doors, threatening us with death. We did not know what to do. That first arrest they packed about sixty-five of us young women into a jail cell made for six people. We had to figure out a way to stay there and coexist. Half the night we told stories, sang songs, and prayed prayers. They shut off the lights, so we couldn't see what was going on or who was in there with us. But God is good; light from the streetlights came through the windows, giving us just enough light to function, and we had a full moon that reflected its light as well. We refused to surrender our dignity for a prison light. We stayed in Camilla County jail overnight and survived. That arrest freed me from a lot of fears, and I knew this would be the beginning of a new me.

The next evening, just before sunset, they loaded us back on the buses and headed us back to Albany. President Kennedy had called the Albany government officials and insisted that we be released. Albany officials said we'd all be considered juvenile delinquents, so they marched us to court and gave us all a record before they released us. When I got out, it was so nice, because Mama gave me *five* candy bars! I thought, *I need to go to jail all the time!* Since we had not eaten at all that entire day, I ate all the candy bars at once. I always remember getting this treat of Butternut candy bars and how they tasted so good.

Marches in Albany were happening almost daily. By the time I was sixteen, I had been in jail seventeen times. My sister Dear, who was two years younger than me, and my cousin Maretta, whom we called Deake and who was a year older, usually went right along with me. The most difficult arrest and jail experience happened after I went on a summer 1963 march organized by SNCC field secretary Willie Ricks. Jean Wheeler, from SNCC, was in the line, too. The Albany authorities had told the Movement that we could not congregate in groups of more than three people, but we marched anyway. At city hall, when we informed the chief of police that we wanted to pray, he told us we were under arrest.

So we all began to lie down and go limp, and the police started to drag us down an alley. We soon named this alley Freedom Alley, because that's the route on which we freedom workers were always taken when we were arrested. There were rocks and broken glass all up and down the alley. Everyone who refused to walk into the jail was dragged over rocks and broken glass and then up several steps. We were asked to get up. Some got up, but I did not. I made them drag me all the way down the alley and then up the steps. My back hit each step, one by one, as they bumped me over them.

When they got me inside, they threw me into a corner. Faith Holsaert of SNCC had been arrested on an earlier day, so she was in jail before we got there. Faith was on the other side of the jail, because they couldn't put "the little white girls" in with us. I remember hearing Faith's voice from the jailhouse as I lay there on the floor of the jail. I hollered something to her.

I continued to sit in the corner, where I sat trying to put my shoes and socks back on. Somehow, my continuing to sit angered two of the policemen so much they punched and slapped and kicked me. And I punched back. They threatened to kill me. They said, "Get up, you black bitch!" I didn't. I continued to sit in the corner on the floor, tying my shoe strings and trying to get myself together. They said, "We'll kill you, you black bitch. You'll see!" I said, "You'll just have to do that, because I will not move." Then they crushed me behind the door, pulled me around by my hair and tried to snatch the rest of my clothes off. One policeman just stood on my legs. Imagine a man who weighs in excess of 230 pounds standing on the legs of a sixteen-year-old! But, through the help of God and a punch to the most sensitive spot on a man, I was able to get him off my legs. He spent two weeks in the hospital, as the sheriff in Camilla angrily told me near the end of my time in jail.

They finally pulled me up to a standing position. Because I had been arrested so many times before, the police went past the booking area, telling the clerk there, "You don't have to book her; we already have all the information we need on her."

We were usually grouped by race and age, but first they threw me into the white-only holding cell. This was the area where Faith was being held. I couldn't see her. I later learned she had been patted down by several policemen, who isolated and surrounded her. I kept calling her name, and she would speak to me. What the police had done to me upset Ralph Allen, another SNCC worker who had been jailed, so much that he started shaking the bars and yelling. I think he was saying, "Leave her alone!" I thought he would injure himself, so I had to keep telling him, "I am fine. I'll be all right." He was yelling and screaming, and Faith was, too.

I heard the police and the detectives talking, saying, "Keep this one separate from the others." Then instead of putting me in with the girls under eighteen, they put me in the cell with SNCC worker Jean Wheeler, a college student. Albany chief of police Laurie Pritchett refused to keep his jail full of Freedom Riders, so he would send us off to the surrounding county jails. Therefore, I was carried off to the Camilla jail again, where they always held us juveniles, leaving Jean and the others in jail in Albany.

I was transported to Camilla in a police car, alone with the two policemen who had earlier threatened to kill me. We trailed the paddy wagon with all the other students. The police talked about me all the way to Camilla. They talked about how they would kill me. The talk was not just one-sided, though. We had a nice conversation.

When we arrived in Camilla, they put all the young ladies except me in the cell downstairs, and I was placed into what is called the holding cell and then upstairs into solitary confinement. They told me that I was on death row. I figured, "If you gotta go, you gotta go."

I think that a lot of the events I have forgotten I forgot because they were just too destructive. I haven't thought or spoken about when I was in solitary in a long time. I remember there were no lights, no mattress. There was a toilet, a sink, and two bunk beds made of steel, with holes as large as an orange throughout the base. I stayed there for two weeks.

While in this solitary confinement I was offered all sorts of foods—foods different from what the other young women received. I would be given large offerings of rice, fried chicken, greens, peas, but I wouldn't eat any of it. I'd just politely flush it down the toilet. The jailer and the local sheriff said, "If you don't start to eat, you black son of a bitch, we're going to kill you." I said, "I'm going to die one way or the other, so you might as well kill me." I can remember the black trusty in the jail begging me to eat. I refused. I knew he'd been told to tell me that.

Some days later, my younger sister Dear, who was fourteen at the time, and my cousin Deake, who was about seventeen, were arrested. Anybody with the last name of Christian was separated from the rest of the population. Both were put in solitary cells across from me. I could not see out, except there was this little peek hole at the bottom of the door that you could kick out, kneel down, and peek around. I could see Dear peeking out, and I could see my cousin. We would yell to each other, back and forth. We tried to stay in contact with each other as much as possible, but then the jailer covered the hole.

We were harassed throughout the night. Through the doors we could hear threats such as, "We're gonna kill all them Christian bitches." Our thoughts were, *If you've gotta go, you've gotta go.* Years later I learned that Dear had been touched inappropriately by one of the jailers.

To further intimidate me, they let my sister and cousin go after they'd been there a week. They also would not allow my mama or my daddy to come see me. Finally my daddy went to see the judge and told him, "I am going today. I've had enough of this. I will see her. I will be there in twenty minutes." That day Mama and Daddy were allowed inside the jailhouse; however, they weren't allowed to come to the jail cell. I was led down from the cell to the jailhouse kitchen. We talked for about thirty minutes, and I was allowed to receive some personal items. Mama was able to get everything I needed past the jailer, even those favorite candy bars. My mama and daddy left, satisfied that I was okay, just a little weak from not eating. I did not tell them of the threats, because it would only cause them more worry.

While in solitary I was threatened every day. One day the police put this huge, vicious black German shepherd in the cell with me. I guess I was supposed to scream and yell, but I didn't. In fact, what I did was to turn over like I was going back to sleep. God Almighty must have shut that dog's mouth. He came over to me, sniffed me here and there, and turned around. Didn't do anything to me.

Every day someone would come up to get me to eat. They came with an apple pie, baked specially for me. I politely flushed it down the toilet in the presence of the jailer. They probably thought I would die, because I wouldn't eat anything. But I knew that the young ladies down in the cell below were only offered jailhouse beans. How could I accept anything any different?

About a week into my stay, attorney C. B. King and Dennis Roberts, a young white law student who had volunteered to come south to work as King's law clerk, came to visit me about sundown. I was just about to go to sleep when I heard the jailer's keys in the door. I didn't know what was about to happen to me this time, so, of course, when I saw them my heart leapt for joy. C. B. sat on the toilet seat and Dennis sat on the steel bunk. The jailer stood in the door, with the dog. To help C. B. I had kept notes in a journal every day of all the things that the police and jailers had said and done to me, so I had written things like "Monday: Officer Such and Such . . ." I had written down what he had said and what I had said. Through the window, I could see the time on the bank clock and I could hear the church bells, so I would write down all the things they did and the date and time. I gave C. B. my notes.

This angered the jailer so much, he said something very derogatory. Dennis respectfully asked, "Attorney King, want me to write that down?" C. B. just looked at Dennis like, *Here we all are in this jail, and you are asking me, a black man, if I want you, a white man, to take that down? Boy, you'd better shut up; we're already in enough trouble!*

C. B. was very impressed with my note taking. It made his job of information gathering easier. We thought we should encourage everyone who was jailed to keep a journal. Before they left they took my notes and gave me some more paper. After they left I felt a test was coming, and I was right. Several days later the Klan surrounded the jail. I was the only one left in there, so they were there because of me—a little sixteen-year-old girl.

Finally the officers came and took me back to Albany, where local juvenile probation officers talked to me without a parent or lawyer present. There, as at the Camilla jail, they told me that I was being held responsible for punching the police officer. Because of this, they said, I would have a record and would be picked up and taken to some juvenile detention center at a later date.

"Home of the Brave"

It was just about sundown. I was leaving downtown Albany after the interview and had to pass Shiloh Baptist Church on my way home. The SNCC workers—or "outside agitators," as the white southerners liked to call them—were all in the church seeking sanctuary, because there had been a massive sweep and arrests of all the civil rights workers. My daddy, James Christian, and my cousin, Monroe Gaines, were sitting at the back door of the church, under a spotlight, with their guns across their laps. Daddy said, "You go on home, Sugar. You can't stay here tonight."

I had just spent two weeks of constant harassment, no food, no mattress, and now I had to observe my father and cousin sitting with guns, trying to protect the lives of students and others. As I rode off I could see them sitting on the steps of Shiloh, sitting under the light. Both of them had worked all day but planned to spend the rest of the night guarding the church, because the Klan had been circling the church at night. I thought to myself, *Oh, what a country; land of the free, home of the brave. My father and cousin are truly "the brave."*

Daddy also told me the Klan had gathered for a rally over across Slappey Drive in a cow pasture where the old Slappey Dairy had once stood. It was about seven blocks from where we and our cousins lived on Holloway Avenue. People who lived near the dairy site told my father and cousin that the Klan had called our family names over their microphone, saying they would get us. I hadn't realized all these things were happening while I was in jail. Daddy didn't want me to worry. But Albany was just about at a point of insurrection, or an explosion, one.

The Movement Prosecuted

The Albany Movement was prosecuted by the federal government starting in the summer of 1963. My sister James Zenna, who was nine, and I were subpoenaed by both sides to testify in Macon. We had a good old time. They kept me on the stand for two solid days, trying to get something on the Movement. They would ask me a question, and I would play with them: "Well, your honor, you know, I went to these segregated schools and I don't understand all these words you're using." The judge and the lawyers would have to take forever, explaining.

When James Zenna took the stand, she was so little, you couldn't see anything but the top of her head until they put some phone books under her. Mama had sewn her a pretty dress in that fabric with the little holes in it and a lining underneath. She had a big bow in her hair. The government was saying Joni Rabinowitz had been at this particular demonstration and that James Zenna was holding Joni's hand. We all knew that it was Joyce Barrett at the demonstration, not Joni. The government kept nine-year-old James Zenna on that stand for two hours, trying to get her to change her story. James Zenna was something else. She talked in this certain, precise way. They couldn't shake her: two hours and a nine-year-old. That was James. She didn't change her story.

Since both sides had subpoenaed us, both sides had to pay us a stipend. We took the money and bought our lunches, then took the rest home and gave it to Mama. After all this, the charges against the Movement were dropped.

Integrating Albany High School

After the demonstrations were over and most of the civil rights workers had left, we continued to push for our rights. In my senior year (1964–1965) I attended formerly all-white Albany High School with several other black students: Mamie Nell Ford, Eddie Maude McKenzie, Shirley Lawrence, Ruby Nell Singleton, and Annette Powell. It was the worst year of my life.

Our registration—at the board of education instead of at the school—was separate from that of the white students. While we were registering, the principal publicly referred to us as "monkeys." I looked him in the eye and smiled and said, "First day of school, we'll be there." After we registered we went over to Albany High to get our schedules. When we walked on campus, it was like the Red Sea parting—everybody moving back from us. I said to myself, "Lord, the power that we have." The administration had spread us out so that we were each in different classes. To take us to school we had one whole bus—just the six of us. Another Albany High School bus drove right past my house, but we were so special, we couldn't ride with those white students. It took all of my strength to finish that year.

At lunch, when we stood in line, we were spat upon. Seeing how we were treated, all the black women who worked in the cafeteria would give us great heaping plates, saying, "Take another one. Help yourself." We organized ourselves: I would sit at one table; Mamie Nell would sit at another table; Eddie Maude at another, and so on. Since the white students refused to sit with us, we would have many of the tables in that cafeteria. We did that every day for the entire school year. We wore their tails out. They never sat with us. Never. The entire year.

We joined the glee club and sang those white southern glee club songs. Whenever we performed, the white members had to stand *very* close to us for the songs to sound right. This made them very uncomfortable and made me laugh. Once, one of the biggest football players took pennies and threw them at me, a gesture meaning "Dance, nigger, dance." I turned on him and knocked him straight through the window that was in the hallway near the cafeteria. The administration called me in and said, "We don't fight over here." I said, "I'm over here and I fight. If anyone ever pitches pennies at me again, you *know* what I'll do." I didn't have any more problems with anybody pitching pennies.

They would have pep rallies at the school in the morning before classes started. If we went and sat in the middle of the crowd, the other students would scatter. We also went to the football games. Our Rev. Samuel Wells, a staunch Albany Movement activist, would take us to every game and sit in the bleachers with us, bless his heart. While we watched the game, people threw liquor, firecrackers, sodas, everything—you name it—at us. Reverend Wells sat through it all with us. We would leave early, before the crowd broke up, to avoid being trapped in the parking lot. We went to every game in town. Every game.

One young white woman became very good friends with Mamie Nell. She would slip away from home and visit Mamie Nell. Somebody saw them together and reported it to the school. The young woman had had a 4.0 grade average her entire high school career, but in the last semester of her senior year, they gave her a 3.5. Her friends had ostracized her. Even her family was criticized. She was expelled from the honor society and put out of the theater club. She lost her scholarships to college. This young white woman was bold, and brave, too. She would call me and we would talk. I told her she had to take care of herself. Do what she had to do to heal herself. She wrote in my yearbook: "No one picks my friends for me."

I saw her sometime later. She asked, "Joann, do you remember me?" I said, "Yes, I remember you." She said, "We had some hard times, didn't we?"

I remember walking out of that school that last day. Charles Sherrod and somebody else came to get me. I was so weak from the hardships of that year, I couldn't walk. They had to hold me up and help me walk. It had been a fight every day of the year: teachers, administrators, students. My grades were ruined, but I still earned a scholarship to Franconia College in New Hampshire. There I found myself surrounded by rich kids, extremely rich kids, without much on their minds. It was a lifestyle I wasn't comfortable with, so I came back and finished my bachelor's degree at Albany State.

Reflections on the Albany Movement

When I look at the successes that occurred in Birmingham, in Selma, and all over this country, I realize that Albany, Georgia, was the testing ground that gave rise to a number of other movement challenges throughout this country. Some people have said that the Movement failed in Southwest Georgia, but no movement can fail when you can get people to realize and understand that they will not be "slaves" anymore. The story of the struggle has to be saved, kept from being lost, protected and taken care of, by us—the ones who lived it and the ones who will live it. Not by strangers.

There were so many of us young women in everything the Albany Movement did. The women were the leaning posts that everyone depended on. We were the strength of the Albany Movement. We grew up fast in those days. At that time black children didn't have an opportunity to be children. There were too many things we had to take care of.

Being the oldest, I felt grown at an early age. Faith says I had a saying about myself that summer: "Nobody bosses this black woman except my mother, Dessie Mae Christian. Nobody." When I think about my father guarding the church, about Dear and me in jail, my mother going to jail at different times, my sister James Zenna, and even my six-year-old baby sister, Loris, I think the calling was a family thing. When one person got involved, it took everybody else along. I went to jail first, but my entire family soon joined the Movement. One time, Faith and I ended up at home with all the babies from two households, because the mamas and the other older sisters were in jail. In the morning we had to plait everybody's hair and feed them—it was a mess! We had all the babies except Peaches Gaines, who was in jail with her mother and my mother. Peaches was jailed because she had not obeyed an officer. She was about two. Her bond was set at, I believe, $125.00.

As I look back I see that the commitment is there, wherever I might live. It is a continuous thing, not just for Albany, Georgia. The Movement continues wherever you find yourself. Over thirty years ago I moved to Lowndes County, Alabama, with my husband and three children. When my husband was elected to the county commission after the first black commissioner was shot, I feared for his safety. I feared for my whole family's safety. I still have those old quirks: I look out of both sides of my face so that I can see what's coming from either side. We still part from one another in certain ways, still sit in a certain way, still listen for beeps on the phone. Some things are starting to come along in the county, none without a struggle. The struggle continues, and we will win with patience, perseverance, commitment, and concern, fighting fires one at a time.

I try not to think about some of the horrible things that happened to me in the Movement. I have never shared some of them with my own children, because these incidents are just too destructive. My husband and I didn't want our children to become bitter because of the things that have been done to us. Although they are already adults and we want the calling to continue with them, I believe that when they are more mature, they will be better able to handle these kinds of racial realities. We cannot fight the fires of today without understanding where we have come from.

Reverend Wells had a saying: "We had no army, no navy, no marines, and no air force, just a group of concerned, committed young folks, and yet we turned this country right side up. It was already upside-down; we turned this country right side up."

Joann Christian married Bob Mants, another SNCC worker. They live in Lowndes County, Alabama, where they are involved in church activities and have developed after-school educational enrichment programs. For the past twenty years **JOANN CHRISTIAN MANTS** has taught social studies to black and white public junior high and high school students in Selma, Alabama. Her teaching has always been enriched by her experiences in the Movement, which gave her a different perspective in terms of how she taught the social studies curriculum. She and her husband have three children and seven grandchildren.

Everybody Called Me "Teach"

McCree L. Harris

A public school teacher finds a way to use her position to support the Movement in spite of the opposition of her school board.

Opposing Segregation

My father was a great source of strength, and he taught us to believe in civil rights. Of course in his day he didn't call it civil rights; he called it the difference between right and wrong. On Saturday nights, when we held family prayer, he would pray, "Teach my children right from wrong. Give me the strength to teach them, and when I teach them right from wrong, Lord, you lead them in the path of righteousness." Always my father said, "Never back down when you are right. We're in the Southland and we're human beings, but they don't treat us like we're human." He was from Terrell County, and he told us he walked from there to Americus in Sumter County because things were so bad in Terrell. "At least you could walk the streets in Sumter County," he explained.

Called to the ministry at eighteen years of age, he first pastored in Jacksonville, Florida, where he met my mother. Then he came to Albany as the minister of one of the big churches in town, Mt. Zion Baptist, where many of the mass meetings took place. By the time of the Movement, however, my father had left Mt. Zion because of his feelings about what was right. Some of his members asked him to establish a mission in the little alley that ran beside Elliott's Funeral Home over on Jefferson Street, where a lot of black people lived. When my father brought this to the church deacons, they were adamant: "We don't bring our mission into an alley." He responded, "If I'm the pastor, you'll take it in the alley, where the people are." This stirred up a whole lot of turmoil. Rather than remain with the members of Mt. Zion, who did not want to be bothered with poor people, my father founded Mt. Calvary Baptist Church in 1932 with the support of a group of women from Mt. Zion who did not want him to leave town.

When I attended Talladega College in Talladega, Alabama, my father's civil rights message was reinforced. Every day the teachers told us, "Don't pay for segregation." We were not allowed to go to any events in town. All of our activities were on campus, because the city was segregated. We usually formed a pool to go to Birmingham and shop, even though the treatment there was not much better. When I returned to Albany, I continued to practice "Don't pay for segregation." I took no part in it. I tried to stress this with my students, that you don't pay toward anything that promotes segregation.

I did break this rule once to take my students to see a very good movie. If a popular movie was showing and it got crowded downstairs in the white section, white moviegoers would come upstairs to the black section and all the black patrons would have to leave. I warned the students ahead of time and instructed them, "A gentleman will come and ask you to move. Don't you move. You paid your money." As I expected, the downstairs filled and we were asked to move several times. We refused to leave our seats until the police came and threatened to arrest us. The children were getting scared, and I decided I should compromise. I took the children home, as I had not asked their parents for permission for them to be arrested.

I did receive one advantage from segregation. In the 1950s the State of Georgia paid my tuition and transportation to Columbia University in New York City for graduate school rather than allow a black person to sit next to white students at the University of Georgia. I attended one of the best teachers' colleges in the nation, simply because I was black.

Get Them Down There

When I returned to Albany from undergraduate school at Talladega in 1955, I went back to Monroe High School, the school I had attended and where my older sister taught. My old principal hired me. I worked at Monroe for the next thirty-six years, teaching Latin and French. I taught my sister Rutha Mae and other students who became involved in the Movement. Annette Jones White was in my class, and the day they arrested her I cried like a baby.

I helped the lines of marchers to multiply. Being at Monroe High was an advantage because I had direct contact with the student body. Every day I told students when the marches would start. I would say, "The meeting starts at Shiloh at twelve noon. I can't give you permission to march, but you know what's going on." Some would go from each class. An active student might come to me and say, "Teach, I've been in the cafeteria, and I told them what time we're leaving, and we're fixing to leave." I would respond, "I don't know anything about it, you know, but get them down there. They need the people for the march."

One day the news media came and asked, "Who do all those students down at Shiloh belong to?" I said, "They are mine." The newsman asked my principal, "Do you know your students are down there?" My principal said, "Yes," and added, "Sometimes a big truck comes and takes my students to work in the fields. Nobody says a word about that."

My involvement with students gave me the strength to play my role in the Movement. Other teachers weren't involved. I was only about twenty-seven years old and considered myself one of them. The students liked that closeness. Before the Movement we had gone to games and other community events together. Children came to my house as if they were at home, and we'd sit and talk. Sometimes they would bring their books and I would help them with their assignments. Some of them met the SNCC workers there. The levels of freedom and respect between my students and me were quite unusual; our bond was almost spiritual. It was too formal for them to call me Miss Harris, and using my first name, McCree, was too familiar; everybody settled for calling me "Teach."

There was a lot of undeveloped talent among the black youth of Albany. We had only one black elementary school and one black high school. My students weren't allowed in the art museum. They weren't allowed to go to the library. I shared my few books that I had brought back from college, but that wasn't enough. There were almost no recreational facilities. I saw no opportunities for my students. I said to myself, *If the doors are to be opened to the youth, then they must help open those doors.* That's the reason I wanted so much for my students to get involved in the Movement—to open those doors.

Lifelong Movement Worker

I didn't attend any of the weekday marches, because I couldn't leave school. At night I routinely met with the SNCC people, often at our house on Whitney, if not at Dr. Hamilton's house. We'd teach the children the nonviolent approach and what to do if they were attacked. At first I wasn't in favor of nonviolence, but I came to feel it was the safest way.

The superintendent of schools told me that if I wanted to remain a teacher, I could not officially be a member of the Movement board or get arrested, but I was on the board of the Albany Movement when it was first organized, and I stayed on the board. I participated in a few marches and public accommodations testing. The first time I went out to test the public accommodations law was in a little hole-in-the-wall coffee and sandwich restaurant down the street from the courthouse where white big wheels would have their coffee at noon. A fellow threw hot coffee on my arm. I remained nonviolent. I'm quite sure, however, if he had thrown it in my face instead, I wouldn't have taken it.

I almost stopped teaching to join that fulfilling movement life, to experience what it means to be a full-fledged citizen instead of a hijacked citizen. I paid a price for the involvement I did have. There was a time, after the Movement, when I just couldn't get out of bed. I could not walk. They ran all kinds of tests. The school system had to hire a substitute for almost an entire semester. The stress of civil rights struggle just took it out of me.

But I recovered and carried on. I have kept fighting since the sixties. When the schools desegregated and I was transferred to another school, I threatened to quit. After talking with me, the superintendent agreed to let me stay at Monroe. There I put together a black history course, which even some white students took. Teaching black history was so exciting and gave me a sense of pride, which the black students felt, too.

My message to young people today has not changed: Get a good education. In getting that education, find out who you are. You must know yourself. Go back to your roots in religion and faith. Return to where we were years ago when the singing and prayers in mass meetings would uplift us. I don't care what kind of religion you choose, but we need profound hope in a supreme being to make it through.

Teaching for me was a calling. My main goal in the Movement was to raise the educational status of black youth in our community. For educational advancement and everything else we need, I feel we must do it ourselves. As we knew in SNCC and the Movement, and as I learned at Talladega, we cannot expect the white man to save our race.

McCREE L. HARRIS was a lifelong resident of Albany, and one of her major interests was preserving the story of the Albany Movement. She was instrumental in the creation of Albany's Civil Rights Movement Museum at old Mt. Zion Baptist Church and served on the museum's board of directors. Active in the Democratic Party, she was a consultant to a number of politicians, including Albany state representative John White and Albany's former mayor Tommy Coleman. Harris served on several other community boards and worked with various groups seeking community improvement, including the Albany Water, Gas & Light Commission; the Albany-Dougherty Economic Development

Council; the Community Relations Council; the National Urban League; the National Association for the Advancement of Colored People; and the Georgia Commission on the Status of Women. In 1999 she was honored as the National Community Leader of the Year by the Black Women's Community Leaders Program and chosen as the Service to Mankind Award Winner for 2000–2001 by the Albany Past Presidents Sertoma Club. She died in July 2000.

"Everybody Called Me 'Teach'" © 2010 by Ruth Harris

I Love to Sing

Rutha Mae Harris

A college student puts her education on hold to join the Movement and becomes a member of the SNCC Freedom Singers.

Joining the Movement

The first time I went to the Albany SNCC office was in the summer of 1961. Before I actually went inside, I had to walk around the block several times. I was home from Florida A & M University in Tallahassee, Florida, and I wasn't sure whether to become involved in the Movement or to continue my education. I just had to walk a little bit so that I could get it in my mind exactly what I wanted to do. I decided that I needed to help myself and that I didn't want anybody else to get my freedom. I wanted to be able to say, "I was involved in this struggle. Nobody did it for me." Although I still wasn't sure whether I should put my education on hold, I went on inside. Later I spoke with my mother, and she told me that as long as I came back to finish my schooling, it was all right with her.

My involvement and commitment to the Movement came from my strongly knit family, particularly from my father, Rev. Isaiah A. Harris, the founding minister of Mt. Calvary Baptist Church here in Albany. In the forties he was encouraging people to register to vote. He set up a literacy school at the church to prepare people to register. He was outspoken and would tell white people what he was and wasn't going to do. My father died in 1951, when I was ten years old, but he remained an inspiration. His being such a strong person trickled down to all of us.

My mother, Katie B. Harris, whom we call MaDear, was a schoolteacher. After my father's death she raised the eight of us. My entire family was in the

Movement: my brothers, Emory, Alphonso, and Elijah, who was known in the Movement as "Peter Rabbit," and, of course, my sisters, McCree, Rosetta, and Juanita. Our house was one of Albany's freedom houses. We provided lodging and meals to many a volunteer from afar during Albany's days of struggle.

Singing for Freedom

I've never been afraid when I am singing. I started singing at Mt. Calvary Baptist Church and began doing solos in the eighth grade. Singing is my joy. Our music in the Albany Movement was so unique. We brought together so many musical traditions. For instance, common meter, congregational style, and devotional songs all found their way into freedom songs. We took our church songs and made them fit the occasion. For instance, in the song "Ain't Gonna Let Nobody Turn Me 'Round," the original version says "marching up to Canaan land." In Albany we changed the lyric to "marching up to freedom land."

Sometimes we created songs for a specific situation. When they were in jail with hundreds of demonstrators, Bertha Gober and Janie Culbreth wrote the lyrics to "Oh Pritchett, Oh Kelley." Bertha Gober also wrote the song "We'll Never Turn Back," to commemorate the death of Herbert Lee in McComb, Mississippi, who was killed for trying to register to vote. This became the theme song of the Mississippi Summer Project after James Chaney, Andy Goodman, and Michael Schwerner were killed.

I was a member of the first group of Freedom Singers for SNCC, which included another Albanian, Bernice Johnson, as well as SNCC field secretaries Cordell Reagon and Chuck Neblett. Now we call this group the "original" Freedom Singers. We traveled all over this country in a compact Buick given to us by a folksinger named Len Dressler. On one tour we managed to go fifty thousand miles in nine months without any fights. We got to see every state in the country, except Washington, Oregon, Alaska, and Hawaii. We sang at colleges, universities, churches, and coffeehouses; sometimes we sang in major concert halls, such as Carnegie Hall in New York City and the Chicago Civic Opera House.

Being a Freedom Singer allowed me to express myself about the wrongs that had been done to black people, about how badly we were treated. I also got a chance to tell the story of both the Albany Movement and the larger movement. Albany, to me was the beginning of the Movement as a whole and a training place for Dr. King. He carried the things he learned in Albany to other areas.

Albany has always been my home. I taught at Monroe High School for thirty years; it is the same school where my two older sisters taught. Since the Movement, there's been a little change in Albany, but there still needs to be a whole lot more. Black folks need to come together. We're too worried about who will get the praise. What's the difference if we all benefit? Sometimes all the suffering we did seems in vain to me. I don't get involved much anymore, except when I am asked to sing freedom songs. I love to sing.

RUTHA MAE HARRIS was a regular participant in Albany Movement marches and demonstrations and was arrested three times. In 2003 she retired from teaching and coaching the school's cheerleaders. She remains an active member of Delta Sigma Theta Sorority. In 2004 she recorded her first CD, *I'm on the Battlefield,* at Bias Studios in Springfield, Virginia. She is a frequently requested singer at churches in Albany and regularly sings with the Georgia Mass Choir, which was featured in the movie *The Preacher's Wife.* She has organized an adult Freedom Choir that performs at the Albany Civil Rights Movement Museum every second Saturday. Albany mayor Tommy Coleman and the city of Albany, Georgia, have twice honored her with a Rutha Mae Harris Day. On various occasions she still sings with other members of the SNCC Freedom Singers. In February 2010 she sang with the Freedom Singers when they participated in the PBS program "A Celebration of Music from the Civil Rights Movement: In Performance at the White House," produced by WETA.

Since I Laid My Burden Down

Bernice Johnson Reagon

A young song leader in the Albany Movement describes how the music she learned in church and school became the core from which freedom songs and singing became a powerful collective voice during mass meetings and in jail.

>
> Glory, glory hallelujah
> Since I laid my burden down
> Glory, glory hallelujah
> Since I laid my burden down
> I feel better, so much better
> Since I laid my burden down
> I feel better, so much better

Since I laid my burden down
Friends don't treat me like they used to
Since I laid my burden down . . .

That's my jail song, I had known and sung it long before being arrested in the wave of demonstrations in Albany, Georgia, December 1961. It was a favorite song of my mother, Beatrice Johnson, who would sometimes say, "I can't sing, but I love to sing," and she did. This is a song she would lead from her seat in the congregation if she was so moved. I have many times shared with others this statement about not being a singer, loving to sing, and raising your voice anyway, to explain the congregational singing tradition in which I was raised. There were no auditions; everybody could sing. One only needed the desire within to be a part of the birthing or raising of a song and the courage to do so. This song, "Since I Laid My Burden Down," describes one of many things I discovered about being locked up in jail. The idea that I would be locked up but not really locked up had never occurred to me before participating in demonstrations against segregation policies throughout the city and county. The idea of being in jail and that being exactly where I needed to be was the antithesis of what had been taught to us by our parents and teachers. "Staying out of trouble" certainly also included staying out of jail. I had not really known that the day would come when I would make the decision that the best way for me to move ahead in my life, jeopardizing everything I, my parents, and my teachers had worked for, would be through the Civil Rights Movement. "Getting in trouble" would really be the best way to move from where I was.

Who knew that being free of a heavy burden could actually be experienced even if the police had taken charge of your body and locked you behind bars? I could express this because there were songs that gave us a way of saying what we were doing in Albany, Georgia, in 1961, as we began to build a movement. I was arrested during demonstrations in December of that year. I was not alone; there were almost two hundred of us—we were in the second wave, because that many had been arrested the day before. And in the jail cells of Albany, where eleven were put in cells made for four, and in the Lee County Stockade, where more than sixty of us were moved, we sang. And in our singing we nurtured this different way of being that we were determined to bring about in our lives.

Mass mobilization actions in Albany began on the Albany State College campus. We moved into young adulthood in the midst of evidence all around us that the world we lived in could be changed if we were ready to confront and demand it. It had been more than seven years since the 1954 Supreme Court decision and six years since the murder of Emmett Till; the

Montgomery Bus Boycott had taken place in 1955; and, under occupation by federal troops, Central High School in Little Rock, Arkansas, had been integrated in 1957. The 1960 February 1 Greensboro sit-in led to an expanding student-led sit-in movement. It was clear that this was a movement with plenty of room for young people.

One of my first mass meetings took place in the college gym; the issues were related to the campus and hostile acts carried out by whites as they drove at high speeds through the street that ran through the campus. When we got in the gym, Marion Blount and I were asked to open up with a song. We quickly agreed that "Lift Every Voice and Sing" would be the right song. When we began to sing, as was and still is the practice, we all stood and sang: "Lift every voice and sing, till earth and heaven ring, Ring with the harmony, of liberty . . ." Many of the students sang along, but there was a noticeable number who did not sing, because they did not know the song. It was then I realized that all Black people did not know what we then called the Negro National Anthem, the song composed by the brothers James Weldon and J. Rosamond Johnson.

I had learned the song at Blue Spring Elementary School; it was also part of the standard repertoire of my junior and senior high school culture. After that mass meeting, I remember thinking a lot about students in college who had never learned the song and the blessing of having teachers who made sure we learned more than was required by the Georgia curriculum. It was the beginning of an important lesson about opportunities available and not available within Black communities and the resulting difference in what we did not know or think about many things.

Singing was a major force in my life; I do not know when I did not love to sing. Most of my early singing was congregational. By "congregational" I mean we learned the songs as we sang them; there was no rehearsal tradition. Each song was started by a song leader; there was no director. When someone started a song, we would join in. We sang at home, we sang at games on the playground, we sang at school, and we sang at church.

When I was eleven I was baptized and joined the Mt. Early Baptist Church, pastored by my father, Rev. Jessie Johnson. There were a growing number of younger people coming into the church, and the decision was made to buy a piano and organize a gospel choir. My oldest sister, Fannie, started Mt. Early's first gospel choir. It was my first experience with a rehearsed choral singing tradition. I, of course, had known about learning and arranging songs through a system of rehearsals. I loved gospel quartet singing and knew the singers had required rehearsals, which served as the foundation for their performances. This was also true for gospel choirs. The early music that formed my foundation was congregational, and I found later that much of it was from the nineteenth century. I loved adding the rehearsed traditions to my singing experiences.

In addition to congregational singing, I also had very early experience singing solo and duets with my sister Mae Frances. Music and singing were very much a part of who I was and who I understood Black people to be. I was twelve by the time I reached ninth grade and high school, where I auditioned and began singing in the high school chorus. I was in the glee club and the sextet. I was the contralto soloist, and I sang with the Angelets, our own R & B "girls" group. I continued all these various kinds of singing in college.

Singing in the Movement changed the way I sang and why I sang. The first march from the Albany State College campus in 1961 was in support of two students, Bertha Gober and Blanton Hall, jailed for trying to purchase tickets at the white-only ticket counter. Annette Jones and I led the march in support of Bertha and Blanton. We left the campus silently, marching two by two up the hill, across the Flint River Bridge to the Albany jail on Pine Street. SNCC field secretaries Cordell Reagon, Charles Sherrod, and Charles Jones were monitors. They rotated their positions, but throughout the march, one was directly in front of the line—walking backwards—while the other two walked up and down each side of our line. After circling the jail twice, we left downtown, but did not return to the campus. We met with the permission of the pastor, Rev. William Boyd, at Union Baptist Church. Charlie Jones looked at me and said, "Bernice, sing a song." I took a breath and started "Over My Head, I See Trouble in the Air." As I moved down that first line, I knew it would not be a good idea to sing the word *trouble*, even though I knew we were in trouble, but did not think it would help. So instead I put in *freedom*, and by the second line everyone was singing, with me placing a new word (*glory, justice,* and so forth) for each cycle:

> Over my head, I see freedom in the air
> Over my head, I see freedom in the air
> Over my head, I see freedom in the air
> There must be a God somewhere.

It was the first time I'd ever changed the text of a sacred song. It was the beginning of my understanding how to use what I'd been given in that body of old songs we had learned growing up in school and church. I'd always been a singer, but I had been singing what other people taught me. At that moment in Union Baptist I claimed these sacred songs truly as my own. They were mine to use for my contemporary journey. I could change the text to articulate and support what we were trying to do in fighting segregation.

The singing tradition in the Albany Movement was primarily congregational. There weren't soloists; there were song leaders. In fact, in most mass meetings anywhere from five to seven of us would be in the front leading songs, one after another, to get the meetings started. When people asked you to sing a song, they were not asking you for a solo, but for you to raise a song—to plant a seed. The minute you started the song, the song was expanded by the voices of everybody present. No one had to say, "Come on and sing." Everyone joined in; there was a wonderful sound expansion, and the originator of the song disappeared into the singing.

In all mass meetings in Albany, I was often a member of a group of singers who led the congregational singing that opened the meeting. This group included some great voices, among them Rutha Harris, Andrew Reid, Charlie Jones, Larry Gibson, Brenda Darden, Annette Jones, Cordell Reagon, and Charles Sherrod. The meetings always started with freedom songs, and the freedom songs were heard in between all of the mass meeting activities. In most of these meetings there was more singing than there was talking. The most essential movement business was nurturing the people who had come. There were two or three people who would talk, giving testimonies of their experiences or updates, but basically the singing was the "bed" and the "air" of everything, and I had never before heard or felt singing do that on that level of power.

The same songs, the same prayers, and the same words were no longer the same. I'd sung "This Little Light of Mine" all my life. In the Movement this song said something very different. "All in the street / I'm going to let it shine"—I'd never even heard that before, because, I mean, who would go into the street? That was not where you were supposed to be if you were an upstanding Christian person. And certainly not in jail, but still we sang, "All in the jailhouse / I'm going to let it shine." These were new concepts of where I as a fighter could choose to be.

This was also the first time I heard the text in some of the old prayers, and it felt as if they were saying exactly what we were going through. "Lord, you know me, you know my condition, and I'm asking you to come by here and see about me" was prayed every second Sunday in Mt. Olive Baptist Church, No. 2, by the mother of the church. But when she did it in a mass meeting just before a march, those words named our situation. It was like an amazing light of understanding opening up within me. That prayer, which had sounded old, was new and immediate; it was about us, pressed down by racism and wanting the power in the universe to be with us as we marched. I became more aware that there are different kinds of knowing. You can know a lot of data, but sometimes the journey you walk with your life allows you to really know what in this case, a prayer, is expressing. Your understanding is deepened because you have been changed by the path you are now traveling.

The Albany Movement conquered my fear of going to jail, and the songs helped to do that. They allowed us to name the people who were using jail against us, like Mayor Asa Kelley and Chief of Police Laurie Pritchett. Not only could we call their names and say what we wanted to say, but also they could not stop our sound. Sometimes the police would say, "Stop the singing." And we would know we were being heard, and we would just sing louder and longer. "I feel better, so much better since I laid my burden down" expressed what I felt like inside the Albany jail cell. There was a clarity about everything. I knew where I was; I knew what I was doing. I did not like being locked up, and it was not easy. It was where I was supposed to be. My life was being used for a purpose—fighting racism—and it lifted me up to find that I could take a stand and make clear what I thought about the way we were treated in this country and in my hometown. My body was locked in jail, but I was free and centered.

When Albany's Black residents marched and went to jail, we expanded the space we could operate in, and that was echoed and supported in the singing. It was a bigger, more powerful singing, because we were bigger and more powerful. In the Movement there was a transformation that took place inside of the people, and the singing echoed it. If people are transformed, they create the sound that lets you know they are new people. It is a sound you've never heard before, and they have never heard it before, because they've never been in that place before.

If you can imagine Black people at our most powerful point, in terms of community and peoplehood, then that's Albany, Georgia, during the Albany Movement. The Movement seemed to focus and concentrate the spirit of our people. One of the strongest ways to witness this was through the singing. The singing was powerful because what we did in the mass meetings and the Movement extended our physical space beyond the territory our bodies occupied.

A woman at Shiloh Baptist Church who could be heard three blocks away would lead "Come and Go with Me to That Land" for so many cycles. People were clapping and the feet were going. The text lines articulated a position of movement and a determination to be in another place, where things would be different. "All is well in that land . . . No more hatred in that land . . ." "We'll all be together in that land . . ." Reverend Holloway would sing, "Shine on me, shine on me, let the light from the lighthouse shine on me." The text is and was about claiming your rightful space. We had been too long out of the light, and it was our time.

This is not about a specific song, but about singing in a way that is beyond words to express. If you walk into the singing with your body, it is not a hearing experience; your ears are not enough, your eyes are not enough, your body is not enough, and you can't block it. The only way you can survive the singing is to open up and let go and be moved by the singing to another space.

In mass meetings I was alive and knew what I was supposed to be doing and where I was supposed to be. That was the way it was in jail and on the marches, too. The voice I have now I got that first time I sang in a mass meeting after I'd gotten out of jail. When I sang "Over My Head, I See Freedom in the Air," the same song I had sung in the meeting at Union Baptist after the first march from Albany State College to the jail, my voice was not only stronger—there was also a oneness about the song and the commitment I felt about this new struggle I had joined. I'd never heard that voice before, but I had never been that "me" before. And I have never let that "me" go—not in my singing, nor in the life I have tried to live since that time.

The biography of **BERNICE JOHNSON REAGON** can be found after her essay "Uncovered and Without Shelter, I Joined This Movement for Freedom," earlier in this same section.

We Just Kept Going

Carolyn Daniels

In spite of almost losing her life, a local beautician and movement host refuses to stop her civil rights activities.

Getting Involved in the Movement

I got involved in the Movement and SNCC because of my son, Roy. At the time, I owned my own beauty shop in Dawson, Georgia. Dawson is the county seat of Terrell County and is located twenty-five miles from Albany. I had made a little money and bought the land. Then I made a little more money and built the shop, made a little more and built my house. This was very important, because black people who did not have their own businesses and homes had to work for white people who were in business. Since I owned my own home and business, I was free to do what I chose. Roy, who was in high school, and I were the only people in my house, so I really did answer only to myself.

I can't really explain why Roy became active. Roy is just Roy. Even to this day, he can't fit into a "Do as I say do, punch a time clock" kind of thing. Early in the 1960s, when Roy was president of the student body at Carver High School, he gave a speech about civil rights that the principal didn't like. The principal called in the police and Roy was expelled. Shortly after this, Roy brought Charles Sherrod to stay with us, saying, "Sherrod wants to spend a night or two." Sherrod would go out and Roy would be with him. At first I didn't know what Sherrod was really there for, but after a while Roy started telling me a little bit about the civil rights work they were doing.

Next they wanted to have meetings at my church, Atoc A.M.E. Church. It was our right as members to ask to hold meetings there, but when I asked, none of the other church members agreed, because we were about voting and civil rights. They said, "You know these white people will burn our church down" (which turned out to be true later on for the churches that did hold voting classes), and they refused to let us use the church.

Still Sherrod kept going. Roy kept going. One day in the fall of 1961, Roy—who was not old enough to vote or drive, really—drove one of their recruits, Mrs. Inez Calloway, up to the courthouse to register. While Roy was waiting outside, the sheriff, Z. T. Mathews, slapped and kicked Roy. When Roy came home and told me what had happened, the hair rose on the back of my head. I knew I couldn't stand by and let things like this happen. The thing I couldn't get over was that Roy was just a youngster who didn't bother anybody, yet he couldn't go into the courthouse, a public building, without the sheriff slapping and kicking him. And I was a taxpayer. That just made me mad. I had no other choice. I started working and really got involved in the Movement. Through anger I became active.

I got out there with Sherrod and Roy. This was the way to make a change, to get people to register. That way the white people would have to hear what we had to say. We knew that if we had gone in and gotten angry, there would have been a bloody battle. So a night or two turned into a week or two. A week or two turned into a month or two, and a month or two turned into years. We held meetings at the churches to teach people to register to vote. We started studying the Constitution and all these long words that we didn't know. I was the teacher, with a blackboard, some crayons, and other materials, which I bought with the thirty dollars Andy Young at SCLC sent me every month for this purpose. After people went through the training sessions, they went down to the courthouse.

Fearing that Roy would be killed if he remained in Dawson, I sent him to his father's in Jacksonville, Florida, to finish high school, which he did, with honors, and then on to Paine College for a year. Finally Andy Young arranged a scholarship for Roy at UCLA. In the summer of 1962 the white segregationists burned down the three churches we did use in Terrell and Lee counties. That didn't stop us. Sherrod put up tents instead, and we kept going and met in those tents. I taught my voter education classes in those tents. The harassment was always there. At one point they suspended my driver's license. I had done not one thing, yet still I had to go three months without a driver's license. They really tried to make it hard for us. Teachers would call me and say they couldn't come to me to have their hair done or they'd lose their jobs, but somehow I kept going.

At that time there were only five registered black voters in Terrell County. The test was so hard that it was difficult for people with limited education to pass it, but even teachers had not been able to pass the test, because the white registrar arbitrarily determined who passed and who didn't. We started going up to the courthouse by ones and twos. I took about four people up with me, and we all passed the test and got on the voters' roster. Even though some people were discouraged by that long, drawn-out test or when they were not passed, enough black people did get registered as a result of our campaign to elect quite a few black officials in Terrell County.

Things changed after people started to register and vote. When the next election came, the students and teachers would call me late at night and whisper, "We have to get this superintendent out." I laughed at all their tiptoeing around. I knew they had to keep their jobs, but I still laughed at their caution. When the superintendent lost, he said, "It was on account of that Carolyn Daniels."

Terrorism in Terrible Terrell

What made Terrell County so terrible before we got the vote was that the white people felt, "This is my county; this is the way things are going to be. And I don't want it to change." They would actually kill black people by lynching and other methods. From the time I was growing up in the 1930s, I would hear stories about beatings and lynchings of people I knew. When a black man who owned the dry cleaners became involved with a white woman, they took him out, beat him, and castrated him. Another man, arrested for a domestic situation, was beaten so badly in jail that when they brought him to court, they had to drag and carry him in. They had to sit him up, because he couldn't sit up by himself. He died shortly afterward. Of course, these incidents were intimidating.

During the Movement, Terrell County white folks shot into my home because I housed young civil rights workers, both white and black, and, of course, this was unacceptable in that area then. From time to time I would have as many as nine SNCC workers staying with me. My house was shot into at least twice when they were there. Once was late in the summer of 1962 when I was over in Albany; two civil rights workers were hit. Prathia Hall was shot in the finger, Jack Chatfield in the arm. Ralph Allen was at the house also. When the shooting started, they all tried to hide: Sherrod under a bed and Roy behind the refrigerator. But we kept going, kept in the streets, kept taking people to register, kept getting people to vote.

One Saturday night in December 1963, about eleven at night, after all the volunteers and my son, Roy, had gone back to school, I had closed my beauty shop and was lying on my bed in my house alone. I heard footsteps and car doors slamming. I thought, *What is going on this late at night?* My bed was right next to the window. Just as I started to peep out of the window, the shooting began. As I rolled over onto the floor and got under the bed, all the windows were shot out. Then a bomb was thrown in and rolled right under the bed with me. All I could think was, *Oh, Lord, what is Roy going to do without me?* I knew this was the end. But somehow the bomb did not go off.

Finally the shooting stopped, and I could hear the cars drive away. I crawled out from under the bed, went into my son's room at the back, turned on the light, and saw that blood was just pouring from my foot. I ran outside to the neighbor's and she took me to the hospital.

When I came back, my house was gone. The bomb had gone off after I left. There was a big hole in the floor where my bed had been. Slats from the roof were everywhere. They never found who bombed my house or who shot into it. Different organizations sent money to repair my house. After it was fixed, Sherrod and the SNCC workers continued to use my house, and we just kept going, we just kept going.

CAROLYN DANIELS remained in Terrell County for several years after her home was bombed. Then she moved to Albany, Georgia, where she opened a grocery store and was an insurance agent for black-owned Atlanta Life Insurance Company. When she later became a resident of Atlanta, she continued to write insurance for Atlanta Life and sold Avon cosmetics for over nineteen years. For many years she was a geriatric nurse and did volunteer work for the Red Cross. She is active in the choir Daughters of Bethel, the stewardess board, and the Sunday school at her church, Big Bethel A.M.E. Now retired, she lives with her son and his family in Atlanta.

Photojournalist Matt Herron moved to Mississippi with his family in the summer of 1963. In 1964 he organized a team of six photographers (including Danny Lyon) to photograph events in the South unfolding around the Mississippi Summer Project and continued to shoot Movement activities until 1970.

Photographer and filmmaker George Ballis photographed with Herron and Lyon during the summer of 1964, most notably the Mississippi Freedom Democratic Party (MFDP) challenge at the Democratic Party National Convention in Atlantic City. He is best known for his pictures of César Chávez and the United Farm Workers.

A contributor to *Hands on the Freedom Plow,* Maria Varela joined SNCC staff in late 1962 and was assigned to Selma in 1963 to develop a literacy project. In 1965 she moved to Mississippi to write, photograph, and produce organizing materials used by SNCC and local leaders. Trained by Matt Herron, she worked as a SNCC photographer from 1965 to 1967.

Fannie Lou Hamer marching in Hattiesburg Freedom Day voter registration demonstration outside Forrest County, Mississippi, courthouse. Sign reads "Freedom Now, SNCC" (Hattiesburg, Mississippi, January 22, 1964). © 1978 Matt Herron/ Take Stock

Tougaloo student Joan Trumpauer was a trainer in nonviolence for a group of northern clergymen who planned to attempt to integrate Jackson, Mississippi, churches (Rev. Ed King, background). A Georgia native, her sweatshirt reads "Just a Cracker from Georgia" (Tougaloo, Mississippi, November 14, 1963). © 1978 Matt Herron/Take Stock

Ella Baker addressing the MFDP delegates at a boardwalk rally during the Democratic National Convention. Behind her is a poster of Michael Schwerner, killed with James Chaney and Andrew Goodman in Philadelphia, Mississippi, just two months before MFDP delegates and SNCC staff rode in caravans to the convention to challenge the all-white Mississippi delegation (Atlantic City, New Jersey, August 10, 1964). © 1978 George Ballis/Take Stock

Mary King, who worked with Julian Bond in SNCC's national office communications department, on phone in Jackson, Mississippi, just before the MFDP delegation drove in a caravan to Atlantic City. © 1978 George Ballis/ Take Stock

Victoria Gray (holding banner), a founder of the Mississippi Freedom Democratic Party, during a nomination rally for President Lyndon Johnson on the convention floor at the Democratic National Convention during the MFDP challenge to the all-white Mississippi delegation (Atlantic City, New Jersey, August 1964). © 1978 George Ballis/Take Stock

Annie Devine, a leader of the Madison County, Mississippi, Movement and of the MFDP, seated on the floor of the Democratic National Convention during the MFDP challenge (Atlantic City, New Jersey, August 1964). © 1978 George Ballis/Take Stock

Fannie Lou Hamer leading protesters singing freedom songs on the boardwalk during the MFDP challenge to the all-white Mississippi delegation at the Democratic National Convention. Foreground, left to right: Emory Harris, Stokely Carmichael, Fannie Lou Hamer, Eleanor Holmes, Ella Baker (Atlantic City, New Jersey, August 10, 1964). © 1978 George Ballis/Take Stock

Denise Nicholas being made up before a performance by the Free Southern Theater at the dedication of the community center. (Also pictured: Gil Moses, director). The theater, organized by John O'Neal, traveled throughout Mississippi with its productions, including *In White America* (Mileston, Mississippi, June 1, 1964). © 1978 Matt Herron/Take Stock

SNCC staffer Casey Hayden (fourth from left) participates with other SNCC staff and local residents as they listen to speeches during the dedication of the Mileston Community Center (Mileston, Mississippi, June 1, 1964). © 1978 Matt Herron/Take Stock

June Johnson during the Meredith March against Fear in Mississippi. She is holding a sign: "I wonder is White power dying?" At the age of fifteen, Johnson, a Greenwood, Mississippi, activist, was brutally beaten in a Winona, Mississippi, jail, along with Fannie Lou Hamer, Annelle Ponder, and Euvester Simpson, after they sat in at the bus terminal there upon their return from a voter education workshop in South Carolina (June 1966). © 1978 Maria Varela/Take Stock

Local activists from the Lowndes County Freedom Organization (LCFO) organize voting during their May 1966 primary. Rather than join the segregationist Alabama Democratic Party, Lowndes County's black residents formed the Lowndes County Freedom Party. An unofficial party, its symbol was a black panther, as opposed to the Alabama Democratic Party's white rooster. The panther can be seen on a ballot at lower right (Lowndes County, Alabama, May 1966). © 1978 Maria Varela/Take Stock

Local black Lowndes County residents voting in the Lowndes Country Freedom Party primary. The party ran candidates from sheriff, coroner, and tax assessor to the board of education (Lowndes County, Alabama). ©1978 Maria Varela/ Take Stock

Local Lowndes County residents voting in the Lowndes County Freedom Organization primary. Although the county was 80 percent African American, no black people had been allowed to register to vote until the LCFO began organizing its political party (Lowndes County, Alabama, May 1966). ©1978 Maria Varela/Take Stock

PART 4

Standing Tall

The Southwest Georgia Movement, 1962–1963

> How could we say to our children that we had
> been alive when it was happening and tell them
> that we had not fought for equality and justice? . . .
> Those southern students, our peers, were standing
> tall and [we] felt compelled to join them.
>
> —Peggy Trotter Dammond Preacely

Like their Albany counterparts, the young northern women who went to work in the Southwest Georgia Project had already been involved in civil rights activities. In addition, they came from groups or settings that had already placed them in direct contact with SNCC's staff. The beginning of a northern network of activists providing both support and personnel to the southern movement is evident in almost all of the following stories.

By the early sixties, most of the young women in this section, like most of the northern women in this book, had already been sensitized to racial issues—either by personal exposure or by something in their family background, travels, or political and religious beliefs—well before they went south. Like almost all of their movement sisters, they felt that joining SNCC was an absolute and compelling necessity; they did not want to miss the opportunity to stand up proudly for civil rights—in Peggy Trotter Dammond Preacely's words, to stand tall. They also believed that the tiny, poorly funded, and barely staffed organization had the potential to effect tremendous social change.

Whether the northern volunteers arrived in Southwest Georgia several months or almost two years after the Albany Movement marches made national headlines, they still found an active movement. The activities carried out by the Southwest Georgia Project were charac-

teristic of SNCC projects in other places and in later years. The major
focus was on canvassing and preparing residents for voter registration,
but public accommodations testing, picketing, boycotts of downtown
merchants, and protest marches were still taking place. Activities more
closely associated with the 1950s were also part of the program. The
Albany Movement maintained a boycott of the city buses and continued
to push for the desegregation of schools. Some of the 1960s efforts
were a revisiting of activities and strategies that previously had been
employed by older Albany residents. Some economic efforts were also
undertaken, including bringing together a pecan growers cooperative.
This was a groundbreaking civil rights program, both in the mounting
of a multi-issue campaign and in employing so many different strategies
at the same time.

All sectors of the black community were welcomed into and contributed to the Movement. However, the overwhelming majority of the
residents in these rural counties and towns were poor; many were sharecroppers, and the economically disenfranchised came to make up the
majority of the movement participants in these areas. This was not just
because of the sheer weight of their numbers, but also because by this
time, following Miss Ella Baker's lead, SNCC had a stated commitment
to organizing the poorest of the poor and those hardest hit by racial oppression. Her views on grassroots organizing and making radical social
change through building a black mass movement in the Deep South
formed the basis of SNCC's philosophy and organizing strategies. Miss
Baker insisted that the members of the resulting local organizations and
movements should determine the nature and course of their struggle
and that these groups should operate in a very democratic fashion with
a broad-based and shared leadership.

An activist since the early 1930s, Miss Baker had worked for the
NAACP in the 1940s, first as a field secretary and then as director of
branches. A number of the people she contacted then were important
in getting SNCC's early organizing efforts off the ground. In addition to
bringing the student groups together to form an organization, providing
SNCC with a basic organizing philosophy, and sharing her community
contacts, Miss Baker kept the group together in the summer of 1961
when the issue of whether or not to accept funds for voter registration
from liberal establishment foundations threatened to split the young
organization in two. Suspicious that this was an attempt to moderate
the student movement's militancy, fearful of aligning the organization
with the programs of white liberals and Democratic Party leadership,

and reluctant to engage in electoral politics, many in SNCC initially opposed accepting the funds and insisted on continuing confrontational direct-action campaigns. Those in support of using the funds argued that voter registration was a key issue for black southern progress and that therefore the organization should take advantage of whatever funds were available. Seeing the importance of both positions, Miss Baker suggested that the group create two wings—one focused on direct action, the other on voter registration—which ended the conflict. After this debate, SNCC field secretaries continued to push for desegregation and address other issues, but almost all of their community organizing projects maintained a focus on winning the vote. In so doing, they also found that pressing for black voting rights in the deep rural South, rather than in the southern cities and Upper Southern states envisioned by the funding agencies, required great militancy and determination.

The accounts in this section contain hints of the controversies that would be more hotly debated in SNCC a few years later. There is an interesting balance between views on nonviolence and self-defense. Movement workers might choose to live with people willing to protect them, sleeping more soundly while Mama Dolly Raines or Mr. James Christian sat outside under a light with a loaded rifle across their laps. Expecting difficulties, SNCC staff might assign local youths to guard sit-ins, as they did in two of the Atlanta sit-ins described earlier, with full knowledge that these youngsters were unlikely to remain nonviolent when movement demonstrators were in danger. Gang members might be asked to provide security, as they were in both the Augusta and Albany actions. In a small town or rural area, where everyone usually knew everyone else, members of a white mob ready and willing to attack nonviolent demonstrators would hesitate, knowing they first would have to challenge the young men providing security. Recognizing the role of authority that gang members held in certain neighborhoods in Albany, SNCC staff recruited them to be part of the Movement in the same manner as the organizers sought the support of local ministers and other community leaders. In Albany some of the gang members worked closely with movement workers and launched their own demonstrations. Finally, long before SNCC spokespersons publicly advocated self-defense, there were a number of occasions when SNCC activists set nonviolence aside and defended themselves.

Two values that later caused deep splits within the organization seem to reside in harmony during the first half of the sixties. The writings in this book indicate that both a belief in the importance of interracial work, relationships, and communities and a belief in the importance of black control of the organization and the Movement are accepted by SNCC women well into 1964. During this period there is no mention of racial tension by either black or white women when describing their work. The white activists, in particular, give the clear impression that they felt fortunate to have participated in the Movement, were fairly treated, and were able to make creative contributions to movement work; they had significant control over decisions relating to their personal actions within the Movement. Furthermore, they felt empowered and enriched by taking on the task of building a more equitable and just society. In these writings about early SNCC efforts, there are only subtle signs of the future racial divides. Notions of the beloved community seem particularly important to some of the white writers. A number of black women enter the Movement partially motivated by a pride in race and black culture.

The southern black college students who established SNCC created a black-led, rather than interracially led, organization. Several writers comment on the reality of a group where, in Debbie Amis's words, "African Americans were in charge." While fighting to change racial relationships in the South, SNCC workers established a racial dynamic that was unusual in the South and quite different from the norm in the North at that time. In the Movement, from the time of the sit-ins, black people, many of whom were southerners, were giving direction and guidance to white participants. The stories of the young white women who went to Southwest Georgia and later to other projects in the Deep South, or who participated in particularly dangerous activities like the SNCC Freedom Rides, suggest they not only took direction from black organizers and community people but also trusted their very lives to the judgment and decisions of these same people.

The goal of SNCC's early organizing efforts was to build a black mass movement in the Deep South rather than an interracial movement of black and white southerners. Yet within the organization, as can be seen in a number of the following accounts, there were some people who were deeply committed to creating a loving, interracial community, "the beloved community," both in SNCC and in the society at large. More than a few of the women writing here believe they found such a community, a community where positive and caring relationships could exist across racial boundaries, within a black-led SNCC.

Before the summer of 1964, white staffers were a fairly small minority within the organization. Those who chose to do grassroots organizing in places like Southwest Georgia lived as an even tinier minority in the heart of black communities, adjusting to different cultural norms and activities. Some black northerners with southern family roots and a familiarity with a black culture rooted in the South and urban black southerners in SNCC found themselves making similar adjustments, especially when assigned to farming communities. In these settings, college-educated women, both black and white, set aside any feelings of condescension they may have had and learned to respect the courage, wisdom, and knowledge of their black community hosts.

In developing an integrated, black-led program in Southwest Georgia, project director Charles Sherrod, SNCC's first full-time field secretary, departed from existing civil rights practices. Civil rights organizations like the NAACP, SCLC, and even CORE at this point had sent only black field secretaries to these areas. Other SNCC projects, most notably the Mississippi Project after 1961, also had been recruiting only black organizers. Considerations of safety and of encouraging local black leadership played a role in the Mississippi decision. Also committed to a movement led by local black residents, Sherrod argued that seeing black people working on an equal level with white people would strike at the heart of notions of white superiority and thus strengthen local black participation.

In Southwest Georgia adult local women sheltered, fed, and protected both black and white northern movement workers and offered them invaluable information and guidance regarding the communities where the organizing efforts were taking place. Younger women in these communities, some barely in their teens, worked alongside the northern SNCC workers, also guiding and protecting them. Local women of all ages demonstrated and went to jail with the northern civil rights workers. Female community activists, young and old, became a major source of strength as well as heroic role models for the young women who went south to join the Movement.

It Was Simply in My Blood

Peggy Trotter Dammond Preacely

Arriving in Southwest Georgia with a family legacy of militant opposition to racial oppression stretching back before the Civil War, a New York activist is transported into a new world.

Connecting with My Ancestors

A lot of civil rights organizing took place around eating and preparing food in Lee County, Georgia, during the summer of 1962. Talking about the vote might be done on porches while shelling beans or drinking lemonade, and sometimes even while picking crops. Sharecroppers had to reach their picking quotas before attending evening voter education classes, and sometimes we would help. Once, my best friend, Kathleen Conwell, who had gone south with me, and I volunteered to work in the cotton fields. Although I grew up in Harlem, I had been out in the country canoeing and camping in New England all my life. I was strong and young and invincible. I figured, how hard was it going to be to chop cotton?

We got up at five in the morning. The experienced choppers were wrapping their legs with flannel and had on long pants and covered shoes. We thought to ourselves, *Hey, we're going out in the summertime, we'll go out in our shorts and our sandals.* We did put on hats. Well, I'm here to tell you there is *nothing* like the Georgia sun. At five o'clock in the morning it is sort of warm, but by ten o'clock in the morning it is a blazing heat! The reason the others had wrapped and covered themselves was for protection from the sun. Kathy and I got the worst sunburns in the world!

People who do that work are to be admired. Chopping cotton is backbreaking labor. You work at an angle with a certain kind of hoe in a special kind of motion. And that's why you sing when you're in the fields, because you need something to break the monotony and to take your mind off the pain and the heat. You look at a row from this end all the way down to the other end, and you think you will never finish that row until nightfall. Somehow you find yourself at the end of that row and coming back. We chopped and chopped and chopped.

This was a heavy emotional experience for me, because my ancestors had escaped from slavery in Georgia not that far from the fields where I was working. Although my great-great-grandparents on my mother's side had been house slaves, not field slaves, at one point I felt I was a re-creation of my ancestors. It was an almost transcendental experience. I stood in the field and felt as if I were actually a slave and not free, but burdened with all the emotions that a slave must have felt. The earth, the dirt in Georgia is very red. At that moment I knew that the color came from blood, the blood of our slave ancestors, who were often worked to death and died right there in the fields.

In 1848 my slave ancestors on my mother's side, great-great-grandparents William and Ellen Craft, made a historically well-documented escape to freedom by disguising themselves as slave and slave owner. My maternal grandmother's brother, my great-uncle William Monroe Trotter, founded and ran the *Boston Guardian* newspaper at the beginning of the twentieth century and provided constant opposition to Booker T. Washington. My grandfather Henry K. Craft had been the executive director of the historic Harlem YMCA from 1932 until 1949. Both my great-uncle Monroe and grandfather Craft were Harvard graduates. My mother told me that my grandmother Bessie Trotter Craft remembered dinner-table discussions at the Trotter home that were usually on subjects related to race and were held with noted visitors like W. E. B. Du Bois and Archibald Grimke.

My father's family had some familiarity with manual labor. My dad, among the first in his family to receive any higher education, worked in the steel mills of Pittsburgh to pay his way through the University of Pittsburgh in the 1930s. His mother was a hairdresser; his father was a house painter, who always wore a light blue shirt and tie under his overalls when he went to work. In SNCC I felt so at home with the black farmers who wore blue denim shirts and ties under their overalls as they drove their tractors in the fields. I got my first driver's license driving a tractor in Lee County, Georgia, the summer I joined SNCC.

Harlem Training Ground

Both of my parents worked in the business world. In 1960 my father, Donald Dammond, began a career with Metropolitan Life Insurance in New York City when he was hired as the company's first black executive officer. In fact, we lived in a Harlem housing development called the Riverton, which had been built for black people by Metropolitan Life Insurance, and my father had been the assistant manager for the Riverton Housing Development. My mother, Ellen Craft Dammond, was the first black personnel counselor for the B. Altman and Company department store until she retired at age seventy.

My parents made sure that my brother, Hank, and I understood how very fortunate we were to have food on our table and a place to live. We were taught to treat everybody with a certain kind of dignity, to be polite and respectful. My dad used to park our car a block or so away from home under the train tracks, near where a number of homeless men used to live and light fires around empty trash cans to keep warm. When these men would walk up to our car, my brother and I were reprimanded if we didn't speak, and speak courteously, and say, "Good evening" or "How are you?"

Both our parents were involved in community work through the Urban League and the Black Achievers of the Harlem YMCA and worked to help black and Puerto Rican families get better employment and housing. My mother stayed involved in the YWCA locally, nationally, and internationally all her life. As long as I can remember, I've known that Uncle Monroe stood up for black people to get what they deserved and that black people should move beyond the context of their own family and their own world of job and home to help their race. This idea was reinforced by my parents, who insisted that their children always do something for our community and concern ourselves with the plight of the underdog and the rights of the poor and the dispossessed.

In the 1940s my brother and I were recruited to integrate The Dalton School, a private school in New York City. The school, whose students came from prominent New York activist families, fostered liberal ideas and stayed on the cutting edge of social reforms. Hank and I also became part of a group of black students from other New York private schools who became involved in SNCC in the 1960s. Our social lives revolved around social justice and political issues and our activism in the Freedom Movement. Of course, my brother and I followed the path of Monroe Trotter and his legacy of protest. It was simply in our blood.

The fifties were a very exciting time for me to be a teenager. I was a member of the National Conference of Christians and Jews (NCCJ), which sponsored several Kenyan students to study in New York and other U.S. cities in response to a request from Kenyan student leader Tom Mboya. Mboya became a major trade unionist in Kenya and was later appointed by Jomo Kenyatta to be independence minister of economic planning and development in 1963. This first international involvement created a sense in me that I belonged in the WHOLE world. My brother and I were also active in the Harlem and New York chapters of the NAACP. Stokely Carmichael, who later became chairman of SNCC, was my brother's pal; together we all formed the Harlem Brotherhood Group under the NCCJ. One of the things we did was to literally sweep the streets of Harlem with brooms, up and down Lenox Avenue, in order to get folks to come out of their houses and discuss correcting some of the unjust conditions. We used to meet at the Harlem YWCA and YMCA, local churches, and other organizations' halls.

Harlem at that time was a friendly and accessible community. It was like a small town. We had our own shoemaker, butcher shop, and other stores. The merchants were Jewish, West Indian, and Italian. I was never afraid in Harlem; we didn't even have to lock our front door most of the time. Bob Moses lived near our home, and so did Ron Brown and Don Harris and others who later joined the Movement. Some of my peers at Dalton also became involved. They included siblings Paul, Geoff, and Holly Cowan; Penny Patch; and Andy Goodman, who was murdered in 1964 in Mississippi along with two other civil rights activists, James Chaney and Mickey Schwerner.

Harlem was an incredible training ground for black activism. There were so many black organizations and institutions, including the Countee Cullen (later the Schomburg) Library, the YWCA's Emma Ransom House, and St. Phillips Episcopal and Ebenezer Baptist churches. We heard Malcolm X speak at the local Muslim mosque, and we hung out late into the night at Micheaux's famous black bookstore on 125th Street.

What did we Harlem teenagers do on a Saturday? We got up, did our homework and our chores. Then we grabbed our picket signs and went down to the local Woolworth's store in support of the southern sit-inners. The people I picketed with in those days were both black and white, from my own Harlem community and from the whole of New York City.

Sit-in on the Eastern Shore

Late one night in early December 1961, Angeline Butler, whom I had met earlier on the demonstrations along U.S. Route 40, called and asked my brother and me to participate in sit-ins on Maryland's Eastern Shore over the Christmas holiday. I had just turned nineteen that November, and Hank was just seventeen. We simultaneously answered "YES, we'll go!" into the phone. I was very excited, because here was a chance to really do something more than just walk a picket line. Christmastime had been chosen for our demonstration in order to make the connection to Mary and Joseph, who had been refused room at the inn for Jesus's birth. Organizers thought we could make the point better during the Christmas holiday that refusal of service to anyone is un-Christian and inhospitable. We thought if we could appeal to the conscience of the oppressor, maybe some changes would be made. We felt strongly that our nation, supporting unequal laws, just needed to be reminded, coaxed into turning itself around.

My brother and I and Angeline Butler took the train from New York City's Penn Station into Baltimore, where we were met by Reggie Robinson, Bill Hansen, Faith Holsaert, and others. First the seven or eight of us who were there received some training in movement rules, codes, and protocols. I felt a bond with my fellow sit-inners, and I imagined I felt something of the way slaves must have felt when they planned their daring escapes from plantations. After a day's drive from Baltimore, we went to a restaurant in Crisfield on the Eastern Shore of Maryland and sat in at five o'clock in the evening. My brother, who was underage for going to jail, was to be the look-out and communications scout. As I sat at the lunch counter in this small back-road town, I was shaking like a leaf, but I also felt brave and strong, as if I were doing something I was destined for. Hecklers shouted at us, and, of course, since we were an interracial group, we were refused service and arrested. In the police car it was even scarier. At the point they put the handcuffs on, it all became real. My fear was mixed with my excitement at being prepared and ready.

After they arrested us they didn't know what to do with us, because the jail was too small to divide us up by both race and sex. Finally they decided to put all the men together and all the women together, but first they cleared out some of the regular prisoners, the prostitutes and the drunks. We fasted the whole five or six days in jail. We were really on a crusade. I've never been so hungry in my life. We let ourselves drink only water and chew gum. When you are fasting you get a little wobbly in your mind. People from the community would come to the jail and sing outside while we leaned through the bars and joined them. Five days went by, and we were able to keep the feeling of being brave and honorable. At first the white guards were very hostile, but we followed our nonviolent training and did a lot of teaching of the guards in the jail. We continued to sing, and a couple of the guards eventually joined us in singing Christmas songs. A few guards actually sang some of the freedom songs with us!

1962 Southwest Georgia Project: Out in the "Rurals"

After my arrest on the Eastern Shore, I continued participating in demonstrations along Route 40. I also went to Highlander Folk School in Tennessee for training in nonviolence and to Raleigh, North Carolina, to learn more about organizing. I went to conferences and meetings all over the South and

North from 1961 through the early spring of 1962. I met Kathleen Conwell when Charles Sherrod and Charles Jones from SNCC spoke at her school, Skidmore College.

By the spring of 1962, Kathy and I were examining ourselves in the light of the Movement, as were many of our friends. Imagine two African American college girls—one at Hunter College, the other at Skidmore—talking late into the night on the phone about justice, freedom, and risk taking and asking, "If not now, when, and if not me, then who?" Oh, sure, we had our boyfriends and our loves and passions for swimming in the ocean and writing poetry and dreaming of visiting Paris, France! But the subtext of our lives was the MOVEMENT.

The big question was, how could we ever say to our children that we had been alive when it was happening and tell them that we had not fought for equality and justice? Our parents had fought in World War II and taught us right from wrong. *Oppressed* and *oppressor* were terms we had grown up with. We knew America's shame of Emmett Till, Bessie Smith, and Dr. Charles Drew. Each one of us had a family tale of racism, of being denied fair treatment. Those southern students, our peers, were standing tall, and Kathy and I felt compelled to join them. We decided to spend the summer working with SNCC's Southwest Georgia Project. Kathy and I were assigned to live in Lee County with an incredible woman, Mama Dolly Raines. Mama Dolly was a farmer who had her own house and raised crops and chickens out back. She was not imposing in appearance at all. She was a short, brown-skinned lady with strong arms, and usually wore a flowered house dress. She was Charles Sherrod's confidante, and her home was like a stop on the Underground Railroad, because so many of us in the Albany Movement came there. She had a tremendous influence on my life.

From her we learned to get our food at the source. Mama Dolly, who was always up at dawn before us, would go out to the backyard, select a chicken, and wring its neck. Kathy or I then had to pluck the feathers. One morning Mama Dolly said, "I have a real surprise for you gals." She had fixed a beautiful breakfast with biscuits and gravy and everything, and we were just eating away, polishing off the meat and sopping up the gravy. When we finished eating, we said, "Oh, Mama Dolly, that was so good; you can sure cook!" Mama Dolly replied, "Well, I am glad you all liked it, because I went out and shot a squirrel this morning. Y'all were eating fried smothered squirrel!"

Mama Dolly was very religious and had strict rules about what "nice young ladies do and don't do," whether they were in the Movement or not. We arrived at her home on a Friday and spent Saturday getting oriented. On Sunday morning Kathy and I got up and put on our shorts to sit on the porch and review the past two days. But Mama Dolly said, "No, no. You girls are in the South now! We don't do any work on Sundays; we go to church, and you do not wear anything but a dress." I think she had to rustle up some dresses for us from one of her daughters. The next thing we knew we were sitting and fanning ourselves in a backcountry church, with long "meter hymns" surrounding us and transporting us to that special world that is the black spiritual Deep South.

We spent a lot of time in church that SNCC summer. A great deal of movement teaching and learning took place in churches, the usual place to hold voter registration classes. Going to church was one way to be more accepted by the community, for it provided not only a place to meet and talk but also a venue to demonstrate our sincerity and common values. It must have been interesting for Jewish SNCC kids to get so much church! For me, church there represented a real reaching back to my original southern roots; from that time on my whole spiritual life was transformed.

I was concerned that I might not be accepted by the black community in Southwest Georgia because of my fair complexion. I didn't want to be mistaken for white, and initially I didn't have a southern accent. Southern black people accepted me very easily, however. Once when I was feeling self-conscious, an old man pulled me aside and said gently, "Daughter, we colored folks is *all* colors of the rainbow! Don't you ever feel like you outta place down here. Just like them flowers, we one garden and we all God's creation!" It brings tears to my eyes still; he was so welcoming and made me feel a part of the people and the life in the South.

Danger All Around

Wherever we were as civil rights workers, it was not safe. The police and the racist power structure thought they could wipe us out—if they could just scare us enough. When it became known that we were holding voter registration classes in a church, some of the churches were burned down at night. Sometimes we could only stay at a certain home for a while and then had to move, because our very presence put the families in danger. Mama Dolly lived alone way out in the woods in a farmhouse. Sometimes we would have prowlers and would hear through the grapevine or from a phone call from the SNCC office in Albany that there might be danger that night. Then we would sleep on the floor in order to be below the window in case someone decided to shoot into the house.

Black folks in these areas had to overcome years and years of thinking of another way to embrace nonviolence. There were people who thought we were crazy and said, "What do you mean, 'turn the other cheek'? You know the white man is evil. Why do you want to embrace him? Why don't you want to fight back?" Several people told me, "Honey, I am *not* getting rid of my gun." Actually, Mama Dolly had a rifle and a shotgun, and she knew how to use them. When we slept at night, we felt somewhat protected. It was ironic and ambiguous all at the same time.

In the summer of 1962 I was jailed twice for marching and praying on the steps of Albany City Hall. Once was to protest the beating of Albany Movement activist Marian King. She was six months pregnant; she was beaten all in the stomach and lost her baby. The longest time I was in jail was for two weeks in a stockade. We were crammed in there with all the regular prisoners. At first there was a distance between the civil rights prisoners and the other prisoners, but we came to recognize that basically the Jim Crow laws affected all of us. We could see that many times the regular prisoners were stealing or prostituting because that was the only thing they could do to make a living. Sometimes we talked with them, and sometimes we sang our freedom songs. When we sang, almost everybody in jail was singing. We took hymns from the church and put freedom lyrics to them—"Keep Your Eyes on the Prize, Hold On," "Ain't Gonna Let Nobody Turn Me 'Round," "This Little Light of Mine." The songs intermingled protest, prayerfulness, and hopefulness. Just as our slave ancestors had used code words in their songs like "Follow the Drinking Gourd," we created our own code songs and recruited some of our best movement warriors from the jails.

The singing in the jail also really annoyed the jailers. Angry, they would start target shooting right outside the windows of our cells to scare us, or they would just take away our food. I was mistreated, pushed around, my bracelets ripped off me, my eyeglasses taken away. I was shouted and spit at, but I never had some of the really severe beatings others received.

Chief Pritchett in New York

After I left the South, I ran into the Albany police chief, Laurie Pritchett, in the lobby of a New York hotel where I was attending a conference. Down south he used to talk so badly about us and how we weren't going to mess up *his* town. He walked over to SNCC chairman Chuck McDew, Mississippi Project director Bob Moses, and me, catching us totally unaware, then sat down and said, "Hi, you guys, what's doin'?" Then we knew he had been playing the game. He said, "Oh, that is how I have to act when I am the police chief of Albany, Georgia. I know things are gonna change. But I have my constituency down there to hold up." So we sat there in the lobby of the hotel and had a civil conversation. The encounter was mind-blowing, especially because he had been the very person who had once thrown me in jail.

SNCC

SNCC was about direct action in combination with community organizing, sit-ins, nonviolence, and voter registration instruction. The central concept was to build empowerment at the local level so that SNCC could then move on to other communities. SNCC was to be a catalyst, an instigator, to hold a sort of mirror up for people to really see what was being done to them and encourage them, support them, and involve them to take their own action. I see now the veritable poetry in that plan. I say *poetry* because it was an essence of freedom that we continued to distill in the communities in which we found ourselves.

SNCC in the early 1960s was a model of democracy. Of course we had leaders, but everyone's opinion mattered. We had many, many staff meetings and other kinds of strategy meetings where men and women, black and white, got to express their thoughts, fears, doubts, and ideas. We were encouraged to put our thoughts on paper for the SNCC newsletter.

In the early movement the camaraderie between white and black participants was very, very strong. I was not a part of SNCC when the Black Power Movement came forward, but I did agree that point of view was necessary to move to the next level. There was a moral high ground that pervaded the organization in 1962. We just wanted to show America what wasn't right and call attention to the wrongs. Then, we felt, it would all just work itself out. We could all be Americans. That naïveté and that hope were driving forces in everything we did.

Our lives seemed to have been seamless in those days. We moved freely around the country and felt at home just about anywhere where there was work to be done, and our personal and our movement lives blended together.

I feel so grateful that I am a child of the 1960s and that in my formative years I had the privilege of being in service to my people. Being a SNCC student set the stage for how I have lived the rest of my life. I will always be reluctant to cross any picket line. I will always be suspicious of the police. I will always have a warm place in my heart for freedom songs and protest lyrics. And I can never think of my teen and young adult years without remembering that we were going to rescue America.

After the summer of 1962, **PEGGY TROTTER DAMMOND PREACELY** fund-raised for SNCC while a student at Boston University, participated in the 1963 March on Washington, and helped write the original Freedom Schools curriculum with her former husband, civil rights activist Noel Day. During the sixties, her mother, Ellen Craft Dammond, participated in the Wednesdays in Mississippi

Project with Polly Cowan, Dorothy Height, and Mary French (Mrs. Laurance) Rockefeller. Also in the sixties, Preacely's Boston home became an underground railroad stop for Vietnam War draft resisters escaping to Canada. After earning a master's degree in public health, she focused on projects related to the health of women and inner-city youth. She helped found the San Francisco Women's Health Center and is the project director of the Health Promotion/Tobacco Education Program in Long Beach, California. Currently she is working on two independent films—one about her great-uncle Monroe Trotter, the other about the Wednesdays in Mississippi Project. Preacely and her husband, Earnest, have four children and nine grandchildren.

"It Was Simply in My Blood" © Peggy Trotter Dammond Preacely

Freedom-Faith

Prathia Hall

Organizing in Southwest Georgia, a Philadelphia woman examines the role of faith in the freedom struggle.

Born and Raised for the Freedom Struggle

When the student movement began on February 1, 1960, there was never a question in my mind that I would become involved in it at the deepest level possible. I had been born and raised for the struggle for human justice, freedom, and equality. My father, who had been my first spiritual and intellectual mentor, died that week. He was a Baptist minister and what has been called a "race man." He was totally committed to God and God's justice on the earth. That justice included full freedom and development for African Americans and all other oppressed people.

My parents were part of the mainstream of the Afro-Christian religious tradition in harmony with the African worldview that the religious and the political are profoundly integrated. Therefore, faith and freedom were woven together in the fabric of life. My parents' ministry was founded on that principle and on their belief that service to people was service to Christ. They fed the hungry, clothed those in need, advocated for the poor, and redeemed lives from the ash heaps of American society. I received their training and respected their example. I always knew that I, too, would serve God by serving people.

During high school and college, I was active with students from across Philadelphia in a center called Fellowship House that had been organized in the 1930s as a place of advocacy for peace and interracial human relations. Dr. Martin Luther King Jr., as well as noted pacifist-theologian and Howard University dean Howard Thurman, frequently spoke there. During the late 1950s we studied nonviolence as taught by Gandhi and Martin Luther King Jr. Most of us subscribed to this philosophy of nonviolence as a personal principle for life as well as a strategy for public protest. We held workshops on nonviolent direct action as preparation for our campaign to support the southern student sit-ins as we had supported the Montgomery Bus Boycott.

My baptism and initiation into the movement of nonviolent direct action occurred during 1961, my junior year at Temple University. With a group of students from Fellowship House, I joined the demonstrations on Maryland's very segregated Eastern Shore. Our group was arrested at the bus station in Annapolis, Maryland, and remained in jail for approximately two weeks.

It became extremely difficult to concentrate on my studies and graduate while the pull of the southern movement upon my heart was so powerful. Attending SNCC's regular conferences, I struggled for the discipline to finish college before going south to join the Movement in full-time service. I almost succeeded, leaving campus in August 1962 with an unresolved dispute about one graduation requirement.

With a major in political science and a minor in religion, I planned to go to law school and become a civil rights attorney like Thurgood Marshall and Constance Baker Motley, whom I so deeply admired. I planned this despite the war being waged in my consciousness against the compelling call to the ordained ministry, a terrifying prospect for me, since I knew almost no ordained women ministers who were taken seriously by the church. The primary exception in my experience was Rev. Mary Watson Stewart, an itinerant elder of the African Methodist Episcopal Church. I attempted to resolve the conflict by fighting racism at home and in the South. I was convinced that was God's work and also my sacred calling, and so I went south.

Without making any prior arrangements with the organization, I arrived at the SNCC office in Atlanta in the fall of 1962 and offered myself as a volunteer.

The Albany Movement

During my second week in Atlanta, I was sent to Albany, Georgia, to work with Charles Sherrod and the Southwest Georgia Project. It was of great interest to me that both Charles Sherrod and Charles Jones, the leaders of the project, were seminary graduates. I said very little about my own theological journey, however, since I was trying desperately to escape or evade the call to ministry.

The Albany Movement was in full swing. I had never in my life been so profoundly moved as I was by the mass meetings that were the central rallying points of the Movement. They began with the prayer service of the black Christian tradition. The raised voices and the rhythmic stomping of feet could be heard far in advance of one's arrival at the church ground. The undulating wave of the old call-and-response lined hymns drew latecomers and visitors into its warm embrace. It was impossible to stand as a spectator outside the circle of this communion. Whatever your faith or your lack thereof, you were included in the amazing kinship of this worshiping community. Interspersed between the lined hymns were the fervent prayers of the deacons, the mothers, and other congregational leaders.

I'd heard those songs before. I'd heard them in the piney woods setting of the churches of my mother's heritage in Nelson County, Virginia. I'd heard them as they were repeated by the daughters and sons of the American Southland in the churches of Philadelphia and other northern cities. Yet, in this place, Southwest Georgia, with hostile police ringing the exterior of the church, they were neither repetitious nor familiar; they were worship that contained within the reality of its expression a power affirming life and defying death. That power with which those songs and prayers were infused transcended the objective reality of our situation, fashioned fear into faith, cringing into courage, suffering into survival, despair into defiance, and pain into protest. Even today, when I am going through a storm, I breathe those hymns and those prayers.

Shot in Terrible Terrell

The staff of the Southwest Georgia Project included several students from northern colleges; we were assigned to the SNCC programs in the rural counties surrounding Albany. I was in the group assigned to Terrell County, known for the abject poverty of most of its black inhabitants and the brutal violence it inflicted upon them. It was called "Terrible Terrell" and "Tombstone Territory." We lived in the home of Mrs. Carolyn Daniels and her son, Roy, in Dawson, the county seat. It was a modest and pleasant two-bedroom house in the middle of Dawson's black community.

This home became a freedom house filled wall-to-wall with people. Carolyn was undisturbed by the perpetual disarray and elevated noise level of students waging philosophical debates, holding serious strategy sessions, and their general, youthful clowning. There was a greater price to be paid, however, for supporting the freedom workers than personal inconvenience or discomfort. One night in early September as we settled down, having made plans for the next day's work of canvassing homes to encourage potential voters, we heard a car driving up. As it slowed in front of the house, there was a hail of gunfire. We hit the floor as we had been trained to do, while a blast of shotgun pellets was sprayed into the house. After the car drove off, we waited several minutes and then called to each other to learn if anyone had been hit.

We were all alive, thank God. But this had been a very close call. Jack Chatfield was bleeding profusely from shoulder and arm wounds. Christopher Allen, a student from Oxford, England, had also been hit. My hand was stinging where a pellet had grazed it. We had been warned in orientation sessions not to go into the field unless we were prepared to die. That night any and all romantic thoughts about our freedom adventure dissolved as we came face-to-face with the real and present possibility of death. The shooting was reported to local and federal authorities, but there was never an arrest or any consequence for those responsible for the crime.

Meeting the Brave Black Residents of Terrell County

Our primary work included voter education and registration as well as literacy training for the effort toward political empowerment. We moved out each morning in small groups to knock on doors or talk to people sitting on their porches. The process was slow without being tedious. Sometimes local residents were in the groups, but most groups were made up of student volunteers who were strangers to this community. People tried hard to be cordial in spite of their fear. A few greeted us with open warmth. Some confided that they had been waiting a long time for the day of this freedom struggle. Others slammed the door in our faces, declaring, "I ain't having nothing to do with that mess." They were not being rude. Fear was an absolutely rational response. After several visits, the fearful and the skeptical usually allowed us to come in or to sit on their porches and visit. The topic of the imminent danger soon made its way into the conversation. They told us of people who had just "come up missing" or had been found floating in the river after some minor assertion of personhood or an infraction such as trying to register to vote. One woman explained that she could not attend the mass meeting because "I had been sick in bed with the flu, and if I go down to that meeting, it might turn into the double pneumonia and that'll kill you." We understood that it was not pneumonia that she feared would kill her. It was the local forces of racist oppression.

The conversations that took place on those porches and inside those "shotgun" houses, where the sun shone as brightly through the cracks in the walls as it did outside in the yard, were a part of a long, cautious, and caring educational exchange. We students had information about voting, political empowerment, and literacy training to share as we sat rocking and talking and listening. The local people had the wisdom of the elders—or perhaps the wisdom of the ages—to share with us. They had lived under that system of domination and brutality for generations. Everyone knew someone whose loved one had been beaten or killed by its violence. They also knew about life and how to live life without surrendering humanity or dignity to those who sought to crush them.

It was an exchange of mutual learning. Some of the most important lessons I have learned in my life were learned from those people in the rural South and people like them elsewhere, many of whom could neither read nor write their names. The primary lesson that I received from those black sages was that of faith for living in life-threatening circumstances. It was a faith first made manifest by our slave fore-parents who defied the teachings of the slavocracy, which distorted the Bible and declared that their slavery had been ordained by God. Those profoundly spiritual women and men developed their own moral critique of the slaveholders' oppressive brand of religion and expressed the slaves' absolute conviction that slavery was contrary to the will of God and that God definitely intended them to be free.

These sons and daughters of those enslaved ancestors continued to hold on to that freedom-faith. The freedom-faith fired and fueled the fight. By that faith and in that faith they finally stood up in the meetings and announced, "I am afraid. It could cost my job. It could cost me my life. But I want to be free, and I want a better life for my children. So I'm going down to the courthouse. I'm going to trust God to take me there, and I'm going to trust God to bring me back."

The continuing presence of African American citizens at Southwest Georgia county courthouse offices pressed the claim of all African American people for the rights and privileges of their citizenship based on more than three hundred years of economic, political, and cultural contributions to this nation. The people of Terrell County attended the mass meetings and the literacy classes and continued to make their way to the office of the registrar.

Dancing to Bullets and Going to Jail

One hazy afternoon in August, as three other SNCC freedom workers and I were canvassing in the tiny town of Sasser, Georgia, we saw a great cloud of dust and a pickup truck speeding down the road. The truck screeched to a halt in front of us. An extremely agitated white man with a very red face jumped out of the truck. He was wearing a tin badge on his chest and screamed that he was a deputy marshal. He asked what we were doing. I answered, "We are talking to people about voter registration, and you have no right to stop us." He began screaming curses at the top of his voice and literally foaming at the mouth. Trembling with rage and calling me a long-haired bitch, he pulled a gun and began firing at the ground around our feet.

I do not remember how we moved from the bullet-sprayed ground to the Sasser jail. I remember the gunfire and then being pushed into the filthiest hole of a building I have ever seen, before or since. It was about three times the size of an outhouse and smelled as bad. The "marshal" opened the rusted locks and pushed us into what passed for a jail in Sasser. There were only two cells. Rather than mix races, the jailer chose to mix sexes. The two white workers, one male and one female, were forced into one cell. Roy and I and two other black workers were pushed into the other. We had no way of knowing if any friendly person had seen our arrest. The thought that we would be left in this vermin-infested slime pit to be eaten by the rats and the monstrous bugs, or taken out in the dark of night and murdered, brought more terror than the bullets splattering around my feet had. We were only there several hours, but the place was so horrible that those hours felt like a full day to me.

I spent many days and even a few two-week stays in jail during the freedom struggle, some of which I have forgotten. That day in the Sasser, Georgia, jail was actually my briefest experience of arrest and imprisonment; however, the sheer horror of that hot, dry day in 1962 is inscribed in my memory. The Sasser deputy was not finished with us. A few days later he chased three of us out of town by firing gunshots at our car and threatening to fill us full of lead and put us all in the cemetery.

We reported the episodes to the FBI and the Justice Department. These federal authorities conducted their investigation. But we were never quite sure if the investigative targets were the criminal violators of our rights or those of us who were working for freedom and authentic justice. Federal charges were brought against the deputy, and the case was tried in late December 1962. During the trial I was called as a witness for the prosecution. I dressed as I had been taught was appropriate for a court appearance. I wore a business suit, hat, and gloves. As I waited to testify, I was approached by one of the Justice Department attorneys and asked to remove my hat, because the local whites were offended by the presence of a black woman dressed in such professional attire.

Church Burnings

The most critical community institutions for the Freedom Movement were those black churches that opened their facilities for mass meetings and literacy classes. For most black congregations the risks were too great. The ministers were not usually completely independent, because in addition to their church responsibilities they held jobs in the white community. Sometimes they were teachers, but in the rural areas they often worked in the mill or held a custodial job in town.

The people in the rural areas were at the bottom of the economic ladder. Most worked in the cotton fields, where they labored all day for the total daily wage of fifty cents. Women worked in the fields or as domestics for three dollars a week. The prevailing economic arrangement was sharecropping, which tied most black people totally to the plantation owners. Black sharecroppers owned nothing. They were forced to buy seed, farm supplies, and food from the planter. The merchandise was usually overpriced. Sharecroppers attempted to settle their debts at harvest time. But when the family's share of the profits was counted and the amount of all credit purchases deducted, the sharecropper was either in debt or, at best, had only a few dollars left for a year's labor by the entire family.

The churches and their congregations were very vulnerable to the oppressive power of the racist plantation system, yet despite their precarious predicament in each community where we worked, at least one congregation stood upon their faith that God was with them and on the power of their own freedom yearnings. It took all the freedom-faith that one could gather to open those churches for the movement classes and meetings, where we affirmed each other in the struggle. Movement leaders from SNCC and from the community clarified the issues and inspired strength and courage in the movement troops. We all reaffirmed our commitment to the freedom struggle at the mass meetings.

Because the mass meetings were places of reinforcement for us, they were under constant surveillance. The police and/or the county sheriff stood outside the churches, taking the names of people as they entered the church. Whenever these authorities chose, they came inside and stood around the back in a threatening posture. Their intention was to intimidate.

It would be insanely dishonest to claim that we were unafraid. Fear was an intelligent response. Fear was a part of the survival kit. The challenge was to use fear as a signal to exercise caution while refusing to allow fear to paralyze you. One night when a gang of local "lawmen" entered the mass meeting and stood behind us with their hands on their guns, we sang our freedom songs with defiant and prayerful fervor. More than once Charles

Sherrod challenged the sheriff by praying for him by name. He asked God to free the sheriff from chains of hate and racism. All of us joined that prayer and we sang:

> Ain't gonna let no sheriff
> Turn me 'round,
> Turn me 'round,
> Turn me 'round,
> I'm gonna keep on a-walking,
> Keep on a-talking,
> Marching up to Freedom Land.

Finally, we joined hands and sang our movement anthem, "We Shall Overcome," prayed the closing prayer—for the safe return of all of us to our homes—and departed the building.

The intimidation continued. Early before dawn on Sunday, September 9, 1962, we were awakened by a phone call that informed us that the Mt. Olive Baptist Church, the site of the Terrell County mass meetings, was on fire. We dressed quickly and made our way to the church. There were no firefighters. The church had already burned to the ground. Student workers and members of the congregation and the community tried to console each other as we choked on our sobs.

As day broke, more SNCC staff arrived. During that night, another church, the Mt. Airy Baptist Church, whose pastor was active in the Movement, had been burned to the ground. Later in the day, representatives of the press from around the country came to report the story. Rev. Wyatt Tee Walker, executive assistant to Dr. Martin Luther King Jr., arrived from Albany with a few members of the SCLC staff. SCLC had decided that the situation in the counties was too dangerous to allow Dr. King to go out there, but he did visit the Mt. Olive site later in the week.

A member of the press suggested that since the SNCC workers had been waging the struggle and facing the dangers in the counties alone, we might resent the appearance of the finely tailored SCLC ministers now. Truthfully, there would be other times and places when such feelings did emerge. Standing before the smoldering ruins of our church that painful Sunday morning, however, I was glad for every helpful presence. Other well-known people, including baseball great Jackie Robinson, visited during the days and weeks following and organized a campaign to rebuild the churches. The reign of terror was by no means over. Other churches were burned in Terrell and Lee counties. The homes of four voter registration workers in neighboring Lee County were shot into. The Shady Grove Baptist Church in Lee County, also a site of project meetings, was burned to the ground late in August.

Faith of Our Mothers and Fathers

Courage and faith were at the heart of this struggle. There's the courage that's lived when one *lays down one's life* for a cause, and there is that other courage that is lived when one *lives one's life* for a cause. This living in the face of death, this constant, perpetual encounter with death in order to *live* the struggle, is, I think, the most powerful expression of freedom-faith. Still, there were those personal moments, times of solitude, when I would ask myself, Why am I here? What am I doing? Am I doing it right? If I am, as an organizer, inviting someone to risk their life, God, do I have a right to do that?

The courage I witnessed in the communities where I worked was beyond reason, beyond the level of the rational! The courage to go down to the courthouse or the courage to open the doors and say, "Let's have the meeting here," was a courage that transcended reason. When somebody stood up and made a commitment to participate in movement activity, that was a religious statement, as profoundly religious as saying a prayer or doing any kind of religious discipline. That came out of a worldview and an understanding of life and of what was ultimately paramount in life. Fueled by their freedom-faith, Southwest Georgia residents were willing to walk face-to-face with the forces of death in the struggle for life.

Praying at the site of one of the burned churches when Dr. King was present, **PRATHIA HALL** expounded on the theme "I have a dream." Dr. King remembered this imagery and used it as the basis for his famous speech at the March on Washington in 1963. Hall continued to work for SNCC through 1966, and a short piece about her work in Selma, Alabama, is included in part 9 of this book. She earned her master of divinity, master of theology, and doctor of philosophy degrees from Princeton Theological Seminary. Beginning in 1978 she pastored the same church her father had pastored, the Mt. Sharon Baptist Church in Philadelphia. She served as a professor and dean at United Theological Seminary in Ohio and held the Martin Luther King Chair in Social Ethics at Boston University's School of Theology. Dedicated to a social gospel, and responsible for the training of many black female ministers, she was recognized by *Ebony* magazine as one of the nation's most outstanding African American women preachers. The mother of two children, Hall died in August 2002.

Resistance U

Faith S. Holsaert

*The child of an interracial family in New York City extends
her political education during a year in Southwest Georgia.*

Both My Mothers' Daughter

My sister, Shai, and I grew up on Jane Street in a Greenwich Village household headed by two women: our Jewish birth mother, Eunice Spellman
Holsaert, and Charity Abigail Bailey, our African American mother by affection. Charity and my mother were the emotional center of each other's
lives, and we four formed a family. Within this family I received my early
political education. In high school I expanded my learning into greater New
York City, and in college to a jail cell on Maryland's Eastern Shore and the
SNCC freedom houses in Southwest Georgia.

Our family lived together for eleven years, facing racial slurs scrawled
on our sidewalk, slashed tires, strained dealings with families and friends,
shopkeepers' remarks, and waitresses who refused to serve us. My sister and
I were raised not to complain about these petty harassments and the fears we
experienced when shoved and called names outside the Catholic school that
we passed every day going and coming from our school. Visiting Charity's
friends in Harlem we were outsiders; because of our "mixed" household,
we were politely but coolly received by my mother's mother and brothers.
Because my parents' marriage had collapsed, it was called "broken." In the
postwar economy, my mother had trouble finding work as a copywriter.
In financial pinches she borrowed from Household Finance Corporation.
Charity paid for many of my lessons—for instance, on the recorder and
piano—and when I was in high school she gave me a clothing allowance.

When I was seven we spent a year in Haiti, where my sister and I were
in the racial minority and our female household was noteworthy. Scene of
a historic slave uprising, Haiti, the first black-run republic in the Americas,
prompted a pride in Charity that I took on because I loved her so. In my
child's heart, Haiti and blackness and rebellion were one. Charity studied
folk songs, drumming, and dance with a member of Katherine Dunham's
Troupe Nacional, and my mother taught English. At night in the Haitian hills,
lit by the soft light of a kerosene lantern, my mother, Eunice, told stories of
Jewish courage and humanism, stoking my sister's and my idealism.

Charity came into our lives when I was four. She taught music at my school, the Little Red School House. The staff there were generous, radically child-loving, anti-racist, mostly women teachers. Since preschool I have loved school, and as I grew I pressed my definition of *schoolhouse* deeper and deeper into the world. In 1954, at the end of the McCarthy era, my ten-year-old classmates and I studied Negro history. We learned "Lift Every Voice and Sing," the black national anthem in which the stormy past gives rise to hope. We rode the subway to Harlem's Schomburg Library. I borrowed books about Harriet Tubman, whose story of courage appealed to me, and John Brown, whose violent righteousness stunned me. That May, we ran a freedom time line from one end of our classroom to the other—from Crispus Attucks in the 1700s, to Frederick Douglass and Harriet Tubman in the 1800s, to leaders and events of the twentieth century. During the last week of class, on May 17 the U.S. Supreme Court handed down its decision on *Brown v. Board of Education*. When we tacked the *New York Times* article about *Brown* onto the end of our time line, we had learned down to our bones: no matter how dire the circumstances, history can be changed by people like the abolitionists, people like us.

I left this protected world to attend a public school, the New York City High School of Music and Art, where I was a diligent student in and out of the school building. There were ugly, haunting, and entrenched cruelties in the 1950s, and they flickered across our television and filled the newspaper: segregation and racial violence in the United States and, among many other examples abroad, the intractable Algerian war. I worked in Harlem and on the Lower East Side with groups loosely connected with the National Conference of Christians and Jews (NCCJ). We surveyed housing conditions of African American and Latino tenants, tutored black children, and met university students from Africa and from the southern sit-ins. Some people I met identified themselves as black nationalists, and several of us read C. Eric Lincoln's *Black Muslims in America* (1960), not to mention Michael Harrington's *Other America* (1960) and Camus's novel set in Algeria, *The Plague* (1948). My two closest friends were black: Sherron Jackson, who later joined the Nation of Islam and changed her name to Amina Rachman, and Candy Keeling, the daughter of a social worker and a transport worker. Candy and I had been born only a day apart in 1943 and lived at either end of the bus line that ran up 8th Avenue from Abingdon Square in the Village past her family's home in the Dunbar Apartments on 149th in Harlem. My fervent closeness to Sherron and Candy resembled the sister-closeness of my family, but it was something entirely new, too. Audacious. Loud. Self-confident. Joyous. We liked ourselves far more than anyone had been allowed on Jane Street. With the loyalty I learned from my family, I remain friends with Amina and was close to Candy until her death in 1991.

Through our NCCJ adviser, sociologist "Dr. Bob" Johnson—son of Mordecai Johnson, eminent black educator and former president of Howard University—I met my first SNCC people. Dr. Bob introduced us to SNCC activists Tim Jenkins, Charles Jones, Chuck McDew, and Diane Nash. People I knew in NCCJ later worked with SNCC: Peg Dammond and her brother Hank, Ivanhoe Donaldson, Don Harris, Doug Harris, and Bonnie Kilston.

In 1961, during my freshman year at Barnard, I went south for the first time—just a little bit south, to a sit-in in Maryland. My mothers were not thrilled, despite their pride in this act of mine. They had fought oppression simply by surviving the 1940s and 1950s with equanimity and good humor. They were reticent about their private lives and avoided drawing attention to themselves. My rising up in the face of injustice terrified them. In the end, they wholeheartedly supported me, the daughter of their household. You can be sure that as that daughter, when I went south I took with me a set of good manners, and those manners stood me in good stead.

The slogan for our Christmas Eve sit-in was "No Room at the Inn." We knew we would be refused service at the lunch counter as Mary and Joseph had been refused in Bethlehem. Our destination was Crisfield, a fishing village on the isolated Eastern Shore, hometown of Millard Tawes, governor of Maryland, where public facilities were still segregated. For the half-day journey from Baltimore, we crowded into a few cars driven by older black men. As we drove over the interminable Chesapeake Bay Bridge, my stomach tightened. Going down the Eastern Shore, we drove past marshy land and stands of pine. The flat boundlessness—the unknown-ness—aroused my jagged fear. We passed Easton, birthplace of Frederick Douglass, and soon after, Cambridge, close to Harriet Tubman's birthplace. Miraculously, I was in a landscape I knew, if only in books, from my year as a ten-year-old in that Greenwich Village classroom.

At a café, we sat at the counter. Asked to leave, we sat tight. A siren. We were read the trespass law and bundled into squad cars. We sang loudly in the patrol car, our voices overriding the police radio. "Oh Freedom!" At midnight, caroling voices from outside floated up to our cells. A dozen people from the nearby "Negro" college had left their warm homes for the cold moonlight below our window. Their caroling voices were soft and sweet, sustaining me as did the entwined spirit of Douglass and Tubman.

In spring of 1962 we returned to the Eastern Shore for our court hearing, and I discovered how various the phenomenon of race can be. We stayed at the home of "Pops" St. Clair, grandfather of Gloria Richardson, Cambridge

Movement leader, and Frederick S. St. Clair, our bail bondsman. Pops told us our white judge was cousin to Gloria and Freddie on the other side of the racial blanket. Our attorney, Juanita Mitchell, a formidable black lawyer of the generation before us, defied segregation's conventions by dressing the part of a professional woman. That morning in the courtroom, she slowly removed her long winter gloves. Spellbound, everybody watched her.

My move deeper south was edging toward inevitable, though I didn't know it. I thought of myself as a woman with organizing to do in New York City, though Peg Dammond and Dr. Bob would both go to Southwest Georgia in the summer. In Baton Rouge, Louisiana, SNCC workers Dion Diamond, Charles McDew, and Bob Zellner were arrested for organizing at a local college. In jail they were threatened with castration with a rusty knife and displayed to hostile spectators. They were charged with criminal anarchy. The charges carried stiff penalties and, in the post–McCarthy era, suggested the three were "extremists." I heard about the case from SNCC people and read about it in SNCC's newspaper, the *Student Voice,* which kept me up to date and strengthened my identity as a member of the Movement. I did not read of the case in the mainstream press, which neglected it.

We decided to walk U.S. Route 40 from Baltimore to Washington, D.C., to draw attention to the Baton Rouge situation. Twenty of us set out, later than we'd hoped, trudging into rain. The shoulder of the road was narrow, and trucks buffeted us as they passed. Our singing and our serious conversations barely offset the conditions. Very late, we trooped into a café where the warmth was as sensuous as the smell of coffee and pancakes, but none of us carried much more than bus fare, so we just drank coffee. We sat with our feet buzzing sorely in Keds and flats. Amina's feet were raw, but she danced to the jukebox with a pain-defying grin. Back on the road, our exhaustion was so intense, it is comical to think about it now. Arriving exhausted in D.C., we went to a mass meeting. Later we spent the night on the floor of a student apartment where Stokely Carmichael lived. Inert bodies stretched from one side of the living room to the other.

The next morning someone went out to buy Sunday newspapers. Around the breakfast table our bleary group sat shoulder to shoulder. Cold juice tasted sweet, even thrilling, to my played-out senses. The person who'd gone for newspapers flung open the door, shouting, "The Algerian war is over." A sip of cold, sweet juice. Someone read the story aloud and we listened, rapt, no other sound in the room but our breath. Our feet and legs ached. If the plague of the Algerian war was over, history could be changed, and if history could be changed, we knew McDew, Diamond, and Zellner would be freed.

Thus I embarked on my life in SNCC, a world-class university: Resistance U. There I met and learned from great thinkers who might be domestic workers in Albany, Georgia, or erudite black students at Howard University.

The Southwest Georgia Movement: The Hub and Spokes of the Wheel

In the summer of 1962 the balance was tipping toward my going south, though I followed my usual New York City groove: I worked as a typist in a travel agency by day and organized tenants and tutored with Candy, Amina, and Hank Dammond in the evenings. In our neighborhood my seventeen-year-old sister and I were accosted by a white man who tried to pick us up. When we ignored him, he asked if we weren't those Freedom Rider bitches. Albany Movement attorney C. B. King was browbeaten with a cane by Sheriff Cull Campbell until C. B.'s head was hooded in bloody lace; in the county jail in Albany, SNCC worker Bill Hansen was beaten and his jaw and ribs broken; in Terrell County, Sheriff Z. T. Mathews invaded a mass meeting in a church and assaulted the Southwest Georgia Project director, Charles Sherrod, in jail; the home of Carolyn Daniels was shot into; arsonists burned three Southwest Georgia churches to the ground. I was convinced: I had to go south. I requested a leave from Barnard, and by mid-September I was on a bus heading to Southwest Georgia, where I would live and work for a year. I was nineteen years old.

SNCC's Albany office/freedom house was at 504 South Madison Street, one of three units in a one-story frame building on cinder blocks. SNCC occupied an end apartment. Up three wood steps to the front door, which displayed a poster with a photo of Frank Smith, Bob Moses, and Willie Peacock at the SNCC office in Greenwood, Mississippi. In the tiny living room was a musty fold-out couch, where three or four male staff slept. In the equally small back room were a single bed and cot, where several women staff slept under donated quilts. The kitchen walls were streaked with soot from the kerosene stove. Files of reports and news clippings spilled from shelves lining an entire kitchen wall. Hardly an adequate setting for the race-mixing orgies fantasized by white racists. We covered each pane of glass with paper at night to keep from being silhouetted targets.

The Albany Movement rented the other end of 504 South Madison. Their office was commanded by Albany Movement secretary Goldie Jackson, who had been fired by Albany State College for her activism. Goldie wielded her phone like a tool of righteous warfare, phoning lawyers, the press, supporters, and families across the region and the nation. From the sandy yard, freedom buses transported black Albany to work during the bus boycott. Drivers and black ministers, some of whom were one and the same, congregated there. When they interfered with Goldie's work, they earned her chastisement.

Our project director, Charles Sherrod, was in his mid-twenties, a former divinity student who had grown up in Petersburg, Virginia. He was one of the original SNCC field secretaries and with others had pushed the organization to open field projects in the Black Belt South. He said SNCC's Southwest Georgia Project was a wheel: work in the town of Albany was the hub, and organizing in the outlying counties of Lee, Terrell, and eventually Sumter, were the spokes. Together, hub and spokes drove the wheel. Sometimes he described it as Ezekiel's wheel within a wheel.

Sherrod's vision, including his rules, structured our work. The most important rule I obeyed was Sherrod's "lynch prevention code." I was never to heedlessly provoke danger for black males or myself. A white woman and a black man publicly walking together in Southwest Georgia could be accused of "fraternization," for which a black man could be lynched. As a new white female staff member, I was at first allowed to work only within a block, and then two, and then three, of the office. I assisted the Albany Movement by checking on the few demonstrators from the previous summer who remained in jail, and I canvassed for voter registrants with public school students— Vera Giddings; Shirley and Patricia Gaines; and Joann, Dear, and James Zenna Christian. For orientation I read SNCC staff reports from across the South and the volumes of the newly established U.S. Commission on Civil Rights. After a month I was allowed to walk outdoors by myself if I carried identification, phoned ahead to my destination, and phoned back when I arrived, but the lynch prevention code continued in effect. Always.

Sherrod believed women must participate fully in the struggle. He said, "All movement soldiers must drive." A New Yorker, I did not know how to drive and thought there were better ways to spend my time as a freedom fighter than in learning. Sherrod, however, sent me for my learner's permit. Inside the squat cinderblock Bureau of Motor Vehicles, twine was strung down the middle of the room. Paper signs clipped to the twine read "colored" and "white." I meant to walk down the "white" side, but it made me sick, so I walked down the other side and got a "colored" learner's permit. Sherrod felt it was not safe for me to use this ill-gotten "colored" permit, so I never did drive in Albany. He was not amused. I had withheld a potential movement resource.

I didn't appreciate it then, but Sherrod was as exceptional in his way as the family in which I had grown up. A man raised in a sexist society, trained in the even more sexist Baptist ministry, and holding some chauvinist ideas about social relationships, he believed that in the fight for freedom, women were his equals. He was successful when he insisted I pull my weight in the movement pulpit, and I grew to like public speaking. He selected a female staff member, Prathia Hall, the daughter of a minister, to preach at the Albany Movement's first anniversary program, a night when Dr. King spoke from the same pulpit. I was bowled over by Prathia—I had not imagined a young woman my age could possess such oratorical power.

That autumn, my head and heart whirled with the people I was meeting, including my lifelong mentor and friend, Anne Braden, of the Southern Conference Educational Fund (SCEF). Anne was a circuit rider for the Movement, writing and publishing the *Southern Patriot* with her husband, Carl. She often visited Southwest Georgia SNCC. In her Alabama twang she told me that in the 1930s Alabama white women had organized against lynching, and black and white tenant farmers and sharecroppers had organized across the color line. That Alabama white women were not uniformly segregationist was a nuance I had not yet appreciated. Past midnight, speeding on instant coffee and fogged in cigarette smoke, Anne evangelically told me that she and Carl shared care of their children, allowing both Braden adults to work in the Movement. Anne seemed to think this applied to me, but I had no idea why—until 1968, when my first child was born.

Mr. Marion Paige, an Albany Movement officer (and our landlord), told me the story of James Brazier. Years before in "Bad Baker" County, Brazier had been beaten to death in jail. Mr. Paige went to pick up the body for the funeral home. When he lifted the body, Brazier's broken bones clicked like dice. The U.S. Commission on Civil Rights listed Brazier's death as "the last recorded lynching in the U.S." There were other Southwest Georgia cautionary tales. There was a lynching tree in Lee County where four men and one woman had been lynched in one day. In Baker County black people weren't supposed to drive through town after sunset. White merchants in Bad Baker would sell only RC Cola, not Coke or Pepsi, to black customers. One night Penny Patch and I were alone in the dark freedom house. From outside, an intruder smashed the window beside our bed. We crouched on the floor while, through the curtain, he ran his hand over our bed, groping through the litter of shattered glass. We called the police, but that man, like many who attacked the Movement, was never arrested.

Everywhere, the rural crossroads of Southwest Georgia were points of power. White men owned the land adjacent to major crossroads and at night guarded those intersections, but we drove past the lynching tree and eased through the intersections on our way to mass meetings in Terrell, Lee, and eventually Sumter counties. In tents on the sites of the burned churches, in the charred rubble of segregation, the black South sheltered a movement that was participatory, black-led, and integrated, a redemptive community. The Movement lived the future in the peanut fields of the past, opposing racism, sexism, elitism. In those tents I understood two things: that I would become a teacher, and that, as Bayard Rustin said at a planning meeting for the 1963 March on Washington, demanding racial justice in the United States was inherently revolutionary.

In mass meetings, we shared organizing news, taught ourselves constitutional and voting rights law, and reported on the Beyond—greater Georgia, Mississippi, Virginia. At my first meeting we ate homemade barbecue from a family who had slaughtered a hog. The space in the tent was illuminated by a low-hanging kerosene lamp like the one on the Haitian veranda that had lit my mother's tales. The tent smelled of wax and canvas, damp and military, and was redolent of barbecue. As I sat on my folding chair, only three of whose legs rested on the uneven ground, I thought, *This is what our work is: moment added to moment, sandwiches and scary car rides, citizenship lesson added to citizenship lesson, staff reports week after week.* The singing turned the tent into a ship flying into the future, the song burning like the lamp at the tent's heart.

There was this intense music everywhere in the civil rights struggle, riding in cars, at mass meetings, and at SNCC conferences, where we shared war stories and held long discussions, made or renewed romances and friendships. We sang. Movement music from Albany, from the tents of Terrell and Lee, from Nashville and Mississippi was taught and blended. We stood in a circle, hands joined, brothers and sisters singing, gazing into one another's eyes, some of us weeping, ending with the song "I Know We'll Meet Again" and knowing it might not be so.

In contrast to the Movement's uplifting music, in October I heard U.S. bombers roar overhead, flying from Albany's Turner Air Force Base to patrol Cuba during the missile crisis. My government patrolled the Caribbean, leaving white segregationists like Sheriff Z. T. Mathews to go marauding in Terrell County. In the spring of 1963 the U.S. government could have exercised its mandated power to protect vote workers during the federal trial of Sheriff Mathews. Sherrod's metaphor of the hub and spokes together driving the wheel of the Movement went "live" for me during this trial; the court's decision drove us to work more openly in Terrell and to open a project in Sumter. Mathews had been charged with violating federal voting laws, after the *New York Times*' Claude Sitton documented Mathews swaggering into a mass meeting and making note of those present. Everyone in the black community knew Mathews had contributed to the county's climate of terror.

The Justice Department's investigation of Mathews took place in the white community, where none of the events had occurred. SNCC workers dealt with local white people only in banks, gas stations, police stations, and the post office, so news of the investigation came to us from black people who worked downtown, in the courthouse and offices, and in the homes of white people. These Justice Department investigators, all white men, mostly southerners, said they could not come into our side of town or they would appear biased in our favor. Their investigation built an ineffective case— perhaps their intent. I told myself, no matter how dire the circumstances, history can be changed, but this time skepticism would win out. Black residents from neighboring counties came to witness the trial in Sumter County, home of future U.S. president Jimmy Carter (we didn't know him—he was white). For each local black spectator, attending the trial was a public act of courage for which each might lose a job or suffer harassment. Mathews was acquitted, as were all white southerners accused at that time, of attacking civil rights workers.

In late spring 1963 we decided Prathia Hall, Chico Neblett, and I would move thirty-five miles from the hub of Albany to live and work with Carolyn Daniels in Terrell County. Under Sherrod's guidelines, over the course of a week we gradually increased our perimeter, working outward from a small square in the center of which sat Carolyn's house. I was shocked when Sherrod called Carolyn a "crazy nigger," but he explained, southern white folks didn't mess with a few intransigent black people who would rather die than lose their dignity. It would be more trouble to control such souls than to leave them alone. Carolyn's teenage son, Roychester Patterson, had this spirit, too.

Carolyn kept us in the know. A woman with a well-decorated home re-fused to look us in the eye and sidestepped our request to register. Carolyn laughed. "She's a teacher and she knows who butters her bread." Another day as Prathia and I walked beside the road, a white man in a truck with a young black man in overalls riding beside him shadowed us; a shotgun hung behind their shoulders. The white man took a long, slow look, drove away, then circled the block and came back for another look. Only one woman responded to our knocks. She claimed that all the adult members of her household had the flu and were unable to go register. Carolyn told us, "Oh, she can't register. Her landlord is so-and-so; and that was her landlord buzzing you."

Prathia and I canvassed out in the "rurals," sometimes with Carolyn, who kept up a patter of local history and gossip, punctuated with her me-lodious laugh. We heard the first yes to our question, "Will you go to the courthouse?" in a wood frame house set in a plowed field. Outside that house I felt free in the open space, but also vulnerable as part of an interracial team that could be seen from the highway. A chinaberry tree shivered its lavender blossoms, and a quilting frame was set up in the room, its wood gleaming with the touch of generations.

To take the women to the courthouse, we drove Carolyn's red and white Chevy Impala, a big and noticeable car. I blithely accepted a dip of snuff from a prospective registrant, though Carolyn and Prathia wisely declined. The tobacco made my eyes water, and its sting was so painful I had trouble focusing. In the courthouse we confronted a seething registrar. A white crowd gathered, and Z. T. Mathews himself strutted around like a rooster. An old white man who was an onlooker barely controlled the hostile crowd. All of this was overshadowed by the pained scream of my mucous membranes, stripped naked by burning tobacco. The registrar's office closed for lunch rather than accommodate us, withholding the right to register. But that day there was the mystery of a lone white man, the onlooker, who stepped up to talk down the crowd.

In late spring, after police attacks on movement activists in Greenwood, Mississippi, some Southwest Georgia staff went to Greenwood. Prathia and I returned to Albany to take up the slack. I was arrested on a march downtown. The black demonstrators were taken to their cells. I was singled out and found myself with six policemen in the booking office. On the pretense of conducting a search, the men encircled me and felt me up. I can still feel the claustrophobic heat of their bodies, and the memory makes me cringe. One of them stepped in to call a halt. I was placed in the cell with white staffers Joyce Barrett and Joni Rabinowitz. Also in the cell was a white drug-addicted prostitute going through cold turkey withdrawal. When I left jail, I felt weak. I thought this was the result of our hunger strike, but I did not recover in the following weeks.

I Want to Know, Which Side Is the Federal Government On?

In late spring 1963 the Albany Movement stepped up its campaign to desegregate public accommodations. The gospel song says Ezekiel saw a wheel within a wheel, but a later verse also proclaims he saw a flame burning within a flame, and this became a more apt metaphor for the Movement as that season progressed. Teenage activists, including the Christian sisters, picketed a discount store in Little Harlem, demanding the merchant hire black people. This led to arrests, which led to marches, which led to more arrests. Albany teenagers were in one demonstration after another and in and out of jail. Roughly a dozen teenage girls were jailed in a rural stockade and photographed by SNCC photographer Danny Lyon.

Southwest Georgia's second summer project began. Albany's black gangs picketed the downtown movie theater, the city swimming pool, and the cloistered homes of Albany officials. Ignoring Sherrod's cautions, gang members acted on their own. At the pool one young man scaled the fence, jumped into the chlorinated water, and swam through the white swimmers to the other side. Having integrated the pool, he leaped over the fence and took flight. One night the stop signs in town were stenciled to read "Stop Segregation!" and we all knew the gangs had done it. An acid "Freedom!" message was burned into the mayor's lawn. One afternoon the young men picketed the library and were admitted. They trooped into the freedom house bearing armloads of books with the word "black" in their titles, including Anna Sewell's *Black Beauty*. The freedom house was shot into. The Albany police tried to arrest every civil rights worker in town, picking us up on sidewalks and out of cars. For a week, SNCC staff took refuge in a church. As a city prisoner, SNCC staffer Willie Ricks was assigned to sweep street trash outside the SNCC office. When Ricks saw us, a slow grin spread over his face. Three years before the slogan gained national attention, he shot his fist into the air, yelling, "Black Power!" The police didn't put anyone else on work detail.

I woke on hot mornings and struggled up from sopping, fever-soaked sheets. Marian King paid for my visit to a local black doctor, a recent graduate of prestigious Meharry Medical College. Seeing me as a patient, the doctor was breaking southern prohibitions. During the exam he could not look me in the eye, much less touch me. I believe he didn't send my specimens out. He could have suffered reprisals for sending the specimens of a white female to the state lab. He was trapped and so was I. I left his office without a diagnosis and with only his advice to rest.

Sixteen-year-old Joann Christian was again in the Camilla jail and was the target of vile abuse. At the request of the Justice Department, I took an affidavit from her mother, Odessa Mae Christian. Mrs. Christian had often sheltered and fed me, and her daughter Joann was one of my closest friends. Joann's mother and I sat in the sooty kitchen at 504 South Madison. I did not hold much hope that justice would result from this affidavit. It was an act of righteous anger on my part. I was enraged that Joann would never receive the protection she deserved. I was enraged that Mrs. Christian, who worked long hours in addition to making a home for her husband and demonstrating daughters, was not popularly heralded as an American heroine. I can see the paper, a cheap legal pad with watery turquoise lines. I can smell the bushel of Georgia peaches that someone had left outside the SNCC door. This image surfaces when I think of myself that year: a twenty-year-old woman to whom words mattered, working at a kitchen table to record the words of her elder. Mrs. Christian perfected her reading and writing in Albany Movement literacy classes. Over the many years we corresponded, she signed her letters to me, "Your mother in Christ." During a Southwest Georgia year of frequent church services, I had grown comfortable with freedom messages couched in Christian terms, but the word *Christ* in this closing did bring me up short. Then I relaxed into Mrs. Christian's intended affection and benevolence.

I was failing physically, sleeping feverishly at night and too weak to complete my organizing work by day. Worse, none of us knew what was the matter with me. As I weakened, southern violence and repression rose in a ferocious wave from the late spring into the summer, from the fire hoses of Birmingham, Alabama, to the police sweep of demonstrators in Danville, Virginia. Southwest Georgia joined in. Following Sheriff Mathews's acquittal, SNCC opened a project in Sumter County, scene of the federal trial. During the summer SNCC, staffers Ralph Allen and Don Harris and summer volunteer John Perdew were charged with inciting insurrection, because they had urged Sumter County's black residents to register to vote. Ralph Allen had been a witness against Sheriff Mathews in the federal case. The insurrection charge carried the death penalty, and while they were in police custody the three men faced threats to their safety, as had McDew, Diamond, and Zellner in Baton Rouge in 1962.

Allen, Harris, and Perdew were arrested and mistreated by local officials for championing a fundamental right of U.S. citizens, but the federal government did not intervene on their behalf. There had been no federal protection during my year in Georgia, despite the instances of intimidation and harassment related to voter registration, which we repeatedly phoned in to the office of U.S. attorney general Bobby Kennedy. Reluctant to let go of my schoolgirl idealism arising from the *Brown* decision, I felt disillusioned, though not entirely surprised, by my government's alleged helplessness. I did not like that my government was in effect complicit in southerners' intimidation and harassment of civil rights workers. I was not amused by the ironic insight that my "helpless" government did find itself capable of flying planes from Albany to patrol the air above Cuba.

My disillusion deepened to estrangement when the federal government joined the segregationist attack on the Albany Movement. Federal officials prosecuted nine Albany Movement activists and officers, including the redoubtable Goldie Jackson and SNCC worker Joni Rabinowitz. They were charged with violating the rights of a federal juror. One of many segregated establishments targeted during the spring public accommodations campaign had been a discount store owned by a man who happened to be a juror in a federal trial. No one in the Movement knew about the trial, much less who was on the jury, because the Movement was boycotting the racist local newspaper. The store was explicitly being picketed because of its owner's racist employment practices, not to influence the outcome of a trial. These absurd and insubstantial charges came out of the blue.

The charges were equally absurd when applied to Joni Rabinowitz, a new SNCC staff member who was never on the discount store picket line. Could she have been targeted because she was Jewish? Because her father was the U.S. lawyer for the nation of Cuba? Joyce Barrett was the SNCC staff member picketing that day. Joyce repeatedly testified to this fact, but this did not budge our government. Joni and Joyce endured a series of humiliating examinations, which included a lab test of each woman's pubic hair, supposedly to see if either had dyed her hair, to establish their distinct physical identities to the feds' satisfaction.

In his speech at the March on Washington in August 1963, SNCC chairman John Lewis noted the lack of protection for voting rights workers in Southwest Georgia, mentioning the federal prosecution of the Albany Nine and the insurrection charges against Allen, Harris, and Perdew. At the insistence of march organizers, John's conclusion was cut from his speech. It had read, "The Albany indictment is part of a conspiracy on the part of the federal government and local politicians for political expediency . . . I want to know—which side is the federal government on?"

When I was back at Barnard College, the FBI interviewed me about the Albany Nine case. I had been in Terrell County at the time of the picket line in Albany and could verify only that Joni and Joyce were different people and that Sherrod's policy of limiting freedom of movement for new white female staff would have prohibited Joni's presence at the picket line. The short, unnerving interview took place in my college library in view of my classmates and teachers. I was dry-mouthed with fear that with my words I might unwittingly harm movement co-workers.

Movement resources and participants' fervor were drained by this case. Joni Rabinowitz's case was separated and defended by her father and Leonard Boudin, who built their case upon exhaustive documentation of the improper and racist composition of the jury. The eight local members of the Movement were defended by a team including our attorney C. B. King, Don Hollowell of Atlanta, and Jack Greenberg of the NAACP's "Inc Fund." Eight of those indicted, including Joni Rabinowitz, were found guilty and appealed. In the end, Rabinowitz and Boudin defended their appeal based upon jury composition before eight federal judges convened *en banc* in New Orleans. They won their case. Charges against the remaining defendants were dropped by the federal government. By then fear and exhaustion had thinned the Movement's ranks, and its coffers had been emptied by the legal defense. The federal government was not required to make restitution for consequences of its misdirected zeal.

At the end of the summer, I left Georgia to lobby congressmen in Washington for Harris, Allen, and Perdew. Up and down the cold, echoing corridors, I was escorted from the office of one congressional staffer to the next. I was so sick I could barely eat, and I saw everything through a feverish shimmer. As Sherrod had ordered, I went to see a doctor while I was up north before joining my co-workers for the March on Washington. In New York my family doctor saw my yellowed eyeballs and ordered lab work. Hepatitis. "Junkie's hepatitis" he called it. Knowing I had never taken drugs, the doctor and I assumed I had contracted this illness in jail. During the month's bed rest, I watched the march from my mother's couch, raging at my unfilled place beside my comrades. In September I was in bed when Candy Keeling phoned to say Birmingham's 16th Street Baptist Church had been bombed. "Children," Candy shrilled, "they're killing the children." I jumped out of bed (where did I think I was going?), but my body betrayed me and I stumbled to the floor.

Though I returned to college at the end of September 1963, the hepatitis drained me for the next year, drained me as had the fear and anger of my time in Georgia: the lynching tree, James Brazier's bones rattling like dice, cars waiting at the night crossroads. I came out of Georgia an experienced fighter—defiant and skeptical and at the same time filled with love for those with whom I had worked, the actors in new southern tales of courage: black gang members risking their lives for a swim; Carolyn Daniels registering voters in "Terrible" Terrell; the Christian sisters going to jail. These memories sustained me that year of illness. I was told the virus had altered my blood. Even if I had a son or daughter who needed a transfusion, my blood was so compromised that no one, including my child, should receive it. Of course, more than my blood chemistry had been changed. I had taken my two mothers' complex and subtle legacy—with its jagged edges, its contradictions, its passion, and its tenderness—and made it my own.

FAITH S. HOLSAERT is a writer and a teacher. Following SNCC's mandate that white activists work in the white community, she moved to West Virginia, joining mine workers' fight for democracy, health, and safety. She has been active in the women's and lesbian communities and has worked against racism and in the endless anti-war effort of the last four decades. With SNCC from 1961 to 1965 she later worked with the Southern Organizing Committee, the

Rainbow Coalition, Durham's Harm-Free Zone, and Eternal Summer of the Black Feminist Mind. She has supported women's health organizing, the fight for adult literacy, and advocacy for people with disabilities. Since the 1970s her fiction has appeared in journals and is featured at OutHistory.com. She lives in Durham, North Carolina, with her partner, Vicki Smith. They share four children and seven grandchildren.

Caught in the Middle

Cathy Cade

A young white woman spends time in jail and struggles with her father, who is worried about her safety and what he believes to be un-American influences in the Movement.

Going South

In 1963, two weeks after graduation from Carleton College in Minnesota at twenty-one years of age, I was in Albany, Georgia, for the first SNCC summer program to use significant numbers of white volunteers. My third day in Albany I was arrested for "vagrancy" along with other SNCC workers. My father came to Albany to rescue me and ended up suffering a nervous breakdown after he tried to traverse both the movement world and the white world of Albany, Georgia. My father was hardworking and respected others for their hard work, but he could be authoritarian and racist. At times he mistreated my mother. I believe that my siblings and I first experienced oppression from my father as children, and this helped us to identify with other oppressed groups.

During high school I lived in the South, attending Memphis's all-white, segregated Central High at the same time that Central High School of Little Rock, Arkansas, was being integrated with the help of the National Guard. My midwestern family had moved to Memphis because my father's employer, International Harvester, wanted him to work on designing better mechanical cotton pickers. These machines were displacing the black labor force in the nearby Mississippi Delta region. In Memphis, while segregationists worried about the new threats to their "way of life," I attended the Unitarian Church and youth group, where there was support for my integrationist ideas but very few black members. During my second year in college my family moved to Hinsdale, Illinois, a wealthy Chicago suburb.

I had some movement experience before I arrived in Albany. As a college junior I had participated in an exchange program at Spelman College, a black women's college. It was my first decision independent of my parents. They were nervous but did not try to stop me; my parents were very pro-education, and my mother, at least, had raised me "not to be prejudiced."

The first week I was at Spelman we had a brief sit-in at the Georgia State Legislature. My Spelman professor Howard Zinn and other white exchange students sat in the upstairs seating section for Negroes. We left before we were arrested. The rest of my semester I attended classes, hung out at the SNCC office, demonstrated, worked on voter registration, and attended a SNCC conference. Back at Carleton the next year, I raised money for SNCC, collected books and clothes for Mississippi, and arranged for the Freedom Singers and SNCC staffer Frank Smith to appear on campus.

The following excerpts—from letters I wrote to my parents and a report and letter my father wrote that summer—illustrate what happened to my parents and me during my brief stay in Albany. These documents give some sense of the day-to-day organizing efforts of the Albany Movement, the flow of events, the racial climate in the city, and the distorted views white officials and professionals in Albany had of black people and the Movement.

FRIDAY, JUNE 21, 1963

Dear Mom and Dad,

As I'm sure you've already heard things are happening down here. There are about 15 white students on the staff. The Movement is using two houses in the Negro community. Cooking for summer staff is done by a neighbor lady—wonderful breakfast—paid for by the community. I'm to stay with a family, I think. Last night I was at the house where the senior staff stays. . . .

As yet, I don't feel I'm ready to go to jail, but it is a definite possibility. I'm becoming convinced that direct action is the only hope. There will be no concessions without pressure and the Negro community has had all it can take. Publicity is now of major importance. I feel awfully naive, but did you realize that even after last summer's demonstrations, the demands for desegregation of the public facilities, an indication of upgrading in jobs, lawful conduct of the police, a biracial negotiations board, etc., have not been met at all, none of them!

If I do go to jail—I won't 'til I feel ready and there will be other white girls in jail with me—there are several things you can do. First of all, I'll be all right. They won't hurt us, for they fear the publicity. Can you find me some news contacts with Chicago newspapers and radio? You can give them the office number.

If I do go to jail . . . the policy is jail, no bail. It usually takes about two weeks for trials to come up. . . .

P.S. Whatever you can do about those publicity contacts will be greatly appreciated.

My Field Notes

THURSDAY, JUNE 20, 1963

I arrived yesterday afternoon. Last night, the shit hit the fan. We went out to a meeting in Terrell County, in a tent where one of the four churches that were burned last summer used to be. We had about ten people from Albany SNCC and twenty-five from the counties. We heard a report from Charles Sherrod, SNCC project director, the gist of which was that the concentration of SNCC this summer would be direct action in Albany. We new workers were introduced. Everyone was very friendly. We met a Mr. Edwards who was trying to start a co-op gas station. Each person is to put up five dollars and the federal government is to give a loan. We heard of a case in Sumter County of a [black] girl getting raped [by several white assailants] and dying a few days later. The family knows who did it, but is afraid to come forward. Some fellows are working on a follow up of this.

When we returned to Albany we were greeted by the news that the people at the meeting in Albany that night had decided to march. Twenty-six were arrested; at least two boys were beaten. A black woman watching on her porch was dragged half a block by the police.

An emergency mass meeting was held at Beulah Church. Some of the boys in the C.M.E. neighborhood, a tough one, threw bricks at a police car and really tore it up. A white man was hit with a brick.

Rev. Wells spoke. He says he has trouble keeping the boys in church. He is a very kindly folksy preacher who works as a civil servant. His daughter, fourteen, went to jail last night.

Sherrod spoke, quieted down the people. He talked a little of nonviolence, but is afraid to say too much, I think, for it is so difficult to get the people to move.

Chief Laurie Pritchett, Albany Chief of Police, walked right into the meeting: big—about 6'2"; 275 pounds; sandy-haired handsome— wearing white spats! Everyone cheered and clapped —a strange kind of "hero." . . .

Slater King, head of the Albany Movement, was last to speak. He spoke loudly, quickly, and forthrightly. Joni Rabinowitz, a white girl from Antioch College who's been here for a while, feels that he'll demand real steps, not wishy-washy compromises. Slater King put it on the line that he was disappointed about the violence. . . .

I'm working in the office today, a good way to get into things. So far have washed dishes. There's no running hot water just a kerosene stove. . . .

Twenty to thirty kids have just been arrested in the Washington housing project. The plan is to have simultaneous movements from all parts of town rather than bringing everyone together for one meeting and one march. This is a fairly new approach. Hopefully it will mean more grass-roots contact. Each area is playing it by ear, seeking advice from leaders living in the area to march, to meet, or ride downtown and sit-in.

Action is now starting in East Albany. About five carloads of people left East Albany to sit in downtown. Six were arrested at Quickie where a customer spilled coffee on them with the police watching. More were arrested at Lee's drug store. Meetings at CME are now in progress. Nine SNCC staff are now in jail.

The white man hit by a brick in a passing car last night has a fractured skull.

SNCC staffer Joyce Barrett just talked to John Martin of the Justice Department. He feels that demonstrations are necessary to channel the tension, and frustration. The community is very aware of Medgar Evers' death, the rape, [the brutal treatment of demonstrators in] Birmingham, Danville, etc. . . . . .

SATURDAY, JUNE 22, 1963

[Written from the Albany City Jail]

Dear Mom and Dad,

Felicia Oldfather and Miriam Cohen just came to join us. Also drunk white woman had been added to the cell next door. I'm fine, am losing weight! Felicia said that Joyce had talked to you and you were great. It was a great relief for me to hear that.

Relationships here are very interesting. Penny Patch, a veteran activist, dislikes policemen so much that she talks to them as little as possible. Joni Rabinowitz, another veteran, manages to keep her dignity while giving the officers a lot of lip. They seem to have a kind of respect for her. There are seven of us now in an 8 by 8 cell—all white females in the Movement. The jail is segregated, of course. . . . There are four sections in the jail: black male; black female; white male; white female. Our cell has two bunk beds and a mattress on the floor for the seven of us.

We can yell to the Negro kids, but it's not too easy. We sing together, have grace together as a group before we return our food uneaten. I'm getting pretty hungry, but temptations are minimal! It's hot in the day and cool in the morning—need blankets.

There are about 120 of us in jail now, some have been moved to other jails.

We're being held for investigation of vagrancy. They can hold us for 72 hours then need to charge us. Our attorney, C. B. King, is very capable and charming. He visits us every day. I'm looking forward to his bringing us books tomorrow.

How's the publicity in Chicago coming? Write me a long letter. Mail will be greatly appreciated. I'll write more later.

It will mean a lot to have your reassurance that both of you are not too upset.

[The rest of this letter was written after my father's telephone conversation with Chief Pritchett that same day.] That nice Chief Pritchett you just talked to just came back to look in on us. He's all smiles and false charm. We asked him how many people he beat last night and he told us, "Why you know we never beat anybody." We heard an old man and a woman beaten last night. The old man was taken out on a stretcher. Joanne [sic] Christian, a sixteen year old, was beaten yesterday, not hurt badly. These are all beatings of Negroes, some more serious than others, but all illegal.

My plan is to stay here as long as I can contribute. If I decide I can't, and I won't decide for a week or more, I'll probably go to Atlanta to work on voter registration.

My purpose here is to try to assist demonstrations to the end of achieving some meaningful desegregation. You say things are getting out of hand. To a degree this is true. That's why SNCC is even more important than ever, for the people are tired, they are beginning to know that things don't have to be the way they are. If this frustration and anger isn't organized and channeled, even more violence will occur with no beneficial results for the Negro community. You begin to realize that this fight isn't something you pick up after you've done your homework, but something affecting the whole way of life for thousands of people, things are changing, but so far they've made little difference in the every day life of the majority of Negroes. Children are still growing up knowing there are vast numbers of experiences never open to them. Just because they're Negro.

Excerpts from My Father's Report from Albany

JUNE 26–28, 1963

After I was arrested my father flew to Albany to convince me to come home. As an engineer he was used to investigating and writing reports about his empirical findings, and he was determined to talk to all sides of the struggle. He was also operating under great fear for my safety and had decided, before he came down, that the Albany Movement was "used" by Russian Communists for their own nefarious ends. The punctuation, capitalization, and so forth are as they appear in his typewritten report, except for my clarifications in brackets. Here is the letter:

> This is an attempt to relate the facts concerning the arrest of my daughter Catherine in Albany, Georgia, as a result of her organizing activities among the colored population there. I suggest that the reader acknowledge the *possibility* that they represent the moves in a "cold war" between the southern white people and a portion of the Negro population. In this "cold war" the ordinary ideas of truth, justice, fact, rumor have been distorted out of all reasonable comprehension. . . .
>
> This story starts about 5:00 P.M. on the 23 of June when I arrived home from a long hard day at the office and my wife handed me the following clipping from the *Chicago Daily News*, "Hinsdale Girl Held in Georgia."
>
> At the suggestion of SNCC my wife had instituted a series of phone calls, person to person, to the Albany jail requesting to speak to Cathy Cade. All had been met with statements that she was not available.
>
> I decided to call Chief Pritchett and ask for permission to speak to her. Chief Pritchett inferred that were she persuaded to leave town, she would be released. He also asked me whether or not we knew that the whites and colored female and male members of the SNCC organization were living together in cramped quarters. . . .
>
> Cathy stated something to the effect of not to worry, the arrest charge was completely false and they would be quickly released by their brilliant lawyer C. B. King. That it was important to contact

him, that we should spread the word, keep calling the jail person-to-person and protest, as it would protect them from police brutality. She would call us immediately upon her release and not to worry, the publicity was wonderful.

We spent an anxious Saturday and Sunday with not a word. On Monday morning, I asked our lawyer to contact someone there. He called back and advised that the firm of Perry, Longstaff and Walters were considered the leading lawyers in Albany. They advised that I come down and see for myself. . . .

After checking into the hotel, I went for a walk around the center of town to get the lay of the land and called Mr. C. B. King's residence. I did this from a pay phone rather than the hotel since the "cloak and dagger" atmosphere was beginning to get to me. Mrs. King answered and stated that C. B. was in Montgomery and would not be home until late, but that he would call me at the hotel. She assured me that everything was OK and that the trial would be Friday morning. She gave me the telephone number of the Shiloh Baptist Church and stated that I need not have called her from a pay phone as her phone was tapped and every move watched! She said she assumed that C. B. would be acting for me as well as Cathy and I said no, I had in mind other counsel. "You mean 'city' lawyers, well that's a switch!"

I continued walking around town for half an hour, saw the jail where Cathy and seven others had been on a "fast" for seven days—somewhat nerve shattering by its very stillness.

I went back to the hotel across the street from the jail and started to relax, I wrote up a number of questions, which I thought needed answering and tried to sleep. On impulse I picked up the phone and called SNCC headquarters. Charles Sherrod picked up the phone and said, roughly, "Who is this?" I introduced myself and started asking him what he could tell me. He said he could tell me anything he would tell any reporter over the phone so I asked how far away the church was . . . about 5 blocks and suggested I give the name of the corner of Jefferson and Whitney . . . I asked the (white) taxi driver to take me to the above corner. "Are you a reporter or something?" He said a white man had had his skull fractured by a thrown brick while taking his maid home recently, and he would not go down there, that there had been a mass meeting that evening and the police had had that area blocked off. I said take me as far as you want and let me off. This was about 1 block from the church. . . .

The next block consisted of a row of typical Negro shacks on stilts with a dirt sidewalk wandering among trees. . . . I saw a long low brick church building. . . . There was a light behind the shuttered windows and apparently much activity. . . . A white boy came to the door and said "Go around the block." I followed instructions although reluctantly because it meant going into the dark adjacent to the housing. The thought crossed my mind that my white shirt might be a "flag of truce." Anyway I "had to know."

The same white boy opened the door. I was introduced to Joyce Barrett, Prathia Hall and the rest. Joyce was a young white girl very pretty, delicate face and good figure. Prathia was a young colored girl about 20–25 with a good mind and very commanding presence—somewhat masculine in her authority, I should say. Sherrod entered, attired in blue jeans with a blue jeans jacket and said, "Did you know you were followed?" I allowed as how I had expected to be, but that I thought it important to talk to them before anyone else in order to get the picture. Sherrod appeared to be an intelligent young Negro about 20 but of not great managerial authority. During the next two hours of conversation interrupted by phone ringing every 5 minutes, Joyce and Prathia constantly said to Sherrod, Don't you think this is right and he always agreed. It was apparent that the two girls were running the show.

During our two hours talk, it seemed we covered everything under the sun. They wanted to know why I was there. I said I was an engineer and wanted to see for myself what was going on, to make up my own mind what was happening. They were sorry I got into town too late for the mass meeting, but that there would be one tomorrow night. I emphasized that I intended to talk to everyone including Chief Pritchett—long silence.

On the subject of salary they said they were being paid $10 per week, but had not been receiving it recently. The church was now their room—they sleep on sleeping bags on the pews—and the colored folks brought them their food.

We discussed the situation regarding bringing white, northern girls into the situation as irritating to the white population and that there was a real danger of great violence on the part of the whites if they were irritated a little too much, that this did not seem to be a nonviolent approach, the situation being what it was. They said that violence might be necessary to accomplish their ends, but that they felt that the white girls being there was channeling the explosion of pent-up emotions into nonviolent action. . . .

Joyce stated that she had been in jail recently for three weeks, had fasted, and while it was unpleasant, it had had no ill effects. She appeared to be in good health.

We discussed that in America it was possible, an example, myself, that whenever I was unhappy with my job I picked up and moved to another part of the country. They said that this was simply unthinkable.

[The next day] I called my wife and decided not to tell her of my visit to SNCC's hideout of the night before and of my suspicions as to its phoniness. It would only worry her the more. . . . I had a strong feeling that Cathy should be gotten out of town!!!!

. . . I had a good breakfast, and went to Attorney Walters' office. . . . By way of introduction he stated that he was a segregationist and believed in the separate but equal philosophy, but that being a lawyer first and foremost he felt that he could work with me. I stated that I understood his position from having lived and worked in Memphis for four years, and that I wanted his advice and help, but probably not his representation in court as C. B. King was the lawyer for the girls. . . .

Mr. Walters offered to call Chief Pritchett over and we could have a private talk. . . . Chief Pritchett came over and we discussed the situation for about an hour. He said that when the particular complaint re: Cathy's organizing activities came in, the detectives went into the area and saw these girls going from house to house. When asked for their identification they would not show it, although the detectives showed theirs, but asked were they arrested and when told that they had to come to the city hall for investigation, they flopped on the ground and one white girl refused to pull her skirt down below her waist. Fortunately she was wearing undergarments. But this behavior, by white girls in front of a crowd of 30–40 Negroes, was simply not rational!!!

He felt that the white people of Albany were being very restrained, that the Negro elite and in fact the great bulk of the Negroes were having nothing to do with the movement, in fact they resented it as making the gap wider between colored and whites. He felt the situation to be extremely tense as witness the fact that the hardware stores had been completely sold out of shotgun shells recently. He urged that the white SNCC organizers be gotten out of town immediately.

I accepted his offer to talk with Cathy in the hotel room. . . . Cathy was brought in dressed as she had been picked up, in culottes, open-toed sandals, and a sleeveless blouse, all somewhat the worse for wear. Once in the hotel room Cathy said in a weak voice that she had not wanted me to come. I explained my position as an interested person, father, and citizen of the USA and I wanted to know what was going on and why, what were the objectives. She complained of police brutality such as the chief eating a piece of pie in front of them and raiding their cells taking toothpaste, soap, books. The books were later returned [and] turned out to be paperbacks of all sorts of revolutionary literature—the titles being unfamiliar to me. . . .

With respect to the effect of this activity on her part on her family and her grandparents, she said that it was simply a question of values, that this situation was disturbing a lot of white and Negro people and that this was necessary. . . . [Cathy added,] "Please Daddy, offer to pay C. B. He works so hard and won't ask for a cent, but a contribution would be very nice." This concluded this conversation and I concluded that in her present state of mind she thought it possible to stay in Albany when she was released.

. . . Walters and I drove over to the post office where we met with the head of the local FBI. . . . After some off the record discussion I said it boiled down to whether or not Chief P. was *honest* with respect to the things he was telling. They stated that he was *honest* and that I could quote them on this i.e. there was not wanton mistreatment and beating of prisoners! They felt that Joni Rabinowitz and Penny Patch, both white, were the leaders of the SNCC operation.

I called Chief P. for more information and he told me that mass meeting would be at Arcadia Church and it would be safe to go there. Arriving at 8:00 P.M., only a few children and older women were around. Prathia Hall started the meeting with a reading from the bible about the torture and martyrdom of the Christians according to Paul. Prathia is an excellent preacher with a beautiful contralto voice. She led several freedom songs and also introduced me as the father of Cathy who was one of the girls in jail. . . . The climax was when the Rev. Jones gave his "monkey dance" imitating of the city judge dancing while the "devil" Chief Pritchett pulled the strings. This brought the house to its feet cheering and clapping. By this time about 140 people had assembled. . . . The meeting was closed by the singing of more "freedom" songs and everyone went home. Several kindly people came up and introduced themselves and one kindly colored woman said she was working weekdays but come Saturday she was going to carry some food to the church for SNCC.

I called C. B. King at home, who . . . in deep, measured tones [stated]: the girls would likely be convicted since the judge has previously demonstrated little or no regard for the basic freedoms. They would probably get 60 days or $200 fine or both. Asked how the girls felt physically he replied, "Their sense of purpose will overcome their physical discomfort." . . . Re: the wisdom of SNCC's irritating the

Albany white population by the use of white, Yankee girls as agitators he felt that getting things changed required irritation and that agitation stands to bear some good ultimately. Only thru agitation has there come progress. . . . The majority of the violence has come from the guardians of the peace. It is true that after the police have demonstrated their brutality some children have hurled rocks and brickbats. That neither the Albany Movement nor SNCC can accept responsibility for violence any more than the white people accepted responsibility for the KKK in days past.

. . . We were allowed into the courtroom with the prisoners: some 12 white boys and seven white girls and perhaps 70 Negroes . . .

C. B. King is a 33 year old, handsome, energetic, intelligent colored man who obviously knows more law than the judge, prosecutor and Chief P. put together. He handled the trial strictly as a show for the benefit of the prisoners to show them how wronged they were. . . . C. B. King addressed the court saying the police had acted in a manner to harass SNCC by picking up the organizers, following them and referring to the girls as "bleached niggers." He moved for dismissal on the basis of no prima facie case. Motion overruled. . . . Cathy Cade came to the stand next. She testified that she was going through the projects knocking on doors and telling of a mass meeting. Seeing her two companions being arrested, she went over, showed her identification and asked if she were under arrest. Informed of her status of being under investigation as a vagrant, she sat down on the ground in protest. "Two patrolmen picked me up and jerked me along the ground and put me in the back of the patrol car." Policemen pushed her into the office at City Jail. . . . . Asking the arresting officers why she looked suspicious she was told that any white girl in shorts, sleeveless sweater and open-toed shoes working in an all-Negro section of town was considered suspicious!!!!

The judge ruled that the 14th Amendment had not been violated, that you girls were doing the city of Albany, yourselves and your families a disservice, that you were guilty as charged and would serve a sentence of 60 days on probation under jurisdiction of parents and the judge added he would suspend the sentence if the girls went back home. . . .

I finally got Cathy to make a decision to come home for the weekend for a rest, if she could come back by plane on Tuesday, this being the best I thought I could do under the circumstances.

I called Edgar to thank him for all he and Mr. Walters had done. He said they were glad to do it, that there would be no bill for their two days work, and that if anything further should come up to please give him a call.

I walked down to Shiloh Church to say goodbye to the SNCC people and to see that Cathy was really coming home!! I almost flipped when Cathy wasn't there, imagining that she had skipped town. They said she was over at the SNCC headquarters . . . I went there, no Cathy, then back to Shiloh fighting panic all the way . . . Finally Cathy showed up at the airport with her baggage. [We had almost missed the airplane because the car we were riding in was stopped by the county sheriff, falsely charged with no title and a defective muffler. The car was driven by the dean of the law school at the University of Kansas and belonged to his daughter.]

Joni Rabinowitz also showed up at the airport. . . . Joni and I got a seat [on the plane] together after the first stop and we had a good talk about what she was doing and why, the fact that she was going to NYC for a [fund-raising] party and to make speeches re: their experiences. Significantly, we talked about her visit to Russia under the Student Movement program, beautiful Leningrad, etc. I concluded that she had had much training and indoctrination in Communist organizing methods.

My Father's Letter to Attorney Walters

[Written on the plane from Atlanta to Chicago]

June 29

Dear Mr. Walters,

We are on the final leg of the journey home. Now the battle for Cathy's mind can begin, thanks to the very wonderful and generous treatment that a group of southerners has given to a complete stranger. At the moment, Catherine does not suspect anything of my complete role and is being very cooperative. . . .

I have all the notes I took and a briefcase full of stuff. I am thinking of giving a report to the Chicago FBI. Perhaps we have devised a way to operate or improve operations. What a completely incredible nightmare this has been. Show this to anyone you wish, but would suggest Chief Pritchett, Justice Department men, and local FBI, and most of all to Edgar who was really wonderful.

If there is anything or any way I can help the peaceful progress, let me know. It seems to me that if all of the good people in this country will only realize the seriousness of the situation and work together we can defeat Communism, but it will take some doing, and we must be as dedicated as they are and as *smart* and clever.

P.S. Here's for more amateur Cloak and Dagger.
Yours, Bill

My Father's Breakdown and My Compromise

When we got to my parents' house in the all-white suburb of Hinsdale, Illinois, I was weak and exhausted. My father called the FBI to come "debrief" him. I fell asleep as my father was talking to these two strange men in the living room. When I woke up, my mother told me my father was in the hospital having a nervous breakdown. I found out later that this was not the first breakdown. He had had one other breakdown in 1942, right after Pearl Harbor was bombed, when my parents were living in Hawaii.

I was in Chicago for two weeks, and then, as a compromise, I spent the rest of the summer doing office work in SNCC's Atlanta headquarters. It was a hard decision for me to return to the Movement. I did not want to harm my father; yet I felt, quite literally, that to save my life, to be alive, I had to be in the Movement. Not to go would be a living death.

I was also scared for my safety in Albany. I had only been there one day when I was arrested. I had no time to feel at home there. It was hard to know if the attention and care I needed from the Negro community was justified by any contribution I could make.

I paid a price for not returning to Albany—in not getting to see if I could indeed make a meaningful contribution. Moreover, there is a built-in contradiction, stress, and marginalization in doing office work in a radical social movement, in not being "in the field."

As early as the summer of 1963, the question of whether white people were useful and appropriate in SNCC was already being raised by some black SNCC workers in and around the Atlanta office. Some who were raising these issues were my close friends, so I took these questions especially seriously.

I found ways to work with SNCC through the summer of 1964. That fall of 1963 I entered graduate school in sociology at Tulane University. While there I remained in contact with SNCC people in Mississippi and New Orleans. Between classes I canvassed on a SNCC voter registration project in New Orleans and hung out with SNCC workers. I went to Jackson, Mississippi, on weekends and witnessed the debates around planning the summer of 1964. That summer I ended up working in communications in

North Gulfport, Mississippi. Back at Tulane, I helped a city-wide group called Students for Integration, also Tulane Students for a Democratic Society, and worked with CORE in New Orleans' Fourth Ward. In 1967 I became involved in the city's first women's liberation group with other veterans of the Mississippi projects.

Understanding My Father

I had never wanted my father to come to Albany. I couldn't believe that he was talking to and trusting the white authorities. Back in Chicago, I was angry with him for tricking me into coming home and for making the racist assumption that Negroes could only be fighting for their freedom if they were duped by Communists.

I was furious with him for interfering in my life, but I could also see that he was very afraid for my safety, as I was myself, and I felt I owed him something for raising me.

I understood that my father's nervous breakdown was caused by fear that I would die before my time, just as his younger brother had died. Putting himself in the presence of *both* sides of the struggle in Albany, my father created deep internal conflicts for himself. As a racist, my father chose to believe and identify with the white male authorities. But while he was experiencing the charm of these powerful southern white men, he also exposed himself to the mass meetings and the charisma of the black civil rights workers like Prathia Hall, Charles Sherrod, and C. B. King. He glimpsed the strengths of black civil rights workers just before he questioned their motives.

Furthermore, the situation of black people challenged my father's most dearly held beliefs. He was unable to understand that an oppressive system could make it very difficult, or even not in your best interest, to put your hopes into individualistic achievement. He believed that capitalism was the best economic and political system possible—anything else would be chaos. He experienced the Albany Movement in July 1963 as chaos. Using all of his investigative and problem-solving skills, honed over a lifetime of engineering projects, he could not create order.

My father never again tried to rescue me or stop me from working for civil rights, and I don't think he and I ever talked about racism in America again. Of course, being a parent now, I have more sympathy for my father's fears about me.

My father and I had our last fight in 1971. I had just come out to myself as a lesbian and was telling the whole world, except him. It was the same old fight, but this time fought to the conclusion with angry exaggerations—me calling him a filthy capitalist and him calling me a dirty Communist. Once said, we never fought again.

In the last years of his life, my father changed more than I ever imagined a human being could change. Though he still had moments of clinging to his old ideas, after heart bypass surgery in the early 1980s his heart and mind opened in a way that seemed miraculous to the rest of the family. He worried about the homeless; he made special efforts to talk with and understand the unconventional lives of his five grown children. He even supported me financially so that I could work part-time and create a book of photographs about lesbian mothering. When I remember these changes in him, I experience great hope for change in the whole world.

CATHY CADE lived a year in Canton, Mississippi, doing the research for her sociology dissertation on whether members of the black community there believed education or direct action represented the best avenue for change. In 1970 she moved to San Francisco and worked full-time in the Women's Liberation Movement and became a lesbian community photographer. She has two children by donor insemination—one black and one white. She currently assists others in writing their personal histories. A longer version of Cathy's experiences in Albany and how being in the Movement affected her parents and siblings is available on line at www.crmvet.org, "Our Stories." In 2003, forty years after her arrest, Cade was invited back to Albany to display her photographs in the Albany Civil Rights Movement Museum. Currently she lives in Oakland, California, and has a personal history and photography business. She also participates in activities sponsored by the Bay Area Veterans of the Civil Rights Movement. For more information on her life and work, visit www.CathyCade.com.

PART 5

Get on Board

The Mississippi Movement through the Atlantic City Challenge, 1961–1964

> Is that freedom train a'coming? Is that freedom
> train a'coming? . . . Get on board, get on board.
>
> —Freedom song

Most women who joined the Mississippi Movement did so with a level of fear and trepidation. The state was known for its exceptionally brutal treatment of its black residents and for its extremely strict enforcement of segregation, yet, early on, SNCC made the Magnolia State its major project. The many women who entered the Mississippi Movement worked undeterred by frightening attacks and the murders of their close friends and allies. Using Denise Nicholas's metaphor, Mississippi civil rights activists got on board the freedom train, gave it some steam, and helped push it down the track.

SNCC staffers believed that if the Civil Rights Movement could defeat racism in Mississippi, other states would fall in line. In addition, SNCC organizers noted, black Mississippians made up 42 percent of the state's voting-age population, presenting the greatest potential for change of any southern state. SNCC's focus on Mississippi stood in stark contrast to other national civil rights organizations which, by the summer of 1961, thought it best to focus on the more liberal southern states and on major southern cities in an effort to surround and isolate the Deep South rather than attack it directly.

However, other national organizations still had members, representatives, and programs in the state. In February 1962, SNCC project director Bob Moses brought together local representatives from the NAACP, CORE, and SCLC. Using the name of an earlier ad hoc committee, they formed the Council of Federated Organizations (COFO). With the largest number of field secretaries in the state, SNCC remained the most influential member of the group and many of SNCC's programs were carried out under the COFO banner.

Mississippi's rigid enforcement of segregation codes and laws frequently captured national and sometimes international attention. During the summer of 1955, fourteen-year-old Emmett Till was beaten to death in the Delta hamlet of Money, apparently because he broke the southern code of black male behavior either by speaking too familiarly to or whistling at a white woman. White Mississippians registered their support for Till's treatment by acquitting and praising his murderers. The memory of the lynching of such a young person, publicized by a picture of his bloated and disfigured body in *JET* magazine, informed the activism of a number of the women in this book.

The nation and the world received another glimpse into the Mississippi way of life when James Meredith desegregated the University of Mississippi in 1962. Spurred on by Governor Ross Barnett's inflammatory defiance, a crowd of several thousand white students and spectators rioted after Meredith, heavily guarded by federal marshals, entered the school. Two people were killed and more than 150 marshals injured, almost 30 of them by gunfire. It took more than 20,000 U.S. Army troops to restore order, and a rotating force of more than 200 soldiers remained with Meredith throughout the school year.

Mississippi has a long roll call of lynch victims and civil rights martyrs. At least five of these killings were of people especially close to SNCC's organizing efforts. In September 1961 Herbert Lee, the father of nine children, a local NAACP official, and one of the first men to work with SNCC's project in the small town of McComb, was killed by a Mississippi state legislator. Two years later, in June 1963, two months before the March on Washington, NAACP field secretary Medgar Evers, who had worked with young people throughout Mississippi, was gunned down at the entrance to his home. In January of the following year, Louis Allen, another early SNCC supporter and witness to the Lee killing, was murdered. Then in June three young men from a COFO project in eastern Mississippi—James Chaney, Andrew Goodman, and Michael Schwerner—disappeared and were presumed murdered. Chaney, a native of Mississippi, and Schwerner, from New York, were experienced CORE activists; Schwerner's wife, Rita, was working on the project as well. Goodman, a summer volunteer, had just entered Mississippi. While looking for these three young men, searchers found the bodies of three other young black men—Charles Moorer, Henry Dee, and an as yet unidentified teenager wearing a CORE T-shirt. All three were lynched by white terrorists who thought the youths were civil rights workers. In early August the bodies of the three actual civil rights workers were finally found buried beneath an earthen dam on a Neshoba County farm. Then in January 1966 three members of the Klan bombed the Hattiesburg home of Vernon Dahmer, a Mississippi Movement stalwart, head of the local NAACP chapter, and another early SNCC supporter, causing his death the following day.

In the accounts that follow, several women discuss their relationships with the older civil rights martyrs and how they experienced the martyrs' deaths. Other writers describe events and emotions surrounding the disappearance of the three young COFO workers. Although the incident is barely mentioned by the authors, all civil rights activists in Mississippi after early June 1963 were also aware of the awful beatings that female civil rights workers suffered in a Mississippi county jail. On their way back from the South Carolina Citizenship School run by Septima Clark, Mrs. Fannie Lou Hamer and four of her younger companions—June Johnson, Rosemary Freeman, Annelle Ponder, and Euvester Simpson— were arrested after several members of their party entered the white side of the Winona bus station. All five women were beaten badly. June was only fifteen years old.

Annelle Ponder and Mrs. Hamer received the worst beatings after the local lawmen identified Annelle as an SCLC staff person and learned that Mrs. Hamer had been urging black people to register to vote in Ruleville. Annelle was beaten mostly about the head and face, after she refused to use "sir," when answering the jailers. Barely able to speak afterward, she chose to utter only one word, "Freedom." The officers ordered two black male prisoners to beat Mrs. Hamer. Taking turns, they used a weighted leather strap and beat her so badly she received lifelong injuries. She recalled being in so much pain during the beating that she wished "they would have hit me one lick that could have ended the misery that they had me in." Neither she nor the young women were dissuaded, though, and they remained staunch civil rights activists in Mississippi. Their treatment underscores the reality, as do Joann Christian's and Prathia Hall's experiences, that movement women were not exempt from physical attacks.

Many women—both students and adults—were in the forefront of SNCC's Mississippi efforts. For example, Joyce Ladner, whose story opens this section, and her older sister, Dorie, had already been expelled from Jackson State College for their movement activities when SNCC arrived. Diane Nash, whose story appears earlier in the book, was among the first SNCC field secretaries to enter Mississippi. High schoolers Brenda Travis and Emma Bell quickly joined SNCC efforts in their hometown of McComb. Young women like Freddie Greene, Ida Mae Holland, and Mary Lane stepped forward when SNCC workers arrived in Greenwood. In her story Mrs. Victoria Gray Adams describes how she and others in Hattiesburg provided support and refuge for the young SNCC workers.

Women from Mississippi, like their Southwest Georgia counterparts, usually came from families that provided them with an awareness of racial inequalities, some protection from racial injustices, and the tools for surviving without a loss to their pride. On their own, they took steps to assert their dignity or to maintain their independence within a racist society. The Mississippi women who joined SNCC projects also had prior protest and organizational experience. Their stories suggest that many black women from the Deep South were savvy and active resisters to racism. Local civil rights activists were softening the ground, as Joyce Ladner writes, long before the sixties Civil Rights Movement began. They saw the sixties movement as part of an ongoing struggle rather than an event with a distinct beginning and ending.

SNCC and COFO efforts to register black voters had begun with accompanying individuals to the courthouse, then groups, then sponsoring "Freedom Days," which attracted even larger numbers of participants. In August 1963, hundreds of disenfranchised black Mississippians had presented affidavits at polling places for the Democratic primary, stating they had been prevented from registering to vote. That fall COFO also sponsored a statewide mock election running long-time NAACP activist and pharmacist Aaron Henry for governor, with white, Mississippi-born Tougaloo chaplain Ed King for lieutenant governor. Prospective black voters cast eighty thousand freedom ballots for Henry and King. Throughout the campaign for the vote, SNCC workers broke with the established civil rights practice of asking for fair application of literacy requirements and instead called for banning literacy requirements altogether. All the while COFO workers kept track of registration attempts and the attendant reprisals, filed voting rights suits, and followed up on the few legal efforts of the Kennedy administration to chastise racist registrars.

In the winter and spring of 1964 the SNCC staff in Mississippi engaged in a highly charged debate about the efficacy of the proposed Mississippi Summer Project, which would bring large numbers of white northern volunteers to the state. Many on the staff were convinced that their existing practice of using mostly black and mostly local staff and of helping to build grassroots community organizations in a step-by-step, deliberate fashion best represented SNCC's organizing goals. Staff members finally agreed to the project, however, hoping the volunteers' presence would focus national public attention on the racist repression and violence in Mississippi. The Mississippi Summer Project sponsored two major programs—the Mississippi Freedom Democratic Party (MFDP) and the Freedom Schools.

Through the MFDP, black Mississippi residents pushed for the franchise by challenging the legitimacy of the Democratic Party in Mississippi, the dominant party in the state. For almost one hundred years the Democrats had comprised the state's entire political power structure. Repeatedly reelected, Mississippi's congressmen and senators chaired important congressional committees, giving them significant power in the national government as well. Throughout that summer, Mississippi's black citizens, assisted by COFO workers, tried to participate in the five-stage all-white state Democratic Party process of choosing delegates to the Democratic National Convention. Anticipating rejection, they simultaneously established a parallel statewide organization that operated from the precinct level to the final selection of delegates at a state convention. Beginning with existing projects, COFO workers fanned out across Mississippi, establishing new projects, thus creating a statewide MFDP organization.

In early August, Ella Baker, who was then coordinating the MFDP's D.C. office, gave the keynote address at the MFDP's state convention, held at the Masonic Temple in Jackson. The nearly twenty-five hundred people present selected COFO activists for key positions. SNCC field secretary Lawrence Guyot was elected chairman of the party; Aaron Henry, chair of the sixty-eight-person delegation chosen to go to Atlantic City; and Fannie Lou Hamer, vice chair. Victoria Gray, a businesswoman and SNCC supporter from Hattiesburg, and Ed King were chosen as representatives to the Democratic National Committee. At least twenty of the delegates were women.

At the end of August SNCC field secretaries and office staff traveled with the MFDP representatives to Atlantic City for the convention. There the MFDP delegation, integrated by gender and race, challenged the legitimacy of the all-white, all-male delegation from Mississippi and asked to replace them on the convention floor. Instead the national party offered to seat only two members from the MFDP—Aaron Henry and Ed King. Citing the seriousness of their struggle for the vote, MFDP delegates rejected this offer, shortly afterward ended their demonstrations, and returned home. Mrs. Hamer played an influential role in the group's decision to reject the two seats, and her heart-wrenching, nationally televised testimony before the credentials committee about the hardships she had endured in her attempts to register to vote was a major factor in creating favorable public opinion for voting rights legislation.

The Freedom School program was formalized and greatly expanded during the summer of 1964. Before the Mississippi Summer Project, SNCC workers had set up small Freedom Schools here and there for local student participants who were interested in learning more about movement issues or who had been expelled from school because of their movement activities. During the summer of 1964, the summer project established a statewide system of nearly fifty schools serving more than twenty-five hundred students of all ages. The schools offered classes in basic skills in response to the vast discrepancies in the state's educational system. Mississippi spent four times as much money on white schools as on black schools. In rural areas local funding was even more one-sided. The Freedom School curriculum reflected its movement origins and also included black history and encouraged political thinking by asking students to define their needs and pose solutions. In keeping with the Movement's organizing style, Freedom Schools employed non-authoritarian, student-focused teaching methods. Many of the women who went south that summer set up the schools and taught in them. Often they also established Freedom Libraries in or next to the Freedom Schools. The Mississippi Summer Project founded other learning and cultural programs as well, including the Free Southern Theater and the Tougaloo Literacy Project.

In response to the plans for the Mississippi Summer Project, white Mississippians increased Ku Klux Klan membership. That summer, individuals, the Klan, and smaller Mississippi groups dedicated to using terror to oppose any advancement in black rights were responsible for the murders of actual and supposed civil rights activists mentioned above, at least thirty-five shootings, eighty beatings, and sixty-five bombings; thirty-five of the buildings bombed were black churches.

Standing Up for Our Beliefs

Joyce Ladner

A young woman learns dignity and courage from her mother, community, and early civil rights martyrs while growing up in Mississippi.

> *[Editors' Note: This piece is based on a keynote speech given by Joyce Ladner on April 14, 2000, in Raleigh, North Carolina, during the SNCC 40th Anniversary Conference, which was dedicated to Ms. Ella Baker.]*

My Community: Palmers Crossing, Mississippi

Race was always the central most important thing in the lives of my older sister, Dorie, and myself. We've always carried both the burden and the blessing of this strong racial consciousness. Perhaps it came from our mother, who taught us that you look white people dead in the eye and don't blink. All the white salesmen, like the insurance collector who came around our house, deferred to her. She always told us that there was a certain way you carry yourself in order to keep your dignity so that white people don't walk all over you.

One day Dorie and I were at the grocery store, a block from our house. Dorie had just bought some doughnuts, and we were looking through the magazine rack. We were just entering puberty, and she had just gotten her first bra. The white cashier at the store walked up behind her and tried to touch her breasts. She turned around, took the bag of doughnuts, and began to beat him over the head. Then we ran all the way home, frightened and worried about what our mother would do, because assaulting a white person was strictly forbidden by the unwritten laws of segregation. My sister's act of defiance might have put us and our family in immediate danger from night riders or the Klan. When we told her what had happened, our mother insisted that we should never tolerate any form of sexual abuse and replied, in all seriousness, "You should have killed him. Don't ever let any white man touch you wrong."

Mother also taught us "Beliefs aren't worth very much if you can't stand up for them." We learned this as well within our all-black community of Palmers Crossing, four miles from downtown Hattiesburg. Here we were taught how to survive with dignity, which was like walking a tightrope. The people around us told Dorie and me that we could indeed stand tall, have the courage of our convictions, and carry ourselves in a certain manner. If, for example, we were faced with the frequent situation of a white man making a pass at one of us, we were instructed to stand proudly, not respond, and walk away like ladies—and it worked. We knew we couldn't beat too many people over the head with a bag of doughnuts, for fear that we might be killed, but we could demand respect.

Even though we lived in a very closed society, it was possible to get certain information. I read the newspaper from the time I was very little, spending a dime a day to buy the paper. I remember the *Brown* decision very clearly and how the local newspaper covered it. After that decision there was no attempt at all to desegregate the Hattiesburg schools, or schools anywhere in Mississippi. What the black community got were new public schools in some places, which was the white Mississippian's way of staving off any attempt to say that we had unequal facilities. WDAM, the major television station in Hattiesburg, was very, very racist in the late fifties, but as an NBC affiliate they would break for Chet Huntley and David Brinkley. This was the one window of national news that we saw.

More importantly, a family friend, an older man by the name of Mr. McLeod, came to our house all the time when I was about twelve or thirteen years old. We called him "Cuz," though he really wasn't our cousin. Other people gave him the honorary title of doctor. He was a "race man" who sold herbal medicine and was a member of the local NAACP. Every week he brought us the *Chicago Defender* and the *Pittsburgh Courier,* and every month *Ebony* and the *JET.* (Black people in the South always called *JET* magazine "the" *JET.*) He also brought books, introduced us to literature on black people, and told us, "You girls are going to have to change things. It'll be your generation that's going to change things when you get older."

Black war veterans also criticized race relations in the United States. I remember when I was a little girl that my uncle Archie, a World War I vet, would sit on the back porch and tell us that going to France had given him a different perspective and that it was disappointing to come back home and see how terrible conditions were. The veterans of World War II, especially, were very important to the Civil Rights Movement in Mississippi. Many of them were the founders of the then-underground statewide NAACP. I cannot emphasize enough the importance of the role these men played. They were the ones who always felt that ours was the generation that would make things different. For them the environment was pregnant with possibilities of all kinds of change.

Ours was the Emmett Till generation. No other single incident had a more profound impact on so many people who came into SNCC. We had seen the *JET* magazine cover of Emmett Till's disfigured and bloated face with one eye missing. It was just an awful picture. When his body was prepared for burial, no cosmetic surgery was done. In the 1980s I asked Mrs. Mobley, his mother, "Why did you have him buried like that, with an open casket?" She told me, "I wanted the world to see what they did to my baby." We were his age and could identify with him. I felt that if they had killed a fourteen-year-old, they could also kill me or my brothers. We knew that men were lynched, but we'd never known of a *child* being lynched before. On a profound, personal level, this reality had a strong, galvanizing effect on all of us. The image is with me still. It became etched in my generation's consciousness.

Prying Mississippi Open

Dorie and I were very fortunate to be closely mentored by several black Mississippi heroes. Three men who had a profound influence on my life all died for their beliefs—Vernon Dahmer, Medgar Evers, and Clyde Kennard. In the mid-fifties when we were first- and second-year high school students, Mr. Dahmer and Mrs. Dahmer (Brother Beard and Sister Beard, as we called them in our church) and Clyde Kennard used to take Dorie and me to Jackson for state NAACP meetings. I think you seek mentors out as much as they seek you out. It's possible that the reason they took us is because they knew we had an interest in race, because we talked about it so much. All the meetings were held at the Masonic Temple, up the street from Jackson State College. At these meetings we saw outside people coming into the state, people like Ruby Hurley, who was the first black woman lawyer I ever met. I don't believe I knew that one existed before then. As Southeast regional director of the NAACP, she would come and speak at these meetings. Gloster Current, the association's national director of branches, also spoke. Our local mentors, especially Clyde Kennard and Mr. Dahmer, helped us to organize our Hattiesburg NAACP Youth Chapter in the late fifties.

When Clyde came back home in the mid-fifties, he had served seven years in the military as a paratrooper and left the University of Chicago in his senior year, after his father died, to help his mother run the farm. Clyde was just in his early thirties. He was a very quiet person and moved easily without your noticing his presence, except there was a profundity there. Determined to complete his college education, Clyde applied to the nearby all-white Mississippi Southern College (now the University of Southern Mississippi) two or three times and was arrested and imprisoned as a result.

Not directly for that, of course. Instead he was set up by local authorities who enticed a young black worker to plant twenty-five dollars' worth of chicken feed at Kennard's farm and say that Kennard had planned a robbery. Kennard was found guilty and given the maximum sentence possible, seven years; the young man received a suspended sentence and was immediately hired back by the man who owned the chicken feed factory. In prison Kennard was required to do hard labor, even after he was diagnosed with cancer and denied necessary medical treatments. I began a campaign to secure his freedom, which was picked up by SNCC and *JET* magazine. Kennard was eventually released, but not pardoned by Governor Ross Barnett, in the spring of 1963. Kennard went straight to Billings Hospital at the University of Chicago but died shortly afterward from the cancer. It was awful. I have never cried, yet I still feel the tears deep down over how terribly they treated him.

When Dorie and I were in high school, there was a network of similarly minded students in the surrounding schools. What facilitated the younger people, my age, joining the Movement was that we were also active in certain high school organizations, which meant we traveled around, mostly within the state. When Dorie and I went to Jackson State College in the fall of 1960, I began to see some of those same students among my classmates. Some of the upperclassmen were people I'd seen at the NAACP office in the Masonic Temple or at the statewide NAACP meetings. We all recognized one another. James Meredith was one of these students; he was older, married, and had been in the military. We knew absolutely nothing about the fact that he had applied to go to Ole Miss.

For first-year college students, every Wednesday afternoon was free time. Most students used this time to go downtown to shop, but Dorie and I would go up to see Medgar Evers, whose office was on the second floor of the Masonic Temple. He would always tell us what was going on in NAACP chapters around the state. One time he told us that there was going to be a sit-in. Without knowing why they were going to sit in, where or when or what, we said, "Really? Can we join?" And he responded, "Well, yeah. You can." We exclaimed, "Oh, that's great. Tell us when." Hesitating, he said, "I'll let you know later."

Each time we went by his office, he would say something vague. We knew not to ask too many questions, because having information could be dangerous if you were ever pressured enough to give it up. Once he told us, "You really can't participate, because I would never be able to explain to your parents why you were arrested, and that's important to me." When I was away at school, he had met my mother one time in the grocery store in Palmers Crossing. She'd given him some money to give to me. By then my mother was used to Dorie's and my activism. She would yell at us, "You know you're going to get us all killed. They're going to throw a bomb in this house, shoot it up because of what you two are doing!" But she never told us to stop.

Finally Evers mentioned that the sit-in was going to be soon and told us, "What you can do is try to organize some students on Jackson State's campus." We began to prepare for the sit-in. Talk about being ingenious; for example, when we had a regularly scheduled meeting one night in the dormitory, Dorie, who was president of the dorm council, asked me to say the closing prayer. Without ever saying the word "sit-in," I talked about, "Oh, dear Lord, there are perilous times ahead. Please protect us as we go into this danger," and so on.

Next morning, we were called before the dean of students, who asked what I meant by the prayer and "perilous times ahead." I said, "What do you mean, asking me about what I said to my God? You have no right to question me about my relationship with Jesus." Dorie, who knew the dean was also an ordained minister, jumped in and said, "As a man of the cloth, how could you?" The dean agreed, "Well, you're right, you're right, you're right." My sister and I walked out of there laughing.

We also carefully spread rumors so that they could not be traced back to us that something was going to happen and that we had to be ready as students to support it when it went down. Then eight or nine Tougaloo students, members of the NAACP chapter on their campus, held a sit-in at the Jackson Public Library. The sit-in was organized and supported by Medgar Evers. They didn't go to Woolworth's or any other five-and-ten-cent store, because they wanted to attack a tax-supported facility. Next we started spreading the rumor that there was going to be a prayer vigil, a meeting, in front of the library at seven o'clock at night.

When we got out there, Rev. Emmett Burns was in the middle of his prayer. Then we heard someone shouting, "Stop it! Stop it! Shut up!" Everybody was looking around, wondering where these orders were coming from. It was the president of Jackson State running through the crowd, arms flailing, absolutely out of control. He was in a frenzy. "What is this? What's going on? Stop it!" He took Eunice, one of my two roommates, by the shoulder and pushed her on the ground. Then he turned on Reverend Burns. The college administration brought a lot of police on campus that night. The next day, as we tried to march down to the courthouse, where the Tougaloo students were being arraigned, I heard someone screaming, "Oh, Lord, they're killing us." Tear gas canisters were being shot into our group, and they sounded like guns. I ran and hid by going into different people's homes.

I knocked on one front door, heard a radio, and reached a hand through a hole in the screen, unlatched it, and ran into the house. I told the older black lady who was there what happened. She responded, "Come on in. Nobody's coming in my house." She kept ironing and listening to reports of the event on the radio. Talking to herself, she kept muttering, "It's a low-down dirty shame, these white folks treating these children like dogs." Some of the other marchers hid in the embalming room at a funeral home. It was bedlam. Eventually we got back to campus. They closed school early the next day and sent us home for spring break. And when we came back, the college administrators expelled the president of the student government.

This is what Mississippi was like before Miss Ella Baker came. There were a lot of people who carried on their civil rights work underground, lest they be killed. It meant, though, that Miss Baker came into a state that was no longer totally closed. The state was being pried open, because there were the Vernon Dahmers, the Moores, Mr. E. W. Steptoe, Clyde Kennard, the local men and women like Mrs. Hamer, and my dear cousin, Victoria Gray. These are people who consistently took stands. By the time the SNCC people came in, even though direct action couldn't be carried out in Mississippi, we'd also matured to a point where we realized that eating at a lunch counter was not as important as having the right to vote. Then we thought, naïvely, that if you get some political power, then you can change things. We hadn't really progressed yet to the point where we understood that economic power was very, very important.

Frantz Fanon said that each generation must define its mission, then fulfill it or betray it. We had our time to stand up for our beliefs. Now my son and his generation have a tougher set of problems to solve than we did, but it is their choice as well.

An activist and pioneering sociologist, **JOYCE LADNER** has taught at Hunter College in New York City and Howard University in Washington, D.C. At Howard she also served as vice president for academic affairs and as interim president. She was appointed to the D.C. financial control board by President Bill Clinton and was a senior fellow in the governmental studies program at the Brookings Institute. Concerned about the importance of improving education for public school students, she has researched successful programs and discussed this topic on nationally syndicated radio and television programs and with interested audiences nationwide. Her publications focus on issues relevant to the black community and include *Tomorrow's Tomorrow*, a study of black inner-city adolescent girls; *Mixed Families: Adopting across Racial Boundaries*; *The Ties That Bind: Timeless Values for African American Families*; *The New Urban Leaders*; and *Launching Our Black Children for Success*.

Inside and Outside of Two Worlds

Jeannette King

A married southern white woman steps out of her expected roles and becomes an activist in her own community.

The White Community

In January 1962 my husband Ed and I moved into a small wood frame house on the campus of Tougaloo Southern Christian College outside Jackson, Mississippi. Ed assumed the job of chaplain on the predominantly black campus, and I set about finding a job as a social worker in Jackson. My effort failed although there were few professionally trained social workers in the state. I was ostracized from the profession because we lived on a black campus and because Ed and I were two of a very small handful of native-born Mississippi white people who openly supported civil rights.

Ed and I were no strangers to Tougaloo College, having gone there on many occasions as students at nearby all-white Millsaps College. We later learned that the State Sovereignty Commission monitored these meetings between Tougaloo and Millsaps students and called our parents to let them know we were attending. These meetings had a profound effect on my life. It was the first chance I had as a white Mississippian to meet in the same room with black people and discuss personal and intellectual issues. In a short space of time, these meetings accomplished what all the religious (do unto others) and social (be kind to everyone) ideas had just talked about.

By the time we arrived at Tougaloo, Ed had made his commitment to civil rights quite public. In May 1961 he had participated in the second wave of the Freedom Rides. When the bus arrived in Montgomery, Alabama, Ed was attacked and beaten by a mob, arrested with the other riders, and had his picture splashed over the front page of the *Jackson Daily News*. The morning of the arrest I received a call from a reporter at the newspaper. He wanted to know if I had decided to break my engagement as well as drop my wedding plans, scheduled for the following summer. The reporter seemed surprised when I said no.

In June 1961 Ed had made an impassioned plea for the Methodist Church in Mississippi to desegregate the churches and the placement of clergy. He made this plea from the floor of the annual meeting of the Methodist Church in Jackson. The conference subsequently sanctioned him and denied him ordination in the conference.

Although Ed had been offered placement in other Methodist conferences in the West, we both wanted to return to the South to participate in the changes that had already begun to sweep across the region. An old friend, Ernst Borinski, who was a Holocaust survivor and head of the sociology department at Tougaloo College, suggested that Ed consider applying for the chaplaincy of the college. This offered us a good opportunity to return to Mississippi without having to immerse ourselves in and be engulfed by the white community in Jackson, which, as capital of the state, was tightly segregated. It was impossible at that point in time to consider functioning simultaneously in both the black and white parts of the community.

Since members of my family lived in and around Jackson, relating to them in the midst of political chaos was often hard. Because of the demonstrations, Tougaloo was frequently mentioned in the newspapers. When Ed and I were arrested, our names were also in the papers. My maternal grandmother, my role model for courage, was a widow who by working as a seamstress had supported three young children during the Depression. She told my mother she was very disappointed in me and gave me the silent treatment. We never regained our relationship, though we saw each until her death at ninety-four.

My two uncles and their wives considered us to be "Commie pinkos," corrupted by too much education and exposure to the North. Mother stood up for Ed and me within the family and continued to see us while we were in Jackson. Even though she disagreed with our tactics, she agreed with the principle of desegregation. The only thing she would say to me was, "I don't know why you have to take the burdens of the whole world on your shoulders," and she would then comment about how tired I looked.

Just how much my mother dealt with because of our high-profile activity was brought home to me on one Sunday afternoon visit. As I started back to the campus, I was followed. This was not that unusual, but someone had obviously followed me from near Mother's house. I took the regular precautions, locked the car doors, and headed for the center of town to make sure the man could not isolate me. When I felt safe, I glimpsed the driver's face and realized he was our next-door neighbor. When I got to the campus, he went on his way. My mother was living alone in this house, where I had lived until graduating from high school. She told me that this man was a Ku Klux Klan member and had once confronted her about our activities, making veiled threats about "nigger lovers" and what should happen to them. Although he did not specifically name us, there was a cross burned in our yard twice when we lived on the Tougaloo campus.

My mother was also visited by the FBI, who wanted to pump her for information about us and our activities. Since we rarely talked to Mother about what we were doing, she could deny any knowledge. Ironically, at a later time she also had a visit from the FBI about her neighbor and his KKK activity.

We were threatened directly one evening in the fall of 1963. Six of us had gone to a small voter registration meeting at a rural church. There were two black students, one white student, and a Pakistani professor in our Pinto station wagon, including Anne Moody, who later wrote the moving story of her life in *Coming of Age in Mississippi*. Without warning, three men in a pickup truck with shotguns visible in the truck rack ran us off the interstate. They got out and surrounded our car. They told us they knew we were "nigger lovers" and said we had no right to come into Madison County to stir up trouble. Ed, who was driving, quickly made up a story and told them there was a visiting professor from Pakistan in our car. If we were attacked, he pointed out, it could create a nasty international incident. After a few more threats, the men left.

I felt a wide gulf between the gunmen and myself, even though I was white and southern and they were white and southern. We might have been "kissing cousins," as we say in the South. How incredible that these white southerners could not see either my black friends or the white passengers in the car as individuals, but instead demonized all of us in such a way that they felt we didn't have the right to live.

The Movement

When we arrived at Tougaloo in the winter of 1962, we immediately joined the Jackson NAACP Youth Group, led by another white faculty member, John Salter. John had reluctantly been made the coordinator of the group over the suspicions of the local adult NAACP leadership, who distrusted his militancy. John and his wife, Eldri, planned to mobilize high school and college students to boycott white-owned businesses in the Jackson area and desegregate public facilities. From 1961 until the June 1963 death of

Medgar Evers, the head of the Mississippi state NAACP, this campaign led to numerous demonstrations and jailings. John and Eldri, Ed and I were to become close friends and movement allies.

Throughout the spring of 1963 the recruited students conducted small demonstrations to desegregate the churches, theaters, and libraries. First demonstrations began with small picket lines prior to an actual sit-in. Eldri Salter, Memphis Norman, Bette Poole, and I had been involved in one of these picketing incidents and jailed. Usually I provided backup as a driver, assisted students in getting out of jail, or brought supplies to them in jail. At the same time movement momentum was building in Jackson, SNCC was undertaking voter registration projects in several Mississippi communities.

The attempt to desegregate the Woolworth's lunch counter was the most violent. Anne Moody, John Salter, and Joan Trumpauer were threatened and beaten for two hours as they sat in at the Woolworth's lunch counter. Our efforts to get the police to intervene during the attack on those three proved fruitless. Ed and Tougaloo president Dan Beittel joined subsequent sit-ins. The unresponsiveness of the authorities ignited the students as well as Medgar Evers, who initially had hesitated to support the Jackson boycott. The NAACP national leadership became more reluctant to support the Jackson Movement as the number of arrests rose into the hundreds and the leadership of the national office was asked to provide bail and legal support.

It took tremendous courage by the student activists to be a part of the demonstrations. Many were afraid, with good reason, about retaliation against their families, most of whom lived in small towns and rural areas of Mississippi. If the identities of the students were known, parents could be physically threatened and/or lose jobs. Even students who weren't demonstrating were afraid for their families if Tougaloo became known throughout the state as an activist center.

Opinion on the campus about the political activity of Tougaloo's students and faculty was divided. Many faculty members believed radical action was the wrong approach. President Beittel created an open atmosphere where the activists inside and outside the campus were accepted. As a result, although Beittel had a written contract guaranteeing his position as president until age sixty-five, he was fired. His ouster put a damper on the student movement. However, many of the most active students, like Joyce and Dorie Ladner, Anne Moody, and Bette Poole, joined SNCC projects. Other Tougaloo students participated in a voter registration campaign in Madison County, bordering the college campus. This county had a majority black population and a particularly violent history in its treatment of black residents. One reason for this level of mistreatment was the especially high level of black land ownership, which created some measure of independence for black farmers and fear on the part of white people.

Following the large-scale demonstrations in Jackson, negotiations took place between the city fathers and the national leadership of the NAACP. The national organization put conservative black leadership in charge of the local NAACP, a move vehemently opposed by John and Ed. During this time, Medgar Evers was shot and killed. The gathering at the church the day after Medgar's death was a mixture of sadness, rage, and solidarity. Three days later, Medgar's funeral was held and a protest demonstration planned to follow. The NAACP and CORE leadership had organized the protest in compliance with nonviolent principles, but when the five thousand people marching began to sing freedom songs and when the singing was met with police violence, the demonstration broke into a riot. In the days that followed, the more conservative NAACP Jackson leadership sought to control the students.

Three days after the funeral, Ed and John were involved in a serious car wreck. The local papers speculated about whether the accident was intentional. However, there was no evidence to back up the claim. Ed, who went through the windshield of the car, suffered the most damage. While hospitalized, he underwent the first of nine plastic surgeries to repair his face. Initially we were unable to find a doctor willing to treat him or to perform the surgery required. Throughout his hospital stay, I feared hospital staff would mistreat him. I had to be there constantly or have friends from the campus present to ensure that no harm came to him. This accident left Ed in a very weakened condition, but it did not stop his activities.

By the end of summer 1963, we knew massive pressure must be put on the federal government to intervene in Mississippi. All efforts by the Council of Federated Organizations (COFO) had yielded little real change in voter registration. In most Mississippi counties, black people were still not getting registered. Either they were simply turned away, or they were being told that they failed voter registration requirements. In October 1963 COFO held a statewide meeting to plan for the 1964 elections. The plan involved developing an alternative structure to the all-white state Democratic Party. This was the beginning of the Mississippi Freedom Democratic Party, which led to the challenge of the 1964 Democratic National Convention. This meeting was extremely exhilarating—black representatives from county after county participated in the planning of this effort. I was elected as one of the delegates to this statewide convention. The delegates chose Aaron Henry from Clarksdale to run for governor in the freedom ballot campaign. A week later, though weakened by recent hospitalization and facing more surgery, Ed acceded to Bob Moses's request to run for lieutenant governor as Henry's running mate. The statewide campaign had to be conducted in little over a month.

COFO decided to bring in more outside help, including large numbers of white students, to conduct a massive voter registration drive leading up to the 1964 national elections. This decision was a very difficult one because of the very strong feelings of black SNCC project leaders who had worked in the state since 1961. Very few white people had been allowed to work on Mississippi SNCC projects, because their presence would increase the danger to white and black SNCC workers, as well as to movement supporters in the various communities. Black male Mississippi civil rights workers also expressed a personal resentment and fear that this would create a potential for white dominance on projects throughout the state, competing with the existing black leadership. I felt very conflicted about the debate, mainly because it forced me to look at my own role. I had always felt very sensitive about my "whiteness" in a black community and participating in bringing about changes "for black people." This position had always made me feel like an outsider taking on someone else's burden. As a result, I could identify with black staffers who did not want to be submerged by white volunteers swarming into the state to "save the situation," even though I often felt insulted by the condescension directed at me by certain male movement heavies.

When I began to understand my own female rage at any form of male dominance, I better understood the strong stance taken by SNCC men in relationship to the possibility of white dominance and the move to "black power" as they tried to change white-dominated political systems.

Early in 1964 I joined the group preparing to establish Freedom Schools across the state. Our curriculum emphasized a real version of history that included information about the contribution of black people to every aspect of American experience. In addition, we prepared materials for working on verbal and math skills. We had contributions from some stellar national educators, like Staughton Lynd of Yale and Robert Coles and Alvin Poussaint of Harvard Medical School.

During the summer, I worked in the Canton Freedom Schools, one of my most rewarding movement experiences. Later, when local people took charge of their own Head Start programs, the schools became the foundation for the federally funded Child Development Group of Mississippi (CDGM). I also helped develop college course work for SNCC workers. These programs demonstrated the Movement's desire to expand the life experience for black Mississippians. The movement leadership understood that beyond getting the vote, the people needed the means for economic power and education and that taking control of their own economic lives was the key.

In late summer 1964 I was elected as an alternate MFDP delegate to the Democratic National Convention in Atlantic City. When the delegation was offered two token seats by the credentials committee, the disappointment and anger the members felt over this cynical treatment cast a dark shadow on the long-term work in Mississippi interrupted by the MFDP campaign. Tokenism was unacceptable. We returned to Mississippi exhausted, feeling defeated and betrayed. For me, this was the beginning of the end of the idealistic phase of the Movement as we had lived it for the previous two years.

In the next year the loose alliance of COFO broke apart as each member organization attempted to redefine its goals. CORE, SCLC, and the NAACP distanced themselves from SNCC, fearful that SNCC's tactics were too radical to be "managed." To me, the Movement in Mississippi was SNCC, but there was no place for a white southerner to fit into the organization as it began to change. I had identified with SNCC's principles of grassroots development and creating mechanisms for change in the economic structure that affected people's lives. Once again, I was on the outside. Over the coming years I worked with CDGM, a Head Start program that covered sixty counties in Mississippi, making it the largest such program in the country. First I directed the social services program. Later I served on the board of CDGM, along with Annie Devine and many other early movement activists.

My most vivid memories of spring 1963 to summer 1964 are those intense conversations held around my dining room table over food and drink. It was the most intellectually stimulating time of my life. We talked about strategy for demonstrations or spun out theories of possible change in the educational system. Tougaloo's campus and our house were safe havens for many of the people coming into the state for part-time volunteer work.

Because I believed in our goals, I pushed myself far beyond my personal comfort level when it was required, though I felt more comfortable being the person who cooked the meals and housed people. Internally, I often labeled myself as a coward, because I could not be enthusiastic about demonstrations and being in the middle of sometimes dangerous situations. Whatever role I played, the Movement was life-changing and life-defining for me. I hope it will cast a long shadow over the generations to come—my children, grandchildren, and all our children.

JEANNETTE KING, her husband, Ed King, and their two daughters left Jackson for New Orleans in 1967, where they spent two years, and then lived in India for a year. Returning to Jackson in 1970, she worked as a psychiatric social worker in hospital settings and managed her own therapy practice. She served as president of the Mississippi Association of Social Workers from 1985 to 1987 and won its Social Worker of the Year award in 1987 for her work dealing with domestic violence and setting up the first rape crisis center in Jackson. She and Ed King were divorced in 1986. In the past several years she has lived in various parts of the United States. She and her partner Jim Russell, an anti-war activist, were together from 1999 until his sudden death in 2006. The grandmother of four, she now resides in the state of Washington.

They Didn't Know the Power of Women

Victoria Gray Adams

A Mississippi businesswoman supports student organizers and becomes a full-time movement activist herself.

These Young People Are Our Friends

I've always been in the Movement. I've always had my own movement, from the time that I was conscious of the situation, both racially and economically speaking. For example, I was very unhappy with the kinds of employment that were available for black women in Mississippi, so I decided to start my own business. When the Movement that you know about came to town, I was a businesswoman selling cosmetics and household miscellany. My mission, as I understood it, was to help people have a better life by providing employment for black people in general but women in particular.

When SNCC people came to Hattiesburg, Mississippi, they represented just one more kind of movement, a way for folks to get a better life. Initially, I got involved from a support stance. At the time the SNCC youngsters arrived, the black powers that be had received their instructions from the white powers that be not to let SNCC in, even though SNCC had been invited to Hattiesburg by a local group, which included Mr. Vernon Dahmer. When the word came down not to let them in, nobody would open their churches or do anything else that might be helpful to these civil rights workers.

I heard that one of the black powers that be was trying to block Mr. Dahmer from inviting the Movement to come to my church. I said, "No, he doesn't control the church that I go to; SNCC people are welcome there. I'm quite sure that if we meet with my pastor, everything will be okay." With the cooperation of my pastor, Rev. Leonard P. Ponder, I arranged for my church to be open so that SNCC workers could have meetings there. That's how the Movement found a place to become a movement in Hattiesburg, in my church, St. John Methodist Episcopal Church, which today is St. John United Methodist Church. For a long time, Reverend Ponder was the only minister who was participating in and supporting the Movement in Hattiesburg.

Arranging a meeting place was the beginning of my involvement. Then the youngsters began to invite me to do other things, including going to Dorchester, Georgia, for the Citizenship Education Program training, an SCLC program run by Septima Clark to train teachers in voter education. I was very excited when I left Dorchester, and back in Hattiesburg I had a voter education class up and going within a couple of weeks.

First I recruited a class of people from my church and neighborhood. Then I went to other churches and invited them to come also. We could not call it "citizenship education"; we called it "adult education" or a literacy program, in order to camouflage what we were doing. Next the SNCC workers invited me to go to a meeting. I took a bunch of kids in my car, and we met with kids from all over the state. That's where I first met Ella Baker. When I met her and that community of youthful civil rights activists, I realized that this was exactly what I'd been looking for all of my conscious existence. Before, I had not found a community of people who understood where I was coming from. It was like coming home.

When I met Miss Ella Baker it was like we had always known each other. She was never a stranger, somebody I had to get to know. She was a very little figure, with a very strong and imposing voice. Our understanding of things was just so similar. Miss Baker and I, only two of the four adults at the meeting, reacted in the same way and were affirming, embracing, and supporting the youth. We also talked about finding ways to involve adults in the process. As a result, I became a mediator in Hattiesburg between the young civil rights workers and the local community.

For instance, when SNCC workers Curtis Hayes and Hollis Watkins were walking the dusty roads, encouraging people to register, people in the black community were afraid of them. Their fear was based on articles in the white papers circulated in the city, the *Hattiesburg American* and the *Jackson Clarion Ledger*. These papers said the SNCC kids were dangerous, talking about Communism, and that their actions would jeopardize the entire black community. Black people were afraid, among other things, of losing their jobs as well as the few hard-won rights we did have.

I would explain, "These young people are here as our friends, as our supporters. But the local white people can't see civil rights workers in a positive light, because for white folks civil rights workers are the enemy." I went to the black churches describing the projects Hollis and Curtis and the others were planning and encouraged people to support these activities.

As I went from place to place for my business, I talked about those young people and why it was important for us to support them. Sometimes the kids had pretty lean days out there. Even though Mr. Dahmer took care of some of their living and shelter needs, he could not do it all. The local white people spread propaganda that the kids had plenty of money. I emphasized that this was just not true. I told the people I came in contact with, "Often-times when these youngsters out here knock on your door, they're hungry. Sometimes the shoes on these kids' feet aren't too solid on the bottom. If you can't do anything else, certainly you could contribute some food."

I recruited women to come to the freedom house in Hattiesburg and cook. Other people brought food. We organized a telephone tree to be certain that someone would come every day to ensure that the SNCC workers would have at least one hot, well-prepared meal. Some of the working men in the community would come to my house at night and give me money, saying, "Take this. We appreciate what you're doing, but we can't help you directly."

We adults provided a little money sometimes and places to stay and work. Mrs. L. E. Woods, a lifelong businesswoman, provided the freedom house. She had the only hotel facility for black people, like the big band folks, coming into the area. She was a very independent and courageous woman, who understood what was going on as soon as the SNCC kids came to work in Hattiesburg. She had always been interested in voter registration and was one of the first to support the Mississippi Freedom Democratic Party (MFDP).

The initial SNCC office was in my brother's place. He and Mr. J. C. Fairlie had a TV repair shop in the downstairs area of the Masonic Temple. SNCC was there, and then the Delta Ministry came. Everybody in the Movement was in that TV shop. Eventually, the Movement outgrew the space. When Miss Woods became aware that the Movement needed a larger space, she opened up the first floor of her hotel across the street from my brother's TV shop for the office.

We Need Something New and Different

The Mississippi Freedom Democratic Party grew out of the frustrations of people attempting to participate in the regular political structure. First of all, we were not getting registered. Our primary effort in Hattiesburg and Forrest County was just trying to get registered. During this time we launched the Freedom Vote campaign. We'd run our own candidates for the purpose of showing the larger national community that people would register and vote if they were granted fair access.

Some of the most significant voting rights suits came out of Hattiesburg. The circuit clerk, named Theron Lynd, was also the voting registrar. He was as obstinate as he was big and tall. He thought all the records, everything, belonged to him. He just did not pay court rulings any attention. Eventually the Justice Department filed a suit against Lynd and his tactics. It was only after that suit was won sometime in late 1963, early 1964, that we began to get registered. When we started to get registered, white officials played all kinds of games. They would say that the precinct meeting was going to be one place at a certain time. We'd get there and there would be nobody there. Or we'd get there and the meeting would be over. Or we'd get there and they just wouldn't let us in.

This is why in 1964 the MFDP emerged. The party came alive for me when we started having our state meetings in Jackson, Mississippi. It was wonderful. It was just the most exciting thing to think that we were going to the Democratic National Convention in Atlantic City to challenge the all-white Mississippi delegation. We were doing our politicking; we were making our speeches. At these statewide meetings I spoke, Mrs. Fannie Lou Hamer spoke, Miss Annie Devine spoke, Miss Ella Baker spoke, as did many others.

Miss Devine, Mrs. Hamer, and I, we talked to each other about everything under the sun. There's not anything we didn't talk about. None of us could remember when we first met; we just clicked. We were just perfect accompaniments for each other. After we had been running up and down the road and meeting in hotel foyers for the MFDP, I said one day, "You know, this doesn't make any sense. We're giving these folks all of our money. Why don't we just rent an apartment for the three of us in Washington, D.C.?" And they agreed.

Each of us had her own key to the little apartment we rented in southwest D.C., on Capitol Hill. Whenever one of us was in town, she went over to the apartment and let herself in. Once in a while, two of us would be there; every blue moon three of us would be there. It was exciting for us, slipping into this apartment one by one.

I don't know where the idea came from to occupy the seats on the floor of the convention during the 1964 challenge. We were outside, picketing and singing. Then we decided to take those seats on the convention floor that had been vacated by the white delegation. They had left those seats because they had received premature and incorrect information that the MFDP had accepted the "two-seat compromise." Incensed by the idea of giving up even two seats to civil rights activists, they walked out.

Some of our friends on the floor, friends in the delegations from places like Michigan and California, sent back their passes to the MFDP members. We entered one by one and sent those passes back to somebody else from the MFDP who would come in and repeat the process. We just kept passing those passes around until finally all of us were inside. Then we unfurled our

Mississippi Freedom Democratic Party banner and sat in the seats vacated by the white Democratic delegation from Mississippi.

I was always opposed to the compromise. We spent hours and hours and hours discussing this, because not all the other MFDP delegates were as clear. There was a lot of pressure being brought from the big guns, such as Roy Wilkins from the NAACP and Dr. Martin Luther King Jr. of SCLC, trying to get us to accept. The big guns thought we should accept the compromise; it would be a victory. They said, "The people have worked so hard, and they need a victory." They were political animals in the sense of how politics worked at that time. But we were not. We were a different kind of political animal, desperate political animals, with our lives and everything staked on this. To add insult to the injury of offering us only two seats, the white government officials and others were so audacious and arrogant as to tell us who they would have sit in those seats—Dr. Aaron Henry and Rev. Ed King. So what kind of compromise was that? It wasn't one. I said, "What kind of a victory? A victory of what? Two seats at-large! Who does that represent? Nobody. We came here with nothing and we leave here with nothing." Oh, it was heavy. It was very, very, very heavy.

I wasn't at all sure which way the vote was going to go. When local people are listening to the big guys, the national figures, the people tend to say, "Well, they're smart. They know." Here I was in the position of saying, "They may be smart, but right now they are wrong."

Rev. Andrew Young, an aide to Dr. King, came to my hotel room and said, "Vicky, why won't you accept it?" I responded, "Andy, because it really is nothing. That's why." I continued, "You need to understand something, Andy. We're not asking you to make this decision for us. We're asking you to support us. You live in Georgia. We live in Mississippi. What goes on in Mississippi is not always the same thing that goes on in Georgia. We're going to make our own decisions, because the decisions that are made here affect *our* lives. All we're asking from you is support, not that you necessarily agree with us. Just support us the same way we support you when you call us to come to Alabama or whatever. That's all we want from you." And he said, "Okay."

During the meeting to decide about the compromise, the big guns talked on and on. Mrs. Hamer and Miss Devine and I didn't say anything for hours. It's amazing how we clicked that day. We were not sitting anywhere near each other in that church in Atlantic City. I think Mrs. Hamer was down near the front, Miss Devine was somewhere at the midsection, and I was near the back. We three just sat and listened and listened. Finally, when I got convinced that something was about to happen, I decided I'd better get on the floor. And I did. I said, "We are here representing people in Mississippi who have everything on the line. And they're looking to us to bring back something that's going to make a difference. Two seats at-large aren't going to make any difference. So I'm not going back to the people and lie. We came here with nothing, so let's go on back with nothing. Quite frankly, if what I've seen since we've been here is what it's like, I'm not sure I even want to be a part of it." That's exactly what I said.

Next, Miss Devine hit the floor. Miss Devine is always very quiet and very deep. Then Mrs. Hamer hit the floor. Of course, once Mrs. Hamer took hold of an issue and went with it, everybody listened. The other point we made that day was that we can go back and fight another day. We'll go back and continue the struggle until we get what it is that we need and what we want. That was the final word on that. I think that's what swayed the MFDP—the three of us up there like that.

I remember clearly that both Dr. Aaron Henry and Rev. Ed King were disappointed. They would have been the persons seated by the Democratic Party, but I don't think that was the source of their disappointment. They were thinking that the MFDP lawyers were the experts on these matters and that they had recommended accepting the compromise. Our lawyers might have been experts, but they were the experts at things as they were. The last thing we needed was things as they were. We needed something new and different.

Ed and his wife, Jeannette, Mrs. Hamer, and I left Atlantic City and went on to New York to keep a speaking engagement. Ed remained enthusiastic about the Movement, but Dr. Henry only kind of lip-serviced from then on. Later, at the 1968 convention, with a truly integrated delegation, both Henry and King were seated.

The Congressional Challenge

The MFDP delegation was seated in 1968. I don't think a lot of people tie together the events that made this happen. I never saw the 1964 exploration as a lost cause, although many other people did. I believe if we had accepted those two seats in 1964, then 1968 would have been the lost cause. Because if we had accepted less than we went for, that's what we would have gotten and it wouldn't have gotten any better. Also, in between the two conventions there was the Congressional Challenge. The Congressional Challenge really frightened the powers that be.

After we were not able to convince the 1964 Democratic National Convention that we deserved to sit in the Mississippi delegation's seats, we had to fight another way—that was the point of the congressional challenge. We came back to Mississippi saying, "We'll fight another day." During the Reconstruction period of the 1860s and 1870s there were federal laws enacted that the Mississippi Constitutional Convention of 1890 ignored. One law stated that people can challenge the seating of congressional delegations if they can prove that the congressional representatives have been illegally elected.

We changed lawyers for this second challenge. We wanted lawyers who gave us the information and let us decide instead of making decisions for us. We took depositions in the process and tried to have them printed in the *Congressional Record.* In fact, I went to jail in D.C. because I went down to the House of Representatives to challenge the clerk, asking why they weren't printing our depositions in time for us to complete our process.

We challenged the seats of all the congressmen from all over Mississippi. When our challenge was voted on in Congress, the close outcome surprised the Mississippi congressmen. It shook them. It really shook them. They couldn't believe that as many of their colleagues stood up and voted on our behalf as did.* That vote just really turned things upside down. John Bell Williams, for example, the white congressman from Madison, the congressional district where Miss Devine was from, went back to the other white Mississippi congressmen and said, "You're going to have to do something, because if they come back again, they're going to win."

When he came back to Mississippi, Williams put the same word out. I believe it was this Congressional Challenge that made the white Mississippians know that business as usual was not going to continue. After that, some of the moderates in the regular Democratic Party began to take courage and reach out to us through whatever channels they thought they had. Their message was "We can talk. We need to talk. Let's see if we can't develop something acceptable." As a result, in 1968 we won the Democratic National Party Convention challenge. Our MFDP delegation was seated that time.

Dangerous Times in Mississippi: Vernon Dahmer's Death

One of my big allies was Mr. Vernon Dahmer, whom I had known most of my life. He drove my school bus when I was a little girl. It was his own school bus, since the county did not furnish black children any buses in the early days. I really got to know him as an adult through my business. When I would be in his community and stop at his house, I would just give up the day, because we would talk forever. We had a very good rapport.

Mr. Dahmer was a significant figure in the community. He was a very successful businessman, farmer, and political activist and had been one of

* Editors' Note: At the opening of the 1965 Congress, over a third of the representatives voted to bar the white Mississippi congressmen. See John Dittmer, *Local People: The Struggle for Civil Rights in Mississippi* (1994), 339–40.

the movers in the NAACP for years. After the Voting Rights Act, he had opened a store to make it convenient for the people in the community to come by and register to vote.

One day in 1966, after we had a meeting in Hattiesburg, Mr. Dahmer said, "Mrs. Gray, I got something I want to discuss with you. It's very important." "Okay," I said, "Can we discuss it when I get back? I'm on my way to South Carolina." He said, "It can wait. Give me a call when you get back. Okay?"

On the way back that Sunday night, Helen Anderson was driving and I dozed off to sleep in the car. I dreamt I had left my baby, Tony, on the riverbank while I went up the hill to get something, and there was a huge explosion. And I said, "Oh, my God! My baby! My baby!" Then I woke up and looked at the clock. It was about two o'clock. I wanted to tell Helen about the dream, but thought better about talking about something that terrible.

We reached Hattiesburg between six and seven o'clock in the morning. I had dropped Helen off and was taking Rev. Osmond H. Brown home when the news came over the car radio that Mr. Dahmer's place had been bombed and that he was in the hospital. When they mentioned the time of the bombing, I almost jumped out of the car, because it was the same time as when I woke up from my dream.

As soon as I got home, I called the hospital. Ann Taylor answered the phone and said Mr. Dahmer was doing pretty well. I asked if he wanted me to go to the hospital immediately, but he said I should get some sleep first. The phone rang after I'd fallen asleep. He was gone. Dead. Just like that.

Voter registration at his store was a threat to the white people. They may have wanted to harm him anyway for all his other civil rights activities, but registering voters seems to be what precipitated this bombing.

Dangerous Times and the Role of Women

When I was moving around the country, speaking on behalf of our challenge to the Democratic Party and other civil rights matters, the issue of women's leadership came up frequently. Many leaders of the MFDP were women. People wanted to know: Why is it that women are out front in the MFDP? Women were out front as a survival tactic. Men could not function in high-visibility, high-profile roles where we come from, because they would be plucked off. There would have been a lot more deaths like those of Vernon Dahmer and George Lee. Think about the black men of the early days of the Movement. Think about how many of them were killed simply because they went down and tried to register to vote or simply because they gave shelter to somebody. The women had to do it.

Dying isn't so bad, but dying and nothing is ever going to be done about it, that's foolish. That's very foolish. You don't sacrifice your life just for the heck of courageousness when you know nothing is going to come of it. Nobody's going to pay the price of having taken your life. Nothing is going to happen to discourage it from happening again and again. So that's what it was all about. That's why the women were out front. The white folks didn't see the women as that much of a threat. White thinking has always been, if you controlled the men, you got the rest of them covered. They didn't know the power of women, especially black women.

Yet the men were involved in less public ways. I knew some of the men in my community who appeared totally uninterested and uninvolved, but when night fell they set up guards at every entry route that could be taken to my house. I remember seeing them sitting there—they sat up on the nearby icehouse, watching. Besides, the men had to be willing for us to be active. Otherwise, you know, as wives and mothers and sisters and sweethearts, we couldn't have done it.

Some of the killings of black people were known and called what they were. Others were called accidents. But your life was in danger; you could be walking down the highway and somebody could come by and purposely bump you off and go on about their business. It would be called hit-and-run, not murder. Sometimes the targets were women. I escaped an attempt like that myself one night.

After I put my kids to bed, I had a habit of going up to see my aunt. I'd just sit and chat with my aunt and her family, relaxing from the day. I lived in a community surrounded by family, so I felt safe. One night I was on my way up there, and I saw a car coming down the road. Initially, I didn't think a thing about that car. Then something said to me, just as that car reached me, "Jump the ditch."

That car swerved out of its way to hit me. But I had jumped the ditch far enough out of the way so he couldn't hit me. He had all kinds of trouble trying to get his car straightened again. When the car passed, I didn't know what to do. I just stood there and I thought, *God, if I hadn't jumped that ditch, they would have found me here in the morning. And nobody would ever have known what happened.* I thought about the high number of hit-and-run deaths around the state, and I said, "That's what's been happening to these people." And I came within a hair's width of being one of them.

I went on up to my aunt's house. I was so shook. I told everyone what had happened. They said, "We done told you about not walking these streets at night!" They knew that I never locked my doors. They criticized me for that as well.

Reflections for Today

On James Meredith's March against Fear in 1966, when we came into Canton, Mississippi, we were gassed. We held a meeting that night. All of the big wheels were there, including Rev. Abernathy and Dr. King. I wondered, "Well, what are we going to ask for?" We were in a good bargaining position. The local authorities had blown it by using the gas. The first thing out of somebody's mouth was, "We want some black policemen."

I was mad as a whip that that's all they asked for, black policemen. I fumed, "I am so sick of people asking for black policemen, I don't know what to do." Everybody turned and asked, "What's wrong with black policemen?" I said, "There is nothing wrong with black policemen. They just don't have any kind of power. That's all. Policemen are nothing but tools in the hands of more powerful people. The people who are really in charge can use black policemen to do the same thing to you as the white policemen have been doing to you. This time they can feel good about it, because it's your own folks that's doing it. If you're going to ask for something, ask for something that can make a difference."

The strength of the Civil Rights Movement was in the fact that there were so many local people involved. We had marvelous high-profile national spokespersons, but the day-to-day work, the hanging in there was done by the local people. Once they were able to rise above their fear, they had the courage to stand up for what was rightfully theirs as citizens of this country. Local people made the difference.

To young people today, I would say, "Get to know everyday people. Make sure you acquire, to the degree possible, the wisdom and knowledge of these people. Everybody has something to say and something to offer. There should be an opportunity for that to happen. Make the information available and all of the sources accessible. Then hear what the people have to say. If you do, you will find, to borrow a phrase from Miss Ella Baker, 'Strong people don't need strong leaders.'"

VICTORIA GRAY ADAMS became head of the Hattiesburg Project and a full-time SNCC worker in 1962, remaining a member of the NAACP and later joining SCLC's board of directors. She was one of the first three women to run for U.S. Congress in Mississippi and the first woman to run for the U.S. Senate. Twice a military wife, Mrs. Gray Adams still remained a staunch anti-war activist. Besides Mississippi, she lived in several European countries; Thailand; Arlington and Petersburg, Virginia; as well as Baltimore, Maryland. She created social justice institutions and programs in all of these places and directed many of her efforts toward young people, including helping her middle son launch a charter school in Baltimore. A compelling public speaker, she traveled widely to share her Freedom Movement experiences. Several books and films document her work, most notably *Freedom on My Mind* and *Standing on Our Sisters' Shoulders*. The mother of a daughter and three sons, she nurtured her oldest son through his journey with AIDS. She made her final transition in August 2006.

"They Didn't Know the Power of Women" © 2010 by Rev. Cecil Gray

Do Whatever You Are Big Enough to Do

Jean Smith Young

A black Howard University student participates in Mississippi Freedom Summer.

The Freedom Vote

In the spring of 1964 I went to Hattiesburg, Mississippi, as part of a SNCC effort to organize a statewide Freedom Vote, one of the building blocks to the MFDP's August challenge of the regular Mississippi Democratic Party. The Hattiesburg Freedom Vote was held on the same day as the regular precinct elections. This very hot day started under the watchful eye of Miss Woods, a black lady somewhere between forty-five and seventy-five years old, who allowed us to use her rooming house on Mobile Street—the colored business street of Hattiesburg—as a meeting place. Sometimes we held special meetings upstairs, in the parlor decorated with thick red curtains and velvet settees, but mostly we used her large kitchen as a regular meeting place. She lived upstairs in quarters that I imagined to be very elegant and to which we were never invited. Miss Woods was a business lady.

Miss Woods was also a very proper lady. She was a thin, handsome, coffee-colored woman who always wore a delicate, white, starched blouse adorned with an old ivory brooch with intricate metalwork or a lace collar. She always had on stockings, no matter what time of the day or night you met her.

She had been political since the 1940s, when she and her husband had joined the "Black and Tan," the black Republican Party in this southeastern part of the state. They joined because of the blatant exclusion of blacks from the Democratic Party at that time. After the Black and Tan, Miss Woods had continued to work for black voting rights. She was willing to support any organization that was for voting, whether it was the NAACP or our younger, brasher organization, as long as we followed her house rules. She didn't want any foolishness. She wasn't the least bit interested in youthful exuberance, and she didn't allow any sexual liaisons in her boardinghouse. Miss Woods wanted you to know that she meant business. But after she thought you had gotten that message, she was a kind and nurturing woman.

On the morning of the precinct elections, Miss Woods came downstairs into the kitchen to wish us good luck. That morning she found just two people in her kitchen, project director Sandy Leigh and myself, eating grits and bacon. Her eyes swept the kitchen to make sure we had kept it clean. She disapproved of my Afro hairdo, but I could tell by the way the lines in her face softened when she talked to me that she actually liked me. Lately, when I had caught her unaware, I'd notice that she was looking at me with a special concern. I think she felt sorry for me because I was going with a man from the Movement who, as far as she was concerned, didn't mean me a bit of good. And I didn't have sense enough to figure this out. I'll call him Paul.

That morning Miss Woods looked at me with sadness as I explained that I was waiting for Paul, who was one of the early and legendary Mississippi field organizers and whose reputation stood ten feet tall. The two of us were supposed to lead the precinct meeting. I'd gotten it into my head that I couldn't start the precinct meeting without Paul.

But I didn't know where he was. I'd spent half the night looking for him in the blazing honky-tonk places that sprang to life after hours in the woods surrounding Hattiesburg. The following morning I sat drinking Sandy's really strong coffee and watching the clock above the stove. Eight o'clock and he still wasn't here; where could he be? Finally, at nine o'clock, Miss Woods got disgusted and said, "It's time for you to go, Jean. You got work to do. Don't wait on no man."

Miss Woods walked with me down the dark center hall that led from the kitchen to the front of her boardinghouse. I glanced briefly at the freshly made beds in the rooms on either side of the hall and hesitated a little. I wanted to stay with her and wait, but she wouldn't let me. With a pat on the back, Miss Woods basically pushed me out of her dark and supportive world and into the bright sunlight of Mobile Street. No more food and coffee. No more discussions. She pointed me toward the Masonic Hall—across the street and to the right, upstairs, above Mr. Fairlie's TV repair shop. It was time for me to go. I had a precinct meeting to run.

At 9:30 A.M. I walked up the stairs to the Masonic Hall and pushed open the door to the second story, which had been the meeting hall for the

NAACP and a center of black resistance for twenty years. The door was not locked, and I had the feeling that the room had been placed just there, waiting for me. It was a simple, rectangular room that could hold more than fifty people. The walls were bare except for a panel of purple velvet painted with ancient Egyptian symbols: a pyramid and the all-seeing eye. Secret orders of black Masons have shared these symbols with the secret orders of white Masons for hundreds of years. In Mississippi there seemed to be an unspoken agreement that within certain bounds the black Masonic halls would be safe from white intrusion. These halls would be places where blacks could meet and talk freely among themselves.

Our meeting was scheduled for 10:00 A.M. It was modeled on the white Democratic precinct meetings being held that month, which excluded black people. This was a historic moment and I was very excited. By this time I was a pretty good organizer, but I had never led a mass meeting. And neither I nor anybody I knew had ever led a precinct meeting to form a parallel political party. The task of the day was to explain, in language that the people would understand, the rationale for these meetings and then to conduct the vote. This was important, and I didn't want to be the one to botch it. Worried, I looked around the hall for Paul. *Where is Paul?* I wondered. *Could he be lying in a ditch somewhere, beaten senseless?*

And being all wrapped up in worrying about Paul, I didn't take definitive steps to take charge of the meeting. Instead I waited, hoping that either the meeting would take care of itself or Paul would miraculously appear.

It wasn't long before Mr. Fairlie came up from his TV repair shop on the first floor. He was a quiet, unassuming man in his fifties, who had been the NAACP representative in Hattiesburg for many years. "Beautiful day to be voting, isn't it, Miss?" he said as he came smiling into the room. "How many chairs must I set out?" This was his way of reminding me that it was time to start. For more than thirty minutes, while the twenty or so black people who had come to form an independent party sat singing and waving fans with vivid pictures of a white, suffering Jesus carrying his cross up a hill, I waited for Paul to come and run the meeting.

I knew that Paul talked in such an intense, powerful way he could move people by brute force. I felt that my orating skills were nothing in comparison to his. My intellectual self sneered at this indecision: "What are you standing around for, girl. It doesn't matter how good he is. He can't get votes if he's not here. You are gonna have to do this yourself." But my heart stood still, staring at the door, waiting.

After a while the farmers and city people started passing their fans down the aisle. It didn't look like any meeting was going to happen that day. I could feel the disappointment in the air, and I felt ashamed.

Then I felt the presence of Miss Woods in the room. I can't remember whether Miss Woods actually followed me from her boardinghouse and down the street to the Masonic Hall, or whether her spirit, her persona, went with me. The thought of Miss Woods—standing there in one of her best starched white blouses and an elegant gray suit from the forties, made of a fine wool blend, with a tailored jacket, fluted at the waist, and a long narrow skirt and carrying her copy of the Mississippi constitution—summoned up memories of all the strong women who had helped me to get to this point in life.

I remembered my quiet, thin anatomy teacher at Cass Technical High School, a science and arts school in Detroit. She was a white woman bent over with age, but with a bright, piercing glint in her eyes, who pulled me aside at the end of class one day and whispered, "Come to the lab before school opens tomorrow, Jean, I've got something to show you." Early the next morning, I stood before a huge beef heart in a shiny metal pan. "This heart is like a human heart, Jean. Examine the chambers. Notice the beauty of the valves and the thin cords that control them." She never told me why she had chosen me for this tutorial, and I never asked. The effect of it was to let me know that my dream of going to medical school could become reality. If another *woman* knew these things, *I* could know them, too. When I did go to medical school, I think this teacher went with me.

Right alongside my teacher came an image of Patricia Roberts Harris, the dean of women when I attended Howard University, who later became the first black head of the Department of Housing and Urban Development. In 1963 Dean Harris gave me a gold chain for my Phi Beta Kappa key from Howard University and told me that she expected I would do great things "for the race."

Finally, standing there in the Masonic Hall, was my mother, who had found herself a widow at the age of twenty-one, with two children under the age of two. My father, one of the Tuskegee Airmen, was killed while strafing a train in Germany, just a few months before the end of World War II. My mother had taken care of us and went on to become a nurse and then a teacher of the deaf. I do not remember one word of complaint from her about the difficulties in our life. She just did whatever she had to do.

In a remarkably short time the images of my mother with her laughing eyes, my dean of women, and my ancient anatomy teacher came to stand with me in the Masonic Hall, alongside the ageless and no-nonsense Miss Woods. In the presence of all these women who loved me and expected me to do well, my job became quite easy. I walked toward the front with the Freedom Democratic Party ballots. I took a deep breath and started talking. I forgot about my limited skills in comparison to Paul's magnificent oratory, and my words took wings. I explained that for months, SNCC—

along with CORE, NAACP, and SCLC staff, and seven hundred student volunteers—had been enrolling black people in the movement-created Mississippi Freedom Democratic Party. The MFDP was to serve as an alternative to the existing state Democratic Party, which excluded all black people, a parallel party. More than eighty thousand black Mississippians had registered to participate in the MFDP's Freedom Vote, thereby showing that large numbers of blacks would be a part of the political process, if allowed. Now we were following the rules for political parties in the state by having a precinct meeting and voting for delegates to the upcoming MFDP state convention to be held in Jackson, again shadowing the actions of the all-white Democratic Party's membership and demonstrating our legitimate right to represent black voters.

I was so excited with these grand ideas that I had to stop and make sure people were listening. Not only were they listening; but they were also rocking and nodding their heads and shouting, "Amen, sister," the sweetest sound I'd ever heard—Amen! to me, with me! I felt wonderful. Thirty minutes before, I had been tongue-tied and helpless. Now here I was connected to all these people; I was them and they were me. We were sharing a great vision.

One by one, those who felt prepared to take the next risk for freedom rose from their chairs and carefully approached the long table to pick up a ballot and vote. Those who didn't feel ready to go that far sat quietly and waited. At the table I explained the ballots and gave help if a person couldn't read and write. I felt a thrill of excitement each time a man or woman who had never voted in their lives stuffed a carefully folded freedom ballot into the homemade ballot box.

I was so excited that I didn't even think about Paul anymore. By one o'clock I had certified about fifty ballots, and by three o' clock I was on my way to carry them to the state capitol in Jackson, Mississippi, for the state-wide MFDP vote count.

That night in Jackson some of the lawyers who were down for the Freedom Vote took me to the black restaurant on Farrish Street. They took notes about the specifics of how I had conducted my portion of the vote. These notes would show that we had carried out the election in an orderly way, consistent with the standards of the national Democratic Party.

Then the lawyers treated me to a wonderful steak dinner. I can still see that steak on its long, white, oblong platter as the waiter brought it from the window in the back of the restaurant. I can still taste that meal. It was the taste of success. I had independently taken responsibility for my organizing assignment, and I didn't need some man to do it for me or with me. I had helped the Mississippi challenge to become an important part of history. Nothing could have spoiled that meal. It was the day I became an organizer in my bones.

Philadelphia, Mississippi

Soon after the precinct elections, in May 1964 I hitched a ride north to Oxford, Ohio, where a thousand volunteers were to be oriented for the massive Mississippi Freedom Summer Project. About the third day of the orientation, I was sitting next to Judy Richardson in the back of the Western College for Women auditorium. The hall was just large enough to hold the two hundred or so volunteers who had come for this training session. It was handsomely decorated in old, dark wood paneling. I scanned the room, trying to assimilate the new, mostly white volunteers into my thinking and feelings, but there were just too many of them. So I tuned in to Judy.

Judy and I know each other in a deep, abiding way. We can't remember ever being introduced or our first meeting. We've just always known and admired each other. My sort of Jungian theory is that we have a special radar system that connects us because of similar events in our pasts. We both had the misfortune of losing daring and creative fathers early in life and the good fortune of having powerful, intelligent, and driven mothers to carry on.

Both Judy and I got these messages: (1) Life is tough, and you can't depend on any man to take care of you; and (2) You are very much loved, but there'll be no pampering around here. Everyone must pull her own weight. From the beginning, Judy and I recognized and related to each other, across crowded rooms and in the middle of the most complicated and frightening situations. This radar that we have lets each of us know that the other can be depended on. There we were in the back of the auditorium in Oxford, just being related to each other and feeling right about it, when Bob Moses, the project director and architect of the Mississippi Summer Project, came out to speak.

Bob explained the project to the volunteers and informed them honestly about the dangers that were ahead. I didn't listen too closely when he talked about what might happen. After a year in SNCC I had gotten used to the atmosphere of danger and didn't think very often about dying. Instead of concentrating on Bob's facts about danger, I was more interested in watching his style and trying to learn how to model his delivery. Bob was good. No matter how determined he was about his own point of view, his presentation was the soul of humility. He rarely placed himself center stage, and this day was no different. He stood on the side of the stage, to the left of the audience. He talked in a conversational tone, so we had to strain to hear him. He paused often to let others speak. He answered all questions at length. He created the real feeling that we would remain in the auditorium for as long as it took to reach a common understanding.

Sitting next to Judy that afternoon, I had just relaxed into Bob's mood of mutuality and consensus when suddenly the atmosphere became electric with tension. Bob was called offstage for a few minutes. When he came back, his body was stiff and it seemed he was being propelled forward by about four staff members, including his wife, Dona. Then these staff members lined up next to Bob as he announced, in an unusually hesitant way, that three of our people—Andy Goodman, Michael Schwerner, and James Chaney— were missing in Philadelphia, Mississippi, and feared to be dead.

Dead! I had been moving around Mississippi in a cloak of denial, thinking that somehow I would be taken care of and wouldn't get hurt. Now the reality gripped me, and I was scared. I felt Judy next to me. She was scared, too. I felt the atmosphere in the auditorium. In the stunned silence the room felt cold and empty. It was awful. Fear had separated us and broken down the significant relationships by which I, at least, was defined. Judy was the only person in the world whom I still felt connected to.

So I said, "Judy, let's sing a song!" I knew she'd agree, because she and I were so much alike. Judy said, "Not me, girl. You do it." It really didn't matter which one of us did it. We were interchangeable. The silence and the emptiness continued. I searched the air for a song that would unite us, and the song came to me. I started walking from the back of the auditorium and toward the stage, singing.

> I don't know why
> I have to cry sometimes.
> I don't know why
> I have to cry sometimes.
>
> It would be a perfect day,
> But there's trouble all in my way.
> I don't why
> But I'll know bye and bye.

Everyone in the room learned that song in about a minute and joined in. By the time I got to the front of the auditorium, the frightened atmosphere had changed into one of resolve and we were together again.

Judy and I went to separate projects after the Oxford meeting. Later in the summer, as it became certain that the three workers were dead, I volunteered to be part of the team that would set up a new organizing project in Philadelphia, Mississippi, the town from which the SNCC workers had disappeared. After the Oxford orientation, Bob Moses had pointed out that SNCC had made a mistake by withdrawing from our position in McComb when Herbert Lee had been killed after he attempted to register to vote. Bob emphasized that we should not do this again.

We civil rights workers in Philadelphia stayed close together and focused on maintaining a presence in the face of organized violence. At first we met secretly in an abandoned schoolhouse in the woods that looked as if it had been built to teach freed slaves just after the Civil War.

Four of us were from CORE, because Philadelphia was in the congressional district where CORE had been doing the most organizing, and two of us were from SNCC. We set up headquarters in Philadelphia's black neighborhood, referred to by its residents as the "colored quarters." The office was on the second floor of a two-story building owned by Charles Evers, the brother of slain NAACP leader Medgar Evers. SNCC field secretary Ralph Featherstone decided that even though we were nonviolent we should do something to protect ourselves. So we strung barbed wire across the narrow stairs to at least make it hard for the Klan to surprise us. During the days, we canvassed the town and countryside, boldly making our presence known. Sometimes in the evenings we sat around in the freedom house and laughed at ourselves for being nonviolent in a place where all the white people wanted to kill us, and we made jokes about how much worse it would be once they got scratched up by the barbed wire.

Every night, Ralph walked me down the street to stay in the community. Because I was the only woman on the project and we were careful to respect the community standards, I didn't sleep at the freedom house with the men. Instead I spent my nights terrified in the front room of a two-room wooden house down the dusty road that was the main street for the "colored quarters." In the evenings my hostess would practically have to break into her own house after she came home from her "day work," because I used to wedge a chair against the door under the doorknob whenever I was alone. There were no such things as locks. The whole place was so fragile that a hard wind would have blown it down. I went to sleep terrified and each morning woke up grateful that I was alive. Each day, I fought my fear and did my work as a SNCC organizer.

After the three workers had been found dead, in addition to maintaining an obvious presence in Philadelphia, our main goal was to get people to try and register to vote and to openly attend a memorial service in nearby Meridian for the three dead workers. In addition, we tried to get the Native American people who lived around the county involved in the struggle. Neshoba County, where Philadelphia is located, had actually been named for the Indian people. Most of their ancestors had been driven out of Mississippi on the Trail of Tears when whites had decided that they wanted to farm the land themselves. The furthest we got with the Indian people was to talk to them at the baseball games that they and the black townspeople played on Sundays. At these times we were able to sit next to the Native Americans and explain why we were in Neshoba County. But they never seemed to get beyond their amazement that people who'd been treated as badly as black Mississippians would ever want to come back to Neshoba.

Fortunately, the white people in the county did not try to kill us. I think that in addition to the presence of the Justice Department and the FBI investigating the deaths of Goodman, Chaney, and Schwerner, the local whites really were so surprised that we'd show our faces after what they'd done to our comrades that they had to stop and think about what to do next. Early on in the project, I was caught alone in town by accident and was paced by silent white men in two sedans. All I had was a walkie-talkie that had no one on the other end to hear me. I put the thing up to my ear and pretended that I was talking to someone, and the cars moved away. To this day I don't know quite why they let me keep on walking.

In about a month we were able to find a church that would allow us to hold mass meetings even though the first church used for this purpose had been burned down. I formed friendships with black people on every block of the colored area. It felt good to know that at least I wouldn't be abducted and killed in silence.

At the end of the month we held the memorial service for our three brothers. The church was filled with local people and with civil rights dignitaries. Dave Dennis, from CORE, gave a heartrending sermon while Ben Chaney, James Chaney's little brother, sat crying into his mother's chest. Leontyne Price, the famous black opera singer, who was from the area, sang a beautiful spiritual. During the service I again felt this powerful relatedness to all my people, even to the Neshoba Indians, who never figured out why we would come there in the first place.

What Organizers Do

My experiences in SNCC strengthened me as a person and taught me some essentials of what organizers do. Although I can't give a road map to organizing, I can share these conclusions about the process. I believe that once they have chosen a righteous goal, organizers must face fear and must model bravery for others. Organizers have to maintain trusting and dependable relationships with the local people and with one another, no matter what else is going on in their lives. Finally, whenever possible, organizers should use music and art to communicate.

I also learned that my relationships with other SNCC workers strengthened me. There is a theory that a woman is functional, effective, and happy in the world to the extent that she is able to call on her strength as one in relation to others, and to actualize this experience. This posture of being in relation to others was the central fact in my organizing work in SNCC, and it has carried on into my adult working life, first as a teacher and then as a psychiatrist.

I would say that to the extent I was successful as an organizer it was because I maintained close and open relations of mutual dependence with the people I was trying to organize and with my co-workers in SNCC. Even though the language may come from women's psychology, I'm sure this was not just a female thing. I believe the men in SNCC valued this relatedness as much as the women.

I also believe it is amazing that SNCC existed as long as it did in light of the powerful historical and political forces arrayed against us. Our survival is testimony to the strength of human bonds and relationships. And when the light went out in SNCC, the signal for the coming darkness was that we began to lose the enduring bonds between us.

I cannot end without saying something about the controversy over the role of women in SNCC: I never felt discriminated against as a woman in this organization. In fact, I felt and experienced just the opposite. SNCC was a liberating experience for me as a woman. The staff, including Stokely Carmichael, always treated me as an esteemed member of the team and always encouraged me to stretch my wings and fly. In the SNCC that I knew the message was "Do whatever you are big enough to do."

JEAN SMITH YOUNG remained a SNCC field secretary until 1967, taking only a short break to finish undergraduate school. In SNCC she served as a field secretary, community organizer, and campus traveler. She returned to Washington, D.C., where she obtained a master's degree and taught at the University of the District of Columbia. She then went to medical school and became a board-certified child and adolescent psychiatrist. She has worked with a number of community-oriented mental health programs serving special populations, such as foster children and mentally ill juvenile offenders. She has instructed medical residents at Georgetown and Howard universities. In addition to her medical work, she is actively and joyfully engaged in the education of her seven grandchildren. Her articles and stories have appeared in *Black-Eyed Susans and Midnight Birds: Stories by and about Black Women*, edited by Mary Helen Washington; *Black Fire: An Anthology of Afro-American Writing*, edited by Amiri Baraka and Larry Neal; and in *Negro Digest*, *Redbook*, and *The New Republic*.

Depending on Ourselves

Muriel Tillinghast

Less than a month after graduating from college, a young woman finds herself in charge of a SNCC project in Mississippi.

Project Director

Three days after I graduated from Howard University in June 1964, I decided I was going to Mississippi. I didn't know what was going to happen after that, but I was definitely going to "the Sip." For years I had let my hair grow in its natural state and was associated with the Movement. That alone limited my circle of friends and immediately cut down all talk in my house to an absolute minimum. By the time I had made up my mind to go south, no one in my family was talking to me.

I was basically a northerner. People from Washington, D.C., like to think they are from the North, whether it is reality or not. By the time of my departure, I had gained significant organizing experience in Washington, D.C., Maryland, and Delaware. I had demonstrated on the Eastern Shore of Maryland and along U.S. Route 40 (formerly the main artery servicing the diplomatic corps who drove between their embassies in Washington, D.C., and their consulates at the United Nations in New York City). The Eastern Shore was a cauldron of racial hostility, but it did not prepare me for the state of Mississippi.

We spent a week at the orientation center in Oxford, Ohio, getting ready for something no one could really prepare for. We were taught to take Mississippi seriously, to respect our hosts and our contacts, to understand the risks they were taking and that they might be the ones to save our lives. Then we headed south in Greyhound buses. People sang and spoke quietly among themselves. Everyone was pensive. These would be the last relaxed thoughts and movements we would have for weeks to come. Once we hit the Mississippi state line there was silence. It was past midnight and we had not been told exactly where we would be assigned. Most of us were dropped off in small groups. The local people whose silhouetted forms met the summer volunteers hurriedly escorted their charges from the pickup point, disappearing silently into the starlit Mississippi night. I was dropped off in Green*ville,* not Green*wood*—both are in the Mississippi Delta, but Greenwood was known for its hard-edged racism and active Klan activities.

Greenville was a river town that enjoyed local distinction as being "liberal"—
that is, liberal for Mississippi. In Greenville I still had hope.

I spent my first two weeks in the upstairs office of the Greenville Project. I was petrified. How was I going to survive Mississippi? It dawned on
me that I would never get anybody to register to vote staying in the office,
so s-l-o-w-l-y I started coming downstairs and cautiously going out into the
town. I walked like a shadow on the wall, edgy, just getting used to walking
in the streets.

The Greenville Project answered to Stokely Carmichael (who later became Kwame Turé), the district head who worked out of Greenwood. My
direct project head was Charles Cobb, "Charlie" to everybody. About two
weeks after I got my "legs," Charlie informed me that he wanted to do something else. It was time for him to move on. So he said, "I'm going to leave
you in charge. You look like you can handle it." I thought, *Right, sure!*

The volunteers, both local and northern-bred, and I developed a routine
of sorts and defined our work and roles. Our day started around 4:30 in the
morning; we wanted to get to the cotton and day workers before daybreak
so that we could talk to them without immediate fear of economic harm.
I didn't realize it at first, but we were under constant surveillance. Once, a
young white volunteer from our project was leaving the city library, which
was located in the same building as the police station. The police chief
stopped her, took her to a room, and showed her a file drawer with pictures of
everyone in our project. They had pictures of every kind of activity, taken by
day and even at night, because they were using infrared. When this became
known, one of the young gay men from our project left, saying tearfully,
"Muriel, I can't have those pictures shown." It was sad for both of us; he
was a good organizer.

The Greenville Project area included Washington, Issaquena, and Sharkey counties. Part of our Oxford training required that organizers learn the
political and physical structure of each Mississippi county—its roads and
every possible means out of town, places to avoid, how the county operated,
people and resources that might be reachable. This you needed to know like
the back of your hand. Your life depended on it.

A rural state, Mississippi's politics were county-based and local. Greenville, the center of our operations, was the Washington County seat. It was
the only town in a county of hamlets. Just down the road from us, about
forty-five minutes away, stood Issaquena County on the river and Sharkey
County on an inland border. Issaquena was a predominantly black county,
and Sharkey County was the home of the Klan in this part of the state.
Learning about Mississippi taught us up close and personal about politics

and power. We learned that power could be monolithic, an inbred, jealously operated means of control, where new ideas and new people were not allowed to participate. That cabal of power would do anything to stay in power, and we were there to encourage opposition to it.

Life in a rural setting is fairly humdrum. Aside from hard work, there wasn't much to break the daily cycle of work, once a week food and dancing at the juke joint, church on Sundays, and then more work. In these little country towns any unfamiliar sound was noticeable. With an unusual car sound, people knew immediately that a stranger was there. Even if the sound came in the middle of the night, someone still knew. "I heard a different motor last night. It stopped about two doors down the street." Then there would be inquiries. Next, on a number of occasions, the police would just walk through folks' doors looking for us. Sheriff Davis and his deputy never said a word to the people of the house; they just moved around checking. The police were not intent on harming us at that point; they were just verifying the information they'd received. Local black people were not supposed to associate with people who weren't local, and this was the way the police issued a warning to those who did.

Encouraging people to vote in Mississippi was unlike most of my prior organizing activity, yet it called on everything I had learned up to that point. Mississippi was proud of its cruelty toward black people and provided such a threatening environment for black residents around the exercise of basic human rights that voting wasn't even on the list of possibilities. For better or worse, however, the vote is a cornerstone of democracy, and without it Mississippi's black population would continue to be outside the political framework. When we started organizing people to register, at first the "system" would only allow for a few people to be registered each day. Sometimes the courthouse closed for unannounced "emergencies." Gradually, as local people came to trust us, they would talk to their neighbors, and the numbers of people willing to try to register swelled.

When we could, we examined the voter rolls and found that many of the names were bogus. In Issaquena, for example, more than half of the names of white voters on the voter rolls were names from the local cemetery.

Into the Heart of the Black Belt

Later I moved from Greenville and into Mayersville, the county seat of Issaquena County. The county is long and very sparsely settled. Counting everybody standing up and a few chickens, Mayersville had about fifty people. Unita Blackwell, a housewife who later became mayor of Mayersville, and her husband, Jeremiah Blackwell, along with the Sias family, were among the first ones to offer SNCC workers a safe haven there. We worked, family by family, person by person. Once a person had a sense of the Movement and of us, they would introduce us to the next contact. We were functioning in warlike conditions. As a rule, we did not talk to anybody unless someone we knew said it was okay. Even at that, people's ultimate allegiance might mean you were still talking to the Mississippi State Sovereignty Commission, an intelligence force that used black and white taxpayers' money to gather and spread ruinous information and lies about civil rights activists to undermine movement work.

We had to be careful about talking to people and about what we discussed when we canvassed, because everything and almost everyone could be traced. Wherever we were staying, those people were just as vulnerable day and night to raids and attacks on the streets as we were. When they allowed us to sleep on their floors or in their beds, whatever the accommodations were, black Mississippians were risking economic reprisals, the loss of their jobs, or worse. We stayed with people who were just barely getting by themselves, yet they were willing to risk all to allow us to bring the message of their rights and the Movement to them.

One family of cotton pickers that I stayed with in Hollandale—two adults and five children—worked by permission on someone else's land. They worked from sunup to sundown with no breaks. It was as close to slavery as I hope I ever see in life. I usually ate elsewhere or not at all, but one night they said, "No, you eat with us." I'll never forget that dinner. It was cornbread and a huge pot of water into which they cut three or four frankfurters. For them that was a special dinner; on other days their meals were even more meager. Rarely have I ever been the beneficiary of such generosity and kindness.

The Impact of a Freedom School

We started a Freedom School. Out of natural curiosity schoolchildren wanted to know, "Why can't we vote?" To answer this, there was a need to put voting and our current registration efforts into a historical context. As we talked about the history of black people in this country, a change took place in our listeners, young and old. Before, they had not challenged what they were taught in school, but with our presence they found the courage and the personal strength to speak up, to challenge certain information, and to bring other information into the classroom. Things were slowly beginning to change in the Plantation South. Even so, every day one or another of these Freedom Schoolers was sent home from the local school and told, "Don't come back!" Before long we had a class of fifteen to twenty children every day.

Why were these black students in black schools expelled? In Mississippi one didn't get to be a principal in a black school unless one was politically acceptable, a known quantity, someone who would not "rock the boat." A principal quickly became *unacceptable* when he or she started having alien thoughts such as, *Why can't we register to vote?* and *What is this grandfather clause anyway?* These thoughts were, by Mississippi standards, alien and subversive. The political cabal with which black principals cooperated wanted to pluck out these "diseased" ones before the cancer of freedom and hunger for democracy took over the rest of the student population.

You Will Not Move Up

Even though Issaquena was a majority black county, all the people who had any power were white, including Sheriff Davis. When our paths crossed, we would greet each other—"How ya doin'?"—because Mississippi is country and people knew each other anyway. The first time I saw Sheriff Davis he had a pickup truck. By the next week the pickup truck had a grated metal cage on the truck's bed. He stopped me and Louis Grant, a black volunteer from New York, hollered out the window, and pointed to the cage, saying, "You like that, you like what I got? Well, that's fo' y'all."

Sheriff Davis's construction continued. He built a one-room jail out of cinder blocks smack-dab in the middle of a field without a branch for shade. "Do you like that?" The "jail" was just big enough to stand up in or sit down; there was no pacing space and, of course, no sanitary amenities like a toilet—just cinder block in the scorching Delta sun. When we told him he was wasting his time, Davis said, "Well, I know you're gonna do something. I know you are, and I'm going to keep up with you." Sometimes when we would walk the county (rides were hard to come by, and cars were even harder!), Davis would ride up behind us and keep pace with us while we walked along. He wanted to see where we were going. Louis and I would stop and admire the scenery, stalling until Davis moved on. Sometimes he would sit in the car and wait. He always tried to guess where we were going. Sometimes we would go past the intended person's house and go to somebody else's house in the back, because we didn't want to lead him directly to our next possible registrant. If we couldn't shake him, we would leave our visit for another day.

It may be difficult to understand today what local people risked when they took those steps toward freedom and equality. The history of black people in Mississippi is written in blood. As soon as a potential black voter went to the courthouse to register, their employers or "bosses" would often be right there. If the "bosses" were not at the courthouse, they were still informed immediately that "their" worker had taken this step—a step too far. If the people worked in the cotton fields, often they were dismissed immediately, losing both their means of employment and their homes. If they were receiving food through the Commodity Surplus Food Program, suddenly they would be cut off. Occasionally prospective black voters were beaten, arrested on false pretenses, or killed. The power system was consolidated, monolithic, entrenched, and resistant to any notion of change. No, no, no, not you. *You* will not move up. *You and your kind* will not change this system; you will not challenge us in any way!

By the fall of 1964 we began to look at other things aside from general voting—for example, how the local power structure obtained its cash flow. There were white gentlemen farmers who planted nothing but made an awful lot of money. Then there were black people who were planting cotton, and if they owned it they were barely able to get it ginned. Early on, we began to deal with the cotton allotment system set up under the U.S. Department of Agriculture. The Cotton Allotment Board determined federal subsidies to farmers. When we ran candidates for local cotton allotment boards, that hit the economic bell, which, in turn, brought out the Klan. In Mississippi the Klan had rivals and almost looked benign compared to some of the more rabid, racist organizations in the state, like the Association for the Preservation of the White Race, who made no bones about pledging to kill a civil rights worker if one were spotted. Nice people!

One time I called a meeting to organize black tractor workers. I walked right dead into a group of white men who had learned of the meeting somehow and were expecting a meeting of white tractor workers. They knew something was wrong because the meeting was at a black church, and they didn't look happy. I kind of looked at them, and I knew immediately that they were the type willing to do harm to civil rights workers; they kind of looked at me, trying to figure out who I was. I said, "You here for the meeting?" And they said, "Yeah. You called the meeting?" I said, "No. I'm just looking for the person who called the meeting." A white volunteer named Russ was with me. He and I, though terrified, walked slowly back to our car showing great confidence, got in the car, backed it up out of there, and deliberately drove off at moderate speed.

All of us learned how to be patient, how to read the situation, because your life could turn on a dime. Later you might laugh, but at the time it wouldn't seem so funny. Once I backed into a police car. Again, Russ was with me. The car was a stick shift and we were on an incline. Being a very new driver, I was not adept at managing the clutch and the brake, so the car rolled back, damaging the police car behind us. I knew I had to play this one or it might turn into a dangerous situation. I jumped out of my car, acting incensed, acting like a crazy lady, carrying on about this and that. Poor Russ just cringed—he knew we were dead meat. The policeman got out of his car, surveyed the damage (and there was plenty); but rather than deal with a crazy black woman, he gave me a look of disgust and just told me to get a move on.

Life Lessons

One of the things I have learned about doing the work of the Movement is that everything is political and each step is serious. You may not know *how serious* the step you're taking is, but when the opposition believes you are trying to shift the "balance of power," they will always attack, and their attack is *always* serious. We had so many near misses, so many close calls, and we had nobody to depend on but ourselves.

As a result of movement activism, Mississippians died by the score. I learned that black people in Mississippi are a very special group. I witnessed incredible wisdom and extreme courage. Sometimes I rode with a local resident who was a placid, nondescript kind of guy. I did not like riding with him, because I felt if we were ever in a dangerous situation, I was going to be on my own. One day we were riding down the road, and I said to him, "Do you have anything in this car in case we get stopped?" With a perfect poker face, he said, "Open up the glove compartment." Then, "Check down underneath the seat on my side, and on your side. Listen, we may not survive, but we sure could blaze a few holes." I said, "That's the way I want to go."

In SNCC we always encouraged people to read and understand things for themselves. We always encouraged people to discuss. Nothing we did was cloaked in any kind of secrecy, which is the way I have continued to operate. On the whole, I think we were very successful. We paid some very, very high prices for our gains—lives lost, mental and physical damage, economic and social destabilization, governmental enmity and invasion—but I think without a doubt most of us would do it again without hesitation.

"And the day came when the risk it took to remain tight in the bud was more painful than the risk it took to blossom"—Anaïs Nin.

MURIEL TILLINGHAST has remained an active advocate of appropriate institutional responses to family violence, especially against women and children, since her tenure as an instructor at Atlanta University's School of Social Work in the early seventies. She was an advocate for tenants' rights, working as an organizer with Jesse Gray and as an administrator in New York City's Department of Housing Preservation and Development. She served as a prison educational administrator at the Brooklyn House of Detention and Rikers Island and as the executive director for a Head Start organization. A charter board member of the National Organizers Alliance, Tillinghast was an active participant in the Green Party, USA, working on environmental and social justice issues and running as Ralph Nader's vice presidential partner in New York State in 1996. She assisted Joanne Grant with the distribution of the film *Fundi: The Story of Ella Baker*. Currently she is the interim general manager of Pacifica Radio station WBAI in New York City. She is the mother of two daughters.

A Grand Romantic Notion

Denise Nicholas

A college student from Michigan finds her calling and her voice during the Mississippi Summer Project.

Getting There

There's a feistiness about people from Detroit that my friends in California recognize. "Oh," they exclaim, "those Detroit women are *bad!*" The life my brother and I experienced growing up in Detroit was enriching and strengthening. As youngsters we saw black people in positions of responsibility and authority: teachers, lawyers, doctors, and police officers. Then there was the music, not just Motown, but extraordinary jazz, also reinforcing a black culture and aesthetic.

My father used to tell us stories about his youth in the late 1930s and early 1940s. He often talked about the Detroit race riot of 1943. He told these stories with humor, saying the white boys tried to do *x, y,* and *z* to us and we did *x, y,* and *z* to them. What he was teaching, without saying it directly and without preaching, was a way of being in the world that you don't allow people to do certain things to you with impunity.

At the University of Michigan I heard other stories, stories of southern student activism. Even though Michigan was a white campus with just a few black students, there was enough information coming in to keep us up to date about what was going on in the South. Michigan was (and still is) a very sophisticated campus, idyllic in appearance, but hardly isolated. Tom Hayden was there; people like Stokely Carmichael came to speak on campus. There was an active NAACP branch in Ann Arbor. My very political friend

Martha Prescod and I helped set up a tutoring project for local elementary and high school students designed to get them on a college prep track. Coming from a place like Detroit and going to college in Ann Arbor, when I read and heard stories about what was happening in the South, that other black people were being denied certain things and being pushed down, it just got me going.

Another highly provocative incident that I never forgot was seeing as a very young girl the *JET* magazine photo spread of Emmett Till. Those images were branded on my brain and remain there as if I'd seen them only yesterday. When I was doing research for my novel, *Freshwater Road,* I went to the library and looked at that issue of *JET* to see if my memory was true. It was.

Everything coalesced for me when I took a semester off to go to New York in 1963. Going to New York—without parents—was a necessary rite of passage for some students. New York was the mecca. We had to go to New York, just as other students had to go to Florida. While in New York, I went to a party where I met Gil Moses and other students who had already spent time in Mississippi and were talking about basing a touring theater there. Gil wrote music and played the guitar, spoke French fluently, and talked about movies I had never even heard of. He had studied at the Sorbonne and had also worked with Jean Vilar in his French touring theater.

Gil believed that this kind of theater would work in Mississippi: take the theater to the people. Infuse that theater with a historical and political point of view and, at the same time, keep the artistic conventions of traditional theater. That's basically the foundation of the Free Southern Theater.

I had no interest in acting when I went to New York. Running into Gil and the other theater people at a party was just happenstance. At that time I had two career plans: plan A was to go to law school, and plan B was to teach. That's what we were told as women in those days, "If all else fails— teach." Then I was at that party and Gil Moses was talking about the movie *Black Orpheus.* Here was this brilliant black man who was an artist. And I thought, *What is this?* It was so extraordinary to me that he was an artist and he was political, a new kind of person to be in the world. I didn't know what that was. I hadn't been exposed to that kind of person in real life or in my reading. Although I was always a reader, very much interested in writing and literature, I thought of these kinds of things as hobbies, not careers. I did have fantasies about being a person of the whole world. I could see myself in the foreign service, in the Peace Corps. I didn't know at that point that I wanted to be an artist, or a person who lives through the arts, but it was pulling me. At school I found myself taking more art history than political science and going to cultural events on campus.

That there was a way to be politically involved and also be an artist was very important to me. I don't really know how much I understood at the time. These were feelings, impressions. There was something grand about the idea of the Free Southern Theater, something idealistic and so romantic. Someone will play the guitar; we'll sing, we'll play, and we'll bring the people in. This was like something out of a dream and was the final pull for me. I was absorbing all of these things, trying to find myself, too, when I went back to Ann Arbor right after Kennedy was killed. I did another semester of school, and in June 1964 I took the train to Mississippi from Ann Arbor by myself, with a little green book bag. I went to Chicago on the train, changed trains, and went south to Jackson, which is the opening geography of my novel *Freshwater Road*.

When I first arrived, alone and scared—my first time in the Deep South—it felt as if I had landed on another planet or stepped back in time. Then I began meeting all these other young people from all over the country, which quickly helped build up my strength and courage. Then I met local people. Pretty soon I was in it. I was home.

Mississippi Spirit

The Free Southern Theater (FST) was in the beginning stages when I arrived in Jackson. We were operating out of Tougaloo College and the Council of Federated Organizations (COFO) office in Jackson. SNCC folk had mixed feelings about a theater. Some people felt the theater and the arts, basically, were frivolous in the face of what needed to be done in terms of voter registration. They couldn't see how it would help or how it could be anything but a nuisance to have us running around all over the place with our sets, props, and costumes. It was an interesting challenge even from the inside. Gil and John O'Neal (co-founder of the FST) and Doris Derby had put out the word that they were looking for people among the summer volunteers who were theater majors or who had an interest in the theater. That's how we got the first group. I wasn't there as an actress; I was reading scripts and writing critiques. After much heated provocation from actress-activist Madeleine Sherwood, John and Gil decided to do Martin Duberman's play *In White America* that summer. They needed a black actress for the play and asked me to read for it. I read, though I didn't know what I was doing. They said, "Well, that's good enough." What a start!

By the time I arrived in Jackson, James Chaney, Andy Goodman, and Mickey Schwerner were missing. We were afraid, but I think because everybody believed very much in what we were doing, we tightened up and we just kept going. We went all over Mississippi that first summer, performing in seventeen cities. They found those boys on August 4. I remember, from pictures or television, seeing these white sheriffs with body bags, like Vietnam body bags, bringing in the remains. I have that in my head, right with the Emmett Till photo. Those visuals never, ever go away. There were other unforgettable moments when Rita Schwerner, Mickey Schwerner's wife, who was also working in Mississippi that summer, came to a number of our performances and spoke at the churches where we were. Her fragile appearance contrasted with her strength as she stood there assuring us that she would not leave Mississippi that summer but would stay and do the work we all had come to do.

That first summer there was violence everywhere. We could feel it in the air all the time. Even when we were dancing and letting off steam in some Dew Drop Inn with a jukebox that was leaning over three feet to the side, danger was always part of the equation. It was always there. In McComb someone threw a bomb at the stage. In another location—Holmes County, I think—men with shotguns sat on the porch all night guarding us while we slept.

Once we performed in a half-finished community center building. Some young builders from California had come out to reconstruct it after the original one had been bombed. When we performed, half the roof was there, the posts were there, but the walls were not up yet. It was incredible and beautiful. We did *In White America* in that space, and local people guarded us while we performed. Our performances were held in the early evening. We had to follow all the regulations and rules coming out of Jackson, just as the COFO and SNCC workers did, as far as being on the road—for example, making sure the cars were serviced, because you didn't want to have a breakdown on the road in a rural area; driving a little bit under the speed limit; and being very, very polite with people all the time. We walked around with our necks so stiff from tension. We were having this extraordinary experience, but at the same time we were also always riding on top of terror, constantly trying to leap up on top of our own fear and do the things we were there to do.

The Free Southern Theater toured towns where there was a COFO project, places like Canton, Greenville, Meridian, and Hattiesburg. People on our staff worked with the COFO people in the towns we went to. Our housing, how things would be set up, what church we would perform in, publicity, all of these kinds of necessities were worked out between our staff, the local people, and the COFO volunteers in that particular town. COFO workers and local people helped us with advertising by handing out flyers. Young people from the town helped us unload the equipment, do the setup, then helped us take it down and load it onto the truck. Older people in these communities housed and fed us; they really took care of us.

In most of the communities we toured to, the local people had no conception of the conventions of the theater. Often people spoke to us from the audience during performances. During one tour we were doing a one-act that Gil Moses had written, and in that play my character, Dottie, is onstage trying to open a jar but can't get it open. The husband character takes it, but he can't open it either and gives it back to her. Dottie tries again. At that point, an older, slightly built man came right up on the stage from the audience and said, "I'll help you," took the jar, and opened it. It was so sweet and kind. Things like that happened all the time.

People reacted with joy to our performances. They were happy to have us there and said so. I think it was all a part of the world opening to them, letting them know that we cared enough to come see about them. It was beautiful. It was beautiful to be in the place, to be there. We had discussions after all the performances, so people had an opportunity to voice what they got from the experience of the play and how it and we connected to their lives and how we connected to the political changes that were going on in the South. The theater, like literature, can be a tool of community, of illumination of the human condition.

There was so much energy that first summer in Mississippi; even backwater, teeny-weeny little places picked up the zeal of what was going on in the whole state. In a sense it was like the entire state was in performance. It was uplifting, very uplifting. That whole summer was an incredible moment. We went to places like Mound Bayou, an all-black town with no paved streets. As a young woman from Detroit and Ann Arbor, I saw how poor, rural, and forgotten some places were, but at the same time I saw how wonderful these people and these places were. The spirit was so strong. It was us picking up their spirit and giving back what we had. It was an exchange, a pure exchange.

I was always very shy. It is hard to believe now, because theater made me into a talker. Theater is a group experience, which gave me courage and helped me to develop a personality. I don't think I projected a whole lot; I wasn't pushed through to myself until I'd worked for a while in the theater. I've heard other actors say this also, that the theater experience, the act of doing it, this group experience, developed them as personalities.

New Orleans

Gil Moses and John O'Neal decided that Mississippi was so hard, so harsh and unrelenting that we would probably do better basing the theater in New Orleans and touring into Mississippi. However, the worst incident I experienced personally took place in New Orleans. We had two apartments in a building on Burgundy Street (Bur-GUN-dy, as black people say). SNCC people would come in and use the apartments for rest and relaxation days. On this weekend there were a bunch of SNCC folk in town, and two SNCC photographers went across the street to a little store to get cigarettes. There was a shoeshine stand directly opposite that the police used. Watching from one of the apartment balconies overlooking the street, I saw the two photographers go over to the corner store and come back out, but they never came up the stairs to the apartment. I thought, "Oh, my God, something has happened!" so I walked downstairs. As I walked out the door, a cop pulled his gun out and put it to my head, saying, "If you take one more step, I will blow your effing brains out." You pay attention to something like that.

I thought, *Oh, God, this is it.* I could see the photographers in the back of the police car that was pulled up on the curb under the balcony. I just stood there. I couldn't move. I've never been so frightened in my life. I remember thinking, *I hope I don't pee on myself out here.* I prayed, *I hope I don't die right here on this street.* After a few terrifying minutes, other people from the Free Southern Theater came downstairs and the cop let me go. Although the photographers had identification and money, the police arrested them for vagrancy. Correctly assuming the photographers were bringing film out of Mississippi to send it north for newspapers and other media outlets, the police broke their cameras and took their film. Of course, the police weren't just getting their shoes shined, they were watching the apartment. They were there to keep track of us and to harass us.

There were funny moments, too. Quite a few times when we, an integrated group from the theater, went to restaurants in New Orleans, the waiters would serve the black members but not the white. They set out the place settings and gave menus to the black people, but not to the white people. When we asked, "What are you doing?" they replied, "The law says we *have* to serve black people, but there's no law says we *have* to serve white people." Of course, we'd leave without eating.

During the first year when we were operating out of New Orleans, we performed in Bogalusa, Louisiana. Bogalusa's up near Poplarville, very close to the Mississippi border. There was a chapter of the Deacons for Defense and Justice there. The police arrested two Free Southern Theater members, one black and one white, and impounded the theater's car and released them in the middle of the night, very much like what had happened to Chaney, Goodman, and Schwerner. So we had to go looking for them at night, which was absolutely terrifying. We didn't know if this was a ploy to get us out and in harm's way as well. When the arrested ones were released, they ran and hid in the woods, figuring the police would call the

Klan or some other similar group and tell them where the Free Southern Theater people were. So with the help of one of the Deacons for Defense, we scouted around, trying to find them, whistling, flashing lights. Eventually they came barreling out of the bushes, scared to death, and climbed into the car, shivering and shaking in fear.

We had heard from local people there that the sheriff was very rough on black people. I went with a white lawyer from the National Lawyers Guild in New York to get the car out of the impound so that we could leave town. We wanted to get the hell out of there. We went into city hall and walked into the sheriff's office. The sheriff picked the lawyer up by the lapels, lifted him right up in the air, and threw him down the hall. He chose the lawyer, whom he'd identified as a "nigger lover," rather than me, just a regular old "nigger." The lawyer's briefcase went flying, papers scattered. I just stood there shaking. Finally we gathered the papers and briefcase and proceeded to get the Free Southern Theater car out of impound.

When we moved to New Orleans, I enrolled in Tulane because I wanted to finish school, but the theater was starting up again, and I thought, *Ooh, I'd rather do that than go to school,* so I dropped out of Tulane and went on tour again. On that second tour I believe we did *Purlie Victorious.* That was great fun. In one town we performed the play right next to a cotton field. There's a scene where a character comes running through the rows of cotton pitching cotton bolls into the air. It was real cotton. It was wild. The theater, *Purlie* in particular, allowed for another way of venting—through comedy—and people loved it. They laughed and laughed.

The next fall we did *Waiting for Godot,* Samuel Beckett's play. When we toured to Ruleville, I stayed with Mrs. Fannie Lou Hamer. Well, we had to sleep on the floor, because her house was being shot into all the time. We slept this way a lot, but it was particularly important in Ruleville and particularly important staying at her home, because she was definitely a target. I remember sleeping on the floor, just out from under the bed. No wonder my mother didn't talk to me for ten years!

Godot is a very difficult play, with sparse language, and there are such stark images in the piece, not the least of which is one of a slave with a rope around his neck being pulled by another man who is as enslaved as the other. During the discussion Mrs. Hamer took over the theater and spoke. She keyed in on the word *waiting* and wound it around in a way to stimulate and motivate people. She began, "Well, we know something about waiting, don't we?" I have never forgotten her opening comment!

Everybody did every job in the theater, carrying sets and props, acting, and audience development. Generally speaking, our duties rotated. Sometimes I drove a station wagon or a small truck; other times I unloaded and set up equipment. Actresses received no special treatment, and there certainly was no star system. The thirty-five dollars a week we received for expenses didn't allow for that.

At the same time, the four people who ran the theater were men—John O'Neal, Gil Moses, and eventually Richard Schechner and Tom Dent. It was male-based, male-dominated in terms of the leadership. Still, I did not hesitate to express my opinion as did the other women. I was very vocal in meetings, and, believe me, we had meetings all the time! Everybody had meetings in the '60s: meetings, meetings, meetings on top of meetings, and talk, talk, talk. Everyone was free to speak at the Free Southern Theater's company meetings; we all voiced our opinions, and the meetings were long!

Pretty much all of my life my way has been to experience the world and be in the world as fully as possible. Learn as much as you can. Do as much as you can. I don't know if it crept in and became a codified kind of a thing before or after the Movement. I guess I was already thinking that way, or I wouldn't have been there in the first place.

When the black power movement took hold in the late sixties, we went through an extraordinary, raging change. The Free Southern Theater had always been a mixed group, and there were a couple of white people who had been integral to making this project happen. People you'd come to know and love were suddenly being excluded. It was a very, very difficult time. The Movement was changing, and we had to change with it. It wasn't long after that, September 1966, that I moved to New York.

Riding the Freedom Train

As a professional actress, I did not take roles that I thought diminishing to me as a black woman or diminishing to the status of black people in the world. My father, Otto Nicholas, taught me this idea. He loved my career in show business probably more than anyone else in my family, but that was one of the rules I had to follow. Another was no nudity. My experience in the Movement supported this kind of thinking. Also the fact that I was a reader, that I had some knowledge and understanding of American history and our history in America, meant I had to discern whether or not a role would cause discomfort for my father, his peers, and really for myself. These films and TV shows don't go away. So there are a lot of roles I didn't or couldn't do. For me that was okay. I reasoned I could always work somewhere. That's the Detroit in me. My dad was fond of saying, "You can always get a job at the post office." That was his way of casting his counsel in a humorous light, but he never stepped back from it. I accepted his view and believed I could always get a job doing something and not have to fool with acting if it wasn't right.

I wouldn't exchange my movement experience for anything. I've had some other wonderful times in my life and some lovely successes. There's the thought that it would have been nice if the Movement hadn't been necessary, and, well, this is true, but since it was, I'm blessed. I don't think anything else is as important as our struggle.

This struggle molded and shaped us. It pulled us in and made us do things that we would not have done otherwise. It's the good part of the bad part of our experience. My time in Mississippi taught me much about surviving, about the essential things in life and in people that can't be taken away. I was part of an extraordinary time in our history. I believe that experience made me who I am.

I think what we had is lacking for young people today. There is no great romantic political theme bringing young people together to change or protect or move the human race forward or move the country forward. It isn't that people aren't individually doing things, but in order for it to be a great, grand thing and a big romantic notion, it has to be massive. It has to be something that is going to change the course of history.

We were a part of such a struggle in the 1960s. We were very lucky to have lived through that time. It's a badge of courage and a badge of honor to have been allowed, in a sense, to have been at that point in history at that age when we weren't really too afraid of too much. We were filled with idealism, and the Movement was right there waiting for us. It is extremely important to me that I was able to find a place in the middle of that struggle. I got on that freedom train and participated in giving it some steam and moving it down the track.

After leaving the South, **DENISE NICHOLAS** joined the acclaimed Negro Ensemble Company in New York City. Within a year Twentieth Century Fox screen tested her for the role of guidance counselor Liz McIntyre on the new television series *Room 222*. She won the role and moved to Los Angeles. She went on to star in many popular television shows and costarred with Bill Cosby and Sidney Poitier in three films. She costarred on the hit series *In the Heat of the Night* opposite the late Carroll O'Connor and wrote several episodes for that show.

Nicholas completed her undergraduate degree at the University of Southern California in 1987 and pursued a second career in creative writing. She worked with author and writing teacher Janet Fitch for five years and attended the Squaw Valley Writers Workshop and the Natalie Goldberg Writing Workshop in Taos, New Mexico.

Her first novel, *Freshwater Road*, a fictional account of the experiences of a Mississippi summer volunteer, received a starred review in *Publishers Weekly* and went on to win the Zora Neal Hurston/Richard Wright Award for Debut Fiction as well as the American Library Association's Black Caucus Award in the same category. Her novel was selected by five major newspapers as one of the best books of 2005. She is currently working on a second novel.

If We Must Die

Janet Jemmott Moses

A young New York teacher leaves her job and joins the Movement.

A Place in the Sun

I decided at twenty-two that I would risk my life to stay alive, to walk in the sun without shame or guilt for not doing what in my heart I knew I should do. A chain of events had brought me to this crossroads in my decision tree. Two years of picketing of Woolworth's stores in support of the campaign against segregated lunch counters didn't seem to be enough when others were putting their lives on the line. So I finished out the school year—I was teaching social studies at Wadleigh Junior High School in Harlem—and made arrangements to go to Mississippi in the summer of 1964.

I spent my first year in Natchez, which had been pried open by Chuck McDew, George Greene, and Dorie Ladner. We were provided lodging in a rooming house owned by George Metcalf, a local NAACP leader. He worked at the Armstrong Tire Company and was badly injured in a car bombing.

The Maziques would feed us at their restaurant, sometimes for free and sometimes on their eat-now-pay-later plan. Annie Pearl Avery from Birmingham joined us sometime during the year. By that time, we had established ourselves in the freedom house that Annie Pearl guarded at night with her .22.

I spent a lot of time working with the young people who were becoming increasingly conscious of their right to a place in the sun. We would go to pool halls, juke joints—wherever the folk were. The community bailed us out when we got arrested for walking down the street with leaflets and for peacefully demonstrating in front of the local segregated movie theater.

One time, Annie Pearl was arrested in the group. Initially a bystander, she placed herself in the procession being led into the paddy wagon and so was hauled off with the rest of us. At the jail the sheriff insisted that Annie Pearl sit down on one of the benches. When she refused a third time, the sheriff started yelling, threatening to shove his foot up her ass if she didn't sit down. Annie Pearl pursed her brow and, in a steady voice, asked what he thought *she* would be doing while he was shoving *his* foot up *her* ass! I don't know if Annie Pearl had ever read Claude McKay's "If we must die, let it not be like hogs, hunted and penned in an inglorious spot."

Whatever inroads we sowed in the community were being rapidly reaped by Charles Evers, who was in and out of Natchez, building a base from which he would later launch his political campaign for mayor in Fayette—a three-block slip of a town in a forty-five-minute jaunt down the road from Natchez. Pressure was coming from SNCC staff/volunteers to integrate the Natchez Project, which had maintained an all–African American staff and which, because of its location in southwest Mississippi, was considered one of the more dangerous projects in the state. By the spring of '65, we had established a beachhead in Fayette and worked to have a voter registration rally.

Two male SNCC workers and I moved into Fayette slowly, tapping into a small network of men whose fearless spirits were not bowed by the aroma of Mississippi's "strange fruit," which lingered in the psyche of all who were born there, of all who worked, and of most of those who passed through. These men—overalled, in dusty boots—were winter trees, deep-rooted, enduring, and unadorned. Their hearts resided in the spirit of spring and sang of renewal and hope. Their tongues spoke widely and often metaphorically in parables of what was important.

After weeks of visiting, a woman I knew as "Ms. Crew" and her husband offered us a place to live. They were raising two grandchildren. One of my jobs was to braid their granddaughter's soft, cottony hair—a very uneven exchange in return for biscuits and syrup in the morning and a safe, warm place to lay my head at night.

At some point we were passed onto others, including Mr. Brown and Mr. Peavine. I recall one evening needing a ride back to Natchez. Mr. Peavine offered to drive me back. We left his house after dark and rattled in his pickup truck through piney woods over unpaved back roads into Natchez.

I had lived on my own since I was twenty-one, renting a small apartment just off Central Park West in New York City. My mother had slowly adjusted to the idea of my living on my own instead of returning to the South Bronx, where I had been born and raised. As I moved deeper into the darkness and silence of the night, not knowing where I was, with a man about whom I really knew very little, I wondered what she would say.

I wondered why she never suggested that I *not* go south. She had spent her formative years in Greenville, South Carolina. I recalled the story she told of her mother having to rush her father (my grandfather) home in fear that he would be lynched after he had bumped into a white woman. He was blind in one eye and had not seen her approach on his blind side. My mother never forgot the terror of the thought that her father might be killed. But whatever misgivings she had for me she kept to herself. Instead she worked with a small group of women in the Bronx to raise funds for SNCC.

That night, driving with Mr. Peavine, I asked not for an answer, but for deliverance—to Natchez of all places—and for deliverance from my fears. Mr. Peavine explained that we would come onto the highway a few miles from Natchez, and we did, much to my relief. Then he returned home the way we had come.

One day I met Mr. Brown and his wife. He listened unemotionally as I told him who I was and why I was there. I knew this was not the first news he had had about voting. I invited myself back—another day, another week— to chat some more. He didn't tell me not to return, so I would go back and he would ask if I had talked to so-and-so, and I would dutifully go and talk to so-and-so. After several months they all agreed, singly, that registering to vote was a good idea and that they would support a voter registration day in Fayette. We set the date.

I don't remember how the FBI got involved; a rumor had been launched that there would be trouble, that a group of Klansmen was planning to stop the demonstration. On the morning of the demonstration, local people began to gather around the courthouse in clusters. Some stood across the street, and others sat at the side of the courthouse lawn. I moved from group to group, greeting onlookers and those who had indicated that they might try to register. We escorted those ready to take the long walk up the courthouse steps into the registrar's office.

I recall that at some point several white men in a pickup truck drove up in front of the courthouse. I watched them from the courthouse steps as they got out of the truck. Trouble was materializing in front of our eyes. There was no place to go, or to run. (Mother had always instilled in my brother and me that we could only be chased if we ran.) The bottom line at that moment was that I not show fear. As they approached the stairs, several other white men—FBI—intercepted their approach and escorted them to their truck.

Mr. Brown indicated that he wanted to see me. He sat on the stone embankment that bordered the side of the courthouse, one among several men with whom we had worked rather closely over the past few months.

He wore baggy denim overalls and held a crumpled brown paper bag in his lap. There may have been another crumpled bag next to him—I'm not sure. Mr. Brown beckoned. I sat down next to him as instructed and gently asked if he was ready to ascend the courthouse steps. He answered by opening the paper bag in his lap. In it lay a large pistol—I surmised a .38 or a .45. "Now, Mizjaunette, don't you worry 'bout a thing. You just keep working," he said. I humbly thanked him and managed to escort a few others up the courthouse stairs.

I don't think Mr. Brown had ever heard of Claude McKay, but, like Annie Pearl, he knew what McKay meant.

In Mississippi, we lived by the grace of God and the love and the vigilance of farmers and day workers who took care of us children, who had no better sense than to believe that we could take white power to the mat.

JANET JEMMOTT continued as a SNCC organizer through 1966, working on other projects in the Mississippi Delta as well as in Selma and Lowndes County, Alabama. Later she married Mississippi project director Bob Moses and accompanied him to Tanzania in the late 1960s when he left the country in opposition to the war in Vietnam. Three of their four children were born in rural Tanzania, where both Janet and Bob worked for the Tanzanian ministry of education. They returned to the United States in 1976, and their fourth child was born shortly afterward. Janet attended Boston University School of Medicine and then worked as a pediatrician in the medical department of the Massachusetts Institute of Technology. Retired after thirteen years of service, she and Bob, now grandparents, live between Hollywood, Florida, and Boston, Massachusetts. Janet served on the advisory board of the Cambridge Young People's Project (YPP), an offshoot of the Algebra Project, which Bob founded in 1982 to promote math literacy.

A contributor to *Hands on the Freedom Plow,* Doris A. Derby worked with SNCC in Albany, Georgia, during the summer of 1962 and with the New York SNCC office from 1962 to 1963. After attending the March on Washington in August 1963, she worked with SNCC in Mississippi until the summer of 1972, where she initiated and implemented numerous projects in education, economic development, the arts, and political reform.

A member of the Una Sewing Cooperative cutting out a pattern for production of black rag dolls. The cooperative was part of SNCC's economic development program begun by Jesse Morris and local black Mississippians (Una, Mississippi, 1968). Doris A. Derby

Fannie Lou Hamer speaking at the 1968 Democratic National Convention. She was also a delegate to that convention, representing the Mississippi Freedom Democratic Party. Four years earlier, in 1964, the Democratic convention had refused to seat the MFDP delegation (Chicago, Illinois, August 1968). Doris A. Derby

Demonstrators gather in Baltimore before being arrested for sitting in at the City Restaurant in Crisfield, Maryland, on Christmas Eve. Standing, left to right: Angeline Butler (with coat), Bill Hansen (middle), Reggie Robinson (second from right), Faith Holsaert (far right). Seated, left to right: Bonnie Kilston, Diane Ostrowski, Peggy Dammond (Crisfield, Maryland, December 24, 1961). Peggy Trotter Dammond Preacely Archives

PART 6

Cambridge, Maryland

The Movement under Attack, 1961–1964

From the early to mid-sixties, two movements in the Upper South associated with SNCC received the same violent responses from state and local authorities as those in the Deep South. In Danville, Virginia, and Cambridge, Maryland, marchers were met with excessive brutality but still kept on protesting. In this section, through telling her own personal story, Gloria Richardson, co-chair of the Cambridge Nonviolent Action Committee (CNAC), describes the demonstrators' confrontations with state and city police forces, including the National Guard, as well as the process of building a movement using SNCC organizing principles.

Cambridge, Maryland, is located on the state's Eastern Shore less than ninety miles from Washington, D.C. Proximity to the nation's capital ensured that movement activism in Cambridge and elsewhere on the Eastern Shore would attract federal attention and intervention. The Eastern Shore was the birthplace of two major black abolitionists—Harriet Tubman, born in a small town right outside of Cambridge, and Frederick Douglass, born in adjacent Talbot County.

CNAC encouraged the support of student associations and the participation of students from colleges within driving range. As a result, students from Maryland State College (now University of Maryland Eastern Shore), Howard, Morgan State, Swarthmore, Goucher, Harvard, and others received their early activist training in the Cambridge Movement. Unlike most of the areas where SNCC organizers worked, Cambridge's black citizens already had the right to vote and held a swing vote as one-third of the city's voting population. Since the mid-1800s they had elected at least three city councilmen from within their own ranks to represent the city's black Second Ward. Besides electoral politics, CNAC's members were also involved in desegregating public accommodations and addressing economic issues.

Cambridge civil rights demonstrators were met with a state-sponsored police response that included tanks and military gases. CNAC members organized armed self-defense to protect their community from night riders shooting into their homes. More closely aligned with the philosophy of Malcolm X, CNAC officers discouraged Dr. King's participation in the later stages of their movement.

Militant and outspoken during the movement years, Gloria Richardson was one of the few women to lead a citywide protest movement during the sixties. She won the admiration of SNCC men and women as she and CNAC waged a hard-fought battle for black political and economic rights on Maryland's Eastern Shore.

The Energy of the People Passing through Me

Gloria Richardson Dandridge

*A soft-spoken local resident with deep family roots
on Maryland's Eastern Shore becomes the militant
head of the Cambridge Movement.*

The Foundation

I was born in Baltimore in 1922. During the Depression my father and mother
moved down to Cambridge, Maryland, to live with my maternal grandparents.
Most of the family on my mother's side were St. Clairs. There were two or
three St. Clair houses, and we socialized back and forth among ourselves.
Members of my father's family, the Hayeses, were living in Virginia.

I came along at a time when a more conservative behavior was expected from children than now. We went out to play for several hours in
the afternoon and then came back home. It was obligatory for our families
to know who our friends were and have a relationship with their parents.
The children I played with could be found within a two-block radius of my
house. Many black families in Cambridge, regardless of income, wanted to
raise their children right and had ambitions for their children to achieve.

In four generations Cambridge had grown from a community of about
fifteen hundred black residents to a major center for black people by the early
1960s, with a population of more than four thousand living in the Second
Ward. The men in my family from my great-great-grandfather on down
were known as race men—that is, they worked to alleviate the oppression
of poor black people—and growing up I absorbed that commitment.

My great-grandfather and grandfather, who both owned grocery stores
supported by the black community, always used to tell me, "You owe something back to people in the black community. Their patronage of our businesses is paying for your way of life and your way to school." Recognizing
the same reality, every winter my grandmother would get food given by the

local canneries and clothing from the Red Cross, which otherwise ignored black families, and give it out to less fortunate black residents. Interestingly, when my great-grandfather had the store, Cambridge neighborhoods were not separated by race and a significant number of his customers were white. By the time my grandfather had the store, Cambridge was segregated and his customers were all black.

My grandparents were very strong, my grandmother as well as my grandfather. The women in our family were never really what is today called gender oppressed. They filled the role of traditional wives, but in terms of pursuing their own ideas and their own civic lives, neither my father nor my grandfather nor my uncles ever tried to control the women in our family. Almost all of my family's women friends may have done most of the household work, but they were more than homebodies. In my mother's time there were quite a few black women who were teachers, pharmacists, or doctors in Baltimore and on up the East Coast. Since I was the only grandchild for a long time, the men and women in my family really wanted me to follow the example of these highly achieving black women and become a doctor, a pharmacist, or other professional and then return to Cambridge.

Everybody in my family, women and men, could speak extemporaneously in public—everybody except me. My mother used to make me go to Sunday school to do all these little recitations, which I never wanted to do. Family members would insist, "You may have to speak in public some time." It was really an ongoing battle. During the Movement, after the first time we had gone to jail, executive committee members had to literally push me out the door to get me to the televised press conference. That day I thought, *Oh, god. I guess my mother's getting vengeance on me now, because here I am, having to speak in public, and I don't have the slightest idea how to do it.* Of course, it became easier for me after that.

I grew up in a totally segregated society. Even my grandfather, a city councilman from the all-black Second Ward in Cambridge, could not escape segregation's reach. When there were council-related banquets and dinners, the white councilmen thought enough of him that they wanted him to have the meal, but only as long as they did not have to eat with him. They sent his food to the house. My grandmother was furious both because he would accept the food and also because he would continue running for city council. My grandfather would say, "Well, this is just the way the times are."

I'm sure from his father's time until his own time, my grandfather probably did think they had made great progress. They had. For example, there had been no black schools, and now there were schools; no black churches, and now there were churches; and oyster-shell roads became paved roads. But in terms of my reality, I thought, *This is just too slow. What is this about?*

When I went to Howard University, black people couldn't try on clothes, not even kid gloves, at Woodward and Lothrop's or any other department store in Washington, D.C. Salespeople did, however, make an exception for one of my classmates, Geraldine Pittman, who was so wealthy that she was buying dresses by the half dozen in different colors. Another of my classmates, Tootie Joyner, was able to ignore segregation laws because she was quite fair-skinned and had long, blonde hair. When we sat together on the bus in D.C., white people would lean over and ask her why was she sitting with "that nigger"—me. She would tell them, "I am black," but they did not want to believe her, because actually she looked really *white* white.

I realized segregation was not inevitable in part because of a vacation my mother and I took to Canada, probably around 1954. The farther north we got, the less racist pressure we felt. When we hit Canada, whatever that thing about color was seemed to disappear. In Canada it was like what happened to my lungs years later when I went to Bermuda, where the air was clear. Boom! I realized that at some point, in certain little spaces in the world there probably were situations where black people were not looked upon as pariahs, or left to wait, or treated discourteously. You really didn't have to think about, Is this going to happen or not? It's as if almost everywhere in the United States you expected something heavy, but in Canada it suddenly became light.

The racism I experienced in the United States was an assault on my psyche. My family members experienced deadly physical harm as a result of racism. My father actually died because medical care in Cambridge was almost totally segregated, and black doctors there did not have hospital privileges. He had a heart attack, and they would not admit him in the hospital. The white heart specialist we found cared for him at home under his forbearance and whenever he had time. My father lived for only about two or three weeks under these circumstances. One of my uncles also died for the same reason; he had what they called "walking typhoid fever," but he could not gain admission to the hospital for the required treatment. Ironically, in most segregated hospitals the few black patients and all the white patients were cared for by black aides.

Medical care was better in Baltimore at Provident Hospital, an all-black facility, a good two-hour drive away. The general understanding in Cambridge was that Johns Hopkins used black people as guinea pigs for various research projects. After my father and uncle died, the people in my family would usually go to Provident, but most people in Cambridge did not have the resources to take their sick family members that far. We couldn't use the white ambulance, so black folks in Cambridge got together and bought their own ambulance.

When I was a student at Howard University from 1938 to 1942, the political, moral, and cultural foundation I received at home was reinforced and expanded. At Howard I gained insight into the world I was living in, not only regarding the evils of its racism, but also about black culture and achievements—increasing my pride in the heritage of black people. It was a time when there was a group of nationally known, highly gifted black professors, such as Alain Locke, E. Franklin Frazier, Ralph Bunche, Highland Lewis, and Sterling Brown—geniuses, really. In almost every core subject, our professors talked about the achievements of black people. In math, for example, when we learned about all the great mathematicians, black mathematicians from time immemorial were included; in sociology we studied the theories of both black and white prominent sociologists. When we left Howard, we felt well prepared and equal to anybody.

When I was on campus there was a lot of civil rights ferment—intellectual inquiry, political exploration, and direct action—usually with faculty support. In an effort to discredit Howard's student activists, they were accused of being Communists. At that time the university did allow Communist clubs on campus. I picketed at Woolworth's to protest the segregation in their stores. Edward Brooke, who later became a senator from Massachusetts, went on some demonstrations. My friend Tootie, the one who was blonde and looked white, really came out and became a serious agitator. She was reading and thinking at a higher level than most of us, even Nietzsche; she was very radical and we all listened to her.

We also demonstrated about conditions at Howard. I don't know what possessed us, because Mordecai Johnson was the president and he was very radical. We protested anyway, because we didn't think we should have curfew hours in the dormitory. There was one time we just turned the dormitories upside down, protesting. The outcome of that was that the school did relax the curfew and some of the restrictions on women students.

The Cambridge Movement and SNCC

Near the end of 1961, SNCC came to Maryland at the request of the Baltimore NAACP, which wanted SNCC to organize against segregated public accommodations in Maryland, specifically on U.S. Route 40. They asked for SNCC because SNCC was known as radical and willing to go into any kind of situation. The governor of Maryland at that time was from Crisfield, which, like Cambridge, is on the Eastern Shore. In the heat of the Route 40 demonstrations, SNCC organized busloads of people to follow the governor to his hometown of Crisfield on Christmas Eve 1961. There they sat in, trying to eat at a white lunch counter, and were arrested. My uncle Herbert St. Clair and his son Freddie provided bail bond for the demonstrators on the Eastern Shore. Coming back from bailing them out, Freddie told some of the SNCC organizers, "Well, Cambridge is so bad, why don't you stop there and see what you can do?" The SNCC workers did come to Cambridge and ended up staying at my uncle Herbert's house.

Until SNCC got to Cambridge at the end of 1961, there had not been any vehicle to change the segregated conditions. At that time I had taken over management of the family drugstore after my father's death. SNCC workers had been in town for two or three weeks, really before I was aware of their presence. A high school group made the first move. My teenage daughter Donna was a student leader before I became involved. One Saturday a group of people appeared at my door, saying Herbert had sent them. They needed local guides to show "outside" demonstrators how to get around Cambridge. I told them that my daughter Donna, who was baking cookies, usually had a lot of high school students coming around. I told the SNCC organizers, "Fine. You can ask the students," and that's how Donna and her friends got involved.

Next, SNCC organized a group of adults to observe the demonstrations. I was an observer off and on. If any incidents happened, we could report them accurately. Also our presence let the police know that adults supported what the teenagers were doing. The kids did the planning, the placards, and the strategizing and still kept their grades up. We were scared for the young people. They locked the students into the restaurants a couple of times. The youngsters were beaten and attacked by the police and white onlookers and jailed on a daily basis in one great demonstration after another. By March the teenagers—going downtown in groups of at least forty and sometimes as many as seventy-five—almost brought the town to its knees economically; their actions so disrupted downtown businesses that even the banks were on the skids. As long as the demonstrations continued, most of the city's residents, white and black, avoided shopping or doing any kind of business downtown—white shoppers out of fear, black shoppers deliberately supporting the Movement. On weekends students from the Northern Student Movement (NSM), the Congress of Racial Equality (CORE), Morgan State University in Baltimore, and Swarthmore College in Pennsylvania came to Cambridge to demonstrate as well.

I went on one demonstration, but I was not nonviolent enough. I just could not stand there, passively going up and down while the white onlookers were saying all kinds of hateful things. Cambridge is small, so I knew half of those people and tried to trip them as they were going to harass the demonstrators. Donna, who was about fifteen then, came and said, "Ma, you're violating the rules. Get off the line." I had to leave. I knew I was wrong in the first place, but I just didn't think she had seen me. I decided that demonstrating was not what I should do. Out of stoicism, you had to gear yourself to face the violence and hatred. I chose to continue gathering information and sending it to the Movement, telling them about what was going on and what I heard from black people in the community at the drugstore.

After the student demonstrations began, the white folks called in the city commissioner, Charles Cornish, a black man, who was now the representative from the Second Ward, as well as the black ministers, who together promised that they would see that things were quiet. The authorities promised they would come to the negotiating table once demonstrations stopped. The young people, who at that time thought they could trust the ministers, agreed, thinking that the theaters and other public accommodations would be desegregated soon. Of course, day after day after day passed with no progress.

At one of the mass meetings in April, movement people asked me to be more visibly involved, partly because they figured that I was least likely to suffer economic reprisals, and, besides, my family could take care of me financially. Family members also provided daily support. Donna or my mother did the cooking and took care of the house. This was the only way I could have managed being a civil rights worker and raising two daughters. I could not have done what I did without my family's help. I replaced my cousin Freddie who had been co-chair of the Cambridge Nonviolent Action Committee (CNAC), along with Inez Grubb. Freddie got to thinking that there might be a conflict of interest in being co-chair and the person supplying bonds for movement demonstrators.

Once I became the public voice of the Cambridge Movement, a black minister from the A.M.E. church brought me the word that the authorities had said, "You can have any job you want" and offered me all kinds of jobs. I thought it was very funny, because they were jobs I had applied for in the past but didn't get. This was not the last time they tried to deflect me by offering me jobs. In fact, before I left Cambridge I refused a federal job offer to run the employment programs for the Eastern Shore of Maryland. Also to lure me away from the Movement, at one point Governor Millard Tawes, a Democrat, sent state senator Verda Welcome with an offer to back me if I would run for state senator.

In the spring of 1962 the community got the money together to send Yolanda St. Clair, my cousin Freddie's wife, and me down to a SNCC conference in Atlanta. Our purpose was to establish a continuing affiliation with the group and learn more about what people were doing in other communities. Yolanda and I both were in awe of the SNCC people, who had done all kinds of movement work. We went down there with little white gloves and full-skirted summer dresses. People at SNCC were looking at us like we were crazy. I'm not sure they were in jeans, but they weren't dressed in white gloves and little dresses, except, of course, for Miss Ella Baker, who wore a dress along with a big hat and gloves. SNCC people were so serious and had so many different kinds of civil rights organizing going on, including direct action, voter registration, and organizing farming cooperatives. Attending the conference was very important to us. We were there to find out whatever strategies or tactics we could use.

Initially, however, most people in SNCC did not think holding demonstrations in Cambridge was going to be that difficult, because it was in the Upper South, not in the Deep South like Alabama and Mississippi. As a result it was hard for us to get enough SNCC field secretaries to work in Cambridge when we needed them, because their attitude was, "You are almost in the North, so what do you need us for?" Of course, that was only until everything broke loose.

After the SNCC meeting we went back to Cambridge and started seriously organizing on a day-to-day basis, talking to everybody, having small meetings, trying to get them larger, going out to churches in the county, trying to pick people who were leaders or had leadership skills or the people who were looked up to in various parts of the neighborhoods and counties. We put together an active committee that became CNAC. Compared to the older civil rights groups, we were more based in the community.

We expanded our picketing to include factories, banks, businesses with federal subsidies, since none of these places hired black people. The only jobs black people could get then were as workers in the crab and oyster factories or as teachers in the schools. College students associated with NSM, CORE, and the Civic Interest Group (CIG), a group affiliated with SNCC in Baltimore, would come in on the weekend to participate in our demonstrations. Inez Grubb and I went before city council with a list of demands: low-income public housing, desegregation in the hospital and health services (in the 1800s black women and white women had set up the hospital at a time when there wasn't the racial dividing line), jobs in the post office (the post office had previously hired black mailmen, but then changed), desegregation of schools and school buses, and a general end to job discrimination. Everybody in the white power structure in Cambridge always told us we didn't know what we were talking about and told the national and local press that Negroes in Cambridge were basically happy.

To support our position and find out how people in the black community prioritized issues, I came up with the idea of a door-to-door survey in the black community, which I designed. The kids, even younger than high school kids, went from house to house, having people fill out large eight-by-twelve-inch cards. The survey was basic to my philosophy of organizing. Its goal was to find out exactly what people in the community wanted—to prioritize what they felt their needs were. Students from Swarthmore College took it to their professors to do the correlations and gave us a report which found that economic issues, rather than desegregating public facilities, mattered most to black Cambridge. The survey revealed that there was more than 60 percent unemployment in the black community; that two-thirds of the community was surviving on less than three thousand dollars per year; that 40 percent of homes had no inside toilet facilities, and that some families were living in made-over chicken coops. We sent this report to the Kennedys, and it actually formed a basis for changing Robert Kennedy's mind later on. He could tell that the government's census figures did not capture how widespread poverty and discrimination were in the United States, and he began to change.

Our organization also continued doing voter registration and voter education. Also this year CNAC helped elect a number of local white officials, based on their perceived policies. When we went to get their support, however, we were told they had to pay attention to their other constituencies. It was a very educational process.

From SNCC workshops we learned that before we went anywhere we should thrash out in our meetings whatever we wanted done and how we wanted to do it. There was so much national press stationed in Cambridge, we wanted to be certain there would be only one movement voice. I never went to meetings by myself. I always took other people from the executive committee or whoever was able to go along with me. This ensured that the power structure could not go around to two or three different movement people and play us off one against the other. With our consensus process and our foundation in the community, we knew where we stood when we went out in public.

The Cambridge Movement and other movements in the South were not based on rhetoric. We really took the pulse of the community prior to the time we took a position. I learned this in SNCC and also from my grandfather, the city council member, who insisted, "You have to find out what the people think. Find the key person on that block or in that neighborhood, the person that people look up to, and see what they're thinking."

The Cambridge Movement respected what the people wanted. This philosophy brought us into conflict not only with local and national authorities but also with those who were considered supporters, with the more conservative leadership of the Civil Rights Movement as well as with folk in the Kennedy administration. The Kennedys were running around the world as the "great human rights people" when there was warfare in the streets of Cambridge. Because Cambridge is so physically close to Washington, we asked ourselves, "First, can we create enough chaos with our movement to force the Kennedys' attention to be focused on this area? And then, what would they be likely to do?"

National civil rights leaders would go to the White House and would be asked if they could calm us down. The Cambridge Movement had three or four conferences battling back and forth with Robert Kennedy. One hot summer day in 1963 they sent for us to come to the White House. About five of us from Cambridge went. We had always heard about these moderate black folks who go to the White House, drink tea, and eat cookies. It was boiling hot outside and they offered us iced tea. We were in a room at a conference table, where we were supposed to be mediating, figuring it out, negotiating. We were just as thirsty as we could be, but we kept refusing the tea.

I had to tell Robert Kennedy, "These national leaders cannot make any agreement with you. They can participate, but they can't have the final say. It's us. It doesn't matter what anybody else says. It's our bodies out in the street. It's our movement. So you have to deal with us, whether you like it or not, or whether you're going to agree with us or not."

Officers from the NAACP national office had gone behind our backs to the Kennedys, telling lies, saying, for example, that the schools in Cambridge were integrated. That time I said, "Well, you just go down there in Dorchester County and show us. You can just walk through the schools there and find out." Even Dr. King criticized us, telling Mike Wallace, who was then on the radio in Philadelphia, that I didn't know what I was talking about. State workers would phone us, repeating negative things they'd heard, saying, "We've talked to Roy Wilkins, and we've talked to Dr. King, and we've talked to this other person."

The major thing, however, as far as we were concerned was for the Kennedys to understand that none of those people had the final say. John Kennedy never quite got it, but Robert Kennedy did. Either that, or because John represented so many different constituencies, he couldn't afford to say that he got it, but John and Robert each had to know what the other was doing. Maceo Hubbard, who then represented the Civil Rights Division of the U.S. Justice Department, became friends with my uncle in college and was in and out of Cambridge on several occasions when I was I child. One of the times Hubbard called, he told me John Kennedy wanted to speak with me. By that time I was so irritated by their previous responses, I responded, "You tell the Kennedy brothers they both can go to hell."

When all was said and done, in the long run Robert Kennedy was very good for Cambridge, though he was very hard-nosed. He helped start needed programs. With housing, for instance, he got the Urban League to do the proposals to build the low-income housing. He ordered the authorities to put black people in the post office and in the state employment office. He ordered desegregation of our schools. He also got Dinez White and Dwight Cromwell released from the Maryland State Reform School, where they were serving indefinite sentences because of their movement activities.

To Vote or Not to Vote

Around 1963 the state of Maryland passed a public accommodations bill; however, all the thirteen counties on the Eastern Shore were able to opt out of this particular law through something called senatorial courtesy. In response, CNAC had asked to have a public accommodations ordinance written into the city charter. The charter itself supported segregation by designating the streets where black people were allowed to live. The city authorities proposed it for a referendum. We had just seen what happened in California when a fair housing referendum lost there.

Our position was that we were not going to put our rights up to a vote. Our rights were not based on the whim of the white majority. We called for black voters to boycott the polls. Black veterans from World Wars I and II and many other people could not understand why, simply because they were black, they had to receive by vote something that all the people who were white got when they were born. Supposedly slavery had been abolished. Moreover, in Cambridge the vote did not make sense as the solution, because we had been voting since the mid 1850s, and in the 1960s Cambridge black voters were only about one-third of the city's voting population. Using the vote had been tried by the black community in Cambridge, and it did not help improve our situation.

Only a few people outside of the black community in Cambridge seemed to be able to understand our position; even King tried to influence us. Somebody whose major goal, though I did not know it, was for Martin to convince me to stop people from boycotting the vote got me an invitation to a Carnegie Hall concert, a fund-raiser for the Movement in New York City. Lena Horne, Harry Belafonte, and Frank Sinatra were performing. At the concert, I sat overlooking the stage with Martin Luther King Jr. and Senator Kenneth Keating from New York. They bombarded me with arguments about why I should get out the vote on the Cambridge referendum. Finally, just before the concert ended, I left because I was really getting angry. I said to Martin words to the effect that he needed to go back south and mind his business. I had wanted to watch Frank Sinatra and Lena Horne on stage, but instead I had to listen to all this advice that I was never going to accept. I was totally disgusted.

When I went to D.C. for the 1963 March on Washington, Charles Evers and somebody else took me out to dinner and bombarded me again. The Black Ministerial Association in Baltimore had been supporting us, but even they threatened to pull out. Members of the press tried to grasp our argument. I remember that the *New York Times* sent their reporter Ben Franklin down. He came back and forth two or three times, trying to understand. Finally the *Times* decided it really wasn't that difficult after all. It was a very simple thing: you're born here; you should be able to use public accommodations. I think the *Christian Science Monitor* got it right away, but almost everybody else, except for those of us in Cambridge, did not get it.

Even SNCC opposed our position and sent a SNCC worker in. Without my knowledge, he went to the CNAC executive committee and told them to get out the vote. In opposition to the previously agreed-upon position, the committee then labeled me as a betrayer, and I resigned from CNAC. People from the community and CNAC came to see me and said, "Don't resign, just for something like this." After about two days of people asking me not to resign, I withdrew my resignation. The national and local NAACP attempted to organize people against CNAC, and the black ministers in Cambridge said that they could turn out the vote. They closed their churches to CNAC, but the church members said, "Then we won't put money in the collection plate on Sunday," so the ministers reopened the churches to us. As we expected, the white majority of voters defeated the public accommodations referendum.

Another Wave of Direct Action: Back in Stride Again

After the referendum, in the late spring of 1963 we began the second wave of the direct action campaign. Usually 150 to 300 people would take part in the demonstrations. There would be two or three generations of families in the jail—the grandmother, the mother, and the daughters—as was true in my case. The police didn't want any teenagers in the jail, so they put the younger people out of jail. After one particular demonstration the students went home, although we had told them they should stay. I was really disappointed, because I couldn't understand why my daughter Donna and Dinez White, a thirteen-year-old local activist, were leaving with the other students. Here we were, all in jail, and the students go and leave because the white jailer says, "Go home." So we parents were arguing about this in the jail.

The fifteen or so teenagers went home, got their toothbrushes, took off their school clothes and put on their jeans, turned right around, and "laid in" at the local movie theater. The police dragged the students out of the theater, beat them, and brought them back to jail about ten or eleven that night. A woman called "Baby Sis" went around like Paul Revere, knocking on people's doors, waking up the black community to tell them about the brutality. Then everybody came down, on foot and in cars, any way they could get there, and surrounded the jail, some still in their night clothes, some bringing guns, knives, and whatever.

By twelve or one that night, those of us remaining in jail heard a dim roar that kept getting closer and closer. It was unbelievable: more than three hundred people coming out at night and courting arrest, knowing they might be the subject of the same brutality the teenagers had experienced earlier in the evening. The police arrested a lot of people. To make room for the new demonstrators, they wanted to send some of us already there to other jails in Easton and Salisbury. The other towns refused to take any demonstrators, so the police had to start turning people out because we had packed the jail.

This time Donna and her group stayed in for two or three days. Those of us who were in there, the older ones, stayed in for two weeks. There were a lot of people in there with me. Every time the police would take me out of the cell to meet with city officials, the officials would not agree to any of our demands, so I'd just say, "Well, I'm going back to jail."

While we were in jail, city judge Laird Henry decided he was going to form a committee made up of people from the city's white power structure. Henry was from the premier white family in the county. His family members had held this position stretching back to the formation of Dorchester County. He believed the city's problems could be solved by meetings and talking, but he was not able to get the committee members to reach agreement. He reportedly had a nervous breakdown before the talks ended. The Maryland Interracial Committee also tried to intervene, but they gave up. Henry was also the presiding judge at our trial. Even though he severely castigated us, me in particular, for being involved in the Movement, he only fined us a penny.

When we left jail we continued to demonstrate. After the "Paul Revere" demonstration, the mayor asked for the National Guard. The governor first sent in the state police, and then shortly afterward, around June, he sent the Guard, which stayed in Cambridge for a year and a half. The Guard was supposed to enforce martial law, which included an early evening curfew. In effect, its job was to keep the black community quiet. Periodically, they'd tell us we couldn't demonstrate, but we would start out every night anyhow, even though we knew guardsmen might stop us at certain points and keep us from reaching our destination downtown. Local whites thought the Guard was there to keep them quiet; the Guard did take over the jails to prevent local police from beating local prisoners.

Tactically we wanted the National Guard to stay there. We believed that as long as the state was spending money for the Guard, there was more pressure to resolve Cambridge's problems. In addition, the press was there as long as the Guard was there. We kept demonstrating and boycotting, knowing we needed to keep that pressure on in as many ways as we could. Ironically, the National Guard tapped our phones, and the federal government tapped movement phones and the Guard's phones. The commanding officer of the Guard, General George Gelston, and I both were aware of the federal tap and would sometimes communicate with notes to avoid it.

Occasionally we used the taps to our advantage or to tease the Guard. People who had been involved in Cambridge would phone periodically to keep up with events. Once, Arnold Goldwag from Brooklyn CORE called to say that members of his group were coming in to demonstrate in Cambridge. Shortly afterward, Gelston called me and said, "Don't you know we aren't allowing any demonstrations?" So Arnie phoned me back and said, "No demonstrations? They're going to stop us at the bridge? Oh, okay. Well, I have these friends, and I think we can get enough boats to come through the long wharf." The Guard heard this and brought out the U.S. Coast Guard. There wasn't any single boat out there, except the Coast Guard boats. We laughed hard that day.

When I was totally engrossed in the Movement, I almost couldn't see how funny some of these war stories were. We were tired of the National Guard popping up in their little jeeps every time we moved. One night we were relaxing at a bar called the Green Savoy. When we came out, the Guardsmen in a jeep asked, "Is everything all right?" I said, "Yes, except we're waiting for some people to come, because we're getting ready to start a demonstration." They believed it, radioed back to headquarters, and soon we were inundated by the National Guard in a bunch of jeeps.

We laughed a lot, but we stayed at a high level of rage also. In addition, there was a constant level of fear that we learned to live with. That rage and fear came with the territory. Once I'd made the commitment to be active, I couldn't stop simply because I was afraid. Otherwise, the racists would win, and it would be a waste of people's energy to stop.

CN2 Gas

That same summer two black children drowned in the Choptank River. Prohibited from using the local swimming pool, they were learning to swim by jumping off Long Wharf, where deepwater boats from other cities and countries docked. Cambridge black folks had internalized the idea so much that it was becoming a matter of pride, going and jumping off the wharf to learn how to swim. The adults hadn't planned to protest the deaths at that time, but the smaller kids in the elementary school started organizing themselves; my younger daughter, Tam, and her friends were making posters. The little kids wanted to go in the swimming pool, and that was their thing. They were having small demonstrations. They wanted the Cambridge Fire Arena opened, because it had a huge swimming pool and skating rink for whites only.

In the midst of these protests, white people had invited former Alabama governor George Wallace, who was running for president on an antiblack platform, to speak in Cambridge. The local White Citizens Council had the nerve to bring him to Cambridge during the protests and, on top of that, to have him speak in the segregated Fire Arena. Prohibited from demonstrating by martial law, we stated that we were holding a rally, not a demonstration. Our goal was to get as close to the arena as we could and get some of the white NSM students working with the Movement into the arena where Wallace was speaking so that they could find out what he was saying and how the audience responded. They were also supposed to protest by raising signs; some got in, but so much broke loose that night, I don't know what happened to them once they entered the arena.

After the rally ended about six or seven hundred people congregated outside the Elks home at Pine and Cross streets. Then the movement leadership discussed whether we should proceed, since I had publicly said that we wouldn't march. Some of the SNCC leadership felt the situation was extremely dangerous. My response was, "No, we're going on."

Then the National Guard stopped us at Race Street, a crossover point from the black neighborhood into the white neighborhood. Although the majority of the demonstrators were from black Cambridge, people from all up and down the East Coast of all colors as well as extra SNCC staff had answered our call to protest Wallace's appearance. They were stretched out, sitting down in the streets; they were not going to move forward unless I said so. I stayed away from the line, stalling so that the students had time to get into the arena before the arrests began.

Military tanks were positioned in front of the demonstrators, blocking access to the streets leading to the arena. Finally I came out and got up on one of the tanks to talk with the governor's brother, Commander Tawes, who was in charge that night. He said, "I want you to tell these people to turn around." I said, "No, I'm not going to do that." "Oh, yes," he said, "you have to tell them to turn around." When I looked down the three front rows of demonstrators, they were all small grammar school kids. I thought, *Where in the hell did these children come from?* Then I had to take a deep breath, regroup, and say, "Okay.

We'll go back." I got down from the tank and asked the parents to take the kids home. The parents got hold of the little kids and almost had to whip them to make them go home. After we got the children out of the front lines, we moved forward again. That's when all the gassing began.

First we sat down. Stokely Carmichael, Stanley Wise, Cleve Sellers, and three or four other people from SNCC were there. The National Guard arrested them and took them away. Then they took me and somebody else away. The Guard looked like men from Mars, because they were wearing gas masks and extra gear.

After we were taken away, we thought we heard gunfire, but it was actually the Guardsmen throwing the gas canisters. They put us in a military truck and took us to the Cambridge armory. General Gelston was not there. We kept saying, "Take us to your commanding officer," but the Guardsmen just stood there stone-faced and mean. When they brought more SNCC workers—Cliff Vaughs, Stanley Wise, and others—you could smell the gas in their clothes, although we first thought they had been shot.

The gas was so strong that it made other people in the army wagon sick. People on line in the demonstration reported that the gas made them throw up and cut their breathing so much they felt they were dying. It was so potent that people ten blocks away from the demonstration got sick. An elderly man and infant in their homes both died from the fumes. Afterward, Stokely took a canister to a lab for analysis and found out that it was CN2 gas, designed for military use. It had never been used on civilians in the United States before. It is the same gas that the Israelis have used against the Palestinians.

March on Washington

That same year, 1963, the March on Washington for Jobs and Justice was held in August. About two weeks before the march, organizers told me that I would be honored as one of the women of the Civil Rights Movement. However, I was treated with the usual disdain at the march. It was more of the same attitude I'd been getting as a SNCC radical from the more conservative civil rights leadership since the beginning of the Movement. It started even before the march itself. Someone from the NAACP called me to say I would be allowed one minute to speak and that it was not appropriate for me to wear jeans to the march instead of the hat, gloves, and dress they expected me to wear. Because we were boycotting the stores closer to home in Cambridge, I had to run all over the Eastern Shore in search of a jean skirt. I think I finally found a jean skirt in Salisbury, and that's what I wore.

Someone said, "Oh, the rest of the people are dressed up with stockings and dress shoes." I thought, *I sure would like to see the police running them down the street with stockings and dress shoes and fancy hats on.*

Lewis Flagg Jr., a man who'd been my playmate as a child and was now assistant secretary in the U.S. Department of the Interior, informed me that people in the department talked about me in the pre-march planning meeting, saying I was a whore and that I would find some way to disrupt the march and turn it violent. Lewis looked white, but he was actually black. Finally Lewis spoke up and said, "Now, let me tell you one thing. I grew up with this woman, and our families were friends. In fact, my mother is her godmother. And I can assure you, she's very moral. I don't think she's going to create chaos, but that's a different question."

I imagine that white folks were obviously putting pressure on the NAACP, the National Council of Negro Women (NCNW), and other moderate organizations not to include me in the march. Really it was only at the last minute that march organizers decided to seek women's participation. When the Cambridge contingent arrived at the march, march organizers took me to the tent for speakers and dignitaries. Dorothy Height, head of the NCNW, was there along with a group of women. They all said they were going to the ladies' room and would be right back. I thought, *Well, I don't have to go to the ladies' room, so I'll sit here and wait.* So I waited and waited and waited. What had happened was they had left me in the march tent by myself.

When march organizer Bayard Rustin came into the tent, a reporter was interviewing me by satellite. Bayard asked, "Don't you know the other women are on the platform?" I responded, "No, they told me they were going to the bathroom."

Bayard then took me through the crowd. When I arrived on the platform, my seat at the front was gone. Lena Horne and Josephine Baker, who were on the front row, said, "They removed your seat. You should raise hell." I replied, "I don't care. I see some people in the back row I need to make contact with. Let them take the seat." In the back I had seen Robert Ming, a black lawyer from Chicago, whom I wanted to do something for the Cambridge Movement. I joined him more or less seething inside and finding it hard to believe that some of the big three—the NAACP, Urban League, and SCLC—had publicly removed my seat and the Cambridge banner from the stage.

Somebody must have said something, because after I had moved to the back, they called my name and I went to the front, picked up the microphone, and all I was able to say was "Hello." Before I could say another word, an NAACP official took the mike away.

Then, just before Martin got ready to speak, we were told that Lena Horne and I would get crushed in the crowd and had to leave—nobody else—just the two of us. They put us in a cab and sent us back to our hotels. They did this, I believe, because Lena Horne had had Rosa Parks by the hand and had been taking her to satellite broadcasts, saying, "This is who started the Civil Rights Movement, not Martin Luther King. This is the woman you need to interview." When I found Lena Horne doing that, I started helping her. We got several national and international broadcasters to interview Rosa Parks. The march organizers must have found that out.

Red-Baiting and Union Organizing

In the CNAC we were not concerned whether volunteers came from the North or South, or what their religion, politics, sexual orientation, or ideologies were. We preferred all of that be ignored, because it would have been divisive for our movement or any other movement. All we cared about was if someone was willing to support us. We found out, however, that the government was investigating people, looking for Communists.

Then one day early in the Movement, General Gelston of the National Guard came to me with the name of one of the volunteers from the North and claimed, "You have a Communist very active in your movement." Hoover in Washington had already identified the Cambridge Movement as being Communist, and the FBI said such leftist associations were a danger to the Movement. At the time, I told Gelston it didn't really matter to us. Red-baiting would not be successful, neither with SNCC nor with CNAC.

I myself was red-baited and threatened in the midst of a local trade union organizing effort at Rob Roy factories, national makers of men and women's clothing. Local members of the International Ladies Garment Workers Union (ILGWU) were holding meetings around wages, since the Cambridge workers were paid a lower rate than ILGWU people in New York City doing the same work. The Cambridge local had both black and white members, but because of segregation, they didn't usually meet together. But this time the black trade unionists, with support from white workers, asked us to come to the meetings. For one large meeting of about two to three hundred people, ILGWU headquarters in New York sent people down who supported the wage discrepancy. In the heat of the conflict over this issue, the New York representatives red-baited me and moved to put me out of the meeting. When they did that, surprisingly, local white ILGWU members, who in the day before civil rights demonstrations probably had been throwing stones at us, got up and said, "Oh, no. If she goes, all of us go."

Later that week national ILGWU leaders came to my house and told me they were going to call Jim Forman and have him stop me from interfering with union business. I said, "Jim Forman is not my boss, and he cannot tell me what to do." The union leaders responded, "Well, somebody must be able to tell you, because you need to just stay out of Rob Roy. This isn't your business." They went so far as to say, "And you better be careful." I replied, "Well, you know, we are used to threats here. If you think you can get Jim Forman to get us to stop, you go right ahead." I didn't hear anything more about that from them.

There was another instance of a union effort in Cambridge with black and white collaboration. When the meatpackers union tried to organize the canning factories, no white clubs or churches would let the white workers from these plants meet in any of their places. The union activists ended up holding their meetings at the black Rod and Gun Club outside Cambridge in the county. While blacks and whites were fighting each other and shooting each other over civil rights in the streets of Cambridge that summer, black and white workers trying to negotiate a contract were meeting together out at the black Rod and Gun Club.

Role of Women

It didn't seem to matter within the local movement and within SNCC that I was a woman. Nobody ever said anything, at least not to my face. However, my behavior as a woman was challenged once by a fifty-year-old white woman, a member of the University of Maryland Board of Regents, who also sat on the Miles Commission, a group that had been established to attempt to bring closure to the Cambridge situation. I was arguing with the committee chair when the female regent became almost hysterical. She said I was a woman: How dare I speak before I was spoken to? She was referring to the fact that I was a woman, not that I was black. I asked, "Well, what do you mean?" "Well, you're insulting this man. You aren't waiting to be spoken to."

I don't remember who was with me, but whoever it was put their hands on my shoulders and kept pressing me into the chair. Afterward, I thought, *Oh, God, maybe that's what's wrong with the Eastern Shore of Maryland.* Then I remembered what Miss Todd, a stringer for the *Baltimore Sun*, once said to me. She was an older white woman, who had married into one of the Eastern Shore's premier white families. She said, "They don't know whether they hate you worse as a woman or as a Negro." She was the only woman reporter on the shore, and I guess in the past they had given her a hard time, just as they were trying to give me.

Nonviolence and Self-Defense

Violence was a fact of life in Cambridge, but we kept the actions at our demonstrations nonviolent. When a demonstration ended, however, participants were on their own. Collaborating with one another at night, we protected our homes and communities. There was always a tension between the violence and the nonviolence. The most dangerous and scary time for us was the period between the end of a demonstration and the time people could get to their homes and get their weapons. During the height of the Cambridge Movement, late in the summer of 1963, white people opposed to the Movement were shooting into the black community every night, and black residents were shooting back. The National Guard was there, trying to stop both, but it didn't always work.

Although I believed in the need to hold nonviolent demonstrations, I did not believe that we were supposed to let people come in and shoot up or firebomb our houses or shoot us and not defend ourselves, because then the white attacks would just keep on. In fact, white folks mostly did the violence at night, because they were not going to tackle those black men on the streets in the daytime. Even with people demonstrating nonviolently, there was always a group of black people present who were not nonviolent and didn't demonstrate. They were prepared to move in at any moment if things got out of hand. Sometimes black people who were not committed to nonviolence would send word to the black movement leadership, saying, "Do you need our help?" or on other occasions, "Either you will get a resolution to this, or we're going to take things into our own hands."

I believe they would have, because there was a lot of gunfire the night that two carloads of white men with five or six men in each car decided to come into our community. I don't know what possessed them besides their own racism. They came through our neighborhoods shooting. As they drove past, you could hear the guns clicking from houses on the street, one after the other. Click, click, click. Black people, movement participants or not, in all those houses, all up and down Muir Street, High Street, and Pine Street. You actually could hear the clicks of guns in the still of the night as black folks prepared to shoot. I hoped they'd get the white shooters. At that point, from the clicks I thought there were so many guns out there that I knew the carloads of white men would be outgunned. When the white attackers came through the community a second time, black people shot the cars out from under them.

By six the next morning, after these men had ridden through the black community shooting and black people had responded by shooting, the entire Second Ward, the city's only black neighborhood, was hanging heavy with smoke and the smell of cordite from gunpowder. The local authorities tried to blame the black community. But the national press was in the black business district on Pine Street and saw the carloads of white men firing the first shot. After the first round of firing, some members of the press went to my uncle's house, coming in and crawling under tables and other furniture for protection. Those who remained on Pine Street phoned in stories and told General Gelston that if he subpoenaed them, they had the film to prove that the whites had come through shooting first. It turned out that the six or seven white shooters were actually National Guardsmen from Maryland who were not part of the Guard stationed there at that time, but they had been stationed in Cambridge earlier. Gelston court-martialed them, making sure they could not return with the Guard for further duty in Cambridge.

It was very dangerous. For instance, Donna almost got shot. Every night black folk would lay out armed in the backs of the yards on the perimeter of our Second Ward neighborhood to prevent white incursions into the neighborhood. On the night that the white guardsmen came through the community shooting, Donna was trying to leave my uncle Herbert's through the backyard and make her way down to Park Lane to get home. She forgot to give the secret whistle signal. The armed lookouts realized in time that it was Donna, but they were getting ready to shoot her. When she got home, she and my mother guarded the house from the second floor with rifles. They used to go out with some of the men in the family and hunt. I was the only one in my family who could not have hit the broad side of a wall if I fired at it. Everybody else was familiar with guns.

On one of the nights when the National Guard had temporarily moved out, there was a riot atmosphere in the city, and the state police were going from house to house, looking for guns in the black community. They were using these big K-9 Corps dogs. In the process of conducting this search, they sicced the dogs on a white newsman and a local black man who was coming home from work. Both men were bitten badly. That night, at the end of one long block, about twelve black men came out of the dark and garroted the dogs, killing them. The state police captain called me in the next morning to complain, saying this was not a civil rights issue. I told him, "Yes, if you continue to send your men down there in the middle of the night looking for guns and hurting people, your men might get killed too."

Minister Malcolm X

During the Movement I met Malcolm X. I knew about him before I actually met him, because people from Philadelphia used to come back home and talk about him. I had heard him on the radio several times and had seen him on television. In the spring of 1964 I went to Detroit for a conference at the church of Rev. C. L. Franklin, Aretha Franklin's father. The purpose of this meeting was to create a northern counterpart to SCLC that would exclude SNCC. Several people approached me suggesting that I really belonged at an organizing meeting sponsored by a militant grassroots group called GOAL (Group on Advanced Leadership) that was taking place down the street at the Shrine of the Black Madonna, pastored by Rev. Albert B. Cleage Jr. There I was invited up to the platform while Malcolm spoke. He was in rare form that night. The title of his talk was "The Ballot or the Bullet."

Later a group of us, some of whom were defectors from the NAACP, asked Malcolm to come to Chester, Pennsylvania. The group included New York activist Judge Wilson Booth, comedian Dick Gregory, and Chicago civil rights activist Larry Landry. We were engaged in an organization called ACT with militant tenant rights organizer Jesse Gray. We wanted to create an alternate northern structure for people who were dissatisfied with the more conservative groups like the NAACP, and we wanted Malcolm to be a participant. He agreed. Moved by the spirit of his Detroit speech, I asked him both to come to Cambridge in the fall of 1964 and to announce as he travelled around that if certain progress hadn't been made in the black community, "Now it's time for bullets. Ballots are no longer working."

As it turned out, Malcolm was in Africa that fall and later invited me to go with him on his second Africa trip. We became friends after meeting in Detroit. One evening, after I had resigned from both CNAC and SNCC and had moved to New York, I was sitting with my husband in a restaurant near 125th Street when Malcolm came in to eat and watch television. As he passed our table on the way to his booth, Malcolm told me I would like what would be on the eleven o'clock news. I couldn't imagine what it was. It was the announcement of his final break with the Nation of Islam. Since I never understood the religious aspect of his beliefs, at first I thought, *Oh, thank god,* but then I worried, because I realized he was probably in more danger than ever. I was also excited, because I thought he had an even greater potential, unrestricted by the Nation's ideology. He had enough charisma, intelligence, and commitment to become more than a sectarian leader. No power structure, black or white or a combination of the two, would be able to control him the way they did some other civil rights leaders. Malcolm could inspire trust and energize people. He was loyal to black people and completely committed to our struggle. I believe this made him such a danger to our country's power structure that they had to kill him.

Organizing

Looking back, I think it's important to remember that organizing takes time, that things don't come together all at once. People think you start a project and are able to have thousands of people step forward the next day. It generally takes around eighteen months, which is how long it took us in Cambridge to get to that moment when local people filled the jail for the first time. That was the moment when all the people, regardless of age, religion, or politics, had come out. Mostly people from the lower income brackets participated; our few middle-class residents did not demonstrate, but sat at home, above it all. On weekends we'd been having students from NSM and adults from CORE coming in to help with demonstrations. Before that the local teenagers, high school students, had been doing a lot of the picketing.

In the course of that eighteen months, if you're working on it every day, it does not really seem that long, because you're having little successes of this, that, and the other along the way. But nothing is easy. I mean, you have to struggle. The opposition's major goal is to do something to make you give up. The longer you go, the better chance you have of winning. Most of the movements that grew into something big started small. The core of people who met regularly in Cambridge was probably between ten and fourteen people. I think it happened this way throughout most of SNCC's projects in the South.

A movement like ours is built more slowly, because people have to trust you. They have to learn what anybody in a leadership position is about. Once people trust you, they will be able to work with you. Also people in leadership need to get rid of the idea that "I am the great leader." Finally, it's important for everyone to know that other people are struggling, too. It's easy to think, "We're here struggling alone." It is significant that others are in almost parallel universes fighting the same racism. Even though these different groups of people may not have day-to-day contact, there is a psychological connection among them as long as they know that the other struggles are going on. In the context of SNCC, we learned from each other because we had a forum, a coordinating body through SNCC, where we could go and meet with people dealing with the same situation we were facing.

In hindsight, there were times we made strides or improvements that benefited the very people in the black community who opposed the Movement. For example, we pushed for equal employment. When jobs opened up, even federal positions, it was hands-off for movement activists, because we felt there was a large unemployed or underemployed workforce pool in Cambridge who should be the ones to benefit. However, some of the people who got the higher-level jobs were those who would not talk to movement workers and were called Uncle Toms or Aunt Thomasinas and wannabes. It made sense that the town's white power structure would pick certain kinds of black people whom they knew they could manipulate or who were not sincerely interested in the welfare of the black community as a whole for these kinds of positions that really had no power. At one of the SNCC conferences, Howard Zinn had told us that we should expect this would happen.

The Value of the Student Movement

I believe what happened to SNCC in the final days was that the government or government-related agencies sent in certain black people from the North to destroy SNCC. Also, for whatever reason, SNCC was not able to attract enough new recruits. After they spend hour after hour, day after day in the Movement, people get worn out and need new blood coming through.

It's necessary for people to have some kind of historical record of what went on in the student movement, because maybe the next time people will have a structure around which to plan better. The history of our struggle is deliberately withheld from our young people, because they are the most likely agents of radical change. The heart of the Movement that turned the South around came out of elementary, high school, and college students, but most young people today don't know that. Recently I was part of a panel discussion, and the young people there were very interested, but they thought black people in Mississippi just were placid and didn't struggle for their rights, that white southerners accepted change readily, and that everything was done by adults and ministers.

Young people today shouldn't be sitting around waiting for old folks to lead them into some new kind of millennium. Young people will have to do it themselves. They have to be willing to make their own way and their own mistakes. And they might as well do it while they're young, before they get into the part of their lives where they are raising families and cannot afford to take the risks. They should listen only to those older people who will support them, or who have some experience that may be useful but will not tell them what to do.

It wasn't Dr. Martin Luther King Jr. who turned Cambridge around; it was all the local students who were out there laying their lives on the line. Early on, people had asked King to come to Cambridge but were told it would cost three thousand dollars to bring him in and that anyway he was so busy, it would be two or three years before he could accept. People were so disappointed, but it was the best thing that could have happened to us, because we had to go ahead and do it ourselves. The only people I knew who were doing anything were SNCC people. When all this hullabaloo arose and the press got there, Martin said he was coming into Cambridge and Danville to see what was going on. We gave out a statement saying we would stop him when he got to the Emerson Harrington Bridge leading into Cambridge, because we no longer needed him. After our statement the members of the press told me that Dr. King said, well, he was catching the flu anyhow.

Leaving Cambridge

The Movement wore me out, but I wouldn't change any of it. I don't think people in that intense kind of activity should come out of it trying to fill a mainstream leadership position. The two kinds of leadership positions are not compatible. Sometimes I wonder if I'd stayed in Cambridge, what would I be doing now? Would somebody have convinced me to run for city council? And for what? The same old thing: week after week after week, fighting establishment politics.

When I left, I missed Cambridge, black Cambridge. In fact, I've gone back there a lot of times; now I go to the annual crab festival. I think the problem in Cambridge now is that there are black people on the governing committees and whatever, but the people I know don't seem to think these black officials are exercising power or have the power to exercise. It's like they've reached another plateau, just like my father and grandfather reached their own plateaus, decades before.

When I first came to Howard University, my classmates considered me a timid, retiring person. When I was in the Movement, I changed. In struggle I became stronger—I became more of a fighter because of the energy of the people passing through me and because of the historical conditions for black people. Philosophically, though, I hadn't changed, because I had always thought like a fighter. There had just never been a vehicle to put my thought into action, but in the Movement there was a way to fight for a level playing field, to open doors for black people.

GLORIA RICHARDSON DANDRIDGE also served on SNCC's executive board while she was active in Cambridge. In 1965 she married Frank Dandridge, a freelance photographer for *Life* and *Time* magazines, and moved with him to New York, where she continued to raise her two daughters. For more than twenty years she has worked as a program officer in the New York City Department of Aging; for more than sixteen of those years she has been the union delegate for Local 371 of the Social Service Employees Union (SSEU). She occasionally speaks at colleges and historical museums about her life and the Cambridge Movement. In 2008 she received honorary doctorates from Washington College and Morgan State University. For more on the Cambridge Movement, see *Civil War on Race Street* (2003) by Peter Levy and *Sisters in the Struggle* (2001) by Sharon Harley. Dandridge's relationship with Malcolm is detailed in *The Death and Life of Malcolm X* (1979) by Peter Goldman. Historian Joseph Fitzgerald is working on her biography.

PART 7

A Sense of Family

The National SNCC Office, 1960–1964

You haven't just joined an organization.
You've joined a family.

—Judy Richardson

From the formation of SNCC through preparation for the 1964 Mississippi Summer Project, SNCC's national headquarters in Atlanta kept growing and expanding. The organization moved from a desk in the corner of SCLC's headquarters to an ever-larger series of offices incorporating more staff and providing more services. During the organization's first year, several people established and maintained SNCC's Atlanta office: Miss Ella Baker; Jane Stembridge, a white Union Theological Seminary student from Virginia; Connie Curry, head of the National Student Association's southern program; Ed King, a Kentucky State University student activist; and Bob Moses, who had come from New York to work for SCLC.

By the middle of 1961, a core staff, which remained in place for several years, was at work. Jim Forman, a Chicago activist, had accepted the job of executive secretary. Julian Bond, a key figure in the Atlanta Sit-in Movement, was SNCC's communications director. Shortly after Forman arrived he hired Norma Collins, a black student activist from Baltimore, as a full-time secretary, and Chessalonia Johnson, an Atlanta native, as bookkeeper. He also brought in Ruby Doris Smith as his administrative assistant. Smith, a Spelman student, had participated in the Atlanta sit-ins, the Rock Hill jail-in, and the Freedom Rides; in 1966 she replaced Forman as executive secretary. Forman's wife, Mildred (whose story is in Part 2 of this book, "Entering Troubled Waters"), moved to Atlanta at the end of the year and also worked full-time in the office. Later Mildred traveled with the second group of Freedom Singers, coordinating their schedules and arrangements.

All the women in the following part also came to work full-time in the Atlanta office. They edited SNCC's newsletter, the *Student Voice;* enlarged the publicity department; established and maintained the office of northern coordinator—who was responsible for keeping contacts with SNCC's fund-raising base and Friends of SNCC groups—and took care of the organization's general administrative needs. Office staff championed SNCC's work to the outside world, generating the publicity and funds the group needed to become a force for social change. The young women who were on the office staff viewed their work as important, significant, and challenging. Those in Atlanta justly considered themselves at the nerve center of the organization, in the midst of the rapid flow of events and of people. They describe the atmosphere in the Atlanta office as quite positive, as one of warmth and acceptance, of being in the center of the beloved community, and in the midst of family.

Young women with journalistic, administrative, and secretarial skills volunteered or were recruited to work in the office. However, in an organization making social change they had to use their skills in new ways and learn new skills, often without any training or guidance. For example, Dorothy Zellner helped organize a workshop on civil liberties and arranged an information-gathering meeting to find out how more conservative organizations planned to undermine SNCC programs. Other women maintained contact with the Justice Department and hosted visiting dignitaries. Sometimes the work required dealing with strong emotions. Jane Bond, who used her secretarial skills to help her husband, Howard Moore, SNCC's lawyer, took care of her family and assisted with movement work while struggling with the fear that her husband might be killed. Office staff taking field reports and affidavits from field secretaries or answering emergency calls from the field on the organization's WATS (Wide Area Telephone Service) line found there were times when they had to keep their feelings in check to do their jobs.

Like the women activists in Southwest Georgia and Mississippi, most of the women in the national office had already been involved in various civil rights efforts. Their earlier activities, however—ranging from going to the Highlander Folk School, to arranging clandestine meetings of black and white southern students, to facing off tanks in Cambridge, Maryland—tended to be within the SNCC orbit. Working in the office did not preclude their participation in more confrontational activities; instead it afforded them opportunities to become involved in demonstrations in Atlanta and other parts of the South. Several women actually demonstrated *in* the office, protesting the expectation that women would always perform certain secretarial tasks.

In the summer of 1964 SNCC's national office moved to Greenwood, Mississippi. Greenwood had been a town with special significance to SNCC workers ever since SNCC field secretary Sam Block entered the Delta town in June 1962. The six-week period from February 19 to March 26 the following year provides forceful examples of the kinds of reprisals civil rights activists faced. First, white racists burned an entire block of businesses in an unsuccessful attempt to destroy the SNCC office. Nine days later a carload of white men, who had spent the day sitting in front of the SNCC office, caught up with a car driven by SNCC field secretary Jimmy Travis, whose passengers were Atlanta-based Voter Education Project director Randolph Blackwell and SNCC state project director Bob Moses. The white men fired into the civil rights workers' car thirteen times, hitting Travis in the shoulder and the neck near his spinal cord, almost killing him. A week later white terrorists fired two shots from a double-barreled shotgun into a car that had just parked at the front of the SNCC office. Greenwood activists Sam Block, Willie Peacock, Essie Broom, and Peggy Marye were in the car. Two and a half weeks later, arsonists did burn the SNCC office, destroying all the records and equipment. Two days later night riders fired three shots into the children's bedroom at the family home of sister and brother SNCC workers Freddie and George Greene. Fortunately, no one was injured in these last three incidents.

In 1964, when SNCC moved the national office to Greenwood for the summer, the town was still a dangerous place for civil rights workers. Nevertheless, women who were on the office staff in Atlanta or in the North faced their fears, entered the state, and found an even more intense activism could be part of their office work. They were under attack just traveling to and from the office. In addition to providing support and publicity for the wide range of programs instituted that summer, they provided security for the staff and summer volunteers and, in one instance, rescued SNCC workers from a large angry white mob.

Staff members had differing judgments concerning the value of the Mississippi Summer Project and the significance of the Atlantic City challenge. Nevertheless, both the staff and the organization emerged from the Mississippi Summer Project more informed and more experienced. The organization that Barbara Jones Omolade joined when she began working in the Atlanta SNCC office after the summer of 1964 was a more substantial and accomplished one than the organization that moved its national office to Greenwood. Through initiating and pursuing a number of creative programs and strategies, office personnel, field staff, and community people worked together and, by the end of the summer, established SNCC as a major civil rights organization. Their efforts brought the horrors of Mississippi to light for the nation, which put enormous pressure on the federal government to intervene against white supremacist violence. Even without being seated, the Mississippi Freedom Democratic Party (MFDP) challenge effectively eliminated all-white, all-male delegations to the Democratic National Convention and put the right to vote at the top of the country's political agenda.

Peek around the Mountain

Joanne Grant

*A New York progressive is revitalized
by the Civil Rights Movement.*

Coming Alive

For me, February 1, 1960, the date of the Greensboro sit-in, was the beginning of racial awareness. Before the Movement I was almost completely divorced from the race issue. I grew up in a small Upstate New York town. There were approximately twelve black people and six Jews in the town of ten thousand people. I do not know if the six Jews felt as isolated as most black people did. I, however, felt included. I was a star: literary editor of the yearbook, person most likely to succeed, president of the French club, a cheerleader!

Still, nobody asked me to the prom—until my freshman year at college when a lovely high school boy I had a crush on asked me to accompany him. And it did wound when the local Italian women muttered *"negretta"* when I appeared one morning to pick up a friend for a walk to grade school. Or after one person made a racist remark in third grade, another student said disparagingly, "She's crying because she's a nigger."

My mother used to gather dandelion greens with our neighbors, elderly women of Italian descent, but I had never even heard of collards. My mother, a Republican—in her words "because Lincoln freed the slaves"—looked with disdain on some distant cousins who were members of the NAACP. I remember my sister saying insouciantly as she sat on the lap of a very black man who was a friend of our aunt, "Your ears are like burnt toast." Just a comment from an innocent.

I came alive in October 1961 when I was sent to Atlanta by the *National Guardian* to cover a SNCC conference. It was a rebirth. Here I was, plunged into SNCC's belief in the establishment of the beloved community and surrounded by a group of people who thought that they were changing the world. And they were.

I went into Atlanta as a northern novice. I had no idea of what I was facing. What, no taxicab could transport an interracial group? No hotel could accommodate black and white guests? No restaurants could serve both races? I found out later that there was one hotel that had formerly been white only that accepted guests of both races and one restaurant, at the airport.

When the delegation from Mississippi entered the conference hall, the entire assembly stood in tribute to those who were struggling in the toughest state. All felt that these arrivals were heroes fighting the good fight on the worst of the battlefields. Later, a group of Atlanta students prepared for a sit-in at Rich's department store downtown with their walkie-talkies in hand and dressed in their Sunday-go-to-meeting best. They sang an old gospel song as they were about to depart: "This may be the last time. This may be the last time, brother. This may be the last time. It may be the last time, I don't know." The recognition of what they were facing sobered me: this might be the last time that they would be together, the last day of their lives.

I went with them to the demonstration. When Capt. L. C. Little of the Atlanta police asked me if I was part of the group, I cravenly said that I was a reporter, so he ignored me. Of course, this demonstration was nothing compared to others that took place later, but it was my introduction.

SNCC Support Work

As one of the founders of New York Friends of SNCC, I became active in fund-raising and general support. The new, young, scrappy, but insolvent organization always needed ever greater infusions of cash. Our New York office provided at least three-quarters of the organization's budget. Besides fund-raising, another major contribution I made was getting the story out, interacting with other reporters who were covering this extraordinary American experience. *Atlanta Journal* reporter Fred Powledge used to corner me outside the SNCC meetings and ask me what was going down. I helped him because I liked and trusted him. Others who were blocked from attending meetings, as I was not, I ignored for the most part. Though if I thought they could help, I fed them bits. Fred told me that in a poll taken by the *New York Times* on campuses across the country, there were three writers whom students read regularly: C. Wright Mills, Herbert Marcuse, and my articles in the *Guardian*. Wow, what company! What was important was that the story was getting out to young people.

Covering the Movement, the newsmen themselves were experiencing an epiphany that shook them out of their objectivity and onto the side of the civil rights struggle. With Stuart H. Loory of the *New York Herald Tribune,* for example, it was the bloody attack on the Freedom Riders in Montgomery, Alabama; likewise, for Murray Kempton of the *New York Post,* it was the tear gas attack on a Montgomery mass meeting; for Claude Sitton of the *New York Times,* it was when the sheriff and his deputies stalked into a Sasser, Georgia, mass meeting with guns drawn.

Providing support for the Movement involved more than simply getting the news out or raising money. I would get frantic calls from beleaguered SNCC workers: from Avon Rollins in Danville seeking my immediate help in getting press coverage of the siege there; a desperate call from Mississippi asking for a neurosurgeon for Jimmy Travis, who had just been shot in the neck while driving the dark and dangerous road from Greenwood to Greenville, and who everyone feared would not be given proper treatment in Mississippi. We got him treatment in New York and hospital beds for others who needed treatment. Jimmy Travis said at the time of his ordeal, "I want to make my home in Mississippi. If I stop now, the segregationists will say, 'Okay, we'll shoot a couple more and the rest of them will quit.'" We offered support to sixteen-year-old Brenda Travis of McComb, Mississippi, helping her to relocate and attend school after she was expelled from her high school and sent to a reform school for taking part in a demonstration. She said she had demonstrated because, "It seems as if I've had the desire to do this ever since I was small. It always seemed as if our people were being kicked around and being mistreated."

In the Deep South

My other role was to look and listen when in the South so that I could adequately provide support once I got back out of the battle zone. To that end I traveled to Greenwood, Meridian, and Philadelphia in Mississippi and to the small, beleaguered group in Albany in Southwest Georgia. Traveling to Mississippi and Southwest Georgia was frightening. While flying over the beautiful verdancy of Mississippi, I wondered whether it was more desirable to crash and meet a white-only ambulance, which would not take black people to a hospital, or to drive along those frightening roads, lined on each side with seemingly threatening kudzu vines that seemed to crawl out to engulf not only trees but people. Also frightening were the drivers of pickup trucks who blatantly displayed their rifles as a challenge to "outside agitators." Cars in which there were both black and white passengers were suspect to the segregationists who patrolled the roads. Therefore, if the occupants of a movement car were mostly black, the white occupants huddled on the floor covered with blankets to hide their presence and vice versa.

My heart swelled when I stopped to ask directions to the freedom house in Albany and was greeted as a long-lost friend by the woman who answered the door. I had stopped with trepidation, because I didn't know how far the reach of the movement workers went, and it was wonderful to feel a part of a conspiracy against the white power structure.

Once at the Albany freedom house, where I was greeted by Faith Holsaert and Charles Sherrod, I got a view of life in the field. The warm and folksy Sherrod ran the freedom house with an iron hand. The women paid lip service to his commands and did their own thing. They wrote and typed their own reports and organized as best they could. They did not cook and clean, nor did they type for others, unless they chose to do so for the Movement. Faith and I slept in the same bed and in the night were roused by noises outside. Scared, but not immobilized, we shone lights and decided that it was a false alarm.

During another visit to Southwest Georgia I met an elderly woman named Mama Dolly Raines. She had gone to register to vote ten years earlier and had been turned away. An active nurse and midwife, she told the registrar, "If I'm not qualified to register, then I'm not qualified to nurse you and never will again." Mama Dolly lived out in the country on a farm and housed SNCC staff, including white workers Penny Patch, Larry Rubin, and Ralph Allen, guarding them with her shotgun. She said, "I grew up on a plantation with white people and always lived with them, so I guess that's why I'm not afraid of them." In her words, she was "the most nonviolent shot in the county."

Once, traveling out of Albany, we went to the Piney Grove Baptist Church, deep in the countryside, where the window shades were lowered because white men on motorcycles were circling the building. Rev. Agnew James of Lee County led us off with the song "Guide My Feet While I Run This Race." For trying to register to vote, he and his wife, who had thirteen children, were boycotted by the gasoline dealerships, which served all the small farmers who needed gasoline on their places for their tractors and other farm equipment. At this meeting he said, "They can boycott and double boycott. I am going to stay right here and work and fight and not give up. I'm not suffering anything; they are just telling me that I am. That's all. They can put every stone in my path; they can put a mountain there, and then I'm going to peek around it and still tell you to go register." When a man in a terror-ridden place like Piney Grove, Georgia, says that, what do you do? You go peek around the mountain yourself.

"We Will Show You": 1964 Mississippi Summer

In Mississippi in 1964, teaching in a Jackson Freedom School, I felt an over-whelming sense of helplessness when I discovered that the eight-year-old I was coaching could barely read because his vision was so bad. He simply could not see the letters, and no one had noticed this, or at least no one had ventured to do anything about it. At such times the situation seemed hopeless.

At other times, such as when I talked with fifty-nine-year-old Hartman Turnbow of Holmes County, I was transported. Turnbow said, "In April I went down to register, and they accused me of being an integration leader. I was written up in the paper. In May they firebombed my house. There were two cocktail bombs in the living room and one in the bedroom. The whole house was in flames." Turnbow ran outside and had a gun battle with the bombers.

That summer I also traveled to the Meridian office, where James Chaney, Andrew Goodman, and Michael Schwerner had been based. When I arrived in Meridian, a black policeman said, "I remember you. I saw you get off the plane in Jackson. You were met in Jackson by Moses." The omnipresence and omniscience of the police were creepy.

At the Meridian office we received a threatening call, which was, as usual, vicious. Moments later we got a second call, which went like this:

CALLER: "Are you one of those white northern bastards?"
RESPONSE: "No, I'm Negro."
CALLER: "Oh."

Then he paused a bit and said, "Uh, excuse me," and hung up. Such were the strange confusions of the white South. It almost made me feel sympathy for the poor soul at the other end of the telephone line. Here he was, ready to spew out hate to a white northerner but was flummoxed when confronted by the reality of the Movement.

It was different with the young thug who leaned into our car and in-vited us up to Philadelphia, where the three civil rights workers were lying under a dam. He said, "Come on up to Philadelphia. We'll show you." And there it was. We will show you. In a sense they did. The killers of the three workers—James Chaney, Andy Goodman, and Mickey Schwerner—went free. Another threatened us saying, "We got Mickey and we will get you."

Despite such threats, the search for the three movement workers was carried on by SNCC almost totally independently of FBI activity, though there was some, rather limited, sharing of information. One night at Jackson's

Sun and Sand Motel a few of us sat discussing developments with the television blaring and all of the faucets turned on full blast to foil any FBI taps that might be in place. Some of the talk was about the only white person in Neshoba County who was a member of the NAACP, who had said that the sheriff, Lawrence A. Rainey, and his deputy Cecil Ray Price had been involved in the murder of the three men.

In the end, I think that the horrible deaths of Chaney, Goodman, and Schwerner prevented the same fate for others. The nation and the world were pointing the finger, shining the spotlight on Mississippi, and this surveillance was some form of protection. These murders had not, of course, prevented the previous killings of so many others, some nameless and some named, like Herbert Lee, Medgar Evers, and Louis Allen. Nor would they prevent the later murders of civil rights workers Jimmie Lee Jackson, Sammy Younge Jr., Rev. James Reeb, and Viola Liuzzo. But I believe that for a time it stopped the wholesale license to kill that the southern segregationists had held. This is not to say that we ever let down our guard, that we ever stopped being vigilant. Only that Chaney, Goodman, and Schwerner did not die in vain.

At the end of the summer, although the Mississippi Freedom Democratic Party was not seated, the party could claim a victory in that the nation took notice. In the end the delegation's stance was responsible for a rewriting of the Democratic Party's rules, which in the future would not permit any delegation to be seated that did not represent proportionately minority populations *and women*.

My Friend Ella Baker

One of my closest friends in SNCC was Miss Ella Baker, the organization's founder, whom I met at my first SNCC conference. Her influence on me has been lifelong and lasting beyond her death in the 1980s. Miss Baker, who nurtured all of us in SNCC, most certainly helped me to grow, to understand, to be tolerant, and above all to take it slow, relax, not take anything too seriously. Soon after we met, we began to share rooms—despite the fact that I smoked. She tolerated the smoking while I leaned out of the motel room windows to puff into the outdoors. We found that we had a lot in common, as almost everyone found in relation to her; our links were New York City, radical politics, and a love of Chablis.

She rescued me on some occasions, as when she got me moved from Atlanta's loathsome University Motel into the home of Grace Hamilton. Another rescue I recall was when there was a serious dispute at a SNCC meeting and a scuffle broke out in the balcony. Feeling sad, I burst into tears, and Miss Baker, who was sitting next to me, stood up, pulled me to my feet, and began to sing "We Shall Overcome," the song she called "old soothing syrup." It worked. She cooled it down. She cooled me down as well after the meeting at Kingston Springs, Tennessee, where the chairmanship of SNCC was snared by Stokely Carmichael from incumbent John Lewis in what I felt was a non-democratic ploy. This incensed me. Miss Baker kept me calm.

I worked with Miss Baker in the New York Friends of SNCC office and in the Fund for Education and Legal Defense (FELD). She set up FELD to provide aid to SNCC workers and local activists. Miss Baker and I collaborated on the first major fund-raising event for SNCC in New York, a star-studded concert at Carnegie Hall in 1963. At the end, the battle-weary SNCC workers came onstage to rousing bursts of applause. There was a glorious assemblage of black and white, male and female, veterans of the struggle on the stage with Thelonius Monk, Charlie Mingus, and Tony Bennett.

The bulk of the money raised by SNCC in New York was garnered through direct mail campaigns run by a committee made up of writers, editors, and direct mail experts in the days when this fund-raising technique was in its infancy. Special events included hundred-dollar-a-plate dinners that featured such performers as Sidney Poitier, Harry Belafonte, Diahann Carroll, and Marlon Brando. Eventually a New York fund-raising office run by Roberta Yancy was established; here my sister-in-law Lucille Perlman was in charge of our large and valuable mailing list.

Miss Baker's contributions to the Movement were on a grand scale. As Chuck McDew, the second chair of SNCC, put it, "She made us in her image." She taught the SNCC students the importance of nurturing local leaders, the value of organizing local groups who would make their own decisions, and the vital concept of a group-centered leadership as opposed to a leadership-centered group. She instilled in them the idea that they were not organized to exist in perpetuity as an organization, that others would come along to continue the struggle, and that the struggle is continuous. "The tribe increases," she always said.

At Miss Baker's funeral, her friend and co-worker Anne Braden said that Miss Baker had the ability to sift through the superficial to find the real human being. "She didn't deal in labels. She wanted to know what people thought, but mostly she wanted them to think." I spoke of Miss Baker's faith in humanity and that she did not distinguish between individuals on the basis of race. We were all her children. While she thought that black is beautiful, Miss Baker never abandoned her belief in black and white together, in the humanness of all humankind.

Good Times

We had good times in the midst of the terror and danger. There was the night I made jambalaya for a couple dozen people in Jackson, Mississippi. Everyone, particularly the men who were in charge of provisions and supplies, rallied to find lobster, saffron, and shrimp for the master work. Once, at my Manhattan apartment on Central Park West, I had a dinner party that kept growing. People kept calling and saying they would like to come, so we kept going out to buy more steaks, until we had fifteen or twenty hardy, hungry SNCC workers lounging around the crowded one-bedroom pad I shared with Faye Goodman. Somehow the grapevine had sent out the message that there were steaks to be had and SNCC people kept showing up.

My contributions to the Movement were of some merit, I suppose, but the Movement's contributions to me were ever so much greater. What did SNCC give us? It gave us a reason for keeping on, for continuing to peek around the mountain, and it gave us the means. We are the inheritors of Ella Baker's teaching that ordinary people can do what is needed to help themselves. It is this tenet that communicated itself to the young people of SNCC and to me.

It is important that much of the organization's overall planning was in the hands of women such as Ruby Doris Robinson and Betty Garman, not to forget Ella Baker. Much of the cooking and cleaning was done by men who worked so hard to make the tasks gender nonspecific: William Porter, who in Atlanta did all of the food ordering and most of its preparation, and Jim Forman, who organized the cleanups and swept the office himself.

As important is the sense of family. In SNCC in 1960 I found another family, my real family, the family that has sustained me throughout the years. Not that I have abandoned my biological family, just that I had found a new one, one that encompassed many people, black and white, who shared my dreams. The Movement gave me a sense of community, of continuity, of brotherhood, which I still take to mean brotherhood and sisterhood. There was a sense of togetherness; we really did want to build the beloved community.

Forty years later we all respond to distress calls from one another. Despite any disagreement that arose then or since, we remain bonded by shared experiences, shared dangers, shared accomplishments, and, yes, shared failures. We did not establish the "beloved community" nationwide, but we have it. We still live as a band of brothers and sisters in a circle of trust.

Trained in history and journalism at Syracuse and Columbia universities, **JOANNE GRANT** worked full-time as an editorial assistant to Dr. W. E. B. Du Bois in the late 1950s. After a stint at *Sing Out* magazine and Folkways Records, she then moved to the *National Guardian* as a reporter and later served briefly as news director for the radical New York radio station WBAI and did publicity for the *Nation*. She authored three books, *Black Protest, Confrontation on Campus,* and *Ella Baker: Freedom Bound.* Grant produced, directed, and wrote the award-winning documentary film *Fundi: The Story of Ella Baker.* An inveterate traveler, Grant traveled many times to Europe, Russia, China, and Cuba. She is the mother of two children born to her and her husband, the late civil rights attorney Victor Rabinowitz, the father of former SNCC worker Joni Rabinowitz and Mississippi Summer Project volunteer Peter Rabinowitz. At the time of her death, in January 2005, she was working on another film, *Rebel in the House: The Life and Times of Representative Vito Marcantonio.*

My Real Vocation

Dorothy M. Zellner

A New York radical learns firsthand in the South the joy of participating in the noble struggle for racial justice.

Going South

On February 2, 1960—a moment I still remember with perfect clarity—I sat drinking coffee at the counter of a mid-Manhattan coffee shop, furiously smoking Pall Malls and reading the *New York Times,* when I spotted a news story from Greensboro, North Carolina, on a back page. The day before, four young black men had sat down at a Woolworth's lunch counter, ordered, and, when refused service, declined to leave. They were arrested. *How inventive and clever,* I thought. *How brave.*

"Equality for the Negro people" had been an axiom of my upbringing as the child of immigrant Jewish leftists; therefore, unlike most white Americans, I actually knew something of black history. I had even glimpsed both the great Paul Robeson and W. E. B. DuBois in person. And I had grown up with the heroic stories of resistance to fascism, particularly of the young Jewish fighters of the Warsaw Ghetto who fought the Nazis in a last spurt of defiance and despair.

At age twenty-two and just graduated from Queens College, I was electrified by the sit-in story. Somehow I knew that for me this was more than just an interesting news story about some heroic young people far away. Within a few weeks I applied to participate in a nonviolent direct action workshop organized by CORE in Miami.

Much to my surprise and excitement, CORE accepted me as a workshop member, and in June 1960 I found myself in Miami, Florida, which at the time was completely segregated. I experienced an immediate kind of recognition and affinity with the other workshop participants. Most of the young black students—like Bernard Lafayette, Rudy Lombard, and Angeline Butler—were already veterans of the sit-in movement. I saw them as heroes, but they didn't act like heroes, which of course made them all the more heroic to me. In the group there were even some young, extraordinary white Louisianans, like Oliver St. Pé, who was legally blind and wore inch-thick lenses, and Hugh Murray, who had defied his family to become involved in the Civil Rights Movement. I felt at home at the meetings, talking in the hallways, spending time with all the other young women in our rooms, laughing and talking while we washed clothes and set our hair, danced, and listened to the radio. They literally fell on the floor, screaming with laughter, when I asked who Ray Charles was.

Our job was to have an actual sit-in, both for training's sake and to challenge Miami's segregated restaurants. After sitting down for an hour at the counter in a downtown eatery, we were arrested as a matter of course. On the way out to the paddy wagon we held hands and sang a freedom song. I felt afraid, yet proud, and even strangely relieved: what I had dreaded was now actually happening. Only at the segregated jail did it dawn on me that as the only white woman I would be held in a segregated cell with white southern women! I was not prepared for this.

The lights were off and everyone was asleep by the time a hefty police matron led me to my cell. I took off a minimum of clothes and slept on the bare mattress. As we lined up in the morning, the matron called the roll. Everyone else said, "Yes, ma'am," in response to their names. I said yes, having never said or heard *ma'am* in my life. She bellowed out my name again. I got it. "Yes, ma'am," I stated meekly. The other women giggled. The matron handed me a mop that I could hardly lift and ordered me to clean the floor of the cell. I did, but certainly not to the satisfaction of the other women, who also expressed dismay that I had slept on a bare mattress. "Don't you know what's *in* these mattresses?" they shouted.

After the workshop ended, I persuaded the New Orleans contingent to let me go home with them, where they were planning to hold the city's first sit-in, at the main Woolworth's on Canal Street. As part of my assignment to obtain support from members of the white community, I visited Rabbi Jules Feibelman at the largest synagogue in New Orleans, Temple Sinai on St. Charles Avenue. In response to my plea as a fellow Jew for some kind of public support from the Jewish community, he sputtered that the Jewish community was already insecure and couldn't support an action as controversial as a sit-in and then ordered me out of his office.

I walked out of the grand synagogue confused and upset; on the one hand, I understood how this small community could feel so threatened; on the other, I was embarrassed that it had abandoned what was surely a main tenet in Jewish culture—the love of justice.

Some days before the actual sit-in, several of us "cased" the Woolworth's, strolling through the store, spotting the entrances and exits. On the day of the sit-in I helped make and bring the picket signs and was appointed to drive one of the cars. I said nothing but was completely terrified by this task, since, as a typical New Yorker, I had been at the wheel only a few times in my life.

As a designated observer, I watched the group seat themselves on stools at the counter. Among them was Hugh, from Hanrahan, a small town near New Orleans. Though nervous, he bravely sat with our other black friends at the counter for more than an hour, as the waitresses refused to serve anyone. Behind the sit-in area, now roped off by New Orleans police, a large crowd gathered, muttering angrily. Then a middle-aged white man tore through the store and flung aside the rope. Screaming, he dragged Hugh from his stool. It was Hugh's father. He had heard a radio report of the sit-in while driving his car and came directly to Canal Street to get his son.

A few moments later, I went up the stairs to the white women's bathroom. As I sat in the stall, I heard the other women at the sink talking about the "disgraceful" thing that was going on downstairs, although "talking" is not the word for it. The supposedly respectable white women screeched to each other that those "niggers would catch it for sure" when the schools were desegregated next week, just as they would catch it downstairs in the Woolworth's restaurant. This was the worst racist bile I heard in the twenty-two years I ultimately spent in the South.

The police arrested those still seated at the counter, and the rest of us jumped into our car, with me nervously at the wheel, racing back to the YMCA to make phone calls and raise bail. I came to a traffic circle, something I had never seen before, and wove from side to side in the traffic. Even though Oliver could hardly see, which was why he had disqualified himself as the driver, he screamed, "We never should have let you drive!" However, we arrived without incident at the Y, and I was so relieved I practically fell out of the car.

SNCC

After my experiences with sit-ins in Miami and New Orleans, I was anxious to get back south. My friends at the CORE workshop had spoken incessantly about SNCC, an organization run completely by young people. I wrote to SNCC but never heard anything. I found out only much later that SNCC at this time was hardly an organization in the proper sense of the word, with no staff to speak of, and thus nobody to answer my letters, which ultimately ended up, I was told later, in the trash.

Not brave enough to just appear somewhere in the South, suitcase in hand without any preparation whatever, I felt I had to have a *job* with someone. As the months passed, I wrote to any organization that might possibly hire me. Finally, in May 1961 I got a letter from the Southern Regional Council (SRC) saying that James A. Moss, a former professor of mine at Queens College, was the new research director, that he had seen one of those letters and would like to hire me as a research assistant. SRC expected me in three weeks! Thus, by extreme luck, my real career, my real vocation—in fact, my real life—began.

In June 1961 I flew down to Atlanta with two suitcases. (My mother helped me pack a trunk with sheets and household utensils and sent it separately.) Les Dunbar, the SRC executive director, assigned me to research and write a white paper to be issued by the organization about the now eighteen-month-old sit-in movement. I found a furnished apartment on Tenth Street on the white side of town near Peachtree Street. Everything in Atlanta was segregated, except for the city buses and Rich's department store, newly desegregated by black student sit-ins. This meant a schizoid existence for all of us at SRC. We worked in an interracial organization, but once we left the SRC offices on Forsyth Street, every single thing we chose to do—whether eating lunch, shopping, going to a movie—was determined by race. My parents had supported my move to Atlanta, my father in particular being quite proud of what I was doing. He had in fact passed around a *Miami Herald* press clipping to all and sundry showing me in jail.

My main object was to get to SNCC, but I could not summon up the courage to take a twenty-minute walk to the SNCC office on Auburn Avenue. The more stories I read about the heroic actions of SNCC workers, the more awed I became. The more awed I became, the shyer I was. While reading and filing newspaper clippings in preparation for the report, certain names kept popping up. A man by the name of Robert Zellner was frequently mentioned: he was unique—a white Southerner who had broken with segregation and worked for a predominantly black organization. I wondered to myself, *What on earth is a Jewish boy doing running around the South and getting arrested?* (Later, of course, I realized he was the son of a Methodist minister, the man who would become my father-in-law.)

Several weeks later, still not having gone to the SNCC office, I finally completed the draft report on the sit-in movement, which Dunbar edited and approved. SRC released it to the press on September 29, 1961, and the *New York Times* ran the story on the front page, reporting that between February 1, 1960, and September 1961, sit-ins or other forms of direct action (what we used to call nonviolent resistance) occurred in more than one hundred cities, in every Southern and border state; 3,600 students and supporters had been arrested; at least 70,000 people had participated in some way (marching, picketing, sitting in, attending mass meetings), and many thousands more had supported the sit-ins; at least 141 students and 58 faculty members were dismissed or suspended; 236 students withdrew from Southern University in Baton Rouge when sit-in leaders were dismissed.

In October 1961 an exceptionally blond Danish journalist named Per Laursen asked me to take him to the SNCC office. No doubt he mistakenly thought that as someone who lived and worked in the small interracial community in Atlanta, I was a frequent visitor to the SNCC office. So, finally, after five months in Atlanta, with a foreign journalist in tow, I actually set foot in the SNCC office, the object of my journey to Atlanta in the first place.

All I remember now of the SNCC office is how small and dark it was. But it was lit up with the immense personality of Jim Forman, SNCC's new executive secretary, a burly man in baggy pants. Upon meeting me, Forman asked immediately, "Can you type?" I did not think then, nor do I now, that this was an insulting or sexist question. Yes, I answered eagerly, feeling lucky to be able to do something needed, and in this way to contribute to and belong to a movement I considered so important. Forman (many SNCC people were called by their last names) was an organizational genius. His brain operated like a SNCC chessboard: he never stopped thinking about the moves that needed to be made and what could or would happen to SNCC if they were. Sometimes gruff and grumpy, his greatest gift was the ability to immediately match each person's skills to the organization's needs. I loved and respected him from the moment I met him until he died in 2005.

For the next several months, I worked at the Southern Regional Council during the day and came to the SNCC office in the evening. When I told Forman that I could write as well as type, his eyes lit up. Right away he told me that he wanted me to work with Julian Bond on the *Student Voice*, SNCC's newsletter. Later that winter I began to share an apartment with Jane, Julian's sister. I became devoted to both of them—for Jane's humor and quick wit, and for Julian's writing talent and wry sense of humor. When he danced at parties, smiling cryptically, he often kept his hands in his trouser pockets and hitched up his pants, his feet twinkling this way and that to the music.

When SNCC field secretaries came to the office, I sat, fingers poised at the typewriter keys, and took down reports from Reggie Robinson, Sam Block, Willie Peacock, Hollis Watkins, Curtis Hayes, or other SNCC workers as they described in a matter-of-fact way what had happened at this or that courthouse when they accompanied disenfranchised black people, mostly sharecroppers or domestic workers, to register to vote in rural Mississippi or Georgia. The story was always the same: after weeks of slow and patient urging by field secretaries, local black people agreed to go to the courthouse to register; stood on line for hours, often in sizzling heat or damp cold; and endured heckling and abuse. The end was always the same: invariably someone was arrested, someone was beaten, someone was shot at, someone was fired, and nobody was registered. Aghast, I typed, trying hard to match their nonchalance, as these young men sitting right next to me talked, "telling the story."

SNCC used this material in two ways: as statements accompanying irate letters to the federal government demanding that it guarantee black people the right to register to vote, and as reports to build a national network of Friends of SNCC groups in northern cities and on campuses throughout the country.

Ruby Doris

When the office on Auburn Avenue soon proved too small, in the winter of 1962 Forman rented a large loft a couple of blocks away on the same street. Here I met Ruby Doris Smith, probably that spring. She was viewed as a hero, and I noticed that the men in particular treated her carefully and spoke of her respectfully. A student at the proper Spelman College, she had been a Freedom Rider and, after being arrested at a sit-in, had been sentenced to thirty harrowing days in jail at Rock Hill, South Carolina, during which she was assigned to a work gang, lifting rocks along the road. She was tough, smart, fierce, and often difficult to approach. Later on, after she succeeded Forman as executive secretary, she was merciless; she forced the mostly male field secretaries to explain their expenses and their whereabouts, and all someone had to do was threaten to say, "Uh-oh, I'm going to have to talk to Ruby Doris about this," and the miscreant quaked. My fondest recollection of Ruby, however, was of a sweet afternoon in the office when she and white field secretary Bob Zellner, who was by then in a pair with me, sang hymns like "Just a Closer Walk with Thee" for a long time.

In June 1962 a worried and drawn Dunbar called me into his office at SRC to tell me that he was letting me go because of "automation." He also mentioned that the FBI had come by several weeks earlier asking about me and had shown him a photo of me at some kind of political "rally." Although he emphatically denied that the firing and the visit were connected, I didn't believe him. Forman promptly hired me. In eight months I had come from being afraid to walk twenty minutes to the SNCC office to being a full-fledged staff member in the organization I loved.

I worked with Julian writing press releases, firing off indignant telegrams to the Kennedys in Washington, and writing letters to northern supporters and articles for the *Student Voice* and SNCC pamphlets. As a new SNCC staff member, I was comfortable being in a tiny minority of white people in a black-led organization in a black world, and I enjoyed being a part of "the beloved community," the lofty expression that SNCC members used in the early days of the sit-in movement to describe not only the goal they were seeking, but their human relationships. Of course there were frictions between black and white, northern and southern, men and women, people in the office and people out on the field, the leadership and the staff. But the ethic of SNCC did not allow discord on these issues to get out of control. The culture of cooperation that valued loyalty, even love and trust for one another, took precedence. Indeed, this small group of maybe thirty SNCC people achieved, for a limited time at least, a community that actually was, to a remarkable extent, beloved.

It seemed to me that SNCC people had total, unwavering belief in American democracy and were fighting for access to what this democracy had promised them. Politically the SNCC folk felt the house was basically sound. The problem was to open the door somehow so that black people could get in. One way to do this was to embarrass the Kennedys to do what was right. This was at the heart of the ceaseless stream of telegrams we sent to Washington reporting each and every atrocity and urging them to intervene. At the time, my more leftist friends pointed out that such faith in the federal government was misplaced. I didn't agree, but they were probably correct, for this probably accounted for SNCC's later shock at the betrayal by the liberal establishment at the Democratic convention in Atlantic City in 1964.

In the next few months we settled into another "new" SNCC office, this time a former apartment on Raymond Street. I spent many hours, along with other staff members, hand-cranking the mimeograph machine, spitting out hundreds of copies of a clemency petition for Clyde Kennard, who was serving time in the notorious Parchman Penitentiary in Mississippi because he had tried to integrate Mississippi Southern College. Occasionally the Freedom Singers, an a capella group of SNCC workers, practiced in the office. There was no way anyone could work when they sang. I would put my work down on the desk and just sit back in my chair and listen to the heavenly sounds of Rutha Harris belting out "This Little Light of Mine."

Sometimes the incessant and fruitless demands we sent to Washington, plus the poverty and hardship of our working conditions, made us giddy. When Forman's birthday rolled around in October 1962, Julian and I sent a congratulatory telegram purporting to be from none other than President John F. Kennedy himself! I thought this was hilarious, but Forman took a very dim view of this prank, dourly suggesting that perhaps we had committed a federal crime.

During the winter of 1962–1963, the temperature dropped to an unheard-of eight degrees in Atlanta. We wore our winter coats and gloves indoors in the SNCC office, because there was no money to pay heating bills. Julian and I once walked through neighborhood vacant lots and empty backyards picking up scraps of wood and other flammable substances to burn in the office fireplace for warmth. On another day, we actually started cannibalizing office furniture; we broke a bookcase apart and fed the wood into the fire.

However, by the spring, the northern support began to mushroom and money began to pour in. It was during such a flush period that I witnessed Forman calling a car dealership and putting in an order for twenty Plymouths (at two thousand dollars per car) for the growing field staff. My mouth fell open. Forman had nerves of steel; he said, "We can get the money now, and we'd better do this while we can."

It was also during this spring that I had an interesting interaction with the FBI (whose visit, I believed, led to my firing from SRC). In films such as *Mississippi Burning* the FBI is shown to be professional and alert when it comes to the Civil Rights Movement; therefore, it is even more ironic that about 9:00 P.M. one night my phone rang at home and the caller identified himself as an FBI agent. "Where," he wanted to know, "is Dr. King?" "What!" I said. "I don't know." "We followed him to the airport and lost him," the agent said, disconsolately. Julian and I giggled about this for quite some time.

The Civil Liberties Workshop

In the spring of 1963 Anne Braden, who led the Southern Conference Educational Fund with her husband, Carl, suggested that SCEF and SNCC work together to plan a workshop on the question of civil liberties: free speech and free association inside and outside of the Movement. I was given the job of helping to organize it under the supervision of Ella Baker, who was on the payroll of SCEF at the time. I had met Miss Baker the year before when she ran an interracial program at the YWCA that included Casey Hayden and Dorothy Dawson. Then in her late fifties, Miss Baker possessed an almost mythical status as the person who had single-handedly preserved SNCC's independence from the NAACP and SCLC.

Though McCarthyism was on the wane in the early sixties, it had not vanished. Members of groups like the Women's Strike for Peace were still being subpoenaed by the House Un-American Activities Committee for so-called subversive activity, and the FBI, which was supposed to be gathering information to support the constitutional activities of prospective voter registrants, spent much of its time instead surveilling suspected Communists. By the spring of 1963 the SNCC staff had already felt pressures from other civil rights and liberal organizations to exclude radicals, both as donors and participants. Anne, a passionately committed movement fighter, was herself the victim of red-baiting in and out of the Civil Rights Movement and felt strongly that SNCC, as the most important civil rights organization, needed to prepare itself for possible attacks from the government.

Miss Baker, as well as Anne, supervised me, which was not easy, since I was then in the throes of my romance with Bob Zellner. One day, in fact, Miss Baker, who normally was quite indirect in her approach to young people and could sit in the back of a meeting room for hours and days without saying anything, reprimanded me for not paying enough attention to what I was doing! However, the workshop, which was really an extended discussion, went well. After many long and difficult talk sessions, the consensus was that SNCC (1) would not cooperate with any federal investigating committee, and (2) would accept assistance and participation from outside individuals or groups regardless of their politics. (It is my belief that word of SNCC's stance of noncooperation quickly got around government circles and that the prospect of subpoenaing noncompliant black heroes of the Civil Rights Movement contributed to the ultimate death of such groups as the House Un-American Activities Committee.)

The idea of non-exclusion caused a most painful discussion. I recall that Bob Moses spoke at length about his fears that local people in Mississippi would be endangered by the presence of Communists or other radicals. It was impossible not to be affected by his concerns—Herbert Lee and others had already been killed in Mississippi—but the group decided that it might ultimately be more dangerous for the Movement to compromise on this question. The decisions made at this workshop were maintained during the Freedom Summer of 1964.

Fire Hoses and Escapes

Forman was always very keen on history and told us at the slightest opportunity (in fact, in tedious detail, over and over), "You must keep everything, you must file everything, you must write it down, you must keep copies—because this is History!" He decided that we needed to write and produce pamphlets about SNCC's work, pamphlets that could be distributed in the North and elsewhere for educational and fund-raising purposes—for the sake of History!

In June 1963 Forman assigned me to write a pamphlet on the big movement battle that SNCC had recently joined in Danville, Virginia. This pamphlet was later edited by Elizabeth Sutherland Martinez and illustrated with brilliant photographs by Danny Lyon, a witty Chicagoan whom Forman had put to work as a SNCC photographer.

In Danville I participated in a nighttime demonstration of black community people led by ministers at the back of the police station, where several movement people were being held. After we began to kneel and pray for the release of the prisoners, we were hit from the side by high-pressure water hoses. The water from the hoses could knock you over in a second. At the time I weighed 106 pounds, because I had been mistakenly diagnosed as being diabetic and was afraid to eat anything. Almost immediately I found myself lying flat on the ground, minus my shoes, which had been washed away by the water. When I tried to get up on my hands and knees I felt a sharp crack on the side of my head, and I saw starbursts of different colors, like a brilliant fireworks display, inside my skull. Until then I had thought that "seeing stars" was just a literary expression. The cop who hit me loomed over me like a white mountain, wielding his nightstick and staring at me blankly, not registering either satisfaction or hatred as I staggered to my feet. Many of the other demonstrators were beaten much more savagely. The next day Danny took photographs of the walking wounded, with their bandaged heads and bodies. These photos went into the pamphlet.

After this, Forman and other SNCC personnel arrived. About forty local people decided to hold a protest demonstration in front of city hall, an imposing granite building with broad stairs sweeping from the street to the main entrance. Vowing to stay all night if necessary, we sat all day on the city hall stairs. Forman captured the attention of this involuntary audience by conducting an impromptu black history lesson at the top of his voice, telling us about Harriet Tubman and other great black figures of the past. When darkness came the police drove the water cannons to city hall and parked them directly across the street, unraveling huge hoses. Several white men grabbed the hoses—the city had deputized practically every white male in sight—and pointed them at us.

Those of us on the stairs, now down to about twenty, prepared for the worst. I held a railing with both hands as tightly as I possibly could, my heart pounding, dreading the moment when they turned the hoses on us. We had heard that some people had been blinded by the blast of water in their faces. Just then, Forman, seeing the hopelessness of the situation, lumbered to his feet and approached the police chief, saying, "Do you want all these people to get hurt?" In the momentary confusion, Forman motioned to us to leave, and we slowly got up from our positions and left city hall, heads held high. I felt that Forman had saved our lives.

The State of Virginia was preparing to use against the Danville Civil Rights Movement the "John Brown law," passed after the insurrection at Harper's Ferry. This law made it a felony to "incite colored people to acts of war and violence against the white population." Forman told Danny and me that defending us against felony charges, if we were indicted, would be a needless expense. In other words, we had to leave. As directed, Danny and I took our luggage to a black church on a hillside. When it was time to go, we climbed out of a back window and into a pink Cadillac, where we lay on the floor of the backseat, covered with newspapers. Out of fear and tension, I began to laugh uncontrollably.

At the airport I switched from laughter to tears, thinking of all the people I had left behind. Danny went up to the airline ticket counter and, in a burst of invention, registered me under a nom de guerre: "Joanne Woodward." It could not have been possible for me to look more different from actress Joanne Woodward, standing there in bedraggled clothes, and I began to laugh maniacally again.

Along with several other SNCC people, including Bob Zellner, Danny and I were, in fact, indicted under the "John Brown law." Later, Bob and I, then married and with our two children in tow, drove through Virginia many times. Until the statute of limitations was up in the 1970s, we never stopped for anything, not even gas.

Massachusetts and Mississippi

In the fall of 1963 Bob and I set up housekeeping in Cambridge, Massachusetts. Forman assigned me to run the Northeast Regional Office of SNCC located in Cambridge, Massachusetts. When SNCC made the momentous decision to organize the Freedom Summer of 1964, I spent much of my time recruiting summer volunteers from the many colleges and universities in the northeast region. My interviewing partner was Katie Clark, the daughter of black psychologists Kenneth and Mamie Clark, whose tests on black children had been a decisive factor in *Brown v. Board of Education*. Our task was to weed out anyone we thought inappropriate for the work in Mississippi, such as thrill seekers or those who were unappreciative of the seriousness and danger of the work or who might not show the proper respect for people in the black community.

I, myself, the chief recruiter for the northeast region, became increasingly terrified at the prospect of going to Mississippi. I thought of ways of getting out of it. But how could I recruit other people and not go myself? Maybe, I thought hopefully, I would be lucky enough to get run over by a car and get my leg smashed up. Then who could possibly insist that I go to Mississippi on crutches? Not wanting to go, not wanting to stay, either I couldn't sleep or I slept too much and couldn't get up.

Finally, I went to Mississippi, which became a summer filled with more terror than I could ever have imagined. In Oxford, Ohio, at the orientation session for Freedom Summer, Julian and I conducted a workshop for the volunteer "communications people." We stood at the blackboard explaining that they must track the whereabouts of the project members at all times. I remember saying, "If people go out and say they are coming back at three, and if it's ten after and they're not back, start calling"—the jails first, then hospitals, and so on. A young woman who attended this workshop was to be the communications person for the Meridian project, and it was she who started calling when James Chaney, Andy Goodman, and Mickey Schwerner didn't come back to the project office on time.

Rita Schwerner was unforgettable. She was then one of the tiniest people I had ever seen—she couldn't possibly have weighed more than eighty-five pounds—but she loomed large in bravery and principle. She refused to weep for the cameras or to answer the question, "How do you *feel?*" and repeatedly told the white press that if her husband were black, as was James Chaney, they wouldn't be covering the story. They didn't want to hear this—they began to ignore her.

I worked a shift on the WATS line in the Greenwood, Mississippi, office, where SNCC had moved its operation for the summer, which meant I took calls from people who had been arrested or abused and made calls to the press and their families. A nineteen-year-old Harvard student, Peter Orris, whom I had recruited, set up a walkie-talkie system in each of the project offices. Once, a desperate call, which consisted mostly of inarticulate cries about being followed by cars full of menacing white people in Tallahatchie County, one of the state's worst, came crackling over our walkie-talkie system. Harry Belafonte and Sidney Poitier, who were traveling the state on a morale-boosting tour, happened to be standing right next to us as we handled this call. Visibly nervous, they watched this process, mouths agape—we stared at them, our own mouths open. Later that evening, Forman ordered Bob and me to vacate our bed so that Harry and Sidney could sleep in it.

One evening, Judy Richardson, a lively SNCC worker who shared the WATS line work with me, and I were crossing the street in front of the office when a car drove by and we heard a loud crack. Judy shouted, "Get down, get down!" We both fell to the ground and crawled through a stubbly backyard to get to the back door of the house we sought. Naturally, since I was completely terrified, I began to laugh hysterically. Judy remembers nothing of this.

After the Mississippi Summer

Back in the Cambridge SNCC office in the fall of 1964—after the stupendous successes of the Mississippi Summer Project and the momentous betrayal of the Freedom Democratic Party at the Atlantic City convention by Joe Rauh and Hubert Humphrey and all the other supposedly "helpful" liberals—something was definitely wrong in SNCC. There were endless staff meetings about tactics and strategy. There was the "freedom high" group, who believed in letting the people decide; there was the "structuralist" group, who believed in a strong central authority. I was in the latter category, as ever the big supporter of Jim Forman, the de facto leader of the structuralists. We talked, we debated. Now, looking back, I see that we didn't really address the real issues—(1) that the house was rotten, (2) the door had been slammed to keep us out, and (3) we didn't know what to do next.

To compound our problems, unbeknownst to us, several prominent organizations and individuals were meeting to discuss minimizing SNCC's authority if a second Freedom Summer occurred in 1965. This I learned accidentally from someone Bob and I had met at a party in January 1965 and was confirmed later when I met with now Congressman Barney Frank, then a graduate student at Harvard, who was present at the meeting. Forman instructed me to write a memo summarizing this conversation, which I did the very next day. It is in the SNCC archives today. In brief, the memo states that major organizations, even including the National Council of Churches and the NAACP, were prepared to set up dual recruiting for a second Freedom Summer Project, essentially a counter-project, if SNCC did not agree to accept the idea of a governing board to manage joint summer activities in Mississippi. The main reason expressed for this concern was SNCC's increasingly radical stance, especially its refusal to accept the compromise at the 1964 Democratic convention in Atlantic City, although some participants at the meetings cited SNCC's refusal to screen out radicals as an additional factor. Of course, another Freedom Summer never occurred.

Later in 1965 I went back to work in the Atlanta office. I worked in the office two days a week, taking with me our six-month-old daughter, Margaret, in a bassinet. Ironically, one of the tasks I completed was finishing another SNCC worker's drawing of a black panther at Stokely Carmichael's request. I made the panther's whiskers fuller and straighter and inked in his body, making him black. Afterward, I handed it back to Stokely, knowing that he and Jack Minnis were going to use it as the emblem of the Lowndes County Movement in Alabama. This same panther became the emblem of both the Black Panther parties of California and Alabama and of black power in general.

Issues

Something new was afoot. Staff discussions, pushed passionately by several members of the Atlanta Project of SNCC, now consisted basically of the demand that SNCC should become an all-black organization. I remember hearing this for the first time at a meeting in Atlanta near the end of 1965. I was quite shocked that first time and simply could not conceive of my life without SNCC. Sometime earlier someone passed me a memorandum about sexism in SNCC, asking if I would like to "sign on." I declined, saying that I thought the discussion would be "divisive," that it would pit the men and women in SNCC against each other. Such was my feminist understanding in those days.

At the final SNCC staff meeting, held at Peg Leg Bates's estate in Upstate New York in late 1966, black SNCC members voted to exclude white staffers. Bob attended the meeting and reported to me that the white people who were present chose to abstain from voting on this issue. I went to see Forman in New York. I sat on a chair facing him and his new wife, Constancia Romilly, who would soon become my close friend. They sat on the couch opposite me. Forman was clearly very upset by what was happening in SNCC but seemed unable to deal with it in a meaningful way.

In the midst of these discussions, Ruby Doris became desperately ill with a form of leukemia and was hospitalized at Beth Israel, two blocks away from my parents' apartment. In the winter of 1966–1967 I came frequently to see my parents in New York from New Haven, where Bob was running an anti-war congressional campaign. I visited Ruby often, as did Cathy Archibald, another SNCC worker. That awful winter I remember trudging through high snowdrifts to the hospital and sitting with Ruby for many hours. When she could, we talked and laughed, and when Forman came we sat, our three heads bent close together, talking, talking, talking, talking, mostly, as I remember, about the foibles of this or that SNCC person, whether so-and-so should do such-and-such. Sometimes Ruby was so weak that she whispered. I can't remember if we discussed all the torrents of racial change raging around us, but Ruby seemed glad to see me when I came, and I felt a great tenderness for her. She died at the age of twenty-six.

In the winter of 1967 Bob and I decided to make one last attempt to stay in SNCC. By then, most, if not all, of the white people had left. Having joined the staff almost five years earlier, thinking this would be my life's work, I did not want to disappear from SNCC without a trace. The Bradens had been after us for some months to come on the staff of SCEF; indeed, Anne wanted Bob and me to take over the leadership of the organization. I wanted to postpone this decision until we defined our relationship, one way or the other, with SNCC. I wrote a short statement to the executive committee of SNCC on behalf of both of us, which proposed that we would live in the white community and organize white people (no small concession for me). But, we insisted, we could do this only in the context of remaining in SNCC as staff members—with a vote. I felt a strong personal need to have rights in the organization I loved so much, but I also thought that white people could not be organized in a vacuum; there had to be some black presence if such organizing were not to degenerate into racist activities.

Bob went to Atlanta to deliver this paper in person. I stayed in Alabama with the baby. He was asked to leave the room during the discussion and then called back in, where he was told, with much regret and emotion, that our proposal had been refused. Some weeks later we went to work for SCEF in New Orleans, where our second daughter, Katie, was born in 1968 and where I lived until 1983, after Bob and I separated.

Leaving SNCC was one of the most painful things that ever happened to me. It meant not only the loss of what I thought was my life's work, but it was also the end of my five-year proud association with SNCC, the most creative, funny, innovative, daring, fearless group of people I ever met. I disagreed then with the decision to ask white people to leave and continue to believe it was wrong. Still, I thought I understood where it came from—how many black SNCC workers felt that after all these years and all the deaths and all the betrayals, an interracial organization was no longer viable in such a racist country as ours.

For many years I did not discuss this with the press, not wanting to play the role of the "wronged" white woman who had been so "terribly mistreated" by "ungrateful" black people. I felt that even saying anything would be interpreted as disloyalty to SNCC. Now I think it has become extremely important to talk a lot about SNCC.

For me, probably the hardest consequence of leaving SNCC was the subsequent breach between many black and white SNCC people, years of distance and chilly separation. But this has changed. Now, so many years later, we are often together, and when this happens, when I am with other SNCC people, I feel a special kind of joy—a feeling of being, at last, complete.

After her five-year stint as a SNCC staff member, **DOROTHY M. ZELLNER** and her then-husband, Bob Zellner, settled in New Orleans and worked for the Southern Conference Educational Fund. In 1972 she became a licensed practical nurse and worked at and organized a union in the New Orleans Home for Incurables. Once back in New York with her two daughters in 1983, she worked at the Center for Constitutional Rights, managing the group's publications and its Ella Baker Student Program, and then at the City University of New York School of Law as director of institutional advancement and publications. Her article "Red Roadshow: Eastland in New Orleans" appeared in *Louisiana History* and won a New York Foundation for the Arts award. Profiled in Debra L. Schultz's book, *Going South: Jewish Women in the Civil Rights Movement*, she lectures frequently about SNCC, the Civil Rights Movement, and blacks and Jews in the Movement. Currently a board member of the Friends of the Jenin Freedom Theatre in Palestine, she speaks against the Israeli occupation of that country. Her most recent articles have appeared in *Jewish Currents*.

"My Real Vocation" © 2010 by Dorothy M. Zellner

A SNCC Blue Book

Jane Bond Moore

Raised in a prominent Atlanta family with strong social values, a young woman makes her contribution mainly through supporting the efforts of other movement activists.

The Test

Writing this essay is like taking a test. A test posed by a caring and concerned professor, but a test nevertheless. It's a test for which I do not have the answers, for which I didn't study enough. The test has questions for a book about women in the Student Nonviolent Coordinating Committee: Who were the local movement people who were in place before you began working in your project? What were the political experiences and history of the community where you worked? When you began your SNCC work, what had been going on, historically, in the community? If you participated in a notable event that hasn't been covered in existing histories, please include it in your story.

I am flunking this test. It's my worst nightmare. There was a course I should have enrolled in. I thought I enrolled, but I guess I went to the wrong lectures and studied the wrong books. I can't answer these questions, because I never participated in a notable event—covered or not. When I should have been "sitting in" in Albany or marching in Selma, I was safe in Atlanta. There are no local movement people I can write about, and my community was small. Yet, as a veteran of many tests, I know that my panic is just test panic. I must know *something* that I can be graded on. So I will tell my story.

How did I become part of the Movement? Through my brother, Julian Bond; my roommate Dottie Miller Zellner; and my husband, Howard Moore Jr. My relationship with SNCC came through other people. I was an outsider and an insider. I loved that time. I was part of the Movement, too.

In 1960, the year the sit-ins started, I was in graduate school at Indiana University. I read the newspapers and got letters from Julian about the Atlanta Movement. I was envious but not surprised that he would be involved with something exciting and interesting compared to my boring and frighteningly baffling graduate school classes. The only "movement" thing I did at Indiana was to march around downtown Bloomington with other students, asking for support for the sit-ins. One old man spat at us, but other than that we were ignored. That was the first time I was amazed and awed by the students who were sitting in. Where did they get the bravery to be beaten, hosed, and arrested? How did they find the courage to do it again and again?

I came back to Atlanta and, at some point, decided to work instead of continuing in graduate school. I got a job at the Southern Regional Council, an organization that works toward interracial understanding in the South. That's where I met Dottie. We were both working, clipping and filing newspaper articles about the Movement, the Klan, the radical right. Dottie had come to Atlanta from New York, and through Dottie, a sophisticated and worldly woman by my standards, I began to be involved in SNCC.

Our apartment was on a side street, parallel to a major street that must be named Martin Luther King Jr. Drive now. You got there from the black community by driving down West Hunter, through a neighborhood of lovely homes of the black bourgeoisie, with manicured lawns and shrubbery, until you reached our neighborhood. Although it was in Atlanta, it had a rural feeling about it. The grass was wild. There were many trees, crowded together.

The flowers were as likely to be in tin cans on the porch as in pleasant little beds on the lawn. We lived in an apartment building, but the other homes on the street could have been in a small southern town. The people who lived there were not like the university professors who were my parents' neighbors in the Atlanta University Center. These were people who worked in factories and as domestics, who rode buses long distances to work. Dottie and I must have seemed a strange and exotic couple to them—two young women, one white and one black, living alone together in an apartment. Still, with the tolerance that was typical of black people then, no one objected or complained.

How Dottie and I scandalized the secretaries at the SRC when we got our apartment! I was the only black woman I knew in Atlanta of my age who wasn't living at home with her parents. The secretaries felt I was daring the fates and defying moral standards. I loved those days, having my own apartment, where I could do what I wanted. I also loved our early SNCC parties. There were people from all over the country, all of like mind, all the same age—we had a lot of fun. We danced and sang movement songs.

The SRC was my first real job and introduced me to the world of work. I thought of it then as a home for eccentrics, but now I know it was just a workplace. I learned about politics and class warfare from Dottie. During the Cuban missile crisis, she picketed in a park, bringing the wrath of the SRC down on her. We went together to the SNCC office on Auburn Avenue, where I met Bob Moses for the first time. Bob was reporting to Forman about a Mississippi trip. Bob immediately impressed me. He seemed so profound, in part because he was so quiet. Most people talk three to four times as much. Bob gave the impression of being mature and knowledgeable, so considering about his opinions and his choice of words. He told me he had been a tutor for Frankie Lymon of "Why Do Fools Fall in Love?" fame. But that's all he told me. Bob never told me much of what that life was like, traveling around with a teenage R & B star and what led him to become part of SNCC.

Dottie and I met many newspaper reporters who used the SRC archives—Fred Powledge, Claude Sitton, and others. Fred Powledge came to our apartment and took pictures of us. I remember mine was the best picture anyone had ever taken of me. I wanted to blow it up and paste it on my face.

Atlanta was still generally segregated. We went to see *Lawrence of Arabia* with Tom and Casey Hayden. The movie was popular, so we bought tickets and then went to hang out in a drugstore. The people in the drugstore thought we were going to sit in, so they started unwinding the tops from the counter seats. They probably called the police, too, but we left before they arrived, because we wanted to see that movie. That was my only sit-in experience.

My Role

SNCC was in the center of Atlanta and national politics. Calls to the FBI and the White House were frequent, as were talks with network news reporters. Dottie had left SRC to work for SNCC, and I left to work for the Southern Christian Leadership Conference. SCLC was very different and a shock to me. The support staff was as supportive and congenial as the one at SRC, but executive secretary Wyatt T. Walker made me address him as Mr. Walker, even though I had called him Wyatt when I worked at SRC. Dr. King and Andy Young were rarely in the office. I never quite figured out what my job was, and no one ever really told me. I left SCLC and went to work at Spelman, then left Spelman to have Grace, my first child.

I was never envious of the people in the field. I thought them brave and stupid—holy idiots. I did not have the strength to do what they were doing—live in constant fear of death, risk being shot at and beaten up. They were my heroes, heroines, and sheroes. That was a powerful time. I still have a special bond with people I met then, although I may not see them for years.

While the SNCC troopers were storming the rural areas and becoming black nationalists, this was my life. I was getting married, having kids, yelling at the SNCC people partying below our apartment for waking the babies, and moving into our first house and then to a house on Kennolia Drive. This is where I think I wandered into the wrong classroom.

I felt a real tug between being a proper, young bourgeois matron or a kind of wild, hippie mother—or often just a wild hippie. I thought children should be brought up in a home with rules and limits, so I tried to make my house conform to the accepted pattern. At the same time, I hated and was bored by rigidity.

I began to have non-SNCC friends: other mothers with children, mothers who were married to men who got up every morning and went to work and expected their wives to be there, preferably in a clean house with dinner ready, when they came home at night. We started an integrated, cooperative nursery school. I put that on my resume for a long time, not that anyone cared, but I did and they should have. It made me angry, and still makes me angry, that all that good work I did back then—starting the cooperative, working in Julian's campaign—counted for nothing in the male world of law.

Once I was married, I typed a lot for my husband, Howard, who was a lawyer representing SNCC workers and taking on a lot of civil rights cases. I was always in his office typing when something important happened. The Chicago convention—I just saw part of it. The 1964 Atlantic City convention—I was typing away. I am sure Howard knows what brief

I typed during each convention. I hated that typing but also felt important, and I loved getting out of the house and being around grown-ups.

Betty Friedan visited Atlanta and interviewed me. I was happy to talk to someone about the tyranny of motherhood and housecleaning. I felt betrayed when some SNCC women said they lied to her about their relationships with SNCC men and led her to believe they enjoyed being told what to do.

All of these people I met in SNCC are part of my life forever—either through friendships like Dottie, Dinky, and Bob or in the news like Marion Barry or Marian Wright Edelman.

Now I am in the middle of the test, and I have filled up half of a blue book. I have explained who I am to the professor, and now I can answer her questions.

I don't think I ever left the Movement, as I have continued in some form of political action, although less and less, ever since. My prison work in Berkeley, walking precincts, even serving on the board of the black adoption agency was, in my mind, movement work. Being a lawyer has cut down on what I do in my spare time, as I have so little spare time. Yet if the Movement is the universal move to recognize and place in operation all human rights, I am still in it.

My intellectual influences came from my family. My father, Dr. Horace Mann Bond,* emphasized the wrongness of slavery and segregation when we were children. He believed and taught us that every person has value and deserves to be treated as such. He deeply loved our race and considered us noble. He constantly reminded us of the terrors and hardships that the race had overcome. With this background, how could I not believe in the Movement?

My Quaker schooling added to this belief. The Friends believe that there is God in every person and that when one engages in serious exchange with that person, you speak to the God in him or her. The Friends also believe that social justice is an important aspect of religion, that striving toward social justice is an integral part of religious observance.

My intellectual and spiritual background—the knowledge that black people are entitled to be treated as human beings and that all black people are more than capable of achieving if given the opportunity—led me inevitably to know that change must happen. Now, whether I believed at the time that segregation would end and black people would get the vote, I can't say. I

* Editors' Note: Horace Mann Bond, a premier black sociologist, served as head of Lincoln University and as the dean of education at Atlanta University. Both Kwame Nkrumah and Nnamdi Azikwe, who became independence heads of Ghana and Nigeria respectively, were students at Lincoln and guests of the Bond household when Dr. Bond was president.

did and do believe that the universe is pushing us forward with a universal imperative and that the failure to struggle will end in spiritual death.

I did not take part in any historical events except my life. I did not sit in or protest. When I rode the bus in Atlanta, I always sat in the front. I am sure that my light skin kept me out of confrontations.

But back to the test: What kept me going? What were my darkest hours? Does the professor want us to write about our personal or movement experiences, or is there any difference? Isn't the Movement an ongoing natural, human striving to move forward, to be human and to ensure that the world knows you as human?

My darkest hours occurred when fear overcame me. I felt it a lot after my children were born. I felt that something would happen to Howard and we would be left alone, with no support and no way to live, thrown back on my parents. I had no faith in my ability to provide for us, monetarily or otherwise. What kept me going was that life went on. You can't stop, curl into a fetal position, and whimper—you have to keep on. Change the diapers, read to the baby, take her for a walk. All those things have to be done.

The best moments were when I felt part of a group in mass meetings in Albany and Birmingham with the crowds, choirs, and organists. The speakers were a stirring, inspiring, uplifting bunch, with Dr. King at the top of the list. Often, after hard and unrewarding labor, black people of all classes came together at mass meetings; to be part of that group, working toward our freedom, was thrilling and inspirational.

I am at the end of the blue book. I have answered the questions as best I can. Will I pass the test?

JANE BOND MOORE moved to Berkeley, California, in 1971 with her husband, civil rights attorney Howard Moore, and their three children. She graduated from the University of California's Boalt Hall School of Law in 1976 and has practiced law in various settings, the most recent being the Oakland Unified School District, from which she retired in 2002. She began teaching—her true love, she says—in 2003 and now teaches such courses as "The Constitution" and "Gender and the Law" to undergraduates at Notre Dame de Namur University in Belmont, California, and to law students at JFK University Law School in Pleasant Hill, California. Her article "My Vietnam" appeared in *Against the Vietnam War: Writings by Activists,* which has recently been reissued. The mother of three children—a nurse practitioner, an art teacher and a lawyer—she still practices law part-time and is currently writing a mystery story based on her experiences growing up in Fort Valley, Georgia, where her father, Dr. Horace Mann Bond, was president of Fort Valley State College from 1939 to 1945.

Getting Out the News

Mary E. King

A recent college graduate joins SNCC's communications department and ponders the significance of that work.

The Moment to Decide

In the heat of nineteenth-century antislavery struggles, a hymn by abolition-ist James Russell Lowell challenged:

> Once to every man and nation
> Comes the moment to decide,
> In the fight of truth with falsehood,
> Twixt the good and evil side;
> Some great cause, God's new Messiah,
> Offering each the bloom or blight,
> And the choice goes by forever,
> Twixt that darkness and that light.

During my postadolescent struggle of self-discovery, the same hymn encouraged me to be decisive and take a stand. When the sit-ins began, it was my moment to decide.

In the dormitory of Ohio Wesleyan University on February 1, 1960, I watched on TV as students in the South sat in at lunch counters, deliberately violating racial segregation statutes. Young men and women—mostly black, but also white students like me—were taking history into their own hands, translating ideas into action. My reaction was strong. I also wanted to act. I had no hesitancy about where I belonged as the sit-ins began and felt that a momentous historical opportunity would pass me by if I failed to seize it. I also believed it would be hypocritical if my actions did not correspond to my beliefs.

Two years passed until I was graduated in 1962. My decision to join the Civil Rights Movement intensified. As an undergraduate I had organized a student committee on race relations in solidarity with the student sit-ins. Just before graduation, I traveled through the Deep South on a study tour sponsored by the Ohio Wesleyan University's campus Young Women's Christian Association (YWCA). There I met Miss Ella Baker, an adviser to both the Y and SNCC, and talked with student sit-in leaders in Nashville and Atlanta.

My view of the Movement then roiling the South was shaped by these black and white activists, who were working hand in hand. Neither burning cigarettes ground into the arms and backs of the students sitting in, nor ketchup and mustard poured into their hair and eyes, nor chewing gum stuck in their hair, nor spittle and slurs would break the protesters' discipline. They were not meek or mild, but the reverse, and they showed formidable strength in exposing themselves to raw violence. The demonstrators' restraint contrasted sharply with the massed legal and coercive power of the aggressively segregationist police and mobs. As the nonviolent protagonists refused to strike back, sympathies of spectators near and far began to flow toward the challengers.

My affinity for words—written or spoken—seemed to be the key to the question of what I might offer the Movement. I had majored in English literature and been elected president of the English Writers Club at the university. Although sure of my decision and thinking I could perhaps contribute, I still had to find my way into a complex mobilization. My first concrete step toward working in the Civil Rights Movement came sooner than expected.

Waiting at the Delaware, Ohio, bus station to go home after graduation, a long-distance telephone call intercepted, asking if I would be willing to fly immediately to North Carolina for an interview with Ella Baker. She and Howard Zinn, then a professor of history at Spelman College, were advising an Atlanta YWCA human relations project designed to encourage dialogue at southern colleges and universities. The contentious topic was to be race relations. When we met they interviewed me, and I soon became a human relations intern. Working under a Field Foundation grant, I replaced a young white Texan named Sandra Cason, who was married to Tom Hayden and known as Casey Hayden.

Miss Baker's original idea had been for a racially mixed team of two young recent college graduates to travel together onto campuses across the South. She paired me with an African American graduate of Barnard College, Roberta (Bobbi) Yancy. In reality, Bobbi and I were rarely able to travel onto a campus together, thus she traveled to black colleges while I went to white campuses. At the white institutions I would speak in chapels on the topic of "academic freedom," since it was impossible to address forthrightly the question of race at that time. We also organized joint seminars and workshops for students of both races who had responded positively to our separate speeches. At these meetings—usually led by Miss Baker and Professor Zinn—black and white students could sit together and discuss highly charged issues of race and racism. The sessions took place semi-clandestinely on black campuses, since white universities would not allow integrated gatherings.

During my stint as a YWCA human relations intern, I would volunteer on weekends at the Atlanta SNCC office. When the year's internship ended, I was able to fulfill my goal and joined the SNCC staff in June 1963.

Reasoning as I Went Along

My family background predisposed me to taking a stand in political defiance. I am a direct descendant of an officer with Nathaniel Bacon in the failed rebellion of 1676 against Governor Alexander Spotswood, the British representative in colonial Virginia. This rebellion served as dress rehearsal for the successful American Revolution a century later. A number of officers ended up at the gallows, although I don't know if my ancestor was one of them. When Governor Spotswood was summoned to Britain for an audience with King Charles II, according to our family oral history the monarch told him, "Governor, you have hanged more men in Virginia than I killed to avenge my father's death," referring to the execution of Charles I. I am also a collateral descendant of Henry Clay, the twice-unsuccessful Whig candidate for president, in 1832 and 1844, who provided for the freeing of his slaves in his will.

In almost a straight line, my father was the eighth minister in six generations of Virginia and North Carolina circuit riders and clergy. Having won a scholarship to study theology in New York and been ordained in what is now the United Methodist Church, he became an expatriate from the South when he realized that he could not be true to his conscience on matters of race while serving southern white congregations. In studies for his doctorate, he worked with two of the towering figures of the twentieth century, the theologian Paul Tillich and ethicist Reinhold Niebuhr, both concerned with contemporary issues of political and social justice. Considering himself a "citizen of the world," he studied seven languages. As I was growing up in my father's parishes in New York City, which he prized for their ethnic diversity, he would often bring social issues from the American South into discussion. Along with my mother, a teacher of public health nursing, my father instilled in my brothers and me a strong sense of social responsibility. Debates on major social justice issues filled our evening meals as children. Here I learned that John Wesley, founder of Methodism, had declared, "The world is my parish," which made an impression on me and is an apt description of how I have tried to live my life.

Based on my background and in agreement with my self-assessment, Jim Forman, SNCC's executive secretary, asked me to remain in Atlanta and work in the communications department, headed by SNCC press secretary Julian Bond. Collegiate experiences aside, almost everything was new to me. Reasoning as I went along, I managed to catch on to the writing of news reports and the answering of journalists' questions. In June 1963 Jim sent me to Danville, a textile center in the tobacco country of Southside Virginia, to handle communications for a SNCC project there. Carl Braden of the Southern Conference Educational Fund gave me a crash course in writing news releases. He had me write one news dispatch after another, until, within minutes, I could produce a credible release on any occurrence.

After several months in Danville, Jim asked me to come back to SNCC headquarters in Atlanta. For a portion of 1963 and 1964 I lived in a basement apartment at the home of Julian Bond's sister, Jane Bond Moore. Other times I shared apartments with white SNCC workers Casey Hayden and Constancia ("Dinky") Romilly.

In December 1963 I went to jail for becoming a sit-inner. When the SNCC headquarters staff went downtown to Atlanta's only racially integrated hotel to meet with Oginga Odinga, a visiting Kenyan minister of government, two of our members stepped out for a cup of coffee next door at the Toddle House. The waitresses refused to serve them. The rest of us joined them in unspoken concord. Based on previous training in noncooperation, twenty-one of us went limp as the police hauled us into paddy wagons.

I spent Christmas of that year in Atlanta's "Big Rock" city jail, within sight of the Georgia state capitol's gold dome. In our group were eighteen black people, one Japanese American, and two white women: Nancy Stearns, now a civil liberties lawyer, and me. In our ethnic makeup we were a microcosm of the Movement as a whole.

Communications

The techno-bureaucratic word "communications" fails to convey the substance or value of what Julian Bond and I did. Basically we managed a Southwide information system. Seven days a week I grasped for every handle I could in order to pump words from movement centers into the circuits of the news media. Not only did this arrangement serve to tell unfolding stories, but by facilitating the news reporting of working journalists, we were also able to provide protection for civil rights workers. This flow of information was as critical to our purpose as organizing demonstrations or voter registration drives, devising mock ballots, or developing alternative political parties.

For this mechanism to work, however, we had to gain respectability as credible sources in the eyes of the national news corps, which could be indifferent and was suspicious of being "used" by propagandists. Julian's inclination toward understatement set the tone. We downplayed anything sensational and underestimated the numbers of people participating in movement activities or any count of atrocities. We attributed facts to named sources. The style was clear and unembellished with no opinions or value judgments.

Today it is widely believed that the news media were unambiguously on the side of the Movement, providing it with heft and authority and with reporters functioning almost as co-workers. This is not true. In fact, the nature of the U.S. news industry mitigated against stories of the southern Civil Rights Movement ever reaching the press. National wire services such as the Associated Press (AP) and United Press International (UPI), whose ticker-tape accounts fed the small and midsize regional newspapers across the country, did not maintain reporters in most areas where the Civil Rights Movement was at its most intense. Such news agencies depended on "stringers" from local newspapers, who would cover events in isolated areas and send the resulting accounts over the wires to them for relay. Moreover, southern reporters from white-owned newspapers were often hostile to the Movement and did not consider acts of brutality, casualties, or attacks on African Americans as sufficiently newsworthy to publish or send through the national wire services.

In order to get accounts from the Movement into the press, Julian and I worked scrupulously to turn out news releases that carried accurate narratives and to take sworn affidavits documenting circumstances that might otherwise seem beyond belief. We also wrote lengthier special reports describing civil rights projects and programs too complicated for one-page releases and published a periodic newspaper called the *Student Voice,* which chronicled movement activities across the South.

Routinely laboring twelve hours or more daily at 8 ½ Raymond Street, NW, on the west side of Atlanta, Julian and I worked the phones in our two-desk office above a tailor's shop, keeping in touch with various press contacts. We fed radio stations with segments that contained voices of civil rights workers recorded directly from the scene of a local movement. Stations could put these recordings on the air, a live "actuality" in radio-speak. Working this way meant a flexible division of labor; as Julian wrote one release, I took an affidavit or vice versa.

In those early years a small number of exceptional professional journalists would battle with their editors to get accounts of movement activities (or reprisals) into print. These reporters were the first we telephoned whenever we had something of import. I inherited a clipboard from Dorothy Miller Zellner, my predecessor, with her list of reliable news contacts and their telephone numbers. Among them were Claude Sitton of the *New York*

Times, Fred Powledge of the *Atlanta Journal*, Karl Fleming of *Newsweek*, and Nicholas Von Hoffman of the *Chicago Tribune*. Some journalists would share with us their own anecdotes about problems encountered in getting editorial approval for their reports. The best in this choice group were white southerners who, with particular insight, cared enough to take the professional and personal risks necessary to get their pieces filed.

After April 1963, when television viewers could see for themselves the live footage of German shepherd police dogs and fire hoses unleashed against unarmed protesters by Birmingham's commissioner of public safety, Bull Connor, it became less difficult for us to get the media to carry legitimate stories. By then, international news organs such as the BBC and London's *Guardian* were covering the Movement. A critical mass of American citizens became so offended by the cruelty exhibited by Connor's police force that his excesses had the effect of changing the nature of news coverage, both here and abroad. Flashier live television crews would soon overshadow the patient *New York Times* and *Atlanta Constitution* reporters, who had traveled alone to cover complicated stories, sometimes risking life and limb, and later hammered out their dispatches on small portable typewriters.

Saving Lives in Mississippi

By 1964 and the Mississippi Freedom Summer, the attention of the national news corps was focused on the moral struggle under way in the South. Even so, we still had to devise creative ways to ensure the flow of accurate information. That summer, the involvement of nearly one thousand volunteers from across the country in projects in Mississippi gave our communications section added leverage for getting out the news. Working in collaboration with Casey Hayden and Betty Garman, who coordinated with Friends of SNCC groups on university campuses and in northern and western cities, Julian and I would receive telephone calls from a staff person reporting an incident from a rural southern county. We would immediately alert the appropriate Friends groups, especially if someone from their city had been arrested or hurt. They would query their local AP or UPI to find out if the wire services were carrying an account of the incident. Roberta Galler in Chicago, or Lucia Hatch in Princeton, for example, might phone to her respective AP bureau, indicating that she had received a reliable report that a volunteer from Chicago or Princeton had been beaten or was being held without charges in a county jail. Such precisely targeted local interest would force the wire services to ask their southern bureaus for the story. Despite the distaste for reporting accounts that southern newsrooms would deem less than newsworthy, they were now obliged to put the reports onto the national wires.

We also had to think about keeping our communications costs as low as possible. Julian and I assigned code names to the towns and hamlets where SNCC had projects and staff, and these, too, went onto the hand-me-down clipboard. To lessen phone charges, the field secretaries would place a collect call to us from a fictitious person, using the name of a tree conferred upon that field office—for instance, a maple or oak. We would refuse the charges but knew from the "maple" or "oak" which office to telephone on the less expensive wide area telephone service, or WATS line. Thus a collect call from "John Maple" meant we should phone Itta Bena, or "Sally Oak" wanting to reverse charges meant we should call the Tupelo office.

Meanwhile in Jackson, the hub of the Mississippi Summer Project, two gifted volunteers from Stanford University, Robert Beyers and Irene Strelitz, worked in our communications shop at the office of the Council of Federated Organizations at 1017 Lynch Street. Francis Mitchell, an able SNCC staff member from Los Angeles, joined us to push the news into publication. By now our purpose was not so much to appeal to our adversaries, but to save lives and prevent injuries among movement participants by throwing the light of publicity on law officers who were operating in collusion with vigilante terror organizations.

The *Oxford English Dictionary* notes that in the medieval period the Latin word *manipulare* meant "to lead by the hand." During the four years I spent with SNCC, this is what I did—led the media by the hand toward the Movement, exposing what some editors wanted to keep hidden.

The Significance of Our Task

Our work reflected an attitude within the organization as a whole—an orientation toward arguing the situation with rationality and facts. SNCC staff operated from the perspective of concreteness and realism. We were physically moving into communities and organizing them, all the while documenting and denouncing the impediments and obstructions encountered. Julian and I wanted our case to be watertight and specific. We were deliverers of facts.

Although organizing communities can be an intuitive process, we didn't dispense with reason. Bob Moses's 1963 mock ballot in Mississippi disputed the argument that black people did not want to vote. The formal challenge to the seating of the Mississippi Democratic Party in 1964 contested the legality of all-white delegations to represent the range of Democrats.

One reason the memory of SNCC survives as well as it does may possibly be due to the work of the communications staff. Dryly, meticulously, tenaciously, we documented events and punitive retaliations. Then, with speed and intensity, we disseminated the information we had collected through the machinery we had created. Our operation continually expanded. By 1964 the tailor's shop downstairs had closed, and SNCC had set up its own offset printing press in the basement and had nearly a dozen trained photographers spread across the South. Their work illustrated our words, whenever they managed to capture a scene.

While I was working for SNCC I was not yet aware of Mohandas K. Gandhi's views on the significance of documentation in nonviolent struggle. He had used the written word as one of his principal tools during campaigns spread over a half century in South Africa and India. When I studied Gandhi years later, I realized that Julian Bond and I had been carrying out the same function: writing, explaining, and describing. Gandhi reasoned that one must start with persuasion, gathering the facts and laying them out in such a way that clear presentation of the grievances might appeal to the sensibilities of one's antagonist, in some cases leading one's opponent to change from within, and increasing the odds of eventual reconciliation. Only when words failed would sterner nonviolent sanctions be employed.

During the glory years of the Movement, between 1960 and 1965, we were also working to touch the national conscience and trying to arouse a sense of moral indignation in order to break the color bars enshrined by law. We wanted our reports and information to cause splits in public opinion, and, in turn, sway policy. In the process, we had been forced to develop an alternative apparatus for getting accurate news carried by the media and to find ways to break stories that would otherwise have been lost, considered inconsequential, or simply regarded as not newsworthy.

Touching History

For each individual, small connections allow us to touch another place and time. None of us are as far away as we might think from historic encounters. Through my personal contacts and work with SNCC, I found more than one connection to Gandhi. During my first year at Ohio Wesleyan, I made friends with a black student named Edward G. Carroll Jr., the son of a Methodist minister who was himself a friend of my parents. In 1935–36 Ed's father and mother, Edward and Phenola Carroll, had gone to India with Howard Thurman, the noted black theologian and dean of the Rankin Chapel at Howard University, and his wife, Sue Bailey Thurman. They had met with Gandhi in India at length. Although almost three decades had passed, I was gratified to know individuals who had seriously engaged Gandhi. The Carrolls were not my only bond. Through the Movement itself, I was often only one person removed from the Indian independence struggles.

As historian Sudarshan Kapur shows, knowledge of Gandhi's theories and techniques traveled from India to the United States through a steady stream of African American professors and clergy who, interested in learning about the Indian campaigns and Gandhi's philosophies firsthand, traveled to the subcontinent in the 1930s, 1940s, and 1950s. Two such individuals, Bayard Rustin and the Reverend James M. Lawson Jr., were close to us in SNCC. A third, James Farmer, headed another action-oriented civil rights group, the Congress of Racial Equality, known as CORE and founded in 1942 explicitly on Gandhian theories. All three had systematically studied Gandhi's strategic thinking and believed in the practicality of his approach. Each played a significant personal role within the larger Civil Rights Movement, including the specific transmission of theories and methods of nonviolent struggle to the Reverend Dr. Martin Luther King Jr. and everyone else in our mass movement. These three individuals were critical conduits of knowledge about nonviolent resistance to the mid-twentieth-century United States. It is an enduring source of strength in my life that they initiated me into the technique of nonviolent struggle, as a SNCC staff member.

SNCC's Egalitarianism: Gender and Race in a Nonviolent Movement

SNCC was an organization of fiercely individualistic young men and women. The qualities that had enabled each of us to embrace personal risks by joining SNCC were the same attributes that made us individually reluctant to accept supervision or direction. Although nonviolent movements require group discipline, they also rest on personal commitment, making such mobilizations inherently averse to top-down command structures. Since the decision to accept the penalties for nonviolent resistance cannot be externally imposed, and no one can force another person voluntarily to accept reprisals for their acts of noncooperation such as civil disobedience, the judgment of a group begins with the conviction of the individual. Decisions tend to be made democratically. Within SNCC we sought to make resolutions by consensus, although rarely achieving perfectly collective agreement. Yet, during the organization's pivotal first five years, although there was always combustible disagreement, rarely was there discord.

Women did what men did in SNCC. James Forman may have been as responsible as any single person for SNCC's inherently egalitarian spirit toward women. Jim would sometimes sweep the floors in the Atlanta headquarters and, without lecturing or hectoring, conspicuously make the point that all work was important and that everyone had to share in it. Gifted at sizing up each individual's strengths and weaknesses, he would deftly make staffing suggestions. Since he had a major hand in assigning responsibilities and chose to give significant responsibilities to women, substantial credit belongs to Jim for SNCC's inclusion of women as full agents in a historic struggle.

Similarly, my co-worker Julian Bond always treated me as a person of aptitude. He never used insensitive remarks or gestures of the sort that allow a woman to know that she is not viewed as an equal. While some men conspire in the restricting of women, others are eager to shed patriarchal burdens and do not want to hold anyone back because of gender. No one has ever treated me more equally than did Julian.

Moreover, even in the vortex of an intense and rapidly changing movement, Julian never showed any resentment of me because I am white. By 1965, within SNCC black voices of verbal violence, nihilism and threatened retaliation were growing louder, calls often directed against whites in the Movement, or anyone—white or black—who was opposed to their separatist outlook. For me, the "black power" refrain of Willie Ricks, Stokely Carmichael, and others reflected an understanding of power that was simplistic and naïve in its hints, threats, and calls for revenge, compulsion, or triumphalism. Despite whatever positive connotations of self-reliance and ethnic dignity may have been felt by those who embraced the credo of "black power," the slogan was like a Rorschach inkblot personality test; it was vague and had as many meanings as it had adherents.

Movement Lessons

What curiously stands out in my recollection of the period is the intertwining of relationships among the various organizations in the Civil Rights Movement rather than the differences between them—of which I was then painfully aware. At the time, I was concerned about tensions between SNCC and SCLC, even grudging of the inordinate attention paid to Dr. King and SCLC. I came in later years to recognize that these two extraordinary social movement formations were complementary. Now I can perceive a division of labor that I could not earlier see.

Ideas on fighting for justice and rights cannot be contained. The grip on power by ordinary people constituted by the Movement flowed naturally into other areas. The best example of the transforming energies that brimmed over from the cause of civil rights to contesting other barriers was the awakening of women. I have chronicled in *Freedom Song: A Personal*

Story of the 1960s Civil Rights Movement how in 1964 I helped to write, with Casey Hayden, one of the earliest calls to contemporary U.S. feminism. It arose from discussions among several women who were working in the Movement in Mississippi. In 1965 Casey and I wrote another appeal, "Sex and Caste." We mailed this manifesto to forty activists in peace and Civil Rights Movements across the country, which sparked the sharing of views by women in consciousness-raising groups during the 1970s, stimulating what is now called second-wave feminism.

The Civil Rights Movement took me into rural homes insulated with pasted-up newspapers and the wearily weatherboarded houses of worship of those who had been among the most physically and psychologically brutalized of all the diverse peoples who have made their home in the United States. The individuals with whom I worked possessed dignity, magnanimity, courtesy, respect for others, and were often contemplating cosmic questions: the meaning of life, whether forgiveness is necessary for reconciliation, and whether there is a force working for justice in the world.

As a result of living and working in the heart of the Movement, I learned that poor people labor harder and longer than the middle class or the rich, and that, contrary to presumption, the shame of unemployment falls more painfully on the poor than on those who have resources and contacts with which to mitigate failure. Of course there were some "bench-sitters," but in the main the diligence and tenacity of black southerners filled me with admiration. What I discovered in the black agrarian communities of the Southland was a people living at subsistence level, whose industriousness, inventiveness, and magnanimity were to me, then and now, unexcelled in a culture that values productivity and cleverness. At the end of the day, with a job that did not pay enough to cover the basics, much less private health care or higher education, individuals were often moonlighting at second jobs, with third and sometimes fourth jobs on the weekend—valiantly working to make ends meet. Such lessons do not fade.

My indifference to careerism probably derives from the savory satisfactions of the Movement. Having experienced the exhilaration of working on issues much grander than my own desires—while usually feeling that I was doing more for myself than anyone else, because of the intertwining of belief and purpose—I later found it almost impossible to think of what would "help a career." My search has been to find again the unity that was part of my movement experience, when we were able to bring ideas into action at the same time that we let our actions give rise to new concepts. I have wanted again the joy of working with others similarly motivated, of being able to act catalytically and see results while working intently in a team.

I probably owe to the Movement the fact that I am neither personally afraid nor fearful of people or circumstances distant from my way of thinking or culture. I retain strong convictions about the ability of ordinary people to act as agents of social change. Remembering the hatred expressed by onlookers to the disciplined sit-ins jeering "riots," "violence," and "Communist plot" reinforces my conviction that transformation of conflict is possible. Over the years and in more than 120 developing countries for my work and research, I have sat with tribal chiefs in Darfur and elsewhere in Sudan, and with Eritrean and Ethiopian guerrillas on the Horn of Africa. I have visited with refugees in camps from Indonesia to Gaza to El Salvador. I have talked with South African laborers in black townships, Palestinian members of Hamas, armed Israeli settlers near Hebron, and have met with more than one person's allotment of totalitarian rulers such as Ferdinand Marcos, Fidel Castro, and Saddam Hussein. I believe that if you want to influence the thinking of others, you must engage and interact with them, not isolate them.

Of my education in the Civil Rights Movement, perhaps I am most grateful to have learned that unexercised choice cannot be counted. Errors do not burn so painfully as regrets over what Robert Frost calls "the road not taken" because of fear or lack of imagination. For each of us comes a moment to decide, as James Russell Lowell's hymn intones, "twixt the good or evil side."

MARY E. KING wrote of her experiences in SNCC in *Freedom Song: A Personal Story of the 1960s Civil Rights Movement*, which won her a 1988 Robert F. Kennedy Memorial Book Award. King's most recent work is a reference book, *The New York Times on Emerging Democracies in Eastern Europe*, chronicling the peaceful transition from Soviet rule and communist order that occurred in the Eastern bloc. She is the author of *A Quiet Revolution: The First Palestinian Intifada and Nonviolent Resistance*. In 2002 New Delhi's Indian Council for Cultural Relations released the second edition of *Mahatma Gandhi and Martin Luther King Jr.: The Power of Nonviolent Action*, originally published by UNESCO. With support from the United States Institute of Peace, she is completing a book on an Indian struggle against untouchability titled *Conversion and the Mechanisms of Change in Nonviolent Action: The 1924–25 Vykom Satyagraha Case*. Professor of peace and conflict studies of the University for Peace, an affiliate of the United Nations, she is also distinguished scholar, the American University Center for Global Peace, in Washington, D.C., and Rothermere American Institute Fellow, Oxford University, England. She has received the Jamnalaj Bajaj International Award for promotion of Gandhian values, the highest award for distinguished achievement from her alma mater, Ohio Wesleyan University; and the El-Hibri

Peace Education Prize "in recognition of her life-long devotion to the field of peace education." After SNCC she worked for the U.S. Office of Economic Opportunity in the "war on poverty." A presidential appointee in the Carter administration, she had oversight for the Peace Corps Worldwide, VISTA, and other national volunteer service corps programs. She earned a doctorate in international politics from the University of Wales at Aberystwyth.

"Getting Out the News" © 2010 by Mary E. King

It's Okay to Fight the Status Quo

E. Jeanne Breaker Johnson

Raised with family members' examples of courage and strength, a Spelman College student chooses the Movement instead of finishing school.

Leave That White Girl's Hair Alone

On my fiftieth birthday, my sister Lois gave me a book edited by Patricia Bell-Scott that contained journal entries by African American women and the companion diary.* As I began to write down my thoughts, one of the things that I kept going back to in my journal was, What led me to SNCC? What were the forces that compelled me on?

I believe there were situations that occurred throughout my life that had an impact on my decision to leave Spelman College in my sophomore year and go to work for SNCC. I am one of six children of Victoria Breaker, a strong woman who raised all of us without the help of my father, but with the help of her family members. I was the first person in my family to attend college, and I always knew I would go to college. My mother still talks about how I was preparing for college, had my bags packed, and was ready to go, even though we didn't have the money for transportation. This didn't stop me, as I was sure we would find the money and I would go off to Spelman as I had planned. We found the money and off I went.

Consequently, it was no easy matter for me to leave school and a more certain future for a very radical group talking about equality. So how did this happen? There are at least three events in my life that I can look back on and say they were important.

* Patricia Bell-Scott, ed. *Personal Writings by Contemporary Black Women* (1995).

Early Racism

My earliest encounter with racists was before I started school. In the South in the 1950s, poor white people lived close to poor black people. In my neighborhood poor whites and poor blacks were separated by a ditch. We played together as children until we went to school. Then they went to the white elementary school, where they were presumably taught their superiority, and we went to the black elementary school, where we were taught our place. One day, when I was four or five, I was plaiting, or playing, in my white playmate's hair when a car with some white men in it drove by. They stopped and yelled at me, "Nigger, leave that white girl's hair alone!" I don't think I had ever heard the word *nigger* before, but I knew it was not something good. This happened more than fifty years ago and I still remember it.

My high school was over two miles away from my home. We had to take a city bus that went past the white high school. Riding the bus was a daily experience in racial injustice. As black people, we were supposed to go to the back of the bus and sit behind the whites. Because a lot of the black students got on first, we used up all the seats in the back and some of the seats in the front. When a white person got on, if we were closer to the front, we were supposed to get up and give them our seat.

My five siblings and I rode the bus every day with our aunt Billie, my mother's youngest sister. Billie refused to let us get up and give our seats to any white person. This was the first instance I can recall of someone actively refusing to give in to racial injustice. For a while there were confrontations almost daily, with my aunt and us being thrown off the bus. These confrontations sometimes became out-and-out fights between black and white school kids. Before the end of my first year at this school, the school system gave us a school bus to transport us to and from school. This helped my family tremendously, because the school bus was free, whereas my mother had been paying public transportation costs for six kids.

Highlander

People always thought my aunt was crazy. As I look back on this today, I realize she taught us all a valuable lesson: "Stand up for what you believe." She was the first person to put the idea in my head that it was okay to fight the status quo. My aunt Billie is dead now, and I never told her how much she influenced me. And I never told her that I didn't think she was crazy.

When I was a sophomore in high school, somehow I learned about a summer camp in Tennessee for teenagers of all races. I applied and received a full scholarship to attend. The year was 1960. I had to sell my mother on the idea, as she was not too happy to have her young teenage daughter go off into what she knew could be a dangerous situation. It was hard, but somehow I convinced her that this was the right thing to do. Highlander Folk School was my introduction into a new world. Here I met black, white, and Native American kids from all over the country, including the children of Rev. Fred Shuttlesworth, a Civil Rights Movement pioneer in Birmingham, Alabama. We played, talked, sang, and lived together for six weeks. My world up to that point had been rather narrow, but at Highlander I met kids who already had a worldview, who had ideas about the world and how they might make a difference. I was very impressed. I believe that summer had the most impact on my decision to join SNCC.

In my second year at Spelman College, I left school to devote myself full-time to working with SNCC. I had worked with SNCC for a few months while attending Spelman College, but it soon became apparent that I would have to make a decision. Spelman's administration didn't approve of its students participating in sit-ins and demonstrations. After participating in my first sit-in, which led to my being arrested and consequently spending a weekend in the Atlanta city jail, I was called before the dean and told, "Spelman young ladies don't do things like that." Leaving Spelman and going to work full-time with SNCC was one of the biggest decisions of my life. My family hated my decision to leave school and tried in vain to get me to go back.

Working for SNCC

My years in SNCC were some of the most exciting and meaningful times in my life. I was so very young and so very inexperienced. One of the first things I did after joining SNCC was to cut my hair into what became known as an Afro. We didn't call it that at the time. I just wanted to let it be natural. This gave me a new look and feeling about myself. I really began to think I could possibly be pretty.

Immediately after joining SNCC, I was sent to a workshop to learn about the Movement and nonviolence. I believe it was led by folks from SCLC. One thing I was taught and never forgot was how to read and evaluate the media, how to tell if a piece is balanced or not, how to look for loaded words. This was excellent training. During my first few months with SNCC, I did a lot of the menial jobs that have to be done in organizations: collating, stapling, mailing the large number of newsletters that went out to Friends of SNCC, and so forth. However, after several months I was sent to work in Jackson, Mississippi, at the central office of the Council of Federated Organizations (COFO). My main job was working as the WATS line operator, keeping in phone contact with all of the SNCC projects throughout the state. I received telephone reports from projects and made calls to check up on staffers who were late calling in. When field workers left their home base to go out into the county or into another county, they called in and told me what time they were leaving and when they next expected to check in, or when they would be back. If they didn't call in at the time they had said, then I would call them. Most of the time it simply was that they forgot or they had car trouble or were just a little late getting back.

In the beginning of the summer of 1964 our worst nightmare happened. James Chaney, Andy Goodman, and Mickey Schwerner left their field office in Meridian to travel to Philadelphia, Mississippi, for some voter registration work. They missed their check-in time. Because I was on the WATS line at the time, I was the first person to realize they were missing. Of course I believed there was a simple explanation, that they had forgotten to call or had car trouble. But I followed protocol and alerted the person in charge that the three had not checked in. This was the first time I really began to understand the danger that we all faced. The days that followed are still a blur to me; I don't remember much of what happened. I do, however, remember experiencing real fear for the first time.

I stayed in Jackson for another five months and eventually ended up in the Atlanta SNCC office. There, everyone seemed to have their niche, and I had no idea as to what I wanted to do. Jim Forman took me in hand and gave me a job. He decided that since Carol Merritt was leaving, I would take her place. Carol was writing to foundations to try to get scholarship money for SNCC people who wanted to go back to school. I was awful; I didn't have a clue as to what I was doing and couldn't even type properly. I just tried to follow Carol's format. I was so bad at this, and those foundations probably got some interesting mail back then. I like to believe I got better as time went on. But as my mother used to say, "What doesn't kill you makes you stronger." So what do I do now? I write grants, am fairly successful at it, and love it!

In the fall of 1967 **E. JEANNE BREAKER JOHNSON** left SNCC and moved to New York, finished her undergraduate work at Hunter College, and did support work for the Free Southern Theater. In 1971 she moved to New Orleans and attended graduate school at Tulane University's School of Public Health and Tropical Medicine. After graduation she earned a living as a writer, developing educational and training manuals for Louisiana family planning programs. In 1978 she began work as an educator with the Genetic Disease Center, a federally funded sickle cell education, screening, and counseling program. She is still working in this field. The program evolved into the Sickle Cell Center of Southern

Louisiana and is now part of Tulane University's Health Science Center, where she is the assistant director and chief grant writer. She has been married to Philip Johnson, an artist, for thirty-five years. They have two adult sons and two grandchildren. Forced to leave their home of twenty-eight years by Hurricane Katrina, they remain committed to living and working in New Orleans.

SNCC

My Enduring "Circle of Trust"

Judy Richardson

A shy African American student from Tarrytown, New York, is transformed by the power—and people—of the Movement.

I saw the national office of SNCC for the first time in November 1963. It was a teeny, run-down office at 8½ Raymond Street, a one-block side street off Hunter (now Martin Luther King Jr. Boulevard), near the Atlanta University Center. The office was located on the second floor above a beauty shop. It definitely did not fit my image of a "national office."

I was nineteen and had gone to Atlanta with Reggie Robinson, SNCC's field secretary in Cambridge, Maryland, where I had been working full-time since leaving Swarthmore College in Pennsylvania. From the downstairs glass door of the national office I saw this large man at the top of the stairs, dressed in overalls and sweeping the stairs. Reggie saw him, too, then ran up the stairs and, with broad smiles and much hollering, they hugged each other like long-lost brothers. I thought, *Whoah, this is truly an egalitarian office,* since I assumed the man to be the janitor. It was only after Reggie called the man's name that I realized this was Jim Forman, SNCC's larger-than-life executive secretary.

There was such joy, warmth, and affection in this moment that I thought, *Judy, you haven't just joined an organization, you've joined a family; SNCC really is a band of brothers and a circle of trust.* And I assumed I'd be in it the rest of my life.

Now, I later found out that Forman often swept up, and not so much to clean the perpetually dirty office (which was good, since he wasn't all that good at it). Rather, he was showing us that, as he often said, no job was too lowly for anyone in SNCC to do, and every job was important to sustaining the organization. Reggie introduced us and, through questioning, Forman found out that I had taken a semester off from Swarthmore and that I could take shorthand (which was kind of like texting, but with symbols) and type ninety words a minute. I never made it back to Cambridge.

My first contact with SNCC began when I joined a busload of Swarthmore students traveling to Cambridge to support locally led demonstrations against segregated facilities. The trips were organized by the Swarthmore Political Action Committee (SPAC), the campus SDS chapter. I initially went on a lark, not out of any great commitment. I was, after all, away from home—and my mother—for the first time in my life, so I figured, Why not?

One of my first demonstrations took place at the segregated Choptank Inn, a dark, smelly bar and grill. I don't remember much about the place, just the big white man standing in the doorway telling me I couldn't come in. For me, all the little slights, all the small acts of racism I'd experienced growing up became bound up in this one man. And I became absolutely enraged. But I had now found a constructive vehicle through which I could struggle against the racism—and that was SNCC.

At that point, for me, the Cambridge Movement *was* SNCC. More specifically, it was Gloria Richardson, the firebrand local leader of the Movement, and Reggie Robinson from Baltimore, the veteran organizer who had been assigned there after the local movement requested SNCC assistance. I watched Gloria—tall, thin, fearless, ramrod straight, and dressed in a shirt and jeans—leading the mass meetings and demonstrations and never backing down, even in the face of National Guard rifles and suffocating tear gas. I watched Reggie Robinson, not much older than me, working in tandem with Gloria, moving the crowd, strategizing with her and others around Gloria's kitchen table late at night (a number of us lived in her house). I decided this was a world I had to join—if only for a while.

It was a world very different from where I'd grown up, in Tarrytown, New York, about twenty-five miles north of New York City. Tarrytown, home of the author Washington Irving, was steeped in tradition. I went to Washington Irving Jr. High and Sleepy Hollow High School, and our high school mascot was "The Headless Horseman." Yup.

I grew up in the "under the hill" section near the railroad tracks. The main employer in town was "the plant," the Chevrolet plant where the fathers of everyone I knew worked: black folks, Italians, Poles—everyone. My father had helped unionize the plant, where he worked on the assembly line and was treasurer of the United Auto Workers local. When I was seven he had a heart attack and died "on the line," leaving my mother to support my older sister, Carita ("Chita"), and me. My mother immediately got a job as a clerk at Macy's in nearby White Plains and managed to keep food on the table and still send Chita a little spending money after she was accepted to Bennington College on full scholarship.

My mother had an eighth-grade education, was amazingly literate, always corrected my grammar, watched *Meet the Press* every week, read the then-liberal *New York Post* religiously, and played a mean jazz piano. On Sundays she read the Bible and listened to a religious radio program broadcast by the Ethical Culture Society. She was extremely distrustful of organized religion, though she never told me why. She also almost never talked about race. This, then, was the world I left when I went to Swarthmore, a prestigious Quaker college in Pennsylvania.

By January of my freshman year I was going to Cambridge just about every weekend, and generally landing in jail. Coming back to campus was like coming back to another life—reality had now become my SNCC/Cambridge world, with all its camaraderie, passion, immediacy, and overwhelming sense of purpose.

I would return to campus on Monday or Tuesday and miss some of my classes, so my studies began to suffer. Adding to my worry, I was on full scholarship and one of only eight African American students in the freshman class. Swarthmore's magnanimous commitment to diversity (ten out of more than three hundred in the entire student body) was a big deal for the college, and they handled it with caution. We eight freshmen were evenly divided between males and females (presumably so we wouldn't have to date outside our group), and the administration roomed all eight of us with children from Quaker families, who I think they believed would accept us more readily.

As it turned out, at least on one issue neither the Quaker children nor the rest of the campus quite lived up to their liberal reputation. The demonstrations in Cambridge absolutely split the school. My white "Big Sister," who had warmly oriented me to the campus those first weeks after my arrival, now passed me in the dorm hall in stony silence. Two friends from my dorm stopped speaking to me. Other white students, referring to segregated facilities, said that a proprietor had the right to refuse service to anyone. One student, who had earlier amazed me in my poli-sci class with references to people, places, and philosophies I hadn't even known existed, now pronounced that the Cambridge demonstrations were forcing integration on southerners before they were ready. And besides, he added with great certainty, Swarthmore's Negro students would do better to stop meddling in things that were not their concern and concentrate on getting an education—this was the best way to help "their people."

In January 1963, the second semester of my freshman year, Penny Patch, a Swarthmore student who'd been on SNCC staff in Southwest Georgia, returned to campus. She encouraged me to take a semester off to work with SNCC full-time (though she cautioned me that Ruby Doris Robinson, who ran the Atlanta office with an iron hand, would first have to approve my application). I decided to make the leap. But first I had to tell my mother—which I truly dreaded.

I finally called her on the hall phone in my dorm. I was amazed—and relieved—at how calmly she took the news. I thought, *See, Judy, that wasn't so hard.* But fifteen minutes later my sister called me, shouting, "What did you tell Ma? She's going crazy! And what do you mean you're leaving school?" Obviously, my mother hadn't argued with me, knowing that she'd just get my sister to talk some sense into me. But once I made them both understand how important it was that I do this—and that it would be for just *one semester* (a semester that turned into three years)—they were really supportive. In fact, my sister left her job and became a fund-raiser for SNCC out of our New York office, and my mother started sending me civil rights–related news clippings.

I recently found a letter my mother wrote me in October of 1964, at the end of a summer of beatings and killings and church burnings. By that time they had also found the bodies of Chaney, Goodman, and Schwerner. The letter reads (in her as-always beautiful script):

> Sunday eve. 10/25
>
> Hi—Nothing much to say . . . Talked to Chita on the phone. She says that she will be too dead tired to have any Thanksgiving dinner. She has 3 SNCC [fund-raising] parties to line up and it is keeping her very busy. We'll have to do something; I don't know what. Well, everything is fine here. Please do not get any colds. Keep away from people who are sneezing and get your rest. Well, I guess I'll go to bed. I haven't had much sleep lately. 'Nite, Mommie, xxxooo.

My mother never let on that she was frightened, never asked me to come home. I don't think I realized then how frightened for me she must have been and how many sleepless nights she must have had.

After my arrival in Atlanta, I worked there for several months in the SNCC office, where I was Jim Forman's secretary. For those who look with today's eyes at that sentence, let me just say that I found no problem with that then, and don't now. Whatever sexism I found in SNCC (and, of course, we didn't use that term then) was always, for me, balanced by an incredible sense of power. And that was nurtured in me as much by the men as by the women of SNCC. In fact, I always felt respected for whatever skills I brought to the organization.

As Forman's secretary I was immediately thrown into the deep end of the pool. I got a crash course in dealing with SNCC's far-flung project staff, their strengths, and their weaknesses (just like a real family). I also had contact with the Friends of SNCC offices that were fund-raising for us in cities throughout the North, with our campus travelers who were organizing campus chapters of SNCC at black colleges in the South, and with the many pro bono lawyers, like Bill Kunstler, Victor Rabinowitz, and Leonard Boudin, and the Lawyers Constitutional Defense Committee.

Thinking back on those days I realize that much of my strength—and my values—was instilled in me not only by my family but also by the movement folks who gave me room to grow and helped form me. I remember sitting one day in the little area outside Forman's office, transcribing a mass meeting speech given by Prathia Hall, a SNCC field secretary then posted to Selma, Alabama. As she described the violence in Selma, the awful beauty of her words—and the intensity of her moral outrage—took me by such force that I remember typing onto that long, green mimeo stencil with tears just streaming down my face. It was as if some force of nature had swept me away to another place. When I think about it now, I'm amazed I said anything to anyone in SNCC—I was so in awe of everyone.

The End of "Ooga Booga"

It was December 1963 and I was still in the Atlanta office. We were in the midst of a staff meeting, and a bunch of folks had come in from "the field." Forman informed us that Mr. Oginga Odinga, then minister of home affairs in newly independent Kenya, was on a State Department tour and staying at the venerable (and only recently integrated) Peachtree Manor hotel in downtown Atlanta. Mr. Odinga's State Department guides had taken him to Dr. King's SCLC office but, as usual, had excluded SNCC from their tour. So Forman called Mr. Odinga at his hotel and arranged for SNCC staff to visit him.

Mr. Odinga greeted us in the lobby with a warm smile. He was elegantly dressed in a long, flowing traditional *buba,* had a bearing that was truly regal, and spoke better English than I did. I was completely dumbfounded. Understand, now, the only "Africans" I had ever seen were those portrayed in Tarzan movies: clad in loincloths and yelling "Ooga booga." It's one of the many instances during my time in SNCC when I thought, *Now, if they lied to you about this, what else have "they" lied about?*

As we all sat in the lobby, Mr. Odinga talked about the history of Kenya's liberation movement and their vision of maintaining a "people's struggle," and we talked about our voter registration work and other activities. We even showed him the traditional SNCC bumper sticker on one of our briefcases: "One Man, One Vote"—the slogan of the African anti-colonial struggle. When Mr. Odinga said he had to leave, Forman suggested we sing a freedom song.

Before we could finish the song, the hotel manager asked us to leave, with thinly veiled anger but forced courtesy, seeming to understand that the State Department wanted no incidents with African dignitaries. This was, after all, the era of the Cold War, when African nations were not to be alienated for fear they'd align with Russia. SNCC folk used to joke that they could get served at a lunch counter if they just put on a *buba* and spoke what the white folks might think was an African language.

As we left, Forman said that since we were all there, we might as well go next door and sit-in at the Toddle House, a segregated southern restaurant chain. The moment was captured in an often-published photo by SNCC photographer Danny Lyon. When I look at this photo now, I think how young and fresh we all look. It also awakens the longing I sometimes feel—for the people, the energy, the passion, the all-night deliberations. In SNCC I really did feel like I'd died and gone to heaven.

My strongest image of this demonstration, however, is of Bobbi Yancy, long the number-two person at the Schomburg Library in New York, who, upon being carried away by the police, shouted, "Watch the fur, watch the fur." She later told me the fur was fake, but the image endures.

In jail the men and women yelled back and forth and sang freedom songs to each other throughout the evening. Eventually our wonderful attorney, Howard Moore, got us all out and we went directly from jail to a church, where the congregation welcomed us with freedom songs and the best fried chicken I've ever had in my life.

Another Kind of Freedom Song

Annie Pearl Avery, from Birmingham, Alabama, was a loner and something of a loose cannon because she was absolutely fearless and was known to carry a gun. She always traveled with a 45 rpm record player and a slew of records, and she could drive you crazy playing them into the wee hours of the morning in the Atlanta freedom house, where some of the female staff from the Atlanta office lived. I was always a little in awe of Annie Pearl.

Both of us were arrested on one of the smaller demonstrations at an Atlanta restaurant, only about six or seven or us. After transfer to the county jail, we were thrown into "the hole," a totally empty cell: no cot, no basin, no toilet . . . no nothing. Only a drain in the cement floor, thus the cell's name. Then they opened the window on us to let in the cold December air. Since all I had was my thin coat, I got really cold.

So, that first night I began to feel sorry for myself . . . and afraid. I'd never been alone in a cell before. Then I heard Annie Pearl. She was on the other side of the cell block and, in that crisp, cold air, she was whistling, "Since I Fell For You" ("Yo-o-u made me leave my happy home. You took my love and now you're gone. Since I fell for you-u."). I listened to her and thought, *I'm okay; Annie Pearl's here.* I didn't shout out or let her know I was awake. I just listened. And then I fell asleep on that concrete floor, feeling suddenly secure. And I remember it now as if it were yesterday.

Drop Kick

The Atlanta office was also involved in demonstrations to integrate Grady Memorial, the municipal hospital. As I was being carried off to the police van on one such protest, I saw John Lewis, then SNCC's chair, being roughly handled as they arrested him, too. I angrily started kicking to get out of the officer's grip so I could help John. In the process I evidently kicked the policeman who was carrying me in a very vulnerable spot. Looking back, it's amazing the other arresting officers didn't retaliate. After I was bailed out of jail, Forman summoned me to his office. He showed me a *New York Times* article mentioning that Judy Richardson from Barrytown [*sic*], N.Y. had kicked a policeman in the groin and asked me whether the report was accurate. I said I didn't remember, which was true. He scolded me, reminding me that we were supposed to be nonviolent and that this kind of negative publicity could hurt our fund-raising efforts. I left his office feeling very hurt by his anger and guilty that I had in some way jeopardized the organization.

That demonstration has remained a strong memory for me, but another memory—of Miss Baker's role in the Atlanta office—came back only when I recently reviewed some of my shorthand notes from the Atlanta office staff meetings (and seeing the names I wrote down of the staffers in these meetings almost puts me back there): Forman, Julian, Ruby Doris, Bobbi, Dinky, Minnis, Mendy Samstein, Jimmy Bolton, Mark Suckle, Tom Wakayama, Ed Nakawatase, and a bunch of other folks. I was surprised to discover how involved Miss Baker could become in even the minutiae of the office—but only if she was concerned about something. For example, we had been organizing high school students for our Atlanta demonstrations, and she questioned us about whether the parents of the students had been contacted and felt comfortable entrusting their children to our supervision. She grilled us about preparations for the forthcoming Dick Gregory national fund-raising tour. She asked about an error in the formatting of a press release and got on us for opening the office late (she reminded us that, among other concerns, the press might be delayed in getting information they'd need to run a story). My favorite section of the notes is where we're discussing organizing on Atlanta's black campuses, and Miss Baker cautions us that we have to "break through the pseudo-sophistication of college students and you can't do it in overalls." One staffer then actually had the temerity to respond that we were doing it to identify with the rural folks we were helping to organize—as if Miss Baker hadn't known this all too well when she pointed out the incongruity of the SNCC "uniform" on Atlanta's urban black campuses.

Then there were the national staff meetings. Every five months or so, all our staff would come in from the field to share information and also to get some R & R (Atlanta might have had problems, but it was not Selma, Albany, or Greenwood). Most were eighteen- and nineteen-year-old women and men, mainly African American, sharing organizing problems, discussing possible solutions, and requesting research from Jack Minnis, our crusty and rather enigmatic white research director. With Jack's research, SNCC folks went into new communities armed with U.S. Census data and other information indicating the number of registered black voters, if any; the levels of poverty; the discrepancy between federal funding of African Americans as compared to white farmers from programs like the Agricultural Stabilization and Conservation Services (ASCS); and the main industries in the area—and all this before the advent of computers. Our discussions also included references to both the national and international events that were swirling around us.

Here I was, a young African American woman coming from a little town in Westchester County with a 10 percent black population, no black folks with any political or economic power, and a high school where I was usually the only black student in my advanced placement classes. I was totally blown away by the brilliance, particularly of all these black SNCC staffers from throughout the South and North who were the same age as I was, but who seemed so intelligent, strong and—amazing. Since I was so totally intimidated by their breadth of knowledge, I usually remained silent.

However, when I read my diary entries from 1964, they in some ways contradict my memory of myself:

April 7   Tarrytown Concert with SNCC Freedom Singers made $1,000—cool.
April 9   Brooklyn CORE announced a stall-in on opening day of the World's Fair. National CORE rejected their proposal.

April 13   Forman left for England—International Conf. on Sanctions Against South Africa.

April 15   Dinky [Romilly] and I saw one picketer in front of the local movie house from Firemen and Oilers Union. Told them maybe we could help out.

April 16   Union guy came to office. UAW guys crossing their lines. Maybe they can use our WATS line to call Reuther [Walter Reuther, president of the UAW].

April 18   Got Stokely at 2:40 A.M. plane from Washington. He'd been to ACT meeting (Dick Gregory, Jesse Gray, Gloria Richardson, Stanley Branche and others). [ACT was composed of the more militant urban black community leaders in the North, organized by Harlem rent strike leader Jesse Gray.]

April 20   5:30 A.M.—been talking with Betty [Garman] about politics. This afternoon got to read New Yorker article on NY SNCC meeting. Read proposals about Miss.—fantastic. Going with Betty now to office. Decided neither of us tired.

April 22   Stall-ins today in NYC. John [Lewis] cancelled engagement in order to keep in touch. Letter from Forman—he's going to Kenya and Uganda (special visit with Mboya on the 1st).

April 23   Up at 9:00 A.M. for union picket with Margaret, Jesse and McCray on Peachtree. Our car just caught fire [this happened frequently with Dinky's car]. Fire Dept. came. It's now 2:30 A.M.

April 29   6:00 A.M. Just got home with Betty. Birds are singing outside. The morning is really beautiful. Have about 7c to my name. Hope we get paid tomorrow. Will have to walk to work (about 2 miles), but it looks like it'll be beautiful day. OH—John Lewis got arrested yesterday in Nashville. Bad cop brutality. Cordell on way there. Ruby Doris leaving tomorrow.

April 30   Talked to Stokely tonight. He's leaving for Cambridge [Maryland] Saturday. Demonstrations against [George] Wallace (he's speaking at the RFC arena there). Could really blow up. Will send off minutes Air Special tomorrow. Mom sent me letter Miss Kenney wrote to the editor of Tarrytown Daily News accusing us all (particularly Stokely and me, since we made what she called "inflammatory statements" at Tarrytown's Women's Strike for Peace meeting) of being communists or, even worse—communist dupes!

May 1   2:30 A.M. Just playing "Walk On By." Beautiful. Have $5.34 to live on for 2 weeks, but spent 90c for this record. John Lewis got punched in the mouth at a demonstration in Nashville today. So afraid somebody will be killed in Mississippi this summer.

May 8   FORMAN HOME! Man, hugged him to death when met him at bottom of [office] stairs.

May 24   2:30 A.M. Mendy Samstein called [from Mississippi] and said Dick Jewett had been arrested. Few weeks ago he was arrested on same charges and beaten severely. I called Mrs. Jewett [Dick's mother] who was very level-headed and has good contacts. Called John Doar of JD who didn't seem too impressed. Hope Dick doesn't get beaten again.

May 25   Dick was beaten in jail—while being booked in the police station. Beaten by sheriff and some guards.

May 28   Must get up at 7:45 A.M. to call Forman in NYC. Septima Clark asked him to appear June 26th at SCLC closing of training classes at Dorchester. Would like to give her quick answer. Chita is coming week-end of the 14th. Be cool to have her here. Can't wait.

June 5   Dinky & Betty in office talking to Forman (in NYC) about minor staff revolt which seems imminent. Decided exec. comm. must come to Atlanta and staff must attend. Miss. people, particularly, should be heard. People feel leaderless and with no sense of direction. During meeting Bob Weil said, very matter-of-factly, that probably 4 or 5 people would be killed this summer. When I wrote it down in the minutes I felt like running from the room.

The remaining entries are from the Oxford, Ohio, orientation session:

June 14   Won't even try to convey the depression, frustration and just plain cold fear which pervaded the whole orientation session.

June 15   SNCC office bombed in McComb [Mississippi].

June 20   Three kids—Mickey Schwerner, James Chaney and Andy Goodman lost after arrest in Philadelphia, MS. No publicity on it, although we contacted JD and FBI (Wash. and New Orleans offices) on Saturday.

June 21   Kids still not found.

June 22   Guys still lost.

June 23   Still lost.

June 25   Still not found. President makes another inane statement about inability to send in federal marshals to protect those working in Miss.

Not noted in my journal is an image that remains with me of that orientation week: Bob Moses starting each morning session after the disappearance of the three by walking slowly to the blackboard on the stage in the auditorium and, without saying a word, writing "The three are still missing." Just those words. Nothing else.

June 27   Bomb threats all night in McComb. 2 calls in Jackson.

This is the last entry in my diary till that winter. The disappearance and murder of Chaney, Goodman, and Schwerner had profoundly changed things for me. Unlike those who had worked in the field and experienced brutality before, for me these murders forced me to realize that my amazing friends/family/colleagues—the people whom I'd grown very close to—really could die here.

The Move to Mississippi

We moved SNCC's national office to Greenwood, Mississippi, for 1964 Freedom Summer. I stayed—as did many of us—in the homes of local African Americans, who, as always, put themselves at great risk by sharing their homes with us.

That summer Dottie Zellner and I shared responsibility for covering the WATS line (like an 800 number). One night, while I was alone in the office, June Johnson came tearing in. June was a teenager from a staunch movement family in Greenwood and had been brutally beaten in the Winona, Mississippi, jail in 1963, along with Mrs. Hamer, Annelle Ponder (SCLC), Euvester Simpson, and Lawrence Guyot. She said we had to drive immediately to the hospital. Silas McGhee, a teenager from another strong movement family in Greenwood, had been sitting in at a local restaurant—even though sit-ins were frowned upon that summer, as all resources were to be focused on building the Mississippi Freedom Democratic Party. When Silas returned to his car, a white man threw a rock through the car window, splattering glass in Silas's eye.

Since I had the keys to a SNCC car, June came and got me. I drove to the hospital as I had been taught—within the twenty-five-mile-per-hour speed limit so that we wouldn't be arrested for speeding. Suddenly we heard a bang, and June shouted, "Judy, they're shooting at us, get moving!" Looking straight ahead, I replied, ever so calmly, "No, June, those are just backfires," and continued at the same slow pace. Now, you would assume that I would listen to her, since she was not only *from* Greenwood but had been in the Movement years longer than I had. But, no, I just kept driving at twenty-five miles per hour. Luckily, no more shots were fired.

When we reached the hospital parking lot, we were met by a small mob of white guys waving baseball bats. They must have followed Silas from the restaurant. June and I made a dash into the hospital waiting room. A picture window faced the parking lot and was the only thing between us and the mob. Six FBI men were milling around the waiting room, doing nothing. I talked to Forman on the hospital's only pay phone (no cell phones then) and began trying to reach John Doar of the Justice Department. June went to see about Silas.

Shortly after she returned, a brick came flying through the picture window. I had never seen FBI agents move so quickly. They immediately ran into the hallway, behind a wall, and away from the falling glass. Since the pay phone was in the waiting room, at some point I went back there to begin calling the Justice Department again. When I returned to the hallway, I found all six agents seated on the floor, like the three "see no evil, hear no evil, speak no evil" monkeys. Now, I knew FBI agents would never do anything but take notes, even while witnessing beatings on federal property. But *experiencing* it incensed me, and I started screaming at them to do something—anything. They looked at me as if I were crazy. Finally, as June Johnson later reminded me, because of all my calls (I'd finally gotten through to the Justice Department), the sheriff of Greenwood arrived. After we confirmed that Silas would be all right, June and I followed the sheriff out past the mob to our car, and he followed us back to the SNCC office.

Unlike the image portrayed in *Mississippi Burning*, that's the FBI we knew. But I learned—from Dottie Zellner and Julian Bond and Mary King in our office—how to deal with them. How to take a call from a worker in the field at 2:00 A.M. about an arrest or a shooting, and then to wake up (real quick) and evenly ask for any pertinent information. I learned how to call John Doar (he was the only one in the upper echelon of the Justice Department to give us his home number) and then to call certain Friends of SNCC folk around the country and raise them from their beds with the necessary information, including the home number of the sheriff, if we had it. The Friends of SNCC offered a semblance of protection. When Mrs. Shaw from Chicago or Mrs. Wilson from Philadelphia called the jail, the southern officials knew that someone outside their town knew about the arrest. Obviously, given the many deaths, even this didn't protect us often enough.

My last call would be to the FBI. Their tone was hostile as soon as they realized I was calling from SNCC, and they routinely implied we'd committed the violence ourselves to gain publicity. Coming from Tarrytown, New York, where "Mr. Policeman is your friend," I had to learn—even as a shy nineteen-year-old—to inject a tone of steel into my voice. I had to call upon a force of will I didn't even know I had just to get them to listen to me, even if, as usual, they did nothing.

At some point that summer of 1964, while Dottie and I were handling the WATS line, I got a call from my sister Chita in New York. As a SNCC fund-raiser she had been coordinating the Long Island fund-raising parties that Harry Belafonte had offered to do that summer. He'd also agreed to appear at a rally in Mississippi—with Sidney Poitier—that had been scheduled for the next night. But my sister called to say that Belafonte was about to miss his plane. I immediately hung up and called New York's Idlewild (now JFK) Airport to try to delay the plane. It is hard to imagine how powerful we felt at that time.

I frantically spoke to someone at the airline counter at the airport, explained the situation, and was immediately transferred to the tower (this truly was a different time). I dramatically explained the problem and asked that they hold the flight. Incredibly, the flight controller was sympathetic to my request (the "disappearance" of Chaney, Goodman, and Schwerner was all over the news), said he loved Belafonte, and would do whatever he could. When he returned to the phone, he said, with what I believe was genuine sadness, that they couldn't hold the plane. Still refusing to give up, I made one final plea: "If you can't give us the vote, at least give us Harry Belafonte." Yes, I actually said this. But to no avail.

I called my sister back with alternate flights, and she put Belafonte on the phone so I could tell him directly. I heard his mellifluous voice and, to my amazement, became totally speechless. My mouth opened, but no words came out. Even when I heard Belafonte say, with some irritation, "Carita, no one's there," I still couldn't utter a word. When my sister got back on the phone and said, "Judy?" I suddenly found my voice again. But she didn't try putting Belafonte back on the phone.

At the end of that summer I was part of the caravan of SNCC Plymouths that were driven up to Atlantic City for the MFDP challenge at the Democratic National Convention. We had dotted every i, crossed every t, as required for recognition of an alternative delegation by the convention. Our lobbying effort, coordinated by Miss Baker and SNCC staffers, was highly organized. But we soon discovered this wasn't enough—not to counter the machine that Lyndon Johnson had revved into action. That's when I realized that politics wasn't what I'd been taught in school: it wasn't about morality or democracy or any of those things—it was about power.

We Shall Not Be Moved: The Role of Women

Looking back on it now, the amazing thing about SNCC was how much we were able/allowed to define ourselves, both as young people and as women. I was given incredible support to do things I otherwise wouldn't have thought myself capable of.

However, this didn't mean you didn't have to fight against racist or sexist assumptions, even within the organization. We weren't always one big, happy family. But SNCC *was* a youth organization and, therefore, less wedded to tradition—even internally. I also think SNCC drew a certain kind of woman (just as it attracted a certain kind of man). And many of the women—like Diane Nash and Ruby Doris—had been leaders and activists in their own right before assuming positions in SNCC. Beyond that, when it came to women's issues, because SNCC was so much on the cutting edge, you could, as we used to say, "raise the contradictions" and force the men to listen—most times.

Case in point: the issue of who did the minutes of meetings. At some point during the spring of 1964, the other women in the Atlanta office and I decided to protest the fact that only women took the minutes and were responsible for office administration. I still have my diary entries recording the days and days it took me to transcribe my notes from my first three-day staff meeting. Unfortunately, because I knew shorthand and had such high regard for all the field staff, I took almost-verbatim notes of the meetings. Since we usually met from late morning to 3:00 or 4:00 A.M. the next day, this meant that those of us (all women) who took the minutes always had pages and pages of notes to transcribe, type up, and put on those horrible green mimeograph stencils. For that first meeting I had thirty-three type-written pages.

So when Forman came back from one of his fund-raising trips, he was greeted by a halfway serious sit-in by five of us in the little area adjacent to his office—Mary King, Mildred Forman (Forman's then-wife), Bobbi Yancy, Ruby Doris, and me—all singing "We Shall Not Be Moved" and holding picket signs that read "Unfair" and "Now" and "No more work till justice comes to the Atlanta office."

He looked baffled and none too pleased when he saw us, but we talked it out and it was agreed that from then on both men and women would take the minutes. Now, this agreement stuck not because all the men understood the justice of the issue, but because the women in the organization would no longer go along with the silliness.

Epilogue: It's July 1985 and I'm in Boston in the middle of production for the first six hours of the PBS series *Eyes on the Prize*. On the train ride from Boston to New York to attend a book party for a new edition of Forman's book *The Making of Black Revolutionaries*, I begin to read a section from his new preface, titled "Some Thoughts on the Emancipation of Women." About that sit-in Forman wrote:

> That sit-in grew out of a discussion between some women in the SNCC national office in Atlanta, Georgia, and myself about the conditions of women in general and in the SNCC. Many of those who worked in the office stated that they felt they could not discuss with some men how they felt about certain matters or grievances they held about various situations.
>
> I suggested at that time that women should begin to become more militant in their demands and that they could start the process by emulating the lunch counter sit-in movement . . . I proposed that they role play, using me as a target. I also suggested they should make a sign or signs and develop a plan of action along with the sit-in in my office.

Now, I will always dearly love Forman. But as I read this section on the train, I angrily wrote, in aqua highlighter, "What?" At the book party I waited till we were alone, and as I gave him my book to autograph, I said, "Forman, how could you have said that crap about suggesting we role-play a sit-in in your office? You know that wasn't what happened." He only smiled and said, "Well . . ." And then he wrote, "To Judy Richardson, With plenty of love and recognition that your (our) work has not been in vain. Sincerely, Jim." What can you say?

Another "contradiction" arose in 1965, on the morning of "Bloody Sunday." Folks were staged at the bridge, backpacks on and ready to go. John Lewis, chair of SNCC; Hosea Williams (SCLC); and Bob Mants (SNCC) were at the head of a line. At 7:00 A.M. John called the SNCC office, concerned that Dr. King, who was to lead the march, couldn't be found. Forman called the Atlanta staff to the office, and it was decided that we would send some of our guys in to join John, even though, as an organization, SNCC was not supporting the march (believing by then that mass marches were antithetical to sustained grassroots organizing).

As we called around to locate the whereabouts of the staff we planned to send in, I asked Forman, "What about Prathia? Why are you sending in just the guys?" Prathia Hall had been a SNCC field secretary in Selma when SNCC originally went into the town three years before. I was ignored each time I raised the question, but I kept on, even while making calls and helping to coordinate booking a helicopter, since no scheduled flights would make it into Selma early enough. Eventually Forman relented and said I could call Prathia (though I had already called her so that she'd be ready once I got the go-ahead).

So what's now called sexism *could* rear its head in SNCC. But it was usually possible to struggle against it—and even win.

The Circle Is Broken

A staff retreat was called for the fall of 1964 in Waveland, Mississippi. The retreat followed the anger and the letdown of losing the MFDP challenge in Atlantic City. We were in the midst of a general malaise, with some folks seeming burned out. I felt a loss of direction—within myself *and* the organization. Also, for the first time since joining SNCC, I was in a meeting that was majority-white, and many were total strangers to me—college students who had come down for the summer project. We'd expected them to return to their campuses, but they hadn't. The students were unlike the white SNCC staffers, who had forged bonds over years of working together with their black colleagues and who were comfortable in what, up to that point, had been a majority-black (and black-led) group. I felt no connection to these new folks. Waveland was the beginning of the end for me, though I didn't actually leave until December of that next year, 1965, to return to college.

What I most remember about this meeting was the almost-constant tension and the confusion. There was the incident where a black female staffer stood on a table top in the cafeteria, waving a knife at longtime SNCC staffer William Porter, who was supervising the cafeteria during the meeting and who had said that you had to be on staff and show a meal ticket in order to eat. This was during the whole debate about who was SNCC staff and who wasn't. We were now at the point of arguing about *meal tickets,* but only because we couldn't get our minds around all those other issues that were tearing us apart.

There was one session where the level of anger was higher than I'd ever seen it. We'd gotten mad with each other before, but what I was seeing now was something new and very frightening. Earlier in the retreat Forman had been able to calm folks down with his usual tactic: singing "Will the Circle Be Unbroken" in his not-so-great voice. And it had worked. But this time the anger was deeper and harder to contain.

In the midst of this, Jean Wheeler, who, like Forman, understood how singing together helped reconnect us, told me to start "I Don't Know Why I Have to Cry Sometime." It was a song she had taught me and another staffer to sing in three-part harmony the day before. I just looked at her as if she were crazy. First, I was very shy then and wouldn't have considered starting a song, even in the best of times (particularly as I've never had a great voice). But this was the worst of times, and I thought we'd gotten beyond the power of song to bring us together.

So *she* began to sing it—alone. First haltingly and then stronger and more beautifully, with her feet planted solid like the roots of a tree, in an aisle of the meeting room. And, to my absolute amazement, others started to join in. And soon that whole roomful of angry and frustrated folks was singing the song, in harmony, and with me joining in on alto as Jean had taught me.

But we soon went back to the anger, because it seemed as if there was no longer enough connective tissue left between us to keep us together. Some of the people who were angriest were relatively new to the organization and didn't have the history with each other that often lifted us beyond the emotion of the moment. The spirit within the organization had changed. But for that moment in time, many of us were brought back to our best selves by the power of the song, and we remembered why we were there and what we meant to one another.

At that meeting Forman had suggested the staff write and distribute "position papers" on any issues they wanted the staff to consider. I remember Ivanhoe Donaldson giving me a paper (which later turned out to be the now-famous "feminist paper") and seriously asking me what I thought. I told him I didn't quite understand it and wondered who had written it. I also didn't understand why we were focusing on sexism when racism was, to me, the larger problem. And why we were now distributing papers when we used to be able to talk with one another. Throughout the retreat I felt lost, as if I were trying, desperately, to hold on to Jell-O.

Following that meeting I headed our Cordele, Georgia, Project and organized a residential Freedom School in Chicago to connect young people from our Friends of SNCC groups and young activists from a few of our southern projects. Then, during the spring and summer of 1965, I worked with Stokely, Ruth Howard, Bob Mants, and others in Lowndes and Wilcox counties, helping to build the Lowndes County Freedom Organization (LCFO). Jack Minnis, head of SNCC's research department, had discovered that Alabama law allowed the formation of an independent political party if it received a certain percentage of votes in the primary. As opposed to the MFDP, the LCFO was consciously organized as an all-black political party. There had always been a nationalist strain in SNCC, which I had not considered myself a part of; however, having personally witnessed the liberal cave-in at Atlantic City and now, internally, what seemed to be the increasing whitening of SNCC, I leapt at the chance to join an all-black project. It worked for me.

Later that summer I was pulled back to Atlanta to work on Julian Bond's campaign for the Georgia House of Representatives. In January 1966 I left SNCC to attend Columbia University. There I began to shut myself off from the white SNCC staffers I had been close to the previous three years, to the point that I didn't talk to any of them for about the next six years.

The Circle's in Me

In December 1966 I attended my last staff meeting—the famous Peg Leg Bates retreat in Upstate New York. The image that stays with me about that meeting is of seeing some staffers from SNCC's Atlanta Project kicking in doors with such rage that I was actually afraid—for myself and for the organization. There had been anger before, but this was even worse than what I'd witnessed at Waveland. There was also now a current of viciousness and hostility that seemed to override any connecting bonds within the organization.

After that meeting many of the black SNCC folk gathered at my New York apartment for a party. It was joyous and went on till daylight (image: Stokely dancing the "Uncle Willy" as only he could). It was as if by eating and dancing and laughing as we had always done, we could shake off the chaos that had engulfed us at the meeting and reestablish the bonds that had, up until then, kept us strong.

The Peg Leg Bates meeting affirmed for me that this was no longer "my" SNCC. Still, when Forman asked me to join the 1967 sit-in against apartheid at the South African consulate in New York City (I was still at Columbia), I did so—as much to fulfill my need to be connected to the SNCC I had known as to protest U.S. support of that violently racist regime. And, of course, because Forman asked me to. It would be my last official SNCC protest.

But that didn't really matter, because my SNCC—and *all* who were part of it—was now an essential part of who I was. Working with SNCC had truly transformed me: it changed the entire direction of my life; it irrevocably changed how I saw my world. It made me understand that if you do nothing, nothing changes. And it connected me to an enduring circle of friends that sustains me to this day.

JUDY RICHARDSON was on SNCC staff from 1963 to 1966: in Cambridge, Maryland; in the national office, both in Atlanta and in Greenwood, Mississippi, during 1964 Freedom Summer; in Southwest Georgia and in Lowndes County, Alabama, in 1965. She worked on the production of the fourteen-hour PBS series *Eyes on the Prize* and was its education director. She produces

African American historical documentaries for broadcast and museums for Northern Light Productions, including the Little Rock Nine historic site and, most recently, PBS's *Scarred Justice: The Orangeburg Massacre, 1968*. She has worked for numerous social justice organizations and writes, lectures, and conducts teacher workshops on the Civil Rights Movement.

Working in the Eye of the Social Movement Storm

Betty Garman Robinson

A young woman rebels against her family's race and class prejudices and becomes a lifelong social justice organizer.

What Will the Neighbors Think?

One summer night in 1958, when I was nineteen years old, I couldn't find my mother anywhere in the house. Where was she? I finally found her sobbing uncontrollably in her small basement workroom. What could be wrong? My brother and I had just finished cleaning up from a party we held for the counselors at the local YMCA day camp where we were working that summer. "You brought a dirty nigger into the house," she screamed through her tears. "I'll never live this down! How could you be so evil? What will the neighbors think?"

My feelings went from concern for my mother to anger and disgust. She often made disparaging remarks about other people, with the most derogatory reserved for people of other races and ethnicities. Both my parents were from working-class backgrounds and the first in their families to go to college. They were anxious to meet what they saw as the expectations of their new middle-class status. My mother had received an undergraduate degree, and my father had earned a PhD in physics from New York University. They were conservative Republicans and both quite prejudiced. During the 1950s my mother, a fervid McCarthy follower, had me sit for hours watching the Army-McCarthy hearings while she called everyone to the left of Eisenhower, sometimes even Eisenhower, a Communist.

I loved going to the "country" to visit my dad's parents on their small farm, but my mother hated going there. She viewed my father's family as backward, foreign, and beneath her. She hated that her Pennsylvania Dutch in-laws did not speak English and bluntly criticized my dad's "country habits," like picking his teeth and chewing loudly, things that "proper and good" Americans should not do.

My mother's prejudices included just about anyone different—especially people of another color. Still, she selected Lucy, the wife of my father's Mexican co-worker, as my godmother. During my early childhood I enjoyed wonderful times with Lucy, who had no children of her own. She cooked good-smelling, spicy food; gave me huge hugs and hellos; paid me lots of attention; and brought me little gifts from her native Mexico. My mother sometimes referred to Lucy as a "dirty wetback" and complained about her "broken English." Puzzled, I would ask, "If you don't like Lucy, why did you make her my godmother?" My mother responded that when I was born, Lucy was the only Catholic she knew.

My mother was also severely critical of my habits. She constantly scolded me for the way I dressed, walked, or wore my hair, saying, "What will the neighbors think?" Or "A proper young lady would not act this way." Her negativity toward me, coupled with the positive experiences I had with my grandparents and godmother, set me on a different path. I rebelled early against my mother's views and her need for me to act a certain way to impress others. I also struggled to be accepted by my schoolmates. Everyone knew that my father was the director of the new "Lab," a subsidiary of a large electronics company, and they assumed we were better off than they were. In seventh grade, in my effort to fit in with my working-class public school friends, I threatened to run away from home when my dad said he was going to buy a Cadillac.

In high school, over my parents' objections, I dated a boy whose father drove a truck and who lived "on the other side of the tracks." I made friends with girls whose families did not meet my mother's standards. One had parents born in Germany, and another's father was a blue-collar worker. As more and more of my choices did not please my mother, my rebellion deepened but was still pretty superficial. I refused to apply to any of the "Seven Sister" colleges, the "snob" schools, and instead chose the second-rung, although still all-female and privileged, Skidmore.

These battles were confusing to me as a child and adolescent. Because my experiences ran counter to what my parents told me, I was frequently in turmoil. Through this process, I formed new values. And in spite of their views, each of my parents modeled characteristics that would be helpful to my future social activism. My father, who grew up on a small family farm in Pennsylvania Dutch country, maintained the habits of hard work he had learned in his youth. My stay-at-home mother volunteered for local charities. Even though I had had little or no interaction with black people, this background helped move me to action when the sit-ins began.

College

My rebellion took a significant turn in college and became political. During the summer of 1958, between my sophomore and junior year, I attended the National Student Association (NSA) Congress at Ohio Wesleyan University. Here I met Negro students from the United States and students from other countries. I was energized by learning about the struggle to end apartheid in South Africa, the Algerian people's fight for liberation from France, and the developing Civil Rights Movement in the U.S. South. Almost immediately, I felt an affinity for those incredibly alive and smart students. A key NSA idea was that students had not only a right but also a responsibility to take part in changing the world. *This really stuck with me!* I did not know that students wanted to or could do something about the burning issues of the day. When I returned to Skidmore that fall following the congress, I changed my major from psychology to political science. In the spring I was elected NSA campus chair for the 1959–1960 school term, my senior year.

In summer 1959 the NSA Congress raised my awareness of world conditions and my desire to fight for social justice even higher. I was determined to bring the issues back to campus. Our first campaign organized students to write postcards to their congressmen opposing a bill requiring a loyalty oath as a condition of receiving federal education loans.* When a letter I wrote on this subject was published in my hometown paper right before I was to come home for spring break, my mother, again out of fear of what the neighbors would think, asked me to stay out of the house until after dark so no one would see me.

Our letter-writing campaign coincided with the February 1960 beginning of lunch counter sit-ins by southern Negro students. At school we watched and read the news with great interest. We were shocked to see black college students demonstrating and being beaten for sitting in at lunch counters. Students across the country began to demonstrate in support. A freshman student, Linda Chase, quite insistently looked to me, a senior leader, to initiate something. Filled with fear, unsure of the outcome, but believing in the cause of the sit-in students, I rose to her challenge.

* Because of the Cold War and the McCarthy witch hunts, the Federal Defense Education Act legislation was passed, which required students applying for college loans to sign an anti-Communist oath.

With leaflets titled "The Right to Eat," and "Let Your Voice Be Heard," we invited all Skidmore students to participate in the decision about whether to back the southern sit-in students. Between sixty and two hundred students attended about a half dozen, long, heated collective discussions—my first experience with grassroots democracy in action. We discussed, debated, shouted, cried, and finally evolved a plan.

On March 22, 1960, holding picket signs, two hundred Skidmore students left the campus for downtown and marched around the shopping center, home of Woolworth's five-and-ten-cent store, which was a big target for the sit-in students in the South. After the march and a heated street-corner discussion of how to continue, we decided to send four students every hour to continue an informational picket at Woolworth's. The first four students who went were "unofficially" arrested. They were brought back to the college president's office with the police pushing to charge them under an old union-busting statute. Skidmore president Val Wilson stood up for our right to picket, although he advised us to stop.

This threat of arrest for trespassing on private property, coupled with criticism from the local press and lectures by the Saratoga police—who said we accomplished our purpose with the march but the picketing would bring discredit to the college—led us to drop the picketing idea. We continued with rallies, letter writing, and meetings. One of those meetings included New York governor Nelson Rockefeller, Skidmore women, and our exchange students from Spelman, a black women's college in Atlanta. We saw this as an opportunity to get a statement of support from a major politician and felt we had an entree because the Rockefeller family had donated much of the money used to found Spelman. After the meeting Governor Rockefeller held a press conference and publicly expressed support for the sit-in students. Local residents and Skidmore faculty, motivated by our efforts, formed a group and continued the pickets at Woolworth's.

Somehow, word of these sit-in support activities reached my family. I remember a scene in the kitchen of my parents' house during spring break. I am standing against the wall by the table, the light is kind of eerie, and my mother is screaming at the top of her lungs at me, "If you love those niggers so much, go back to Africa!" My father is pacing and silent but definitely not supporting me. I am scrunching myself closer and closer to the wall, trying to be as small as possible, terrified that one or both of them will begin hitting me. *What were they so afraid of?* I wondered.

After college graduation, I remained active in NSA and attended the 1960 summer congress. There a powerful debate occurred on a resolution to officially support the southern sit-in movement. It passed after a passionate speech by Sandra Cason (Casey Hayden), a white southerner, who later became a close friend. I joined a progressive caucus, the Liberal Study Group, which quickly became a recruiting ground for the infant Students for a Democratic Society. One of my jobs the next year, while working in Philadelphia as the assistant to the president of the NSA, was to organize its August 1961 national meeting. At this congress the Liberal Study Group was the nerve center of discussion. There Tom Hayden, Al Haber, and other leaders of SDS were organizing for grassroots democracy; the elimination of poverty; and an end to nuclear testing, cold war diplomacy, and imperialism.

Immediately after the NSA Congress, I began graduate school at the University of California, Berkeley. Along with other students, I launched a civil rights support group after receiving eyewitness accounts from Tom Hayden and Paul Potter of SDS about groundbreaking work being done by the Student Nonviolent Coordinating Committee in McComb, Mississippi. At the first meeting, we chose the name Provisional Student Committee for Civil Rights and decided to make SNCC's work the focus of our fund-raising and support. Our group soon joined a national support network, the Southern Student Freedom Fund (SSFF), initiated by NSA and SDS.

We set up a table at the UC Berkeley entrance on Telegraph Avenue, collecting money, clothing, and books. Our activities increased each time we received blunt letters from Casey Hayden and Jim Forman in the Atlanta office: "We are broke and in debt, without any sure knowledge of how or when we will meet our payroll." We hosted speakers on campus, held fund-raising parties in wealthy Berkeley Hills featuring the SNCC Freedom Singers, and occasionally held support demonstrations. I especially remember one that was hastily organized at the FBI office in downtown Berkeley to protest arrests and beatings of SNCC workers in Selma, Alabama. Chuck Neblett of the SNCC Freedom Singers, who were in town for a benefit that night, indignantly carried a sign saying, "My Brother Was Beaten in Selma While the FBI Watched." We marched and sang freedom songs, like "Ain't Gonna Let Nobody Turn Me 'Round," and "Ain't Scared of Your Jails," bringing attention to the FBI collaboration with southern officialdom.

During this same period, I joined a study group of political science graduate students who were trying to understand the history of social change in the United States. We read historical accounts of the abolitionists, the suffragettes, the populists, the farm-labor movement, the Garveyites, and the labor movement of the 1930s. The basic question we sought to answer was why these movements were not able to bring about the fundamental system change they initially sought. It became clear that when the U.S. system incorporated the most immediate demands of each movement, the majority of the participants felt victory had been won. We concluded that the only people who were not complacently accepting second-class citizenship were African Americans and that the southern Civil Rights Movement held out the most hope of bringing fundamental change to America.

Near the beginning of my third year in graduate school, in the fall of 1963, Casey, then in SNCC's Atlanta office, and Jim, SNCC's executive secretary, urged me to come to the November SNCC conference at Howard University. It was a powerful experience for me to hear firsthand stories of struggle and discussions of history, strategy and tactics. There, amid the singing and debating, I made my decision to go south.

Leaving the "ivory tower" life and graduate school wasn't difficult. Passionate about the part of the SDS platform that challenged university education to be more relevant to the real world, I was already looking for a way to be more involved. I was really troubled by an essential contradiction in U.S. society: we were supposed to be living in a democracy in which the people make the decisions, but people with wealth and privilege were really running things. As soon as I finished up the semester at Berkeley, I packed my bags and boarded a cross-country train to Georgia.

SNCC

I arrived at the Atlanta SNCC office in March 1964 and worked with Dinky Romilly, the northern coordinator. We developed and sustained relationships with Friends of SNCC groups and other prospective supporters. I modeled my work on the example of Casey and Jim when I was a SNCC supporter. They consistently wrote and called to stress the importance of the support work we were doing in Berkeley and urged us to continue.

Through the careful process of nurturing our Friends of SNCC groups, we built an impressive network of dedicated college and community allies who could respond quickly to crises. In the spring of 1964 there were a few dozen well-organized Friends of SNCC groups. This number grew to over sixty in late 1964 and 1965. Our mailings to the groups in the North suggested mass marches on local government buildings to protest police brutality or demand the right to vote, and picketing at federal buildings to insist on passage of a strong civil rights bill. At the height of SNCC's work, we could organize large coordinated demonstrations in fifty northern cities simultaneously, with only a few days' notice.

We knew intuitively that support work, although difficult, was one key to SNCC's survival as a militant, front-line organization. It was easier for Dr. King and the Southern Christian Leadership Conference, which had a more respectable image than SNCC, to raise funds. On occasion, SCLC, as the better-known civil rights organization, would even get the credit and the funds for work SNCC was doing.

One of the most important memories I have is of the SNCC staff meeting at Gammon Theological Seminary in the spring of 1964. The album *Freedom Singers Sing of Freedom Now* was recorded at this gathering. I still feel immense pride that I am one of the many background voices on that album. When I was growing up everyone told me I couldn't sing. I actually believed them and subsequently was afraid to try in anyone's presence. In the Movement it didn't matter if you couldn't carry a tune; you got the spirit of the song and sang it with feeling like everyone else. I memorized every freedom song we sang and still know them all by heart. Both my daughters remember me singing freedom songs and union tunes to them when they were babies—along with the usual lullabies.

Behind the Scene in Mississippi

In June 1964, when SNCC moved its national office to Greenwood, Mississippi, for Freedom Summer, I went along. Greenwood was a large town by Mississippi standards, but there were probably no more than six or seven dozen houses in the Negro section, because most people lived as sharecroppers on the plantations. The small frame houses of the community, usually clapboard, were painted white with green trim and lined up in rows on either side of narrow dirt roads. Sometimes there would be a smaller house in back of the main house.

My host and hostess lived in a house like this with only three rooms. For the whole summer they slept on the living room couch and chair, giving me the only bedroom. Overwhelmed by their generosity, I was respectful, but worried for years that I had not thanked them enough or been sufficiently conscious of their sacrifice.

The SNCC office was on the first floor of an old building on Avenue N. It had three old wooden desks, each with a typewriter, a telephone, and a chair. I worked the national phone line, the WATS line (like an 800 number of today) and communicated with northern support groups, mobilizing them to give political support, contact local press, and send funds for voter registration and Freedom Schools. We spent many hours typing stencils for the mimeograph machine to reproduce the WATS line reports, detailing all the activities in Mississippi on a particular day. Four of us—Judy Richardson, Dottie Zellner, Ed Rudd, and I—worked around the clock in long shifts with no particular schedule, getting four to six hours of sleep per day.

Each week we received a check for $10.00 ($9.64 after taxes) from the Atlanta office. We used the money to purchase our essentials—cigarettes, cupcakes, candy, and female supplies from the small corner store—and to pay for our one regular meal of the day at Blood's. Mr. Blood, the African

American owner of this restaurant, welcomed the freedom fighters to his establishment at some risk to his livelihood. Here I ate my share of turnip and collard greens, grits, cornbread, fried fish, and smothered pork chops. I am certain there were times that Mr. Blood fed us without being paid, since the SNCC Greenwood staff *and* our visitors managed to eat there daily on our meager salaries.

In the Mississippi office our main work was to protect the field staff. Leaving the office unattended was something we dared not do lest a call come in reporting that a COFO worker had run into trouble. Civil rights workers who ventured onto Mississippi's roads could disappear, be beaten, arrested, or even killed for challenging the segregated system. Upon hearing of an arrest we called the jail, thereby giving notice to local authorities that we knew they had someone in custody. We then proceeded to call the rarely cooperative local FBI office, the Justice Department in Washington, families, and our northern contacts—ministers, elected officials, Friends of SNCC groups—to inform them and, among other things, ask them to make follow-up calls or organize local actions.

My parents voiced their objections to my working with SNCC by calling me every few days to say I had been duped by Communists and insisting that I leave the South. They were definitely influenced by Fulton Lewis Jr., Fulton Lewis III, and Rowland Evans and Robert Novak, right-wing journalists, who repeatedly accused the Civil Rights Movement of being under Communist control.

My parents threatened to bring me home with a deprogramming organization, and my father insinuated that if I did not come home I would make my mother have a heart attack. "You'll be the cause of her death," he would bellow through the phone. Though I knew this was a scare tactic, sometimes I believed it really could happen. Paradoxically, my mother sent care packages through this period and even purchased an air conditioner for the Greenwood office. On one hand I was sure my parents knew we were sweltering and sent the air conditioner out of genuine concern, but I could not help wondering if they thought such gifts would bring me home or help undo the imagined brainwashing.

Going to jail was a badge of honor in the Movement. It seemed to me if you had not been arrested and spent time in jail, you did not count. Up to midsummer I shied away from active participation in demonstrations— they usually resulted in arrest—because of the pressure from my parents. A part of me was relieved that I could hide behind my office responsibility and not get arrested. As the summer progressed, the pressure to go to jail mounted inside of me. With the intent to be arrested, I joined the next large gathering of people attempting to register to vote: Greenwood Freedom Day,

July 16, 1964. I went to the demonstration at the courthouse but chickened out and left the line at the last minute.

Once I went down to the Greenwood police station with George Johnson, a law student, to bail out a summer volunteer and local youth. After being given the run-around about the amount of the bail, George was thrown bodily out of the station. Then, when I went in to try to post the bail, a large white man with a red face and a baby in his arms literally pushed me down the four or five concrete steps of the station, screaming at me, "Go home, nigger lover." I still find it ironic that a man could cradle a baby in one arm and react so violently to another human being. Bruised but not seriously injured, anger welled up in me and helped me to understand how much discipline was required for SNCC staff to remain nonviolent when physically confronted.

While working in the office one early August night, we were warned by phone that several carloads of whites, presumed Klansmen, were driving straight for the office where we were working. Fearing for our lives, we ran to the back of the office, wondering, *What if they begin shooting? Will they put up a cross or firebomb the building?* Pretty soon we heard cars slowing down as they reached the front of the office. Next we heard loud voices and rifle fire. The four shots seemed like a dozen. Then silence. No one was hurt. We waited awhile and carefully peeked out. The bullets had ricocheted off the brick wall at the front of the office, leaving it badly chipped.

Our determination in the fight for equal justice was something we talked about to our supporters. Some shared our values while others simply responded to the bravery of the field workers and local people who faced water hoses, cattle prods, church bombings, beatings, and arrests. Throughout the summer, our mailings about the Democratic National Party Convention challenge by the Mississippi Freedom Democratic Party told a political story, not a sob story. The MFDP hoped to unseat the all-white Mississippi delegation. We hoped the challenge would bring about a liberal realignment of the Democratic Party and eventually wrest the chairmanship of congressional committees from the conservative and racist southern Democrats. Among other things, we asked supporters to get a list of their local Democratic Party delegates, learn whatever they could about them, visit them to express support for the MFDP, and send us the names with comments about where each delegate stood on the convention challenge—that is, the unseating of the all-white Mississippi delegation.

This work definitely contributed to the MFDP's strong grassroots support among Democratic delegates in Atlantic City, support that Democratic Party power manipulations outrageously subverted. I will never forget the passionate speech Mrs. Fannie Lou Hamer gave to the credentials committee or what she said at the meeting of the MFDP delegation when they learned of the proposed two-seat compromise. Expressing a desire not to settle for anything less than full justice, and remembering the pain and costs of their struggle, she stated, "We didn't come to Atlantic City for no two seats!" Heartbroken and angry, these extraordinary men and women tapped in to a deep well of resistance to oppression as they returned to Mississippi to continue their struggle.

Return to Atlanta

After the MFDP challenge, the summer staff packed up the Greenwood SNCC office and moved back to Atlanta. Dinky went to work in the New York SNCC office, and I assumed the job of northern coordinator. Mostly I remember how hard my staff worked that year and the creativity and energy that came from people engaged in fund-raising all over the country. From concerts to house parties, from walk-a-thons to street collections, extraordinary amounts of money were raised. As people sent stories of their successes, we passed on the details to other cities.

I still have handwritten notes of my northern coordinator report to Jim Forman, John Lewis, Bob Moses, Courtland Cox, and others from September 1964. It said there were twenty-three full-time SNCC staff in nine northern offices, volunteers running solid Friends of SNCC groups in twenty-two more locations, prospects for strong fund-raising groups in twelve additional cities, and fourteen cities where we were organizing people to build new groups.

The northern coordinating staff continued to call northern offices and major Friends of SNCC groups almost every day, write personal letters to supporters, send out a weekly news summary analyzing the political situation of the time, and educate supporters about the importance of building local leadership and fighting to make the U.S. Constitution a reality. This network continued to raise funds and generate political support through demonstrations at federal buildings, phone calls, and other forms of pressure on national elected officials. As the fund-raising infrastructure was built through late 1964 into 1965—attributable, I believe, in large part to Jim Forman's vision—we were able to better plan for the regular needs of the organization.

Fall of 1964 into 1965 was an exciting time for me in SNCC. We were learning how to build and manage a large organization. When we had problems with finances, a financial oversight committee formed and developed principles to govern us. For issues of personnel, we selected staff to develop standards and procedures. Few of us had any experience running organizations, but we tackled this with the same energy we used to defeat the segregationist power structure. There was also a lot of political debate with its accompanying tension, argument, agitation, and resolution.

All staff in the organization attended staff meetings, held about every four months. During the first meeting after Freedom Summer, held at Waveland on the Mississippi coast, the staff faced deep, fundamental issues about our continuing community organizing and the maintenance of our organization. Dozens of staff wrote position papers on challenging questions: What is the direction for SNCC now that the convention challenge has been lost? How do we consolidate the gains of the summer? What is the relationship of local people in the projects to staff? How do we best organize in a way that brings local people forward and develops their leadership, power, and resources? What does the system mean when it decides who is "qualified"—to vote, for example—and how are such standards regularly used to keep people oppressed? Who makes the decisions in SNCC? Who should be on the staff? What is to be done about volunteers who want to be staff, new staff, or continuing staff who are burned out? What is the role of women, and what role should white people play in the Movement?

Debates regarding the SNCC structure intensified in seemingly endless internal discussions. Two distinct factions debated the question of tight or loose structure. I was firmly in the "tight structure" faction, believing at the time that you first needed a governing body, elected democratically, that would make decisions about future programmatic direction.

My desire to see a strong executive committee came from my belief that this would bring fairness to our decision-making process. Field staff often came to me requesting funds and/or supplies because of my connection to the Friends of SNCC. Non-Mississippi staff and I perceived that Mississippi projects, still in the limelight, were getting the lion's share of the available resources. I felt that distribution of scarce resources—which had the potential to divide people if not done equitably—could not be carried out under the loose local autonomy model that the "freedom high" supporters advocated. At times I spoke out or wrote letters to Mississippi volunteers bringing supplies back from the North, insisting they think about broader organizational needs rather than just their own projects. The struggle over structure was more complex, however, than resources. At another level it represented different overall views of how to win victory, who should be in control, how to develop our base, and how best to develop local leadership.

I excelled at solving practical problems in smaller working groups and did not often participate in the large group debates. If I had a clear point to make, my thoughts were often jumbled by the time it was my turn to speak. However, these large meetings, where we worked to achieve consensus, were the crucible that nurtured my beliefs in citizen participation and in the right of people to make the decisions that affect them. They also developed my commitment to collective decision making.

D.C.: A Change of Pace

In late summer 1965, because I wanted to be closer to the work in the field, I wrote a letter to the SNCC executive committee asking permission to work on federal programs outside of Mississippi. The idea of working on federal programs was to spread the word about federal programs that local people could take advantage of and to insist that the federal government distribute resources in a nondiscriminatory manner with transparent procedures for what one needed to do to receive the benefits.

Several staff had already established a strong base for this work, especially in Mississippi, by organizing people to demand nondiscriminatory distribution of food stamps, welfare, and crop subsidies, for example. Hundreds of local people traveled to Washington in early 1965, met with federal agency heads, and told their stories of injustice. As a result, agency personnel promised to be more active in monitoring the distribution of benefits, but there was still a need to continue our education process in the field and collect stories in order to hold the government accountable.

I went to Washington to learn about the various programs and their rules firsthand, as well as to establish contacts in the different agencies. Then I went from project to project informing staff and local leaders about the programs and gathering the details, in affidavit form, of how people were being kept from accessing them. I started in Arkansas, where I found people very concerned about the desegregation plans that local school districts had to file that fall. I collected information and written testimony from the people I met with and headed back to Washington.

To learn more, I went with Washington SNCC office head Marion Barry—SNCC's first chair and later mayor of Washington, D.C.—to the U.S. Office of Education (OE) to get copies of the desegregation plans of specific school districts in Arkansas and Mississippi. Under Title VI of the Civil Rights Act of 1964, each district in the South was required to make a "substantial good faith start" at desegregation by the fall of 1965, already more than a decade after the 1954 landmark *Brown vs. Board of Education* decision. Surprisingly, we were given unlimited access to the files, which we read through for several weeks. The plans we reviewed were so contrary to the statute they were supposed to be enforcing that we wondered at times if they knew what we were seeing. I felt like a spy behind enemy lines gathering intelligence that I hoped would seriously cripple the opponent.

After we left the OE each night we worked to categorize and compile our findings, vacillating between exhilaration, outrage, and anger. The records revealed two important patterns: the Office of Education was not enforcing the law, and the local white-controlled school districts were evading the law in collusion with their national lawmakers. We found letters from congressmen insisting that their districts be exempt from the desegregation order and OE replies accepting plans that outright protected the all-white schools from any black attendance. The vast majority of plans provided "freedom of choice," a few grades at a time, where black families would have to choose to send their children to all-white schools. These plans placed the burden of desegregation on black parents, because local white people could, and did, intimidate any family who decided to transfer their children. They fired people from their jobs, threw them off the plantations, or firebombed their homes.

We detailed our findings in a report titled "SNCC: A Special Report on Southern School Desegregation," complete with illustrations of plans, quotes from letters, and nearly thirty pages of statistics and descriptions of harassment experienced by local residents. We also included our recommendations and model school desegregation guidelines, which John Lewis, SNCC chairman, presented at a press conference. Several months later, when nothing had changed, we called for the resignation of the head of the OE, a congressional investigation, and for funds to be withheld from those school districts in violation of the law.

By November 1965 I had become a permanent part of the Washington, D.C., staff and an elected member of the SNCC executive committee. January 1966 began with a trip to Tuskegee, Alabama, to protest the murder of Sammy Younge Jr., a college student who had recently served in the U.S. Army. Sammy tried to use the segregated men's room at a gas station and was killed by the white station attendant. I marched with hundreds of students and supporters to downtown Tuskegee. The young black militant marchers, most of whom I did not know, were angry and ready for action. Tension between black marchers and white onlookers was extremely high, and as one of just a few whites participating, I felt very vulnerable when confronted with the stares and taunts of the white segregationists. "Race traitors"—no doubt what the white crowd thought when looking at me— were often the first to be attacked.

A few days later the SNCC executive committee met in Atlanta and issued a militant statement on Vietnam, linking our opposition to the war with Sammy Younge's lack of freedom at home. The underpinning of our anti-war proclamation was the slogan, attributed to Muhammad Ali, "No Vietnamese Ever Called Me Nigger." When the Georgia legislature refused to seat Julian Bond because of his identification with the SNCC statement on Vietnam, I stayed in Atlanta to help with publicity and mobilization of support for his case.

Several months later, after I had returned to the D.C. SNCC office, a serious internal rift developed. A middle-age white stranger appeared and gained the confidence of the office director. We organized a very successful D.C. bus boycott to protest higher fares, but the phone system our stranger was responsible for went dead at a critical time. Slowly the office went from being people-centered to leader-centered, and we were shut out of the decision making. Believing as I did that those who do the work should participate in the decisions, I resigned.

At the time I left SNCC I identified fully with the black community—including speaking black English and using slang expressions like *cat, pig, honky,* and *dig it*—and was actually in denial about being white. While I was passionate then about opposing the laws used to uphold segregation, I remained uncomfortable about meeting the class and gender expectations that were laid out for me. Still, I had a college education and was part of the dominant culture. I could leave Mississippi in the 1960s or the factory where I worked, "organizing the proletariat," in the 1970s.

It has taken me years of anti-racist/anti-oppression work to fully comprehend the system of white privilege and how I benefited and will continue to benefit from it. Even after dismantling most of the legal barriers to equality, institutional racism remains firmly embedded in our culture—through policies and structures that entitle white citizens over people of color. These understandings have reconfirmed my belief that fighting racism is critical to bringing about any radical change in the United States.

A Coming-Alive Time

SNCC gave me so much! I loved my years in the Movement. It was a coming-alive time. Upon hearing my story, a woman friend of mine once said to me, "Oh, you just worked in the office," as if to say that I was oppressed or played an insignificant role. Neither is true. In SNCC I was accepted as an equal—for who I was and what I gave.

Because I did not see women playing significant leadership roles as I grew up, I was drawn to the black women who were an integral part of SNCC. Everyone, from Miss Ella Baker to Mrs. Fannie Lou Hamer, both of whom I idolized, to the black women with whom I became friends, influenced how I saw my ability to fight for social justice. In SNCC I also found a situation that was very different from early SDS, where the men did the theoretical work and the women literally served the coffee.

During my childhood the contradictions between the theory and practice of American democracy and equality came out on a personal level when I had to fight to associate with people of another class or color. This contradiction appeared again at Skidmore when, as demonstrators, we had to fight for our own free speech rights and emerged again and again in the Movement as we fought for basic justice. In SNCC we operated out of a simple theory—that for all people to be included in American society, the existing system itself had to change dramatically. Then and only then would disenfranchised and oppressed people control the decisions that significantly impact their lives.

SNCC was much, much more than the daily work of canvassing for voters, running Freedom Schools, organizing a mass meeting or a Freedom Day. SNCC was a family with profound love as well as intense struggles. We did not give up on principles! We questioned "why" at every turn. We were insistent when our elders wanted to go slow. We were both the cutting edge and the conscience of the Movement. It was a special time—living and working in the eye of this social movement storm.

After her two years on the SNCC staff, **BETTY GARMAN ROBINSON** remained involved in civil rights work in Washington, D.C., and was active in the anti–Vietnam War and women's movements in D.C. and Boston. In 1972 she moved to Baltimore, Maryland, and joined ten thousand other young people around the United States who went to work in factories. Beginning in 1980 she worked for seventeen years in public health as a researcher and project director at Johns Hopkins School of Public Health. In 1997 she returned to full-time organizing work as the lead organizer for Baltimore's Citizens Planning and Housing Association. The Open Society Institute awarded her a community fellowship in 2003 to popularize the history of social justice organizing in Baltimore and to bring organizers together across issues and constituencies. She is currently a member of the Charm City Labor Chorus, a volunteer with the Baltimore Algebra Project, and a strong supporter of local initiatives. The mother of two daughters, she has two grandchildren.

In the Attics of My Mind

Casey Hayden

A longtime staff member comments on the SNCC women's memos, SNCC culture, and the style and feeling of working with SNCC.

While it's necessary to situate my story in my SNCC history in order to write about the topics I've chosen for this book, it proved difficult to condense the years I spent in the South. They seemed to deserve so much more attention than I can give them here, and I to deserve so much less. I found the right tone in this autobiographical third-person format:

Casey Hayden was born Sandra Cason, fourth generation in her little Texas town, where she was raised by her grandmother and her single-parent working mom. Attending the University of Texas in Austin as an undergraduate, she was a national leader in one wing of the Student Christian Movement and was selected for Mortarboard, the national senior women's honorary society of the day. She joined the successful Austin Movement in actions against segregated downtown restaurants in the spring of 1960 while a teaching assistant and graduate student in English and philosophy. The following fall she initiated Students for Direct Action, which integrated college area movie theaters.

Casey worked with and for SNCC from 1960 until the fall of 1965. She attended SNCC's second organizing conference in 1960 and worked for Ella Baker out of Atlanta as a campus traveler for a human relations project across the South, taking minutes at staff meetings, helping out in the SNCC office, and riding on the Albany Freedom Ride on her off days in 1961–1962. She joined Friends of SNCC in Michigan and returned to Atlanta as SNCC's first northern coordinator in early 1963. She staffed a literacy project in Mississippi, where she also helped administer the Freedom Votes and the MFDP, and strategized, researched, and wrote organizing materials for the challenge to the seating of the Mississippi delegation to the Democratic National Convention in 1964. In 1965 she initiated a Mississippi photo project and organized poor white welfare women in Chicago.

Casey co-authored two papers that root second-wave feminism in SNCC.

About the Women's Papers in SNCC

The first of the two pieces of writing about women in which I had a hand was composed at the Waveland SNCC conference in the fall of 1964, an important setting. We were in disarray after the summer of '64 on all fronts. The field staff needed to regroup and plan, and the Atlanta administration needed to manage the overgrown staff and raise the money to support us. These needs arose as conflicting, although they weren't necessarily so. I could see both sides. I spoke up for power to the field and decisions to the workers. On the other hand, as Bob [Moses] has said, "We should have helped Jim raise money." While he wasn't talking specifically about the Waveland meeting, this comment strikes me as a good synopsis of this whole event.

In this setting the Waveland women's position paper was definitely an aside. Still, as Bernice Reagon has said, "SNCC was where it could happen." Organizations like the Y, in the Student Christian Movement, had educated us on the changing role of men and women back in the fifties, and I'd been involved with the Y as a national leader before coming to SNCC. But the Waveland women's position paper represents a breakout into public political discussion in this generation. It was precipitated by the list at its beginning, noting gender inequalities in work within SNCC, all concerning black women, as far as I can tell. The list was probably drafted by Mary King over the months following the women's protest on exactly this topic in Jim Forman's office the year before. The openness of SNCC and the Movement in theory and reality, the sheer spaciousness of understanding race as a cultural construct, as well as the invitation to critique the organization, which led to many papers at this time, provided the arena. The paper entered the historical landscape when Sara Evans published her book *Personal Politics* in 1979, and much of the subsequent conversation was about the ideas in that book rather than the paper itself.

So, looking at the actual document, I notice matriarchy is mentioned. I had learned somewhere in one of those human relations seminars I organized or attended that the black community was matriarchal. I don't know if that was true or not, and, in fact, it may be a theory in great disrepute by now. At the time, because I was from a multigenerational matriarchal family, I identified with the notion and with black women in SNCC. I saw them as powerful and primary, regardless of their formal leadership status, and I saw the Movement itself as basically matriarchal. I thought if men had titular power positions, then black women wanted them to be there, and I followed suit. Alice Walker, in the title to her 1983 book, *In Search of Our Mothers' Gardens,* called her writing "womanist prose." I didn't have that language, but I think now that I saw SNCC then as womanist, feminist with a black twist. I'm not arguing for this position, but that is how I observed SNCC to be at the time. I also had a more white feminist perspective, which by then had become more commonly discussed following publications by European women on the left. That is the perspective of the position paper's critique.

I was into outing that perspective now, for much the same reasons I came forward in our larger debates, because I believed deeply that honesty builds trust. But I was uneasy.

I used to think this paper was angry and that I wasn't, but as I read it now it doesn't seem angry. Perhaps a bit scolding, a family squabble. I used to think I was disinclined to write because I was fearful the writing would exacerbate racial tensions, but that wasn't quite it, either. The girl I was then was accustomed to hearing colleagues discuss their racial feelings. In fact, she had run workshops designed to elicit such feelings from blacks and whites. And her friendships inside SNCC were intact. I think we were all anxious at this time, overwhelmed by the size of the movement we had created and the new racial imbalance following the summer project. The more invested we were, the more anxious we were. But my conflict about this paper lay elsewhere.

I was aware that the perspectives and priorities of white women and black women, for the most part rooted in racial and cultural identities, were different. I was anxious to be coming out on one side of this divide, when in fact I straddled them, understanding and identifying with both. My mom, single and working, left my grandmother's house with me when I was eight. My grandmother's house was safety, the old home place after Mom's turbulent remarriage, and my grandmother was the center, raising me and running the home as she had raised her own siblings and her five children. Mom was a single working mother, liberal and commenting on the news at the breakfast table as she read the paper and smoked cigarettes, complained about the absence of equal pay in her professional life. So the capacity to see women's roles as valuable from different perspectives goes deep in my family history. The girl I was at Waveland faced into these insights, bravely taking the lead in putting the paper together, perhaps, in this instance as in others, beyond her capacity to handle the stress it occasioned.

So that was Waveland. Then I started a cultural project with Emily Adams and Mary King, a woman's move, all photographers in SNCC having been male heretofore. There wasn't a single darkroom in the black community in Mississippi. The project first aimed at building one and putting cameras and photography into the hands of local people. We ran into some problems with SNCC photos in Atlanta about fund-raising. After that I took seriously the notion that whites should work with whites, which was now being tossed around quite a bit. Ivanhoe Donaldson said to me years later, "Casey, when we said whites should work with whites, we didn't mean you. You just didn't want to go through all that." He's right on the latter. No one said the former to me at the time.

I chose the Uptown neighborhood in Chicago, officially SNCC staff on loan to an SDS Economic Research and Action Project for the summer, to experiment with organizing poor whites, Appalachian migrants. Gender contradictions inside the project—that is, contradictions in the interests, and even in the safety, of the women I was organizing and the street thugs SDS was organizing—led directly to the memo "Sex and Caste," which sparked organizing among white women on the left. I had to have some help, get some other women involved. The paper critiqued the culture from a feminist perspective and then argued for conversations among women inside the Movement as a way to strengthen it, hoping honesty, openness, and mutual support among women would strengthen the radical momentum we had generated so we could all keep going together. I don't know why I said that when it wasn't working for me. Maybe because it wasn't and because I didn't know what else to do, I drafted this piece with a pencil on a train ride back east from Berkeley, where I'd traveled with Mike James of SDS after Chicago, en route to a labor organizing workshop at Highlander in the fall of 1965. Mike paid for my ticket.

So those were the women's memos. The second memo is not usually credited to SNCC, but it was written as a direct result of work for which SNCC was paying my salary, a generous move toward interracial class solidarity that has also not been recognized.

Social movements are chaotic and ambiguous and creative. And so was I.

About SNCC Culture

At the first of our historical reviews of SNCC in the mid-eighties, I was on a panel discussing women in SNCC. I cried all the way through my talk. That's how much the loss of SNCC still represented to me at that time. The other women were coherent and spoke to the topic. I talked about SNCC culture—rather incoherently, as it turned out, because of all my weeping. I had a purpose in this approach, however. I thought our culture was where the women in SNCC were truly revealed and that this was what made SNCC unique. Since that time I have come to see the many ways that what we see is both what we get and what we bring to our experience, and also the extent it represents what we need to see. SNCC was a great fit for me, reconciling many competing needs on my part. I could be good by being bad and vice versa. I could be powerful by deferring. I could break taboos effortlessly, and I could escape the claustrophobia of my experience of the culture of the white South.

Being an elder means one has some wisdom, which shows up uninvited, and not always pleasantly, mostly as a result of hard-won self-understanding and -forgiveness. So, having owned my life more completely, I don't write about "we" much anymore or talk about essences, and I try to avoid generalities. When I wrote the words below fifteen years ago, I thought I was writing history. Now it seems more mythical than that. But myths are both true and untrue. I've carried this one around in the attics of my mind for years, and talked about it for years, too. I couldn't write it now, but it captures the vision and the experience of the young woman I was, inside SNCC, in the South in the sixties, back in the day:

The SNCC I knew was radically humanistic, placing human values above those of law and order, insisting that values could and should be acted out to be realized. One's actions were in fact the source of the unity of ends and means. Nonviolent direct action was a transforming experience—a new self was created. We assumed a new identity and this new identity was, I believe, the essence of SNCC. We actually experienced freedom and equality—in race, in gender—not completely, but perhaps as close as it gets. We actually experienced integration. We may have been the only people in this country who ever really have.

Relatively free of our socially defined identities, we found our identities in the community with each other. Mirroring each other, we could see ourselves in this new way. I saw the people I worked with as my tribe, my family. We lived communally, sharing living spaces and funds and food. We were almost totally without personal possessions or lifespace. Both our lifestyle and our work style were supportive and loving. It really was the beloved community, grounded in nonviolence and the southern black world of the church. It was womanist, nurturing, and familial, springing from the underlying philosophy of nonviolence, which was neither western nor patriarchal. Loving each individual ensured loyalty, which was both a means and an end.

Nonviolent civil disobedience created a new community of folks willing to risk everything for their beliefs. Together as this community, I thought, we were new people, free of the old stereotypes of gender, class, and race. This was the beloved community and the point was to organize it everywhere, redeeming the culture, undermining the old power structures. Women's culture and black culture, merging for me in the southern freedom movement, especially in SNCC, free of the constraints and values of the white patriarchy, would lead the way.

Strategically, nonviolence had to do with where you put your weight. If you didn't have any weight, you had to figure out how to throw yourself around to catch the other guy off base. We acted this out as volunteers and then we started doing it full-time. We created a profession for ourselves. We gave it a name—we called it organizer. We funded it. We also funded ourselves to be publicists, theorists, mythmakers and speakers, printers, and car mechanics. To be an organizer was very asexual. What you could do, you did. There really weren't any limits.

Part of the SNCC style required us to reshape time. Restless and impatient with the pace of external change, in contrast we slowed time and reshaped it to meet the needs of our own internal work. Everyone should take all the time they needed to formulate and present their ideas. All basic disagreements needed to be ironed out before we took action, so we could act in unity. You couldn't ask someone to risk his or her life without agreeing on what they would risk it for. We worked by consensus, because people should choose the way they might die and because we were all of equal value.

This kind of decision making fostered mutual trust and strengthened us. When we trusted in ourselves we could afford to distrust and question everyone and everything else. We especially didn't trust the press, and tried hard to live inside our own vision of ourselves. Trust kept us going, preserved us from selling out, and held us together. Holding together was our first order of business, so we had little hierarchy. Didn't need it. Didn't tolerate it. In this regard we were like a family of siblings.

As a white southerner, I considered the southern Freedom Movement against segregation mine as much as anyone else's. I was working for my right to be with whom I chose to be with as I chose to be with them. It was my freedom in question; however, when I worked full time in the black community, I was considered a guest of that community, which required decency and good manners, as every southerner knows.

I viewed myself as a support person; my appropriate role was to work behind the lines, not to be a leader in any public way. In fact, one of the major goals of SNCC was to create a new kind of black leadership. This idea of new and uncorrupted local black leaders could be traced to Ella Baker. Traditionally, as soon as leaders rose up, they were no longer of the class they sought to represent and couldn't be trusted. So new black leaders were needed.

I chose not to work in the field except in the comparatively safe setting of Tougaloo, on a literacy project, for which I had a background in English education. Being a white woman meant that wherever I was, the Movement was visible, and where there was visibility there was danger: my presence carried with it the possibility of lynching for my male colleagues.

Working in an office in no sense meant that I did office work as it is traditionally understood. I carried weight, and in all my numerous roles in SNCC, I did the work all the way up and down: the headwork of research and strategizing as well as the footwork, the physical work. That means I did my own typing and mimeographing and mailing, and I also did my own research and analysis and writing and decision making, the latter usually in conversation with other staff. I was self-directing, although often in consultation and community with others. I thought we in SNCC stood the division of labor on its head.

As we said at the time, both about our constituencies and ourselves, "The people who do the work should make the decisions." There were no traditional secretaries in SNCC, with the exception of Norma Collins in the Atlanta office, and there was no office hierarchy. I was at the center of the organization, unlimited except by my own choices and challenged at every turn to think and do and grow and care. The need was great in the Movement for skills of all kinds; I had some and I was happy to be useful.

During these movement years, angry white men chased me out of Haywood and Fayette counties in Eastern Tennessee at gunpoint. At the trials following the Freedom Ride to Albany, Georgia, on which I traveled as a designated observer, city police dragged me from a courtroom after I sat in the black section. White men rear-ended my car and ran me off the road outside of Greenwood. I worked in offices without air conditioning in the summer and barely heated by tiny open gas heaters in the winter. In Atlanta I lived in a rat-infested garage apartment near Five Points and a tiny hot apartment in a black project. I lived in the bucolic, funky Literacy House in Tougaloo, Mississippi, as well as on various couches and in and out of suitcases. I often owned only the clothes I wore, usually denim, usually had no money, and was often fed by kind local people. I hitchhiked and drove, took trains, buses, and planes and sometimes hid under blankets on the floor of integrated cars. I worked hard, partied hard, laughed a lot, loved a lot, was often frightened and was sometimes lonely on the road.

The worst stress was knowing that only I and a very few others at the phones in the offices, with the contacts to the press and federal agencies and our far-flung supporters, stood between the people we loved in the field and their injury or death, and that there was little, and sometimes nothing, we could do for them. This was especially true when our three co-workers were killed in early summer 1964 and our calls out of Jackson could not save them.

I both found and helped create in SNCC a world that worked for me: all for one and one for all, organizing rather than directing and dominating, a model I believed could work for deep social change. Like children we were wild, pragmatic, spontaneous. But we were supported by our nurturing family structure, which enabled us to keep going and circumvent, overthrow, and organize a mass movement right out from under the established order, both black and white.

Sisters and brothers. And, as Chuck McDew first said, many minds, one heart.

For more on **CASEY HAYDEN** see her essay "Onto Open Ground" in part 2 of this book.

Building a New World

Barbara Jones Omolade

A new SNCC staffer explains her decision to join the Movement in a 1964 letter to her parents.

Working for Change

I left New York City to work in the Atlanta SNCC office in September 1964. My father had raised many objections to the Civil Rights Movement, SNCC, and my activism. My parents expected that I would teach school in New York after graduation. My mother cried and my father stared in silence and anger the night I left to work in Atlanta. The following is a shortened version of the letter I wrote them the next month.

Dear Mommy and Daddy,
    I decided to work for SNCC because I am a Negro. I've always been very conscious of the fact of my being a Negro. In high school, I knew the reason I never went out on dates was because I was one

of few black girls in a predominantly white school. And the Negro girls I knew in my high school sorority were running so hard from being Negroes and trying to be white, I didn't want to live like that. My grandparents were farmers; most of my relatives are farmers in the South. I am proud of that and I don't want to run from it.

Last summer, I used to watch civil rights demonstrators in Greenwood, Mississippi, on television. I used to cry because I knew I should be there. But I also cried because I was relieved to find people trying to change what I thought was unchangeable. In addition when I worked in the day camp, two counselors there decided to go to jail for integrated construction work sites in New York City. I couldn't believe it, for here were young white people, just ordinary people who risked going to jail for their beliefs. (One of those counselors was Michael Schwerner, martyred during the 1964 Mississippi Summer Project.)

You see I thought that the people in those demonstrations on television were extraordinary people like Martin Luther King Jr., but they are ordinary college kids and old people. Then I went to a rally where I saw a film with SNCC field secretaries telling of their experiences in Mississippi. There were also some older people like my Uncle Archie, my grandfather, and my aunt Estelle, telling how they were beaten, jailed, and fired because they dared to go down to register to vote. Registering to vote is a task that takes two seconds in New York where a whole bunch of old women volunteer and act extra polite because they have nothing else to do. No tests, no policemen, no jails—that's the way voting should be and if it takes all my life I want it to be like that in Mississippi, Alabama, southwest Georgia and in other areas in the South.

Yes, Daddy, I am brainwashed like you said; brainwashed by the fact that I'm black and I have nothing to lose in this fight against the chains that bound me and my people. Going to college, living in a comfortable house, having clothes, even being able to get a job in New York is not going to change the fact that I'm a black girl in a white man's country and I have nothing to lose by fighting racism. Sure I can teach in New York, but that isn't good enough. The system is corrupt all over and it shortchanges the Negro and Puerto Rican kids and provides better schooling for the white kids. If I taught I could change the conditions in only one school, one classroom. But in the movement, I can help to bring about more basic changes which can allow me to go back to the south that I love and live there with my friends, white and black, building a new world and living a life with meaning. SNCC is a funny group. I guess everyone in it is running from their parents who don't want them to be in the Movement.

This year we are going to have a Black Belt Project, like the Mississippi Summer Project.

But I know you want the concrete results of our work.

1. The nation has begun to pay attention to the Negro in the Deep South. When there is an incident like in McComb, this past week—a couple of places were bombed, we got groups all over the country in a matter of days to start sending telegrams and demonstrations in front of the local Justice Department offices. A trio of mothers from McComb went to see the President and the FBI opened an office there. A contingent of ministers also went to McComb. These actions are some of the things which are needed in the Deep South to protect the very lives of Negroes trying to change their society.

A federal presence is needed because the government is responsible to us and should protect our lives. But they won't do anything unless we push them and we are pushing them.

2. Another result of our work is the beginning of the rise of local indigenous leaders who will voice what Negroes in the Deep South feel and want. There are Negroes in the Black Belt who are running for public office or trying to run. These Negroes aren't scared of anybody and they have guts.

I was so proud of our delegation from the Mississippi Freedom Democratic Party at the Democratic Party National Convention. I kept thinking how I wish you were there to talk to them.

3. We have begun a system of education, through the freedom schools and community centers, in the Deep South that is meaningful. I remember when I was a kid, I always wanted to know who I was. Where Negroes came from. I didn't learn it in school and you never told me. But I wanted to know. We must teach black children that being black is not bad. Community centers have been built in many communities in Mississippi and in these centers are libraries, citizenship schools. The centers also offer nutrition classes and provide birth control information and pre-natal care. These community centers are being built by local Negroes and white volunteers.

4. We are successfully building a political organization outside of and challenging to the regular Democratic Party. This is what I was working on this past summer.

Freedom in Mississippi, like freedom anywhere, means to have schools that teach you about the world, not just the white man's concept of the world. It means freedom to vote for people who will be responsive to you and your problems. We are simply working for change in the conditions of the life of Negroes in the Deep South. We have had some success and we keep on pushing.

SNCC started out with thirteen kids who decided to take a year out of school to work in the South. We are now an organization of 180 people. Nationally known, we pulled off two fantastic things. We had a summer project and asked for people to risk their lives working in the Deep South and got a favorable response. We made the entire nation stand up and listen to us at the national convention of a national party. The President even noticed for the first time the Negroes of the Black Belt south.

Who put this challenge together? Miss Baker, a fantastic woman who is the backbone of the Civil Rights Movement in the United States in this century. Walter Tillow, a white guy from New York. Frank Smith, a Negro guy from Georgia and me, their secretary. This was the staff of the Washington Freedom Democratic Party office which carried out the strategy of the Congressional Challenge and mobilized the Congressional and delegate support for it. Of course, all the black people in Mississippi who weren't afraid to walk those dusty roads, and face the police to register, and became a member of our party were central to the Challenge.

We had very little money, not because any leader was sitting on the money. But because we have to hustle for our money from all those people in the North, white and black who just don't know, or have some little inkling and guilt about what it means to be free. Also our funds are small because we are a group which refuses to compromise with the president like Roy Wilkins and Martin Luther King Jr.

One last thing, Daddy, I didn't come south and work for SNCC because I wanted to be around white folks so much. But I do want to have the freedom that you don't have, to choose who my friends should be. Nobody, not you, or some white sheriff, or some stupid law, is going to tell me who my friends shouldn't or can't be. I know some white people, some I hate and some I love. I have gone out with some white guys; some I want to see again, some I don't ever want to see again. But I feel the same way about some Negroes.

This is simply what this movement is about, liberating people so they can be people, not just white and black, not denying what you are, but looking for the qualities that count: integrity, honesty, and companionship. FACT: SNCC IS PREDOMINANTLY NEGRO AND SOUTHERN NEGRO AT THAT.

I know in many ways it is too late for you to change your ways and I can understand that; but remember it isn't too late for this country to change and I am going to try to make it happen. There *are* things you can do: go to some of these civil rights meetings, hear what they are saying. I am going to send you a book about SNCC and I don't care how long it takes, I want you to read it.

I am working as Assistant Northern Coordinator which means that I help to mobilize Friends of SNCC groups, raise bail money, send material and thank yous. It may seem somewhat removed from the things I have talked about. It's not too removed when you realize that we are in the South to stay and those people in the South need all the support from the North they can get. We need people to respond to the conditions of life in the South, not because we don't know about the conditions of life in the North.

I am working in Atlanta. I'm one of the few Negroes in the organization who doesn't mind working in the office, so I am here. But don't be surprised if I write you from one of those small towns in Mississippi—don't be ashamed either. Because this is what I went to college for, to know and be able to work at what I like best. I was a history major because I wanted to make as well as teach history. Besides there are too many historians who concentrate and live in the past. I live in the present and the hopes of the future. I want to help make history as well as study it.

Remember: "If you can't go, let your children go."

I'm on my way to Freedom Land.

Barbara

As a Woman

One of the most distressing views I heard in post-SNCC political work was from many feminists, both black and white. They saw SNCC women as passive and dominated by the men in SNCC mainly because of a statement attributed to Stokely Carmichael, the late Kwame Turé, about the prone position of women. Yet, for me, powerful feminists I met later in life were more about talk and never quite measured up to the power of women like Casey Hayden, Prathia Hall, and Ruby Doris Smith Robinson. I used to tremble at how these women both analyzed and worked for the Movement. In SNCC I learned that women need courageous involvement in community, not just talk, in order to change themselves and the world. It is a shame that more black and white feminist and activist women don't know about the bravery of the white women and the courage of black ones in SNCC.

Though I was not a leader or popular person in SNCC, from my vantage point as a typist on the support staff, I grew politically, intellectually, and personally. It is hard to express what the experience of being a member of SNCC meant and did for a rather naïve college-age girl like me. I had just left a family that emotionally silenced and socially restrained me. My education was devoid of the opportunity for critical and creative thinking. I felt liberated in SNCC.

I learned to travel easily from place to place. For the first time in my life, I felt personally free and loved to work with groups of men and women whom I admired. SNCC radicalized me and made me daring, sharp, and, most of all, conscious and concerned.

The Search for the Beloved Community

The spirit of SNCC shaped my life after I left the South. For nearly twenty years I continued to search for and attempted to recreate the "beloved community" of SNCC. In 1964, when I thought of myself in the future, I thought I would still live in a freedom house with all my SNCC comrades. Yes, I truly was that naïve, because I believed in the promise of the revolution that SNCC seemed destined to lead. To this day, I don't know why I left SNCC on the spur of the moment, abruptly leaving via the segregated section of a bus station in Natchez, Mississippi. I can only say that I was spared by a merciful God the subsequent events of SNCC's struggles with nationalist factions.

Although I left SNCC formally in 1966, I was determined to remain connected to SNCC. First I moved to the Lower East Side of New York, because a group of ex-SNCC staff members lived there. Then I moved into a California freedom house where Mary King and four or five other people lived. I lived on a kibbutz in Israel for almost a year, then submerged myself in the second Harlem Renaissance of the arts. I danced, wrote poetry, and hung out at black shops, by now feeling fairly desperate for the connections of a beloved community like my SNCC. From there I went to Jackson, Mississippi, for a few months to work on a media project headed by an old SNCC member. Then with my movement husband and children, back to New York City, where I lived in a firehouse in the Lower East Side with other family members and friends. For a time, I was willing to believe that blackness alone could be the connection holding a community together.

However, even living in a community united by blackness did not re-create the connection, mutual support, and sharing that I knew in SNCC. I started to feel that I would never be able to find that SNCC-like group of risk takers and visionaries crossing racial, gender, and personal boundaries for the higher call of social change and justice.

In the years afterward I continued the political mission of SNCC, albeit without its sense of community. I joined groups and organizations struggling for women's rights and black community empowerment, fighting against police brutality and apartheid. I organized demonstrations and led sit-ins. I challenged racism within the white left, sexism in black organizations, and the marginalization of working-class women in all political groups. I made speeches and wrote about the Movement. Through it all I carried the memory of SNCC and tried to capture its power and emulate its heroes.

SNCC was a borning struggle that helped to birth me as a woman and that continues to push itself into my life and consciousness. I continue to look for that unseen combination of timing, human will, personality, and historical moment, when a small group of young people will be powerful enough to change society, but even more importantly, will be inspired to build a beloved community strong enough to change all our lives.

Through my lens of being a Christian, I can also see the way faith moved among the believers responsible for the "spirit" of the Movement. Their prayers, songs, and sacrifice taught me the true meaning of faith as a "substance of things hoped for, the evidence of things unseen." As an adult, I finally understand what gave Ms. Hamer and the others such courage and such power in their songs—it was their faith and their prayers. For after all the ideologies, histories, and policies are analyzed, written, and tried out, it still takes a leap of faith in the hearts of people to make social change.

BARBARA JONES OMOLADE is a retired professor of sociology of the City College Center for Worker Education and a retired dean of multicultural affairs of Calvin College in Grand Rapids, Michigan. She is the author of *The Rising Song of African American Women* (1994), a volume that includes "Ella's Daughters" and "Origins: The Roots of the Black Feminist Intelligentsia," two essays that focus on women and SNCC. An Afro-Christian scholar, she is currently writing *Faith Confronts Evil*, a study of African American Christian women. Her son and daughter have given her seven grandchildren.

PART 8

Fighting Another Day

The Mississippi Movement
after Atlantic City, 1964–1966

> After we were not able to convince the '64 National
> Democratic Convention that we deserved to sit in the
> Mississippi delegation's seats, . . . We came back to
> Mississippi saying, "We'll fight another day."

—Victoria Gray Adams

After the MFDP rejected the Democratic Party's offer of two seats in
Atlantic City, Mississippi's civil rights activists continued to focus on
the franchise but also pursued an ever-broadening range of projects
and programs. At the same time, SNCC women dealt with issues of
gender and race and wrote about organizing strategies and goals. All
the accounts in the following section describe this key period in SNCC's
history, as do several stories in previous and later sections.

Though disappointed by the Democratic Party's actions in Atlantic
City, in Mississippi the MFDP enthusiastically endorsed the Johnson/
Humphrey presidential ticket, in contrast to Mississippi's white Democrats, who stood almost solidly behind Barry Goldwater, the Republican
nominee. The MFDP also held another mock election, this time running
Annie Devine, Victoria Gray, and Fannie Lou Hamer for Congress, collecting more than sixty thousand ballots, and arguing that the MFDP candidates should be seated instead of the white congressmen from those
districts. In Washington, using Section 2 of the Fourteenth Amendment,
the MFDP challenged the seating of the five Mississippi members of the
U.S. House, asserting that the representatives had been illegally elected,
since most of Mississippi's black residents were not allowed to vote.
When the vote was taken, more than one-third of the members of the
House (149) voted against seating the white Mississippi congressmen.

Continuing the challenge, MFDP lawyers and SNCC workers collected more than three thousand pages of affidavits documenting the stories of prospective black voters punished economically and physically when they tried to register to vote. Although the challenge was ultimately voted down the following September, that so many congressmen initially opposed the seating of Mississippi's representatives generated concessions on the part of Mississippi white politicians, who, among other things, urged an end to violent acts in the state while the affidavits were being collected. Additionally, the large compilation of affidavits, distributed to members of both houses, was used to support the need for a strong national voting rights bill.

After Atlantic City, Mississippi activists continued to protest racial injustices—holding marches and sit-ins, boycotting downtown merchants, supporting efforts to desegregate schools, and always canvassing for voter registrants. While Mississippi civil rights workers kept recently established projects like the MFDP, Freedom Schools, freedom libraries, and the Free Southern Theater going, they also began economic projects, reflecting concerns raised in earlier COFO demands. Along with local farmers and community members, they maintained an okra growers co-op, pushed for nondiscrimination in federal economic assistance programs, and attempted to desegregate the Agricultural Stabilization and Conservation Service Committees. These committees, which historically had discriminated against black farmers, controlled the number of acres individual farmers were able to plant. In addition, SNCC activists sought training in media—photography, printing, and slide shows—to produce materials that both documented movement activities and could be used as organizing tools.

They also maintained and initiated projects in a few white communities in Mississippi, another program started during the summer of 1964. This suggested an organizational interest in building an interracial movement in the South. Some of the people working on these projects were indeed guided by the vision of a new Populist movement, one in which large numbers of black and white southerners bound by common economic interests would come together. None of these projects lasted very long, but they represented an interest in a southern interracial movement that had existed in SNCC, albeit with much less influence, from the beginning of the organization. For example, at the same time that Miss Baker centered her work in southern black communities and urged SNCC workers to do the same, she also participated in interracial activities at Highlander Folk School and worked full-time for the Southern

Conference Educational Fund (SCEF), a progressive, southern-based, interracial group. There she joined her friends and SCEF field secretaries Anne and Carl Braden, who were also very supportive of SNCC.

SCEF funded SNCC's first white field secretary, Robert Zellner, who was hired to recruit white southern students, which he did briefly before becoming deeply involved in SNCC programs and demonstrations centered in black communities and on black college campuses. In Mississippi, although the Mississippi Freedom Democratic Party was firmly based in the black community, a very small number of white Mississippi residents were active members—four were delegates to Atlantic City in 1964. This history might also reflect a belief in a more limited interracial movement, rather than a new Populism—a southern black Freedom Movement that would seek out and be open to the few white southern progressives in the Deep South at that time.

There was no mention of the overall racial character of the movement SNCC workers expected or desired at the two staff meetings held in the fall of 1964, but discussions were held about the racial composition of the staff. Decisions made at the October meeting in Atlanta indicated that future organizing in the black community would be done on an interracial basis when a group of eighty-five, predominantly white, summer volunteers were accepted on the staff. At the same meeting Moses and Forman's proposal for a Black Belt Project in the summer of 1965 using only black college students was tabled. Subsequently, however, white workers felt increasingly uncomfortable around Mississippi staff and in the Atlanta office. Feeling unclear about what to do and where to go, yet reluctant to leave SNCC, white staff members searched for what they considered "safe" places to work, started supportive projects that didn't involve direct community organization or much interaction with other SNCC staff, or tried to organize in white communities.

In November, when staff members gathered for a seven-day retreat in Waveland, Mississippi, one of the issues addressed was whether it was better to use both black and white or only black organizers. Almost forty SNCC workers submitted papers on various topics related to SNCC's internal organization and goals. SNCC staff present stated their opinions about what kind of organization SNCC should be, how decisions should be made, and who should make them. Women were among those voicing their opinions and submitting papers. The debate about whether SNCC should be more or less hierarchical, centralized, or structured was highly charged. Sometimes fairly disparaging terms were used—those in favor of less hierarchy were dismissed as "freedom high," and those in favor of more structure were unfavorably referred to as "hard-liners." These issues remained unresolved and were raised again at later staff meetings.

Several white female staffers submitted a paper titled "SNCC Position Paper: Women in the Movement." Four women in this book—Emmie Schrader Adams, Elaine DeLott Baker, Casey Hayden, and Mary King—participated in preparing it. In this section and the previous section they describe the paper's origins and purpose along with their own varying opinions about the level of sexism within SNCC, whether the sexism within the group was greater or less than that in the society as a whole, whether to hold black men or white men more responsible, and the relative importance of gender and race issues. In 1965 King and Hayden wrote another paper, "Sex and Caste: A Kind of Memo," which became a founding document of the ensuing Women's Liberation Movement.

When the views of the memo writers and the other women writing in this book about gender issues are taken together, they suggest that within SNCC there was little of the more brutal and harsher forms of sexual oppression extant in the society at large and that for the most part working with SNCC was an empowering and egalitarian experience for staff, volunteers, and community women as far as gender was concerned. Yet, there were situations when women felt they must remind the men that traditional male expectations concerning women's roles would not be tolerated. All along, working side by side with their brother activists, SNCC women defined and redefined women's place in the Movement.

The wealth of projects in Mississippi after the Atlantic City challenge illustrates that in Penny Patch's words, a "blossoming of activity" was taking place in the state. During this period, women in SNCC found themselves in an environment that, in contrast to the society at large, fostered thinking about and discussing many of the fundamental issues relating to how social change should be made and what issues the Civil Rights Movement should address. Like Mrs. Gray, rather than being stymied by the Democratic Party's refusal to seat more than two members of the MFDP, Mississippi civil rights activists moved forward and chose to fight another day.

A Simple Question

Margaret Herring

A young woman changes her life's trajectory after
a brief exposure to Mississippi Movement stalwarts.

Before and After

I arrived on the planet in 1936 at Ashland, Kentucky, and was raised in Winston-Salem, North Carolina, where my father was the pastor of the First Baptist Church. I was the youngest in a family of three older brothers. At age nineteen I married a medical student, and we had two sons. Later, after my tenure with the Student Nonviolent Coordinating Committee, I accepted the challenge of working in the white community to carry on the goals and ideal of SNCC: an end to racism, an end to the Vietnam War, and economic justice for poor and working-class people of all races.

In response to this challenge, in early 1967 I went with my second husband, Alan McSurely, to East Kentucky to work with the Southern Conference Educational Fund, headed by Anne and Carl Braden. That year the local officials in Pike County, where we were living and organizing, arrested us. They seized all our books and papers. We were charged with sedition against Pike County, the Commonwealth of Kentucky, and the United States of America. The prosecutors were particularly infuriated by our connection to SNCC. The following year we were called before the Senate Permanent Subcommittee on Investigation, chaired by Sen. John McClellan (D-Ark). This same committee had become well known in the 1950s when Senator Joseph McCarthy headed it.

On the way to our appearance before this committee, we filed a civil suit saying that the committee was violating our Fourth Amendment rights. After refusing to cooperate with the committee, we were cited for contempt of Congress. An eighteen-year legal battle over First and Fourth Amendment rights ensued, during which we were represented by Mort Stavis and the Center for Constitutional Rights. In the end, all criminal charges were overturned, and in the early 1980s our civil suit was successful.

When I think about how I got into the Movement, I realize it all began with a simple question.

The Question

In the summer of 1964 I was milling around with the crowd outside the Gem Hotel in Atlantic City when an elderly man came up to me. It was Mr. E. W. Steptoe. "Have you had enough to eat?" he asked. "Yes, thank you," I answered as the true meaning of the question began to sink in. What did it mean? It meant that among those people there was a concern about getting enough to eat. Right there in Atlantic City, New Jersey, at the Democratic National Convention—there were people who were hungry. How could that be? It was a condition I had not ever worried about, but now I had walked right into it. Although I had questioned the customs and racist attitudes in my southern white society when I was coming of age in the 1950s, I just hadn't seen the reality of hunger.

Suddenly there was a shift in my consciousness, like changing your focus from the surface of the ocean and suddenly seeing the depths, the rocks and sand, the fish, the colors, the action. Layers of new meaning and awareness suddenly dawned in my muddled brain. Here, just under a thin veneer of convention glitter, was a completely different scenario. Before, I knew there was discrimination, but now I understood there was suffering. The fog began to lift as I mingled with a crowd of people from the Mississippi Freedom Democratic Party, poor farmers, sharecroppers, maids, SNCC organizers. I began to take a hard look at my life and the way I was living. I didn't like it.

My Life

At that time I was in my late twenties and a secretary to nationally known columnist Drew Pearson. My salary was low, but there were benefits. In this instance he had paid my way to the 1964 Democratic National Convention in Atlantic City and was putting me up in a very nice hotel. It was my job to work from 8:30 to 5:00, typing correspondence and his column and answering the phone.

Back in Washington it had been my job to open and distribute the mail and even answer the fan mail, to type up his diary—daily notes of meetings with friends on the Hill and in the White House. Every day that summer, mailings had come in from the SNCC office in Atlanta with accounts of what was happening in Mississippi and Southwest Georgia. I read them carefully. When I got a chance, I had talked to my boss about them, urging him to write something to help the poor people and the SNCC organizers, but he wouldn't do it. A close friend of President Lyndon Johnson, my boss had access to powerful people. After all, hadn't I typed in Pearson's diary a quote from Johnson saying, "I never deal with a man unless I have his prick in my pocket." Didn't that apply to my boss, too?

Once or twice that summer, however, Pearson had taken me to fund-raising parties for the MFDP, and it was at one of these that I had first met John Lewis and Mr. Steptoe. Oh, those nice houses of famous people where the parties were held, sincere and well-meaning people. And the prestige of being there with the boss. I had been seduced by the idea that I was with powerful people. But something was wrong, and I didn't know what it was.

My boss's friends at the convention were big shots like Hubert Humphrey, about to be nominated as candidate for the vice president of the United States; Pat Brown, governor of California; and Katharine Graham, owner and publisher of the *Washington Post*. Pearson took his advice from them, and they told him that these SNCC organizers and local people from Mississippi were troublemakers, and worse, even revolutionaries, and that the real story at the convention was the jockeying for the vice presidency.

In Atlantic City my boss had said to me, rather impatiently, "If you think so much of these people, when you finish your work, go out and interview them, write something up, and I'll see about putting it in the column." It was then that I made my way to the Gem Hotel, milled around in the crowd, and met up with Mr. Steptoe again.

Later on I talked with Jack Minnis, the research director for SNCC, who told me the story of the MFDP challenge and how black people had been excluded from the regular Democratic Party since the days of Reconstruction by a racist system that included the terrorist attacks of the KKK. He told me about Mrs. Hamer, who was the congressional candidate from the Third District of Mississippi. I was able to go to the sessions of the credentials committee and hear her testimony. Mrs. Hamer was a sharecropper in the home county of Sen. James O. Eastland. She had been viciously beaten in the Winona, Mississippi, jail after attending a voter registration conference in South Carolina. It was a sickening story. The room was silent except for the whir of the TV cameras. Later we found out that President Johnson had blocked out this broadcast by calling a press conference.

Mrs. Hamer moved me deeply. I decided that I wanted my life and my energy to be spent with her and people like her, rather than with my boss and my liberal friends in Washington. I saw in the people from Mississippi a different, more honorable and authentic power than what my boss and his friends in Washington, D.C., enjoyed.

Jack Minnis said that I should come to Mississippi and see for myself and make whatever contribution I could. He said that in the not too distant future, it would be inappropriate for white people to do this. I decided I would go.

After meeting and talking to several people, I had made a complete change in my life. It was rather sudden and happened within a few weeks. Before, I had thought that I had all that I needed, but now all of that looked empty and shallow. I am sure my friends and family thought I was crazy. I tried not to burn any bridges and to leave doors open, but it was hard, because I was eager to move to a new and more meaningful life.

I called home from Atlantic City and asked my babysitter to remove all the LBJ and other Democratic Party candidates' bumper stickers from my car. Once home, I called my ex-husband and arranged for him to take care of our two young sons. Then I resigned my job, arranged with SNCC and the Council of Federated Organizations to go to Batesville, Mississippi, packed my suitcase, and walked out of my house, leaving everything behind.

MARGARET HERRING worked for SNCC until the end of 1966, first collecting affidavits in Mississippi for the MFDP's congressional challenge and then in Atlanta helping Betty Garman coordinate northern support work. During Herring's long legal battle, she worked as a nurse. Afterward she returned to college and earned her bachelor's and master's degrees from American University and worked as a teacher of English as a Second Language. She also raised her two sons. Now she resides in Wilmington, North Carolina, the home of her ancestors.

The Mississippi Cotton Vote

Penny Patch

Organizing in Panola County, Mississippi, in 1965,
an experienced SNCC worker still meets fearful situations.

The Decision

Long before I was old enough to do anything about it, I resolved to be a person who would take action in the presence of evil. I was eighteen years old and white when I first came to SNCC in 1962. I had no background in community organizing and only limited knowledge of American racial history. On the other hand, I brought with me a bone-deep understanding of genocide and political oppression based on ethnicity. As the daughter of a diplomat, I had spent most of my childhood living overseas in China, Czechoslovakia, and Germany. Growing up in post–World War II Europe and Asia exposed me to the desolation left by the war and to intimate relationships with people who had lived through that war, including Jewish survivors of the Holocaust and Germans who had been perpetrators and bystanders. I knew, at a very young age, that the world was a dangerous place. I knew that millions of people, including children, had been murdered in Germany only because they were Jewish and that many of the people I knew and even loved in Germany had either participated actively in the slaughter or simply watched.

Back in the United States as a college student, I immediately volunteered when SNCC workers Dion Diamond, Chuck McDew, and Bob Zellner came north in the spring of 1962 recruiting SNCC workers from the ranks of the students involved in weekend Route 40 sit-ins along the Eastern Shore of Maryland. Out on bail and charged with criminal anarchy for their civil rights work in Louisiana, Diamond, McDew, and Zellner were facing the death penalty.

First I worked on voter registration in Southwest Georgia for a year and a half, and then I moved to Mississippi in early 1964 to work in the Jackson Council of Federated Organizations office. In September of that year I was assigned to the project in rural Panola County, and that winter I helped to organize the "cotton vote" in that county.

Sheltered and Supported in Panola County

We were one of the twelve counties COFO selected to run candidates for the county Agricultural Stabilization and Conservation Service Committee, a federal program. Farm owners, tenant farmers, and sharecroppers could vote for the people in their communities who would decide each individual farmer's cotton allotment for the coming year. The county ASCS Committee wielded substantial economic power, because it essentially could place top limits on family farm income in the Mississippi Delta. In contrast to the electoral vote, there was no registration requirement, no literacy test, and no poll tax.

Panola County had plantations as large as 5,000 acres that were farmed by black sharecroppers with an average yearly income of about two hundred dollars. The county, made up of hill country as well as Delta flatland, also contained a sizable number of small, independent black farmers. That fall of 1964 I lived with other civil rights workers on the farm owned by Mr. Robert Miles and his wife, Mona. Mr. Miles, an intensely quiet, kind, and soft-spoken man with a tenth-grade education, was one of the founding members of the Panola County Voters League, organized in 1959 when five independent black farmers first came together to attempt to register black voters. He owned 167 acres, 24 of them in cotton, and was among the first to volunteer to run in the ASCS election.

The recent years had been difficult for the Miles family. On different occasions their home had been shot into, bombed, and tear-gassed. By the time I came to live in the Miles household, neighbors had taken to guarding the house all night, every night. If you drove into the driveway at night, you had to be sure to blink your headlights three times or you risked being met with a shotgun blast.

Mrs. Miles welcomed us into her home with a blend of intelligence, cheerfulness, and humor, mixed in equal parts with anxiety and pessimism about what the local white folks would do. She was a college graduate and had been a teacher until she became too ill to continue working. She suffered from a kind of paralysis, a traumatic effect, we learned, from all the attacks on her home and family.

Mr. and Mrs. C. J. Williams, also Panola County Movement stalwarts, participated actively in the ASCS vote that fall. I lived out on their forty-acre hill farm when we were working in the southern part of the county. Mr. Williams also had tried to register to vote in 1959 and, along with Mr. Miles, had founded the Panola County Voters League. Mrs. Williams was born in Grenada County, not far from Panola. In the 1920s her grandfather had established a black-owned cotton gin, which ginned all the cotton for black farmers in the area. The Klan came one night, burned down the gin, and tried to kill Mrs. Williams's grandfather. He and his brothers fought back with guns and survived. Mrs. Williams, only four years old at the time, remembered watching from the window of their home, seeing the cotton gin burning, and hearing the shots. After this event the family moved to Pennsylvania, although Mrs. Williams returned in later years to marry and settle in Panola County.

Sheltered, fed, and supported by these Panola County residents, Chris Williams, a white co-worker, and I worked as a team organizing the ASCS vote in the county. It often rains in the fall and winter in Mississippi, and during the rainy season the mostly unpaved roads are deep with mud. Sometimes the mud comes up to the hubcaps of the cars. We drove a rattly, old 1954 Pontiac, and when that broke down we borrowed a pickup truck. We rode up and down the dirt roads of Panola County that month, talking to black farm owners and sharecroppers and distributing leaflets. Chris and I organized farmers' meetings in five communities and made daily visits to key contacts like Mr. Roland Nelson, who sharecropped with his wife, Rosie, and their five children on the Hays plantation.

Mr. Nelson was born in Mississippi and then spent some years living in Detroit, where he became involved in union organizing. He eventually returned to Mississippi and married. Unlike the Miles and Williams families, who farmed their own land, the Nelsons became sharecroppers on Carlin Hays's plantation. The Nelsons were among the first to join the Panola County Movement, despite their extreme economic vulnerability as a sharecropping family. Carlin Hays, the owner of the three-thousand-acre plantation where the Nelsons lived, was chairman of the Crenshaw community ASCS Committee. Mr. Nelson didn't feel it would be wise to run directly against boss-man Hays, but he actively supported the candidacy of Melrow Curtis, a black farmer running as a write-in.

When Chris and I visited the Nelsons' home, a tiny, unpainted wooden shack provided by Hays, we usually traveled with our lights out while entering and leaving the plantation and parked our car behind the house so it would not be seen. Even though we were welcome visitors at the Nelsons', Mr. Hays, as the owner of the property, retained the right to determine who stepped foot on his plantation. He would not welcome our presence and had the right to remove us forcibly, since we were definitely trespassing. The interior of the Nelson home was undecorated except for two posters: one of President Johnson, the other of Mrs. Fannie Lou Hamer. On our last visit before the election, Mr. Nelson told us that many of the sharecroppers would vote.

People sometimes gathered at the Nelsons' to meet with us. Chris had grown up on a small farm and knew a lot about farming. Although we both talked with men and women as we organized on the plantation, he spent much of his time with the men while I developed stronger relationships with the women. I am at heart a shy and quiet person, but I was comfortable communicating one-on-one and in small groups. One evening several women on the Hays plantation approached me and asked if I could educate them about birth control. I was twenty years old and it was 1965. I was not nearly as well informed as a twenty-year-old might be today, but with the help of a co-worker I gathered information and we ran small classes on the plantation. As with most civil rights work, this was one more case of learning on the job.

Election Day

ASCS Election Day was cold and wet, which was good because it wasn't a day to pick the last of the cotton. Many black farmers, tenant farmers, and sharecroppers voted. At one of the voting sites, in a county courthouse, a group of white planters sat in the rear of the courtroom. They had checklists and runners, who were kept busy making phone calls to which the white community responded. One planter was overheard to say that in past years they could never get enough votes to make this election legal, but it was no problem this year. Any white person who presented himself or herself was given a ballot, no questions asked. Black people, of course, were strictly questioned and asked to present proof of land ownership or tenancy. By the end of the day, white people had outvoted black people by almost two to one. Not one black person in Panola County secured a place on the county committee.

On that Election Day I was poll watching at another site with a young black woman who was active in the Panola County Movement. In a tiny country store on a dirt road, we two sat together surrounded by hostile white men. The store was dark and cramped, with a counter and shelves lining the walls floor to ceiling. There was a small wood stove. Two men sat behind a table with election materials on it, and we sat in two chairs next to the table. People, mostly men, mostly white, drifted in during the day to vote and to check us out. It was terrifying to be so totally isolated in that little store, surrounded by people who hated us. Sometimes a small group of black men came in, quietly gave their names, and voted. The white people in the store watched, not saying a word. Their silence was menacing. We wondered who would be attacked, whose houses bombed or burned in the next days.

No one physically harmed us or any of the black voters, a clear indication of some change in Mississippi after the Mississippi Summer Project just a few months before. Finally, there was a measure of federal pressure.

The word was out: do not hurt these people while they are engaged in ASCS election activities. But the Mississippi white folks still harassed us.

At one point three or four white teenagers walked in the door and threw a live snake at our feet. While we sat frozen in our chairs, the white female proprietor of the store, who disliked snakes as much as we did, ran out of the store yelling at the perpetrators. The snake slithered under the wood stove. I only wished I could as easily escape notice.

I was very scared. After almost three years in the Movement, I was always on edge. I became more afraid, not less, as time went by. This incident, which was less life-threatening than any number of earlier ones, remains etched in my memory because of the terror I felt. By the end of the day I was a mass of nerves.

Blossoming Activity

We kept working and the Movement grew in strength and autonomy. In February 1965 I wrote the following positive report to the Atlanta SNCC office concerning civil rights activity in Panola County:

> What are we doing? Or rather what are the people of Panola County doing? For the Negroes of Panola County, young and old, are now beginning to run their own movement. We now ask Mr. Robert Miles, Chairman of the county FDP for advice, rather than the reverse. (Actually that was always the case.) The sharecroppers of the Hays plantation ask Mr. C. J. Williams, FDP delegate, to come and help them organize their voter registration drive. We haven't worked ourselves out of a job yet, but the time is coming.
>
> The voter registration drive is booming . . . 93 people passed the registration test last week. Ike Shankle, the registrar, is angry and frustrated, and had Chris Williams, COFO worker, arrested last Friday for trespassing on courthouse property. (Chris is out of jail and the case is now on appeal.) Mass meetings in connection with the registration drive are being held in all parts of the county, and for the first time the entire county is being worked and most of the people reached.
>
> We finally have word that our hearing on the congressional challenge will be held next week. Negroes from all over the county will be testifying, as well as several hostile witnesses . . . ex-sheriff Darby, Sheriff Hubbard, Ira Seals, District Attorney Finch, and certain plantation owners who have kicked people off their plantations for registering to vote. We are expecting it to be quite a show, and we are also

expecting an increase in harassment as soon as the hostile witnesses receive their subpoenas.

The small farmers are organizing themselves around a petition demanding a higher price for their okra crop (they all sell to one man here in the county, who markets the okra in Memphis), and there is talk of forming a marketing cooperative—this will be discussed tonight at a farmers' meeting at the freedom center.

The plantations constitute the biggest problem. We have done a great deal of work on one particular plantation, the Hays place. About fifty Negro families live on this plantation of 3000 acres. Leaders have emerged and almost the entire plantation has gone down en masse to register to vote. Forty-five adults signed a petition demanding more pay, shorter hours, better housing, the right to see plantation records, etc. and presented the petition to Mr. Hays himself. So far Hays hasn't kicked anybody off. He is simply slowly squeezing people out, not giving work to those people on his plantation who are active in the Movement. Where do they go from here? A strike this spring would probably mean eviction and a chance for Mr. Hays to buy himself a mechanical cotton-picker. The problem is that the people have nothing to bargain with. At this point they have decided that they should concentrate on organizing the neighboring plantations—maybe if four or five plantations get together . . .

The students in the county are also beginning to come into their own. Jr. Voters' Leagues in the small county towns have been functioning for months now, working to get the adults registered to vote. But only recently have they come together from all over the county to plan a course of action for themselves . . . they plan to 1) hold sit-ins in various white cafes, restaurants, libraries, movie theatres 2) petition the superintendent of schools for better teachers, smaller classes, more courses, better equipment, etc. and if he doesn't come through they plan to boycott and perhaps hold demonstrations outside his office. Also, a good number are planning to file for transfer to the white school next fall.

United, these kids can be the most important and vital force in the county. Freedom school sessions are often painful for all concerned, as all of us try to honestly talk and think about the political, economic and social implications of life in Mississippi and the U.S. Last week we listened to the record of *In White America*, picked out certain parts and discussed them: Booker T. Washington vs. Dubois (whom none of the students had heard of), Thomas Jefferson's statement on the inferiority of the Negro, leading into a discussion of the various myths about Negroes, etc. The students are beginning to tear down myths and see who they are, where they came from, and how important they are . . .

We SNCC organizers had played a part in this blossoming of the Panola County Movement. But the Movement was there before we came, and it went on after we left. It was an enormous privilege for me to live and work with such immensely courageous and creative people. Although I left the South in August 1965, my memories of Mr. and Mrs. Miles, Mr. and Mrs. Williams, the Nelson family, and many others with whom I worked there have sustained me throughout my life and inspired me in all the work I have done since.

PENNY PATCH worked with SNCC from 1962 to 1965 in Southwest Georgia and Mississippi. She helped with community voter registration and election campaigns, organized and participated in demonstrations to desegregate public accommodations, and taught in Freedom Schools. Presently she is a nurse midwife living and working in Vermont and has long been involved in maternal and child health work. She is also active in anti-racist education projects in her community. For more on her life and movement work, see "Sweet Tea at Shoney's" in *Deep in Our Hearts: Nine White Women in the Freedom Movement* (2000).

The Freedom Struggle Was the Flame

Elaine DeLott Baker

A sociology student finds herself in rural Mississippi organizing an okra co-op.

Joining the Movement

There was no single moment when I decided to join the Movement. Mine was not a deliberate decision to enter the struggle for social justice. It was a confluence of events that began one day in May 1964 when SNCC field secretary Jesse Morris came to see me at Tougaloo College on the outskirts of Jackson, Mississippi. I had arrived there a week earlier with a group of

Harvard students who had volunteered to teach Tougaloo summer school classes. We were part of a Field Foundation project that provided regular Tougaloo College faculty with the opportunity to work on their postgraduate studies at northern colleges over summer term.

Jesse Morris was an enigmatic character of the times, his complex and thoughtful intellect struggling with what he saw as the unfolding economic future of the state's black population. Jesse remained in Mississippi working on economic initiatives for the next several decades, but that summer the focus on economic issues was overshadowed by the more immediate issues of voter registration and direct action. When Jesse heard I had worked with Harvard sociologist Tom Pettigrew on a survey of Boston's African American neighborhoods, he asked me to help him develop a survey that could be administered by volunteers during the summer. I enlisted Pettigrew's support by mail and began work on the design. In a few weeks I found myself, still working on the survey, at the Freedom Summer orientation in Oxford, Ohio. A week later, when the bus returned to Jackson, I had become part of the swirling energy and moral purpose that was the Movement.

Opening the Door to Federal Programs

In the chaotic aftermath of Freedom Summer, an effort that joined more than five hundred volunteers, mostly white, with veteran SNCC staff, I found a place to work that suited my skills—as a technical resource for the Federal Programs Initiative of the Council of Federated Organizations.

Federal Programs was an umbrella for a broad group of organizing efforts that included leveraging federal funds for local initiatives as well as forcing the federal government to pay attention to the institutionalized racism that characterized the administration of Mississippi's federal programs. Using federal programs as a platform for organizing was not a dramatic tactic, like demonstrations or voter registration, but it was a powerful way of connecting with people's everyday struggles for equal treatment under the law. That fall, Jesse handed me an advance copy of the poverty bill and asked me to come up with a proposal that the nearby community of Canton could submit. I was understandably skeptical about any effort whose success was dependent on the cooperation of local agencies. In my weekly report to Jesse I proposed a more activist strategy, which would later be termed "welfare rights."

OCTOBER 11, 1964

After a review of these types of programs it is my personal feeling that little can be done directly through the community and the federal agencies sponsoring these programs . . . Our job is to put pressure on local agencies to cooperate with federal men . . . As to how to apply this pressure, I have a few ideas. One is to organize a large-scale welfare-type organization, staffed by local people and administered through the political organization of the Freedom Democratic Party (FDP). Using the blocks as units, I would like to train about ten people in the basics of the Social Security Act, disability provisions, plus unemployment laws, plus welfare programs like Aid to Dependent Children and Old Age Assistance. They could get around to all the families in the Negro communities and . . . advise the people [on] what programs they are eligible for, and help them apply and appeal denials. If we do not win our just appeals, we have a legal leverage in Washington.

I began at the State House in Jackson, where I made copies of state regulations for different federal programs. In the fall and early winter I visited projects around the state, answering questions on eligibility and documenting incidents of systematic discrimination. I often traveled alone, borrowing vehicles from other civil rights workers and appearing at projects on an as-needed basis. In the summer we had taken care to travel in pairs, in daylight, and to stay in close communication with base operations. But the summer was behind us, discipline in the field was unraveling, and my impatience outweighed good sense.

As the evidence of systematic discrimination in federally funded state programs continued to mount, I started thinking about how I could get the attention of the Washington agencies that oversaw these programs. An opening appeared with an upcoming trip to Washington that the Mississippi Freedom Democratic Party was organizing. It was an opportunity to bring disenfranchised Mississippians to Washington to challenge the legitimacy of seating the all-white Mississippi congressional delegation. Visits to federal agencies weren't part of the MFDP's original plans, but the MFDP recognized the value of such visits and gave me the approval to begin setting up meetings at Washington agencies, like the Department of Health, Education, and Welfare; Veterans Affairs; the Department of Agriculture; and others.

Along with several busloads of MFDP members, in January 1965 I headed to Washington for the congressional challenge. Scores of MFDP delegates moved up and down the avenues in front of Capitol Hill, picketing the seating of the Mississippi delegation, while others, accompanied by staff escorts, filed into the offices of highly placed federal officials. With the national conscience sensitized by the violence of Freedom Summer, it had not been difficult for me to arrange these visits. Once inside these offices, people stood up and told their stories—a veteran's pension denied, an application for old-age assistance ignored, aid to the blind cut after an individual was seen participating in a demonstration. With each story I felt the fear that was woven into the fabric of segregation begin to unravel.

During those few days I found time to locate the Division of Cooperatives, a small office tucked away in the Department of Agriculture. I had spoken to the director of the division by phone earlier while I was doing my initial research on the poverty program. As we talked, he seemed intrigued by the idea of a Mississippi co-op and encouraged me to go forward with a poverty program application. I knew a little about co-ops from the time I had spent on an Israeli kibbutz, or collective, in the year between high school and college. It was not a great deal to go on, but coupled with the awareness that the farmers in Batesville were struggling to find a new market for their okra crop, it was enough for me to move forward.

The Batesville Co-op

In northwestern Mississippi, Batesville's black farmers had been asking the Jackson COFO office for help in organizing a farm cooperative. The local white agent, who had been buying their okra for seven cents a pound, lowered the price without cause. When the agent refused to negotiate, the farmers began investigating ways to market the crops themselves.

By the time I arrived in Batesville, the groundwork for the co-op had been laid and leadership was in place. As odd as it was for a white woman with no understanding of farming to be advising the prospective co-op, the community somehow found a way to incorporate me as an adviser, as if it made perfect sense. When it came time to introduce me at meetings, the pastor would begin, "We've been calling down to Jackson and asking for someone to help with starting a co-op up here in Batesville, but they've been real busy down there with voter registration and all, so in the meantime they sent us this white girl."

I visited different farms, sometimes with Chris Williams, a white COFO worker with some understanding of farming; sometimes with the part-time pastor and full-time okra farmer, who had taken on the co-op as a personal mission; and sometimes alone. The community formed an organization, elected officers, and pooled resources to buy seed. The meetings grew larger. Our contact in the Washington co-op office helped us secure a seventy-eight-thousand-dollar poverty program loan for the purchase of farm equipment. The farmers bought and distributed seed, planted, and trucked their crops to Memphis. The co-op was operational.

Being out in the field, without a communications office, many of us took on the job of photographing as a way of documenting local project events. Armed with my 35mm camera, I began to photograph the different stages of the co-op's development. When I left Batesville, I turned over my photos to Maria Varela, a SNCC field secretary who had visited the project earlier and had a similar view of using photography as an organizing tool. Maria continued taking photographs and eventually incorporated them into a slide show called "How to Organize a Farm Co-op," which she distributed to other activists. Other black-run co-ops were formed across the South in the next decade. The Federation of Southern Co-ops was formed, and the Batesville co-op itself lasted for well over fifteen years.

One of the reasons I left Jackson for Batesville was to avoid the politics and the escalating negativity of black/white relationships that was particularly pronounced in Jackson. In the field, tensions were less pronounced. If an individual was an effective field worker, black or white, male or female, he or she was likely to be given a certain degree of respect. In Batesville I was able to work without the major distractions of movement politics, but I couldn't avoid the disintegration of working relationships between blacks and whites. As the co-op moved forward, I began to reassess. I was an organizer who knew little about farming or marketing crops. I no longer felt that local farmers were peering anxiously down the road, waiting for the appearance of a male, preferably black, but as organizing gave way to the day-to-day reality of crops and markets, I felt less and less connected.

In May my Harvard colleague Johnny Mudd, who had remained in Mississippi after the Tougaloo Summer Project, arrived in Batesville to keep things moving while I investigated outlets for the co-op's okra in New York. It soon became clear that Johnny and the local farmers were comfortable with each other and that Johnny had the skills to move the co-op forward. The farmers finally had their man.

I left Mississippi in May 1965. I never felt unwelcome in the Batesville community, but the rising nationalist sentiment among the movement leadership and rank and file was unavoidable and emotionally devastating to me. I believed passionately in the civil rights struggle as a *human* struggle that was mine to share, but I couldn't reconcile my continued presence with what I heard and felt from my movement brothers and sisters. It was time for me to leave.

I left the South, but the experiences of that year have had a profound effect on my life. My political values and core values became the same—a respect for the integrity of ordinary people and a belief in the ultimate redemptive nature of principled action.

Race and Gender

Being a white woman in that time and in that context posed unusual challenges. The ideals of social justice and racial equality that were central to the Movement did not extend to the issue of gender equality, an issue that was buried deep within the heavy sexism of the times. Strong black women played pivotal leadership roles, but as a white woman in a black movement, the scope of my work was always constrained by race and gender. It would have been naïve to think a white woman could simply be another worker in the freedom struggle when the sanctity of white women played so heavily in the violence and intimidation that surrounded the convoluted logic of segregation. Yet, even within this context, I was given tremendous latitude to contribute to the work. The strength to continue, in the midst of violence and in the midst of doubt, came from my work in the field, where I was generously embraced and genuinely appreciated by the local people in whose homes I lived and whose lives I shared.

My awareness of gender issues began well before I arrived in Mississippi. In the year between high school and college I had lived in Israel, where I saw women driving tractors, serving in the army, and working as equals beside men. Having seen Israeli women successfully take on these nontraditional roles gave me the confidence to challenge the stereotypes of my own culture. At the same time, challenging these cultural norms in the context of the Movement showed me the depth of sexism in our country—that even within the struggle for equality, sexism would remain a second-tier issue.

Mississippi provided me with a time and place to exchange ideas with other women and to read and reflect on the writings of the feminist authors of the day—Anaïs Nin, Doris Lessing, Betty Friedan, and Simone de Beauvoir. Living down the road from the Tougaloo Literacy House placed me in contact with a remarkable group of women and helped bring me to a greater understanding of gender issues. During the day, we worked at the Jackson office, and at night we talked and read and laughed. Literacy House was a cross between boardinghouse, salon, revolutionary outpost, and commune, a place of intellectual exchange where women spoke freely, argued, and laughed together. Our conversations were a lively blend of our personal experiences, friendships, and frustrations, stimulated and provoked by the movement tradition of questioning and challenging the status quo.

The Waveland Memo

In the fall of 1964, at a SNCC staff meeting in Waveland, Mississippi, I stood with several of these women, huddled around a mimeograph machine in the middle of the night, crafting a position paper titled "The Position of Women in the Movement." The document, which became known as the Waveland Memo in feminist discourse, and which was widely viewed as an early expression of second-wave feminism, was one of more than thirty position papers presented at the November SNCC retreat. As authors we were challenging what we saw as sexism in the Movement, objecting to the "assumption of male superiority," to women being called "girls," to women being left out of key decisions, to women's talents and skills being underutilized, and other realities that were emblematic of sexism in the Movement.

In my travels across the state working in federal programs, I had collected examples of sexism (at the time, we called it "discrimination") that were incorporated into the text of the memo. In the analysis section, my voice was one of the more strident. We spoke in different voices and tones, but together we formulated a passionate statement, challenging the sexist assumptions and practices of a male-dominated political organization whose basis was in the struggle for racial justice.

We did not list our names as authors. Instead we typed "Name Withheld by Request" in the upper right-hand corner. It was a notation I had used to hide my identity on a position paper that I had submitted as an individual. That position paper, which I had titled "Semi-Introspective," was a way for me to express my thoughts and feelings on issues of movement policies, strategies, and leadership, because the prospect of speaking publicly as a white woman was emotionally risky. As the Waveland Memo said, "Think about the kinds of things the author, if made known, would have to suffer because of raising this kind of discussion . . . the kinds of things which are killing to the insides—insinuations, ridicule, over-exaggerated compensations." As an individual author and as one of the co-authors of the Waveland Memo, I struggled to balance the need to speak my mind along with the awareness of the backlash that would surely follow.

These were the days when emotions bled into politics. Looking back at my participation in authoring the Waveland Memo, I can see the blend of thought and feeling. The words and logic came from my mind; the belief that I had the right to speak came from the SNCC climate of challenge; but the raw emotion that drove me to speak came from my experiences as a white woman in a climate where interracial relationships were disdainfully termed "backsliding," where these relationships were viewed as an affront to black women and black culture, where the relationship between myself and a black staff member had to be kept secret from his colleagues in accordance with the political/social conventions of the day. As a woman, I looked around at the work that women and men performed in the Movement and saw pervasive gender discrimination; but it was the sense of betrayal emanating from my personal relationships that ignited the logic, transforming it from an intellectual argument into an emotional assault on the attitudes and practices of sexism. Privately, it was easy for my friends and me to identify the sexism we experienced and witnessed as workers in the struggle, but we seldom talked of the other, the emotional rejection we felt from the brilliant and courageous black men we admired and adored.

Feminist historians have sometimes asked why more of us "early feminists" did not go on to be leaders in the women's movement. I can only speak for myself. Despite the intellectual clarity and the anger I felt when confronting sexism, it was the freedom struggle that held me. It was unthinkable for me to shift my identity, commitment, and energy from the freedom struggle to the struggle for women's rights at a time when I was still grieving over my separation from the Movement. The freedom struggle was the flame. All else was shadow.

I left the South with two powerful realizations. The first was a deep appreciation for ordinary people and how they understand the world. Mississippi taught me to listen with my heart and to speak with my actions. My teachers were the people whose faith, intelligence, and willingness to risk everything were the heart of the black freedom struggle. The second realization was a frightening, gut-level understanding of racism and a terrible awareness of its corrosive and pervasive legacy. As a civil rights worker, I underestimated the lengths to which our society would go to preserve its privilege. In the midst of the struggle for racial justice, I found that I and my movement brothers and sisters had lost the ability to move beyond race in our personal relationships. There were moments when race and gender did not separate us. I know that to be true. For me, Mississippi was a state of grace, one that remains with me in memory—and in the work that I do in honor of that memory.

In 1974 **ELAINE DELOTT BAKER** received her BS degree with a concentration in alternative education from the University of Massachusetts, University Without Walls. After several years in New York City and California, she moved to southern Colorado, where she developed community-based education projects, including a series of oral history projects to document the region's unique history. In 1984 she and her husband built KSPK, an FM radio station whose motto was "Community radio makes a difference." In 1989 she moved to Denver, where she developed a series of community college programs designed to increase the success of underprepared youth and adults, an effort that she continues to be engaged in at the national level. She and her family, including husband Chip, children, and grandchildren, live in Denver.

An Interracial Alliance of the Poor

An Elusive Populist Fantasy?

Emmie Schrader Adams

*Radicalized by African anti-colonial independence struggles,
a Minnesota native joins the southern Civil Rights Movement.*

From America to Africa

When I went south to work with SNCC in the spring of 1964, it never occurred to me that I would end up working with poor white folks in northeast-
ern Mississippi after the Mississippi Summer Project ended. This experience
forced me to examine the role of race in any attempt to organize in the white
community. About the same time, I was examining another key issue, what
would later be called women's liberation, with other women in SNCC.

Although I am a white American, born and raised in St. Paul, Minnesota, my path to SNCC was via revolutionary Africa, which had become
the center of my universe by the early 1960s. Having grown up in an all-
white neighborhood and attended all-white schools, I was pretty naïve about
anything relating to race, other than knowing that most white people were
prejudiced. I was, however, interested in learning about other people and
other cultures abroad. I studied French for seven years and briefly thought
about a career in international affairs. After I graduated from high school
I spent the summer living with a French family in the town of Sens, in the
Burgundy province, under the auspices of the Experiment in International
Living. This program emphasized total immersion in the culture and daily
life of the host country as the best way to learn a foreign language.

When I entered Harvard-Radcliffe in 1959, Africa, particularly the
Congo, had been in the news all that year, as the Belgians were finally forced
to accept Congolese independence. I decided I would apply to the African
American–led Operation Crossroads Africa my sophomore year and that
in the meantime I would learn about modern Africa. Africa represented for
me another chance for total immersion, more people and cultures to get to
know, and very different languages to be learned. I got a summer scholarship
to American University in Washington, D.C., to take a graduate seminar on
Africa, as there were no such courses yet at Harvard. I spent the summer
working on a paper about the history of the Tutsi-Hutu caste system in
Rwanda-Urundi. There were students from Nigeria and the Congo in the

seminar, and we all went downtown to cheer for the new Congolese president, Patrice Lumumba, when he came to visit President Eisenhower.

Back at Harvard that fall, I joined a new interdepartmental field of concentration in the social sciences, with my major called "Problems of Underdeveloped Countries" and my minor in Middle Eastern history. Since Harvard offered no courses in African languages, the school granted me independent study credit to learn Swahili with the help of Kenyan students. Meanwhile I was accepted by Crossroads Africa to spend the coming summer in Kenya.

When we arrived in Kenya, still a British colony in June 1961, the draconian military rule that had begun in 1952 with the Declaration of Emergency had just been lifted, but Jomo Kenyatta and other political leaders of the banned Kenya African Union (KAU) were still in detention, and several thousand Kikuyu militants were still hiding in the forests of Mt. Kenya. Inspired by the Kenyan freedom struggle, I did not return to the United States with the Crossroads group in the fall, but spent the entire year in Kenya teaching high school. On my six-week inter-term vacations and at the end of the school year, I hitchhiked through Kenya, Tanzania, Burundi, Zaire, Uganda, Sudan, and Egypt.

While teaching, I met many of the African "returned detainees" flooding the country after many years of unspeakably inhuman conditions in concentration camps established by the British to suppress the so-called Mau Mau rebellion. Tens of thousands of suspected supporters or sympathizers had been locked up. On some weekends I walked barefoot, because of the mud, to nearby villages and listened to the elders testify about the events that had led up to the revolt and the horrors of the civil war that ensued. I also heard many tales from my students of the brutal and deadly tactics the English used to defeat the freedom fighters in their home villages. My young mind was deeply impressed by the spirit of liberation sweeping across Africa, and I returned with tales of the heroic sufferings of everyday people in the face of what can only be called genocidal attempts to repress their struggle for land and freedom.

After another school year back at Harvard with some canvassing work in Roxbury for the Boston Action Group, I returned to Africa in the summer of 1963, this time with a Ghanaian student, Ayi Kwei Armah. We traveled to Algeria, newly independent after a bloody ten-year war against the French and now the headquarters in exile of many of the movements for the liberation of southern Africa. We hoped to enlist with the military arm of one of the Angolan liberation movements with representatives there, the MPLA or the FLNA. To earn a living while we waited, we worked as translators for the Algerian pan-African magazine *Revolution Africaine,* which shared information on the anti-colonial struggles in each country and documented the human cost of the Algerian war, which ultimately resulted in almost a million causalities. In the end, thwarted in our attempts to join the Angolan military struggle against the Portuguese, we returned to the States in January 1964 to pursue our separate paths: Armah began writing novels, and I became involved in the African American freedom struggle.*

In Algiers we had been receiving articles from the *Harvard Crimson* written by Armah's roommate, Peter de Lissovoy, who had gone to join the Freedom Movement in Albany, Georgia, where Charles Sherrod was heading up SNCC's first interracial field project. Hearing that down in Dixie black and white young people were fighting *together* against segregation and racism was very good news to me. There was no such diversity in the Kenyan struggle, in which the Kikuyu and their neighbors had fought alone, with only a tiny handful of Asian allies. Meeting up with Peter in Cambridge, I decided to accompany him back to Albany in April 1964. When I heard that workers were needed in Mississippi to prepare for the upcoming summer project, I backtracked to the SNCC office in Atlanta and was sent off to Jackson in a car with SNCC worker Larry Rubin. I was ready to work wherever I was needed. I had no idea what a big operation the summer project was going to be until I got there. In Jackson I worked in the Council of Federated Organizations (COFO) office throughout the spring and summer at various clerical and writing tasks, first with communications and then with the Mississippi Freedom Democratic Party until I got sent to Atlantic City on the buses as part of the MFDP staff to the Democratic National Convention.

"Poor Whites and the Movement"

After the disillusioning defeat of the MFDP convention challenge, I decided to try to work in a white rural community in northeast Mississippi. Given my personal history, I had never questioned that I belonged anywhere but on the black side of the color bar. Aside from Ed King and his wife, Jeannette, the only white Mississippians I had met all summer were cops and jailers. In Africa I had lived and socialized only with black Africans, not with English Kenyan or French Algerian settlers. Perhaps I should have known that as a Yankee who had spent the last couple of years in parts of Africa radicalized by anti-colonial wars, I was probably a totally inappropriate person for the job. But nobody else was interested at that time; various people encouraged me, and since the Atlanta office had recently changed

---

* Editors' Note: Armah did become a noted and prolific novelist, poet, and essayist. Among his most well-known novels are *The Beautyful Ones Are Not Yet Born* (1968), *The Two Thousand Seasons* (1973), and *The Healers* (1979).

my status from volunteer to staff, my project was in effect financed for the cost of my ten-dollar weekly paycheck.

During the summer COFO had already had a relatively large white organizing project in Biloxi and Moss Point, headed by two white Tennesseans, Ed Hamlett and Sue Thrasher. The two were also founding members of the predominantly white Southern Student Organizing Committee (SSOC) launched in the spring of 1964. The Biloxi Project attracted twenty white volunteers, many of whom were SDS folk from the University of Texas. Two divergent organizing strategies evolved on that project. The main body of the group identified themselves as COFO workers and tried to bring together sympathetic, hopefully influential white Mississippians who would attempt to convince their communities, churches, schools, and labor unions to support ending segregation and granting voting rights to Negroes. However, the climate in Mississippi was so polarized that the staff could never get any of these moderate white people together to even meet with each other.

Sam Shirah, a white Alabamian on the SNCC staff, moved into a white working-class neighborhood and tried to recruit ordinary white folks to join the MFDP. To me this approach was reminiscent of the elusive populist fantasy of undercutting white supremacy by organizing the poor, hopefully into some kind of interracial alliance. I think it was at an August meeting at Tougaloo College that I was enlisted by Sam or a member of his group to consider pursuing this strategy in a backwoods white rural community where there was no civil rights presence at all. I picked Itawamba County in the northeast corner of Mississippi for my exploratory white folks project, because it was poor, rural, and about 95 percent white. It bordered on Alabama on the east and Lee County/Tupelo on the west.

At the beginning I considered organizing people I might reach through union contacts. From Atlantic City I hitched a ride to New York, gathering names of left-wing union people who might be able to supply me with union contacts in Mississippi. I hitched another ride to Jackson with COFO worker Harriet Tanzman. We stopped on the way to meet union people in Tennessee and northeast Mississippi. Unions were limited to organizing factory workers, however, and there weren't any factories in Itawamba County. Rural folks, sharecroppers, and small farmers fell outside of this union net; it was this rural group at the bottom of the heap whom I was planning to approach.

On my return to Jackson someone introduced me to Ike Coleman, the black project director for the new COFO project in Tupelo, in the First Congressional District of northeast Mississippi. I asked him if I could use Tupelo as my base for probing into the white community in rural Itawamba County. He said, "Sure, no problem." Ike, who was from Tennessee, rarely got ruffled by anything. He and Stu Ewen, a New Yorker, were the Tupelo COFO staff.

I lived in the freedom house with them: an African American man, a Jewish man, and a Waspy white woman. It didn't seem to faze anyone in Tupelo, which had, for Mississippi, a somewhat "liberal" reputation; in other parts of the state, though, our living arrangement might have brought bombs.

In the mornings I would go over to Itawamba and drive around back roads all day talking to people in their homes. Many of these folks were still plowing their fields with mules, did not have running water or indoor toilets, and lived in unpainted tumble-down wooden houses. This was like my stereotypical image of Appalachia, but without the coal mines.

The towns were very small, but I avoided them because I felt too exposed there. I wanted to be inconspicuous, and this was easier in the deep rural areas, stopping at separate family farms. It was the fall before the presidential election of 1964, and I used the pretext of canvassing for Johnson and Humphrey against Goldwater as a way to meet people. It was distasteful to me after the Democratic Party rejection of the MFDP at Atlantic City, but for me, deep behind enemy lines, it seemed a necessary front. I was a Yankee. How else could I explain what I was doing there? I always tried to broach the subject of race in the course of our conversations, but race was not a major issue with these people; their concerns were economic.

A few weeks before the November election, Bob Williams, Dove Green, and Nedra Winans arrived to work with me. Bob and Dove were working-class white southerners from Biloxi and Arkansas, respectively. Bob had been recruited by Sam Shirah and had been elected as one of three white MFDP delegates to the Democratic convention in Atlantic City. Nedra had been working with COFO since the early spring and was descended from destitute "Okies" who had migrated from the dust bowl of Oklahoma to California during the Depression. I felt these three were better suited to carry on this work.

A mundane incident led to my leaving the project. One afternoon in late October while on my way back to Lee County, my VW Bug broke down. Where could I call but to the freedom house in Tupelo? The only person available to come get me was Harold Roby, the most active local black COFO worker. A black man and a white woman leaning together into the rear engine of a VW Bug was bound to attract someone's attention, and the highway patrol arrived quickly. I was arrested for trying to steal my own car—maybe I didn't have the papers with me. When I was arrested the police took the letter C on my driver's license to mean "colored," whereas I had thought it meant "Caucasian." One policeman yelled to another, "I've seen some blond-haired, blue-eyed coloreds before, but this one beats them all."

I was jailed in Tupelo and bailed out the next morning. They didn't hold Roby. They knew him already. They had needed a felonious pretext to photograph and fingerprint me. My cover was definitely blown. I was now known by the police to be a COFO worker. I could no longer work underground traveling the back roads of the county in my little green VW Bug. Besides, with the election over, there was no longer an acceptable pretext for us to be canvassing among the white folks in Itawamba County. The others remained committed to this kind of organizing, but in the end they, too, threw in the towel in 1965, after attempting a project in Tishomingo County, over the Alabama line.

Following my arrest I pretty much gave up. I began going to meetings in the black community and hanging out in Tupelo's colored café with Ike, Stu, Harold, and James Harris, who led the Tupelo Freedom Singers. We brought this group to Jackson to sing at a post-election MFDP rally and I never went back. I concluded that living in the black community, trying to pass while working in the white community, was impossible. It's amazing I pulled it off for as long as I did. I had to be someone I wasn't, to keep up a false front. You can't hide who you are; it's in your eyes. Racist whites take one look at you, and they know you are the "Enemy." They used to tar and feather and have a lot of nasty words for women like me who associated with black men.

After my two months of work in Itawamba County, I made what I called "some very tentative and roughly stated conclusions" in my report, titled "Poor Whites and the Movement," for the upcoming SNCC staff meeting in Waveland, Mississippi. I wrote that it was impossible to do this kind of organizing as a COFO worker. Once the white southerners realized that COFO was part of the Civil Rights Movement, they hated us, they felt angry and betrayed. "Then people did not open their screen doors when we came back, or they went for their guns or the telephone. They were afraid. And they felt they had been taken in by us, remembering how we sat in their homes or how they shared food with us, remembering all the things they had talked to us about."

The only conclusion I could reach highlighted one of the major contradictions in the situation: "Since we are at present indelibly branded as race mixers, perhaps the only way we can relate, however negatively, to poor white people is on the subject of race. Which, we must remember, is not one of their major concerns." My report emphasized that "economics rather than race is the main issue for Mississippi's rural white population facing the tremendous problems of rural decay, automation, and unemployment. Itawamba County's white residents have bitter memories of decades of experience with politicians, parties, and promises. They are very cynical about politics as a means of solving their economic problems." In contrast, SNCC had a focus on winning the right to vote as the prerequisite for making any kind of social change. In addition, SNCC was ill-prepared to address these economic concerns. I asked, "Where would we be in the

Negro community today if we had to confront the economic issues head on and produce some tangible results?"

Surprisingly, I found Itawamba County white folks were liberal by Mississippi standards on race matters related to the vote and violence. "They think Negroes ought to have the vote, at least in their area. They say they oppose the violence this summer brought to other areas of the state." On the other hand, "Most oppose school integration, but many know it is coming one day soon. Some are not afraid of integration because their children have gone to integrated schools up north. They all fear race mixing and economic competition from the Negro in the future." I concluded, "The most striking thing is that to most poor rural whites in Itawamba County, the racial questions seem irrelevant. They live in a white world. . . . The few [Negroes] who live in the county are clustered in little pockets outside the towns. . . . Furthermore, there is no KKK or Citizens' Council in the area. So, many of them can't see that Negroes have any particular problems and do not understand this summer's ferment."

Black and White Organizing: Together or Apart?

Underlying my report were two fundamental questions raised by the work in Itawamba County. The first was how to organize there and what to organize around. The second, perhaps more important, was on what basis could we expect to bring these white communities together with black Mississippians, especially when the black community was engaged in an all-out political struggle for the vote and other civil rights? We would have had to include a generalized war on poverty as one of our political aims, and clearly we were not yet ready to widen our narrower focus on the vote to include mammoth economic issues.

Casey Hayden once remarked that white people never get past racial prejudice by talking to other white people; they start to break out of it by means of a positive relationship with somebody black. Nineteen sixty-four was not the time, 1966 even less so, I dare say, to find anybody black who would be interested in trying to work in the southern white community to create an interracial alliance of the poor, though Dr. King had taken up the idea by 1968 with his Poor People's March on Washington. There was an *underwhelming* lack of interest in SNCC for such projects, if for no other reason than that nobody really believed it was possible. At the October 1964 staff meeting at Gammon, Ruby Doris Smith Robinson did speak in favor of SNCC-sponsored organizing efforts in the white community using only white staff. Black nationalism may have been a motivating factor here, as it was when the question resurfaced in late 1966 at the Peg Leg Bates staff meeting debate on the role of whites in SNCC. "Go work in the white community" was often a smokescreen for "Get lost!" Why kid ourselves about this?

In June 1966, a year and a half after I wrote my report, Anne Braden of the Southern Conference Educational Fund (SCEF) sent an untitled memo on this general problem to SSOC. Anne put her finger on what had been my main problem: trying to hide my identity as a civil rights worker. I believe Anne was right that the only possible way such projects could have made any headway would have been with teams of black and white organizers. Anne accepted that "it might be desirable for Negroes to be organizing the black people in that community in an independent organization." She insisted, however:

> When you go to talk to and organize the white people . . . you have to say to them in front, from the very word go, that if they are going to be effective and solve their problems they are going to have to team up with those black people over there and find terms that are acceptable to the black people to do it on. And . . . you should go to these white people with teams of black and white organizers working together.
>
> In other words, I am saying that I think you have to confront the white Southerner you are trying to reach with this whole question of racism and what it has done to him [or her] *from the very beginning*.

Anne warned, "If organizing efforts arc not done this way, you may be creating a Frankenstein." In the future, white groups organized by white organizers "might become active anti-Negro groups."

A year after Braden's 1966 memo to SSOC, Project Grow (Grass Roots Organizing Work) was founded in New Orleans. In several ways this project put into practice Anne Braden's concrete suggestions for black and white organizers working together to undermine racism in the working-class white community. Codirected by former SNCC workers Bob and Dottie Zellner, Grow staff openly admitted their background, training, and connections with both SNCC and SCEF. This project focused on economic issues, including supporting an already ongoing interracial wildcat industrial strike in southern Mississippi. Anne Braden herself continued along these lines—for example, organizing against toxic dumping near poor and minority communities in the South. These white-founded attempts at interracial organizing among the southern working classes were brave experiments in the period after the end of interracialism in SNCC.

We used to hold hands and sing, "Black and white together . . . We shall overcome someday-ay-ay." Maybe we need to get out the old SNCC buttons with the joined black and white hands. To me, it was exactly SNCC's black-led "black and white together" organizing period that was a critical ingredient in the dynamite that ultimately blew apart the old southern "way of life." Was it really wise of us to jump ship so soon, or were we prodded in that direction by FBI infiltrators bent on splitting up the organization? We may never know the answer to that question. But now that the 2008 Obama campaign has demonstrated that dynamite again, it should be clear, at least to those of us who experienced it fifty years ago, that it is the black leadership of interracial movements that is key to unleashing this explosion of organizing energy.

The Women's Memo

The women's memo was presented at the same Waveland retreat in November 1964 where I submitted my report on my white folks project. Many women, black and white, had contributed to the informal discussions of the preceding year, dating back to the women's sit-in led by Ruby Doris Smith Robinson at the Atlanta office of SNCC in January 1964. These discussions and the sit-in underlay this initial written effort, this attempt to force some attention to an issue that had never been seriously addressed at a staff meeting. Position papers were being sought for the retreat on all subjects of concern to the staff, so a group of us who had been discussing women's issues at the Literacy House in Tougaloo decided to submit a memo.

Already upset by the societal double standard that surrounded male and female sexual behavior, I had begun to discover feminism while in Algeria by reading Simone de Beauvoir, whose French socialist circles supported the Algerian revolution. I came to see that white supremacy and male supremacy were coiled around each other like two snakes. I hoped that if women took a stand against male supremacy, perhaps this would open the doors to white women dividing themselves politically from their menfolk and opposing white male world domination—in other words, colonialism and racism.

This initial women's memo has been much misinterpreted by some historians of the Women's Movement. They focus too much on the question of "sexism in the Civil Rights Movement," suggesting that it was especially egregious there. One of the causes of this perception is probably Stokely Carmichael's joke about the position of women in the Movement being prone.

There seems to be some confusion about the underlying tensions that led to this memo. In the months preceding that Waveland meeting, only a very minor part of our discussions concerned incidents within the Movement. Most of our talks, which often included sympathetic men, were cosmic—about the nature of our socializing and brainwashing as women; our self-concepts; our behavior toward one another, especially when men were involved; and our sexual oppression. Any of these cosmic symptoms that manifested in the Movement were only there because the men and women in the Movement belonged to that male-dominated outer world that was the source of the oppression.

When we were writing the memo, in order to be relevant to a SNCC staff meeting we had to use examples taken from the daily lives of female COFO workers. We never said that male SNCC or CORE workers were in any way worse than men in the world at large. My impression was that women had more opportunities in SNCC and CORE than in the more traditional SCLC and NAACP, the four groups that made up COFO in Mississippi. This was largely a function of age, younger folks being open to change of all sorts. In fact it was the contradiction between the traditional stereotypes prevailing in the society at large and the liberated work we were able to do as gender-neutral civil rights workers that forced the issue to the forefront of our consciousness and made us want to weed out negative attitudes in our own ranks.

In 1964 SNCC was still an environment that fostered all types of "freedom thinking." We were rethinking the world, and all injustices were valid targets. The strategic thinking of the freedom struggle gave us the ideological tools to analyze our own personal oppression. To quote Bob Marley, "Emancipate yourselves from mental slavery!"

Finding a Place

As the Movement began to split apart along racial lines in 1965, I went to study photography with Matt Herron in New Orleans in order to assist Casey Hayden, Mary King, and Jane Stembridge in the production of two filmstrips, one based on the MFDP and the struggle for the vote, the other a visual version of the "interracial alliance of the poor" scenario titled *The Peoples Wants Freedom* [sic]. In midsummer I left Mississippi and moved to New York with SNCC supporter and musicologist Alan Ribback, who later changed his name to Moses Moon. I did odd jobs involving photography and produced a filmstrip about the Vietnam War for the burgeoning peace movement— Vietnam had been an obsession of mine since my days in Algeria.

I moved to southern Vermont in 1967 and, in company with various other former southern movement folks, helped form an organic vegetable–growing commune called the Huggs Family. I had no place in the black power movement, but neither did I fit in with the red-flag-waving type of white radicalism that now advocated violence against the system. From my early experience in the aftermath of two bloody wars in Africa, now reinforced by the believers in nonviolence I met in the South, I had become convinced of the radicalism of nonviolence. After the Movement, I was never at ease in a predominantly white world. I was most comfortable with my identity as a white person in a black world, and that is how I have lived most of my life.

EMMIE SCHRADER ADAMS spent twenty years in Jamaica, where she married a black Jamaican, raised a family, became a Jamaican citizen, and wrote a best-selling book on the Afro-Jamaican language called *Understanding Jamaican Patois* (1991). In Jamaica she and her husband, Dada Adams, farmed land belonging to a seaside estate in an area beyond Robin's Bay. Their community grew into a Rastafarian squatters' colony. In 1992, when their children were ready for college, her family moved to Vermont, where she worked at odd jobs like house painting, driving, and bartending so that she could study ancient African and Middle Eastern history. Adams has served on the board of Northern Counties Health Care, a network of community-based rural clinic and home care agencies there for the past nine years. She returns to Jamaica every few years, and like most Jamaicans, she and her family plan to retire to the green hills of Jamaica. She has written a longer essay about her life and movement experiences, "From Africa to Mississippi," which appears in *Deep in Our Hearts* (2000).

"An Interracial Alliance of the Poor: An Elusive Populist Fantasy?" © 2010 by Emmie Schrader Adams

We Weren't the Bad Guys

Barbara Brandt

A white volunteer initially welcomed into the SNCC staff is later driven away because of racial hostility from black co-workers.

The Atlanta Office

I went down to Atlanta in July 1964, the week after President Lyndon Johnson had signed the Civil Rights Act requiring racial integration of all public facilities. My family, having heard on the news about some racial violence at a sports event in Atlanta, was afraid for me to go, but I was determined. I only intended to go for a week or two at most, just to help out a little. I ended up working for the Movement for a year and a half. When I first arrived in the South, the black SNCC workers treated me and the other white volunteers as friends sharing a deep dedication to the cause of freedom, but by the time I left, many of the black staffers had completely stopped talking to the white workers and wanted us white people out of the Movement.

I grew up in New York City, and in 1963 I was a twenty-year-old graduate sociology student in Boston. One of my fellow grad students, Danny Foss, had gone down to Danville, Virginia, to work for the Freedom Movement, gotten arrested, and ended up in a jail cell with SNCC staffer Bob Zellner, who had joined the Civil Rights Movement early on. Bob had been jailed and beaten up once too often, and he was tired. Through Danny, Zellner made arrangements to take a break from the Movement and came to our school to study sociology.

During the year that Bob Zellner was in grad school with us, he told us about the upcoming 1964 Mississippi Summer Project. Bob said that SNCC could use all kinds of help, including office work. And they would take people who could help out for only a week or so. He was so brave and idealistic that he got us all fired up, and I just had to go.

My mother was very idealistic and had strong opinions about politics and what was right and wrong, especially about how badly black people were treated in this country. Other members of my family, who had marched and organized with unions in the 1930s, had similar beliefs. So even as a young child, I knew there was much in this country that was not right and I wanted to help solve some of these problems. It was only natural that when I heard about the Civil Rights Movement—almost by personal invitation—I would jump at the opportunity to get involved.

While I was considering just how I wanted to be involved, I had an image of myself in a car with a bunch of other young people, driving fast at night down a dusty country road between two cotton fields, being followed and shot at by the Ku Klux Klan. I would have been proud to be able to boast to my stay-at-home friends and family back north that I had been through—and survived—such adventures. But I also knew I was not very emotionally mature and that in such a situation I would probably start yelling and getting everyone confused. I had already been in peace demonstrations in New York City where I saw mounted police charge in and beat up nonviolent demonstrators, and it really scared me, so I felt I should work somewhere where my still immature emotions would not mess up other people's good sense. When Zellner said they needed people to do research at the SNCC office in Atlanta, far away from the front lines, I felt that this was how even I could make a contribution. Maybe it wouldn't be terribly exciting, and no one would think I was a great heroine, but they wanted someone to do research, something I was already doing in my sociology classes, so I offered to do that and they said, "Come on down!"

I walked into the SNCC headquarters, which was in a bunch of old wooden buildings in the thriving black business district in Atlanta. It was filled with black and white students who worked in shifts, twenty-four hours a day, seven days a week, answering telephone calls from the field about the latest successes or violence; they were rushing about putting out newsletters to SNCC's northern supporters and sending press releases to the national papers, running a printing press, and developing photographs rushed in from the front lines. All of this was supervised by a few old-timers—veteran civil rights workers, mostly black men and women, some just a few years older than the rest of us.

It was an intense, exciting atmosphere, made brighter by the constant humor and hopeful spirit we shared, and by the rhythms of the freedom songs we often burst into during occasional quiet moments. And the sounds of the community came in all around us: the jukebox from the shoe-shine place in back of us; the music school upstairs, where they practiced tubas and trumpets, funny and tinny-sounding; and the sing-song chants of the children playing in the street outside.

In the research department my job was to clip and file newspaper articles from the Mississippi papers about the state's reactions to our summer project. The mayor of Jackson brought military tanks to his city in preparation; they were arresting people on charges like "watching a parade without a permit." Anything like this I put into the files. When news reporters or other interested people wanted to know what was going on, we could provide instant documentation about the real state of affairs in Mississippi, contradicting the bogus accounts in the Mississippi papers.

The most exciting thing about being there was meeting the other civil rights workers in the office and from the field. It seemed as if every day we heard a new story of heroism, or met another freedom worker who had gone through some kind of hellish experience and, after a brief rest, went right back out to fight some more. Sometimes it felt like we were at the staff headquarters in a war. It felt like we were creating it as we went along, but we also knew that what we were doing was changing America. Sometimes the local black people from Mississippi would come to the office. We saw them as heroic figures. It was hard to imagine how the white people in their hometowns would consider our heroes an inferior branch of the human race.

My week turned into two, then three, and then I decided to stay the whole summer. At the end of the summer, the regular SNCC staff asked me if I wanted to stay and be an actual SNCC staff person! This was what I really wanted to do rather than go back to graduate school—to work in the real world, helping to make things better. Of course I said, "Yes."

I felt more confident by now, so I volunteered to become the WATS operator on the night shift. I sat in the office from six in the evening until two every morning, sometimes the only person there. Each day I called up every one of our projects in Mississippi, Alabama, and Southwest Georgia to find out about the latest shootings and bombings and voter registration figures and typed them into written reports, and in emergencies I called the FBI, the Justice Department in Washington, or our supporters up north and badgered them to help us.

Since evening was when most emergencies happened, I gradually became known among the field workers as someone they could always count on to be there and come through in a crisis. And since I was the last one in the office each night, I was responsible for writing up and sending out the daily informational mailings that we distributed to each field project and northern support group, and I also wrote and sent out many of our press releases. When reporters from national magazines, the wire services, or even the *New York Times* came by the office to find out what was going on, I was often the person assigned to talk to them, which did wonders for my ego. In a crisis I was often the only person there to handle things. Once I called up the U.S. assistant attorney general for civil rights at his home in Washington, D.C., at two in the morning to tell him the Klan was about to lynch Stokely Carmichael. (Obviously they were not successful.) Another time, when one of our workers in Indianola, Mississippi, had been arrested for some blatantly ridiculous trumped-up charge, I called right into the jail and put the fear of God into the sheriff, letting him know that if anything happened to his prisoner, the whole United States would know about it.

The Movement Spirit

Shortly after the summer project ended, there was a big staff meeting to discuss the new direction of the Movement. It was attended by the young kids from the rural towns, the middle-aged Mississippi women in their worn cotton dresses, the farmers in their faded overalls, and the student field workers, both men and women wearing blue denim overalls, work shirts, and heavy boots. True to our goal of total equality, everyone was free to speak out at staff meetings, regardless of their background, education, or rank in the organization. I was a little disappointed to see that the college students—both black and white—soon took over the discussion and turned it into an almost abstract debate about the definition of an organizer, the qualifications of a staff member, and possible restructuring of the organization, now that they had to incorporate the dozens of new volunteers who, like myself, had stayed on.

In the middle of this long and complex discussion, a tiny young black woman of eighteen or nineteen wearing a pink dress jumped up out of her seat. "My name is Amanda Bowens," she said loudly and clearly, "and I'm from Southwest Georgia. And I just want to say, I don't understand everything you're arguing about, but I do know I'm black, and I'm down here suffering!" Everyone sat stunned for a moment, then the entire group burst into applause. Amanda had reminded us what we were really all about, and after that, people tried to make the discussion more concrete. From then on, if a speaker started getting too abstract, we would yell out, "Break it down, brother." And when someone spoke out clearly, we would call supportively, "Tell it like it is!"

The staff meetings magnified both the beauties and the tensions of the Movement. Everyone was encouraged to say whatever they felt, so we had sessions late into the night filled with hostile accusations between black members and white, or between educated and unschooled, about "manipulation" and "intimidation" and "trying to take over." But we ended each meeting, despite the fighting and mistrust and failures of communication, with hands joined in song, in the anthem of our movement that someday we'd overcome, we'd all be free, we'd live in peace.

Just before the 1964 November elections, the Atlanta office staff was recruited for a week to aid in the Mississippi Freedom Vote. I finally felt ready to go to the field, and was sent to the small delta town of Indianola, Mississippi, a hot, dusty town in the middle of flat, muggy cotton-planting country. It was a town divided into two halves. In the white section the streets were paved, the homes large and beautiful, with lawns and trees spreading out before them; the people were well-dressed, the stores modern and prosperous. In the black section the streets were dirt, the homes often no more than small shacks without plumbing, their front yards filled with broken-down cars or just bare packed dirt; the people tired and plodding in their old clothes, the stores no more than hole-in-the-wall groceries.

The freedom workers in Indianola were white college students, and the project director was a young black man from Los Angeles. They excitedly told me what they were doing. They had turned the old "colored" school building in town into a Freedom School, where the volunteers and local women were teaching the children and adults who dared to attend about political participation and black history. We were also encouraging people to try to register at the courthouse as well as take part in the Freedom Vote of the Mississippi Freedom Democratic Party.

In Indianola the freedom workers lived together in the middle of the black section in the home of Mrs. Magruder, a warm, sturdy old woman who seemed unconcerned with the whole thing, spending her time chatting with the other old women in the shade of her pecan trees, as they pieced red, green, orange-speckled, and black-striped rags into beautiful quilts. She cooked us biscuits, cornbread, collard greens, and spaghetti and meatballs; she also encouraged us to pick and eat the sweet pecans that fell from the tall trees in front of her house. I was always in awe of her. If not for the courage of Mrs. Magruder and women and men like her all over Mississippi, there would have been no summer project. No one ever talked about it, but everyone knew her home could be firebombed any night.

We always sang and shouted and clapped. At our freedom meetings, the church rocked as we sang those old songs taken from the labor movement, like "Which Side Are You On?" or the classic black-gospel-turned-freedom-songs, like "This Little Light of Mine, I'm Gonna Let It Shine." But it wasn't just song. The whole church was alive with bodies packed together in the pews, clapping, bobbing, bending, and swaying against one another with the rhythm. It was ecstasy. And we SNCC folks also felt terror. Walking through the black section of town, canvassing for the Freedom Vote, we ducked behind parked cars every time the Klan members with their rifles drove by on regular patrol. Halloween fell during that last week before the presidential election, and we knew that if the segregationists were going to pull anything, it would be on Halloween night. Sure enough, that night the headquarters in Sunflower, the next town over, was bombed, and one of the freedom workers, in his rush to get out, jumped clear through a plate-glass window, tearing a big hole in his leg. He and his co-worker managed to pile into their car and drive down to Mrs. Magruder's. No sooner had they arrived than we discovered that our own Freedom School was on fire. The Indianola Fire Department took their time about coming; they watched the building burn, and then they drenched what had not been ruined by the fire with water, just to make sure the damage was complete. We went back to Mrs. Magruder's and huddled together, certain we would be next because they all knew where we were, but nothing else happened.

That was the scariest thing that ever happened to me while I was working in the South. But my funniest memory also happened in Indianola (although I suspect it wasn't so funny for the other people involved). During the week I was there, we heard that some of our co-workers had been arrested and were in the Indianola jail. A white volunteer named Karen and I were the only ones at Mrs. Magruder's house at the time, and we discussed what to do (after calling the incident in to Atlanta, of course). Our only experience with people being in jail came from Hollywood adventure movies: What do you do when the hero is in jail? You bake him a pie and hide a file in it.

Well, we didn't have a file, and the sheriff probably would have caught on if we had walked down to the jail with an apple pie for the prisoners, so we decided to sneak in a secret message instead. Karen and I made Spam sandwiches, and in between two pieces of meat, surrounded by lots of mayonnaise, we buried a tiny note wrapped in waxed paper. It said, "Don't worry. I'll get help." We signed it "Jim," who was our assistant project director. After we brought that sandwich over to the jail, we heard that Jim had also been arrested. Karen and I couldn't stop laughing, thinking of Jim's face when he bit into that sandwich and found the note supposedly from himself.

The Mississippi Summer Project had come and gone. The northern students, shaken up and radicalized, had returned to their schools. As we sat in Atlanta, we read about the new student activism suddenly spreading across the campuses. But in the South things were the same as ever. Black people were still poor; homes and churches were still burned; freedom workers were still beaten.

In March 1965, on what became known as Bloody Sunday in Selma, Alabama, we knew something big was going to happen. The civil rights marchers gathered on one side of a bridge, and the local police, armed with clubs and tear gas, stood facing them on the other. The Atlanta office was usually empty on a Sunday afternoon, but this day all the Atlanta staff crowded into the room while I sat at a typewriter with a phone to my ear, taking down the report relayed to us by one of our members, who stood in a phone booth just next to the bridge, where he could see what was happening.

"The civil rights marchers are now starting over the bridge . . .," he said. "They're slowly marching across, four abreast . . . Now the police have begun to charge them . . . They're swinging clubs! . . . People are falling down on the bridge! . . . They're running back to this side! . . . The police are after them, hitting people, knocking them down, hitting the women and children, clubbing them on the ground, clubbing the people lying on the ground." He could hardly speak, and my hands were shaking, my jaw trembling. I was trying to keep from crying as I typed.

As soon as the report was finished, the whole office went into action. While some people put the eyewitness account onto stencils and ran it off for an emergency mailing to the North, others were on all the various telephones, calling key supporters, press contacts, and the wire services, telling them about the horror at the bridge.

Black Power and a Changing SNCC

After the events in Selma, SNCC began to change. Despite all those years of nonviolent self-sacrifice, the oppression and brutality were still going on. The people had not gotten their freedom—they'd just gotten another crack on the head. The black staff in the Atlanta office began to make increasingly bitter comments about "nonviolence" and "love" and "brotherhood." When I first went down south, SNCC had a lapel pin that showed a white hand and a black hand clasped. I still have this pin. After Selma, SNCC staffers began joking that the SNCC button should show two black hands shaking.

I understood why the black SNCC workers were now saying they didn't want white people in the Movement, that black people needed to run their own movement and get themselves together. By the summer of 1965 the black staffers were expressing these feelings by suddenly refusing to talk to their white co-workers and treating us as if we did not exist. It was just sad that people who for almost a year had been treating me like a friend and appreciating what I was doing suddenly stopped talking to me and the other white kids, as if *we* were somehow the bad guys. I believed then, and still do believe, that black power was the right direction for the Movement to take then. But to be treated so cruelly, so suddenly, that I finally had to leave the Atlanta office was one of the saddest, most heartbreaking experiences of my life.

I still believed in the Movement and still wanted to be part of it. I heard that black-white relations were still friendly in Mississippi, so in October 1965 I went to Jackson to work in the office of the newly created Mississippi Freedom Democratic Party. Their office was on Farrish Street, in the heart of Jackson's black business district. At first I did the same kind of work I had done in Atlanta, phone and press communications. Then I worked with Kay Prickett, a white student from Chicago, on the Agricultural Stabilization and Conservation Service project to help black farmers and sharecroppers take part in local elections for the county committees that determined cotton allotments.

Kay and I were assigned to write some educational manuals and publicity brochures, translating the U.S. government bureaucratese into ordinary English so that even poorly educated people could understand their rights and could participate in the ASCS elections. We went out to Mount Beulah, a former black college or seminary near Jackson, where we worked on this project under the direction of Mr. Henry J. Kirksey, an older black gentleman who published a freedom-oriented newspaper in Jackson. (He later was elected to the Mississippi state legislature.) Mr. Kirksey taught us how to do layout and make headlines with paste-on lettering—this was long before computer graphics. In about two months or so we had finished the instructional materials and brochures, and they were being distributed around Mississippi and were being used in training workshops.

Not only did this project help to get many black farmers and sharecroppers involved in ASCS, but also in a few counties they actually got elected to the local committees. We also found out later that the U.S. Department of Agriculture had seen our work and, as a result, had simplified their own ASCS materials to make them more understandable to ordinary people.

By January 1966 I felt I had done all the work I could for the Movement. I moved back north, to the East Village in New York City, where a lot of other former SNCC workers, both white and black, were now living. I was sad to leave the Movement, sad to give up that exciting feeling that I was making a difference. But I really needed to be in a more peaceful environment to rest and recuperate.

However, I still remembered the mission that many of the black staffers gave us white members when they made it known they no longer wanted white people in the Movement. "Go back and organize your own community," they told us. When I left SNCC, I began to examine what this new mission meant for me. What was my community, and what issue or issues should I organize it around? That challenge has guided me to this day.

BARBARA BRANDT has spent most of her life in the Boston area and has continued to work for social change, helping to organize successful resistance to an eight-lane highway through Boston's inner city, and is active in community education and urban environmentalism. In the early 1980s she founded and directed the Urban Solar Energy Association, the largest of its kind in the country. Since 1989 she has worked for the Shorter Work-Time Group. She is a member of the national board and the Boston coordinator of the Take Back Your Time movement. In the 1980s she helped organize The Other Economic Summit (TOES) in Toronto and Houston. She is the author of *Whole Life Economics: Revaluing Daily Life,* which uses feminist, environmental, and populist approaches to describe models that are more just, democratic, humane, and sustainable. She is currently co-authoring *Changing Your Mind Can Change the World: Why Now Is the Time to Transform Our Future,* about positive patterns of personal and social change now taking place.

Sometimes in the Ground Troops, Sometimes in the Leadership

Doris A. Derby

Raised by nurturing family, church, and community members also steeped in the culture of the African Diaspora, a New Yorker spends nine years in the Mississippi Civil Rights Movement.

New York: Preparation

I grew up in the Bronx—a diverse cultural, ethnic, racial, and socioeconomic environment. The area was mostly Italian but also included a close-knit black community with people from South Carolina, Virginia, Connecticut, Massachusetts, and Maine as well as from the West Indies and Puerto Rico. There were Italian, Jewish, black American, Jamaican, Guyanese, Trinidadian, and Chinese merchants who offered a variety of ethnic and American products and services, which made for a very multiculturally flavored community.

Unlike most men on our block, my father, born in Massachusetts, held a university degree in civil engineering from the University of Pennsylvania. As the only black student in his civil engineering class, he faced discrimination and isolation. My mother, born in Bangor, Maine, into a community with about twelve middle-class black families, graduated from Bangor High School. My parents met in New York City after they both migrated there, and married in the mid-1930s. After facing discrimination in the engineering field, Dad became an employment specialist with the New York State Employment Service. During my youth Mom took care of a few children at home in the daytime.

During and after the Second World War my parents raised chickens, fruit trees, and vegetables just as their parents had done. We actually lived in the "country" part of the Bronx, on the outskirts, in a community called Williamsbridge, where there were streams, thick woods, and wild animals when I was growing up. The neighborhood was quiet, and front doors were not locked until nighttime.

Economic self-help and entrepreneurship initiatives were very important values in our family. My father and his father, in the evenings and on weekends, did cabinet making and other carpentry in the neighborhood to earn extra money. My maternal grandfather was a well-known and successful businessman in Bangor, as were his sons. The value of economic self-help rubbed off on me early. I began asking my next-door neighbor and my "play" aunt for work. I did ironing and housework from the fourth grade on and babysat from seventh grade until after college. In the sixth grade a male friend and I sold catalog Christmas cards to his newspaper route customers, and from the seventh grade on I worked weekends in my uncle's record shop. By the time I was in fifth grade I had a savings account and was happy to have an income, especially to buy Christmas and birthday gifts. By the fourth grade I learned about gardening, sewing, and cooking from my mother and by the sixth grade simple woodworking and painting techniques from my father. The family often worked together on various home improvement projects.

Black churches were a glue that, along with black friendship and kinship ties in the neighborhood, cemented the black community in Williamsbridge. There were three solid-black churches, and I participated in all three, as did many other neighborhood youths. Having been christened and confirmed in St. Luke's Episcopal Church, my father's church, I attended Sunday school and religious instruction there after school. I was active in this church's youth group, summer bus rides and picnics, the NAACP, which met there, and the church's Willing Workers group. The latter consisted of young girls and women who came together whenever "Mom Pairadeaux," formerly a market woman from Guyana in South America with a strong commitment to the church, a great sense of humor, an entrepreneurial spirit, and wonderful culinary skills, decided we should perform some job for the church or have a fund-raiser, which always entailed great West Indian food.

In addition I went to Trinity Baptist Church with my three best girl-friends—Barbara Johnson, Elaine Goss, and Harriet Gibbs—and sang in the youth gospel choir at the 11:00 A.M. service. We participated in the Baptist youth group on Sunday evenings and joined the Baptist Bible school in the summers during my elementary school years. My friends and I attended special occasions at Butler Memorial Methodist Church. We went to all of the weddings, revivals, funerals, fish fries, prayer meetings, fund-raisers, and so on that occurred in the neighborhood, and we helped out with many of these activities. We regularly visited people in the "old folks home" that Trinity Baptist Church helped support and brought them flowers from our yards. We did errands for elderly or shut-in members and attended wakes in neighbors' homes. Civic and community activities such as the Girl Scouts, to which I belonged for years, also took place in these churches.

The elementary schools in the neighborhood were predominantly white, with a few black students in each class and a handful of black teachers. The classes and extracurricular activities in which I participated crossed cultural and racial lines, yet I felt the stark absence of black images in textbooks, and outside the school in movies, advertisements, other media, and visual arts. At an early age I started to seek answers as to why and to see how I could make changes.

During elementary and junior high school I formally studied ballet and tap dancing and sang in a female quartet. Because of my training and need to see a public black presence, I gravitated toward African-centered cultural activities in the larger community of New York City, where I won a scholarship to study at the Katherine Dunham African dance classes at the Harlem YMCA. The dance class marched in the annual African Liberation Day parade down Lenox Avenue and across 125th Street in Harlem. I wrote poetry and attended meetings at the Harlem Writers' Guild, which exposed me to black writers like John O. Killens, Rosa Guy, and others who wrote for *Freedomways* magazine. While attending Hunter College in the Bronx (now Lehman College), I joined and attended meetings of the American Society of African Culture with black artists, writers, and scholars from throughout the African diaspora. I held monthly discussions at my home on issues relating to Africa and the Caribbean. In addition, I traveled to Nigeria as an exchange student with the Experiment in International Living and resided with host families throughout the country.

These experiences were very inspirational and exciting to me. They made me interested in research issues related to the effects and influences of African culture in African as well as non-African countries. They contributed to my continued love of and involvement in African diaspora culture and the arts. As a result I expressed myself through reflections and interpretations of our rich black heritage in my paintings, photographs, written images, and the dance. I experienced many new realities through the arts, defined and shaped them myself, and continued these forms of expression throughout my work in the Civil Rights Movement.

Higher education and travel for firsthand knowledge were stressed by my parents, grandparents, extended family, church, and community members. My great-aunt Jessie Maxwell, a missionary in a black church denomination, lived in Liberia, West Africa, for more than twenty years and adopted two Liberian children. Liberia was the first black-run republic in Africa, and almost all of its early presidents were African Americans. My aunt's letters to my grandparents about her experiences there had a great influence on me and my outlook on life and career goals. My grandfather's sister, my great-aunt Julia Noble, the International Grand Matron of the Daughters of the Eastern Star, traveled to Ghana in 1957 to witness the independence celebrations held in the first African country south of the Sahara to win its independence from a colonial power. My paternal grandparents traveled to Haiti for their fiftieth wedding anniversary to experience life in the first independent black nation in the Western Hemisphere. Whenever relatives would get together, we talked about travel experiences, as well as issues affecting African Americans and African people.

By the time I graduated from college in 1962, in addition to spending a summer in Nigeria, I had spent a summer on a Navajo Indian reservation at an Episcopal mission in New Mexico and a summer with the Encampment for Citizenship in Riverdale, New York. At the camp, American and international students lived together attending workshops and holding discussions on issues related to citizenship as well as civil and human rights.

Early Activism

My involvement in the Movement began in the mid-1950s when I joined the NAACP youth branch in my own community. While issues of northern discrimination were not the same as issues of southern segregation, they were still race issues that developed my awareness of political injustice and heightened my senses to the roles and responsibilities of a young black girl and her peers in a mostly white environment. During my years at predominantly white Hunter College, I joined many campus groups, such as the Anthropology Club and the African Scholarship Committee, which financially assisted African students who came to the United States with President Kennedy's African airlift. I remained active in the local NAACP and, on campus, joined the Christian Human Relations Club, the Northern Student Movement, and the Students for Democratic Action. All of these groups had speakers, rallies, and fund-raisers related to various civil rights, student, and political issues. Through these groups and other civic activities, I related to African students, scholars, and artists living here in the United States and learned more about African culture and politics. It was during this time that I also developed my love for Afro-Cuban music and learned New York salsa dancing.

From 1958 to 1960 my father, along with a handful of others in the New York State Employment Service, established an organization, the New York State Careerists, to fight discrimination in civil service jobs. He and his colleagues met on weekends at our home to strategize and compare notes. My father's activism and the related stress that led to his heart failure and subsequent early death in the fall of 1960 also influenced me to fight even harder for equality.

During my last year at Hunter College, some members of the integrated Christian Human Relations Club traveled by bus to talk to sit-in students and civil rights leaders in Durham, North Carolina, about the southern student movement for civil rights and what we could do in the North to support them. We began consciousness-raising on campus, and Hunter students started to get involved with southern sit-ins. Because of my activism and my student teaching requirements, I stayed in school an extra semester. I graduated in January 1962 and began teaching third grade in Yonkers, New York.

Albany, Georgia: Summer Connection

Peggy Dammond, a fellow Hunter College activist, was the first student I knew who went to Albany, Georgia, in early 1962. That summer vacation I planned to travel by bus to visit a friend and fellow anthropologist, Elizabeth Sanchez, in Mexico and explore opportunities to research the African influence in Mexican art. However, when I heard that Peggy was in jail and sick in Albany, I decided to stop to see her before going to Mexico and learn about the southern movement in person. I felt a sisterhood with Peggy and wanted to be a part of the collective struggle of the southern black community where rights were being violated the most under the legal system of segregation. To get to Albany, I was advised to go to the Atlanta SNCC office first. I spent a week there meeting SNCC folk and waiting until SNCC's executive secretary, Jim Forman, and white staffer Bob Zellner were ready to go to Albany and take me with them.

During my stay in Albany, I saw the power of the Movement reflected in the religious convictions, songs, and mass meetings, but mostly in the people working together regardless of economic and social status—leaders and grassroots people, local students and outsiders, black and white, old and young, northerners and southerners. I spent the summer in Albany and never did go to Mexico. I worked with SNCC and SCLC on voter registration, integration of churches, and whatever else was needed in the Albany Movement. I also received nonviolence training in case there were any problems or violence at demonstrations. I was told to be careful, carry identification, obey all traffic signals, and especially not to jaywalk when I went downtown in the white community, because one could easily be arrested for vagrancy or jaywalking. I was uneasy about that, but I remember feeling secure knowing God and right were on our side even if the local law officials were not. Moreover, we were living in the black community, where people were very protective. They opened their homes to outsiders, and we all came together in prayer, song, and commitment to the struggle at mass meetings.

I also spent time going to the city jail to talk to SNCC folk who had been arrested for demonstrations and trumped-up charges. I would spend an hour a day looking up to their second-story jail window bars. I gave them news and they would shout down news about their well-being. I also worked in the Albany Movement office. While there, I would listen to Andrew Young,

Septima Clark, Dorothy Cotton, and Annelle Ponder talk about their work with SCLC Citizenship Schools. I would hear Reverends Martin Luther King Jr., Ralph David Abernathy, Samuel B. Wells, Charles Sherrod, Andrew Young, and C. T. Vivian, and Albany Movement leaders such as C. B. and Slater King, Goldie Jackson, Carolyn Daniels, and William G. Anderson, and Jim Forman, Bill Hansen, and other SNCC staff members talk about movement issues. I learned freedom songs led by Bernice Johnson, Cordell Reagon, the Harris brothers and sisters, Chuck and Chico Neblett, Matt Jones, and Charles Sherrod. Some of the songs were traditional spiritual and gospel hymns, and others were newly created songs of freedom. We loved singing about how our minds were on freedom and how we weren't going to let anyone turn us around, and how "We shall overcome, someday."

Sherrod, Bob Zellner, Charles Jones, and others planned strategies for demonstrations, mass meetings, and voter registration activities. They talked about the jailings, police brutality, the need for money, legal assistance and fees, all kinds of pro-movement people who were coming into Albany, and the media and the coverage we were or were not getting. One day there was a call for a black Episcopalian to try to integrate the white Episcopal church in Albany. Since I had been raised in the Episcopal church, I volunteered. I was picked up by a movement person and taken to the church for the 11:00 A.M. service. The media had been alerted, but the Episcopal church officials did not know about our plans. I alone went up the steps to the church doors, and the white men outside those doors let me walk past them. I sat in the middle section and participated in the service without incident. At its conclusion, I left nervously, not knowing what I would face outside—policemen; angry, jeering faces; or what; however, except for the blank stares of the churchgoers, nothing negative happened. My ride was waiting for me; I was picked up and went back to headquarters to report my success. The *New York Times* carried the story the next day. That Episcopal church, as far as I know, was the only one to be successfully integrated without incident that year.

At the end of the summer, I returned to New York to continue teaching elementary school and publicize the Albany Freedom Movement. I was committed to raising money and other resources and to working with SNCC's New York office. During this time I was in close contact with SNCC members from Atlanta, Albany, and Mississippi. I worked with people who were involved in the 1963 March on Washington the following summer. I worked with Ivanhoe Donaldson, James Farmer, Joanne Grant, Bill Mahoney, Bayard Rustin, and Julie Prettyman. I attended national SNCC meetings and conferences and met with SNCC folk when they came to New York. I was one of the initiators of the New York Artists for SNCC support and fund-raising group, which involved such actors, writers, and artists as Harry Belafonte, Danny Glover, Sidney Poitier, James Baldwin, Lorraine Hansberry, John O. Killens, Romare Bearden, Ernest Crichlow, Roy DeCarava, Jacob Lawrence, Norman Lewis, Hughie Lee Smith, and a host of others. Joanne Grant included a picture of me with some of these artists, SNCC supporters, and SNCC workers in her book on Ella Baker titled *Freedom Bound* (1998).

Nine Years in Mississippi

Bob Moses eventually recruited me to work in Tougaloo, Mississippi, as a SNCC field worker and teacher in a yearlong pilot adult literacy project that was to be overseen by the administrators of the Diebold Group. Although I was hesitant to go at first, I changed my mind after talking with my family, reading the newspapers, seeing the violent oppression in the state on television news, watching the brutality—jailings and attacks using dogs and fire hoses against peaceful protesters—and the escalation of student demonstrations. After the March on Washington in August 1963, I relocated to Jackson, Mississippi, to teach school, just as I had been trained to do.

When I first went to Mississippi, Bob Moses arranged for me to be a full-time SNCC field secretary, based in the COFO office in Jackson until the adult literacy project got started. Among other things, we worked for the Mississippi Freedom Democratic Party and prepared for Freedom Summer. I also made all the preparations to get the adult literacy project up and running, including recruiting staff and prospective student participants and locating housing for the female staff. In addition, in order to get around more efficiently and independently, I learned how to drive. I worked with people like Millicent Brown, Charlie Cobb, Dave and Mattie Dennis, L. C. Dorsey, Fannie Lou Hamer, Curtis Hayes, Jesse Harris, Aaron Henry, Henry Kirksey, Dorie and Joyce Ladner, Worth Long, Jessie Morris, Ian Tomlin, Carolyn and Jimmy Travis, Maria Varela, Hollis Watkins, and many others. Once the literacy project was fully staffed and under the management of New Yorker Burrill Cronin, I worked with it full-time and with SNCC part-time.

In Mississippi I was taken in by local grassroots families, by SNCC and COFO members, and by Tougaloo College faculty and staff. Those of us who worked and lived together in the adult literacy project—Casey Hayden, Hellen O'Neal, and me—lived as a family for a year. People in the Movement, generally, were an extended family of adopted brothers and sisters, cousins, and friends who learned from each other and who were committed to each other and to the struggle. The work, commitment, joys, songs, battles, tragedies, strategizing, gains, losses, and the horrors of violence and intimidation glued us together, and the circle kept getting bigger. As in the African American tradition, there was always room for more.

I initiated and participated in various cultural activities in Mississippi. Around mid-October, John O'Neal, who also worked on the literacy project; Gilbert Moses, editor of the *Mississippi Free Press;* and I began talking about the need for a theater based in Mississippi and connected to the Movement. The three of us brainstormed, wrote the prospectus for the Free Southern Theater, and traveled to New York to do recruitment, public relations, and fund-raising. During the 1963–1964 year, Worth Long, Jimmy Travis, and I pitched in to help organize the music and the art facets of the Mississippi Folk Festivals. Since I was a painter (a group of us regularly painted in a classroom set aside as a studio by art history and German-language professor Ronald Schnell of Tougaloo College), I agreed to take care of collecting the visual arts for the folk festival exhibit held at the Holmes County Community Center coordinated by Henry and Sue Lorenzi. During this time I interacted with local artists, including William Anderson, Marcus Douyon, Maria and Lawrence Jones, and Hugh Stevens.

In June 1965 I began work with the Child Development Group of Mississippi. We initiated one of the earliest Head Start programs in the United States, which was a model for preschool programs throughout the country. SNCC workers, grassroots folk, movement people, educators, health professionals, clergy, administrators, students, black and white people worked together on this vital, innovative, and exciting educational program.

After working briefly at Rust College in Holly Springs, I was assigned in July to the Head Start program in Durant to become a troubleshooter and teacher trainer. Durant was a rural area where there was strong black community support for CDGM and much opposition and violence from the white community. Early in my stay there, when the center director and I were returning from shopping in town and passed the church where Head Start was first held, I saw something strange on the ground. There was a fire slowly moving up a cord that ran up the path to the church steps, onto the church's porch, and through the doorway of the church. I yelled for the director to stop. We jumped out of the car, stamped out the fire, and headed back to the newly built center.

I stayed with Mrs. Hattie Saffold, the leader of the Durant Head Start program. At night the men kept watch with their rifles, because white people had shot into the house on several occasions. Rifles were also kept in the corner of the Head Start center in case of an attack, because white people hated the idea of there being a newly built center for black children and wanted to destroy it. Durant's white residents also hated the idea that the black community donated the land, labor, and materials to build the center. A crew from Indiana University made a film, *Chance for Change,* about CDGM, which featured the Durant center and aspects of my work there.

In the fall of 1965 I became a consultant for Head Start, because the federal grant had ended for the majority of the staff. During this time Jesse Morris, SNCC field secretary in Jackson, was organizing the Poor People's Corporation, an economic self-help program to train people to start their own cooperatives and other economic activities. In the ensuing years until 1972 I volunteered and subsequently worked on staff with the Poor People's Corporation and its components: Liberty House Handcrafts Marketing Cooperative; Education and Training for Cooperatives; and Southern Media, Inc., a documentary film and photography unit that functioned until 1972.

From the time I began my work with CDGM, I took documentary photographs of various aspects of my work in Mississippi, building up an extensive collection; my skills increased tremendously as I learned from the professional photographers who worked with southern media. During my more than nine years in Mississippi, I also advocated for widespread knowledge of African culture and taught African and African American art at Jackson State College (now Jackson State University). This advocacy was fueled by two additional trips I took to the West African countries of Senegal, Nigeria, Ghana, and the Ivory Coast combined with my continued reading about the continent and involvement with organizations associated with African affairs.

Reflections

In my work in the southern Freedom Movement from 1962 to 1972, sometimes I was in the ground troops and sometimes I was in the leadership. In these activities I worked largely with SNCC, grassroots people, students, and professionals, as well as various civil rights activists and organizations. Philosophically or politically, my job level was of little consequence to me; it depended on what needed to be done, my talents, and how I and others defined the situation and the alternative solutions available. I had a lot of energy and I was used to multitasking while holding a job, undertaking church and community work, and pursuing artistic interests.

I left Mississippi in the summer of 1972 to attend graduate school. I believe my work with the Movement and indeed my life's journey fall into the womanist tradition as defined by Alice Walker, whom I knew and photographed when we were both doing civil rights work in Jackson. In *In Search of Our Mothers' Gardens,* published in 1983, she describes a womanist as someone who is responsible, in charge, and serious. She appreciates women's strength, community struggle, the wholeness of an entire people, male and female. A womanist is traditionally universalist and capable; she loves struggle, the folk, and herself.

My experiences growing up in New York City within the tradition of family, kinship, friendships, church, community, and with strong male and female role models, as well as my experiences traveling within the United States, the Caribbean, and Africa, prepared me with a black womanist philosophical framework for taking on many roles and responsibilities in the Civil Rights Movement. My path was just one out of many taken by black women and men who converged at the same point in time, at the same place, for the same cause. It was one of the most significant periods in my life and certainly the most far-reaching one. It is a foundation upon which I continue to build my current life's work, service to the community, and personal and family relations.

DORIS A. DERBY focused on African and African American studies in graduate school, earning a master's and a PhD in cultural and social anthropology. She has been the director of African American Student Services and Programs at Georgia State University since 1990. Many of her department's efforts have included establishing cultural and educational ties between African, Caribbean, and African American students. She has also taught at the College of Charleston, the University of Illinois, and the University of Wisconsin. She has maintained her interest in documentary photography and painting and still exhibits her photographs, slides, and oil paintings. She belongs to Sistography, a black women's photography collective, as well as a number of professional and community organizations, including the Atlanta chapter of the Links, Inc., J.U.G.S. International, and Zeta Phi Beta Sorority. More about Derby's work can be found in Polly Greenberg's *The Devil Wears Slippery Shoes* (1990) and Clarissa Myrick-Harris's "Behind the Scenes" in *Trailblazers and Torchbearers* (1993). Derby lives in Atlanta with her husband, actor Bob Banks.

PART 9

The Constant Struggle

The Alabama Movement, 1963–1966

> They say that freedom is a constant
> struggle. They say that freedom is a
> constant struggle. . . . We've been struggling
> so long, we must be free, we must be free.
>
> —Freedom song

Television footage and newspaper photos depicting helmeted law enforcement officials attacking nonviolent demonstrators crossing the
Edmond Pettus Bridge on March 7, 1965, are the nation's most memorable images of the Civil Rights Movement in Selma, Alabama. The
day before, George Wallace, the governor of Alabama, had announced
that his state troopers were "to use whatever measures are necessary
to prevent a march." State troopers and a posse deputized by Selma's
sheriff, Jim Clark, decided to attack rather than arrest the protesters.
The troopers, wearing gas masks, waded into the middle of the march,
beating the demonstrators with nightsticks, including those felled by tear
gas. The men in Clark's posse who were on horseback rode over and
through the crowd, attacking demonstrators. They helped the troopers
drive the civil rights activists back to Brown's Chapel A.M.E. Church,
the march's starting point. So many people were injured that day that
it became known as Bloody Sunday.

The demonstrators were beginning a fifty-four-mile march from Selma
to the state capitol in Montgomery to protest the disenfranchisement
of Alabama's black citizens. The march was prompted by the murder of
twenty-six-year-old local resident Jimmie Lee Jackson. During a February
17 night march to the courthouse in Marion, Alabama, Jackson and his
mother had sought refuge in a café, hiding from the state troopers who
were ferociously beating the participants. A trooper spotted them anyway

and attacked Jackson's mother. Jackson interceded, the trooper shot him in the stomach, and the young man died a little over a week later.

Three days after Bloody Sunday, another civil rights demonstrator was murdered. Rev. James Reeb, a white clergyman from Boston, was beaten to death when he and two other ministers walked past a café where white racists congregated. Eighteen days after Bloody Sunday, marchers finally reached Montgomery and held a rally on the state capitol's steps. That night, march participant Viola Liuzzo, a white Detroit housewife and mother of five young children, was killed by shots from a car carrying Klansmen and an FBI informant as she drove back to Montgomery with Leroy Moton, a local SCLC volunteer.

Bloody Sunday and the March to Montgomery brought national attention to an SCLC campaign under way since the beginning of the year, a local movement that had been in activist mode for two years with the assistance of SNCC workers, and a decades-long struggle of Alabama black residents to win the right to vote. After the Atlantic City challenge, SCLC leaders had decided to follow SNCC's lead and enter the Black Belt of Alabama. They also adopted SNCC's Mississippi model of focusing on the vote and joined it with SCLC's usual mass mobilizations and demonstrations.

At the February 1965 meeting, SNCC staff, determined to keep the focus on grassroots organizing, voted not to support the SCLC campaign but granted individual members the right to do as they chose. By this time SNCC chair John Lewis and field secretary Robert Mants had already traveled to Alabama to participate in this effort and later were in the front line of marchers on Bloody Sunday. After Bloody Sunday, SNCC workers from all over the South, horrified by the carnage, rushed to Selma. They were determined, as were the members of SNCC's Alabama staff, many northern supporters, and Selma's African American residents, to take up the march to Montgomery right away. On the next attempt to resume the march, however, after holding a prayer service at the far end of the Edmond Pettus Bridge, Dr. King led the more than two thousand resolute marchers back to Brown's Chapel rather than across the bridge. Greatly disappointed by SCLC's refusal to risk a federal injunction prohibiting that march, and feeling that this decision harmed the campaign's momentum, most SNCC staff ended their involvement and somewhat derisively referred to this march as the "U-Turn March." Some SNCC staff went to Montgomery with executive secretary Jim Forman to assist and augment student protests there. A few SNCC workers did provide logistical and tactical support when the march to Montgomery resumed.

Since the beginning of 1963, SNCC workers had maintained a presence in Selma and had made some forays into adjacent counties. In February 1963, SNCC field secretaries Colia and Bernard Lafayette, a married couple, arrived in Selma. With significant assistance from local businesswoman Amelia Boynton, they based a portion of their activities in the preexisting Dallas County Voters League and recruited a group of already militant high school students. Charles Bonner, Bettie Fikes, Cleophus Hobbs, Willie Emma Scott, and Terry Shaw formed the nucleus of a group of local high school students who worked enthusiastically for civil rights well into the late sixties. Other SNCC staff assisted the Lafayettes. The first was Prathia Hall, from the Southwest Georgia staff, who describes some of her experiences in Alabama in this section.

In spite of repeated arrests and physical attacks, some with electric cattle prods, SNCC activists were able to hold voter education classes, accompany significant numbers of people to try to register to vote at the courthouse (including a group of teachers), sponsor a Freedom Day when 350 people attempted to register, organize sit-ins and protest marches, and support the high school students' efforts to desegregate the schools. SNCC workers held mass meetings attended by hundreds of Selma's black residents with speakers like Jim Forman, Ella Baker, SCLC field secretary and former SNCC staffer James Bevel, comedian Dick Gregory, and writer James Baldwin. A large Freedom Chorus made up of Selma youth provided musical inspiration at these meetings. As the singers in Albany had done, they introduced a new sound to the Movement. In this section, Bettie Fikes, the organizer, director, and lead vocalist of the chorus, describes how this musical style developed.

Two years before Bloody Sunday, SNCC and CORE workers had attempted a march through Alabama also provoked by a murder. On April 23, 1963, William Moore was shot and killed on the highway near Gadsden, Alabama. Moore, a white postman raised in Mississippi and a member of Baltimore CORE, had decided to make a solo "freedom walk" from Chattanooga, Tennessee, to Jackson, Mississippi, where he expected to deliver a letter with a civil rights message to Mississippi governor Ross Barnett. Annie Pearl Avery was among the first to rush to the spot where Moore was killed and begin walking. She was arrested within the hour. Ten SNCC and CORE workers, all male, started from Chattanooga several days later, dodging rocks, bottles, and physical attacks as they went through Georgia. They were arrested as soon as they crossed the Alabama state line.

For the most part the young women who write about their experiences in Alabama were a decidedly militant group composed of seasoned southern civil rights workers or women with fairly radical backgrounds. The organizational context they found in SNCC was also militant and unambiguous about the group's target community. At the February 12, 1965, staff meeting in Atlanta, SNCC chairman John Lewis, who never wavered from his commitment to nonviolence as a philosophy and way of life or from his belief in "the beloved community," announced that SNCC's "primary concern must be the liberation of black people." To be effective in reaching that goal, he added "the civil rights movement must be black-controlled, dominated, and led." Lewis's position echoes Diane Nash's statement that as early as 1961 she and her husband planned to spend the rest of their lives working for the liberation of black people. Nash also believed in nonviolence and the creation of the beloved community. Their views illustrate how nonviolence, a belief in the beloved community, militancy, and black control could and did exist together as ideological references within one individual or organization.

The Alabama staff usually relied on the early Mississippi model of an all-black, mostly southern staff with strong local representation. Additionally, there was general agreement among the Alabama staff, at least from 1964 on, that using only black organizers in the black community was preferable. Unlike later Mississippi staff, Alabama SNCC workers did not attempt any kind of organizing in the white community of Alabama. (After Bloody Sunday a group of white Alabama clergymen did march in support of black Alabamians' right to vote.) Still, members of the Selma staff sometimes worked closely with Father Ouellet, a white Catholic priest assigned to Selma's black parish. SNCC staffers did recruit Maria Varela, whose story follows, to set up a literacy school for Selma's prospective black voters at his church. SNCC staff also accepted the help of a small group of white volunteers who arrived in Selma during 1965 and welcomed white Episcopal seminarian Jonathan Daniels and priest Rev. Richard Morrisroe at a Lowndes County demonstration. Technically, the Lowndes County Freedom Organization's Black Panther Party remained open to white voters.

During the SCLC-sponsored demonstrations, women working with SNCC focused on community organizing in the five wards of Selma and in adjacent counties, especially Wilcox and Lowndes. They ran a Freedom School in the city and participated in and sponsored mass meetings. Other women planned and carried out demonstrations in nearby Montgomery. These protests were only one aspect of a more complete civil rights program pursued by activist Tuskegee students described in the following sections. Alabama SNCC workers sadly remembered the 1963 Birmingham church bombing that killed four little girls—Addie Mae Collins, Denise McNair, Carole Robertson, and Cynthia Wesley. Several witnessed the August 20, 1965, murder of Jonathan Daniels and shooting of Father Morrisroe. SNCC staffers' grief was compounded by the January 3, 1966, murder of their colleague—U.S. Navy veteran, SNCC worker, and Tuskegee student, Samuel Younge Jr.

The spirit of the women writing in this section is noticeable in their singing. As the movement progressed, they tended to choose the movement songs with more measured beats and determined lines like "They Say That Freedom Is a Constant Struggle" and "We'll Never Turn Back." They championed independent black politics under a banner with a pouncing black panther and embraced self-defense. They sought to connect with Malcolm X and advocated extending SNCC's official reach beyond the Civil Rights Movement—urging the national organization to issue statements opposing the war in Vietnam and supporting armed struggles against oppressive regimes in other parts of the world, especially in colonized Africa.

There Are No Cowards in My Family

Annie Pearl Avery

Raised on stories of southern racist terrorism, a Birmingham
resident becomes a dauntless SNCC activist.

Predestination

It was just predestined for me to get involved, one way or the other. I was
born in Birmingham, Alabama, but when I was a child I spent a year in
Pittsburgh, Pennsylvania, with my great-aunt, where I read in the newspaper about the lynching of Emmett Till. I returned to Birmingham when I
was about ten years old, and I heard about a black fellow, Greg Aaron, who
was castrated by a Klan mob right in the city of Birmingham. One of my
father's brothers, who we called "Uncle Doc," was lynched and found dead
in the woods. Also, Rev. Fred Shuttlesworth and Rev. Charles Billips were
beaten within an inch of their lives when they tried to integrate the high
school. Both men were taken to the hospital, but nobody wanted to treat
them. Around that time I learned Mack Parker was dragged out of jail and
lynched in Mississippi.

One night right after Mack Parker's death, the police came looking
for my brother. He used to run with these hoodlums in the neighborhood.
The police knocked on the door to our home and barged right on in to look
for him. I thought about it. What if they had decided they wanted to do
something to him because they insisted he was involved? After the Parker
lynching and incidents with my brother and uncle, I happened to pick up
a *Muhammad Speaks* and began attending a few meetings of the Nation of
Islam and became a member of the Nation, even though I never did change
my name and get an X.

My father's father was a slave in Alabama, and he used to tell us about
this hard slavery. Granddaddy died in the early 1960s; he was at least 110. My
father was 54 when I was born and 96 when he died. My great-grandfather

on mother's side was a slave, too. Mama comes from Hale County, Alabama, where Indians and black people married; she's part Indian.

It was the Freedom Rides that got me involved. My friend Candace Grimes, whom I knew from a child, was a niece of Rev. Ralph Abernathy's. We had been looking at the Freedom Rides on TV and listening to the news when the ride came to Birmingham. Candace said, "Annie Pearl, let's go down to the bus station." But we had to wait until the evening, when her husband came home to be there with the baby. We walked all the way to the bus station downtown. At that time it was nothing to walk a couple of miles. They had everything blocked off; the police were all over the place. We couldn't get as close as we'd like to, but we got close enough to see some things. The next evening we decided to walk back to check it out again, but she couldn't go, because the baby was acting up. So I went alone.

Later on, at the end of 1961 or the early part of 1962, I met SNCC workers Wilson Brown and Nathaniel Lee at the A. C. Gaston Lounge. They approached me and began talking about the situation. They said, "If someone hit you, what would you do?" I said, "I'd hit them back!" "Well," they said, "you have to go to one of these meetings!" I said, "What meeting is that?" And then they told me about a Student Nonviolent Coordinating Committee meeting in Atlanta.

I had to decide whether to go to this meeting. I had two children by then, and I was working as a dishwasher. About two weeks earlier a white girl had gotten hired as a waitress. Soon afterward, the manager started acting hostile toward me. I couldn't figure out what was going on. The black girl who was working with me in the dishwashing area said, "Do you know anything about a missing wallet?" They assumed I took the wallet and they threatened me. But actually it was the white girl who took it. When they found out the truth, the manager never did come to me and say, "I'm sorry." Anyway, I was off for two days the weekend of the SNCC meeting, so I went.

After the meeting, we got lost on the way back and got stopped by the police in Marietta, Georgia. We had a white girl with us who wanted to go with us to meet Rev. Shuttlesworth. Wilson Brown was driving, and they arrested him and threatened to do something to us. Since it was beginning to get dark, we decided to go to the Greyhound bus station. A mob came around the bus station and threatened to kill us. We phoned the SNCC office and they contacted the Associated Press, and the Associated Press called us on the pay phone. Howard Moore showed up to get Wilson out of jail, and some people escorted us out of the bus station. We finally made it to Birmingham. I felt kind of like a Harriet Tubman!

Next we had a sit-in at Woolworth's in Birmingham, organized by Rev. Shuttlesworth. I was working on the nonviolence. It was a foreign language to me. I didn't understand it at all. A man was spitting on the demonstrators and pouring ketchup on them, and I exclaimed, "Lord, if that man spits and pours ketchup on me, I'm just gonna have to go off." Rev. Shuttlesworth heard that and said, "Come here and stand with me!" The movement people were watching me; they were reluctant to let me participate. I imagine Wilson had informed them that I wasn't sure about this nonviolence.

On the way to the sit-in I had both a gun and a knife. When one of my godmothers, Mrs. Maggie Cummings, who owned a beauty shop at the time, told me, "You can't carry this knife and this gun!" I took the gun home. I came back and told her, "I still have this knife. I've got to take something." "No," she said, and took my knife. She has the knife to this day. She still has the beauty salon, and she still has the knife. I was just hoping that nobody would get me—that's all! I didn't know how I would react. I was hoping that I would be able to restrain myself, but I still wanted protection, just in case I couldn't.

I Made This Decision within Myself

I went to Albany, Georgia, and was in jail for two weeks after being arrested. Also sometime in 1961 I went to Talladega from Birmingham, because there was a movement meeting there. I got as far as Anniston and found that I couldn't get a bus to Talladega until the next morning, so I had to wait in the Anniston bus station overnight. The shell of the bus bombed in the Freedom Rides was sitting in the parking lot. At that time the station had a white side and a black side. I decided to go to the white side and have a cup of coffee. The guy sitting next to me dumped his coffee on the counter and yelled, "Nigger, get up and get out of here." I refused to go. I paid him no mind and just finished my coffee. Afterward I sat in the white waiting area and a police officer approached me, saying he couldn't be responsible if anything happened to me.

Sometime after midnight, I decided to call the Atlanta office to let them know what was transpiring in case something did happen to me. I spoke to Jim Forman, and even he told me to get out of there. But I stayed in that white waiting room all night. When white people came by, noticed me, and made all kinds of racial slurs, I just sat there. I even went to the white bathroom. I really think the only reason I survived was because I was female. If I had been a black male, I probably would be dead by now. I just totally refused to go. I made this decision within myself. *They're going to do whatever they have to do. I'm going to sit here. I'm going to stay in spite of all the risks.*

Not long after my night in the Anniston bus station, a white postman, William Moore, was marching through Alabama for civil rights and got killed right near Gadsden. At the SNCC meeting discussing how to finish the march that Moore had started, as far as I was concerned it was all a lot of talk, but nobody had come up with a plan. So I decided to go on my own. I didn't tell anybody except my friend Betty Hill. There was a girl from Gadsden who was driving back there. I spent the night at her house, made a sign, and she dropped me off right where they had found Moore's body. Three other women attempting to finish the march had already been arrested and jailed. I decided to pick up where they left off. Well, of course, after I was walking about thirty minutes, the police picked me up.

Later on the men from SNCC and CORE made a freedom walk that got a lot of publicity, but I didn't get any publicity, because it was just me. When they put me in the Etowah County jail, I was in a separate cell. Diane Bevel got arrested a couple of days later and was also in a separate cell. I was isolated. Still I could hear them over in the other area. I was more angry than afraid. The guards tried to intimidate me, but I said, "I am *not* afraid of you people." They wanted to know who sent me and how I got there, and I wouldn't tell them anything. A lot of things were happening in Birmingham—the hoses and the dogs—but I never saw all that, because I was in jail in Gadsden for about six weeks.

They moved the women demonstrators out of Gadsden to Wetumpka, telling us that white people were threatening to come and take us out. When we got to Wetumpka the authorities put us in the hospital area, because they were afraid we were going to disrupt the prison, so they didn't want us talking to the other prisoners. A woman who was in there for life brought us our food trays in the hospital area. When she first came in, she asked all of our names and where we were from. She said she was from Tuscaloosa, Alabama. I told her I had some people there, Corinne Bates and her son Ozell Buster Bates Sr. She said, "Buster killed a white man!" We had always heard this in grown folks' conversation but thought it was exaggeration, that maybe Buster beat the man up but didn't kill him. Now I knew it was true. It never dawned on me that it was true; I thought it was just a folktale the whites were telling.

Buster got caught, but he never served time; by me being a child I never knew what happened. His mother, Corinne Bates, who had raised a lot of children, black and white, probably got someone of importance to get Buster off, since he was only defending himself. After the white guy kicked Buster, Buster hit him with a two-by-four. The blow was lethal because Buster was very strong, having lifted railroad ties when he was a boy.

This told me something about my past. There are no cowards in my family. That's just something that wasn't there on both sides of the family. My mother's brother beat the hell out of a white guy in some dispute and left the South.

After my release, I continued working with the Gadsden Movement. We organized demonstrations and marches and went out into the community. We were marching every day. At first we were marching and not getting arrested, but then there was a massive march and we all got arrested together. They didn't keep us very long, because they didn't have enough space.

Before one of the marches in Birmingham, I went to see Betty, who at the time was working for the *Birmingham Mirror,* a local black newspaper. I said, "I'm going on this demonstration tomorrow." She replied, "They're going to put you in jail." "Probably will," I said. I marched that day, and when we got in front of the post office, they arrested us. Later on that evening, Betty came to jail, too! She said, "You went in; I didn't want to be out there by myself!" I thought, *Well, we had partied together, I guess we should be in jail together!* We were in there for about a week before they made bail for us.

Mama didn't know I was in there until after the fact. I didn't tell her a whole lot. My mother was opposed to what I was doing, very adamantly opposed then, but she agreed to watch the children. My children then were about two years old and about four years old. I felt, What kind of a world will they be in if I don't do something to contribute to a revolutionary change? My mother was very afraid for me. The first time she found out that I had been arrested, she read about it in *JET* magazine after someone told her in the drugstore. Later on, however, she came to the demonstrations herself.

Not long after, I went to Danville, and that's where I met Matt Jones, Avon Rollins, and all the other civil rights people there. We had a demonstration in front of Dan River Mills where the people laid down in the street at the front of the buildings and blocked the traffic. The police knew Matt and I were involved, but they couldn't pinpoint it. They didn't get us right away, but at a later trial they arrested us out in the hallway. We laid down and went limp, so they carried us to the elevator and dropped us on the floor and started to beat Matt. I jumped in front of Matt and told the police, "Don't hit him no more"; then they hit me too, but at least they left him alone for a few seconds. They took us to jail and put us both in solitary confinement. One night a policeman came into my cell. Thinking he wanted to mess with me, I took off my shoe and beat him on the head until he left.

During that year I went back and forth from Birmingham to Danville to Atlanta. In Atlanta we were arrested at several places, including the Toddle House. Over the Christmas holidays, I was arrested with Lillian Gregory (Dick Gregory's wife), Ruby Doris Robinson, Phyllis Martin, and Judy Richardson. Everyone was in there together. Ruby and I were friends and hung out together from time to time. By then everyone was getting ready for the summer of 1964.

Organizing in the Deep South

I went to the Oxford, Ohio, orientation for the Mississippi Summer Project. I met Lucy Montgomery there, and she sponsored me to go to Mississippi. I also met Lafayette Surney, and he asked me to come to Clarksdale, a very scary place. It was also scary going there from Oxford on the bus. As we were getting closer to the South, things started happening. We stopped at a bus station in Tennessee, and there was a crowd of whites there.

In Mississippi we dropped people off in different areas. When we got to Clarksdale, the police were waiting when we got off the bus. Unfortunately the people who were supposed to meet us were late, so we were dropped off in front of Dr. Aaron Henry's drugstore, but it was very early in the morning and he hadn't arrived. We really didn't have anywhere to go. We didn't know where to go or anything. The police were harassing and hassling us, telling us we couldn't stand around or have our luggage on the street. During those times churches were always open, and there was a black church on the corner, so we took refuge in the church until someone came around.

In Clarksdale I stayed with a Mrs. Holder the whole summer. The police followed us everywhere. We tried to do some voter registration outside the city; we were harassed there and followed out of town. One night in Clarksdale a white crowd and police surrounded the SNCC office and shone floodlights and car lights on the front. They threatened to do all kinds of things to us, so we couldn't go in or out of the office that night. This was the first time I had been in Mississippi. It's worse than Alabama in some areas.

When the summer ended I went to Atlantic City for the Mississippi Freedom Democratic Party challenge, and then I came back to Mississippi and went to Natchez with some other SNCC people. We were supposed to have a freedom house, but somebody blew up the house next door by mistake. Whoever was sent out to do the job blew up the wrong house! Of course, the freedom house owner wouldn't rent to us. We found a lady who allowed us to sleep in her room; we SNCC women slept there during the night while she worked in a café. SNCC ended up buying a house in Natchez, because nobody would rent to us.

I've always stayed with community folks who had weapons, but this was the first time I had been with a SNCC group who had guns. The Natchez SNCC staff decided to get some protection because it seemed ludicrous just to lie there and not do anything under the circumstances. This helped do a little "mind adjusting" in the white community. When we bought the house, the white telephone installer came to put in a phone. We had the guns sitting out, the shotguns over here and the rifles over there, and he had to take a note of that and report back to his buddies! We knew he would tell his buddies that this is a different type of group here. They've got weapons! They say they're nonviolent, but they've got weapons! We knew this was a shift in SNCC policy, but we didn't talk about it; we just did it. Forman found out we had guns at the Waveland meeting and he was pretty upset, but we didn't give them up.

All the press had left and the volunteers had left after the summer project, and it was much more dangerous. We had floodlights around the house. White people were coming past the house and pulling up in front of the house. They would call and threaten us, and we'd say, "Come on," but they didn't ever mess with the house!

From Natchez, Mississippi, I went to Hale County, Alabama, where I worked until the end of 1965. I came up to Selma to help organize the March to Montgomery. Cynthia Washington and some other SNCC workers were in Hale County, too, as well as some people from the Medical Committee for Human Rights. Mrs. Virginia Wells of the medical committee dropped me off at the bottom of the bridge. The police wouldn't let me go up to the bridge, because by this time there was pandemonium. The police and I got into it, and they carted me off to jail. I don't know what I was charged with! Maybe attacking an officer, because I was up around his neck! Brother Sunshine, who was with the Southern Christian Leadership Conference, was the only person around who knew who I was and saw me get arrested. He told somebody who sent attorney Peter Hall to get me out. The police waited until it got dark to release me. It was the same night Viola Liuzzo got murdered.

In all the projects I worked in, black women were very important. In the South, black women were more able to exercise their rightful privileges than black men. On SNCC projects there was sexism toward women, because this was a way of life for all women. Sometimes I felt limited because we weren't allowed to drive the cars. At first all the fellows were driving, but they wouldn't teach us how to drive! Eventually, Sammy Younge taught me to drive a stick shift in his yellow VW Bug. The male chauvinism was there, but I don't think it was intentional. It wasn't as dominant in SNCC as it was in SCLC, which Miss Baker told us about.

I'm pleased with my work and with what I contributed. SNCC laid the groundwork for all of the movements around the country, especially in the South. After the Civil Rights Movement, we should have started educational, cultural, and economic projects directed toward controlling our communities and building economic power. I think if SNCC had gone this way after the Civil Rights Act and the voting rights bill—I mean, added a cultural and economic direction—the organization might have survived.

ANNIE PEARL AVERY lives in Selma and Birmingham. She retired from her work at a nursing home but continues to be involved in voter registration drives and in the National Voting Rights Museum in Selma. She also mentors young people. She lived in Atlanta for more than twenty years, where she drove a cab and served on the city's taxicab commission as the representative of the United Taxicab Drivers of Atlanta, which she headed; the organization attempted to form a union of city taxicab drivers. She participates every year in the annual commemoration of the Selma to Montgomery March.

Singing for Freedom

Bettie Mae Fikes

A singer steeped in gospel, blues, and rhythm and blues brings her distinctive musical style to the Selma Movement.

The Music Grabbed Me

I was raised around music, and all my family members wanted me to be a singer. I started singing gospel solos in church when I was four years old. At six or seven I started singing with my mother's group, the SB Gospel Singers. During the week my mother would work, but she and I would practice together at least once a week on Monday or Wednesday nights. On the weekends we would both sing. Later, as a young teenager, I sang with my father's uncle's gospel group called the Pilgrim Four. All of my relatives on my father's side were either preachers or good gospel singers. My great-uncle had a perfect-pitch tenor voice and was responsible for my early musical education. He taught me how to expand my singing range, singing higher and higher a little bit at a time. I would practice as I was doing my errands, walking here and there. People would be sitting out on their porches while I was going by practicing and practicing, but nobody complained.

My church was El Bethel Baptist Church, and I sang in the choirs there, progressing from the children's choir, the Sunbeams they called us, to the senior choir by the time I was eleven or twelve. It wasn't that I wanted to sing; I had no other choice *but* to sing. The music grabbed me and turned me on. For example, we often went to sing at a country church named Bethel; we could hear the people singing as we turned off the main highway toward the church. It seemed as if the music, especially when they sang hymns, was everywhere; it was coming off the leaves of the trees, and I couldn't wait to get up in the church and be a part of it.

In those days we had church almost every day of the week. We went all day on Sundays, and there would be programs through the week, like Bible study on Wednesday and choir practice on Friday. Two or three times a year my uncle's group would travel outside of Selma to places like Montgomery, Birmingham, and Mobile to sing with different groups and join in fellowship. On a Sunday we might sing in churches from eight o'clock in the morning to ten or eleven o'clock at night, sometimes in seven or eight different churches in one day.

For years I took piano lessons from a local minister, Reverend Galloway. He was a musician who played all up and down the piano, like Carleton Reese of the Birmingham Freedom Choir. When gospel groups came to town for special events like church anniversaries or to present their own programs, we opened up our homes to them, since there were no hotels in the city for black people. So we were very used to having celebrities in the house whom a lot of people only heard on the radio, singers like Cleophus Robinson and Joe Mays as well as groups like the Staple Singers and the Angelic Gospel Singers, who sang, "Sweet Home, Sweet Home, Sweet Home, My Lord." These musicians would also practice in our house. A lot of times it wasn't even practice, it was spirit, whatever the spirit led them to do. Somebody would be sitting up and just lead out in a song, and pretty soon everybody in the house came and joined in. This is the kind of music I know, and that's what I tell people today. It is the song in your heart that's important.

I became known for singing "Oh, Lord, Help Me to Carry On," which had the words "I am a stranger and a long way from home. I'm begging you Heavenly Father, help me to carry on." Then I would also sing a duet with a young lady, nicknamed Toot, who used to live next door to me. We sang, "I know a man from Galilee. If you're in doubt, he will set you free. He's the son of David, seed of Abraham. Oh, oh, do you know him." That was an old one. Those were my two trademarks, my two pets in my younger years. From there I moved into "Precious Lord" and some of the other standards. But my absolute favorite was "Touch Me, Lord Jesus," which I think the Angelic Gospel Singers recorded. "Touch me, Lord Jesus, with Thy hand of mercy. Make each troubling heartbeat feel Thy power Divine." There's one more, which I can hardly remember now, "Jesus, My King."

About as early as I learned gospel music, I learned the blues. It was my father who turned me on to the blues. Every Saturday night we could hear him singing as he turned the corner on his way home: "When you see me coming, go get my rocking chair." Daddy was the partier, the one they used to call the devil of the family. He was a normal man until Friday and Saturday, when he became somebody else. On the weekend he would play the blues so loudly that everyone could hear it all up and down the street. He was unwilling to give up the life that he was living just to go to church. "Preachers eat too much anyway," he used to say. "I'm out there working too hard for my food, for my wife to stay up all Saturday night, cooking for the preacher to come on Sunday like he's the man of the house."

There was a club in Selma called Small Street Inn known for their chitlins. It was a small place, but they served the biggest dish of chitlins. I was too young to go inside, but there were chairs outside where I could sit next to the door just to hear the blues. I would save a quarter or a dime for someone to play me my special records on the Rockola jukebox inside. On my way home from football games, I would be over there listening to records and dancing outside at the Inn.

The people of that era, most of them are dead and gone, but their music is still alive. When I was young the Clara Ward Singers fascinated me, not just because they had beautiful voices, but also because of the way they wore their hair and dressed. Most of my friends and family thought it was the blues people who opened me up to the world, but it was the gospel people. They had more style. They looked as if they had already made it in by the way they dressed and carried themselves and by the cars they drove. The church supported gospel groups more then, but when you were a blues singer, you were out there on your own.

There was a Green Street Hall in Selma. On a Sunday afternoon, big-name gospel singers would perform, sometimes preachers, too. I'll never forget when Rev. C. L. Franklin came and preached "The Eagle Stirs Its Nest." Mahalia Jackson came through and sang at Clinton Chapel. She was in a Cadillac. I liked her hair. I wondered how she got those waves going across. She was singing, her head back, and people would get off, shouting. Those were good times. Those people were spreading the word of the Lord, but I was also caught up in the flair, the robes, and the dress.

When I was fifteen a gentleman with a rhythm-and-blues group called the Martinis heard me and asked my people if I could sing with his group. At first they didn't agree with him, but finally, since they knew him personally, knew he was a churchgoing man and a band teacher in the schools, they agreed as long as he took personal responsibility for me. Before this I had just listened to R & B like any other teenager, but I had never tried singing it and I had never sung with a band. It was just like gospel singing in that we started out going to the country to perform.

I still wasn't old enough to be in the clubs. I had to stay in the dressing room until it was time to sing and go back there when the performance was over, even when I sang for Selma's former mayor Joe T. Smitherman. My first national recording was as the female vocalist with Bobby Moore and the Rhythm Aces, a group out of Montgomery. "Searching, Searching for My Baby" was a hit, and all of a sudden, at twenty-two, I was traveling as far away as Chicago. In those days we didn't have concerts, we had revues; all black performers, all the people who worked for Chess Records would appear together. Ike and Tina Turner, Chuck Jackson, Laverne Baker, and Joe Tex were in the revue, and my group, the Rhythm Aces, would play for everybody. The musicians treated me as if I were their little sister. Even when I was twenty-one and twenty-two, they would not let me come to the bar or stay in the club. It was not ladylike, they said. So I had to go back to the dressing room. I could never come out and socialize. The groups I sang with were all men, but I never had a problem. Nobody tried to take advantage of me. Also I was never in a club when something bad happened, like a fight breaking out. I had the time of my life.

Although my parents wanted me to be a singer, I never looked at myself as a singer. On the other hand, the usual options did not appeal to me either. I didn't see anyone in Selma whom I knew I wanted to marry. My parents taught me not to work in homes of white people or in restaurants. At that time, with training, all young black women could aspire to be was a nurse or a schoolteacher. I didn't want to be a nurse, because I didn't like blood, so that left schoolteacher.

Singing wasn't easy for me either. I would start shaking when I knew I had to sing. I shook so much, I thought people would see it and laugh at me, but they didn't and I always sang. Other times I would be so nervous that I thought I was going to pass out, but I stood there and sang. I am still nervous today, especially when I'm singing a cappella. I sang so long with a band that now it's hard to go back to a cappella singing. I can hear the instrumental music in my head, but there's actually no music there, so I have to try to make the vocal sounds fill in. I've learned how to talk to myself before my time to perform and calm myself down.

My Early Life

As a child I lived with my parents in Selma. Later I moved with my mother when she went to Birmingham and then Detroit. Usually I spent two weeks every summer with my grandparents in the country, outside of Selma. I had never heard the term "sharecropping," and I really did not know there was a race problem. The only thing that frightened me was being in the country. It got so dark at night, and I could hear those wild animals. So I was always fearful when I visited my grandparents or when we sang in country churches off the main roads. My grandparents lived on the land of a white man who was my godfather and always treated us like family. Later he was one of the white men deputized on Bloody Sunday.

I lived a happy and sheltered life. Our family did not go to restaurants where we had to use the back door. We thought black people's home cooking was always much better than the food in the white restaurants, even when the ones cooking there were black. So why would we want to go in the white places through the front door or the back door? My mother taught me to say "yes" and "no," not "yes, ma'am" and "no, ma'am" to white folks. I did see the white and colored water fountains and drank out of the white fountain to see if the water tasted any different. I have never understood why Selma, with a population of only two thousand people, needed those designations, colored and white.

I did not think of going to all-black schools as a problem. When I lived in Detroit, I went to all-black schools, just as I did in Selma, so I figured it was the same everywhere. In Selma there were three segregated theaters, but we had our own swimming pool and our own places to buy hamburgers—Fred's and the Canteen. We were taught that we didn't want to be anywhere we were not wanted. That's how we survived life in segregated Selma. As a young person, I didn't know that black people in Selma didn't have the right to vote or that Alabama was any different from any other state. I certainly had no idea that the white people in Selma had such strong feelings about segregation that it would lead to the kind of bloodshed we experienced during the Movement. If anyone had told me, I wouldn't have believed it.

I never had a childhood. Selma was a center for tobacco manufacturing, and my mother worked the night shift and my father worked days. My mother was a strong-willed woman, but physically weak. Since she worked at night and was sickly, I tried to do everything I could possibly do. By the time I was in first grade, I fixed the meals. By the time I was eight or ten, I could iron my father's shirts. My mother taught me many things, so there wasn't anything about a house I could not do. As a result, when my mother died when I was only ten, my relatives fought over having me come to live with them.

I learned color prejudice from my family. Once, when my mother got laid off, I stayed with my great-grandmother, aunt, and some cousins. I had always been the only child and was not too pleased with the change. In my great-grandmother's house I was the darkest child. The others had long hair and light complexions. Making fun of my skin color, they called me "Black Gal," "Black Beauty," and "Moonshine." After my mother died, I was shuttled from home to home; my father kept his lifestyle and stayed in the streets, so from him I never felt the kind of love that she had given me. As a result, I became extremely shy and withdrawn and had a huge inferiority complex. Really, I feel I was emotionally abused. I did not come close to the kind of love I experienced as a young child—a mother's love, the greatest love—until the Movement. When I graduated from high school, my family wasn't there, but movement people were. They came around, came to see about me, and were there for me.

The Selma Youth Movement

When I went to R. B. Hudson High School in Selma, I hung out with Evelyn Mann, Thomasina Marshall, Willie Emma Scott, Charles Bonner, Cleophus Hobbs, and Terry Shaw. We were only at the high school half a day; the other half a day we were supposed to be in the beauty or barber shop, learning how to become cosmetologists and barbers. We were already radical and militant at Hudson High, but we didn't know it. SNCC saved us, kept us from going too far, by offering us a way to express these feelings. In 1961 I met Bernard Lafayette and Worth Long; they were the first people I knew from SNCC. They were trying to reach the adults, but only two people responded: a teacher named Miss Margaret Moore and Mrs. Amelia Boynton, who had an insurance and employment office downtown. When movement people first came to town they would stay with either of these women.

All my friends and I decided to help Bernard and Worth. Our first job was to pass out the leaflets they had made urging the adults to come out for mass meetings. We knocked on doors throughout the black community in Selma, but there was no response. A lot of people wouldn't open their doors to us. I couldn't understand why we were having such a hard time getting the adults to participate. I just thought people were unnecessarily scared and fearful. I wasn't aware that people were afraid of being hurt, of losing their jobs or their lives. I had no idea that was going on.

Most of the churches were afraid to open their doors for movement or mass meetings. Rev. L. L. Anderson was the first to open Tabernacle Baptist Church, next Rev. M. C. Cleveland from First Baptist on Jeff Davis, then Brown's Chapel on Sylvan Street, an A.M.E. church pastored by Rev. P. H. Lewis. Brown's Chapel is now a historic site, but it wasn't the first place to open its doors. It was used a lot because it was in the middle of the projects. Rev. F. D. Reese from Ebenezer Baptist Church and Rev. Ernest Bradford from the Presbyterian church on Range Street came to movement meetings, but we didn't use their churches.

After school we would go to the church and meet with the SNCC people. We would take what they had told us back to the students we were working with, and eventually we pulled together a Selma youth movement. We wanted to desegregate Hudson High. Even though a lot of students, just like the adults, were scared, in September 1963 we turned the school out. Almost all the students left classes. Teachers like Miss Carter and Perry Anderson assisted us. On the day of our walkout Mr. Anderson said he was going to the window and turn his back, and if anyone was left when he turned around, they would be sure to fail. We marched from Hudson High to Tabernacle Baptist Church for the first student meeting. At the tender ages of fourteen, fifteen, and sixteen, we were taught how to protect ourselves from the police. We decided we would have sit-ins, marches, and boycotts.

Understanding that one of the best ways to get the white man's attention is through his pocket, we decided to begin a boycott of the stores downtown that same day by picketing them. We also sat in at several lunch counters downtown. Our parents were afraid; however, we weren't frightened until we got initiated at Carter Drugs. Willie C. Robinson went in to sit in at the counter and asked why could he spend his money in the rest of the store but not buy a hamburger at the counter. The owner, Mr. Carter, hit him in the head with some kind of club and split Willie C.'s head open. Worth Long was beaten that day by Deputy Turner, and sixty-four students were arrested. Afterward we boycotted the buses and shut the bus system down. Actually they don't run to this day, because when the city put the buses back, nobody used them. People had gotten so used to making other arrangements, they wouldn't take the bus.

Next we concentrated on voter registration so that people would have more of a voice in what went on. We wanted desegregation of the high school, and we knew that to make that happen we needed black voters who would have the ability to demand change. We also went out to the county, where most of the people were not sharecroppers but lived on their own property and had more of a say-so in their own lives than the people in Selma. I got arrested in Selma and spent three weeks in jail for accompanying people to the registrar's office. I might have gotten out sooner, but I refused to say "yes, sir" and "no, sir" to the judge. By this time so many students had been arrested that the Selma jails were full, and they sent some of us out to jails in surrounding counties. One day Jim Clark pushed and slapped Miss Annie Cooper, an older woman trying to register. She responded by punching him and knocking him out.

When people started attending the mass meetings, young people provided the music. Since these meetings were being held in a church, we followed the same order of service as for a church service, beginning with a prayer and opening with a song. So we formed a young people's freedom choir and a children's freedom choir, and we put songs together. We began with our regular gospel songs, but then I started changing the music, the tempo, and the lyrics. One of my classmates, Walter Harris, was a piano player, and together we would improvise right off the top of our heads in mass meetings. That's how the Selma version of "This Little Light of Mine" came about. Our version was more upbeat and contemporary sounding than the traditional gospel version. Then when we got to the lyrics, I changed them, too. I was thinking about Selma's sheriff, Jim Clark, and so I sang, "Tell Jim Clark, I'm going to let it shine"' next I used the head of the state troopers, Al Lingo, and put him in the next verse. After that, everybody was calling for it in that order. I've been doing it that way for so long, I can't sing it the other way.

We also put the words from our struggle into "If You Miss Me from the Back of the Bus," a gospel song already turned into a freedom song. We sang, "If you miss me from Hudson High and you can't find me nowhere, come on over to Selma High, I'll be studying over there." Sometimes we even made fun of the city officials in this song: "If you're looking for Jim Clark and you can't find him nowhere, come on over to the crazy house, he'll be resting over there."

As soon as the adults started participating, city officials established a 10:00 P.M. curfew for children. When we were coming home from mass meetings after the curfew, we did not want to get arrested. Most of the houses in the black community of Selma were raised several feet off the ground. If the police came by, we would slide under the houses and hide. We always had homes that we knew we could go to, and we always had lookouts. When the police left, somebody would whistle an all clear, and we would come out from under the houses.

From 1961 to 1965, youth carried the full load of the Selma Movement and had to make adult decisions. John Lewis, Worth Long, John Love, all these people had pulled this thing together with the youth. There were a few adults working right along with us from the beginning, like Mr. Anderson and Miss Carter, both teachers. During these years the Selma Movement got bigger and bigger, mostly because of the actions of young people. We were the ones passing out leaflets, organizing the boycotts, taking people to register to vote, singing at mass meetings, and risking our lives to do the work of the Movement. It took a long time before the adults of Selma really stood up.

Selma was a hard nut to crack. I felt so good when finally our black adults, like the teachers, started to stand up and started to march. But then they pushed the young people out of the way, because we were too militant and they had come up with another agenda and didn't need us anymore. I find it so strange now that people are writing stories just as if they were there from the beginning. The Movement was on its final stages by the time they stepped out, yet they've taken all the credit. All the young people, like my classmate Cleophus Hobbs, have been written out of the Selma Movement.

Bloody Sunday

March 7, 1965, "Bloody Sunday," is a day I will never forget. All throughout the week before, I had an uneasy feeling. The closer it got to the march, the worse I felt. I thought something bad was going to happen, but I didn't anticipate anything as bad as what actually did happen. I knew that Worth Long had been seriously beaten again at one of our protest marches. I was remembering the bombing in Birmingham that killed those four little girls. Of course, people in Selma, especially the young people, were very upset about the recent killing of Jimmie Lee Jackson; his death was the reason the march was planned in the first place, to give us youths a nonviolent outlet for our rage over his murder. We wanted to do more, to fight harder, because now we had to fight for Jimmie. I still had difficulty believing that white people would resort to murder just to keep things the way they were. At the same time, I wondered how many of us would have to die for freedom.

After the freedom marchers came from all over the country to join the Selma marches, Jim Clark started deputizing white men, just taking them off the street to have them patrol the city. A lot of these men were just plain rednecks who really hated black people. Now, as deputies, they had the authority to pretty much do anything they wanted, including beating up folks.

Before an earlier march, I had seen my godfather in a deputy's helmet walking down the street. I was taking a shortcut, coming through the alley to get to where the marchers were gathered. It hurt me so bad. All I could do was look at him and say, "Poppy?" He said he'd been told that it was every white man's responsibility to stand up for his country, and even though he felt it was wrong, he had to be there to keep from being ridiculed by the other white men. After he saw me, however, he just took his helmet off and put it down under his arm. He told me he just couldn't participate anymore after he saw me and retreated through the alley.

Anyway, I decided to play an auxiliary role on March 7. Movement activist Marie Foster asked me, "Will you be leading the line?" I responded, "No, Ms. Foster, not today." I walked from Brown's Chapel to the foot of the bridge, giving verbal updates to the captains of the march, and then returned to the church. I was standing there in front of Brown's Chapel, right where the steps begin, and all of a sudden there was an unusual stillness, just like before a storm. I was asking myself, *What's going on? What's happening?*

Then there was a sound like an earthquake. All I could hear was this rumbling. The next instant, people were everywhere, running and hollering, followed by white men on horses with billy clubs and cattle prods, just running over the people and beating them. Those white men came right into the black community, right up on the steps of Brown's Chapel. The media always say it happened at the foot of the bridge, but they didn't see the brutal beatings that happened in the city. Seeing so much bloodshed made me understand just how serious our struggle was.

Cleophus Hobbs told the story of a mentally retarded friend of his who went on the march. On the way to the march, his friend, catching the spirit of the day, was yelling, "Me want freedom, me want freedom." When Cleophus found him after the beating, the man was hiding under a house on Jeff Davis with a big gash in his head where the deputies had hit him with a club. When Cleophus tried to get him out from under the house, thinking Cleophus wanted him to keep demonstrating, the man began hollering, "Me no want no more freedom. Me no want no more freedom."

The following weekend Viola Liuzzo, who came down to participate in the March to Montgomery, was killed. A young man I grew up with named Leroy Moton was riding in the car with her. He was really skinny, dark-skinned, and tall, so we called him Snake. As we heard the story from him, he and Liuzzo had already made one trip to Montgomery and back carrying supplies. Since it was already dark, they didn't think going again would be a problem. Like most young people in Selma, Leroy was radical and didn't think first. Anyway, they were on the way back from their second trip when Leroy noticed that a truck was tailing them. They knew right away they were in for trouble. A car pulled up beside them, and the passengers started hollering racial slurs. The next thing Leroy saw was the barrel of a gun, then gunfire. The white men in the car kept shooting and then passed.

When the men in the car came back around to check on them, Leroy had to play dead. After they left he was able to hitch a ride home. I can't imagine what it must do to a person to be next to someone who was just killed and have to play dead. After telling his story, Leroy left Selma—had to be that night, because no one saw him after that. Since he was a witness to a murder, his mother was afraid for his life or any other kind of retaliation, and so he got out of Selma immediately. He's been back a couple of times, because he's trying to do a book. The last time I saw him was in Hartford, Connecticut. I was walking down Albany Avenue and walked right into him.

The Movement made me see just how vicious and ugly racism could be. It was a wake-up call. It seemed as if a light turned on inside of me revealing the injustice in how black people had been and were being treated. I was filled with a burning desire to help my people overcome this kind of adversity. Once in the Movement, I just worked hard. I believe part of the reason I participated so regularly and faithfully had to do with my church background, of having to go to church seven days a week and all day on Sundays.

After the Movement got under way in Selma, people in the black community experienced a sense of power, closeness, and self-worth that we had not known before. I saw how important music was in the freedom struggle and became a voice for freedom. I have been singing for freedom ever since.

Since the 1960s **BETTIE MAE FIKES** has filled numerous engagements singing songs of personal and political struggle. Her singing at mass meetings may be heard on *Voices of the Civil Rights Movement: Black American Freedom Songs 1960–1966* and *Sing for Freedom: Lest We Forget, Vol. 3,* both released in 1980. She has also recorded two blues CDs, *Blues Holiday* (2006) and *How Blue Can You Get* (2010). During the 1960s she sang with both groups of Freedom Singers and from the 1990s on she has performed with the revived SNCC Freedom Singers and has sung for and traveled with the national leadership group Faith in Politics. She returns to Alabama every year for the celebration of the March to Montgomery. Fikes has also been invited to sing at several Newport Jazz Festivals and at a number of events sponsored by the Smithsonian Institution. She is the mother of three children and a grandmother of four.

Bloody Selma

Prathia Hall

An experienced SNCC field secretary is horrified by conditions in Alabama and other civil rights workers' attitudes.

Early Organizing in Alabama

In early winter 1963, SNCC field secretary Bernard Lafayette was beaten and jailed in Selma, where he and his wife, Colia, had been working alone. Immediately afterward Forman came to Southwest Georgia and said, "Come on, Prathia, we need you in Selma." The members of the Dallas County Voters' League had been working there for ages; they were part of that longtime movement struggle. They had done some voting rights work, and small numbers of schoolteachers and other middle-class black people had been registered. League members also had filed some related lawsuits.

When Colia and Bernard Lafayette arrived in the early 1960s, they began work with high school students in the projects. I lived in the projects with a family as Bernard and Colia had been doing. The 1965 Selma Movement could never have happened if SNCC hadn't been there opening up Selma in 1962 and 1963. The later, nationally known movement was the product of more than two years of *very* careful, *very* slow work.

Alabama was extremely dangerous. For instance, in Gadsden the police chased a group of young protesters barefoot over a field, knocking them down and beating them. Here the police used cattle prods on the children's torn feet and stuck the prods into the groins of the boys. In Alabama there was a sadistic kind of joy in inflicting pain that I had never seen in Georgia.

Selma was just brutal. The threat of violence was constant. Civil rights workers came into town under the cover of darkness. We were blessed with the support and visits of people like Dick Gregory and James Baldwin. During one mass meeting, the church was surrounded by Sheriff Jim Clark and his men on horseback, displaying their instruments of brutality—batons, cattle prods, and guns. It was an extremely threatening atmosphere. The sheriff and police came into the church. Dick Gregory made some of his outrageously bold statements, addressing them directly, calling them names even though they had their guns drawn. His actions inspired courage, because Gregory made those kinds of statements and lived.

Bloody Sunday and Its Aftermath

On Bloody Sunday, March 7, 1965, I was at the Atlanta SNCC office when a call came from the church in Selma. Over the phone we could hear screams of people who were being attacked. SNCC immediately chartered a plane so that people could go to Selma right away. As the group was ready to leave, Judy Richardson said, "Wait a minute, there are no women in this group. Where's Prathia?" And so I went.

It was a very traumatic time for me. When we got there we saw what had happened. It was a bloody mess; people's heads had been beaten; they'd been gassed. Of course we held a rally. At the meeting people were angry; they, too, had been traumatized. One man stood up and said, "I was out on the bridge today because I thought it was right. But while I was on the bridge, Jim Clark came to my house and tear-gassed my eighty-year-old mother, and next time he comes to my house, I'm going to be ready." Everybody understood what that meant. People had lived their lives basically sleeping with guns beside their beds—that was just a part of the culture. These were people who were struggling to be nonviolent, who in their hearts and spirits were not a violent people, but they also had notions of self-defense.

The SCLC staff members were also a part of the meeting, and they were afraid that the anger would turn to violence. They began leading songs like "I Love Everybody." At one point I remember one of the SCLC staff saying, "If you can't sing this song, you can't see Jesus when you die." As a person who came to the Movement embracing nonviolence as a way of life, I was horrified: this view, I felt, was heresy.

I understood the anxiety that led to that statement, but to me it was like spiritual extortion. If a person has spent all of his or her life living and suffering in the expectation of seeing Jesus at the end, it is troubling to be told if you cannot sing this song right now, you will not be saved. In that particular moment the words did not ring true. Most people in the church were not feeling love for Jim Clark or any of the white Alabama authorities usually mentioned in that song. Folks were not feeling very loving, and they were not singing.

This was a theological crisis for me. I went into a period of very deep silence after that. I withdrew. I was deeply traumatized. I soon left the South. To me the March to Montgomery was a parade. I was not sure that I would ever return to the South. I did, however, go back that summer and worked in Mississippi with families who were desegregating the schools. When I finally did leave the South, I took with me the memory of the tremendous courage I had witnessed in the communities where I had worked, a courage beyond reason.

The biography of **PRATHIA HALL** can be found in an earlier piece, "Freedom-Faith," in part 4.

"Bloody Selma" © 2010 by Betty Hall

Playtime Is Over

Fay Bellamy Powell

A former member of the United States
Air Force becomes a soldier for freedom.

Bringing Malcolm to Selma

I had been working in Selma, Alabama, for a few months when we heard that Malcolm X was going to be speaking the next day at Tuskegee Institute about eighty miles away. It was early winter 1965. The staff delegated our newly elected project director, Silas Norman, and me to travel to Tuskegee to see if we could get to Malcolm and ask him to come to Selma to speak to the youth at Brown's Chapel. We both thought it would be a good idea to expose the young people to Malcolm's thinking and teachings.

Silas and I got more information on Malcolm's itinerary and then headed out to Tuskegee. Although the auditorium was filled to the rafters, we were able to get into the assembly where Malcolm was speaking and hear his lecture. Malcolm, seeming larger than life, spoke and taught as usual. He spent more time addressing questions after his speech than it took to give it, dealing thoughtfully with all questions, whether praise or criticism. Malcolm's actions suggested that he believed that when he put forth ideas, he should be willing to have those ideas critiqued or it wasn't worth the effort.

Several hours after the lecture and questions were over, Silas and I were able to speak to Malcolm and make our request. Malcolm responded immediately that he would be glad to come to Selma to speak with the children. He invited us to spend the night with him at Tuskegee's guesthouse on campus, promising to return to Selma with us the next morning. Joined by a couple of other people, we walked together across the campus to the guesthouse. The talking and discussion continued; it was a thoroughly enjoyable experience.

I asked Malcolm about a mutual friend. He responded that she was okay but that she needed to be here where I was, doing the work we were doing. I was more than a little surprised, because the word was that the Nation of Islam and Malcolm felt that our work in the South was totally irrelevant. Malcolm's opinion was an eye-opener for me and a pleasure to hear. It meant a lot to learn that this man, himself respected and admired by so many, myself included, also respected and admired the work I was doing.

Malcolm talked to us for another hour at the guesthouse before we went to our rooms. The wisdom, the knowledge of this man was truly something to behold. When he talked to us, little doors in my mind would literally just pop open; I could feel the impulses in my brain pulsating with energy. It was visceral and astonishing. Again Malcolm repeated his admiration for our work and for the Student Nonviolent Coordinating Committee.

The next morning Malcolm rode with a lady friend of his from Tuskegee to Selma in a two-seater red sports car. Silas and I rode behind them in our SNCC car. When we arrived at Brown's Chapel we parked in front; Malcolm unfolded his long, lean body from the tiny car and stood up next to it. He had on a New York winter coat and one of those brimless fur hats that he was fond of wearing in the winter.

A group of reporters from the United States and Europe were standing across the street. When they saw such an imperial person emerge from the car, they began to get agitated. They knew he was someone important, but they couldn't place him. You know how when you are used to seeing someone in uniform or on a particular job, you always recognize them in that situation, but nowhere else? Well, Malcolm was the last person in the world the reporters expected to see in the Deep South or at a civil rights mass meeting in Selma, Alabama.

We realized immediately that the reporters had not recognized Malcolm and walked quickly to the side door of the church to get inside before they did identify him. Just as the door was closing, the newsmen began to run across the street in our direction. We didn't allow them in, but told them he would be speaking to the young people later that morning in the chapel and they could speak with him at a press conference afterward. All the reporters went into the sanctuary and listened to Malcolm. Silas and I were on the podium with him while he spoke and had a clear view of everyone. Many of their faces became bright crimson as he talked about the essence of racism and bigotry.

Each morning Brown's Chapel would fill with elementary, junior high, and high school students. They were the core of the Selma Movement and took part in all the demonstrations. Usually these morning sessions were lively and noisy. On the day Malcolm spoke, although the church was packed with young people, there was no noise, no shuffling of feet, no coughing, no squirming. Only Malcolm's voice could be heard.

When Silas and I went to the small Montgomery airport to see Malcolm off later that day, we had another opportunity to talk with him. Malcolm said he and his new organization, the Organization of Afro-American Unity, were planning to come south and wanted to know if SNCC would work with them. This was a startling question to me, because when he was with the

Nation of Islam, I'd understood that he didn't approve of our nonviolence. Well aware of the respect so many SNCC people had for this man, Silas and I answered Malcolm's question with an enthusiastic "Yes!" and asked that he return in the not too distant future. Three weeks later, Malcolm was assassinated. That was a dream deferred.

My Road to SNCC

I came to SNCC after a stint in the U.S. Air Force, several years in New York City and San Francisco, and after attending business school. At that time, Harlem and San Francisco were great places for a single woman out on life's adventures. I was born and raised in Clairton, Pennsylvania, a small, segregated, steel mill town, where a great many of the men had come from Georgia, Alabama, and Virginia to jobs in the mill. Crime was so rare that most people didn't bother to lock their doors. There were no signs separating black from white, but local customs directed black residents to be served take-out only and kept us from sitting on the stools in the white-owned drugstore.

I grew up in a family of many strong, independent women and a few strong, independent men. My sense of self was intense, and my sense of being a strong, intelligent young woman was constantly reinforced by those around me. They were always telling me, "You can be what you want to be. You just have to go for it." They seldom talked about racial matters, injustice, or white people, but they did talk about being strong, being in charge of oneself.

When I was seventeen and working as a clerk in a black-owned drugstore, I picked up a *JET* magazine and read about Emmett Till, a child fourteen years of age who had been kidnapped, mutilated, and lynched by men who acted worse than any beasts of the field. Till might have been the brother of any one of us. There is no way to describe my feelings after reading that article. A heavy weight descended upon me, but not so heavy I couldn't bear the load. My spirit allowed me a glimpse of my future, saying, "Don't worry about this. You will have an opportunity to address this madness. You will assist in showing the world this face of evil."

At twenty-five I had these same feelings when I heard that a church in Birmingham had been bombed, killing four little girls. The spirit spoke to me again and said, "Playtime is over. Time to be about reaching for the source of power. Time to start working your way south, girl." This made me wonder, *What do I do? Where should I go? How can I play a part in the changes that will and should occur? What organization or group of people do I contact? How do I identify them?*

First I headed east and moved in with my play-cousin Vivian Morton in New York City. As it turned out, her husband, Lee Morton, was spending six months in Mississippi, helping to set up a SNCC print shop in Jackson. When he returned, he described the various civil rights organizations to me. I asked him, "Which of these organizations is the baddest?" He said, "SNCC." I responded, "Well, that's the one I'm going to join."

Soon after this conversation, my cousins gave a party for a number of SNCC people attending a meeting in New York. Twenty-five to thirty men and women showed up, and a good time was had by all. What was most striking to me was that I found myself surrounded by a group of highly intelligent, attractive, fun-loving yet serious, committed young women and men who were confronting dangerous situations on a regular basis. They were not beaten down or depressed, however; instead they were bubbling with energy, ideas, and enthusiasm for what they believed the future would be because of their efforts—and they partied hearty.

Not knowing I had already decided to join SNCC, several of the guests talked with me about going south. They told Ruby Doris Smith Robinson about me, and not long after that Ruby Doris called from SNCC's national office in Atlanta. She introduced herself and asked if it was true that I wanted to join SNCC and inquired about my skills and interests. When she asked where I wanted to work, I said wherever I was needed. She said someone was needed in Selma, Alabama, to keep the office open on a consistent basis. I agreed to go.

When I told my cousin who had been in Mississippi where I was going, he exclaimed, "You don't want to go there; that's an extremely dangerous place!" Then he went to his bookshelves, pulled down a copy of Howard Zinn's *SNCC: The New Abolitionists* (1964), and opened it to the section on Selma. I read it and it did put a little tinge of fear in my heart, but I was ready. The die had been cast. Fearful though it might be, I had to go forward. I had to face the beast of racism.

Alabama

Ruby made arrangements to bring me south. I arrived in Atlanta on New Year's Eve 1964, and around midnight John Love, the Selma Project director, arrived in Atlanta and drove me to the SNCC freedom house in Selma. On New Year's Day John took me to the SNCC office, where I immediately became the entire office staff: the manager, the secretary, receptionist, and typist, as well as the media specialist. SNCC's effort in Selma was geared toward voter registration, and it was a time of intense struggle. It was a tense environment and a totally new experience for me. Within days I was writing press releases, although I had never written one before. I was talking to reporters from around the globe who came into the office or called from various countries about the daily goings-on in Selma. We also had twenty-four-hour access to world news organizations via their toll-free lines, because they all wanted to know what was happening in Selma. Selma was what some of them called a "hot spot," and indeed it was that.

For me it was an experience unlike any other. The women and men of SNCC were an exceptional group of people, and this time the spirit said, "Hey, you are in the right place and with the right people." Within two months the Alabama staff chose me to represent the project at SNCC's annual meeting in Atlanta at Gammon Theological Seminary.

In Selma, SNCC was coordinating activities with the SCLC staff. SNCC and SCLC were conducting demonstrations two and three times a week, and field workers from both organizations were traveling the rural areas in the county, organizing. SNCC field secretaries would meet with the field staff of SCLC every weekday morning at 7:00 A.M. in the SNCC office, to make for a smoother working environment and so that each organization would know the areas where the staff of both organizations would be working. I continued to run the Selma office.

Shortly before the Selma to Montgomery March began, Jim Forman, Stokely Carmichael and I left Selma to go to Atlanta. We had decided we were not going to participate in the march, and along with other SNCC folk feared that there would be a knockdown, drag out assault by the police forces on defenseless people, which we did not want to witness. We did, however, hear the attack when another SNCC field secretary, Lafayette Surney, called us from a pay phone on the side of the Edmund Pettus Bridge. We could hear people screaming and sirens blaring; it sounded like a soundtrack from a war movie. Forman and Stokely became extremely upset and agitated and decided we needed to return to Selma. We arrived in Selma late at night taking back streets to avoid any run-ins with Alabama state troopers and were informed that there was not going to be a second march because SCLC would be served a federal injunction forbidding another march. Forman and Stokely both agreed that the injunction had to be broken and contacted Andy Young requesting an urgent meeting with Dr. King and other SCLC representatives. The meeting was held at about 3:00 A.M. I remember that Dr. King and Reverend Abernathy both had on similar blue silk pajamas with red trim. SNCC representatives argued that the community was outraged by the beatings and that there had to be a march that very day. They insisted that Dr. King call the U.S. attorney general and let him know SCLC was going to break the injunction and march. One of the SCLC staff got the attorney general on the phone and Dr. King went into another room to speak to him. We left the meeting with the understanding that SCLC would ignore the injunction.

The march took place that afternoon, March 9, 1965. James Farmer and Floyd McKissick from CORE, James Forman, Bob Mants, and Ivanhoe Donaldson from SNCC joined King, Abernathy, and Young at the head of the line of the thousands of marchers determined to make it to Montgomery. I was also at the front. When we marched across the Edmund Pettus Bridge, we were met by a phalanx of Alabama state troopers and directly behind them a sea of troopers' cars were lined up next to each other across the highway for as far as the eye could see. It was a rather amazing sight. The only way marchers could get to Montgomery that day was to climb on top of the troopers' cars and jump from car to car. Dr. King said a prayer, several others said a prayer, and then Dr. King said, "We're going back to the church." When Dr. King turned, the people at the front followed him, and the people in the back of the line began to scream and cry and ask what was going on, why were we turning back. But really, in all actuality, we were effectively cut off from proceeding that day and they did it without attacking us. I always wondered exactly what was said during that phone call to the attorney general and how the Alabama state troopers got organized and thought up the blockade so quickly.

Near the end of 1965, with SNCC's permission I decided to take a leave of absence from the Selma office to work in the field so that I'd have a better understanding of what that work entailed. I didn't want to leave the South without the experience of working in a totally rural environment, which was obviously more isolated and much more dangerous. I was not looking for more danger, but I really believed that I shouldn't do less than what I would ask others to do.

I went to Greene County, Alabama, with Cynthia Washington, the SNCC project director there, and three male staffers. In an isolated area about two miles off the main road, we found an old house that had been built by an eighty-year-old black man. It had two rooms, a wood stove, electric lights, and a well; we dug our own latrine. The rooms were too small to put beds in for five people, so we all slept at various angles on the floor in sleeping bags.

Every morning when we went out for breakfast, the sheriff of Greene County would be there waiting for us. He had let us know the first day we came in contact with him that he would be watching us. He told us that as long as we didn't bring any white people into the county to work with us, we would have no problems out of him. When a male SNCC worker who had a light complexion came to visit us, the sheriff stopped us because he thought the new worker was white.

Once, the three males on our project left Greene County to drive to Atlanta, leaving Cynthia and me in the county alone. That evening, we heard a knock on the door and opened it to find a young black man from a nearby farm standing in our doorway with a loaded shotgun. He explained that he knew we were there alone and that he had come to make sure we were safe. We assured him we were. He assured us we weren't, that he knew this county and the people in it; therefore, he would be spending the night on our doorstep with his gun at the ready. It was a beautiful summer night, and Cynthia and I talked with him for a long time. He showed us how to use his gun. He stayed there all night, outside our house, making sure we saw the next day. We gained real strength from the strong people in these southern communities.

Unfortunately, the three guys had an accident that totaled the project truck. Since it was impossible to work such a rural area without transportation, we closed down the Greene County project temporarily.

Atlanta: Nonviolence Was Not My Forte

After a little over three months in Greene County, I transferred to the national SNCC office in Atlanta and had another totally new experience. Being in Atlanta afforded me the chance to work with more people on a daily basis and see how the organization was formed and maintained. The printing presses and car repair were in the basement. We published our posters and newsletters and research materials and repaired our own SNCC cars. In the beginning I was Jim Forman's secretary. By this time I was also on the SNCC executive committee and attended other SNCC committee meetings. No one was taking notes, so I asked to record and transcribe meeting notes to have a record for posterity. The Atlanta office was now housed in a large office building with huge windows and carpets on some of the floors. I noticed that the field staff and even the staffers in the basement felt isolated from the central organization two flights up. I proposed putting together a staff magazine to bridge the gap. I called it the *Africanamerican* and produced the whole thing myself. It included staff members' speeches and poems, information about their activities, anything to make people feel connected to one another.

I also decided to participate in the local demonstrations. At my first Atlanta demonstration on the steps of the state capitol, a state trooper attempted to hit me with his stick and knock me down the stairs. Although this was a nonviolent demonstration, I immediately found myself locked in mortal combat fighting the trooper. Never in a million years would I have thought that I, Fay Bellamy, would be in the street fighting hand to stick with a policeman in the Deep South—or anywhere else for that matter. This incident showed me a side of myself I didn't know existed.

The next day a photo of this incident appeared in the local daily. When I arrived at Paschal's restaurant, one of our hangouts, people were applauding me and expressing pride that I had defended myself. I said to myself, *Maybe nonviolent demonstrations are not your forte, or maybe this was just an exceptional incident.* However, I was involved in another confrontation when a revolt broke out in an area of Atlanta known as Summerhill.

In the summer of 1966 a policeman shot a young black man, who made it to his mother's front porch, where the policeman followed and put a gun to the youth's head. The young man's mother intervened and successfully pleaded for her son's life. When the community of Summerhill learned of this incident, hundreds of people poured into the streets. I was at a SNCC central committee meeting when we heard about these events; many of us immediately left the meeting to go to Summerhill. Mayor Ivan Allen appeared and addressed the community, but his words only enraged the crowd further.

People began throwing things. The police began to chase people running from the area. I saw one white plainclothesman running after a thirteen- or fourteen-year-old child. I became alarmed when I noticed that the policeman had unbuckled his holster and had his hand on his gun. I caught up with the policeman and said, "Don't you dare even think about drawing that gun on that child." As a result, he and several other policemen grabbed me by the arms and legs, picked me up, and put me in the paddy wagon. As they were arresting me and carrying me to the wagon, a black policeman did pull my mini-dress down so I would be better covered.

The next morning I was waiting for arraignment in a holding area behind the courtroom. The jailer in this back room was a giant of a man, probably weighing about 350 pounds. He escorted each prisoner from the back room to the courtroom holding him or her by the arm so the reporters covering the rebellion could take his picture with each prisoner. When it was my turn, he grabbed me by the upper arm. As the two reporters were getting in position with their cameras, I told them not to take my picture. Of course, they ignored me and the jailer just held me tighter, pinching my arm. I told him he was hurting me, and he responded by putting even more pressure on my arm. I reached back with my other arm and hit him with all the power I could muster and with such force that he turned my arm loose and fell backward. Next, I punched one of the reporters; he hit the wall and slid down to the floor, his camera going in another direction.

Then I reached for the other reporter's camera, trying to protect my back at the same time.

While all this was going on I had the presence of mind to scream for dear life, because I knew where I was—in a southern jail. The last thing I wanted was to be isolated in that environment and possibly have someone do me real harm. I hollered our attorneys' names as loud as I could, "Len Holt! Howard Moore!" still punching and fighting, trying to keep this jailer off me. Other policemen entered and halted the fray. When I was finally taken to court, the jailer who had grabbed me had taken out an assault warrant against me. From these experiences I finally learned that being nonviolent is not one of my strengths. But I could also see that even if one cannot be nonviolent, there are still things one can do in a nonviolent struggle.

About Movement Women

In every rural area where we worked, strong women in those communities would rise up like cream rising to the top. They were the force within their communities. People whose names never appeared in the national press or never had documentaries made about them were the people who started what we now know as the Civil Rights Movement. They were the folks who remained in those communities when many SNCC people returned to their home states.

Within the organization there were the obvious gender disparities that would occur from time to time, but I don't remember women in SNCC bowing down before anyone. I learned that, as a woman, when we were in a large meeting that consisted of men and women, women had to take a different tactic in order to be heard by the men—but we dealt with it. If a meeting got rowdy, we women got rowdy right with it. Oftentimes when a woman made a suggestion, put forth a solution, or expressed a unique idea, the men could not hear her. In that same meeting a man would make the same suggestion, put forth the same solution, or express a similar idea, using almost the same wording, and he would be heard by most of the other men and women. That was the time to get rowdy, and to point out the contradiction and raise the question, which was done on many occasions.

Many of the women in SNCC sincerely believed it would be hypocritical to talk about fighting for the freedom of others and then allow yourself to be enslaved inside your organization. My assessment and experience with the women in SNCC was that they were exceptional. They did not feel less than anyone. They were strong women, and as women they certainly did not always agree with each other. The only thing required, be you female or male, young or old, was to be about bringing something to the table. One had to come with something that made sense, and it didn't matter what your gender was. If it had not been for women and young people, there would have been no movement.

There were a few men in SNCC who felt it was not a woman's place to be a project director because it was "too dangerous" or "a woman would not be able to handle that kind of responsibility," but they were the few, not the many. Most men realized that women worked in the same dangerous areas of the country, on the same projects they did, and were involved in the same struggle for the exact same reasons: freedom of African people and poor people here and everywhere.

Lessons Learned

I really did land in the right spot. The women and men I met in 1965 and years after will always live in my thoughts. They were just magnificent. I was impressed by their intellect, their organizational capabilities, and their willingness to try the untried. From them, I learned organizing skills that have allowed me to participate in creating many new community organizations after the Movement.

I also learned an attitude toward struggle. In SNCC we would argue our points and ideas and sometimes arrive at conclusions and other times go away with the commitment to research the problem. Sometimes we found solutions; sometimes we found confusion. Even when we disagreed, we learned from each other and we didn't stop trying. In addition, I became aware that even in an organization where everyone is working for a common goal, you have to constantly struggle with internal organizational conflict—that's just the way it is. I believe it is wrong to rally against the oppressive forces without but become an oppressive force within. We in SNCC tried to prevent that.

Our organization was a mixture of the young and the old, but the discussion never hinged on how old or young you were, but on what you had to offer. SNCC no longer exists except in our hearts and minds. But for many of us our work continued, just in different forms.

Along with other sixties activists, **FAY BELLAMY POWELL** helped found several organizations: Radio Free Georgia (WRFG-FM 89.3), an independent, nonprofit radio station in Atlanta, Georgia; the National Anti-Klan Network (now known as the Center for Democratic Renewal); the Fund for Southern Communities; and the We Shall Overcome Fund. At WRFG she was producer and host of *Inside and Out*, an on-air program of local, national, and international news, interviews, and jazz for twenty-seven years. In the early seventies she worked at the Institute for the Black World, a black intellectual think tank, when it was under the direction of Vincent and Rosemarie Harding. She worked with the entertainment management firm David M. Franklin and Associates for more than thirty years. She is a photographer and a writer. Recently she has written a collection of short stories about her early life from a child's perspective titled *Being Me Is a Gas*, which she plans to self-publish in paperback and spoken word.

Captured by the Movement

Martha Prescod Norman Noonan

Defying her parents to join the Movement, a black University of Michigan student struggles with her fears.

"You Don't Know Those White Folks"

The Movement came and got me, at least it seemed that way. When I was still in high school, I encountered picketers supporting the southern sit-in movement at the downtown Woolworth's in my hometown of Providence, Rhode Island. I didn't know anything about the sit-ins—or picketing, for that matter—but I surmised it meant something good for black people and did not cross the line. The following year, in a household where the television was rarely turned on, I happened to see an episode of an NBC *White Paper Series* on the Nashville sit-in movement. It touched me so deeply that I wanted to attend Fisk University to be close to the Movement, but my parents had already chosen the University of Michigan.

Michigan was my mother's alma mater. Her father, a barber in Ann Arbor, had died when she was nine. She had put herself through college while helping to support her family and still graduated at the age of seventeen in 1924. She wanted me to attend Michigan, pledge the same chapter of the sorority that she had joined, and ideally finish law school there as well. (My mother was certain that she and some of her black law school classmates had been unfairly failed halfway through their program at Michigan's School of Law.) Determined to make my educational road easier than hers by paying all my college expenses, my mother found a job and moved to Michigan by herself at the start of my junior year in high school in order to meet the two-year qualification period for the lower in-state tuition.

I reluctantly acceded to my family's wishes and went to Michigan in the fall of 1961, certain I would be light years away from the southern movement. Yet the Movement found me there as well. Crossing the center of campus, "The Diag," several weeks after I'd arrived, I heard a speaker describe a group that had fought discrimination at the university. He seemed to look directly at me when he called for people to sign up. I did, becoming a member of VOICE, a fledgling Students for a Democratic Society chapter, and found myself surrounded by intense political discussions about students' roles in social change.*

A few months later, the Methodist Student Center Guild House, which I had joined for religious purposes, sponsored a luncheon talk by Curtis Hayes, a SNCC worker from McComb, Mississippi. He told the story of the courageous movement there. Meeting a civil rights activist face-to-face who was about my same age increased my desire to be a part of the Movement tenfold. A few months after that, SDSer and Michigan alum Tom Hayden, fresh from the movements in Mississippi and Southwest Georgia, returned to speak about his experiences. Talking with me at the VOICE office after his presentation, he echoed Curtis's sentiment that I should become involved in the southern movement. All these contacts left me almost giddy with the idea that someone my age could take action that might change the overall racial situation in the United States.

I was completely captured when I attended a joint SNCC/SDS conference at the University of North Carolina at Chapel Hill in the spring of 1962. During the scheduled sessions SNCC folk told stories of struggle interspersed with freedom songs. In between sessions, SNCC workers talked to me about Miss Ella Baker's ideas of becoming a catalyst for change in the development of a radical grassroots mass movement in the Black Belt South; building "vehicles of power" was the term they used. If black people won the vote in these areas, they could change national politics by unseating the powerful Democratic representatives who consistently blocked liberal legislative efforts, especially those relating to civil rights. Applying pressure in the Deep South was a strategic way to reshape the national political landscape. I was immediately convinced of the logic and practicality in this vision and was also attracted by the welcoming spirit of the SNCC activists. I felt I had found my real home and my real life in this community, where

* Along with classmate Jill Hamberg, I also spent quite a bit of time in the VOICE office typing stencils of SDS materials to be mimeographed, including Tom Hayden's pamphlet on the early Movement, *Revolution in Mississippi,* and early versions of *The Port Huron Statement.*

it was the norm to be black, political, and radical. I left determined to join the southern Freedom Movement.

My parents had other ideas. Well educated themselves, they had made tremendous sacrifices to provide me with an even better education and more exposure in the face of a major family disaster. In addition to living apart for two years to be able to afford sending me to Michigan, they had supplemented a scholarship my mother arranged for me at Lincoln School, an all-girls Quaker school in Providence. This came at a time when my father, an optometrist, had lost his sight and income, making my mother the major family breadwinner. She supported us on a welfare worker's salary that barely met our basic needs.

Near the end of my freshman year in college, when I was seventeen, I told my parents I wanted to go to Mississippi to become a full-time civil rights organizer. In response, they developed a routine that they used to dismiss this plan. Every so often, when they knew I was listening, my mother would turn to my father and say, "Taffy, did you hear that Martha Susan wants to go to Mississippi?" "Yes, Alice," he'd answer, "I heard; but who in their right mind wants to go there?" "But that isn't all," my mother would continue. "She thinks she can help get Negroes registered to vote." "What!" my father would exclaim, his slight West Indian accent becoming more pronounced as his emotions deepened, "Negroes can't vote in Mississippi. They can barely walk down the street and live to tell about it!" Delivering the crowning blow, my mother would state, "What's more, she thinks she can do this civil rights work NONVIOLENTLY!" "Oh," they would both moan, shaking their heads at the total absurdity of such a plan. "She just doesn't know those white folks down there."

Instead of going south that summer, they insisted I stay in Detroit, attend summer school, and find some civil rights activity close to home. Under age, I acceded and randomly chose two summer classes at Wayne State University. As it turned out, both classes were taught by local radicals, Seymour Faber and George Rawick.[†] Both were members of a group called Facing Reality, led by the West Indian intellectual activist C. L. R. James. I left these classes every day breathless, my mind filled with stories of community activism and of great historical social change.

Before I identified any local activity, SNCC field secretary Bernard Lafayette contacted me, explaining that for the first time SNCC was sending field secretaries north to raise money and that he had been assigned to Detroit. Almost every day after summer classes, I met with him; former Freedom

[†] Faber later became a member of Detroit Friends of SNCC. Rawick later put together a multivolume collection of slave narratives and wrote the introductory volume, *From Sundown to Sun-up.*

Rider Elizabeth (Slade) Hershfeld; and a small, pretty radical group of SNCC supporters. Most of the white members were children of leftists; many of the black members later became central figures in the Detroit-based League of Revolutionary Black Workers and other movement formations. In the summer of 1962 they were reading about and aiding groundbreaking activists like Robert Williams and Mae Mallory from the NAACP chapter in Monroe, North Carolina, whose members chose to display weapons to prevent attacks by white mobs. Informal discussions of all kinds of protest movements in the United States and abroad were held on the way to Friends of SNCC meetings and when we socialized afterward.

At the end of the summer, our fund-raising and publicity efforts culminated with a mass rally featuring a very pregnant Diane Nash giving a speech titled "My Baby Will Be Born in Jail." That Bernard, a minister and excellent speaker himself, chose to focus our work and public attention on Diane reinforced for me the important role women played within early SNCC and how powerful the women were who had cast their lot with the organization. By that time I had heard Miss Baker's ideas treated like gospel at the Chapel Hill conference. While doing support work, I had relayed the bravery of Ruby Doris Smith in the Rock Hill jail. My family had hosted Brenda Travis, who in 1961, at sixteen, had the courage to participate in pioneering demonstrations in McComb, Mississippi, and remained active even though the authorities had sought to dampen her spirit by sending her to reform school. I had seen Diane's confrontation with the mayor of Nashville in the NBC *White Paper Series* and knew she had played a major role in keeping the Freedom Rides going after the first two buses were bombed.

Our little group accompanied Diane through a full schedule of events in the city; then she flew to Albany to be with her husband and delivered her daughter less than twenty-four hours after she left Detroit. Her ability to heighten the level of her activism during her pregnancy was a forceful statement to me that being a woman placed no restrictions on full and significant participation in the Movement.

Back in Ann Arbor for my sophomore year, I spent almost all of my waking hours in the Student Activities Building doing support work for SNCC along with Helen Jacobson, Jill Hamburg, Ralph Rappaport, and Sue and Laurie Wender. (Sometimes our little group would reconstitute itself into an ad hoc committee for other political purposes like peace demonstrations and support for various international causes.) Now there were two civil rights veterans on campus: Tom Hayden had returned to pursue a graduate degree, accompanied by his wife, the former Sandra Cason, whom we called Casey. Encouraged by a letter from Bob Moses, aided by upperclassmen like Nancy and Andy Hawley,‡ who had collected food for aspiring voters in Fayette and Haywood counties in Tennessee two years earlier, our group sponsored a citywide food drive. We convinced Michigan State University students Ivanhoe Donaldson and Ben Taylor to drive the food to Mississippi. When they were arrested shortly after arriving in Clarksdale, we spent the winter raising bond money and generating publicity to get them out of jail.

That year we also hosted a concert for the newly formed SNCC Freedom Singers—Bernice Johnson, Rutha Harris, Cordell Reagon, and Chuck Neblett. Bernice and Rutha possessed especially strong voices; they exuded the power of movement activism. The concert was an overwhelming emotional experience for my parents and me. It was the first and only time in my life I saw my father cry. I believe the dream of freedom meant so much to him and to all our parents, who had to keep it suppressed to function in a racist world, that when it burst forth from the music he could not contain his feelings. At that moment I think he also knew that the pull of the southern freedom struggle was greater than my family's hold on me and that he would lose the battle to keep his only child safe, and not just from southern racists. Among other things, my parents had been active in the Progressive Party: my father, a naturalized U.S. citizen, was threatened with deportation and family friends were called before HUAC (House Un-American Activities Committee).

Hoping that someone else could convince me I could be of greater service to the Movement with a professional degree, my mother somehow arranged for me to meet Judge Constance Baker Motley in New York City. Motley had a stellar civil rights record that included working on *Brown vs. Board of Education*. This plan didn't work, however. The same weekend that Judge Motley graciously invited me to breakfast at her home, New York Friends of SNCC held a concert at Carnegie Hall, which only strengthened my connection to the Movement and my sense of alienation from a traditional middle-class path. Even though my parents had made it clear I would no longer be welcome at home if I went south, I left at the end of the school year. My roommate, Denise Nicholas, who went south the following year, was the only one there to wave good-bye.

"You're in the South Now, Baby"

During the times I was in the Deep South working for SNCC, I was always scared—terrified, actually. Nothing awful happened to me directly, but the realities of violent southern racism surrounded all of us every day. Dealing

‡ Nancy Hawley later became one of the six editors of the well-known guide to women's health *Our Bodies, Ourselves* (1973).

with the fear was difficult for me, but almost as hard was acting as if I weren't afraid. SNCC workers then, especially field workers, appeared fearless and cool, very cool. They communicated mostly through gestures and succinct conversation. Constant chitchat is like breathing to me, so much so that even when I am alone, I keep up a steady stream of conversation with myself out loud. Often, on southern SNCC projects, I felt as if I were in the middle of a Western movie, straining to keep quiet and remain calm and expressionless so that I wouldn't be seen as a babbling, whining East Coast greenhorn.

I rode from Atlanta to the SNCC 1963 summer orientation in Southwest Georgia with Casey Hayden, who had left Ann Arbor a few months earlier; Ruby Doris Smith; and a white female volunteer. The volunteer kept asking question after question. Ruby Doris answered them all with the same refrain, "You're in the South now, baby."

By then familiar with the SNCC way, I resisted the temptation to ask the many similar questions on my mind and mimicked Casey's and Ruby's expression of friendly, mild annoyance. Ruby's refrain ran through my mind over and over; each time it was followed by the inclination to run back to Ann Arbor rather than face the dangers ahead. This desire grew stronger as we drove up to the gates at the Koinonia farm in Sumter County, Georgia, where the summer orientation was to be held. The entrance sign was riddled with bullet holes. "They don't like integration much around here," Ruby intoned, and I wondered if I would make it through the first week.

Southwest Georgia Project director Charles Sherrod guided the orientation, emphasizing that we were not to think of ourselves as knowledgeable or as leaders because of our college education. We were there to assist in a struggle rooted in the community, and community people were to determine the nature and direction of their movement. We were to listen, learn, and take our lead and direction from them.

A day or two into the orientation, everyone on the Southwest Georgia staff looked especially troubled as they withdrew from our larger group to hold a closed meeting. I tagged along. Through tightened lips a staff member reported that a black girl in her early teens from the county had been raped by thirteen white men. One was the Sunbeam bread delivery man, who had left his truck parked in front of the young woman's house during the ordeal. She had died of infections resulting from this attack. It took all my energy to suppress a cry of shock and to take on the resigned but pained expression of the staff members planning a campaign to have the men arrested even though they knew such efforts would be futile.

My fear and understanding of racism took on another dimension. From the SNCC stories I'd publicized and from the little information I'd gleaned from the news, I had left Michigan with the notion that excessively cruel rapes and lynchings like Emmett Till's were things of the past, albeit the recent past of the 1950s. Being the victim of such deadly and excessive brutality myself now loomed in my mind, and I was struck with how brave black people in these communities had to be to live with incidents like this rape as part of the fabric of daily life in the Deep South.

Well, I thought, *You have faced fearful situations before. If you reach back, maybe you'll find something to help you.* When I was six years old, my parents moved into a former funeral parlor in an all-white neighborhood in Providence. We were not at all welcome. Other residents frequently threw stones through our windows, and once someone tried to set the house on fire. I understood quickly that I was fair game for taunts and occasional beatings from the older children, who also enjoyed reminding me that we were living in rooms where dead bodies had been kept.

There were two particularly frightening incidents. Late one night a man leaving the local bar entered our house drunkenly yelling epithets, urinating in our back hall, and shaking the door to my first-floor bedroom. Certain it was the ghost of one of the funeral home's former clients, I was paralyzed, unable to cry for help. A few moments later, the noise woke my parents and they chased the intruder out and cleaned up the hall. The other incident happened during the middle of a day when my father and I were out working in the yard. Another patron of the bar came into our yard brandishing a gun and drunkenly demanded over and over, "Get out of here, you goddamn niggers."

I tried to guide my father toward the house, but he stood his ground, informing the intruder, "This is my house and *my* property, and you can't tell me what to do here." Thinking that with his fading sight my father was unable to see the gun, and still trying to get us both inside the house, I whispered, "Daddy, that man has a gun." This made my father even madder. With his West Indian accent in full force, my father replied angrily, "I don't care what he has, he must leave my property this instant." I was certain that the intruder, still ranting and raving about "niggers in the neighborhood" and waving the gun, was going to kill us. Deprived of the frightened response he expected, though, he put the gun away and left. My father said nothing else, and we went back to our yard work. I didn't take any lesson about standing up to bullies from this—just that I never wanted to feel that close to death again.

Going to the white elementary school about ten blocks away every day in some ways took more of a toll than these two short incidents. I was never sure when the name-calling or attacks would happen. I didn't know when the teachers would accuse me of some phantom wrongdoing or ignore my raised hand. The first day of school my mother explained that I would face these kinds of difficulties, adding, "You're black; this is America. Get used to it." In fact she was the first person I heard use the term *black* to refer to Negroes and to connect it to pride. She also warned me against responding to racial epithets with the corresponding ethnic ones. She said, "When they call you a dirty black nigger, don't call them a name back; that wouldn't be polite or Christian. You respond, 'Yes, I'm black and proud of it.'"

By the time I entered high school, as one of the school's two black students, I handled the discrimination I experienced there by thinking of the young women who were going through screaming mobs to integrate schools in the South at that time. I was ecstatic when college approached and the task of "representing the race," as we called it then, was over. Yet even at the University of Michigan, as one of fewer than three hundred black students on a campus of more than thirty thousand, there was continuing discrimination and stereotyping.

After learning of the rape in Sumter County, I revived my childhood habit of living and functioning with a low level of almost constant fear. When the orientation was over, I felt ready to go to work in Mississippi, but Sherrod maintained that Mississippi was too dangerous for northern black women, since Medgar Evers had just been killed there, so I stayed in Southwest Georgia and became part of the Albany Project.

There I met more movement heroines—Prathia Hall and the Christian sisters. Prathia had been arrested and shot, yet still remained in Southwest Georgia. Although only a few years older than me, she was a poised and an especially gifted orator, with spiritualism so strong that it was almost palpable. The Christian sisters, Dear and Joann, a few years younger than me, were already civil rights veterans of police brutality and had been to jail more times than they were old. In Albany both the heat and the music were incredible. The temperature was over one hundred degrees the first two weeks I was there. For the first time, I experienced being in the midst of the black community's intricate lining of hymns. Although I came from a musical and religious family, this was something new. I knew the words of the hymns, but this rendering was so intense that sometimes I would have to leave the meeting to get away from it.

One day we went to court and witnessed attorney C. B. King defending arrested civil rights workers. In a deep resonating voice, King rolled out his voluminous vocabulary, uttering one impressive legal phrase after another. "Uh, C. B," the judge had to say frequently, "would you break that down for us?" It was delicious. I gained new respect for my father's eloquence when he and King spoke on the phone. I'd asked King to plead my case with my parents, which he did quite persuasively. My father must have been even more persuasive, because when the conversation was over, King turned to me and said, "Go home, Martha."

My mother also had a way with words. At one point, after many of the civil rights workers in Albany had been arrested, those of us remaining took sanctuary in a church. Joann Christian's father and another relative, Monroe Gaines, sat out on the church steps under a light with rifles across their laps, one gentleman at the front entrance, the other at the side, to protect us from hostile white men circling the church at night.

In spite of disowning me, when my mother learned of the situation, she also moved to protect me. She contacted a high school associate, Neil Staebler, who had become a Democratic committeeman, and told him I was in danger. He put her in touch with a low-level official at the Justice Department. As the evening wore on, my mother talked her way up to Burke Marshall and finally to Robert Kennedy. When Kennedy assured her that he was looking into the situation and that no harm would come to me, she responded, "Well, I hope so, young man. I would hate to have to talk to your brother about this."

Just like Mr. Christian and Mr. Gaines, Sherrod and people on other projects practiced what I would term preventive nonviolence. Even those, like myself, who were committed both philosophically and strategically to nonviolence in this struggle, still moved to minimize attacks from white racists. We might share our demonstration plans with Albany's black gang members, who would position themselves between us and white onlookers. Out in the rural areas, we would ride around or live with the local black residents who usually carried weapons. In Albany and other places I worked, I noticed that most homes in the black community had rifles hanging over the mantel, for "hunting," I was told.

About a week after we left the church, I called over to the Mississippi Project and talked to Bob Moses. "Where are you?" he asked. "We've been waiting for you and Jean Wheeler." Jean was another summer volunteer from Detroit whom I had just met at the orientation. Sherrod, as he confessed later, had just thought up an excuse to keep the only two black women at the orientation on his project. Riding in the back of the bus, Jean and I immediately made our way to Greenwood. Sam Block and Willie Peacock met us at the Greenwood bus station in a black and yellow car and drove through the city at such a high speed I wondered if we would reach the office in one piece. All the way there I was thinking, "My mother told me not to come. My mother told me not to come." On the outside, though, I was quiet and tried to look relaxed. I was barely able to maintain my composure a few days later, however. We were in downtown Greenwood buying mimeograph paper when Peacock pointed out Bryan de la Beckwith, who had killed Medgar Evers at the beginning of the summer. Beckwith, walking across the street from us, was being greeted as a hero by white people as he went by. "Oh, he lives here," Peacock explained off-handedly, "and Beckwith pretty much knows who all the civil rights workers are in this area."

Besides Jean and myself, no other northern women worked there, and along with three northern white male summer volunteers, we were the only novices. One of the men was sent home shortly after we arrived. Several staff members told me this was because his parents were associated with the Communist Party. The other two white volunteers rarely left the office that summer. They slept there at night and worked there during the day doing office work and taking affidavits. They never canvassed or organized in the black community. Near the end of the summer, SNCC photographer Danny Lyon, who is white, came to Mississippi. He took a photo of one of the men, Mike Miller, Bob Moses, and me talking to an unidentified couple in the small town of Ruleville. Usually that photo is captioned as if we were canvassing for voters. Actually we had stopped to ask directions. It was the only time I rode in an integrated car in Mississippi, and it was one of the few times Mike left the office. I suspect that since Bob was taking Danny around, which made the car integrated, he figured he might was well take Mike, too.

Rather than accompany small groups to the courthouse to try to become registered voters, the idea was to have a voter registration day near the end of the summer involving a large number of people at once. With George Greene's help and a map, I learned the various neighborhoods and made a street file, like the one I'd seen Democratic Party workers use in Ann Arbor, to avoid duplication of canvassing efforts. There were informational and training workshops on subjects like Mississippi politics and public speaking. Most evenings I was simply too tired to attend mass meetings.

I did go when about twenty SNCC workers were released after serving sixty days in Parchman Penitentiary. Deprived of mattresses, without heat when it was cold, beaten and abused, they were in rough shape. Some were running fevers, others were just worn out; Lawrence Guyot, usually robust, was as thin as a rail. In spite of their condition, everyone walked to the mass meeting from the office. All the way there, people came out of their houses and clapped in a moving tribute to these civil rights heroes.

On another day, Mrs. Hamer came to the office to dictate her affidavit about her arrest and beating in Winona. Other younger female civil rights workers—June Johnson, Annelle Ponder, and Euvester Simpson—who worked out of the Greenwood office, had been arrested and beaten at the same time. Mrs. Hamer's telling of the story was so moving that all activity ceased in the office, her extraordinary strength and determination inspiring us all. (Annelle and I share enough similar facial and behavioral characteristics that people would frequently ask if we were sisters. I would be extremely flattered to think I had anything in common with such a great civil rights heroine.)

There was a small church congregation that met in a small room at the front of the office. They often sang pleadingly, almost in a moan: "Shine on me. Oh, shine on me. I wonder will the lighthouse shine on me." After hearing this song, whenever the condition of black people in this country and our world comes to mind, I think of it in those words—I wonder will the lighthouse ever shine on us.

Hostile white men regularly drove by the office with their guns hanging out of the car, so my heart was in my mouth every time I walked out of the office to canvass in Greenwood, not knowing if this would be the time one of those men would raise his rifle and shoot. Once I went to canvass outside Greenwood at a plantation that looked as if it had been plucked from the history books—big, white-columned main house and off to the back and side a row of small, unpainted cabins, some on stilts, a common type of structure in the South. Near the end of our time there I went into one of those houses up on stilts. Inside there was a small central stove and hardly any furniture. I found myself talking with a young woman my age with a fretful baby. "Is the baby not feeling well?" I asked. "No," she answered, "I think my baby has pneumonia for the third time." "Oh," I said chitchatting along, "what did the doctor say?" "I didn't go to the doctor, this time," she responded. "The boss-man wouldn't allow it, since I'd already gone twice, but the baby seems even sicker this time." My sense was that she had pursued all her options and there was a good chance her baby would die and that there wasn't anything she could do about it. Overwhelmed, I left quickly and went around to the back of her house and vomited, my head spinning from the reality of the plantation owner's heartlessness and filled with thoughts of generations of black babies denied such basic care and their mothers' pain. Just as with the Sumter County rape, I gained a deeper understanding of the horrors of racism. I imagine that I told the veteran staff members and they arranged some kind of medical care, but it is the house, the mother, and the baby that have remained etched in my memory. It gives me great sorrow to know that same kind of callousness, exercised on an individual and collective level, means that in communities here and all over the world, black mothers still lose their children to hunger, preventable diseases, and unnecessary violence.

The mass voter registration day was remarkable; more than three hundred people came out to go to the courthouse. Quite a few members of the press were present, and the day proceeded without incident. The only concessions to fear that I noticed among other SNCC workers that summer were that there was a lot of Pepto Bismol around and that Bob and some of the other well-known staff members were careful not to live in one place too long. At the end of the summer, most of us went north for the March on Washington. We set up our own pickets at the Department of Justice and sat in places at the front of the march that had been reserved for people coming from Mississippi. Although I was impressed with the history-making turnout, I felt the march was too polite, too restrained to reflect the hard struggle we were experiencing.

I stayed for a short stint of fund-raising on the East Coast, which included a stop in Providence, where my high school prom date, Allan Noonan, and Cliff Monteiro were sorting and packing a truckload of food to go to Mississippi. Then I went to Detroit, hoping to reconcile with my parents. Shortly after I arrived, my mother collapsed and was hospitalized. As a result, I did not return to Mississippi, but stayed at home and took classes at Wayne State again, this time purposely selecting wonderfully relevant classes on black literature and history with the campus's most radical professor, David Herreshoff, and an exciting course on Reconstruction with a young southern historian, Charles Dew. I got involved in Friends of SNCC again. Women like Dorothy Dewberry, Peggy Frankie, Martha Kocel, and Judy Quick—along with photojournalist and future SNCC worker Francis Mitchell—were the backbone of this slightly more mainstream, more campus-based group. In preparation for the summer of 1964, we successfully lobbied the Michigan Democratic Party's convention on behalf of the MFDP, making our state's party the first to support the MFDP.

I decided not to go south for the summer of 1964 for two reasons: I didn't understand the logic of the Mississippi Summer Project, and I realized if I took summer classes, I could finish college in December. I had expected the summer project would expand, not change, the composition of the staff—involving more black southern college students from Mississippi especially—rather than recruitment of large numbers of white northern college students. Things were still tense with my parents, and I hoped to improve them through fulfilling one more of their major wishes. So I went back to Ann Arbor; signed up for classes, including one with senior historian Dwight Dumond on the post–Civil War period; and spent most of the summer buried in my books.

At the end of the summer I went to Atlantic City, found a place on the floor in a room with some other women at the Gem Hotel, and picketed on the boardwalk. I went to the meeting in the church where the MFDP delegates heard the heads of various national organizations, like the National Council of Churches, urge acceptance of the two seats proposed by the Democratic Party. Some of these speakers, all men, were so ashamed of their position that they looked down at the floor while they spoke. When Mrs. Hamer and other female MFDP delegates responded and schooled the national civil rights leaders on the meaning of democracy, it was a particularly sweet moment. The delegates voted against such small representation.

I left elated that the delegates had not caved and that our small group of college students and Mississippi sharecroppers had put the issue of black voting rights at the top of the national agenda. Despite my earlier misgivings about the summer project, I had to recognize that in the course of a year, the formation of a statewide organization challenging the seating of the white Mississippi delegates at a national convention represented so much triumph over Mississippi's racial terrorists, so much progress over the previous summer's mass voter registration day—accompanying three hundred people to the Greenwood courthouse—that I could only feel joy.

With the kind of organization the MFDP had put in place, I didn't think it mattered whether the Democratic Party recognized it or not. Mississippi's black residents unified inside or outside of the Democratic Party could have a great influence on politics in Mississippi and the nation. (I do remember hearing some talk that once rejected by the Democratic Party, MFDP members might form an independent party.) Because of the life situation and views of the people who made up the MFDP, I thought the organization could be a true radicalizing force in politics.

After Atlantic City I returned to Ann Arbor, finished my classes, and attended the January graduation. Thurgood Marshall was our commencement speaker. I began working in Alabama a month later.

"I Love Everybody"

The Alabama Project in the winter of 1965 was quite similar to the Mississippi Project I'd worked on a year and half earlier. The staff was all black, almost completely southern, and many were Selma residents, including some of the young people who had been active since 1961. Shortly afterward, a number of people from the Mississippi staff arrived, mostly northerners, some if not all expressing the desire to work in a nonintegrated situation and to keep the Alabama Project all black. Some stayed only a short while, but others became permanent members of the Alabama staff. Two northern white couples and a single white guy, all somewhat oblivious to the project's racial climate, also came and lived in the Selma freedom house, listening to Woody Guthrie records at night and working wherever they were accepted during the day. That summer more black students from the North and South joined the project.

Just as in Albany and Greenwood, everybody worked hard. Some people set up projects in the adjoining counties—Lowndes, Wilcox, Sumter, and York. Others like myself organized one of the five wards in Selma where we held ward meetings and continued the ongoing task of taking people to the courthouse to try to register to vote. In one ward, black workers at the Pepsi plant wanted to organize a union, which involved secret meetings with the AFL-CIO representative from Montgomery, who slipped into Selma under the cover of darkness. The ladies in my ward petitioned for a streetlight and sought employment at Dan River Mills in Selma. Shortly before I left Alabama, we had launched a county-wide effort to take poverty funds out of the hands of Selma's white city officials.

If the Alabama Project's money ran short, which happened frequently, there would be no electricity or hot water in the Selma freedom house. Even with water and electricity there was, of course, no air conditioning in the summer and only small space heaters and donated electric blankets in the winter. Still, I counted myself lucky because the freedom houses out in the counties often lacked indoor plumbing of any kind. On the other hand, no regular arrangements were made for our meals in Selma. Stretching $9.64 to cover personal needs and a week's worth of food was no mean task. On occasion people in my ward like Reverend Echols, Miss Thomas, or members of the Young family would invite me to dinner; sometimes I was so hungry that I found excuses to visit them shortly before mealtimes.

During one of the first weeks I was in Selma, I rode out to Gee's Bend in Wilcox County for a night meeting with four or five members of the Selma Project, all men. Willy Squire, who raced cars on the weekend, was driving his Pontiac Le Mans, which in those days was a muscle car. In the car the fellows talked about how ordinary white men, including the local police, did not go into Gee's Bend at night unless invited. Most of the families in the Bend were named Pettway, and the Pettway men had a reputation for being mean. Not far from our destination, we passed a state trooper, who put on his siren and pulled out after us. Squire stepped hard on the gas and flew down the dirt road. I could hear my heart pounding. *This is something that only happens in the movies. Who runs from the state police?* I thought. I wanted to scream, "This is not a good idea. We're going to get hurt when he and his buddies catch up with us." Aware that the other people in the car were closely observing me to see how I would react, I worked my face into its calm position and just stared out the window as if not much was going on. When we arrived at the beginning of Gee's Bend, the trooper dropped back just as if we had crossed the state line. "Oh," Squire said, "I didn't know it worked for the state police, too." All that on a humble I thought. Evidently my stoicism was deemed appropriate, because after that I was one of the few people Squire asked to accompany him when he drove out into rural areas.

Another night I went out into Dallas County with Mrs. Amelia Boynton as part of the effort to have poor people control federal poverty funds. I was supposed to do a short tutorial on poverty at a meeting. When I asked the farmers and sharecroppers in attendance, "What is poverty?" Someone answered, "Poverty is not having enough to meet your basic needs for food, housing, and clothing." I went on to my next question: "Why are people poor?" Another person responded, "Because someone steals their labor." This, of course, was not the answer I expected. My text was geared toward disabusing the attendees of the stereotypic view that the poor are lazy, and so forth. So, winging it, I asked, "Who steals someone else's labor?" Then I received a ten-minute description of the crisscrossing of economic and political power in the county along with how these people were related to one another by blood and through marriage. That was the last time I attempted to teach any kind of political education class in Alabama.

In Alabama we worked through one murder after another, regularly passing the locations where people had lost their lives: Rev. James Reeb, killed in front of the bar near Walker's Café, where we often ate; Jimmie Lee Jackson, who actually died at the black hospital in the middle of Selma; Jonathan Daniels, out in Hayneville, where we went with people to the courthouse; Viola Liuzzo, on Interstate 80, the highway we used to travel back and forth from Selma to Lowndes or Montgomery; and Sammy Younge, at a gas station next to the Greyhound bus depot over in Tuskegee, where we went to relax and party. In fact when I was regularly going to Selma by bus from Tuskegee, before Sammy was killed, students told me not to even walk on the sidewalk in front of that gas station, because the person there held such a deep hatred for black people.

During this period there were ongoing demonstrations in Selma and Montgomery. Some of us on the Selma staff went over to Montgomery several times when Tuskegee and Alabama State students were demonstrating with assistance from the Atlanta office, mostly in the person of our executive secretary, Jim Forman. Once I went because students from the University of Michigan had come down to support the Tuskegee students. (The two schools had some kind of formal connection.) A lot of the members of the Ann Arbor Friends of SNCC chapter and SDS chapter on campus were in this group. I stayed and visited with them until it was clear that the police were ready to charge. The Montgomery police were on horseback and had long night sticks, like polo mallets. Before making arrests, the police rode through the demonstrators in a figure-eight formation, beating people with these long mallets. I couldn't bear to watch, and many of us on the Alabama Project had sworn off demonstrating.

My friend Helen Jacobson, who had co-chaired Ann Arbor Friends of SNCC with me, was arrested that day and then let out in the middle of the night with several other white University of Michigan students. When they got in the car sent to pick them up, they were surrounded by about ten white men, who began beating on the car with sticks and bats. Helen remembered that in our conversation earlier in the day I had told her to seek shelter with a black family if a situation like this arose. She shouted to the driver to gun the car and head back toward the black community. Closely pursued by the attackers, the students stopped at the first house they came to, and the residents took them in and kept them safe until daybreak.

Most of SNCC's Selma staff pretty much ignored the increasingly large demonstrations in Selma, though sometimes when we canvassed we would pass out SCLC's leaflets announcing the demonstrations. More often we joined the crowd that would gather in front of Brown's Chapel during the times the city police would not allow marchers out of the black community. People remained in front of the church, praying and singing all day long. One of the songs that rang out frequently was a traditional gospel song with the words, "I love everybody. I love everybody. I love everybody in my heart. I love everybody. I love everybody. I love everybody in my heart." The next verse is "You can't make me doubt it. You can't make me doubt it." Often when Chief of Police Jim Clark came to the line, the young people would lead off this song adding a verse, "I love Jim Clark. I love Jim Clark," whereupon the chief would beam. There was a rumor circulating that Jim Clark had a black girlfriend who lived in the housing projects that surrounded Brown's Chapel. If some of the cheekier young people were present, they would sing the next verse putting in the girlfriend's name, and Clark would turn beet red.

We had an interesting relationship with the city officials in Selma. The SNCC office was directly across the street from the building that housed the city hall, police station, and city jail. When our paths crossed, Mayor Smitherman or Sheriff Clark might greet us in a friendly fashion: "How ya'll doing?" They did see us frequently and followed us around now and then. Some of us had their home numbers. I kept director of public safety Wilson Baker's number with me all the time and actually used it one Saturday night. Visitors to the project from Latin America offered to take a few of us out for dinner to thank us for showing them around Selma and discussing the history of the Movement with them. I had heard that Dr. King had integrated the Holiday Inn and so suggested we go there, not thinking about the fact that it was Halloween and probably not a good night to push for integrated service. After we placed our order, everybody else in the room disappeared and two angry white men from the bar entered the dining room and began harassing us. Everyone in the group thought we should leave, but reluctant to defer to the hecklers and not wanting to give up a meal that did not come out of my $9.64, I insisted on staying. So I called Baker at home, saying simply, "We're having some trouble over here at the Holiday Inn." He immediately sent over two squad cars. When the police came, our food appeared and the troublemakers went back to the bar. We ate; I think I ate two entrees—my food and the food of one of my companions who was too nervous to eat. The police in the squad cars waited until we finished and then escorted us back to the freedom house.

Even with the police present, there was so much tension that evening that I decided for the rest of my time in Alabama I would confine most of my socializing to the black community. On Saturdays staff out in the counties would return to Selma, and we might go hear Bettie Fikes sing at the Elks Club, two doors down from the office. Her incredible voice was both very soft and very strong, and she had her own style, which permeated the sound of the Selma Freedom Chorus that she founded and led. She was one of the few brave souls who had started her activism in high school years earlier and still remained active with the Selma Movement.

Other nights we might go and play the jukebox at the Chicken Shack or travel over to the Elks Club in Tuskegee. Sometimes on the weekends people would have fun playing the dozens. I gained great admiration for Fay Bellamy, who had served in the military, when I saw her frequently outplay the men. Listening to these exchanges, I learned a whole new vocabulary. I also enjoyed the evenings at the freedom house when we had enough energy left from the day to talk and get to know our brothers and sisters in struggle. There I began a lifelong friendship with Gloria Larry House, a black graduate student from the University of California at Berkeley. When she first arrived in Selma, dressed professionally and speaking in soft, cultivated tones, I wagered that she wouldn't be able to take more than a month of our rough-and-tumble existence. But she was a lot tougher than she looked and worked out in Lowndes County long after I left Alabama. Bringing an international perspective and a familiarity with political literature, Gloria played a major role in defining SNCC's nationalism and globalism, particularly our opposition to the Vietnam War.

It was also a very romantic time. With so much intensity, purpose, and danger in our lives, relationships seemed that much more beautiful. I got to know my first husband, Silas Norman, there. Endowed with a wonderful speaking and singing voice, a leader of the Paine College sit-in movement in his hometown of Augusta, Georgia, he had left his PhD studies in medical microbiology at the University of Wisconsin to join the Alabama Movement, eventually becoming the state project director. These formidable qualities were not the main reason I was initially attracted to him, however. Really, it was because he was the only one on the project, male or female, who did not drive at breakneck speeds (practicing, they said, for when it was needed), so I always wanted to ride in the car he was driving.

After the Selma marches were over, the voting rights bill passed, federal registrars came to Selma, the Lowndes County Freedom Organization was up and running, and Sammy Younge was killed, I felt we were settling in to the protracted struggle my parents had often mentioned. Visions of building and linking the grassroots movements connected to SNCC were on the table along with making the most of the newly won franchise. Being in the middle of this history-making movement only made me want to study more history. I was accepted at the University of Alabama in Montgomery, but when I visited the campus I thought it wouldn't be safe for me, as a civil rights worker, to go to and from the college, which was located in a fairly deserted factory area.

I chose instead to enter the master's program at Wayne State, expecting to return to an active movement when my studies were complete. Leaving Alabama in the spring of 1966, I had no sense that SNCC was an organization in disarray; rather, I believed SNCC was growing in scope and organizational power.

"Vehicles of Power"

When I left the South, I also had no sense of being mistreated as a woman. Even looking back through a contemporary prism of a sharpened gender consciousness, I still see that time as one of the most liberating experiences in my life and treasure the sense of working hand in hand, side by side with my brothers in struggle. I was surrounded by strong, powerful female role models, who played significant and important movement roles and whom I hoped to emulate in some small way. I was treated respectfully by my male co-workers, including Stokely Carmichael, and encouraged to participate in all aspects of movement work.

I also had no sense of SNCC at any time, early or late, as the integrationist organization some have described either racially or politically. The organization I experienced was not just black run and black led; its projects and programs took place in the heart of the black community. That some people of other races stayed in this movement for years and that many people of other cultures joined at various times did not change the overall color and tone of the Movement for me. I saw it as a black Freedom Movement—in fact, as a southern black Freedom Movement, where the important decisions about the nature and course of our struggle resided with the residents of the black communities where we worked. It seemed just and right that southern black residents and southern black students should be in charge of this struggle. Northern and white participants, I believed, had a voice, but not a vote in this struggle. Ours was an auxiliary and supportive role.

I still identified with the people in these southern communities, and the high level at which they struggled gave me a sense of pride and empowerment. These feelings were not based in or accompanied by any sense of anger or hostility toward my white counterparts. In fact, the clear plan of action SNCC provided made those kinds of feelings disappear. I felt closely connected to the individual white SNCC workers who were also risking their lives and their futures, and I never stopped speaking to them or welcoming them into my home. To this day I don't know what the logic was that said it was necessary to break off relations with our white associates. At the same time, after spending so much time in white schools and white communities, I found myself more attracted to the projects with all-black staff.

I never thought that simple integration, just entering or joining American society, was our goal, even in the earliest days of the Movement. As college students we were poised to enter mainstream America, albeit on an unequal basis, but still with a guarantee of a certain level of success of economic security. Some, like Peacock, Silas, and Gloria, turned away from professional school to become activists. For me, the whole point of leaving the university, of joining with southern sharecroppers and domestic workers in such a dangerous battle, was to make radical social change, to build those "vehicles of power" Miss Baker talked about and help them coalesce into a mass movement in the Deep South.

Back home in Detroit, when I heard the "Black Power!" cry on television, it represented not a new direction for me but, rather, a catchphrase for what we had been doing all along: building vehicles of black power. Then in the era of black pride, as black people explored what the effects of living in a racist society had on our psyches, there did not seem to be anywhere near the same kind of widespread introspection on the part of white society or even among most white civil rights workers, exploring what inaccurate assumptions or harmful attitudes they might hold from growing up and living in a fundamentally racist society. When the women's movement emphasized the need for consciousness-raising and for women to meet with other women without men present, I expected a greater understanding of SNCC's position to have an all-black field staff. A significant number of our white co-workers did understand this, but in general the organization was—and still is—denounced for taking this position.

I married Silas Norman in 1967 when he was on the furlough given to soldiers with orders to Vietnam. Thankfully his application for conscientious objector status was approved and we started a family. When our first son was still a toddler, we decided to work with Sherrod's huge farming cooperative in Southwest Georgia. I changed my mind, however, during a preliminary visit to the farm when Sherrod took us to the main house and mentioned it had just been shot up. I did not want my child to grow up with the constant fear that I had known, and I didn't know if we had the right to risk his life as well as our own.

Silas and I both came to believe that we should return to the South with a professional skill level. Instead of moving to Southwest Georgia, we remained in the inner city of Detroit. Silas went to medical school, and after we had two more children I returned to school and finished my master's at Wayne State and began the doctoral program in history at the University of Michigan. My desire that my children not live in a fearful situation was not fulfilled, though. By the time our middle son reached high school age, living in the Detroit area turned out to be dangerous for everyone, but especially for young black men. Our sons have been harassed and attacked by police, held up by armed robbers, and present at random shootings. Someone shot into our home, and we all got used to hearing repeated gunfire every weekend. Most difficult has been taking our sons to the funerals of their friends and of the children of our friends knowing that there was no consolation for the slain youths' parents and that racism was the root cause of these deaths.

Aside from the friendships and connections made in struggle, I have maintained a tremendous admiration and respect for my SNCC colleagues and the thousands of black southerners who stepped forward to become a part of the Movement. Their actions removed from my thoughts and words forever all those stereotypical adages about how black people can't stick together, act in their own self-interest, or are too passive. I know I come from a community of people, especially those in the Deep South, who out of necessity and choice have been extraordinarily brave.

Canvassing in black communities in the South, when I was asking, "Would you like to try to register to vote or come to such-and-such meeting?" the unspoken questions were: "Are you ready to lose your job, go to jail, or get beaten up? Oh, do you know that your house might be bombed and ultimately you might lose your life, right?" There were people, thousands of them, who actually answered "Yes" to these terms, some of them earning twelve dollars a week or less, some living in homes with walls covered by newspaper to keep out the cold. I don't know where they found that kind of courage. Maybe they were a little bit like me, used to living with fear and aware that being black in America can be so dangerous anyway that it makes sense to risk everything and enter an even more fearful situation whenever there is some small chance that freedom might be won.

MARTHA PRESCOD NORMAN NOONAN remained a community organizer, developing and directing various programs including an anti-hunger project, a large inner-city food-buying club, and a supplemental education program for young people with sickle cell disease. She also retained her interest in history, completing most of the course work for the doctorate at the University of Michigan and teaching various courses in African American history there and at the University of Toledo and Wayne State University. She has helped organize several major retrospective conferences on the 1960s Civil Rights Movement and presented papers on this topic at many others. Two of these papers were published: "Shining in the Dark," in *Black Women and the Vote* (1997), and "How We Stood," in *A Circle of Trust* (1998). All three sons took their grandmother's advice, followed their father's example, and completed a professional education—one is a lawyer in Atlanta, two are doctors employed at the University of Michigan Medical School. She is now married to her high school sweetheart, Allan Noonan, a public health physician.

We'll Never Turn Back

Gloria House

An African American graduate student from UC Berkeley joins the Alabama Movement, witnesses the murder of a fellow civil rights worker, and stays on to help build independent political parties.

Berkeley Free Speech Movement

In 1964 I was a graduate student at the University of California, Berkeley. One morning as I neared the campus, I turned the corner onto Telegraph Avenue and was shocked to see city police and National Guardsmen lined up for blocks. Approaching the mall outside the administration building, Sproul Hall, I was stunned to find policemen dragging fellow students down the marble staircase and into wagons. Close to a thousand students had sat in at Sproul Hall the day before, demanding to meet with university officials to negotiate a more reasonable policy on student political activism. Instead of negotiating, the university administration called in hundreds of policemen and National Guardsmen to remove the students and to police the campus. Walking through those police forces that morning, I could no longer see the university as an ivory tower sheltered from the politics of the outside world.

This was the turning point in the Berkeley Free Speech Movement and for me. Outraged at the brutality of the city and state "law and order" forces, I joined other teaching assistants in organizing the campus-wide strike. We shut down classes, won the support of the major labor unions represented on campus, and pressured the administration to negotiate with us. We demanded seats for students on the board of regents, thereby ensuring a role for students in university policy making. We secured our right to be politically active and to fund-raise in support of political causes. Moreover, we organized the first union for university teaching assistants in American labor history.

The issue at the root of the Free Speech Movement was whether students would have the freedom to exercise their political convictions within the university community. The university administration had outlawed students' soliciting of funds on campus to support the Civil Rights Movement. Under the leadership of Mario Savio, who had just returned from the 1964 Mississippi Summer Project, and other graduate students, radical students maintained that we had every right to aid the fight and that, moreover, it was our responsibility to do so.

Those of us who participated in the Free Speech Movement learned the exhilaration of striving together to protect our human rights. During that time student solidarity was high, and we saw that with this unity we could demand that powerful institutions change. This victory empowered us as activists; however, we also felt sadness, for we discovered that once one takes a position and fights for it, nothing remains the same. Friendships may be broken, jobs lost, and other valuables placed at risk. The lightheartedness of college days was set aside—for some of us, definitively.

I had come to Berkeley as an undergraduate familiar with racial oppression. In Tampa, Florida, where I was born, the schools were still segregated. Though there were many disadvantages we faced as children in a neglected school system, we were fortunate to have a learning environment staffed by people who knew us and our families well, took an interest in our progress, and celebrated our achievements. Black teachers, principals, maintenance workers, nurses, children, and parents were all part of a single community. The schools up north, where my mother and I moved with my stepfather, a U.S. Air Force career man, presented a very different experience. In Salina, Kansas, my first home outside the South, white children were hostile to their black schoolmates, and white teachers assumed a condescending missionary attitude toward us. When I was an eight-year-old third-grader, Kansas introduced me to the meanness of racism in America.

At a very early age I had understood, as I believe most black children do, that we are an oppressed people in the country of our birth. I think this understanding comes to us as an unconscious absorption of the strain we see our parents suffering as they meet daily hardships. As children we are deeply aware of the unfocused misery that engulfs our folks' lives. My childhood memory of this feeling of oppression is associated with the church, where it seemed particularly tangible in the low, moaning, magnificent raising of old hymns, and in the Sunday evening communion circle, where we joined hands and sang "We Shall Overcome."

As an undergraduate I was active in several groups and campaigns concerned with social justice. After graduating in 1961 I traveled to England and France, remaining in Paris for nine months. During my stay in Paris in 1962 I met Congolese and Algerian students who helped make the idea of revolution real for me and convinced me that the hope of revolution is the only one black people and all other oppressed peoples have. At Berkeley we had studied Marxism, so I was familiar with socialist theory, but here my new friends were not engaging in theoretical discussions per se. They were attempting to use the theory to advance very real liberation struggles. I remember many conversations at the cafés along Boulevard St. Michel, where my friends' intense engagement with ideological and strategic issues related to their struggles on the African continent inspired me deeply.

Tattered Angels of Hope: The Selma Freedom School

Back home, events reinforced my politicization. First, in 1963, a church in Birmingham was bombed and four little girls murdered. That atrocity obsessed me for months, leaving me convinced that the whites who held power in this country clearly endorsed genocide against black people. Then, in 1964, three civil rights workers were murdered in Philadelphia, Mississippi. On my way home from the library one evening, I bought a newspaper that featured a photograph of several policemen dragging the young men's dead bodies from the mud and putting them in large black sacks. My work as a graduate student of comparative literature paled in light of this horror.

A little more than a year after the Mississippi murders and the Berkeley Free Speech Movement, I met a group of students from San Francisco State College who were conducting a book drive for Freedom Schools in the South. They were also planning to go to Selma, Alabama, in June 1965 to set up a Freedom School. I happily joined them, agreeing to spend the summer teaching English and French, though I doubted that the kids would have any interest in learning French. As it turned out, French became the most popular subject at the school because of the children's fascination with things foreign.

That summer Selma was still a center of movement activity. Movement culture was thriving; attendance at mass meetings in Brown's Chapel was high. The children were bright, spunky muses of revolution, and the church-rocking music of the Movement took my breath away! The round of murders of Jimmie Lee Jackson, Rev. James Reeb, and Viola Liuzzo had not killed the people's spirit. Voter registration work was ongoing. The Southern Christian Leadership Conference and SNCC both had state headquarters in Selma. SNCC had begun organizing projects with sharecroppers in a dozen Alabama counties.

Inspired by the children attending our Freedom School, I wrote a poem entitled "Selma 1965":

> Amid the ghosts of civil rights marchers
> in Selma
> in the summer so hot,
> the children sang in the paths
> of the afternoon showers,
> "Before I'd be a slave,
> I'd be buried in my grave . . ."
> From the freedom school window
> We watched them come
> across the lawns of the housing projects
> down the rain-rutted dirt roads,
> through the puddles waiting cool for bare feet.
> (Touch the dripping bush, break a leaf and smell
>   the pungency of green.)
> They were tattered angels of hope,
> plaits caught at odd angles
> and standing indignantly,
> a ripped hem hanging like a train,
> grey knees poking through denim frames.
> Dancing the whole trip,
> they performed their historic drama
> against the set of their
> wet brick project homes.

Murder in Lowndes

On the night of my arrival in Selma, a fellow teacher introduced me to Stokely Carmichael (who later changed his name to Kwame Turé). Then he was a SNCC project director in Lowndes County, some twenty miles away from Selma. At Stokely's invitation I visited Lowndes County, made a tour with him of the families involved, and started to attend the weekly mass meetings held in the rural churches around the county. Stokely had also introduced a white seminarian, Jonathan Daniels, to the Lowndes County community. I became friends with Jonathan and with the West family, Selma Movement activists who had sheltered many other civil rights workers and that summer had offered Jonathan a room in their project home near Brown's Chapel. When Jonathan discovered that I was a member of the Episcopal Church, he asked me to accompany him and a group of local children to the segregated Episcopal church in Selma. The priest and parishioners were hostile to us on several Sunday mornings, and I believe their rejection caused Jon a good deal of pain.

By the end of the summer, I had become a part of the Lowndes County SNCC group and was jailed in Hayneville, the county seat, for picketing a grocery store to demand hiring of black people. Approximately thirty demonstrators, including Jonathan, were arrested, some of them teenagers. We were herded onto a garbage truck and taken to the small two-storied Hayneville jail, the men put into cells upstairs, the three women—Ruby Sales, Joyce Stokes, and myself—put into a cell on the ground floor. Filthy water covered the floor, the mattresses on the bunks were lice-ridden, and an overwhelming stench enveloped everything.

We three women sang freedom songs so loudly that the men upstairs heard us and joined in. In this way we passed the time in a fairly good frame of mind while we waited for the SNCC staff to raise our bail. After two weeks, on August 20 a guard came to open our cell and tell us we were being released on our own recognizance. We hadn't had any word from the SNCC office in Selma and didn't believe what we were being told. We refused to leave the jail, suspecting there might be foul play. The guards then forced us out at gunpoint, off the county property, and out onto the road.

We walked about half a block to the main street of Hayneville and turned toward a little store only a few feet away. As we approached the store, we heard gunfire. All of us were horrified to think we were being fired upon. The youngsters, who knew the area, scattered hysterically, seeking shelter. Not knowing what else to do, we older ones hit the pavement where we had been standing. Jonathan was shot down immediately, murdered before our very eyes.

We were terrified, thinking we would all be killed. The only other white member of our group, Father Richard Morrisroe, a Catholic priest from Chicago, was shot in the back, wounded and unable to move. When the shooting stopped, we went up and down the street pounding on the doors, begging for someone to call an ambulance. No one in that white community would open the door or respond. Eventually someone from the SNCC office came to pick us up and care for Father Morrisroe, who had been injured so badly that he required years of physical therapy before he was able to walk again.

At the trial the man who killed Jonathan revealed that he was a marksman who had been deputized for the occasion of our release from jail and that his assignment had been to kill Jonathan and Father Morrisroe. Nevertheless, he was acquitted. The white community of Lowndes had been alerted to this murderous plan and collaborated in silence, because they viewed whites like Jonathan as threats to their illusions of superiority and the very real privileges they derived from racism and segregation.

After Jonathan's murder and the brutality of my short jail experience, I could not see how nonviolence would be effective in the African American struggle for liberation. Over the years, my memory of Jon lying dead and Father Morrisroe moaning in pain a few feet away from me on a curiously deserted main street in Lowndes County has served to reinforce this belief. I came to know Jonathan as a man of extraordinary warmth of spirit and commitment to justice. His murder represented a great loss to the Movement, his family, and friends.

Staying in the Movement: The Party of the Black Panther

Intending to complete my master's thesis and resume my job as a teaching assistant in the French department, I returned to Berkeley after attending Jonathan's funeral. However, once I was on the Berkeley campus I knew I no longer wanted to be there. Within a week I was back in Alabama, ready to work, and in September 1965 Silas Norman, then head of Alabama SNCC, hired me as a field secretary to be assigned to Lowndes County. During my two years in Lowndes, the SNCC staff consisted of Stokely Carmichael (before his election to SNCC chair), Bob Mants, George Greene, Janet Jemmott, Courtland Cox (off and on), myself and occasional volunteers.

In the 1960s we SNCC workers found black sharecropping families eking out a living, in perpetual debt to the white landowners. Many black areas lacked essential services such as indoor plumbing and electricity. We lived among the folks with whom we worked, our housing often provided by local activists. In Lowndes County the Jackson family, one of the few families who owned their own property, allowed the SNCC staff to live in one of their houses. At the back of the house was a pump for water and a bit farther away an outhouse.

The political and social bond forged between SNCC workers and the local communities was extraordinary. College-age students, some of whom were urban and northern, formed respectful, enduring working partnerships with local rural people of their parents' generation and older. Meeting in churches, where the Movement was based, these partners prayed together, reflected, strategized, resolved, and inspired each other to transform southern politics. Our relationship thrived on the courage and wisdom of our elders as well as our vision and determination. We can never forget this phenomenal embrace in which we were loved, nurtured, and protected by the communities that received us. Some SNCC workers, like Bob Mants in Lowndes County, never "went home" again but settled and raised their own families among the folks with whom we had fought for change.

Getting people registered to vote—a priority of our work—involved workers canvassing daily along long stretches of white-owned plantations. We rose early to find the sharecroppers as they left their homes for the fields. In the small towns we did door-to-door canvassing to encourage people to register. We prepared for weekly mass meetings on Sunday and evening meetings during the week. We taught people to read and write; we conducted political education workshops for those aspiring to run for office. We maintained a Freedom School and library for the children. We helped to organize food co-ops and crafts co-ops; we distributed information on government-sponsored farm programs whose benefits had been withheld from black farmers for generations.

As SNCC field secretaries we had to make use of the meager funds made available to us from the Atlanta office. We were responsible for the maintenance of vehicles and other equipment used in our daily work. We also documented developments of the Movement in written reports and photographs. We were busy from early morning to late at night.

We were always conscious of danger. In Lowndes County we learned to hit the ground or find cover when white men drove by at night shooting at the freedom house, or at the tent city where we lived with sharecropping families who had been evicted because they registered to vote or took part in the Movement. Fortunately, no one was wounded in these terroristic assaults in Lowndes when I was there, but they happened regularly enough to keep us alert.

In Lowndes we organized the Lowndes County Freedom Organization, which initiated the formation of an independent black political party. Influenced by the defeat of the Mississippi Freedom Democratic Party, we chose to create a separate political party instead of seeking admission into the Democratic Party. Jack Minnis, a researcher in SNCC's Atlanta office, discovered a provision in the Alabama Administrative Code that allowed independent parties to enter county elections if certain stipulations were met.

Many potential southern black voters had concluded that there was no distinction between the Democrats and the Dixiecrats. Indeed, in Alabama the emblem of the Democratic Party was a white rooster on a banner that read "White Supremacy." In contrast, we chose as our symbol a pouncing black panther. Using this symbol ensured that even those voters who could not read would recognize their party on the ballot. I believe our effort to create an independent party reflected an overall change inside SNCC that began with the failure of the MFDP challenge. This defeat and our work in the Black Belt counties of Alabama marked the demise of a generally integrationist orientation and the emergence of a new spirit of nationalism.

The creation of a political party meant additional tasks for the SNCC staff in Lowndes. Voter registration took on a new intensity. We had to explain the legal requirements for party organization to the community and teach the political history of the South. In short, we were helping to equip the people with the information and skills essential to running the county government. In the independent freedom parties, people hoped to prepare themselves not just as new voters but also as political leaders. We found that a review of African American and African history, giving a strong sense of historical identity, was of immeasurable significance in this process.

There was tremendous political potential in our efforts. At that time black people made up 85 percent of the county population, but white residents had held all the political offices and had kept black people from voting for generations. If black people were elected to county offices, the local political structure would be radically altered and black residents could share more equitably in the resources of the county.

SNCC workers spread the idea of independent black political parties from Lowndes County to other Alabama counties where black people constituted sizable majorities. Later I moved into Selma to help other SNCC organizers establish the freedom party of Dallas County. The fruits of our labor in the Alabama independent parties were not immediately reaped in the 1966 elections, but rather in 1970, when black people in a handful of counties won positions in local governments. These officials subsequently organized a statewide coalition of independent parties, determined to win representation for black voters on a state level.

The Vietnam War, Race, and Gender

By 1965 there was a faction in SNCC to which I belonged that called for a stronger international orientation and self-determination for oppressed nations around the world, including our own nation of thirty million black people in the United States. This new direction grew out of our deepening knowledge of our history as a people in Africa and the diaspora as well as our identification with liberation movements of the period in Asia, South America, and Africa.

Our subsequent demonstrations of solidarity with the Vietnamese people were part of this internationalization of consciousness. SNCC's statement against the war, which I drafted, was a close documentation of the thoughts and arguments that were articulated primarily by the nationalist faction within SNCC. Our objection to the war was debated heatedly and finally adopted at a national staff meeting in Atlanta.

This statement was written sometime after the voting rights bill had passed and shortly after yet another murder of a civil rights activist who worked closely with us in Alabama. Sammy Younge, a Tuskegee student and resident, was killed by a gas station owner in his hometown for attempting to use the white restroom. The statement tied our opposition to the war to Younge's murder and questioned our country's commitment to the rule of law. We contended that:

> Samuel Younge was murdered because U.S. law is not being enforced. Vietnamese are being murdered because the United States is pursuing an aggressive policy in violation of international law. The U.S. is no respector of persons or law when such persons or laws run counter to its needs and desires. We recall the indifference, suspicion, and outright hostility with which our reports of violence have been met in the past by government officials.

Throughout, we pointed out the hypocrisy of the country's stated dedication to freedom and democracy, again tying the country's actions abroad to our experiences as civil rights workers at home, stating:

> The United States government has been deceptive in claims of concern for the freedom of the Vietnamese people, just as the government has been deceptive in claiming concern for the freedom of the colored people in such other countries as the Dominican Republic, the Congo, South Africa, Rhodesia, and in the United States itself. . . . [SNCC's] work, particularly in the South, taught us that the United States government has never guaranteed the freedom of oppressed citizens and is not yet truly determined to end the rule of terror and oppression within its own borders. . . . We recall the numerous persons who have been murdered in the South because of their efforts to secure their civil and human rights, and whose murderers have been allowed to escape penalty for their crimes.

The statement ended by urging opposition to the draft, suggesting instead that "those Americans who prefer to use their energy in building democratic forms within the country . . . work in the civil rights movement and other human relations organizations [although we know] full well that it may cost them their lives, as painfully as in Vietnam."

Later, at a national SNCC staff meeting at Peg Leg Bates Resort in New York, the same group that pushed for release of the Vietnam statement urged that we vote to require white SNCC workers, of whom there were still a handful, to work only in white communities or in our offices. We did not vote to expel white staff members from the organization, as was widely reported in the media. The insistence that only black field secretaries should work in black communities reflected our evolving black consciousness. How could we send white organizers to black sharecroppers to convince them we could be self-determining as a race? We thought this was an obvious contradiction that had to be corrected, but our position cost us a serious loss of support from liberals in the North. Before SNCC took these positions, our fund-raisers had done fairly well, and we field secretaries had received our ten-dollar weekly paychecks intermittently. Afterward we received them very rarely, if at all.

There has also been an ongoing debate concerning the roles and status of SNCC women. I did not experience male domination in SNCC. I felt my ideas were respected, and I felt free to take on any aspects of the projects in which we were involved; neither my work as a field secretary nor my personhood was ever diminished or disrespected by SNCC men. Moreover, during the years I was in SNCC, I witnessed women playing key leadership roles. Ruby Doris Robinson commanded genuine respect from everyone in her role as SNCC program secretary; the women of the Atlanta Project were instrumental in the anti-war work, in arguing for release of the statement against the war, and in pushing for the strong nationalist orientation that emerged in 1966. And of course there were individual women, like Annie Pearl Avery, whose strength and charisma everyone respected—not to mention the powerful leadership of local women like Mrs. Fannie Lou Hamer in Mississippi. On an interpersonal level, women were supportive of each other and respectful of one another's relationships with men. In addition, we were concerned and protective of each other, especially where illness or emotional distress was involved.

The SNCC Legacy

The social environment that SNCC engendered was one of equality in many spheres. There was equality across class lines, and North-South background lines. There was equality across levels of formal education. SNCC's concept of leadership was also egalitarian. We didn't think of ourselves as the "talented tenth," for example, a concept of elite leadership that was still prevalent in black communities. Ours was a much more progressive way of recognizing and encouraging people's skills and abilities, no matter their social status outside SNCC.

Another aspect of SNCC's culture was its legitimization of political organizing as full-time work—the organizer as worker. In our work we shouldered exceptional responsibilities for twenty-year-olds. We tried new things and became good at them. We left with a sense of competency and discipline that most of us have put to good use in our subsequent endeavors. SNCC's approaches to organizing gave us a culture, a way of being, a way of resolving social, political, and personal problems.

In 1966 I married another SNCC worker, Stuart House, at the Episcopal church on the campus of Tuskegee University in Alabama. The reception, our rather modest get-together at the Selma freedom house, was an occasion for a reunion of SNCC staff from various projects. As we sat on the porch after dinner, Rap Brown (now Jamil-Al-Amin) lifted our spirits with his keen political analysis and brilliant wit. When I became pregnant, I was so malnourished that a movement doctor advised me to go somewhere where I could get three meals a day or I would not carry the baby to term. Stuart and I left Alabama to ensure the health of our child.

My experience in SNCC and in Lowndes County had an enormous impact on my development as a human rights advocate. I can see the effects of that experience when I compare my attitudes, expectations, perspectives, and aspirations with those of my peers who did not spend those years in the southern movement. The SNCC experience disciplined me for a lifetime commitment to struggle. In the end, one is never a "retired" civil rights worker.

Forty years have passed since our stay in the Hayneville jail and the trauma of witnessing Jonathan's murder and hearing Morrisroe's pain-stricken cries for help. No one turns back to a life of indifference to human rights after experiences like these. Interacting with others who were engaged daily in the effort to change a repressive system, I learned from close encounters how the mechanisms of power and oppression work and also saw firsthand the enormous human capacity to resist and transcend them.

At the end of SNCC staff meetings, we used to form a circle and sing freedom songs. The one that I have kept close all these years, "We'll Never Turn Back," was written by Bertha Gober, an Albany State student active in one of SNCC's first community organizing efforts. Her song is an affirmation of our commitment to struggle. The lines that moved me most deeply are: "We have walked through the valley of death. We had to walk all by ourselves. But we'll never turn back. No, we'll never turn back. Until we've all been freed. And we have equality."

GLORIA HOUSE did complete her master's degree at Berkeley and went on to earn a doctorate in American cultural history at the University of Michigan. Since leaving SNCC, she has been actively engaged in community issues and international solidarity causes and has written poems and essays that have appeared in numerous journals and anthologies. She has published three poetry collections—*Blood River* (1983), *Rain Rituals* (1990), and *Shrines* (2004)—as well as a study of the political uses of public spaces, *Tower and Dungeon* (1991). She has been an editor at Broadside Press for many years. House is professor of humanities and director of the African and African American Studies Program at the University of Michigan, Dearborn, as well as professor emerita in the Department of Interdisciplinary Studies at Wayne State University, where she taught for twenty-seven years. From 1992 to 1996 she was a visiting professor in the English department and director of the Partnership with Township High Schools at the University of Witwatersrand in Johannesburg, South Africa. She and Stuart House have one son.

"We'll Never Turn Back" © 2010 by Gloria House

Letter to My Adolescent Son

Jean Wiley

A mother explains to her son how her SNCC experience influenced the rest of her life.

Dear Cabral,

I am writing this letter to answer the question I sometimes see in your adolescent eyes. Usually your youthful amusement shines through, but the silent question is no less intense: "Who are you, Mom?" You wonder why all these books everywhere and what's with the long fiery political debates with friends. You marvel at my utter lack of regard for most government institutions. And you bewail to anybody who'll listen, even after we've returned from Grenada, "Only my mother would choose to move to a country with no television at all."

Well, the thing is, I am most notably a mother to you; but I am also a lot else: sister, aunt, niece, cousin, friend, lover, colleague. Still, the single most defining thing about me is this: I am a SNCC woman, come to maturity and womanhood in SNCC, in the fire of the southern freedom struggle, bathed in warm waters of collective and mutual trust and respect—a committed and unrepentant progressive and activist. To understand this woman, you have to glimpse the people and the struggle that produced her, and the magic that binds us still.

Yes, a SNCC woman. For me, SNCC was always more than its individual parts, more even than its collective history. It was and still is a way of life, a lens to life, a way of rejecting certain attitudes and behaviors while applauding and promoting others. An enthusiasm for life's contradictions. A style and posture. An ATTITUDE.

Did we have attitude! Don't we even today! When you've spent your adolescence in the 1950s and watched children your own age being spat upon in Little Rock, when you've listened to the fervent prayers in your quiet Methodist church for the folks in Montgomery using their feet instead of the buses, when you've suffered months of nightmares because you've stolen a glimpse of the mutilated body of young Emmett Till in the *JET* magazine that all the adults were trying to hide from the children, when you have walked past three schools and halfway across the city to get to the closest grade school you're allowed into, then you are more than ready for ATTITUDE.

The opportunity to emphatically express that attitude came on February 1, 1960, with the Greensboro sit-ins. The student sit-in movement and the rapidity with which it spread to every black campus was a stunning surprise to everybody—except to the members of my generation. After all, we were the young people who as children had watched and cringed as the South went wild, bombing black homes and churches, shutting down whole school districts. But we had also seen the Montgomery Bus Boycott, a real mass movement waged by ordinary black people. February 1, 1960, was the dawn of a new decade for us, one in which we were determined to write our own chapter in the history of black resistance. Yes, although we dressed in Sunday church clothes to confront racism and arrest, we were ready to kick ass—nonviolently, of course.

I've always been grateful to SNCC, to SNCC people for saving my life, and to the freedom struggle for enriching my life in ways I am still discovering. When I ventured South in June 1964, I had just finished a master's degree at the University of Michigan and before that a brief stint as a Morgan State student in a filthy Baltimore jail. It was the news that Howard students were on their way to join our protest demonstrations that persuaded the city to release us and open the segregated theater. Can you imagine—a theater sitting just two blocks away from a historically black college, refusing to admit us! So, by dint of demonstrations, jail, and countless strategy meetings on campus, I already considered myself a SNCC person. Still, I had to see the real thing—the southern freedom struggle.

And I had to get there with my own resources. The first college graduate to emerge from two large clans in Baltimore, the Boyers and the Wileys, and now the first to hold a graduate degree, I couldn't very well borrow money from struggling relatives, especially not to go to the Deep South! Everybody thought I'd lost my mind just to consider going. The standard response from friends, family, and neighbors: "Well, Baltimore isn't exactly a picnic for our folks, nor Philadelphia or Washington or New York either." All true, of course, but it was in the Deep South where the Movement was on the move, and it kept calling me.

So when I was offered a position in the English department at Tuskegee Institute, I jumped at it. Without any idea how demanding and exciting the first months of teaching would be, I was on a plane to Alabama in early June. This was the same time that thousands of black and white students, activists of all stripes, were converging on Mississippi for the 1964 Freedom Summer. Well, I consoled myself, I'm at least nearby.

I soon discovered there was no need for consolation, that just a few miles away SNCC was already organizing in Alabama's Black Belt counties. Soon I was attending mass meetings in Selma. I was to see and be a part of SNCC at a different but no less intense stage of its history. Some consider Alabama the best stage of all, where the issue of power rose above the din of integration and nonviolence and even civil rights. No more petitioning, no more waiting for the liberals, white or black, to scatter a few crumbs, no more. Alabama was about taking power in those counties where black people were the majority.

Picture this, Cabral: It's my first SNCC meeting. We are in a small hotel room in Montgomery. I don't recall why I'm there, probably because nobody tells me to leave. In fact, no one pays the slightest attention to me, an entirely new face. The room is stiflingly hot and the tension is as thick as the cigarette smoke. Bodies are flung over every inch of space, weary bodies, just disembarked from groaning wrecks of cars that have sped up from Mississippi. The loud, angry argument finally reaches a crescendo and explodes into vivid, imaginative, totally insulting curses. I've never heard such abominable language, never imagined it. Faces frozen in anger, eyes flashing—it's terrifying.

After a few hours of what looks to me like sheer pandemonium, a tall, slender guy rises slowly from the floor, stretches and mutters something I don't catch. Everybody bursts into hearty laughter and the meeting breaks up. Smiling faces descend the narrow stairs to the restaurant. Well, I just want to go home. These people are clearly nuts. I have just witnessed SNCC fighting it out with SNCC. I am both impressed—and not.

But I had been very much impressed the day before when a dozen or so SNCC workers mysteriously showed up and sprang into action to guide and thereby protect a large student protest demonstration that I had helped to organize. It occurred less than a week after armed white Alabama state troopers had stopped the first Selma to Montgomery March by viciously attacking the marchers with clubs, tear gas, horses, and guns on what would henceforth be known as Bloody Sunday. Teachers and students from Tuskegee had organized to meet that march and fortify its ranks as it moved into Montgomery. Well, the bloodshed stopped those marchers, some injured so severely they had to be rushed to the hospital. In the best tradition of the freedom struggle, we at Tuskegee decided to keep our schedule, head straight for the state capitol in downtown Montgomery, and stand in for all those prevented from coming. "Ain't Gonna Let Nobody Turn Me 'Round."

Now we are finally in Montgomery en masse, a thousand strong. Our long motorcade of buses and cars stops a few blocks from the capitol, the seat of the Confederacy. We've brought along a petition to Governor Wallace, essentially a demand for "Freedom NOW!" and we're determined to stay until he accepts it. Amid the general disarray of grabbing our signs and lining up for the march, SNCC workers appear to act as marshals. What a tremendous relief to see them! Dressed in denim overalls and thick combat boots, the SNCC workers yell out a crash course in nonviolent direct action as we're moving: what to expect, where to steer the march, when to cover our heads, how to go limp on arrest, how to ignore the armed state troopers when they threaten to charge, and how to hold the ranks when they actually do.

The worst moment for me comes late in the afternoon, when several squadrons of troopers on horseback move to a triangular attack position and threaten to charge if we don't leave. The SNCC people order all women on the ground, hands covering their heads. Mind you, some of those doing the ordering are themselves women, seasoned veterans of many civil rights battles. I feel both shock and relief at seeing them among the men. Now, there is no question in my mind that the horses will charge, but this is an order I cannot follow. After all, these are my young students, whom I'd worked hard to get here. I'm the one who should be protecting them—the young men as well as the women. Somebody points and yells at me to get down. As I'm trying to explain, somebody else throws me to the ground, where I lie terrified and helpless, surrounded by the sounds of snorting, stomping horses, and cursing armed white men.

Well, the police don't charge, that time; they don't charge us at all, though they repeatedly threaten to. But they don't let us into the capitol either, not even to advance up the tall steps leading to its doors. Anybody who leaves the demonstration to use a restroom or drink some water is not allowed back in, so we stop trying. Along with hundreds of students from Alabama State College stuck on the side streets and barred from coming any closer to us, we stay through the night, students from both campuses breaking out in freedom songs when it all gets unbearable. Since we are surrounded and trapped, we're forced to either leave the demonstration permanently or stay and relieve our bladders right where we are. It's not a difficult decision for us; after all, was there ever a more appropriate place for a public pee-in? While we were trapped in the capitol, state and local police rampaged through the black community, breaking down doors, harassing and threatening everybody in sight. The next day, a furious Jim Forman would utter one of the more memorable and vivid quotes of the nonviolent Movement: "If we can't sit at the table, we'll knock the fucking legs off it!" Yes!

SNCC relished breaking the rules. It wasn't just that we broke them; we *relished* breaking them. In personal style and collective culture, we never met a rule we didn't try to break. Lord, was it fun! This wasn't adolescent rebellion; this was young adult revulsion at the white middle-class rules that governed all manner of conduct and cloaked the rampant hypocrisy that advanced the most repugnant practices, like segregation and slavery and genocide.

SNCC taught us to live with contradictions, even to savor them. For example, we risked our lives to win the vote while keenly aware that the same vote had done precious little for black people in the North. There we were, singing away our fear and rage as burly, racist cops beat our heads and loaded us into wagons heading for jails that would shortly ring with more defiant singing. There we were, debating nonviolence in the midst of the most violent region of the most violent society on the planet.

By the time I got to the South, SNCC was not "Student," former students having graduated to full-time field organizers, or "Nonviolent," at least not in the pacifist, philosophical sense. Many field organizers began to carry guns to defend themselves against the horrendous wave of terror in 1964. Self-defense was consistent with the common sense of the common folk we were helping to organize. As Malcolm X and the Deacons for Defense insisted, self-defense is a right and often a necessity. SNCC was also not a "Committee," but a hardened cadre of veterans of battles big and small. Oh, yes, also gone were the Sunday church clothes of the student protest demonstrations and Freedom Rides. As SNCC had fanned out across the hard-core rural, racist South, the uniform of choice had changed to the overalls and denim worn by black sharecroppers, the people closest to all the venom and violence of the white South.

"Upping the ante" was a SNCC mantra. It meant increasing the pressure, broadening the resistance, driving the enemy wild, really. When white folks thought their mobs, beatings, burnings, and arrests would stop the Freedom Rides, SNCC sent wave after wave of riders, many targeting the trains and train stations as well as the buses! Never forget, Cabral, that segregation was a form of apartheid, written in law. We were in the forefront of fighting for "freedom," not, as the white media still insists, to sit beside a white person in a classroom or at a lunch counter. People do not risk injury and death for a hamburger.

The Freedom Movement was unstoppable. It was positively delicious knowing that nobody could stop it—not the president of the United States, not the Congress, not the courts, not the FBI, not the black preachers or teachers, who warned us to go slow. The most any of them could do was delay a protest demonstration, but only until other students arrived to carry it on. And they always did arrive. Imagine the sense of power we felt!

Fueling this euphoria was the certainty that we were part of a worldwide movement of liberation. Algeria, Vietnam, Angola, Cuba, Guinea Bissau, Guatemala, Kenya, Mozambique, China—all over the globe people were asserting their right to determine their own destinies, with arms if necessary. The year 1960 was such a pivotal year for African people everywhere: in the United States it ushered in the massive black student protest movement that would ignite the rest of the country; and it heralded the end of European colonialism in much of the African Diaspora. There was a sense of expectancy, of finally realizing dreams too long deferred. Like peoples the world over, we wanted to change the power relationships that governed the sense of ourselves and restricted the mobility, livelihoods, and aspirations of our black people here and everywhere.

But everywhere we looked, something, some law or practice or cherished tradition, was poised to shackle black people. The more we pushed, the more we understood that we weren't the only ones being shackled. Before the decade ended, Native Americans, Puerto Ricans, and Chicanos were organizing and arming themselves. Students black and white were waging pitched battles in the streets and on the campuses to stop the American war on the Vietnamese people. Northern cities were smoldering. And women were organizing. What a time!

SNCC's irreverence was legendary. During the early part of the Vietnam War, with black soldiers already stationed on the front lines and therefore dying in disproportionate numbers, SNCC created and distributed an effective anti-war poster, a black-and-white drawing of Uncle Sam staring ominously out, forefinger pointed at the viewer. The caption: "Uncle Sam wants you—Nigger!" SNCC speakers intoned, "No Vietnamese ever called me nigger," and "Hell, no! We won't go."

SNCC also taught us to keep on moving, to grab any opportunity to advance the Movement, to go where you were called, taking the knocks, the setbacks, and applying the lessons as you moved forward. Now, this could get a little hectic, if not downright chaotic. In retrospect there was a strong strain of anarchism, but we were too young to know much about anarchists and would probably have poked fun at them, too, had we known. We distrusted "isms" profoundly, since those very "isms" had gotten black people the world over so very little. We also resisted hierarchy and bureaucracy—two things we felt had frozen other organizations. Some would say we also fought discipline. So what?

Which brings me to the subject of women in SNCC—a subject that historians and academicians now writing our history persistently get wrong, and, I think, deliberately so. I won't speak for others, but I can emphatically declare my own experience: I wish to high heaven I had found in my life before SNCC, or in the years since, the freedom I as a woman found there. That my gender should prevent me from a role in SNCC was unthinkable. By the time I got to the South, SNCC women were driving the cars and riding the mules, organizing the plantations and directing the field staff, writing the reports and mobilizing the northern campuses. How could it not be so? Ella Baker gathered and mentored us. Fannie Lou Hamer was one of our most eloquent spokespersons. And Ruby Doris Robinson would soon become SNCC's executive secretary. Yes, SNCC was the first and only time in my life that my gender was not a barrier to my aspirations. I'd love it for that, if for nothing else.

In the summer of 1965 I found myself at Julian Bond's desk, suddenly in charge of SNCC's national communications while Julian campaigned for a seat in the lily-white Georgia state legislature. I had never called a radio or television station in my life, much less given a live interview. I had never written a news article, or even a news release, but there I was, hammering them out for the media, the *Student Voice,* and for Friends of SNCC groups on northern campuses. Somebody please tell me what to do and how to do it! Whenever I felt overwhelmed, I thought of Julian, who was probably as disoriented in his new role as young campaigner/politician as I was there at his old cluttered desk.

The strange thing is, everybody knew that I didn't know what the hell I was doing! I don't remember my mistakes; I just know there had to have been a lot of them. But nobody said, "Oops, sorry, you're out of here." There was an expectation and a confidence that I would learn, and learn fast, just like everybody else; all of us were learning as we went. No matter what the role, work in SNCC was demanding: long hours, heroism, intensity, sincerity of commitment, madness of a sort. The sweetness was that acceptance into the group was immediate and genuine.

Well, the articles got published and the radio news broadcasts went out to stations around the country. Wilson Brown, SNCC's genius printer, gave me a crash course on the new printing presses that were his joy. I knew before I returned to Tuskegee that someday I'd be a reporter, a career virtually closed to women in the mid 1960s, even more closed to black women!

Eighteen months later I was strolling confidently along the corridors of the United Nations, an international male enclave of privilege in those days. It tickled me to be walking those halls, though my purpose was dead serious. I was there to follow up Forman's efforts to win nongovernmental status at the U.N. Thanks to the West Indian and African diplomatic corps, we got it. SNCC thus became the first civil rights organization to have official NGO status at the United Nations and access to its invaluable documents, debates, and gatherings.

Do you get the picture yet, Cabral? We were determined to free ourselves from many prevailing prejudices. We didn't always succeed, but we tried and succeeded often. The attempt bound us closer. We were irreverent and we were passionate young men and women. This is important, because the combination of passion and irreverence is rare, in individuals and organizations alike. SNCC people were passionate about the "local people," as we called them. Gentle, generous, and proud, these were the black men, women, and children who lived in the counties and on the plantations and who risked their lives to open their doors to us with no reward promised or expected. In Lowndes County, Greenwood, Selma, Hattiesburg, Lexington, and many other rural places, whole families of several generations welcomed, fed, and sustained us, marched and organized with the "young freedom fighters." Not one of those families was without a gun. Most had several, cleaned, loaded, and ready for use if needed.

I will always think of SNCC as a safe place. There we were, fighting against racism, defying the most cherished practices of the racist South, and standing up to its most horrendous violence, nobody daring to hope to reach the age of thirty. It was safe because it was a place to stretch, learn, and grow. There was no "line" to toe, no leaders to blindly follow, no ideology to mouth and proselytize, only freedom and struggle.

Of course, there was no end to disagreement, debate, or stomp-down, drag-out argument. That tense meeting I described earlier was the first of many. But the kind of brutal personal attack and humiliation I would witness in later political work, the terrible turf battles, tirades, and betrayals I saw in the North and West could not and did not take place inside SNCC. Thank God. As a result, after all these years SNCC people, white and black, feel close to each other, welcome one another, embrace as sisters and brothers. We know we are profoundly fortunate. Our bond is indeed magical.

Grief and tears are also part of SNCC's story, part of the freedom struggle itself. And these, too, bind us. We were facing entrenched, state-sanctioned terrorism, and despite all the heroism and youthful bravado, we sometimes paid a very high price. Friends were maimed and killed. I wasn't always able to protect my students. One of them became the first black college student to be killed in the southern movement—Sammy Younge Jr. A U.S. Navy veteran who had returned to college, Sammy quickly became one of the most active and dedicated of the crop of Tuskegee students who went out into the rural counties to organize.

And then there was Ralph Featherstone, a veteran of both Alabama and Mississippi and one of my dearest friends. "Feather," as we all knew him, was killed in a car bomb blast as he neared Cambridge, Maryland, the scene of earlier movement battles and the site where H. Rap Brown's trial was to open the following day. By then it was 1970, and the FBI's murderous COINTELPRO (counterintelligence program) was in full force. Its publicly stated goal was to stop by any means the Black Liberation Struggle that had come out of the southern Freedom Movement. It largely succeeded.

So there you have it, Cabral, for now at least. These are some of the experiences that shape and influence the woman you know as Mom. Your very name comes from my involvement in SNCC. Where but in SNCC would I have learned about and studied Amilcar Cabral, the brilliant and courageous liberation fighter from Guinea Bissau? Not in college, not in graduate school. Where but in the southern freedom struggle would my lifelong dedication to Pan-Africanism have been rooted? That's what I am trying to explain here: dedication to the struggle takes you to places, causes, and people you'd never have dreamed of. I hope you find your rightful place within our struggle and among the kinds of dedicated activists I found—people with vision, courage, and respect for one another. The struggle continues. It must.

Much love,
Mom

JEAN WILEY left the Deep South after two and a half years, but not the Movement. She continued the teacher-activist role she'd performed at Tuskegee, teaching at the University of the District of Columbia, the Center for Black Education in Washington, D.C., and later at the University of California at Berkeley. She was also an editor at the Institute of the Black World in Atlanta, Georgia. She then shifted to advocacy journalism and covered national and international news at Howard University's radio station, WHUR-FM, where she interviewed several visiting African and Caribbean heads of state and traveled to interview others across the African diaspora. During the Movement, Wiley saw that ordinary people have transformative stories of personal, political, and spiritual significance. With this in mind, she founded Collage Literary Studio to help people write and publish the books inside them. She is also a member of Bay Area Veterans of the Civil Rights Movement (www.crmvet.org), an informal organization dedicated to exploring and sharing with others the soul and power of the Movement. Wiley lives in Oakland and is writing a more complete memoir of her involvement in the freedom struggle.

PART 10

Black Power

Issues of Continuity, Change, and Personal Identity, 1964–1969

> In Atlantic City, we learned the hard way that even
> though we had all the law and all the righteousness
> on our side—the white man is not going to give up
> his power to us. We have to build our own power.
>
> —Fannie Lou Hamer

With the passage of the 1964 Civil Rights Act outlawing segregation in public accommodations and the Voting Rights Act of 1965, which suspended literacy tests and sent federal registrars to certain southern counties, the goals of the early movement appeared to have been won. Yet for many SNCC workers, rather than a time for relaxation, this was a period of intensified activism and increased militancy.

Understanding that the federal legislation represented victories for the Civil Rights Movement, SNCC workers still remained concerned about the pace of change in the South and the federal government's willingness to enforce the new laws there. In spite of the federal legislation, public accommodations and interstate transportation facilities remained segregated in almost all of the communities where SNCC had projects. The social codes of segregation also remained in place, along with the harsh punishments meted out for breaking them or the state segregation laws, as the murder of Sammy Younge Jr. proved.

Acknowledging that the voting rights bill reflected SNCC's position regarding literacy tests and other voting rights issues, SNCC workers felt the law still did not address one of their major concerns—offering protection to people who attempted to register and to people involved in voter registration work. This omission obviously concerned prospective black voters, too. In the first few years after the voting legislation had passed—even in counties where black people of voting age were the overwhelming majority and federal registrars were present—most movement election efforts were unsuccessful. Ongoing terrorist attacks and economic reprisals against black registrants continued, and white elected officials crafted ways to dilute the black vote. Besides the slow pace of change and continuing danger, the other, perhaps even more significant backdrop to SNCC's work in this period was the series of uprisings in major cities across the country that began in the Watts section of Los Angeles the same month that the Voting Rights Act passed. From 1965 to 1968, black residents took to the streets, initially burning and looting white businesses in their communities and bringing regular commerce to a halt. Many SNCC workers began to reflect this urban militancy in their views and statements and sought to give voice to the protests, some interpreting the uprisings as revolutionary acts.

In June 1966, as William Moore had done in 1963, James Meredith decided to stage his own personal walk to Mississippi's state capitol. Meredith, who had integrated the University of Mississippi in 1962, wanted to show Mississippi's prospective black voters that it was safe to register and to vote. After he had walked less than twenty miles into Mississippi, a white bystander from Memphis fired three loads of buckshot at Meredith, causing many superficial wounds. As a result, many black registrants decided it best to stay away from the next day's primary election, in which the MFDP was running a slate of candidates.

SCLC, SNCC, and CORE members resumed the march in Meredith's stead, attracting more marchers along the route and recruiting black registrants. When the march reached Greenwood, newly elected SNCC chair Stokely Carmichael decided to use an expression fellow SNCC worker Willie Ricks had been using since 1962, "Black Power." Previously at mass meetings and rallies, a speaker would ask, "What do you want?" and the crowd would respond, "Freedom." "When do you want it?" the speaker would continue, and the crowd would answer, "Now." This exchange would take place two or three times and end with the crowd and the speaker chanting, "Freedom now! Freedom now! Freedom now!"

With Ricks's expression in mind, Carmichael asked the same question, "What do you want?" but encouraged a different response: "Black Power! Black Power! Black Power!" This phrase was immediately picked up and denounced by the national press and more moderate civil rights groups. Many white liberals also deemed the phrase offensive. Nevertheless, the expression and Carmichael's subsequent speeches and writings garnered considerable support in both northern and southern black communities.

A month before the march, at a May 1966 meeting held in Kingston Springs, Tennessee, Stokely Carmichael replaced John Lewis as SNCC chair and Ruby Doris Smith became executive secretary, replacing Jim Forman. SNCC activists also discussed the role of white staff at this meeting. After the Atlantic City challenge, some members of SNCC had wanted to return to the earlier Mississippi practice of using an all-black, mostly local, staff in the field and the accompanying slow and steady program of community organizing, believing it the most effective way to build a movement. After the passage of the voting rights bill, other SNCC staff, with another perspective, argued that SNCC had to rid itself of its integrationist past in order for the Movement to succeed. Using white staff as organizers in the black community was contradictory, they insisted, in a movement for black self-determination.

Evidently without much dissent, SNCC adopted the policy that only black staff members should organize in black communities and that white staff members should organize in the white community against racism. At this point there were approximately forty white people on staff. However, at the next meeting, held in December at Peg Leg Bates's resort in Upstate New York, with only seven nonblack staff members remaining, this issue was the subject of prolonged and intense debate. This book's contributors disagree on whether or not the final decision at that meeting was to expel or keep white staff, limit their powers within the organization, or require them to form their own organization. Several women in this book describe the meetings where the debates regarding race took place as well as their political and emotional responses to this issue.

After the summer of 1965, SNCC workers, their community supporters, and organizational allies were more public in their use of self-defense. Some SNCC field secretaries regularly carried weapons and displayed weapons in their freedom houses. Lowndes County residents displaying rifles guarded the freedom house and county voters. On the Meredith March, SNCC workers insisted on being protected by the openly armed Deacons for Defense. Near the march's end in Canton, state troopers launched an attack on the demonstrators that was more vicious than Bloody Sunday. Afterward, Carmichael, borrowing a phrase from Malcolm X, renounced nonviolence as the only method of struggle, asserting instead that black people have the right to fight for their liberation "by any means necessary." Yet it appears that SNCC staffers never actually fired weapons in self-defense or organized armed attacks against the white community.

During this time some SNCC workers maintained programs in the field in Mississippi, Alabama, and Southwest Georgia, still focusing on the vote as well as creating new programs and projects. In Mississippi, for example, they assisted with the formation of a black farmworkers union, the Mississippi Freedom Labor Union (MFLU); a black high school association, the Mississippi Student Union; more farming cooperatives; and a large craft cooperative, the Poor People's Corporation. SNCC and COFO played pivotal roles in the creation, design, and maintenance of the Child Development Group of Mississippi, one of the country's first Head Start programs. Along with black power, SNCC workers increasingly promoted the need to build self-sustaining black economic programs and institutions and for black people to exert organized influence over the other programs and institutions central to their lives.

As SNCC abandoned interracial organizing and promoted self-defense, the organization maintained its traditional position of being the most radical civil rights organization and of addressing the needs of the most disenfranchised. Early on, SNCC distinguished itself from the more mainstream civil rights organizations by adopting a policy of nonexclusion and working with individuals red-baited by these groups. Also SNCC tended to be more critical of Democratic administrations, a difference underscored at the March on Washington. More moderate civil rights leaders at the march objected to the speech John Lewis proposed to give challenging the Kennedy administration by asking, "I want to know which side the federal government is on." SNCC workers were upset by the federal government's filing charges against nine civil rights workers in Albany and by the unhelpful action of FBI agents. In addition, many in SNCC believed federal authorities were complicit in the murders of Louis Allen and Viola Liuzzo.

The urban rebellions brought another oppressed black population with significant potential for political power into SNCC's view. An enthusiastic black urban vote could represent the balance of power in several states with the highest number of electoral votes. Several SNCC workers moved to urban centers, participating in electoral politics and establishing community projects. SNCC speakers began addressing the concerns of a national audience, rather than just those of the South, and added the task of black consciousness-raising to community organizing. Women on the Atlanta Project and in Alabama were among the first to promote the idea that building a positive black consciousness was a needed first step in organizing.

In the political process of redefining race relations in the South, the young women in SNCC redefined themselves. From the early years of the Movement, black SNCC women rejected white standards of beauty and stressed a black identity by wearing their hair natural. Altering their expected social identities, SNCC field staff and administrators stopped dressing like other college students and graduates expected to join the middle classes, instead adopting cotton dresses and overalls to signal their identification with the poor and disenfranchised.

During the black power period, racial self-identification and its meaning were important issues for civil rights workers. Some white women in this book ceased to identify with the white community. Others, like three of the women in this section, discussed alternatives to a black/white perspective. Some, like Gwen Patton, considered the social and political significance of having a black identity.

Neither Black nor White in a Black-White World

Elizabeth (Betita) Sutherland Martinez

*Racial debates within SNCC spark a
Mexican American woman's Chicana identity.*

A Hidden Place

One evening almost forty years ago, I was with Jim Forman, the former executive secretary of the Student Nonviolent Coordinating Committee, at a friend's house in Puerto Rico, where I had been helping Jim prepare a first draft of his book, *The Making of Black Revolutionaries*. We had gone there to get away briefly from the pressures of SNCC work and concentrate on the book. That night we were talking about the Puerto Rican people and how they seemed to come in every color from vanilla white to ebony.

"We're all black, don't you see?" Jim said. "African people and Puerto Rican people and Mexican people; we are all black in the eyes of racism."

I thought to myself, *There's a lot of sense in that—and a reason to unite in common struggle.* I knew that more enslaved Africans had been brought to Mexico than the number of Spanish invaders who went there and that over time they mixed in. But Mexicans and other Latinos also have their particularities. Language, culture . . . We don't want to give up all that. So I said nothing to Jim, because the truth seemed to be somewhere in between his thought and mine, in a hidden place we had yet to find.

Yankee No!

I have spent a lot of time looking for that place, going back to childhood. I was born in Washington, D.C., where my immigrant father had finally found a clerical job at the Mexican embassy. Like most Mexicans, he was *mestizo,* mixed—a combination of indigenous, European, and African. From a respected Oaxaca family, he was quite dark. My mother, a Spanish teacher with strong feelings against injustice, was fair-skinned, blue-eyed, of working-class Scotch-Irish descent.

For my first twenty-five years or so, I was Betita (a Latino nickname for Elizabeth, like Betty). My parents and I made yearly trips to Mexico every summer to visit relatives there and renew a sense of belonging. But there were very few Mexicans in Washington, D.C., at the time, so Latino consciousness lacked a sense of constant, interactive community. No people of color lived in the suburb where I grew up, and our white next-door neighbors would not allow their daughter to play with me. I went to all-white schools from kindergarten through college. In elementary school, where the children could not pronounce my name, Betita, they called me "Potato" (a real winner). They asked, "Are you Hawaiian or something?" I felt anger against a racist, Eurocentric society that did not believe in the value of learning Spanish and made fun of Mexicans, but I did not have the words for it then.

One day when I was a small child, I took a trip to downtown D.C. with my father. We were sent to the back of the then-segregated bus, past many empty seats. The message came across loud, although confusing: something is seriously wrong with you. At home, though, we always spoke Spanish at dinner, and my father recalled with pride the Mexican Revolution, which he had witnessed as a young boy in 1910, and heroes like Emiliano Zapata of the peasants' land struggle. His enthusiasm, combined with anger at the United States Marines for bombing the Mexican city of Vera Cruz four years later to stop the revolution, made an unforgettable impression on me. Life did not have to be like that bus.

In my first job out of college, my Yankee-No spirit expanded into a global anti-imperialist consciousness. I worked for five years at the United Nations as a researcher on European colonialism in Africa: more racism, more reasons for resistance. Then, in 1959, I went to Cuba a few months after the revolutionary victory against Cuban dictator Fulgencio Batista. The luxurious lobby of what had been the Hilton Hotel, today the Havana Libre, was filled with peasants who had come into town from the countryside, sitting in chairs covered with gilt and enjoying a sense of liberation. These peasants were the same kind of *campesinos* my father had seen riding victoriously into Mexico City decades earlier. For me, that image defined a dream of liberation, of those at the bottom of society rising to the top. Soon after I began working with the Fair Play for Cuba Committee in New York. By 1961, after the infamous Bay of Pigs invasion, when Cuba declared itself socialist, so did I.

In the Movement

As black anti-racist protest intensified in the United States after the mid-1950s, I understood that to fight militantly against racism and for social justice, the black Civil Rights Movement was the place to be at that time. I first joined in supporting the defense of Robert Williams, the NAACP leader in Monroe, North Carolina, who had the nerve to organize armed resistance in his community against Ku Klux Klan attacks in 1960.

Next I served as a volunteer with New York Friends of SNCC. The group included several book editors. I was then an editor at Simon and Schuster. By then I had become Liz Sutherland, taking the surname from my mother's side when I began writing for publication and thinking "Betita Martinez" just would not make it in the New York literary world. I finally convinced Simon and Schuster to publish *The Movement,* a powerful photo book with text by Lorraine Hansberry. The royalties went to SNCC. After the unspeakable 1963 Birmingham, Alabama, church bombing by Klansmen that left four young girls dead, I found it was impossible not to work in the Movement full-time.

Jim Forman hired me to run SNCC's New York office, and SNCC people soon became my fellow soldiers in a passionate war on injustice. In SNCC I did not grapple with my particular identity, with being half Mexican and half white. The work said who I was. I had joined people, white alongside black, who were giving their lives to end a monstrous social evil—more than that, really: to humanize our entire society.

During the 1964 summer project in Mississippi, I traveled around the state to urge summer volunteers and community activists to go to the Democratic National Convention in Atlantic City at the end of the summer and to support the Mississippi Freedom Democratic Party challenge. I did not think about my personal identity. I did think, when driving at night in areas like the Delta, that I could get killed for civil rights work. One day that summer in Jackson, walking with Jim Forman down the street near the office of the Council of Federated Organizations, which directed the summer project, some white guys in a yellow convertible gunned their engine from behind us. We jumped several feet to avoid being hit. That was a reminder.

Back in New York, no one white-baited me to my face. My work consisted primarily of fund-raising, public relations, the media, and other support for the struggle in the South. As a nonblack person, I did not believe that I should make policy and personnel decisions. I attended meetings at Harry Belafonte's home to plan SNCC fund-raisers, for example, but not in any leadership role. All this seemed perfectly acceptable to me; after all, I wasn't black. My whiteness may have mattered when SNCC field secretary Willie Ricks got pissed off at me in the New York office for nagging him about going to see a dentist. Or did he see me primarily as a woman? Or primarily as a bureaucrat? Or all of the above? It was hard to tell then, and so it is in retrospect. Maybe I just didn't want to perceive the racial hostility.

My age may have helped me to escape racist hostility and also sexism. I was forty when most of the SNCC staff were in their early twenties, and I had a position of some authority in relation to the outside world. My work included, for example, trying to maintain SNCC's largely Jewish funding base (even after SNCC took a pro-Palestine position). Doing my job of notifying the press about events in the South, my identity had not mattered. Helping Stokely Carmichael write an article for the *New York Review of Books* or edit the book he wrote with Charles Hamilton, *Black Power,* my identity did not matter. Representing SNCC on the 1966 United Farm Workers march to Sacramento, it did matter, but in a useful way, since I spoke Spanish. The same was the case for a 1967 trip to Cuba with Julius Lester, George Ware, and Stokely Carmichael to attend a huge gathering of Latin American revolutionaries.

I was a SNCC worker; that remained my self-definition. In fact, I deeply regret neglecting another identity: being the mother of a young daughter who needed much more attention than she received in those years.

White SNCC Workers: A Major Issue

Sitting together at a 1965 staff meeting, Ella Baker and I whispered almost the same words to each other about SNCC: "I think we need an ideology." It's a heavy word, *ideology,* but I think we both meant "an analysis that provides guideposts to fundamental social change, a worldview accompanied by principles, strategy, and tactics." For me, such a worldview would be founded in Marxism, with a Cuban revolutionary accent.

Headed in a very different direction, a faction of black SNCC members focused on the presence of white people on SNCC's staff as a major problem, even *the* problem. SNCC took its first organizational step on that issue at the Kingston Springs, Tennessee, staff meeting of May 1966. White activists should organize in the white community while black activists continued in the black community, everyone agreed. Since SNCC wasn't organizing in the white community, this decision signaled to white staff: go do your own thing; it is necessary but not for SNCC to do.

Some months later, at the full staff meeting held on the New York estate of black entertainer Peg Leg Bates, a louder note was sounded. An hour or two after midnight, those staff still present voted to expel white staff members.

Several black SNCC leaders opposed the decision, and the next morning Jim Forman dramatized his concern by moving to dissolve SNCC and hand over its assets to help newly independent African nations. This motion failed, but the meeting did agree that whites could stay after all—however, without voting rights. In any case, only seven white staffers remained.

The message came across: SNCC should and would be an all-black organization. This did not disturb me at the time; it seemed clear to me that SNCC should be all black. I had no problem arguing for SNCC's stand. For instance, I met with Jack Newfield of the *Village Voice*, explaining "black power" to him with no hesitancy. I simply believed in SNCC. Looking back, I wonder if there was a nascent Chicano/Chicana nationalism in my fierce defense of what could be called black nationalism.

It also helped avoid conflict that the New York office staff was primarily composed of female volunteers, especially between the time of Marion Barry and Ivanhoe Donaldson, who succeeded me. Our work rarely went beyond office-type functions, planning fund-raisers, helping mostly male warriors visiting from the South—all within the natural domain of women, right? No problem, then, if women ran everything. And by the way, this was a marvelous group of women, including several full-time white volunteers who put in long hours daily. They included Judy Ruben, Eve Osman, Lucille Perlman (Tireless Queen of the Mailing List that produced much of SNCC's income), Mary Britting, and others whose names escape me now at age eighty—please forgive.

In retrospect, I think SNCC's struggle over its white staff actually veiled the larger, profound question of vision and strategy: How to work justly against injustice. How to accomplish justice within an unjust system. How not to brutalize individual humans in the course of humanizing a brutal society. How in hell to make revolution in these United States. To put it in immediate terms: having won the vote and a certain desegregation, where on earth do we go from here?

Black, White, and Tan

The white staff debate signaled an identity crisis for SNCC, and I gradually stepped up to questions of my own. There were two Chicanas on SNCC staff then, Mary (Maria) Varela and I. As far as anyone seems to remember, we were classified as white, even though I did not consider myself either white or black. I also do not remember identifying myself as Mexican American until I wrote a long paper to SNCC's Atlanta headquarters titled "Black, White, and Tan" in June 1967. It was my first attempt to air some thoughts as a Mexican American (the term Chicano/Chicana was not much used on the East Coast as yet). In that paper I described the racism experienced by Mexicans, with the goal of showing linkage between the black and brown struggles.

No response to that paper ever came. I do not remember being surprised or hurt by the silence. I knew that almost everyone in the United States at that time saw race relations in strictly black-white terms. A blinding ignorance about Latino/Latina Americans, Asian/Pacific Island Americans, and Native Americans marked the whole society. Among most black people, other peoples of color might be seen as allies, but rarely as part of the fundamental racial paradigm. I don't remember how SNCC viewed Arab Americans; the belief in Islam may have made a difference there.

Later that year I stepped down as head of the New York office, yet I continued working under Ivanhoe Donaldson and with Kathleen Cleaver, who was also new on the staff. But after the trip to Cuba with SNCC, I left SNCC to write the book *The Youngest Revolution: A Personal Report on Cuba*. Thinking about a Spanish-speaking revolution consumed me. The ground of my life was shifting, stretching. Then came August 1968—the season of global revolutionary movements.

On June 5, 1967, in New Mexico, twenty armed *Mexicanos* active in the land struggle had taken over a courthouse when police violated their right to organize. A year later a friend asked me to go with him to northern New Mexico and start a bilingual movement newspaper about the land struggle there. Something clicked. But still: could I do a newspaper in the Southwest, where I had never been? That would be really arrogant, but why not go visit for a week or two?

On the day of my flight to Albuquerque, a crisis involving SNCC and the Black Panther Party exploded in New York City. Plans for a joint press conference at the United Nations demanding freedom for Huey Newton collapsed in the face of unresolved conflicts between the two organizations. The plane left with me on it, upset because I had wanted to spend my life tearing down the prison called white supremacy and there was no better place to do it than alongside African Americans. Working for SNCC from 1961 to 1968 had therefore seemed perfectly natural. What would be natural now?

When the plane landed late that night, you could see the soft, mysterious shape of the Sandia Mountains nearby in the moonlight. The warm air reminded me of a nighttime landing at La Paz, Mexico. A voice inside me said, "You can be Martinez here. It feels like home!"

Later another voice would say, "This New Mexico has its own prison of white supremacy. It is more of a colony, where the police and judges and many officials are brown, but real economic and political power is in white hands. The brown people were born colonized, not enslaved like blacks, but white supremacy dominates both."

"So the two prisons are really one. And the fight is really one," said the last and loudest voice. "Let us tear down all such prisons together. Go liberate!"

That was the hidden place of truth I sought in that earlier conversation with my beloved friend Jim. That is where I have tried to live ever since. That is tomorrow's great meeting place.

Another Path

Life teaches us that we are all creatures of our times—both individuals and organizations. I went to New Mexico as an individual. It was time for me to extend the battle against racism and start finding myself in new, Chicana ways. I started a Chicano movement newspaper, *El Grito del Norte* (The Cry of the North), and later a communications center. From SNCC's "Liz Sutherland," I became Betita Martinez again, overnight. Nevertheless, I never separated the two in my mind. If Sutherland was Martinez, then Martinez was Sutherland, and Liz was Betita and so be it.

As an organization, SNCC also began in the same period to extend its view of the anti-racist struggle and find itself in new ways. It was becoming much more "Third World"—Asia, Africa, Latin America—conscious and committed to the struggle for human rights "not merely in the United States but throughout the world." Other organizations founded to fight for black peoples' rights, like the Black Panther Party, had taken or were taking the same stand.

In response, I wrote:

Is SNCC embarking on a sincere but formalistic rhetoric? Will there be new contradictions? For example, Latin America, a major part of the Third World, contains people of many colors. There are those who look absolutely white; there are those who look absolutely black, and everything in between. If SNCC is to establish contact with Latin Americans it must understand that it will be working with white-looking people sometimes.

Another problem: most Latin American revolutionaries, especially leaders, are socialists or communists. Given the need for land reform and the nationalization of United States' industries, they can hardly be anything else. But black youth in this country have often seen Marxism, socialism, communism, as a white thing, forgetting that such is the ideology of most Third World revolutionaries. It seems much easier, then, to stick to purely nationalist struggles and color issues than to sort out class and other political complexities. But SNCC must begin to do the second thing.

SNCC's acts of cross-racial solidarity dated back to 1965 when Stokely Carmichael met with César Chávez of the farmworkers and an exchange of staff was arranged. In that same spirit, field secretary Ralph Featherstone came to Albuquerque representing SNCC in 1968 to meet with Reies López Tijerina, leader of Alianza's land grant struggle. In June 1969 Phil Hutchings (then program secretary of SNCC) came with "Brother Crook" (Ron Wilkins) of Los Angeles SNCC and Sam Petty of the Black Liberators in St. Louis to support a major Alianza protest on land issues. They were all arrested, along with my daughter, Tessa, by state police, who swooped down on the crowd with guns drawn.

Back in the New York area, SNCC had begun developing close relations with the Young Lords Party of Puerto Ricans for independence. We were talking nationalism, but not just one nationalism. We also related to individual Asian American radicals like the family of Yuri Kochiyama, Pat Sumi, and Chris Choy, as well as Arab Americans. Another indication of the change came when the Third World Women's Alliance, initiated in New York by Fran Beal and others from SNCC, expanded to include not only African American but also Puerto Rican and other women of color.

In 1969 SNCC changed its name to the Student National Coordinating Committee and said in effect that it was open to any person of color. That opening resulted from the increasingly urban work by SNCC. How swift the change from 1966, when SNCC's white staff seemed such a hot issue and my "tan" so irrelevant, to 1968, when solidarity with the "tan" and other colors had become desirable! Two short years. If SNCC had survived, it might have led us beyond the prevalent black-white vision of race relations to a new and much more powerful vision of potential revolutionary forces in the United States.

A Few Last Words

For some twenty-five years I've thought about the price of revolution, the human toll of righting wrong. The price seemed worth it because the toll of accumulated injustice over the years was infinitely greater. I went to Cuba, Hungary, Poland, and Russia in the 1960s, to find out about the price to be paid and whether I personally could pay it. Could you work in a struggle that destroys your friends? On a grimmer note, could you kill your father as "a traitor to the revolution" if ordered to do so? These questions were not abstractions, not in the 1960s-1980s. Revolution could mean a moratorium on humanism (sometimes in the name of humanism). The unrelenting power of the external enemy stimulates internal de-individualization (what a word!—I mean denial of separate, individual reality). Humanistic values may tremble in the balance. Is this inevitable? I hope not. I think not. But how do we make sure?

I failed to do so in my political work from 1976 to 1985 in the San Francisco Bay Area when I joined what was called "the party-building movement" of ultra-left organizations. Most called themselves Marxist or Maoist, although I think Karl and the Chairman would have turned over in their graves watching us at work in their name. Didactic in demanding the "correct line" every minute, sectarian toward everybody else, our party was the only one led by women, but that did not make much difference in the long run. At our best, we did some great work among poor and working-class people of color. At our worst, let us just say that we became a classic example of the anti-humanist struggle for a humanist society—until we finally woke up to the truth and self-destructed. My work today says I did learn from all of that. I learned there is no denying respect for the individual in the process of uprooting individualism, child of capitalist combat. Our human oneness with all living creatures and the land itself cries NO to any definition of social justice that does not affirm that oneness.

What some have called "revolutionary Third-Worldism" lives in my heart. My struggle for identity should now rest.

We could say that SNCC had a long struggle with its identity, that it had to grow stronger through change. As an organization it could not do so, in the end. But as righteous commitment that united thousands of human beings in a way rarely found in this country, SNCC lives. SNCC still lives in my heart, as in so many others', for its militance, courage, and dedication—and as something very personal that I can only call a feeling of family. Not an exclusionary family whose members feel superior to those outside, but a collectivity. At its best, SNCC held up a mirror to U.S. society that reflected back what this nation could become.

I see SNCC's inspiration grow in today's youth, especially among young women of color. For their sake, I have tried to learn from the past while being part of this book. Thank you, all my SNCC sisters, for making that happen. *Gracias, con todo corazón.*

A Chicana activist, author, and educator, **ELIZABETH (BETITA) SUTHERLAND MARTINEZ** has written several books, including *De Colores Means All of Us* and *500 Years of Chicana Women's History*, and edited *Letters from Mississippi* (reissued in 2002). She has taught ethnic studies and women's studies in the California State University system, conducted anti-racist training workshops, and worked on Latino/Latina community issues. As an anti-war activist, she traveled to North Vietnam in 1970, and in 1983 ran for governor of California on the Peace and Freedom Party ticket. In 1997, still believing that racism is not only a black-white issue, but one that embraces brown, red, and yellow people, she co-founded and began directing the Institute for Multi-Racial Justice in San Francisco, a resource center that aimed to help build alliances among people of color. She was one of one thousand women from 150 countries nominated for the 2005 Nobel Peace Prize. Her alma mater, Swarthmore College, awarded her an honorary doctorate in 2000. Martinez celebrated her eightieth birthday in 2006.

I Knew I Wasn't White, but in America What Was I?

Marilyn Lowen

A young Detroiter defines her own identity
as she confronts American racism.

Discovering My Identity

One afternoon in 1950 I was walking home from first grade with my best friend, Cookie. Suddenly we were joined by some older boys. Cookie grabbed my elbows from behind and attempted to pin my arms back while the others began to beat me. Furious at this betrayal, I broke loose from Cookie and landed a good blow to her lip. The words "dirty Jew" caught my attention, a clue, perhaps, to the ambush. We were the only Jewish family in our Lincoln Park, Michigan, neighborhood. Cookie, I learned later, was Catholic. The friendship was over, and I began to wonder about the words "Catholic" and "Jew."

I wasn't at all prepared for such an experience, and I've always been glad I fought back. I didn't know at the age of six that I was a member of a hated, persecuted race. When I got home, I asked my mother, "What is a Jew? Is it some kind of animal?" This incident made me aware of how even as a very young child, a Jewish or black person has to start putting these things together, figuring out what's going on, and trying to understand what it is all about.

By the time I was seven years old, we had managed to move to a safer, predominantly Jewish neighborhood on Detroit's west side called Russell

Woods. Old trees graced the area of well-constructed, two-story brick houses. Soon afterward people of color began moving in. It was hard for me to understand what was meant by "black" or "colored" or "Negro." Our neighbor, Mayo Partee Sr., was about my complexion; his wife, Jennie Partee, was brown-skinned. I began to learn that this colorizing of the neighborhood was causing some consternation among some of our white neighbors. This was upsetting me. I would stare at the black and white octagonal tiles in our bathroom for hours until I became dizzy. The patterns and shapes were contiguous—black and white, white and black. Where did one leave off and the other begin? What did those words have to do with *people*?

For Sale signs were popping up on the lawns all over our Russell Woods neighborhood. I considered them evil toadstools, poisonous mushrooms that sprang up in the night and taunted me on the way to and from school. I would try to kick them off their little wooden stakes and pull these signs out of the ground. This was probably my first civil rights activity.

I would hang up on frequent calls from blockbusting real estate agents exploiting racial fears for profit: "Do you want to sell your house? Better do it soon." Rather than give in to this pressure, my family became part of a group called the Russell Woods Neighborhood Association; its purpose was to preserve the neighborhood with its mix of families and peoples. We were already social friends with black families, visiting back and forth. I especially enjoyed going two houses down to spend time with my "other mother," Jennie Partee, a Spelman graduate, who introduced me to Langston Hughes's stories and poems.

Detroit was an extremely racially segregated city. There were some Jewish families in my neighborhood who identified with being white, perhaps out of fear or from a desire to be upwardly mobile. I knew I wasn't white, however. I knew my family and where we came from. My parents were first-generation children of refugees. My grandparents and ancestors had lived in exile in various European nations for centuries as outsiders without citizenship or other human rights. In Europe our physical appearance was distinctly different from that of most of the people among whom we lived. Trying to figure out where I fit in, I understood by the time I was nine years old that Jews were not white, but some kind of "middle" race, not fitting precisely into the American racial categories of black or white. I felt it was insane for Jews to think otherwise, because just a few years before, we had been designated "the most inferior race" (by the 1935 Nuremberg laws) and were being systematically wiped out of existence by a self-styled white "master race."

At about age ten I helped organize the youth contingent of the Russell Woods Neighborhood Association. Our goal was to strengthen ties between black and white youth living there, in the hope that we could keep the community a place where we could all live. We would meet at my house and talk about how important it was not to let the commercial interests who were promoting "white flight" divide and conquer us and how we had to stick together.

From about the age of ten through thirteen, several days a week after public school I attended the I. L. Peretz Kinder Shul, named for the popular Yiddish writer who lived in Poland at the turn of the century. Peretz was a secular modernist who stressed the need to maintain a Jewish culture and identity. Our tiny *shul* (school) was nonreligious, a place to study *Yiddishkeit* (Jewish folk culture) and *mamaloshen* (the mother tongue), the language of our ancestors. Our identification was with the history and culture of Jews who lived in Eastern Europe and had for centuries been "no class" citizens—meaning they couldn't own land, farm, go to the "other people's schools," or join professions. Long before the Holocaust, Eastern European Jews were ghettoized, restricted, raided, burned, and chased from border to border. There were only five of us, all girls, in my class. I have kept in touch with one friend from that class, Andrea Shapiro, who recently became a member of an organization called Not in My Name, which seeks peace with justice for both Israelis and Palestinians. Another classmate and friend, Peggy Goldman, was active in Detroit Friends of SNCC in the sixties and now defends the Cuban Five.

At the *shul* we also learned about the Warsaw Ghetto uprising when Jews fought back for forty days with bricks and bottles against Nazi tanks and armed soldiers. At home my mother would point out aunts, uncles, and cousins in family photographs who had been shot down in Europe by Nazi white supremacists. It was a miracle that any Jews survived (the Holocaust or the previous centuries of oppression). Our *lereryn* (teacher) Lisa Podolsky told us of how one night when the Cossacks came to burn her family's village in Poland, her sister had gone back into the family's hut to retrieve a loaf of bread to carry into hiding in the woods and was never seen alive again. Miss Podolsky taught us songs with words such as, "Let us sing with joy of a free, new world." Another had the chorus, "White, brown, black, yellow / Mix the colors all together / All humans are related / From one Father, From one Mother."

So I grew up feeling that racism was insane, something to be gotten rid of, that we were one human family. This is what shaped my life as a SNCC person. I never felt like I was a white person. I didn't grow up that way. From a very young age, as a Jew, I always felt my purpose was to be involved in fighting injustice, fighting for freedom, especially fighting racial oppression. I was born in 1944, and later when I read biographies of Jewish women resistance fighters in Eastern Europe, I felt as if I knew them and as if I were there with them.

By the time I was around twelve or thirteen, whenever I went to visit our black neighbors, the Partees, it seemed that my parents would call telling me to come straight home almost as soon as I arrived. The Partees had a son about my age nicknamed "Shorty," in direct contrast to his six-foot height. We were getting kind of sweet on each other; he used to come whistle the "Swinging Shepherd Blues" at my window, and we sometimes walked home from school together. The girls I usually walked home with, most of whom were Jewish, began ostracizing me, not walking home with me or speaking to me. It was clear that I had broken a taboo. My parents' and these girls' reactions were strange and upsetting to me. I'd heard about how in the segregated South black and white children were allowed to play together until adolescence, and then they were separated. I was trying to figure out if something like that was happening to me.

During this time, I put up a bulletin board at my school, Tappan Junior High School, about the recent 1954 *Brown v. Board of Education* Supreme Court decision against segregation in public schools. Although it was controversial, my social studies teacher, Mr. Sariego, didn't stop me, because I was a good student. Soon afterward, however, he sent me to the principal's office for reading Lillian Smith's *Strange Fruit* in class. On the cover of the book was a picture of a white man and a black woman in a loving embrace. Because Mr. Sariego was my favorite teacher, someone I felt close to, I experienced his action as a betrayal. The principal, whom the students called "Terrible" Terry Bannon, was said to be the brother of a warden of the Michigan State Penitentiary. The principal asked if my parents knew I read books like this and sent me home, suspended. I distinctly remember my lost feeling, walking home alone in the middle of the day while all the other children were in school. My parents supported my being an avid reader; I was certain that I had the right to read whatever I chose and that I had done nothing wrong.

In the fifties Detroit was in the throes of McCarthyism, and there was a lot of fear among the adults whom my parents knew. I was confused by this atmosphere, because the adults did not explain what was going on. I understood later that both of my parents were what used to be called "progressives," people who hated fascism and Nazis by nature, as natural to them as the right of people to keep on breathing. Both were descendants of Jewish refugees from Eastern Europe and had struggled their way through college and graduate school. My father, Leslie, earned a PhD in chemical engineering and invented something that made planes seal up when they were bombarded, rather than explode like they did in the Red Baron cartoons. My mother, Ethel, earned a master's degree in psychology. The fate of Ethel and Julius Rosenberg was distressing to my family. The Rosenbergs' names, occupations, religion, and culture were so similar to ours.

Because of McCarthyism, people would hide certain newspapers if visitors came to the house; some people stopped speaking to one another. A friend of ours who was a schoolteacher was fired from her job for refusing to testify before investigating committees or being suspected of being a Communist. She lived with us for a while after she lost her job and before she moved out of state. Once at a concert, when I went to speak to two friends whose parents had been hounded by the House Un-American Activities Committee (HUAC), my mother and father snatched me back because there were FBI agents around with cameras. My parents, who saw people losing their jobs and their reputations, were absolutely terrified of my being involved in any political activity.

Getting Closer to the Movement

Despite my parents' fears I remained active, joining an integrated youth group, the Detroit Brotherhood Youth Council (DBYC), sponsored by the Trade Union Leadership Conference (TULC), headed by Horace Sheffield. TULC was establishing an official black caucus within the United Auto Workers union. Influenced by black southern students' resistance to segregation, we wanted to confront segregation in the North. Our youth group was holding swim-ins to integrate a white-only swimming pool, Crystal Pool, located slightly outside Detroit's northern border—Eight Mile Road—where Northland Mall is located today. Some of the other DBYC members, like Frank Joyce and John Watson, became supporters of SNCC and long-term civil rights and labor activists in Detroit.

Also in 1960 and 1961 there were many days when I would walk about a mile from my high school to the downtown Woolworth's and join the picketing in solidarity with the southern student movement. Local NAACP youth initiated and ran the demonstrations. On the line we sang, "If they can't in the South, then we won't in the North," referring, of course, to the segregated lunch counters at the Woolworth's in the South. We had seen the photos of students, not much older than we were, getting beaten in their Sunday best for sitting down at the lunch counters, cigarettes burned into their skin, mustard and ketchup smeared on their clothing.

We sang a lot of union songs turned into civil rights songs, such as "Which Side Are You On?" and "We Shall Not Be Moved." We would sing in pouring rain, sleet, and snow, marching round and round in front of Woolworth's. A memorable sign carried by a black soldier read, "If we can die together in war, why can't we drink a cup of coffee together in peace?"

By 1960 I was a sophomore at Cass Technical High School in downtown Detroit. I wasn't admitted as was usual at the start of ninth grade. I believe that Mr. Bannon, who had suspended me for reading *Strange Fruit,* so disliked me that he withheld my entrance examination results. Cass admitted students by examination, drawing its student body from all over Detroit. It was the most racially and ethnically diverse high school in the city.

When I was in high school, around the age of fourteen, I went out to hear Miles Davis at a club called The Minor Key with another Cass student, Gerald Bray. My mother was very upset. I don't know if it was because Gerald was black or because I went to a jazz club at that young age. Whatever the reason, the next day she was upset enough to call the Detroit police to "talk some sense into me." Two Polish cops chastised me at my front doorstep, warning me about the dangers of associating with a black guy and what "good girls do and don't do." It took me a long time to let go of my disappointment with my mother. I felt as if I'd been turned over to the enemy. She'd taught us that the Poles had participated in confining our people to the ghettoes and sending them to concentration camps where our families had been massacred, so I felt betrayed. Later I did learn that some Polish people participated in the resistance to German occupation and saved Jewish lives at the risk of their own lives. Even though my parents had chosen to remain in a changing neighborhood and had given me a progressive education, as Jews in the context of McCarthyism and the then-recent Holocaust they felt vulnerable. Apparently they feared the potential power of white supremacy and wanted to protect our family from hostile social pressures.

The Northern Student Movement

Throughout high school I continued working actively with my friends in support of the southern student movement and also participated in the nuclear disarmament movement and the early protests against the war in Vietnam. In the fall of 1962 I enrolled at Bennington College in Vermont. During that semester I spotted a notice on the college bulletin board about a conference in New Haven, Connecticut, sponsored by the Northern Student Movement (NSM), stating that SNCC workers from Southwest Georgia would be there. I was very excited to see this, as it was a connection to what I'd been doing for years in Detroit. We'd been reading SNCC's *Student Voice,* so the names of the SNCC folk from Georgia were familiar to me. I had to go. With no money or transportation, I walked and hitchhiked from Bennington to New Haven and found Yale.

The first person I saw when I arrived at Yale was NSM activist Joan Countryman, wife of one of the organization's founders. She was nursing her son, Matthew, in the cafeteria. At that time Yale was an all-male, almost exclusively white school, yet here was a brown-skinned woman doing a very female thing in this bastion of white privilege and male supremacy. Joan's courage and self-confidence affected me profoundly. At the conference the SNCC workers from Southwest Georgia, including Ralph Allen, Peggy Dammond, and Charles Sherrod, led us in singing freedom songs and shared some of the experiences they had gone through. I had learned some of these songs in Detroit, but singing with my young heroes and heroines of the southern battlefront forged a deeper, more unbreakable bond between me and the Movement.

Here in the midst of like-minded people from the North and the South, I heard Carl Anthony, director of the Harlem Education Project (HEP), deliver the conference keynote speech. He talked about growing up in Philadelphia and explained why we needed a Civil Rights Movement in the North. He was recruiting college students to join NSM. Listening to Carl, I saw a way that I could usefully connect with the Movement. I called Bob Fletcher, my boyfriend in Detroit, and told him that we had to join NSM. Shortly afterward, Bob, who was in graduate school, connected with Frank Joyce, one of my fellow Crystal Pool demonstrators, and became involved in the Detroit branch of NSM, the Detroit Education Project.

I spent my winter nonresident work term in New York City at a regular job. Evenings and weekends I worked with two black radical organizations—the Harlem Anti-Colonial Committee, which supported anti-colonial movements in Africa, and the nascent Freedom Now Party, which advocated third-party politics. The following summer, the summer of 1963, both Bob and I went to Harlem to work with NSM's Harlem Education Project. The project was also black led, but followed the NSM practice of inviting white students from nearby colleges to tutor black inner-city youth.

As a full-time, unpaid staff member living in an area of Harlem with a flourishing drug trade, it could be an unsafe situation—especially for me, since my color identified me as an outsider. We didn't always have enough to eat; on occasion Bob's cousin would supply us with grape jelly, grits, and scrapple—government surplus commodity foods. At the end of the summer Bob remained in Harlem. I returned to school but was only interested in my cultural anthropology class. I organized a Bennington civil rights group, and the professor gave me the opportunity to study this organization's effect on our small rural college community. Members of the group traveled to Harlem to support the NSM project there; we also supported SNCC efforts like the Mississippi Freedom Democratic Party and the Mississippi Freedom Labor Union. I couldn't concentrate on my other three classes, because my heart wasn't in it. By then I felt that college wasn't contributing to the education I needed. My consuming purpose was to change conditions in society, especially to get rid of racism. I felt I could only learn what I needed by participating directly in the Movement. I perceived that this was a unique historical moment, an opportunity to make effective change. So when the semester ended in December, I joined Bob at the Harlem Education Project, where I worked as a tutor, tutorial organizer, and dance teacher.

We both left school to make education real for more people, including ourselves. In Harlem we met and associated with members of the Umbra literary group, which started the Black Arts Movement, among whom were David Henderson, Calvin Hernton, and Joe Johnson. We also met Sherron Jackson, an associate of Malcolm X. Theresa Del Pozzo, who later went to work for SNCC, was on the HEP staff in the summer of 1963. Stokely Carmichael, already on the SNCC staff and who, like Theresa, was from the Bronx, spent time around HEP. In the spring of 1964 Dorothy Zellner came to Harlem recruiting for the Mississippi Freedom Summer Project. Bob went on down after attending the Oxford orientation. His parents thought he'd lost his mind. Bob's father was born and raised in Yazoo City and left Mississippi in a legendary hurry to escape the Klan. His mother was from South Carolina.

I chose not to participate in Freedom Summer. HEP was similar to the Mississippi Summer Project in that it invited white college students into the black community. I'd seen some problems with the organizing strategy of bringing outsiders into a community; there were inevitable tensions based on culture, class, and race. So I decided not to go south until I was clear on what constructive role I could play and had more concrete skills to offer. Instead, during the summer of 1964 I worked in a summer camp program for inner-city Jewish youth in Brewster, New York, and learned more about education and caring for young people. When I did eventually go south, I worked in education.

In the South

I went south in March 1965, right after the Selma-to-Montgomery March. I arrived in Atlanta, in the predawn light of a spring morning, after riding all night with a stranger—a student who had posted a notice looking for passengers to share a ride south over the school break on a campus bulletin board at Wayne State University in Detroit. I'd been at Wayne since the fall of 1964, halfheartedly attempting to resume life as a college student and reconnecting with the Detroit Movement, especially Friends of SNCC.

Now, at last, I had made the journey south. I immediately began working in SNCC's photo department. Since Bob had been working as a SNCC photographer, he was already part of this department. He traveled back and forth between the field projects in the Deep South and the Atlanta office. The department's mission was to keep our own photographers shooting in the field and providing accurate images to the national and international media. After I'd been at the office for a while, Jim Forman asked me to set up an archival system for the photographs. Jim wanted SNCC staff to document the struggle ourselves to ensure that future generations would not have a distorted view of our history. Bob and I did travel to New York City for archival training at the New York Public Library's main research institution.

I worked in the tiny photo office down in the basement of the SNCC building at 360 Nelson Street. I kept in touch with SNCC photographers throughout the South, reminding them to send their film to be developed in our Atlanta darkroom. The rest of the basement crew consisted of SNCC photographer Rufus Hinton, then about seventeen, who worked in the darkroom; Wilson Brown, who ran the big printing press; and Alton Pertilla, who laid out pages for SNCC's newsletter the *Nitty Gritty*. Having no actual place of residence, I often slept there.

At that time I read the Vine Street Project's position paper, which I understood to say that to organize effectively in the Vine Street community it was necessary that the project be black led and the staff be exclusively black. Believing that our goal was to change unjust and inhumane conditions as quickly as possible, it was easy for me to agree with a clearly workable approach. There were only a few white people left in the Atlanta office, and there was intense discussion over the future role of white participants. Jim Forman said he wanted me to stay because of my skills. An African American woman on staff from York, Pennsylvania, I think, pulled my hand, urging me to leave for my own happiness and sanity. Although she cared about my personal welfare, I was glad Jim thought I could still be useful. Beyond all other considerations, I had left Detroit, college, and my birth family to build the free, new world of my childhood songs. Outside the movement family, there was nowhere else to accomplish this. The Movement had become my life, my family, my work. The world we were in the process of creating was still in progress. So I stayed on.

In June 1965 Bob and I decided to settle in Tougaloo, Mississippi, where he had been living and working since the summer of 1964. We were driving westward across Highway 80 through Alabama when the tire blew out and the car ran off the road into a ditch. I was taken to a hospital for black patients in Selma, Good Samaritan. I spent a month there in casts and slings; I had a broken leg and shoulder as well as lacerations on my head. This was very soon after the Selma march. The white doctor who came to see me, dressed in cowboy hat and boots, bragged about being a close friend of the town's sheriff, Jim Clark, a notorious enemy of the Movement. The quality of my medical treatment was questionable. Hooked up to various pulleys in the hospital bed, I still tried to organize the staff, African Americans who were making about two dollars a day, into a union.

Somehow the Medical Committee for Human Rights got word that I was in the hospital in Selma, notified my family, and had me shipped back up to Detroit. My long-suffering and intensely loyal mother got me patched up in a Detroit hospital, where my injuries were treated with more modern surgery and my bones were reset; however, the injuries had life-altering effects on my work as a dancer and have lessened my mobility in general. Nevertheless, in August, within days after the cast came off my leg, I was on an airplane to Mississippi, determined to rejoin Bob and the Movement.

I arrived in Mississippi at an odd time in the evolution of the Movement there. The Council of Federated Organizations and its member organizations were winding down their operations. Many of the SNCC staff and summer volunteers had left the state. The Movement community in Tougaloo at that time included Maria Varela, who had set up Flute Publications, which published the poetry of Charlie Cobb and Jane Stembridge, and prepared educational materials for the okra co-op up in the Delta and voter education projects. Bob and I worked with her to create other audiovisual materials for the Movement and lived together in Mississippi in open defiance of state miscegenation laws.

Sometime in 1965 or 1966 I made an all-night journey from New York to Mississippi to help the Pacifica Radio Network and WBAI, its New York affiliate, establish a movement radio station called Radio Free Mississippi. Since the person driving was a black man, when we were traveling through the South, I rode on the floor of the backseat under a blanket. This was a common strategy used by civil rights workers to protect themselves from racist attacks. Somehow the project obtained a radio tower, but it was never used for broadcasting. I remember the tall metal structure lying stretched out in Maria Varela's backyard, eventually becoming a structure for tomato and bean vines. On the shortwave radios that we used for communication, Varela's home was identified as "Radio City" because of this effort, and our home was called "Ace Base," a tribute to Bob's being an ace photographer.

Almost immediately after arriving back in Mississippi in August 1965, I began work with the Living Arts Project, sponsored by the newly established Child Development Group of Mississippi. Through CDGM, the federal government's Office of Economic Opportunity (OEO), the poverty program sent money to Mississippi's black community for preschool education and social services. At that time there was only a very small number of preschools for black children in the state. As part of the arts project, I traveled around the

Delta and northeast Mississippi with a group of local black students and two white male northern students, doing theater and puppetry performances for children at community centers. Once, after we had stopped at a white-only Dairy Queen in Clay County, two groups of white men in pickup trucks with gun racks in the back sandwiched us in as we drove away, one in front of our station wagon and one in back. I felt especially responsible for ensuring that no harm would come to the local students. Fortunately my SNCC driving skills kicked in. Driving very fast, I managed to get us away from the pickup trucks.

CDGM ended that summer. For six months Mississippi communities fought to get OEO to continue funding the program. In the spring of 1966 I lived in Batesville with the Miles family, long-time local activists, and, in the hope of receiving funds for these schools, helped establish three preschools in Panola County, in the towns of Sardis, Macedonia, and Batesville. Because of years of racist attacks, whenever cars passed near the house, Mrs. Mona Miles would tremble and her son Vernon would run and hide, yet they continued to be active in local movements and to shelter movement workers. I continued to work with CDGM through 1967 in teacher training and curriculum development. The leadership of CDGM was often identical to the leadership of the local movement and Mississippi Freedom Democratic Party infrastructure, spanning eighty communities in Mississippi from up north in the Delta down to the Gulf Coast. Although there was controversy within the larger movement community about the dangers of accepting money from the federal poverty program, local black activists enthusiastically welcomed it.

I believe CDGM was the federal government's concession to the MFDP's organizing attempts. Clearly it was a concession to the power of Mississippi's black activists who had risked their lives and organized throughout the state. Because of this movement connection, the programs were administered at the grassroots level by elected community boards. Many of the teachers and social service staff hired by the local committees were women who had previously been MFDP activists. Their only source of income had been as low-paid domestics and farmworkers. CDGM presented a rare opportunity to earn higher wages; sometimes the community board would allow women to share a position to spread the benefits among more people. Also the work was purposeful and immediately improved everyday life; the staff was helping to educate their own children and other children in their communities. Furthermore, community people were establishing their own institutions as they set up these schools, which also provided social services. The overall purpose of the program was to give children a strong reading readiness and socialization program to prepare them for success in their future education.

I felt we were raising the next generation of movement children, self-confident, skilled, unafraid to be curious, and excited about learning. Evidently my feelings were shared by many of the CDGM staff. Whenever the federal government withheld the poverty money, the unpaid staff and community supporters held statewide demonstrations calling for reinstatement of the funds and used their scarce resources to keep the schools going, even taking produce from their own small garden patches to provide food for the children attending the program.

Mississippi's traditional white political power structure gradually destroyed CDGM by creating a parallel organization cynically named Mississippi Action for Progress (MAP) without movement ties or orientation. These Mississippians were able to use their considerable political influence in Washington to divert federal funds from CDGM to MAP. My using tunes from freedom songs in CDGM schools was one small example used to bolster their demand that CDGM funding be cut. Movement folk managed to regroup and create Friends of the Children of Mississippi (FCM), which continued in the spirit of CDGM. Through the fall of 1968 I traveled for FCM to rural schools in Leake and Newton counties, located in the center of the state. Mrs. Winson Hudson of the Harmony community, outside of Carthage, Mississippi, was in charge of the teachers in these counties and became my main companion and colleague. Mrs. Hudson had worked closely with Medgar Evers and was the president of the Leake County NAACP. She was also a key activist in COFO, Freedom Summer, MFDP, and a tireless advocate for the improvement and safety of her Harmony community.

Leaving SNCC

I left Mississippi toward the end of 1968 for the sake of my unborn child. Bob and I thought that if our child were born in a Mississippi hospital, the baby would be at risk of mutilation or worse from racist doctors. I arrived in New York City eight and a half months pregnant and have remained there ever since.

As women, both black and white, local or outsiders, we struggled to survive as women always have, by being supportive of each other and handling the problems as they came along. SNCC women had a special kind of freedom. There was a tremendous amount of respect among freedom fighters for each other, men and women. In the Movement we became part of the nature and struggle of each place where we lived and worked. We were pretty much on our own, and we were pushed to the max. Everything we had—our physical and intellectual abilities, our survival skills—were constantly challenged in our effort to build a free new world.

SNCC may no longer exist in a formal sense with an address and a board of directors, but all of the people who were ever part of SNCC acknowledge each other and our common dreams and visions. We still feel connected. We remain part of an ongoing struggle we call the Movement.

MARILYN LOWEN eventually finished college through Goddard's adult degree program and went on to earn a master's degree in literature and creative writing at the City University of New York. A dancer and a poet, she has also been a teacher for most of her working life, instructing students from preschool through graduate school. She often uses the works of Langston Hughes and Lorraine Hansberry and teaches the Civil Rights Movement in her classes. Lowen assisted in the preparation of Mrs. Winson Hudson's unpublished autobiography, *A Lonely Walk to the Courthouse*, and is the mother of two sons and the grandmother of a boy and a girl.

Time to Get Ready

Maria Varela

*A Latina describes her tour of duty in the
1960s southern Civil Rights Movement.*

Once Zuni (my husband, Lorenzo Zuniga Jr.) and I lived in a different country from our young daughter, Sabina. Zuni enlisted in the U.S. Marines in the mid-1960s and did two tours in Vietnam. I served as a field worker for SNCC between 1963 and 1968, working first in Alabama and then in Mississippi. When I moved to New Mexico in 1968 there were few people with whom I could share my movement experiences. The exception was Vietnam veterans, especially those of color. We had each faced death. We had seen racism in its most lethal forms and felt let down by this nation's complicity. For many of us, our respective experiences in the 1960s separated us from this nation; "The Star-Spangled Banner" brings no hand to heart. Our view is from the vantage point of a country within a country. This other USAmerica is made up of people who recognize that assumptions of privilege bestowed by skin color or wealth belong to a few at the expense of the world's many. And that we live in this world to do something about it.

Sabina, a brown-skinned, brown-eyed, long-limbed woman, was "binational" during her teen years. While she saw the chasm that exists between the few and the many, she was a tolerant and trusting soul, who seemed color blind. Now in her early thirties, while still much more tolerant than her parents, her feet are planted firmly in this "other country." Part of the reason, she tells me, is what she learned from us, her parents, and from "the incredible people I met growing up . . . the SNCC veterans as well as Latino and Native American activists and artists." But I think what sealed her citizenship in this other country was when she acted on what she learned from all of us. She has used her artistic talents to work with at-risk youth, immigrant women, low-income and sometimes homeless middle school students to bring their anger at injustice into powerful performance pieces that give voice to those at the margins.

Swing Down, Sweet Chariot, and Let Me Ride

I looked down at the speedometer. It hovered at 115. My 1957 Packard hunkered down and propelled the three of us down Mississippi Interstate 55. As I glanced to the side, I saw the two-toned 1962 Chevy with its white occupants trying to pass us . . . yet again. The barrel of a long gun poked up between the two men in the front seat.

It seemed like an eternity since we had left Memphis and got on the interstate. Earlier that day, my companions, an older black woman and her daughter, and I had left a Student Nonviolent Coordinating Committee gathering at Highlander Center in Tennessee. We were on our way to the Mississippi Delta. Traveling in an integrated car in daylight had left us all a little tense. When we stopped for gas in Memphis that evening, I thought the cover of darkness meant the worst of the journey was over. Then I turned from the gas pump and saw the white male occupants of the Chevy staring at us. It was the fall of 1964, open season on civil rights workers.

The Packard moved effortlessly up to 120 mph. It ran as if made for this speed, not a shake or shimmy. My companions were deathly quiet. I closed my mind to thoughts of danger: gunfire from the pursuing car, a collision, a flat tire, a blown rod, or what would happen if the Chevy managed to pull in front and stop us. It was a moonless night, and my eyes were glued to the black strip of asphalt that stretched before us. One thing I knew for sure—I would sooner risk pushing the car to the end of the speedometer than stop on this desolate stretch of road in the far northern reaches of Mississippi.

Up ahead we saw a semitruck. The lack of any traffic since Memphis had made the pursuit lethal. If I could stay with the semi, perhaps the pursuers wouldn't make their move. We were now at 125, shooting down the road, trying to catch up to the tractor-trailer. As I pulled alongside the truck, the Chevy was on our tail. It was a delicate maneuver, slowing the Packard enough to allow me to slip in front of the semi, yet going fast enough to shake off the Chevy. Once in front, the trick was to stay close to the semi so that the Chevy could not come in between. The truck slowed way down and so did we.

Then the trucker tried to pass us. I sped up, staying as close to his front bumper as I dared. The Chevy tried unsuccessfully to move ahead of us both, but finally fell back behind the semi. We hovered close to our "guardian" semi for another few miles. The panic welling in my throat was held at bay by my companions' silent composure. Signs to the Batesville exit emerged. I shot back up to 125. I made the exit with neither truck nor Chevy in sight, cut the lights, and floated down the exit ramp into welcome darkness. The semi and the Chevy roared over us into the night. There was not a word spoken as we continued through Batesville on our way down to the Delta. The terror gradually subsided. Finally, in small murmurs, with a few tenuous chuckles, we dared to believe it was over. I thought that the Packard company must have been God's chariot maker.

My "chariot" got me into more trouble after the 1965 Selma-to-Montgomery March. Sixteen-year-old June Johnson, from Greenwood, had slipped out of Mississippi to participate in the Selma march. Her mother wanted her back home, *now*! Stokely asked me if I would take her. I gave him the "Is this a good idea?" look, which usually made him at least stop and think. But Stokely was more afraid of Mrs. Johnson's wrath than my look. He said he'd be in real trouble with her if he didn't get June back home. Never mind the trouble that June and I could get into.

And trouble we did. Right over the Mississippi state line, driving well under the speed limit, we were pulled over by a state patrol officer. The Packard's automatic load leveler was broken, leaving its trunk riding low. The officer ordered, "Open the trunk." It was empty. It didn't matter. I was arrested for "speeding" and spent the next three days in the Meridian, Mississippi, jail staring at the graffiti on the cell walls. (*"Billy left me and that's why I'm here."*) Resourceful June found her way back to Greenwood.

Terrifying encounters such as these became "normal" to those of us in the Movement who were new to the South. They had been "normal" for generations for those born and raised under southern U.S. apartheid. As civil rights workers, we had to be prepared anytime, anywhere to walk the killing fields. We learned a variety of responses to danger: sometimes to fade into the background, assuming local accent and dress; sometimes to emotionally play dead in hopes the stalker would lose interest; or sometimes to do something so bold as to catch him off balance, enabling flight. We learned how to overcome the paralysis of fear and developed finely tuned survival senses we never knew we had.

For example, one Sunday afternoon in the fall of 1966, Willie Ricks, Stokely Carmichael, and I were coming back from a meeting in the Delta in my "new" chariot, a 1959 Buick roadster. I was trying to get them to the Jackson airport to catch an evening flight back to Atlanta. All of a sudden the Buick lost power and began sputtering down the highway. We agreed that I would try to find someone to fix the car and they would look for a safe place to stay (this being shortly after Ricks and Carmichael had been propelled into the headlines as architects of "black power"). I was in my usual SNCC guise—an unremarkable dress with "going to church" shoes. My approach to survival was always to attempt to be unnoticed. But the highly noticeable sputtering, punctuated with backfires down the main highway in Sunflower County, called for a survival strategy that would have to be created on the fly. Ahead I noticed some young white men working on their cars at an otherwise closed gas station. I drove up and, putting on my best southern accent, breathlessly explained how I was "just rushin' to pick mah Daddy up from the airport" and how he would be "just SO upset if ah didn't get there on time."

With patronizing, knowing grins, the young men popped the hood, clustered around the engine, and found and replaced a cracked spark plug. Gushing gratitude (which at this point was heartfelt), I went looking for Ricks and Carmichael, who, not having found a place out of sight, were grimly walking down a dirt road back toward the highway. They quickly jumped into the car and we sped to the airport, almost unwilling to believe our luck.

The Roots of Resistance

How did this young, naïve, middle-class woman end up working in the Civil Rights Movement and living in the South for nearly six years? My roots of resistance ran deep into the rich soil made up of family, spirituality, and personal identity. As I was growing up, we moved so often (five times by the time I was nine) that I would joke I was from a '52 Pontiac station wagon. Our family became our tribe, nation, and state. My father was a Mexican national born in the state of Zacatecas. During the Mexican Revolution his father brought the family across the border to San Antonio, Texas, to wait out the war. But the revolution persisted, and because of severe anti-Mexican sentiment he moved the family to New Jersey, where my father met my mother (of Irish-German descent) in high school. My mother's mother worked in an embroidery factory in New York before she married and eventually died of tuberculosis when mom was eleven years old. In her eighties my mother told me that she had only recently remembered how, after her mother died, her childhood memories were laced with hunger.

Ethnic identity came primarily from the stories told when our tribe gathered and uncles recounted the adventures and pranks of Los Rodriguez-Varelas' childhood in Mexico. Grandfather forbade the use of Spanish in the house, because children of immigrants were punished for speaking their language in the classroom. Yet even years later, phrases and songs in Spanish would still escape. I don't remember anyone from my mom's side of the family telling us stories. Thus the Mexico stories loomed large, filling the gap and sealing the identity of my tribe.

I once volunteered in the fourth grade that I was Mexican, and the angry response of the teacher frightened and shamed me. "No, you are not! We're *all* Americans here," snapped Sister Rosita, her piercing eyes boring through me as I tried to disappear into the old wooden desk. While her reaction silenced any further discussions of identity, it only reinforced my allegiance to my tribe. It was an internal identity that, along with other personal information and feelings, I had learned to keep to myself.

Although we were a traditional Catholic family, my spiritual growth came largely from participating in the Young Christian Students (YCS) organization in both high school and college. YCS had its roots in the Belgian worker-priest movement of the 1930s and the resistance to European Nazism in the 1940s. By the 1960s YCS was a worldwide student movement, especially concentrated in Africa, Latin America, and Europe. Many YCS leaders were involved in independence movements and resistance efforts in the third world. Several were disappeared or killed. We were shaped by liberation theology, which holds that as Christians our vocation is to be actively engaged in dismantling racism, economic injustice, antidemocratic forces, and unjust wars.

After graduating from Alverno College, I joined the national staff of YCS in Chicago, where we made seven dollars a week and the organization took care of housing and travel expenses. My job was to organize YCS chapters on college and university campuses in the Midwest and Northeast. I also represented YCS at summer conventions of the National Student Association. There I met the founders of the Students for a Democratic Society. In late 1961 SDS founders Al Haber and Tom Hayden invited me to meet with them in New York to discuss the interest of SDS in creating an ecumenical effort of like-minded organizations to write a student manifesto critiquing U.S. social and foreign policy and lay out a vision of participatory democracy to achieve new policy directions. Looking for more diverse views, Hayden and Haber wanted to involve progressive religious groups and thus invited me to represent YCS at the Port Huron Conference in June 1962. Among the leaders I was drawn to was Sandra Cason (Casey) Hayden, who had worked for the Young Women's Christian Association in Texas and was married to Tom Hayden.

Several months later I was lying in the bottom bunk of a dormitory at a Catholic college in Green Bay, Wisconsin, taking a break between meetings with student leaders. I was agonizing over a decision that needed to be made. In my suitcase was a letter from Casey that was several weeks old. She asked if I would consider leaving YCS to work with her at the SNCC headquarters in Atlanta. I couldn't make up my mind. This request to join SNCC came at a time when I was organizing Catholic students in the North to support Freedom Rides and sit-ins in the South. These demonstrations were real-life illustrations of how Christians should apply the gospel. Yet, when called, I just could not bring myself to answer. It was too scary. Stories of people beaten, jailed, bombed, pursued by the KKK, and sometimes killed were vivid in my mind. Stories of flying cockroaches (that got into your hair) were equally as terrifying. I don't know what I was more afraid of, bugs or beatings. For weeks I struggled with the decision. My gut said no. My mind was undecided. My conscience prevailed: How could I, a YCS staff member, continue to exhort students to support fellow students in the South if I refused to go? In the summer of 1963 I boarded the bus to Atlanta.

Plans to work with Casey in the Atlanta SNCC office were detoured, however, when I was asked by Connie Curry and Paul Potter of the NSA to help staff a leadership summer school in Atlanta for black youth across the South. These high school students had spontaneously organized sit-ins in their rural communities in response to demonstrations organized by college students in urban areas. SNCC and NSA helped fund and organize the summer school because of their concern about the students' safety. Many were targeted for beatings and jailing almost weekly. The leadership program included black history, nonviolent resistance, and organizing principles to enhance leadership skills and provide students with effective organizing strategies. SNCC leaders were brought in as role models.

SNCC field secretary Frank Smith, complete with a battered straw cowboy hat, arrived at the leadership school from Selma, Alabama, in a beat-up brown station wagon with hay caught in its side trim. As he questioned me about myself, he suddenly focused in on descriptions of my YCS work. At the time, I wondered why he was so interested. Frank spoke of the Selma Movement and how the terrorism of the white power structure was extremely successful in preventing the black community from organizing voter registration. One key community leader was a young French Canadian, Father Maurice Ouellet, who was the pastor of a black Catholic parish. Bernard Lafayette, director of SNCC's Central Alabama Project, had been unsuccessful in persuading black ministers to open their churches for voter registration meetings. He was finally introduced to Father Ouellet, who, because of his support of the Civil Rights Movement, agreed to open St. Elizabeth's Mission for voter education meetings and adult literacy classes. SNCC wanted to find ways to support Father Ouellet's commitment. When Bernard showed up at the summer school later that week, he and Frank hatched the idea of my going to Selma to work with the pastor. They assured me that I would be underground the whole time. The people in Selma were used to missionary types working out of St. Elizabeth's. Up until then the plans were for me to work in Atlanta. Going into the field had never been presented as an option. It was too dangerous. I had been willing to put my toe in the water, but didn't want to jump in all the way. However, both Frank and Bernard were compelling in their belief that this was an essential move to strengthen the Selma Movement. Bernard commented: "None of us are Catholic. His bishop is against the Movement, and some in his parish have doubts about his involvement. He needs support from his own." Once again my conscience reluctantly made the decision. They handled the discussion with the Atlanta SNCC office and made calls to Father Ouellet.

In October 1963 I found myself, with great trepidation, on a Delta DC 3 to Selma. Coming toward me on the tarmac was a tall, charismatic priest whose belief in the Movement came as much from his heart and soul as from his head. He paid for the heart he put into the Selma Movement, however. Throughout 1964 and 1965 Lowndes County sheriff Jim Clark escalated the violence and retaliation on the black community. Internally conflicted, the black community tried, not always successfully, to pull together in the face of this deepening repression. Ouellet was unable to affect either white or black community leadership. He ended up in the hospital seriously ill from bleeding ulcers. But the dearest payment of all was his removal in 1965 from St. Elizabeth's by Archbishop Thomas J. Toolen because of Ouellet's involvement in the Selma Civil Rights Movement.

St. Elizabeth's became the meeting place for me to connect with SNCC staff. That fall, Worth Long, SNCC field secretary from North Carolina, had taken Bernard Lafayette's place. Our first meeting is etched in my memory. Worth came to the back door by way of a sidewalk edged with riotously colorful flowers surrounded by a deep green lawn with hundred-year-old shade trees. But the look on his face was in grim contrast to the surroundings on that beautiful fall day. His body was tense and his face frozen like an infantryman walking through a minefield. I opened the door for him.

As he stepped into the room, the mask splintered. His face lit up in a warm smile. He didn't know me from Adam. But the parish hall was sanctuary.

Worth and I devised a literacy project geared toward the twenty-one-question voter registration test required by the state of Alabama. The project would recruit and train African American college students to come to Selma and teach literacy in black churches and homes. The summer of 1964 was our target date. It was understood that the literacy test for voter registration was not the main barrier to black people's voting. Literate people, including African American teachers, were flunking the test. We believed that if enough people could read well enough to take the test and all were flunked by the county clerk, it could lead to a successful class action suit.

Part of my research on literacy programming included tutoring Mrs. Caffee, an older woman referred to me by Father Ouellet. Twice a week at Mrs. Caffee's house we began reading lessons with the Bible. It was her favorite and only book. However, since she had memorized most of it, it was hard to distinguish what she was reciting from memory and what she was reading as a result of our lessons. While she did want to learn to read, she *really* wanted someone to go fishing with her. And she found a fishing partner in me. We would sneak away to a small pond west of Selma, her favorite place to catch bream. Sometimes Mrs. Caffee would point out what looked like a weed to me. She would tell how it could be used as a medicine or maybe as a tonic that could conquer that lazy feeling that came with spring. I learned a lot more from Mrs. Caffee than I think she ever learned from me. Through teaching, fishing, and visiting, I began to get small insights into this rich culture of the Deep South with its persistent traditional African practices.

In preparation for the Selma Summer Project, I spent the fall of 1963 researching existing literacy materials. Within a very short time I realized those materials would only make the problem worse. Written by white authors about white life, they were framed in simplistic, childish wording. During the NSA-SNCC summer leadership program, I had seen African American students' eyes shine and their heads lift proudly when they read stories of accomplishments of African civilizations and African American heroes. If SNCC were going to develop a literacy program that would not just teach reading but build pride and hope, materials rooted in black culture and history would have to be created from scratch.

At the same time the Selma literacy project was in the planning stages, Bob Moses and others in the SNCC leadership were planning a volunteer project in Mississippi for the summer of 1964. It would target students from the top schools in the nation and bring "the influential U.S." into the feudal South. To some in SNCC, it didn't matter what the volunteers did. Their presence would open the jaws of segregation. If white kids were beaten, jailed, or even killed, then perhaps the United States would finally notice its apartheid.

I was among those in SNCC who did *not* support the Mississippi Summer Project. As I struggled with the logistics of the Selma summer literacy project, where only four black volunteers would be involved, it seemed madness to think about managing and protecting nearly a thousand white volunteers *and* the local people who would be endangered by their presence. But most of all I feared the impact of volunteers on the emerging black leadership within the communities where SNCC worked. SNCC's philosophy of organizing was, in a nutshell, "let the people decide." We believed that the best solutions to mobilizing people and solving local problems would come from those whose voices were not usually heard. People were used to preachers and teachers speaking for them. It often took intensive work before ordinary people began to raise their voices and speak for themselves.

Could we expect this nascent local leadership to oversee or work in a peer relationship with the more articulate and affluent northern volunteer, whether white or black? And while a local project might be able to absorb one volunteer without disruption, what would be the impact of several volunteers? By the time race, class, ethnicity, and urbanity were factored in, the summer project seemed like chaos looking for a place to self-destruct. From my point of view, common sense dictated that the project be scaled down and tested on a smaller basis.

But logic yields to the inexorable forces of history. Nineteen sixty-four was a presidential election year. Dismantling segregation required more than fielding volunteers to focus national attention on southern apartheid. New civil rights laws and federal interventions were needed to protect voter registration efforts. Utilizing summer volunteers, SNCC proposed founding the Mississippi Freedom Democratic Party, a majority black party open to whites in direct challenge to the all-white Mississippi Democratic Party delegation at the national convention in Atlantic City. The idea quickly found support both among local communities and northern supporters. It would bring the struggle north, providing an opportunity, we thought, for our liberal allies to overcome the Dixiecrats' ability to maintain apartheid at the congressional level. While we weren't staffed up or adequately funded to handle the project, clearly this was an idea that couldn't wait another four years.

The Mississippi Summer Project went forward at the same time that the Selma Summer Project hit the ground. What was remarkable about this era was how young people with little or no experience could materialize raw ideas into concrete projects. Equally remarkable was that women in SNCC were supported in taking leadership roles. While initially I was destined for a traditional woman's role in the Atlanta office, that destiny changed when Frank and Bernard had the idea that working in Selma was more important. I had many doubts but drew my strength from their belief that I could do this. When I developed a proposal to fund the Selma Project, I had to bring it for approval to Jim Forman, SNCC's executive director, and his assistant director, Ruby Doris Robinson. Ruby Doris scared me. She was a tough, brusque, and no-nonsense African American woman. To my surprise, when I presented the proposal, she championed it through the approval process and continued to support my work in SNCC. In these early years, the support of SNCC leaders for men *and* women to translate ideas into action resulted in the piloting of innovative programs that would influence the fields of policy, education, and community development all over the country for the rest of the twentieth century and into the twenty-first.

By early spring of 1964 I had raised funds for the project and recruited four black students: Silas Norman from Augusta, Georgia; Karen House from Washington, D.C.; James Wiley from Gary, Indiana; and Carol Lawson from New York. With some help from innovative adult educators in the North, a literacy training program was drafted for us to test. We held two weekend training sessions in the North and one weeklong session in Tuskegee, Alabama, to prepare teaching methods and materials. By the time the four students arrived in the middle of June, we were ready to schedule test classes.

Two weeks into the program, Lyndon Johnson signed the 1964 civil rights bill, which included the desegregation of facilities serving the public. Unbeknownst to me, the staff decided to celebrate by going to the local white-owned Thirsty Boy for ice cream. After they were refused service, Sheriff Jim Clark strode in with cattle prod in hand. They were immediately arrested and put in jail. Since there wasn't anyone in the SNCC office, I was going to have to drop my cover to get them out. Screwing up my courage, I put on my most feminine summer dress and went down to the jail. If I hadn't been so afraid, it would have been almost enjoyable to watch the expressions on the guards' faces as they tried to figure out who this light-skinned girl was and why she was there. Getting nowhere, I left. The next couple of days were spent coordinating release efforts with the Atlanta SNCC office. SNCC bailed out the staff days later, but the literacy work ground to a halt. Because of their arrests, the staff and I had become targets of Sheriff Clark and his posse. We could no longer hope to test the literacy program without endangering participants.

Angry about how they were treated in jail, the students began spending most of their time at the SNCC office working on demonstrations and mass meetings. James Forman, executive director of SNCC, invited Silas to join

SNCC staff. In the minds of the students, the literacy work became irrelevant as they faced the outlaw sheriff Jim Clark. (Silas Norman eventually became Alabama Project director for SNCC.) Testing the literacy program blew up, because it didn't matter to the racists whether we stood in their face in demonstrations or quietly tutored someone to read. All of our actions were assaults on apartheid. Our attempts to create an orderly, sequential way of challenging the literacy tests disintegrated. But it almost didn't matter. Direct action and the violent responses by segregationists resulted in the passage of the 1965 voter rights bill, which included provisions to outlaw literacy tests.

Radicals to the Roots

The radicalization of SNCC was foreseen by our godmother, Ella Baker, who once said: "We are going to have to learn to think in radical terms. I use the term radical in its original meaning—getting down to and understanding the root cause." While she was godmother, the midwife of this radicalization was the Democratic Party and liberals who put politics above the law. As we mobilized during 1964, most of us working in the Black Belt South still believed that the United States Constitution would require the federal government to intervene quickly and massively to end segregation in the South. I, for one, looked up to the political leaders of this country and believed that once they understood the situation, they would not leave us defenseless as we labored to bring the rule of law to the feudal South.

But 1964 irrevocably broke the faith between many in my generation and mainstream USAmerica. The complicity of the FBI in shielding the murderers of summer volunteers Andy Goodman, James Chaney, and Michael Schwerner broke the faith. The federal government's refusal to protect voter registration workers organizing to form a *legal* political party made up of a majority of black Mississippians open to white people, as opposed to the illegal all-white Democratic Party, broke the faith. The 1964 Democratic National Convention in Atlantic City broke the faith; lawfully elected delegates from the MFDP were unlawfully refused delegate status. And the gatekeepers withholding these seats were not the racist Dixiecrats. They were liberal Democrats, union leaders, and the old-guard "Negro" politicians who couldn't or wouldn't grasp the amount of blood and daily terror that had gone into this magnificent expression of grassroots democracy. Heroes were toppled; trust in the system was shattered. We believed that reforming moribund, corrupt institutions would not eradicate racism and poverty in this country. Going to the roots brought many of us to a radical perspective.

My citizenship in the other USAmerica was sealed. I don't remember ever asking myself after Atlantic City, or the chase down the interstate, or the jailing in Meridian, "What am I doing here?" My initial indecision had disappeared. There seemed no place else to be but in this other country. In the mainstream they believed they lived in a democracy: heroes were white and male; culture was the ballet, symphony, and art museum; religion was about attending church or synagogue. Life was the pursuit of "happiness" purchased by a college degree, a career, or, for women, a good marriage.

In the other USAmerica it was a reverse image. Our leaders were African American men *and* women. Our heroes were local people who began the process of dismantling this country's system of apartheid and forced the nation to begin to live its Constitution. Their lives and economic security were at daily risk. Their spirituality brought the Old and New Testaments alive as they faced the possibility and reality of homelessness, torture, and even death because they stood up for their beliefs. In this USAmerica we got down to the roots of an authentic life: sacrificing safety, security, and even life itself for one another.

By the end of 1964 the stakes had been raised: the beatings, bombings, and spilled blood fed the blood lust of the segregationists. In February 1965 in Marion, Alabama, state police "rioted," attacking a group of demonstrators attempting a night march to the courthouse. Twenty-six-year-old Jimmie Lee Jackson was shot and killed while attempting to protect his mother from being clubbed by the state police. A Selma-to-Montgomery March was called. Local youth along with some civil rights workers assembled at Edmond Pettus Bridge on Sunday, March 7, preparing to make the fifty-mile trek to Montgomery. Blocking the bridge was Sheriff Clark's posse and a contingent of heavily armed, mounted state police, who proceeded to mercilessly gas and beat marchers. SNCC chairman John Lewis sustained a fractured skull. Fifty others were hospitalized. Although expected, Martin Luther King Jr. had not shown up.

Outraged at the carnage of what became known as "Bloody Sunday," SNCC staff came in from all over the region. Pressure mounted to initiate a second march to Montgomery. SCLC returned to Selma.

On the morning of the second march, as I stood at the door of Brown's Chapel I was struck by the fact that coming up the steps were mostly middle-aged and elderly black men and women. Listening to them, it became apparent that they were angry and ashamed that the children had taken the beatings for protesting the denial of the vote to adults. I remember one woman in particular. No bigger than five feet tall, she appeared to be in her seventies. She wore a black overcoat with flimsy "going to town" shoes and brought a thin cotton bedroll tied up with her toothbrush and umbrella. That was all she brought for a march that, if we made it across the bridge, would go on for days. I don't remember ever seeing her before at any of the mass meetings in Selma. My guess was that this was her first time coming out for anything. She came for the children. And she seemed to really believe that she was going to survive that wall of mounted police and walk the fifty miles to Montgomery.

While people sat in church, prayerfully preparing themselves to march, the SCLC leadership was huddling around how *not* to march. A federal injunction had been handed down against the second march. Martin Luther King Jr. would not disobey a federal injunction. The Johnson administration appeared to believe that another blood bath would create more militant public opinion and jeopardize a voter registration bill that Congress could buy into. SCLC was proposing the lifting of the injunction and federal protection provided for the march to avoid a blood bath. None of this was resolved by the morning the second march was scheduled to begin. The church was packed and hundreds of people were outside, awaiting the start of the march.

Then King took the pulpit. He exhorted the crowd to rise up and march, prayed to God for protection, and led us out the door toward the bridge. Once at the bridge, he stopped and told us all to kneel and pray. SCLC staff then ordered us to turn around and return to the church. None of us knew that this was the plan. None of us knew why we were being turned back. Stunned by this arrogant manipulation, I stood outside the church watching angry locals confront SCLC leadership about turning the march around. One man finally said in disgust, "I'm going to get my gun," and disappeared into the crowd.

Angry as we were with SCLC, two weeks later many of us from SNCC went on the "approved" March to Montgomery. There was no other place to put all the simmering rage, frustration, and powerlessness that began with the murders in Mississippi of Chaney, Goodman, and Schwerner, hardened in Atlantic City, left us despairing with the murder of Jimmie Lee Jackson, and enraged us at the Pettus Bridge in Selma.

Two days after Bloody Sunday, three white clergymen who came to Selma to demonstrate were attacked and beaten by local whites. One, Rev. James Reeb, died two days later. Viola Liuzzo, another white protester from the North, was shot and killed while driving to Selma from Montgomery at the end of the march. Finally, *finally,* USAmerica noticed. Yet we watched cynically as the president sent a plane to bring Mrs. Reeb home to Boston and sent flowers to the family of Mrs. Liuzzo. The mother of Jimmie Lee Jackson, the black victim of racist violence, was ignored. If the MFDP experience in Atlantic City was the baptism of our radicalness, Selma was our confirmation.

Mississippi: "We're Not the Only Ones"

By 1965, SNCC projects expanded across a four-state region, as did my work. The Selma literacy project evolved to one of providing organizing materials for movement staff in the region. As Mississippi was the center of the region, I moved to Tougaloo in the winter of 1965. Although I had seen poverty and violence in Selma, I was unprepared for the extremes of violence and poverty in Mississippi. Or maybe I was finally immersed in the reality of this place, this other country. To keep sane, I wrote poetry:

> mississippi winter......
> is
> black-body choked rivers
> that fertilize each spring
> thick lynching trees
> reaching with stark fingers
> into cold brilliant dawns.
> mississippi winter
> is like last night where
> two were found
> dead
> in a bed where damp,
> 50-year-old cotton quilts
> refused to get warm
> and instead became
> a frozen-cotton death sheet.
> born in a cotton field,
> worked 70 years in cotton fields,
> and, finally,
> to die under cotton.

In addition to the political organizing, the SNCC and Congress of Racial Equality staffs were also organizing cooperatives and farm workers' unions. I helped staff in Holmes County put together a manual on organizing local elections and worked with organizers in Batesville to develop a filmstrip and booklet on an okra farmers' co-op they had organized. Because some SNCC staff were attempting to organize a union of plantation workers in the Delta, I created a filmstrip in consultation with César Chávez and other farmworker leaders on how they organized the United Farm Workers Union in California. Continuing my interest in developing reading materials portraying African American heroes, I persuaded Fannie Lou Hamer to tape several conversations for her autobiography, *To Praise Our Bridges.*

These materials all required photographs. I could find nothing in the published world that showed black people taking leadership to change their communities. In pursuit of strong and appealing photos, I endlessly nagged SNCC photographer Bob Fletcher about accompanying me to the communities where I was working. Finally he asked, "Why don't you take your own photos?" Dumbfounded, I replied, "But I don't know how." "Well, learn!" he said. "Matt Herron in New Orleans trains photographers for SNCC."

Matt Herron, a student of photographer Minor White, was influenced by WPA photographers who in the 1930s and 1940s had captured dust bowl refugees, migrant workers, and the rural poor in Appalachia, the Deep South, and California. All around Matt's studio were haunting images from this era, which I attempted to disregard. All I wanted, I thought, were pictures showing "how to" for the organizing materials. But in the darkroom, these ghostly silvery images challenged me to see differently. The resulting photography was immediately useful in books and filmstrips but also created a record of the practical work and resistance events of these times.

The photographs did more than help communities to act. They opened up a view on the world to many who had never traveled outside the region. Father A. J. McKnight, an African American priest who founded several southern cooperatives, invited me to a meeting in Louisiana of black farmworkers from all over the region. Among the filmstrips I showed was the one about the unionizing efforts of farmworkers in California. Flickering up on the parish hall walls were photographs of Mexican American union organizers and field workers being assaulted by white growers and hauled away to jail by white police officers.

When the strip ended there was a long silence. In the audience was an older gentleman who had worked all his life on a plantation in Tennessee and was now homeless, evicted as a result of his participation in the Movement. He rose and with tears in his eyes said, "You don't know how it feels to know that we are not the only ones." It was as though his life's burden of racism was now shared with other people of color. Racism was no longer only white versus black.

Black Power through My Lens

My experiences teaching literacy and supporting SNCC staff's organizing efforts in local communities laid the groundwork for my eventual support of SNCC's transformation from an integrationist to a black power movement. In Selma I came face to face with the terrorism of southern segregation. I also witnessed the social customs that southern segregation required in black-white relationships. Black people much older than me could not look me in the eye or call me by my first name. "Yes, ma'am" and "no ma'am" were said with eyes on their feet. I wondered how integration could result in black people defeating the mental and physical violence of racism. Every assumption and institution in southern society was founded on the belief of the "inferiority" of the African American race. My doubts about integration as *the* solution were beginning to grow.

Many chroniclers of the Movement ascribe the origin of the black power phenomenon in SNCC primarily to northern, urban-raised African Americans. But SNCC's growing insistence on black self-determination and power was seeded by the persistent resistance found in the southern black experience, fertilized by encounters with overt racism in the South and, equally important, by the covert racism exhibited by some of our "allies." In late 1965 Mrs. Fannie Lou Hamer shared with me the conclusions she had reached:

> When we elected our [Freedom Democratic Party] representatives to go to the National Democratic Convention in Atlantic City, we learned the hard way that even though we had all the law and all the righteousness on our side—the white man is not going to give up his power to us. We have to build our own power. . . .
>
> The question for black people is not when is the white man going to give us our rights, or when is he going to give us good education for our children, or when is he going to give us jobs. If the white man gives you anything, just remember, when he gets ready he will take it right back. We have to take for ourselves [from *To Praise Our Bridges*, 1967].

By the winter of 1965, as pressure built toward the "black power" ideology, I believe we were emotionally running on empty. Marches, beatings, protests, murders, and counter-demonstrations began to suck the life out of the organization. Local work was suffering, and some local leaders felt abandoned by the organization. Funds were beginning to dry up, as SNCC was perceived as more militant than the other civil rights groups. Internally SNCC was conflicted. In addition to black nationalism versus integration, the organization's leadership was divided about supporting local programs, the role of those whites who decided not to go home after the summer of 1964, instilling more discipline, and prioritizing the issues we would speak to nationally.

The transformation of SNCC was set in motion at a December 1966 staff retreat in upper New York State where a discussion was forced on whether white staffers should vote or not. Although it was contradictory to the "one man, one vote" ideology of SNCC, the proposal resonated. Empowerment meant not having to ask for a vote from a white person to make a decision. The ensuing strife over the rest of the weekend began a fundamental transformation from an organization that valued participatory democracy and was driven by local community work to one driven by ideology. The programmatic creativity that had connected SNCC to its rural grass roots was virtually abandoned.

Coming to terms with my Mexican American identity, I wasn't going to ask permission or seek approval from either black or white co-workers of what I knew I was inside. As my work was determined by local organizers and supported by my own fund-raising, it would go on no matter how anyone voted in SNCC. I remember passing a note to Stokely saying that I felt SNCC was a part of Third World resistance movements that I had felt a part of before even joining SNCC. Since SNCC was already a black-controlled organization, it would come full circle with limiting the vote to black staff. I envisioned those of us who were not black remaining in technical assistance roles where, at least to me, voting was not essential. He looked over at me and nodded.

As the meeting wound down, the veteran SNCC staff left or withdrew from the debate, which was then taken over by a small minority of cultural nationalists, new to the organization. The discussion had gone beyond who could vote to a demand for white expulsion. A minority of the staff passed the exclusion policy. White staff members left the meeting. I stayed, as did Phyllis Cunningham, a nurse whom I had known since YCS days. In my view, many of the cultural nationalists who had pushed the issue were notorious in the organization for their inability to do anything—but talk. Back in Mississippi, the work would not radically change because of this decision.

After the 1966 staff retreat I returned to the South to continue my work. Some in SNCC didn't consider Mexican Americans white and therefore didn't exclude me. Others working with me at the local level ignored the apparent new direction. Still others, whether aware of my identity or not, stopped speaking to me. In the darkroom the hurt and anger were pushed to the edges and work went on.

In addition to creating educational materials, as a SNCC photographer I also had the responsibility to attend marches on the theory that the presence of cameras might protect marchers. I photographed the 1966 James Meredith March against Fear in Mississippi and witnessed firsthand the impact of black power on the march. Many young people who previously would not march under the nonviolent ideology joined the march after black power became the mantra. The media implied that black power was imposed on the march by urban-raised black militants. Through the lens, I saw it differently. Mirrored in the eyes of these youth was a strength and pride that had been freed from within. For many on that march and many who followed it in the media, black power would bolster a quest for black empowerment that would eventually materialize in building alternative institutions rather than begging for integration into existing failing institutions. While SNCC's hands-on leadership in local communities would wane, black power influenced many local leaders over the next decades to build alternative health care centers, schools, businesses, and financial institutions. At the same time, the synergy of these ideas of empowerment influenced the direction of many Latino, Native American, and Asian organizations that developed innovative social, educational, and economic programs rooted in cultural values and practices. And although many of these programs failed, they still stand as models, creating a legacy from this era when people took their identity and their community back into their own hands.

Passport to the Homelands

My identity strengthened as SNCC, under the ideology of black empowerment, networked internationally with other movements in the Third World. During this period, groups of SNCC workers traveled to Africa. Stokely Carmichael and others went to Cuba, and Charlie Cobb and Julius Lester visited North Vietnam. As they recounted for us their experiences, we were made to feel welcomed by and connected to other revolutions across the globe. Between 1965 and 1967, SNCC also reached out to other movements of color in the United States. For example, two SNCC staff, Marshall Ganz and George Ballis, were financially supported to work with César Chávez and the United Farm Workers in California. SNCC also lent cars and citizen band radios to the predominantly Mexican American farmworkers union.

In 1967 the leader of the Southwestern Hispano Land Grant movement, Reies López Tijerína, was invited by SNCC to the New Politics Conference in Chicago. Julian Bond called me in Mississippi to ask if I would come to Chicago to hostess Reies, "so he would feel more at home among us." Meeting this charismatic land grant leader was the beginning of my education about Spanish and Mexican land grants and how the U.S. government and land speculators had stolen the grants from the *mestizo* (mixed-blood Indian and Hispanic) Mexicans who had lived for hundreds of years in the region.

Impressed with SNCC leadership, in the fall of 1967 Tijerína invited SNCC to send a delegation to the *Convención Nacional de la Alianza Federal de los Pueblos Libres,* a "treaty-signing" summit of Native American, Mexican American, and African American leaders to be held in Albuquerque, New Mexico. This historic meeting also included black activist Ron Karenga from Los Angeles; Thomas Banyaca, a Hopi Indian leader; and other Mexican

American leaders from the Southwest. The SNCC delegation was made up of Ralph Featherstone, Willie Ricks, Freddie Greene, Ethel Minor, and me. After the convention the SNCC delegation traveled three hours north to the Tierra Amarilla Land Grant in the northern New Mexico mountains. Willie Ricks and Ralph Featherstone posed on horseback as I snapped a photo of them with borrowed gun belts crisscrossing their chests and rifles held high in the air.

The visit to New Mexico intensified my thinking about where I wanted to go next. My work was finishing up in Mississippi. Even if I wanted to continue, many key funders discontinued their support because I did not renounce the decisions of the New York staff retreat. While considering alternatives, I received a letter from Reies Tijerína inviting me to come to New Mexico to work with him. He remained deeply interested in maintaining connections with the black Civil Rights Movement and wrote about how minorities divided and fighting among themselves "helped the Anglo maintain his power structure." He ended the letter, "It would be very nice if you could come . . . and spend some time with your people."

There were also invitations from a Mexican American organization in the Rio Grande Valley of Texas and from the United Farm Workers in California. But Mexican Americans in Texas and California had been stripped of most of their land and now worked for those who owned it. I didn't want to spend the rest of my years helping improve working conditions while the land stayed concentrated in the hands of the wealthy. Certainly a worthy cause, but I was tired of piecemeal solutions to economic inequity.

The New Mexico struggle was and is about land. In Mississippi, toward the end of SNCC's work in rural communities, we were beginning to realize that the loss of black-owned land would economically disenfranchise black people in the region. I observed how ownership of land affected the way a people organized and defended themselves. Land-owning black farmers in Holmes County took firm control of county politics and elected the first African American Mississippi legislator in 1967. Farmers in Lowndes County, Alabama, were among the founders of the Lowndes County Freedom Organization, also known as the Black Panther Party. It was the first African American third party in the Black Belt South. The Klan didn't ride as freely in these counties as they did in areas where people didn't own the land. Churches and homes were well guarded by armed farmers determined to protect what they owned. I began to feel that owning land was a key requirement for defeating poverty, taking control of community, and reclaiming culture.

My belief was growing that if something was not done to maintain the land and water rights of *Mexicanos* in the Southwest, then our homelands would be lost, just as Native Americans had lost theirs in the last century and African Americans were losing theirs in this century. Even though the majority of African, Mexican, and Native Americans live in urban areas, the small land base held by our respective peoples represents our homelands within this nation. Within these homelands are the taproots of our cultures where the stories, medicinals, ceremonies, music, dance, and art find their continuation and replenishment. African Americans, Native Americans and *Mexicanos* are, at origin, "people of the land." We have no future in this country or on this continent if we lose our homelands.

In 1968 I closed up my house in Mississippi and moved to New Mexico to work with Reies Tijerína. In 1969 I photographed the start-up of an agricultural co-op and clinic in the Tierra Amarilla Land Grant for the northern New Mexico newspaper *El Grito del Norte,* co-founded and edited by Betita (Elizabeth) Martinez (Sutherland), who had also worked for SNCC. Several months later, the phone rang at 5:00 A.M. with the news that the co-op's recently purchased clinic had been torched by hirelings of Anglos threatened by the success of local land grant leaders in buying the clinic. It was a flashback to the South. I decided to move to this community high in the mountains of northern New Mexico and work full-time for La Cooperativa Agricola and La Clinica del Pueblo. Several years later, with the birth of Sabina, I left the clinic but was soon drawn back into work by my neighbors. Land ownership was being threatened by plans to build a ski resort. We created Ganados del Valle, a model showing how local people could use their land, resources, and cultural assets to create a different kind of culturally and environmentally sustainable economic development model.

Tides of Liberation

In my family and professional life I'm privileged to be involved with many twenty-to-thirty-five-year-old young people. I'm a firm believer that in the liberation movements to come, they have the potential to do better than we did and take the Movement farther down the road. This is the faith that Ella Baker had in us. This is my faith in Sabina's generation and those coming up. When she read this, Sabina commented, "You need to write more specifically about what you expect from future generations." I asked her what she thought I should expect. She said, "We need to care about future generations like you did. We need to give honor to the struggle that went before us. We need to understand that we are privileged and we owe for that privilege. And that when we do give back, a great gift is given: It is not the 'help' we give others. It is that they teach us about the real world and about ourselves in ways that could never happen if we didn't give back." My generation learned this *as a result* of our movement experience. If the generations coming up enter the next liberation movement with this consciousness up front, they will go far beyond us.

Liberation movements are like the tides. Tides can't be forced to come in. When they do come in, they can't be stopped. Just as there will always be tides, there will always be movements. There are signs now, in the new millennium, that the tides are gathering. Like nature's tides, the impending movements will both destroy and create, wound and heal. They will raise heroes and sometimes destroy them. They will be full of dysfunction, soaring creativity, violent rage, and profound love. They will be imperfect, like family, imperfect, like life. Time to get ready.

MARIA VARELA continues to live in New Mexico since moving there from Mississippi in 1967. Awarded a National Rural Fellowship in 1980, she acquired a master's degree in community and regional planning from the University of Massachusetts (1982). From 1982 to the present, in addition to her community organizing work, Varela has held adjunct professor positions at the University of New Mexico and Colorado College. Her SNCC photos have been featured in several exhibits, including at the Smithsonian, Eastman House, and the Howard Greenberg Gallery. Varela was awarded a MacArthur Fellowship in 1990 for her work in community development, specifically for collaborations with Mexican American and Native American artisans and livestock growers in the Southwest desiring to preserve their pastoral cultures by creating sustainable economic development strategies.

Born Freedom Fighter

Gwen Patton

*Born into a race-conscious family, a young activist
continually seeks to understand the significance of race.*

Growing Up

"Breathe. Push," the nurse said to the laboring mother. The baby assisted with her own delivery as she backpedaled with her infant feet inside the womb. After an eternity, the baby's head finally eased out of the womb, the doctor gently pulling the baby into the world. No need to spank the baby. She came into the world with the yelp, "Freeeeeeeee-dom!" This is the way the story of my birth in 1943 has been told to me all of my life.

As a young man, my father had decided that he could not tolerate the "up in your face" racism that was heaped upon black people in Montgomery, Alabama. A hundred times too many, he had witnessed his father being humiliated by banks and suppliers when attempting to get a line of credit for his business. "Nigger, you certain you doing jest nigger work in building houses and churches?" the bank officer would ask. "Yes, sir," my grandfather would reply, "and I have collateral to stand for the loan."

Jim Crow allowed black people to handle some services and limited infrastructure building in the black community. My grandfather could build homes, churches, and business offices in the segregated black community. Soft-spoken and a man of few words, he was very religious and never smoked or had an alcoholic drink in his life. The family believes to this day that my grandfather's disciplined life was a buffer to weather the anarchist whims of racists who had absolute control over black lives. My father, however, could not tolerate the constant indignities, so he left for Detroit in 1940 with no thoughts of ever returning to resettle, even after retirement.

First landing a job as a city bus driver, a position not held by a black man in Montgomery until thirty years later, my father then went into the Cadillac factory and was chosen as a welder's apprentice. Very popular with his co-workers, he was eventually elected a United Auto Workers committeeman and enjoyed respectful camaraderie with union officials.

Unbeknownst to my father, my mother had also left Montgomery and moved to Detroit, where she attended the predominantly black Lewis Business College for Women. On the advice of her mother, who had raised three children essentially on her own, my mother was determined to get an education and be independent.

In Detroit my father, by chance, ran into my mother coming out of the movie theater frequented by Alabama transplants. They married and set up housekeeping in Inkster, a black community some twenty miles west of Detroit. The majority black population resided on the south side of Inkster and the minority white on the north side. Rarely did the races mix except in high school.

My father taught us to be race conscious from an early age. "Colored is on TV," my father would yell, calling my brother and me into the living room. We saw the first game that Jackie Robinson played with the integrated Brooklyn Dodgers and we were in front of the TV later when Al Downing pitched his first ball for the New York Yankees. It was mandatory to see Rochester outwit Jack Benny, Kingfish concoct schemes, and the *Nat King*

Cole Show. Watching Ed Sullivan was a Sunday family ritual. He would often have black people on his show, especially the musician Louis Armstrong. We had all of Armstrong's records.

We lived in a three-story home, with a two-car garage housing my father's new Buick and a Ford coupe convertible. Our "American Dream" home, however, was on a dimly lit, unpaved street. My father mobilized the support of our neighbors; together we not only got paved streets and signs, sidewalks, more streetlights and traffic signs, but we also had new schools built. This was my first movement. I was seven years old.

Every summer, as soon as school was out, my mother packed foot lockers and my brother and I spent the entire summer with relatives in Montgomery. I loved Montgomery and looked forward to these vacations. There I played "real" school by assisting my paternal grandmother with her living-room class where she tutored neighbors in how to fill out the literacy test, the prerequisite to becoming a registered voter. With my maternal grandmother, who was a block captain, I canvassed the neighborhood to encourage neighbors to attend the citizenship schools.

Once, when we children took our usual bus ride, I decided we should get out of the bus at the downtown square and buy ice cream cones. After we ate our cones standing up, I ordered a cup of water for three cents and sat down at the Leggett's drugstore counter. The soda jerk called me a "pickaninny" and rudely told me to get off the stool. I felt it was a dangerous situation, but, nevertheless, I poured my cup of water on the counter, summoned the others, and stormed out of the drugstore. I was nine years old. I told my grandmother about the incident. She looked searchingly in my eyes and said nothing. For subsequent summer vacations, we never had Sunday rides on the city buses.

In Michigan at breakfast and dinner, our family, led by my father, discussed current events and the progress of our race. I attended Urban League socials at the Latin Quarter in midtown Detroit. We were members of the NAACP. Whenever possible, we purchased services and goods from black businesses—from groceries to dry cleaning. *Ebony* and *JET* graced our living-room coffee table and were stacked in the magazine rack in our den.

"Emmett Till Brutally Murdered in Money, Mississippi!" the 1955 *JET* headline screamed. This event wracked the national black community. My brother, who never liked the South, no longer had to spend summers in Montgomery. Soon after the Till murder, the Montgomery Bus Boycott erupted. Buoyed by the elusive 1954 school desegregation decision, black people were fighting back. My grandparents and family on both sides were very active in this bus protest. My paternal grandparents were financial supporters and suffered reprisals from the banks and suppliers. To compensate, my father purchased materials in Detroit and drove them down to Montgomery to my grandfather's construction business. Often he would stay for a stint to help with the work. We in Inkster had weekly telephone calls to our family in Montgomery to learn firsthand about the progress of the protest movement. I was twelve years old.

My father made reports to the community about the Montgomery Bus Boycott after each of his returns. He also continued his race tutoring with my brother and me. A Muslim minister gave us private lectures on the philosophy of the Nation of Islam. My eighth-grade civics project was on the Montgomery bus protest. My tenth-grade world history term paper protesting U.S. support of European colonialism in Africa was titled "The Balance of Terror Is Dead," written about the death of Secretary of State John Foster Dulles and the mysterious deaths of United Nations Secretary Dag Hammerjold and President Patrice Lumumba of the Congo. The daily experiences of living as a black child shaped my thoughts and behavior. These experiences consolidated into the constant, nagging question now etched into my consciousness: What does it mean to be a Negro in America? The very essence of my being was to find an answer to this question.

Montgomery Resident

While I was in high school my mother died from breast cancer. A year later in 1960, at sixteen, I moved to Montgomery. By this time I wanted to be in the South, where I knew a movement would eventually occur. All of my life I was being prepared to be a freedom fighter. After settling in with my great-aunt and her daughter, both schoolteachers, I was offered the option of attending a private boarding school or a public school. I chose the public school, named after Dr. George Washington Carver, the subject of my sixth-grade science project. It was a thrill to attend an all-black school named after a famous black scientist.

The highlight of my activities was volunteering in the Montgomery Improvement Association (MIA) office. After the successful bus boycott, the organization focused on voter registration. I became an apprentice to some of the most outstanding leaders and effective organizers from the bus protest: Mrs. Hazel Gregory, secretary to Dr. King; Mrs. Idessa Williams-Redden and Mrs. Bertha Smith, precinct captains; Rev. Solomon Seay Sr., MIA president; and Coach Rufus Lewis, head of the voter registration project. Lewis, a librarian by professional training, kept detailed, meticulous records and files on who attempted to register to vote and those who were registered voters. He later became the first black U.S. Marshal in the middle district of Alabama. My grandmothers were still active. I worked with them canvassing neighborhoods and encouraging people to attend citizenship schools to learn how to fill out the literacy test.

My other responsibility was to recruit youth. We needed youthful hands to pass out leaflets about mass meetings and other pertinent information. I assisted in forming the youth arm. I became a youth speaker in many churches, urging young people to join our voter registration movement. This movement did not have all the excitement of the bus protest. It was slow, methodical, and tedious. Fear of economic or physical retaliation was always present. When a person would go to the registrar time and time again and could not get registered, disappointment was deep. Much of our work was motivational, to keep the prospective voters from blaming themselves. We would stress our collective intelligence and that it was the racist recalcitrance of registrars who deliberately denied us our right to vote.

Coach Lewis, a businessman and co-owner of a funeral home, opened up the Citizens' Club, a nightclub where only registered voters and those who attempted to register could be members. The Citizens' Club also hosted fund-raisers to pay the poll taxes of voters in need. When a person finally became a registered voter, what a celebration we would have! We would celebrate not only at the Citizens' Club, but also in the neighborhood with tea parties and repasts, as well as in the churches on Sundays with the new voters' names printed in the church bulletins.

Each time I rode the bus, I would plop in a front seat next to a white person. My maternal grandmother, Mommy, would always sit in the back of the bus. One day when there were no white people on the bus, I sat in the back with Mommy. "Mommy, why do you sit in the back after you walked for over a year?" I asked. "Gwendolyn, the protest was not about sitting next to white people; it was about sitting anywhere you please." I gained a new and insightful perspective on our struggle. Mommy, who had nursed a white baby at her breast, did not define herself in juxtaposition to white people.

A week or so after Mother's Day 1961, the Freedom Riders came to Montgomery. My great-aunt, who had a car, would not take me to the bus station to lend support. Her refusal did not stop me. The next day I invited them, both black and white, to our home. The Freedom Riders had taken refuge at Reverend Seay's home, which had been built by my grandfather. I wanted to discuss the growing student sit-in and Freedom Ride movements with them. My great-aunt was outraged when she walked through the door, coming home from school.

"Gwen, come with me," she said. In the kitchen she prepared lemonade and cookies to serve to the Freedom Riders. "Gwen, I don't want any white people in my home," she said. "They are a different kind of white people," I said. "They are our friends." As she carried the snack tray to the Freedom Riders in the living room, she replied, "As long as I have to go through the back door of white homes, white people are not to enter the front door of mine."

That night, I accompanied Mommy to the mass meeting at First Baptist Church, which was organized to lend support to the Freedom Riders. The standing-room-only congregation was held hostage for fifteen hours while the Klan encircled the church, threw rocks, screamed obscenities and threats, and set cars afire. At no time did I feel fear, only a resolve to find the answer to the question "What does it mean to be a Negro in America?"

That summer I moved in with Mommy. She was a deep thinker, insightful, and eccentric. She had no phone or television. She read a lot and we would read together. She taught me how to knit, crochet, and make lace. We embroidered blouses, napkins, and pillow cases. She showed me how to cook fancy dishes and to host tea parties. She stressed the importance of being positive and firm, of standing on principle, of following through on commitments, and, above all, of being a lady in demeanor and decorum in all areas of life. There was no contradiction between being a freedom fighter and being a lady. We were soul mates. I truly loved her and still lament her death.

"Mommy, if I could give you anything in the world, what would it be?" "A round-trip bus ticket to Mound Bayou," she replied. "What and where is Mound Bayou?" I asked. "It's an all-Negro town in Mississippi, run by Negroes, and they just got their first fire truck." The love my grandmother had for our people, with no malice toward white people, became the bedrock of my personal philosophy. While I was living with her, I came to know that I was what we called a race person.

Tuskegee, Tuberculosis, and SNCC

In the summer of 1961 several SCLC workers came to Montgomery to rebuild the Montgomery Movement. They eventually came to live in my grandmother's house, which they rented for a nominal fee. I came to feel that the Movement's greatest hope lay with college students rather than the adults and the high-schoolers that SCLC was targeting. When I left for Tuskegee that autumn, I knew I would eventually break with SCLC, even though my grandmother's house continued to be an SCLC freedom house.

Tuskegee had a close-knit, intellectual student movement. I became a part of this circle, playing chess and reading sociology tracts by E. Franklin Frazier and W. E. B. Du Bois. George Ware, who later became a SNCC campus coordinator, was the leader and facilitator of our discussions. He was a chemistry graduate student, exceptionally brilliant in analyzing the matters of the day.

Again I was a cheerleader and active in campus activities, most notably the Tuskegee Little Theatre. In my sophomore year, however, I became ill with tuberculosis. Never in my life did I encounter more debilitating racism on a constant basis than when I was in a Lafayette, Alabama, sanitarium for over a year. Racism especially rears its implacable head when its victims are most vulnerable. Having a person lying on a sickbed is an ideal situation for racism to take full advantage and ravage the very soul of its victim.

The front of the sanitarium was very impressive, but the ambulance drove me on to the back door, and there I was helped up rickety steps. I was still in the sanitarium the following September when the news that four little black girls had been killed in a church bombing in Birmingham came on, and the television quickly went on the blink. We looked at each other, said nothing, went to our beds, and cried silently. The same question in my mind and heart now weighed heavily on my emotions: What does it mean to be a black child in America?

After these events I marshaled the strength to fight for certain reforms in the hospital, where the living conditions and food were poor: one bathtub for thirty-one patients, no recreation room, and no library with books and magazines for medically captive patients. I did win access to the library in the building. Although I was successful, the only two people who used the library were me and a young girl who had been placed in the adult ward because of overcrowding. No other patients dared to make the trek up the hallway to the white-only section. Though we scored small victories in making a dent in the sanitarium's wall of segregation, the repeated daily humiliations that remained just wore me out. I was finally released from the sanitarium in March 1964.

For the remainder of spring 1964 I emotionally convalesced at Mommy's. By August I was ready to resume my studies at Tuskegee Institute. When I returned to campus, SNCC organizers were everywhere, mainly brothers. Students provided housing and meals for them on and off campus. When SNCC's sister organizers came on campus, several of them would stay in my room. The fact that I had had tuberculosis was no concern to them, even though the disease was still considered a plague in the sixties. The SNCC women's attitudes more than anything else strengthened my self-esteem.

Listening to them, I agreed with all of my heart in SNCC's philosophy "to not underestimate the intelligence of grassroots people" and "to let the people speak" to determine the agenda. SNCC's concept of organizing was for its workers to serve as assistants in the development of indigenous leadership and to build up trust in the community. Tuskegee students formed the Tuskegee Institute Advancement League (TIAL) as an independent entity, which enjoyed an equal partnership with SNCC. TIAL targeted its own Black Belt county, Macon, as its organizing focus for voter registration, but also assisted SNCC's voter rights struggles in Lowndes and Dallas counties, nearby counties also in the Alabama Black Belt. Movement work became as routine as going to classes, an everyday responsibility to beat back racism and push forward toward freedom. The Movement became an inextricable part of my existence and shaped my being, purpose, and outlook on the world, as well as my role in it. It was in my self-interest to be consciously involved.

TIAL students tested the 1964 Public Accommodations Act with sit-ins at restaurants that exchanged their White Only signs with For Members Only signs. Before leaving, after not getting served, we would ask for job applications; if we received them, we would fill them out and leave them on the counters. Our written complaints to the Justice Department included job discrimination. Seeking jobs, we went to every business in Tuskegee. We thought it was unfair that we had to go to New York to get summer jobs when we should have the opportunity to work right in Tuskegee or in Montgomery, the Alabama state capital, only forty miles away.

We held deep discussions around our sit-in work. Some of us felt that the Public Accommodations Act would mostly benefit northerners who motored south to visit family but could not stop along the way to eat, sleep, or even go to restrooms. We knew this law was important, but perhaps more importantly, why not fight for the expansion of black-owned motels, notably those owned by A. G. Gaston, along the highway?

All along, voter registration was the heart of our work. In pushing for the right to vote, we championed the eighteen-year-old's right to vote. It was in our self-interest to be voters. Then we were not being paternalistic when working with grassroots people. We were not doing anyone a favor, for we were working for ourselves as well, to be full participants in the political process.

A short while after President Lyndon B. Johnson signed the Voting Rights Act into law on August 6, 1965, I joined SNCC's efforts in Lowndes County, working in the Benton community. We lost our first independent party election in Lowndes County, November 1966. I am convinced to this day that the election was stolen. My first published article was on the election fraud, "No Clouds in the Sky," appearing in the *Liberator* magazine in December 1966. In Macon County, however, with students being the swing vote, we did elect Lucius Amerson, the first black sheriff of the county since

Reconstruction. We had to out-campaign not only the white establishment but also those light-skinned Negroes who touted superiority over other black people within the county's caste system.

In the midst of these developments I was elected student body president at Tuskegee Institute. SNCC had a permanent presence on campus, and in alliance with TIAL, community organizing was ongoing. A fledgling anti-apartheid movement was in progress at the college as South African exiles, now professors at the institute, told us of the horrors on the continent. They recommended reading anything and everything on and by Nelson Mandela and the African National Congress. Stokely Carmichael, later Kwame Turé; Willie Ricks, later Mukasa Ricks; and Winky (Bill) Hall already had a special interest in African revolutionary developments. They urged Tuskegee students to read Jomo Kenyatta's *Facing Mount Kenya* (1962) and Franz Fanon's *Wretched of the Earth* (1965). Later when I was in New York they suggested reading Amilcar Cabral's *Return to the Source* (1973) as well as Kwame Nkrumah's *Consciencism* (1970) and his *Handbook on Revolutionary Warfare* (1968). The internal discussions between SNCC and TIAL at this time were on the people's right to self-defense and self-determination. Plans were on the board to issue a call for a Congress of African Peoples to unite the diaspora.

Vietnam and Black Power

As student body president, I had to concentrate on campus problems. The draft for the Vietnam War was ravaging its toll on male students who were not doing well in their studies or who had to drop out of school for financial reasons. I contacted anti-war activists Bettina Aptheker and David Hawk for their assistance in setting up a draft counseling center on campus. Our students' opposition to the war heightened when a black soldier killed in Vietnam could not be buried in his hometown of Wetumpka, Alabama, because the black cemetery was filled and the white cemetery refused to inter him.

That same year, Sammy Younge Jr., a U.S. Navy veteran and Tuskegee student, was killed near Tuskegee's campus by a white gas station attendant for trying to use the white restroom of the downtown Standard Oil station. Sammy was a key TIAL organizer and liaison to SNCC and an enthusiastic supporter of the notion of an independent party for black people in Alabama. Sammy came from a middle-class Tuskegee family and was a doo-wop singer. He would stand out on the dorm's fire escape and croon to the coeds. They would almost swoon when he sang one of Smokey Robinson's love songs. Sammy had a sweet, lilting voice and was damn good-looking.

On the night of January 3, 1966, a group of us were gathered, discussing movement issues, studying, and relaxing, when someone realized there was no mayonnaise for our staple late-evening snack of bologna on white bread. Sammy, one of the few students who had a car, a blue Volkswagen, was dispatched for the mayonnaise. When he didn't return, I thought he might have stopped to sing; it didn't seem likely, however. Concerned, I left the group and went back to the dorms to see if he was there. But he wasn't. Finally I drifted off to sleep only to be awakened by a midnight phone call from the dean of students, P. B. Phillips. The dean told me the circumstances of Sammy's death and reminded me that as president of the student body, it would be my task to inform the other students. I just couldn't deal with it. I went back to sleep thinking, "What does this mean?"*

After Sammy's death, movement activities escalated in Tuskegee. At the peak of this escalation, Stokely Carmichael and Willie Ricks proclaimed "Black Power!" when SNCC joined SCLC and CORE on the March against Fear the following June. The march was started by James Meredith, who was shot his second day on the road. The call for black power touched the depths of my soul. All my personal experiences came tumbling forth. If we had had black power, my uncle would be alive; my grandfather, an unbent businessman; my father, a prosperous businessman and a city father in a predominantly black city; my mother, alive in cancer remission with the best of rehabilitation treatment; and me, never to have suffered the mental and emotional humiliation of being captive in a sanitarium. *Yes,* black power was the answer. The revolution to free black people was on the horizon; in fact, for my peers and me, the revolution was just around the corner.

Black power resonated in the voting rights struggle with its objective of electing black people to political office. With black people as a crucial voting population, they could affect public policy within the ideal of participatory democracy. Via black power the American Dream could be legislated into reality for black citizens.

I concurred that white organizers should leave SNCC and form their own organizations to fight racism. I did not see the separation as divisive, but rather complementary. Black power demanded a strategy in which black people would transform the powerless black community into one that could exert its human potential to be an equal partner in the larger society. Fighting white racism from within the white community was absolutely essential if the notion of a pluralistic society was ever to be a reality for black Americans. Who better to do this—to debate the contradictions among whites about their psychological need to feel superior to all other human beings as a measure for their own humanity—than the white people who had been in the SNCC trenches?

* Younge's story is told in Jim Forman's book, *Sammy Younge, Jr: The First Black College Student to Die in the Black Liberation Movement* (1968).

The Southern Conference Educational Fund, led by veteran activists Carl and Anne Braden, did not resist the call, but rather accepted the challenge to organize white people to undo racism. I became part of the beginnings of a revolutionary nationalist core that welcomed black power as a pro-black, not anti-white, premise; we earnestly studied the nature of the country's economic system along with the societal relationships it spun among peoples at home and abroad that included, yet went beyond, race.

Race, Class, and Gender

With the myriad debates raging, and at this point as an adherent to the race and class analysis, I decided to share my time with the now all-black SNCC and the Southern Student Human Relations Project (SSHRP), pronounced "sharp." Forty-one Exchange Place in Atlanta, the movement office building, housed SSHRP, the American Friends Service Committee (AFSC), the Field Foundation, the Southern Regional Council, and other progressive organizations. I was SSHRP's field organizer and had negotiated a salary equivalent to that of a first-year high school teacher. I plunged into drawing up a field program that included SNCC cadre as paid consultants, conference planners, and facilitators to implement a dialogue on black power.

The SSHRP director took exception to my program, but I won out with the help of Connie Curry, a white woman formerly associated with SNCC. Connie worked upstairs with AFSC. She had also accepted SNCC's challenge as a white person to fight racism in the white community. She was pivotal in directing funds to groups that saw the complementary centrality of black power and the fight against racism.

When I moved to Atlanta, I lived in the freedom dormitory, a large house donated by the Mennonites. My roommates were Ethel Minor, who became a communications expert with *Muhammad Speaks* newspaper; Freddie Greene, a wonderful organizing administrator; and Myrtle Glasgoe, who later became a curator for an African American museum in South Carolina. Other SNCC women who had a positive impact on my thinking were Fay Bellamy, Gwen Robinson, Ruby Doris Robinson, and Cynthia Washington.

The women of SNCC were tough-minded yet sensitive, grounded in a vision that freedom was not only external in terms of defining our own space in the SNCC collective and larger society, but also internal in terms of defining who we were as females. I can see Muriel Tillinghast, a chief administrator, demand accountability from all field organizers. I can see Annie Pearl Avery nonviolently snatch a billy club out of a policeman's hand as he attempted to crack it against her head. The policeman stood frozen and stunned as Annie Pearl walked away with the billy club in her hand.

In SNCC meetings, as we planned strategy, Fay Bellamy always pointed out the importance of the black woman's view, based upon our socialized experiences and circumstances in a racist society. Later, Frances Beal, after she moved from Paris to New York, provided the most profound insights and analyses of our triple jeopardy—gender, race, and class status.

We all had boyfriends, either inside or outside the SNCC collective, or both. We were courted and we dated. I do not remember spending time primping with the sole objective to please my boyfriend, SNCC or otherwise. Conversations between us, men and women, were of substance, deep, not superficial. Lifetime commitment to the struggle was the greatest attraction for relationships.

For SNCC women, SNCC men were people just like we were. The beauty of SNCC was that we could let our guard down and comfort one another. We were free to be vulnerable with each other without the threat of being ridiculed or our emotions being trampled upon. This fortified us to go out the next day to battle the conditions that may have made us cry the night before.

Black Is Important and Beautiful

At the same time that black power discussions were being carried on, the blood of the Vietnam War was spilling over in our living rooms via television coverage. As the war escalated, astute white organizers like Connie Curry and Anne Braden described the racist nature of the war, such as the drafting of young black men who could not afford college or who were locked out of higher education because of poor racist public school backgrounds while white males escaped the draft because of the students' privileged, 2-S deferment available to college students. The predominantly white anti-war movement responded to implied charges of racism by characterizing itself as single-issue oriented. "Moreover," the anti-war activists said defensively, "to add racism will drive some mainstream white protesters away from swelling our ranks."

"Racism," I countered, "is not an additional issue. Racism permeates your single issue." Drawing from the above analysis, I wrote an article, "Black People and Wars," which was published in *Liberator* magazine in February 1967. I also wrote two internal position papers to SNCC's central committee, laying out the rationale to establish a black anti-war movement. More than a year later, when I was sitting on the central committee along with John Wilson and Mae Jackson, SNCC organized the National Black Anti-War Anti-Draft Union.

The black power discussion continued and was fleshed out with the articulation of "Black Is Beautiful." Stokely and SNCC's next chair, H. Rap

Brown (later Jamil Al-Amin), traveled the breadth and length of the land extolling black pride and pointing up white Americans' invidious hatred of our people embedded in every facet of society. They would ask, "Why is angel food cake white and devil's food cake black?" Rap and Stokely urged black people to rid themselves of internal oppression and self-hatred. These themes were expanded upon in Rap's first book, *Die Nigger, Die* (1969). Rap urged his readers to resurrect themselves as new people, to free themselves from the white man's internal and external bondage and to get ready for revolution. Hundreds of thousands joined this consciousness-raising movement. Negroes became black people, full of pride.

A black power discussion-conference, partially underwritten by SSHRP, was scheduled for February 11, 1967, at Tuskegee Institute. By this time my grandmother's home in Montgomery had become a way station for young men who refused the draft and were seeking political asylum in Canada. On the eve of the conference, I was driving a friend who was fleeing the draft from Tuskegee to Montgomery. En route we had a terrible, mysterious, one-car accident. The axle rod broke. When I awoke I was in the school's infirmary with a cast on my left leg and wires laced in my left jaw. Several students and SNCC members had donated blood for my operation. My friend had a broken arm and had been released.

After six weeks in the infirmary the doctor came to my bedside and said, "We have to amputate your leg." Rather than agree to the amputation, I left the hospital and embarked on a three-year campaign to save my leg. Living most of this time in New York City, I was aided by members of the Medical Committee for Human Rights. During the ensuing hospital stays, a stream of mostly black and some white movement activists visited frequently, often discussing issues of race and class. For the first time in my life, I met Puerto Ricans and other people of Spanish descent, Asians, and Europeans. I had met Africans, both black and white, while a student at Tuskegee. It was heartwarming meeting so many people from different ethnic backgrounds, all of one accord—the Revolution was just around the corner.

On a special release from the hospital, arranged by Jim Forman, I visited Ruby Doris Robinson, a revered SNCC organizer, who was in a downtown hospital reportedly dying from a mysterious disease she contracted while imprisoned for civil rights activity in the infamous Parchman Penitentiary in Mississippi. Ruby and I talked about life and death in the context of commitment to the Movement. We talked several times on the phone, she in the downtown hospital and me uptown. While hospitalized, with help from the nurses, I also got into a wheelchair with an IV pole attached and rolled all over the hospital supporting the efforts of Hospital Workers Union 1199 to organize the hospital's housekeepers. In addition, I wrote SNCC position papers on various issues and the need to build coalitions, and critiques of movement shortcomings such as the lack of insurance and vacations for organizers. I read political and economic tracts of all persuasions from Adam Smith to James Boggs.

My mentor, Forman, and I engaged in long and probing discussions. When I left the hospital with a cast and on crutches, I traveled throughout the country speaking on the themes "Capitalism, Christianity, and Caucasoids" and "Money, Might, and Militarism." Forman's themes were "Control, Conflict, and Change." During this time I worked with Forman on his effort to transform the Movement from civil rights to human rights. We began to make regular treks to the United Nations to present our case and to attend United Nations receptions, where we met African diplomats and Betty Shabazz, widow of Malcolm X.

In the summer of 1968 I was to experience another car accident and fight another hospital battle. This car accident broke my leg again and forced my leg closer to my ankle. The doctors proposed that since the gap was now smaller they could take a bone from my hip and transplant it in the ankle opening. Instead, I asked my doctor, "Is there such a place as a bone bank like there is an eye bank?" He replied, "Yes, but it's owned by the navy in Bethesda, Maryland. I have already tried, but they turned me down, saying Vietnam casualties had priority." "Well," I concluded, "I guess we have to mount an offensive. I'm a casualty of the Freedom Movement."

Two movement friends, Diane Jenkins, a bright high school student, and Maxine Orris, organized a letter-writing campaign to the U.S. Navy's high brass, arranged press conferences at my bedside, and held demonstrations outside the hospital with signs demanding that a movement soldier have equal access to the bone bank. Members of Hospital Workers Union 1199 joined the demonstrations. My doctor was then able to procure bone. The success of the operation was written up in the annals of orthopedic surgery.

When I left the hospital in October 1968, I was walking with a heel case and later with a patella brace. Maxine took my crutches as souvenirs. I went right back into activism; I continued to organize black support for the anti-war movement. Each Friday, after working through the week with an array of organizations, from SNCC to the newly formed National Welfare Rights Organization, to the National Black Anti-War Anti-Draft Union, I boarded the New York Central train and traveled to Peekskill to work with the youth and report on the Movement there to *Muhammad Speaks*.

SNCC organizers and I were frequently invited to speak to the black student unions cropping up on black and integrated college campuses across the country. These students had found their student government associations lacking in the struggle. To unite these new black student unions, I helped found the National Association of Black Students (NABS), headquartered in Washington, D.C. NABS challenged the leadership of the predominantly white National Student Association to make reparations for past NSA errors and to restructure NSA to have greater accountability to students, especially black students.

After ten more years of activism in New York and D.C., feeling disillusioned about my activities in the North, I decided to return home. My activities seemed less and less connected to a broad grassroots struggle. All of my life's experiences, from the day I was born to the present, had taught me that the Movement was part and parcel of the everyday vicissitudes in the struggle against racial and human indignities. The Movement was not an abstraction, isolated in an insular, sectarian form, parading as the "vanguard" of the people's movement.

When I told Stokely Carmichael about my decision to return home, he asked hopefully, "To Africa?" "No, to Montgomery." I said. By the time I got back to Montgomery, I had learned the answer to my question. Being black in America meant always being involved in struggle. I had also learned that one's life is a movement when one becomes conscious. My grandparents, pioneers and veterans in our struggle for freedom, needed my account as to what I had done to advance our movement. They accepted my report.

GWEN PATTON still lives in Montgomery and works as the archivist for H. Councill Trenholm State Technical College, where she has established special collections of the pioneers of the voting rights movement. She is Montgomery coordinator for the National Historic Voting Rights Trail and serves on its national advisory council. Over the years she has remained active in a variety of political and social causes and earned a doctorate in political history and higher education administration. A member of Delta Sigma Theta Sorority, she is a fourth-generation member of Hutchinson Missionary Baptist Church, where she serves as Sunday school teacher and is on the Board of Christian Education.

"Born Freedom Fighter" © 2010 by Gwen Patton

Postscript

We Who Believe in Freedom

> We who believe in freedom cannot rest.
>
> —Ella Baker

After the 1966 Meredith March, SNCC chairman Stokely Carmichael and his successor, H. Rap Brown, traveled the country giving speeches reflecting both what they considered the radical spirit of the ongoing spate of urban uprisings as well as their own growing militancy rooted in the harshness of the southern struggle. They insisted on defining the black community's attacks on white businesses as "rebellions" and were among the few voices insisting that these acts represented legitimate grassroots protests against existing racial injustices, especially police brutality. The press and most white Americans, on the other hand, called these incidents "riots" and saw them as irrational and violent criminal acts. Police and other governmental representatives agreed with this latter view and further determined that the unrest was the result of black militant conspiracies and intensified their attacks on SNCC.

As SNCC workers spoke and established footholds in northern and southern urban areas, local, state, and national governmental figures blamed SNCC organizers and speakers for the urban unrest, levying arson, destruction of property, and other charges, although SNCC staffers did not instigate these actions or participate in the looting and burning of buildings. In the summer of 1967 the U.S. Congress joined the attack enacting legislation, nicknamed the "Rap Brown law," making it a federal crime to cross state lines to incite a riot. A barrage of extremely serious local, state, and federal charges closed down several of SNCC's urban efforts at community organizing and tied up SNCC representatives, especially Rap Brown and program secretary Cleve Sellers, in a series of arrests, jailings, and trials, which pressured the organization to raise money for bonds and legal fees.

Movement women also filled speaking engagements describing SNCC programs and discussing the staff members' increasingly radical perspective. By 1967, believing the rebellions represented the beginning of an even more serious impending struggle, many SNCC women, along with their male counterparts, thought the country was entering a revolutionary period and came to consider themselves revolutionaries. Giving rhetorical support to armed struggle at home and abroad, they prepared themselves by reading black liberation material, histories of anti-colonial struggles, and various social change theorists. The organization defined itself as part of a world struggle *for* human rights and *against* racism, colonialism, and imperialism. More frequently than in the past, SNCC workers attended international Third World conferences and visited leaders of countries where decolonization struggles and armed revolutions had taken place.

Women field secretaries took positions on international issues and sought international forums in which to present African American grievances. Motivated by the irony of black soldiers risking their lives abroad for a country that denied them rights at home, SNCC women, several of whom are contributors to this book, helped frame the organization's stand against the War in Vietnam and against this country's draft and assisted in the creation of SNCC's National Black Anti-War Anti-Draft Union. SNCC women were also involved in pushing SNCC toward support of the Palestinian cause and were enthusiastic participants in the organization's actions and statements against South African apartheid. They were part of SNCC's unusual and successful effort to obtain nongovernmental organization (NGO) status at the United Nations.

During this time, SNCC maintained a focus on some of its more traditional projects. The organization sought to build on its original base—students attending southern black colleges and universities. There SNCC campus travelers expected to find new recruits to staff SNCC projects. This worked well in Alabama, particularly with Alabama State and Tuskegee students, but similar efforts were stymied by the extremely violent response of southern police forces. Students at black colleges and universities launched very large demonstrations in cities and on campuses across the South. Although they used the militant language of black power and black consciousness, in the instances described below their goals reflected fairly moderate concerns, such as changing campus regulations and gaining access to segregated facilities.

In response to the SNCC presence and magnifying the significance of minor incidents of rock and bottle throwing, police and, on occasion, National Guardsmen attacked students. Officers invaded black college campuses, which had traditionally been off limits to lawmen. They shot at students and their supporters, which represented a much higher level of violence than the arrests, beatings, and gassings previously used against civil rights demonstrators. In the spring of 1967, police wounded student protesters in Nashville and Houston. During the Houston demonstrations, police fired several thousand rounds of ammunition into the occupied dorms at Texas Southern University. That same spring police bullets wounded several Jackson State student protesters and killed a former SNCC staffer, Ben Brown, who was walking nearby. The most deadly attack, now known as the Orangeburg Massacre, took place early in 1968 on the campus of South Carolina State College. On that evening in February, hundreds of state and local police, along with National Guardsmen, lined up in front of the students gathered around a campus bonfire. Without warning, state and local police shot at the students, who tried to run away when the attack began. At least twenty-seven people were seriously wounded, including Cleve Sellers, who was shot in the shoulder. In addition, three students were killed—Henry Smith, Delano Middleton, and Samuel Hammond Jr.

In this period some SNCC staff, including women in this book, were still working in southern SNCC projects or their offshoots in the South. In Mississippi, for example, SNCC people were involved with the Poor People's Corporation, remnants of the Mississippi Freedom Democratic Party, and the SNCC-inspired Child Development Group of Mississippi. Southern community work remained life threatening. In the fall of 1967 two SNCC field secretaries—George Bess, a Tuskegee student and friend of Sammy Younge's, and Henry McFarland, a newer recruit—were drowned, according to SNCC workers, when their car was forced off the road by Klansmen in Clay County, Mississippi. The following spring, Dr. Martin Luther King Jr. was assassinated in Memphis.

As usual, in spite of the grief and intimidation, members of the organization continued to find new and creative ways to proceed, mostly in terms of seeking out and building alliances. In 1968 SNCC officials were involved in a short-lived attempt to build a working alliance with the newly formed, California-based, Black Panther Party, named after SNCC's Lowndes County political party. In 1967, following a 1965 exchange of staff with the United Farm Workers Union, SNCC sought alliances with other Hispanic groups and their Native American associates. Working in concert with primarily white reformist groups like the National Conference for a New Politics, SNCC officers required that minority black representatives, as the leaders of the struggle, have 50 percent voting power. In 1969 Jim Forman, then head of SNCC's International Affairs Commission, initiated calls for reparations from white churches to fund community institutions, especially economic ones. He made these demands at the National Black Economic

Development conference in Detroit and again at Riverside Church in New York City. Women in SNCC gave birth to a feminist group for women of color, the Third World Women's Alliance.

All of these activities were carried out under the watchful eye of government agencies. Throughout this period, Selective Service draft boards intensified their targeting of SNCC's male organizers. Those seasoned organizers who chose to serve were, of course, removed from SNCC projects; those who refused found themselves facing legal charges with long prison terms. In the summer of 1967 the FBI incorporated black activist groups they were already following into the agency's counterintelligence program, COINTELPRO. The agency lumped SNCC, CORE, and SCLC, the Deacons for Defense, and the Nation of Islam under the heading of "Black Nationalist Hate Groups." Agents infiltrated SNCC at every level, including northern support groups. Instructed to use disruptive and illegal tactics, these operatives succeeded in destabilizing the organization by intensifying divisions within the organization and ejecting experienced SNCC activists. The agents harmed SNCC's already strained relationships with other radical black groups by planting false rumors that encouraged violent confrontations. Bureau chief J. Edgar Hoover himself led the public attack and revealed his fairly warped view of the civil rights landscape when he declared Dr. King "the most dangerous man in America."

In early March 1970 a seasoned SNCC veteran, Ralph Featherstone, and a recruit from the Black Economic Development Conference, William H. (Che) Payne, were killed by an explosion that tore their car apart a mile from the Bel Air, Maryland, courthouse where Rap Brown's trial was to be held. Many SNCC veterans believed the bomb had been planted in the car and intended for Brown. Featherstone's Washington, D.C., funeral was the last large gathering of current and former SNCC staff during the movement era.

By this time there was only a tiny skeleton of a SNCC group. The organization had stretched itself to the breaking point by attempting to organize on a national, even international, basis, leaving few people to staff its preexisting southern projects. SNCC members and officers were overburdened by numerous unfounded legal charges, police attacks, as well as the relentless and unpunished murders. These circumstances made the cost of activism so high that it was extremely difficult to attract new recruits. Already under attack by white liberals and moderate civil rights groups after the summer of 1964, the organization had taken more and more radical positions and found that its funding base in the white community evaporated. In SNCC's final years, the staff's ongoing attempt to establish discipline and find the right radical or revolutionary path and methods to make social change resulted in more time spent with internal conflicts and debates and less in the community-organizing projects that had proved successful in SNCC's early years.

For a variety of reasons chronicled in this book, by the time of Featherstone's funeral, most of the authors, like most other SNCC veterans, were no longer involved in SNCC projects or programs. The organization that SNCC women had been a part of was one in which they had been central figures. This was quite an unusual situation in the early sixties, when most other major civil rights groups, businesses, universities, and even churches marginalized their female members and associates. Women had helped determine SNCC's philosophy and political positions. They had participated in all aspects of SNCC's organizational planning, programs, and projects. Initiating and maintaining major movement efforts or suggesting new ways to carry out the work, in ways great and small, women had played a role in determining the character and flow of the Movement. Sometimes women led by example, setting the levels of courage and sacrifice extremely high.

Women in SNCC had experienced an unusually democratic movement, one linking college students and sharecroppers, a movement that respected and admired the wisdom and courage of everyday people, and an organizational model that opposed authoritarian and centralized decision making. Moreover, almost all of the women, both northern and southern, who had joined SNCC's efforts brought with them a social consciousness that allowed them to value this kind of movement. Their consciousness, in turn, linked sixties civil rights activism to other current and past struggles of African Americans and Africans, white liberals and progressives, social justice theologians, and international efforts against Nazism, fascism, and colonialism.

SNCC women knew they had played a vanguard role in sixties activism, which made segregation illegal and the right to vote the law of the land. Through confronting white southern terrorism individually and collectively, they had shortened its reign. SNCC's "Black Power" cry prompted the formation of numerous black caucuses in all kinds of organizations along with a push to create independent black institutions. Together with black consciousness-building, black power ushered in an explosion of black art and culture and strong feelings of pride and dignity. Entertainer James Brown's "Say it loud, I'm black and I'm proud" rang out across the country. Many of SNCC women's pioneering strategies and positions formed the basis for radical discussions throughout the remainder of the century.

SNCC women saw their movement's impact reach far beyond their initial targets. The southern Freedom Movement played a significant part in a general liberalization of U.S. social and political life. It created an environment where appeals for women's and gay rights, prisoner and welfare rights, as well as the rights of other people of color could be pursued and heard. SNCC's calls for black power and black consciousness resulted in a rethinking of education in the black community and the inclusion of black studies programs in university offerings, which in turn was followed by Chicano and women's studies and, later, diversity courses. SNCC's views on the significance of race informed various struggles in Africa and the West Indies. The anthem of the southern Civil Rights Movement became the standard anthem for similar movements around the world where "We Shall Overcome" has been sung in hundreds of different languages.

SNCC women knew they had served their age well, risking life and limb in counties with high Ku Klux Klan membership and doing hard time in southern prisons, receiving incredibly low and unreliable pay, and living in freedom houses that often lacked plumbing and heat. Taking time away from educational, career, and other mainstream opportunities, they had stood on the front lines of the civil rights struggle.

The movement experience was pivotal in the life trajectories of the women in this book. As their biographies attest, when the era of the sixties was over, they kept their hands on the freedom plow. Lifelong activists, SNCC women went on to energize a host of other movement-related activities and organizations. They took the SNCC legacy with them, specifically Miss Ella Baker's radical, democratic ideas regarding movement building, along with a wealth of social change knowledge and experience. Accustomed to working tirelessly under difficult and dangerous circumstances, they lived their lives guided by a passionate commitment to human rights. Movement women remained inspired by Miss Baker's admonition, memorialized in "Ella's Song" by Bernice Johnson Reagon, "We who believe in Freedom cannot rest until it comes."

Index

Beyers, Robert, 338
Billips, Charles, 453
Biloxi Project (Miss.), 420
Birmingham, Ala., 331; bombing at 16th Street Baptist Church, 194, 451, 475, 505, 533, 578; and Freedom Rides, 35, 454; mentioned, 138, 141, 266, 353, 453, 460, 461, 463; violence, 192, 194, 198, 337, 451, 456
Birmingham Freedom Choir, 461
Black and Tan (Mississippi Republican Party), 240
Black Arts Movement, 547
Black Belt Project, 390
black colleges, 34, 315, 588; white students enrolled in, 18, 22, 40, 42, 67, 68, 76, 196. *See also* influences; *specific institutions*
black history. *See* African American history
black institutions, 141, 148, 437; colleges and universities, 33–34, 141, 276, 334; newspapers and magazines, 63, 218, 219, 220, 258, 574. *See also* influences
Black Liberators, 538
black national anthem. *See* "Lift Every Voice and Sing"
Black Panther Party (Cal.), 324, 536, 537, 589
Black Panther party (Lowndes County, Ala). *See* Lowndes County Movement
black power, 264; as continuation, 191, 501; and positive impact, 568, 581–82, 584, 591–92
Blackwell, Jeremiah, 252
Blackwell, Randolph, 301
Blackwell, Unita, 4, 252
Blaylock, Olivia, 105, 120
Block, Sam, 301, 491
Bloody Sunday, 464; and SNCC, 262, 447–49, 563; and violence, 433, 468, 471, 517, 527, 564
Blount, Marion, 148
Bogalusa, La., 262
Boggs, James, 585
Boldern, J. D., 114
Bolton, Jimmy, 354
Bond, Horace Mann, 330

Bond, Jane. *See* Moore, Jane Bond
Bond, Julian, 44, 115, 120, 569, *Illus. 1, 2*; and Dottie Zellner, working with, 315–18, 322; and Georgia House of Representatives, 329, 365, 378–79, 521; and Jane Bond, 327, 329; and Mary King, working with, 335–39, 341; SNCC Communications Director, 57, 299, 315, 354, 359
Bonner, Charles, 449, 465
Booth, Wilson, 293
Booyer, Anne, and Albany Movement, 104, 108, 110, 111, 114, 117
Booyer, Mary, 117
Borinski, Ernst, 224
Boston Action Group, 418
Boudin, Leonard, 193, 352
Bouknight, Gloria, 72
Bowens, Amanda, 431
boycott(s), 193, 282, 306; buses, 15, 36, 98, 106, 128, 148, 158, 173, 186, 397, 515, 574–75; stores, 34, 95, 114, 158, 225–26, 285, 287, 396, 408, 466–67
Boyd, William, 109, 149
Boynton, Amelia, 449, 465
Boynton v. Virginia, 34
Braden, Anne, 82, 187, 583; and civil liberties, 318–19; and Ella Baker, 309, 397; and white organizing, 325, 399, 424, 582
Braden, Carl, 335, 397; mentioned, 82, 187, 319, 325, 399
Bradford, Ernest, 465
Bradley, Mamie Till, 62
Branche, Stanley, 356
Brando, Marlon, 309
Bray, Gerald, 545
Brazier, James, 187, 194
Breaker, Jeanne, 344–48
Breaker, Victoria, 344
Britt, Travis, 68
Britting, Mary, 535
Brooke, Edward, 276
Brooks, Paul, 43, 65
Broom, Essie, 301
Brown, Ben, 589
Brown, Eddie, 118
Brown, H. Rap, 513, 523, 583–84, 587

Clark, Jim, and Selma, 447, 466–68, 471–72, 498, 549, 558, 561–63
Clark, Katie, 322
Clark, Kenneth, 322
Clark, Mamie, 322
Clark, Septima Poinsette, 43, 375, 440–41; and Citizenship Schools, 40, 114, 213, 231
Clark College, 17
Clark Memorial Church, 41
Clayton, Carey, 27, 30, 31
Cleage, Albert B., Jr., 293
Cleaver, Kathleen, 536
Clement, Rufus, 47
Cleveland, M. C., 465
Clinica del Pueblo, La, 571
C.M.E. (Christian Methodist Episcopal) Church (Albany), 116
Cobb, Charles (Charlie), 251, 442, 549, 569
Cochran, Janiece, 40
COFO (Council of Federated Organizations), 211–12, 229; and Mississippi Summer Project, 27–29, 31, 32, 213–15, 227–29, 259, 260, 338, 346, 373, 396, 403, 419–22, 426, 551; after Mississippi Summer Project, 404, 407, 412
COINTELPRO, 523, 590
Coleman, Ike, 420, 422
Coles, Robert, 228
Collins, Lucretia, 43
Collins, Norma, 110, 115, 299, 387
Committee on Appeal for Human Rights (COAHR), Atlanta, 17, 46, 57, 58
Communism, assumed influence, 200, 206–8, 373; Cuban-tinged Marxism, 534; to discredit, 21, 224, 231, 276, 289–90, 324, 528; government investigations of, 289, 317, 319; Maoist, 539; SNCC on, 319, 324; and SNCC staff/volunteers, 55–60, 492, 528, 534. See also McCarthyism
community center(s), 28, 30, 216, 390
Congress of Racial Equality (CORE), 340; and Cambridge, 277, 279, 285, 294; and COFO, 27, 211; and Freedom Rides, 35; Freedom Walk, 449–50, 456; and Meredith March, 526, 581, 590;

and Miami, 44, 312; in Miss., 64–66, 76, 212, 244, 247; and Selma March, 478; and SNCC, 81, 161, 314, 426, 565; stall-in, 355–56. See also COFO; Mississippi Summer Project
Connecticut College for Women, 18
Connor, Bull, 35, 337
Convención Nacional de la Alianza Federal de los Pueblos Libres, 569
Conwell, Kathleen, 163, 168
Cooper, Annie, 466
Cooperativa Agricola, La, 571
co-ops. See economic development projects
Coppin Chapel A.M.E. Church, 53
CORE. See Congress of Racial Equality
Cornish, Charles, 278
Cotton, Dorothy, 114, 441
Council of Federated Organizations. See COFO
Countryman, Joan, 545
Cowan, Dennis, 39
Cowan, Geoff, 166
Cowan, Holly, 166
Cowan, Paul, 166
Cox, Charles, 64
Cox, Courtland, 375, 508
Craft, Bessie Trotter, 164
Craft, Ellen, 164
Craft, Henry K., 164
Craft, William, 164
Craig, Calvin, 46
Cromwell, Dwight, 282
Cronin, Burrill, 442
Cuba, as influence, 192, 193, 439, 519, 532, 534, 536, 538, 542, 569
Cuban Five, 542
Cuban Missile Crisis, 188, 328
Culbreth, Annie Mae, 114
Culbreth, Janie, 115, 145; and Albany Movement, 91–100, 104, 106, 108, 110, 111, 114, 116
Culbreth, Ross, 98
Cunningham, Phyllis, 568
Current, Gloster, 219
Curry, Constance (Connie), 36, 557, 582, 583; and NSA, 49, 299; and SNCC founding, 48

Grubb, Inez, 278, 279
Guyot, Lawrence, 215, 358, 492

Habcr, Al, 370, 556–57
Haberman, Karen, 18, 25
hair. *See* natural hair
Haley, Richard (Dick), 64
Hall, Blanton, 106, 108, 114, 125, 149
Hall, Peter, 459
Hall, Prathia, vii, 4, 58, 392, 449, *Illus.
1;* and Albany/Southwest Ga., 155,
172–80, 189, 202, 208, 213, 490; ora-
torical power, 187, 204, 352; and Selma,
352, 362–63, 470–72
Hall, Winky (Bill), 580
Hamburg, Jill, 484, 486
Hamer, Fannie Lou, vii, 405, 442, 525,
565, *Illus. 2;* on Black Power, 567; and
MFDP, 215, 233–35, 374–75, 395, 401,
495, 567; as role model, 379, 394, 512,
521; and Winona beating, 213, 358, 492
Hamilton, Charles, 534
Hamilton, Dr. (Albany), 142
Hamilton, Grace, 308
Hamlett, Ed, 420
Hammerjold, Dag, 575
Hammond, Samuel, Jr., 589
Hansberry, Lorraine, 533
Hansen, Bill, 129, 167, 185, 441, *Illus. 3*
Harding, Rosemarie Freeny, 14, 483
Harding, Vincent, 14, 15, 23, 26, 483
Harlem Anti-Colonial Committee, 546
Harlem Brotherhood Group, 166
Harlem Education Project (HEP), 546–47
Harris, Alphonso, 145
Harris, Don, 166, 183, 192–94
Harris, Doug, 183
Harris, Elijah, 145
Harris, Emory, 108, 441, *Illus. 2*
Harris, Isaiah A., 144
Harris, James, 422
Harris, Jesse, 64, 79, 442, 460
Harris, Juanita, 145
Harris, Katie B., 144
Harris, Luther, 40
Harris, McCree L., vii, 4, 86, 118, 145
Harris, Patricia Roberts, 243
Harris, Rosetta, 145

Harris, Rutha Mae, 108, 141, 150; and
Freedom Singers, 88, 145, 318, 441, 487
Harris, Walter, 467
Harvey, Claire Collins, 64, 75
Hatch, Lucia, 337
Hattiesburg, Miss., and movement, 27,
213–15, 218–19, 230–32, 237, 239–42,
260, 522
Hawk, David, 580
Hawley, Andy, 486–87
Hawley, Nancy, 486–87
Hayden, Casey, 328, 333, 423, 426, 557,
Illus. 2; and Albany Freedom Ride,
110; mentioned, 16, 335; and northern
support, 337, 370, 371, 486, 557; NSA
speech, 49–52, 369–70; and Tougaloo
Literacy Project, 66, 381, 387, 442; and
women in SNCC, 342, 392, 398; and
YWCA Project, 319, 333. *See also* femi-
nism; gender roles; leadership; "Sex
and Caste: A Kind of Memo"; SNCC;
SNCC Position Paper on Women;
women; Women's Liberation Move-
ment
Hayden, Tom, 52, 110, 328, 556, 557; and
support for southern movement, 257,
333, 370, 484, 486
Hayes, Curtis, 231, 316, 442, 484
Hays, Carlin, 405–6
Haywood County Movement (Tenn.). *See*
Fayette County Movement (Tenn.)
Head Start, 551. *See also* Child Develop-
ment Group of Mississippi
Height, Dorothy, 172, 288
Henderson, David, 547
Henry, Aaron, 235, 442, 450; and Free-
dom Vote, 214, 227–28; and MFDP,
215, 234–35
Henry, Laird, 284
Herndon, Angelo, 56
Hernton, Calvin, 547
Herreshoff, David, 494
Herron, Matt, 426, 566, *Illus. 2*
Hershfeld, Elizabeth, 486
Highlander Folk School, 108, 300, 414;
and Fisk students, 40–42; workshops,
167, 345–46, 384, 553
Hill, Betty, 456–57

Hinton, Rufus, 548

historical documents: Barbara Jones Omolade 1964 letter, 388–92; Casey Hayden, NSA speech, 49–52; and Cathy Cade family from Albany, Ga., 196–205; Joan Trumpauer's freedom rides diary, 69–73; Judy Richardson's 1964 diary, 355–58; Penny Patch's Panola County field report, 407–9

Hobbs, Cleophus, 449, 465, 468–69

Holder, Mrs. (Clarksdale, Miss.), 458

Holland, Ida Mae, 214

Holland, King, 40

Hollandale, 253

Hollowell, Don, 193

Holmes, Eleanor. See Norton, Eleanor Holmes

Holmes, Hamilton, 105

Holsaert, Eunice Spellman, 24

Holsaert, Faith S., 132, 133, 139, 167, 306, *Illus. 3*

Hoover, J. Edgar, 590

Horne, Lena, 282, 288–89

Horton, Myles, 41, 43

House, Gloria Larry, 499, 501

House, Karen, 561

House, Stuart, 513

House Un-American Activities Committee (HUAC), 195, 319, 487, 544

Howard, Ruth, 364

Howard University: campus protest, 276; D.C. protest, 275–76; mentioned, 11, 52, 173, 183, 185, 243, 296, 339; and movement, 67–68, 240, 250, 271, 371, 516

Hubbard, Lonnie, 43

Hubbard, Maceo, 281

Hudson, Winson, 551

Humphrey, Hubert, 323, 395, 401, 421

Hunter, Charlayne, 105

Hurley, Ruby, 47, 106, 108, 219

identity: and coming out, 208; and race, 303, 379, 427, 529, 531–32, 533–40, 555–56, 568–69; and skin color, 169, 464. See also feminism; gender roles; influences; interracial; Jews; movement; SNCC; women

I. L. Peretz Kinder Shul, 542

Inc. Fund. See NAACP Legal Defense Fund

influences: black cultural traditions, 140–41, 148, 165–66, 182, 218, 257, 276, 311, 330, 438, 445, 577; family, church, and community, 9–11, 62–64, 91–92, 100, 128–29, 140, 164–65, 168, 172–73, 181–83, 195–96, 217–18, 243, 245, 268, 273–74, 303, 311, 330, 334, 344, 349–50, 366–67, 383, 399, 403, 428, 436–39, 445, 453, 456, 460–65, 470, 475, 483–85, 487, 489–91, 531–32, 540–44, 555–56, 573–77; international, 165, 181, 330, 368, 403, 417–19, 438–39, 444, 505, 532, 536, 556; movement mentors, 213, 219, 379; religious/ spiritual, 67, 172–73, 195–96, 311, 330, 334, 555, 556. See also African American history; black institutions; churches; identity; interracial; racial codes

Institute for the Black World, 483, 523

Interdenominational Theological Center, 17

International Ladies Garment Workers Union (ILGWU), 289–90

interracial: dating and societal disapproval, 545; experiences, 436–38, 464, 468, 576–77; marriage/family, 56, 181–83, 531–32, 555–56; movement relationships, 29; non-movement fears and perceptions, 25, 29, 127, 185, 186, 202–3, 205, 314, 328, 333–34; student meetings, 36, 46–47, 223, 319, 332, 333–34, 381

Issaquena County, Miss., 251–52, 254

Itawamba County, Miss., 420–23

Itta Bena, Miss., 338

Jackson, Goldie, 185–86, 192, 441

Jackson, Jimmie Lee, murder of, 308, 447–48, 468, 497, 506, 563–64

Jackson, Mae, 583

Jackson, Mahalia, 462

Jackson, Miss., 223–24; and Freedom Rides, 35, 64, 68–69, 72, 75; mentioned, 29, 79, 229–30, 231, 310;

Kennedy administration, 280, 317

Kenyan liberation movement, 165, 352–53, 418

Kenyatta, Jomo, 165, 418, 580

Kilston, Bonnie, 183, *Illus. 3*

King, C. B., and Albany Movement, 103, 107, 108, 110, 116, 119, 134–35, 193, 199, 201, 203–5, 208, 441, 490

King, Coretta Scott, 58

King, Ed (from Kentucky), 299

King, Ed (from Miss.), 419, *Illus. 2;* and Miss. movement, 214, 215, 223–29, 234

King, Jeannette, 235, 419

King, Margaret, 110

King, Marian, 112, 191

King, Martin Luther, Jr., 371, 389, 391, 575, 590; and Albany movement, 88, 94–95, 113, 130, 145, 179, 187, 441; and Cambridge Movement, 273, 281, 282, 295–96; and economic issues, 423; and Fellowship House, Philadelphia, 173; and March on Washington, 16–17, 180, 289; mentioned, 34, 58; and Meredith March, 239; and MFDP, 234; and Prathia Hall, 180, 187; and Selma, 362, 448, 477–78, 498, 563–64

King, Mary E., 359, 383, *Illus. 2;* and educational materials, 383, 426; mentioned, 16, 115, 393, 398; women in SNCC, 361, 382

King, Slater, 107–8, 112, 198, 441

Kirksey, Henry J., 434–35, 442

Knight, Pauline, 43

Kocel, Martha, 494

Kochiyama, Yuri, 538

Koinonia, 115, 116, 488

Ku Klux Klan, 87, 135, 136, 430, 533, 547; in Ala., 453, 570; in Atlanta, 46, 54–55, 58–59; and Freedom Rides, 35; in Miss., 26, 30, 31, 216, 217, 225, 247, 251, 262, 374, 405, 433, 589. *See also* nonviolence; self-defense; white violence

Kunstler, William, 65, 352

Ladner, Dorie, 213, 226, 266, 442; with Joyce Ladner in Miss., 217–21, *Illus. 1*

Ladner, Joyce, 213, 214, 442, *Illus. 1*

Lafayette, Bernard, 64, 312; and Nashville, 40, 42, 43; and Selma, 449, 465, 470–71, 558, 561

Lafayette, Colia Lidell. *See* Lidell, Colia

Landry, Larry, 293

Lane, Mary, 214

LaPrad, Paul, 40, 42

Laurel Project (Miss.), 26–32

Laursen, Per, 315

Lawrence, Shirley, 137

Lawson, James Morris (Jim), Jr., 41, 47, 340

Lawyers Constitutional Defense Committee (LCDC), 66

leadership, 384, 398; and conflicts over, 58–59; and different styles, 29; and gender, 29, 58–59, 237–38; and local African Americans, 30; by women, 237–38, 290, 361, 379, 382, 392, 414, 486, 512, 521, 591–92. *See also* SNCC; SNCC Position Paper on Women; women; *individuals*

League of Revolutionary Black Workers, 486

Lee, George, 63, 237

Lee, Herbert, 145, 212, 247, 308, 319

Lee, Nathaniel, 454

Leigh, Sandy, 241

LeMoyne College, 25

Lessing, Doris, 414

Lester, Julius, 28, 40, 534, 569

Lewis, Fulton, Jr., 373

Lewis, Fulton, III, 373

Lewis, Highland, 276

Lewis, John, 354, 356, 378, 419; and Black Power, 468; mentioned, 16, 40, 115; and Nashville, 40, 42, 43; and Selma, 362, 448, 467, 563; and Stokely Carmichael's election, 309

Lewis, P. H., 465

Lewis, Rufus, 575–76

Liberal Caucus (NSA), 52, 370

liberals, racism of, 30, 323–24, 401, 526, 562

Liberator, 579, 583

Lidell, Colia, 449, 470–71

Moses, Dona, 246, *Illus. 1*
Moses, Gilbert (Gil) 258–59, 261, 264, 443, *Illus. 2*
Moses, Janet Jemmott. *See* Jemmott, Janet
Moses, Robert (Bob), 46, 166, 170, 269, 382, 486; and disappearance of Chaney, Schwerner, and Goodman, 26, 245–46, 358; and Freedom Vote, 228, 338; and Miss. movement, 65, 185, 211, 245–47, 301, 307, 328, 442, 491, 492, 494; and SNCC leadership, 245–46, 299, 319, 375, 397, 599
Moss, James, 314
Motley, Constance Baker, 173, 487
Moton, Leroy, 448, 469
Mound Bayou, Miss., 63, 261, 577
Mount Beulah, Miss., 434
movement: community base, 95, 141–43, 196, 218–22, 232; community fears, 175–76, 231, 254; costs of participation, 18, 87, 97–98, 143, 223–25, 254–56, 558; dealing with fear, 247, 251, 487–90, 502; family responses, 17, 19, 24–26, 132, 139, 183, 223–25, 263, 314, 351, 369, 373, 388–92, 485–87, 490–91, 494; joining, 36, 127, 144, 152, 277, 327; lessons and assessments, 97–98, 171, 229, 264–65, 294–96, 513, 539, 533, 571–72; northern support, 258, 266, 545; racial diversity within, 16, 99, 129, 195, 531, 533–40, 576, 584; and religious diversity, 169, 192, 313, 536; and religious faith, 47, 67, 176, 180, 394; and role of whites, 49–52, 264; and southern white support, 33, 46, 138, 223–25, 312, 386. *See also* SNCC, *individual communities, events, and people*
Mt. Airy Baptist Church, 179
Mt. Calvary Baptist Church, 141, 144–45
Mt. Early Baptist Church, 148
Mt. Olive Baptist Church, No. 2, 150
Mt. Olive Baptist Church (Terrell County), 179
Mt. Sharon Baptist Church, 179
Mt. Zion Baptist Church, and Albany Movement, 99, 108, 118, 129–30, 135–36, 140–42, 151, 201, 206

Mudd, Johnny, 413
Muhammad Speaks, 453, 582, 585
Mulholland, Joan Trumpauer. *See* Trumpauer, Joan
Murphy, Carl, 43
Murphy, Curtis, 43
Murray, Hugh, 312

NAACP, 293, 303, 544; attorneys, 75; mentioned, 47, 161, 247, 308; movement base, 27, 55, 57, 70, 87, 98, 100, 158, 166, 212–14, 218–21, 225–27, 241–42, 257, 266, 437, 486, 533, 551, 574; national office conservatism, 255–57, 266, 281, 283, 287–89, 293; relations with SNCC, 81, 106–8, 211, 229, 244, 276, 319, 323, 426
NAACP Legal Defense Fund, 77, 78, 193
NAACP youth branch, Queens, 439
NAACP Youth Chapter (Hattiesburg, Miss.), 219
NAACP Youth Chapter (Jackson, Miss.), 225–26
NAACP Youth Council (Albany, Ga.), 104, 106, 107, 122, 125
NAACP youth organization, Memphis, 13
Nakawatase, Edmond (Ed), 16, 354
Nash, Diane, 35, 53, 65, 213; as leader, 361; mentioned, 88, 115, 183; and Nashville, 40, 41, 43; and nonviolence, 76–83, 450, 486
Nashville Christian Leadership Council, 41
Nashville Friends, 40
Nashville Movement, 40–44, 53
Nashville Student Movement, 35, 40–44
Natchez, Miss., 266–68, 393, 458, 459
National Association of Black Students (NABS), 585–86
National Black Anti-War Anti-Draft Union, 583, 585, 588
National Black Economic Development conference, Detroit, 589–90
National Conference for a New Politics, 589
National Conference of Christians and Jews (NCCJ), 165–66, 182–83
National Council of Churches, 494

racist violence. *See* jail; racial codes; sexual violence; white violence

Radio Free Mississippi, 549

Rainbow Coalition, 195

Raines, Mama Dolly, 4, 159, 168–70, 306

Rainey, Lawrence A., 308

Rambaeau, Janie Culbreth. *See* Culbreth, Janie

"Rap Brown law," 587

Rappaport, Ralph, 486

Rauh, Joe, 323

Rawick, George, 485

Reagon, Bernice Johnson: and Albany Movement, 104–6, 108–10, 114–15, 119–28; and "Ella's Song," 592; and Freedom Singers, 88, 145, 441, 487; and singing in Albany, 146–52; on SNCC Position Paper on Women, 382

Reagon, Cordell Hull, 127, 356; and Freedom Singers, 85, 105–6, 108, 111, 122, 123, 129, 149; and nonviolence, 125; organizing Albany, 85, 105–6, 108, 111, 122, 123, 125, 129, 149; singing in Albany, 88, 106, 108, 122–23, 150

Red baiting. *See* Communism; McCarthyism

Reeb, James, 308, 448, 497, 506, 564

Reese, Carleton, 461

Reese, F. D., 465

Ribback, Alan, 426

Richardson, Donna, 277–78, 283–84, 292

Richardson, Gloria, and Cambridge movement, 4, 183, 184, 271–72, 349, 356, *Illus. 1*

Richardson, Judy, 299, 457, 471, *Illus. 1*; and Greenwood, 323, 358–59, 372; and Jean Wheeler, 245–46, 363

Ricks, Willie (Mukasa), 15, 132, 191, 555, 570; and Black Power, 341, 526, 534, 580–81

riots. *See* urban rebellions/uprisings

Roberts, Dennis, 134, 135

Roberts, Leviticus, 104, 105

Robeson, Paul, 311

Robinson, Betty Garman. *See* Garman, Betty

Robinson, Cleophus, 461

Robinson, Gwendolyn (Zoharah Simmons), 9, 582, *Illus. 1*

Robinson, Jackie, 179, 573

Robinson, Reggie, 167, 316, 348–49, *Illus. 3*

Robinson, Ruby Doris Smith, 23, 457, 488, 582; and Freedom Rides, 64, 70; illness, 324–25, 584; mentioned, 354, 356; and Rock Hill, S.C., 486; roles in SNCC, 16, 57, 115, 299, 310, 316, 351, 361, 392, 476, 512, 521, 545, 561; on whites, 325, 425; and women's sit-in, 425

Robinson, Willie C., 466

Roby, Harold, 421–22

Rockefeller, Nelson, 369

Rock Hill, S.C. *See under* sit-ins

Rollins, Avon, 305, 457

Rollins, Metz, 41

Romilly, Constancia (Dinky), 324, 375; and SNCC office, 330, 354, 356–57

Rooks, Joseph, 40

Rosenberg, Ethel, 543–44

Rosenberg, Julius, 543–44

Rosett, Jane, 68–69, 71–72, 75

Ruben, Judy, 535

Rubin, Larry, 306, 419

Rudd, Ed, 372

Ruffin, Suzie, 27

Ruleville, Miss., 213, 263, 494

Russell Woods Neighborhood Association, 541–42

Rustin, Bayard, 340; and March on Washington, 17, 188, 288, 441

Saffold, Hattie, 443

Sales, Ruby, 507

Salter, Eldri, 225–26

Salter, John, 225–27

Samstein, Mendy, 354, 357

Sanchez, Elizabeth, 440

Sariego, Mr., 543

Sasser, Ga., 176–77, 305

Savio, Mario, 504

Schechner, Richard, 264

Schnell, Ronald, 443

schools: and desegregation, 48, 63,

137–38, 377–78, 472, 490; and racial disparities, 80–81, 86, 218

Schrader, Emily (Emmie Adams), 383, 398

Schwerner, Michael, 389. *See also* Chaney, James, Michael Schwerner, and Andrew Goodman, murder of

Schwerner, Rita, 212, 260, 322

SCLC. *See* Southern Christian Leadership Conference

Scott, Willie Emma, 449, 465

SDS Economic Research and Action Program, 384

Seals, Ira, 407

Searles, A. C., 114

Seaton, Esta, 14

Seay, Solomon, Sr., 575, 576

Seeger, Toshi, 88

segregation. *See under* racial codes

self-defense: by black communities, 30–31, 135–36, 139, 159, 170, 205, 238, 247, 256, 260, 269, 306, 404–5, 455, 458–59, 466, 479, 486, 491, 519, 533, 570; after Bloody Sunday, 471–72, 564; in Cambridge, Md., 272, 284, 291–92; on demonstrations (Atlanta), 20, 53–55; and SNCC, 266, 451, 458–59, 527, 580, 582

Sellers, Cleve, 287, 587, 589, *Illus. 1*

Selma Freedom Choir, 499

Selma literacy project, 557–59, 561–62, 565

Selma Movement, 83, 269, 362–63, 434, 465–70, 470–72, 473–74, 476–78, 495–500, 505–7, 510, 516–18, 554, 563–64; and Prathia Hall, 352, 362–63, 470–72

Selma Summer Project, 560

"Sex and Caste: A Kind of Memo," 384, 398

sexism, 30, 398; experienced by Zoharah Simmons, 30–32; and female ministers, 97, 173; sexual harassment policy, 29, 31; and women's autonomy, 79. *See also* feminism; gender roles; leadership; "Sex and Caste: A Kind of Memo"; sexual violence; SNCC; SNCC Position Paper on Women; women; Women's Liberation Movement

sexual violence: in jail, 59–60, 112; by white men, against African American women, 86–87, 103, 119, 122–25, 126–27, 197, 213, 217–18, 488. *See also* jails; white violence

Shabazz, Betty, 585

Shady Grove Baptist Church (Ga.), 179

Shankle, Ike, 407

Shapiro, Andrea, 542

Shapiro, Miriam, 198

Sharkey County, Miss., 251

Shaw, Frank, 105, 107, 108

Shaw, Geraldine, 24, 25

Shaw, Terry, 449, 465

Sheffield, Horace, 544

Sherrod, Charles, 168, 502, *Illus. 1*; and Albany/Southwest Ga. movement, 85, 93, 105, 106, 108, 116–17, 121, 122–23, 125, 129, 138, 149, 150, 153–55, 161, 168, 173–74, 178–79, 185, 186, 188, 189, 191, 193, 194, 197, 201, 202, 208, 306, 419, 441, 488, 491, 546; and gender, 186–87, 306, 490

Sherwood, Madeleine, 259

Shiloh Missionary Baptist Church, 99, 118, 129–30

Shirah, Sam, 115, 420–21

Shrine of the Black Madonna, 293

Shuttlesworth, Fred, 53, 346, 453, 454, 455

Sias family, 252

Simmons, Aishah Shahidah, 9, 32

Simmons, Gwendolyn Zoharah. *See* Robinson, Gwendolyn

Simon, Barbara, 18, 20, 22

Simpson, Euvester, 213, 358, 492

Sinatra, Frank, 282

singing, 546; adapting songs, 149–50; and Ala. movement, 449, 460–63, 498, 499; to combat fear, 93, 178–79, 246; on demonstrations, 17, 18, 304, 544; at mass meetings, 150, 152, 188, 432, 466–67, 505–6; in jail, 71, 72, 146–47, 150–51, 170, 507; in response to crisis, 246, 363–64. *See also* Albany Movement/Southwest Ga. Movement;

mass meetings; *individuals and specific song titles*

The University of Illinois Press
is a founding member of the
Association of American University Presses.

University of Illinois Press
1325 South Oak Street
Champaign, IL 61820-6903
www.press.uillinois.edu